Jews and Other Differences

Jews and Other Differences

The New Jewish Cultural Studies

Jonathan Boyarin and
Daniel Boyarin, Editors

University of Minnesota Press
Minneapolis
London

The University of Minnesota Press gratefully acknowledges financial
assistance provided by the Lucius N. Littauer Foundation Inc., New York.

Chapter 2 first appeared in *Visual Anthropology*, 6, no. 3 (1994): 303–22,
reprinted by permission; chapter 5 first appeared in Ann Pellegrini,
Performance Anxieties: Staging Psychoanalysis and Race (New York:
Routledge, 1996), reprinted by permission of the publisher; chapter 9 first
appeared in Chana Kronfeld, *On the Margins of Modernism: Decentering
Literary Dynamics* (Berkeley: University of California Press, 1996),
copyright 1996 the Regents of the University of California, reprinted by
permission.

Bob Kaufman, "Bagel Shop Jazz," from *Solitudes Crowded with Loneliness*,
copyright 1965 New Directions Publishing Company, reprinted by
permission.

Published by the University of Minnesota Press
111 Third Avenue South, Suite 290, Minneapolis, MN 55401-2520
Printed in the United States of America on acid-free paper

Library of Congress Cataloging-in-Publication Data

Jews and other differences : the new Jewish cultural studies /
    Jonathan Boyarin and Daniel Boyarin, editors.
        p.   cm.
    Includes bibliographical references and index.
    ISBN 0-8166-2750-9 (hc). — ISBN 0-8166-2751-7 (pb)
    1. Jews—United States—Intellectual life.   2. Jews—United
States—Identity.   3. Jews—United States—Public opinion.
4. Public opinion—United States.   5. United States—Ethnic
relations.   I. Boyarin, Jonathan.   II. Boyarin, Daniel.
E184.J5J655   1996
305.892'4073—dc20   96-14966

Contents

Introduction / So What's New?

Daniel Boyarin and Jonathan Boyarin

Cultural studies is the name of a creative turbulence in a moment of crisis for the "modern West" and the liberal academy within it. It represents a struggle to provide an answer (or at any rate a response) to this crisis through discovering ways to make history, literature, and other cultural practices "work" better for the enhancement of human lives. Jews and Jewish culture both are obviously in their own state of crisis. Thus there is room for a Jewish cultural studies, one that will function in two ways: first by seeking to discover ways to make Jewish literature, culture, and history work better to enhance Jewish possibilities for living richly; and second by uncovering the contributions that Jewish culture still has to make to *tikkun olam,* the "repair of the world." The question that Jewish cultural studies raises might be said to be this: Is Jewishness up to the challenge?

Cultural studies has various sources, intellectual and political, but as a named field it is readily traceable to the writings of Raymond Williams (Williams 1973) in England during the middle of the twentieth century—a time when intellectual Marxism was still more or less linked to something identifiable as an English working class, but also a time when the dismantling of the British empire was beginning to force a reshaping and rethinking of the British university system. In its earliest formulations, cultural studies questioned the (itself fairly recently) established world of literary production, reception, and transmission that had come to be known as "English literature," insisting that popular and working-class cultural productions were worthy of and demanded study on their own terms, and often with the same tools used to understand elite literary productions.

In the generation or two after Williams's pioneering work, cultural studies in Britain broadened to include both participation by and studies of populations who had come to enrich and complicate British identity from various parts of the crumbling empire. In the process, cultural studies encountered and was enriched by the reflexive anthropology of the post-1968 generation, especially in the United States (Asad 1973; Hymes 1972; Marcus and Fischer 1986). The growing field of women's studies and feminist theory has been another important conduit, helping to introduce key aspects of the contemporary French interrogation of the subject into what otherwise might be a fairly pragmatic Anglophone discourse (Marks and de Courtivron 1980). The continuing appeal and still-increasing scope of cultural studies are indicated by the recent voluminous reader simply titled *Cultural Studies* (Grossberg, Nelson, and Treichler 1992).

While exciting work plausibly identifiable as Jewish cultural studies has been done in recent years (e.g., Neusner and Frerichs 1985; Gilman 1986; Goldberg 1989; Friedlander 1990; Eilberg-Schwartz 1992; Silberstein and Cohn 1994; El-Or 1994; Goldberg and Krausz 1993; Dominguez 1990), the work of establishing a "Jewish place" within the shifting field of cultural studies has barely begun. To a profound extent, a retrospective devaluation of Jewish difference in exile has been a key component of the dominant historiography of Jews since World War II. The conception according to which the Holocaust and the establishment of the State of Israel constitute a Jewish return to history (Fackenheim 1978) reinforces a conception of premodern, post-Exilic Jewish experience as being primarily of antiquarian or philological interest, rather than critical resources for the necessary refashioning of Jewishness in the present.

In order to understand what is new about Jewish cultural studies, it is also necessary to begin to articulate the politics of Jewish identity in the American academy. Whereas instructors in many other "culture areas" are not a part of the culture they are specialists in, faculty in Jewish studies have themselves been predominantly Jews for decades. The result is that scholars in Jewish studies have certainly been allowed to "speak in their own voice," but few outside of the Jewish community have imagined that anything they said was worth listening to. Jewish studies in the modern academy grew largely out of the *Wissenschaft des Judentums* developed in nineteenth-century German-language scholarship, and is broadly linked to the Reform movement (Eilberg-Schwartz 1990; Lambropoulos 1992; Goldberg 1993). Its defining corpus of materials for study remains the vast, and vastly instructive, body of Jewish texts dealing with interpretation, ethics, authority, and practice developed over thousands of years. Its predominant though no longer exclusive method remains that of painstaking philology, in which the contemporary concerns of the researcher are bracketed rather than articulated and mobilized. Because of the depth of the textual tradition and the relatively long pedigree of this particular "ethnic studies" rubric, those who staff Jewish studies programs may see programs such as Latino, African American, or gay and lesbian studies — those "particulars" where the most exciting work in cultural studies often gets argued through and articulated — as overly presentist, and may even see these rubrics as dangerous when histories of discrimination are sometimes directly or obliquely blamed on Jews and Judaism. On the most immediately practical level, Jewish studies programs are commonly supported by funds raised from local Jewish communities, whereas other ethnic studies programs, as well as those in women's studies and gay and lesbian studies, tend to be broadly tied to demands for affirmative action and diversification as a general mandate for universities at the end of the twentieth century. On the other hand, many scholars of Jewish background who were trained and hired to research and teach in areas with no particular relevance to Jewish culture (such as English literature or international ethnography) find themselves becoming interested in studying Jewish culture as their careers continue.

This leads to some very specific and local tensions among scholars with different disciplinary *and* ethnic identities. In a certain public university on the East Coast, the administration is promoting a move to reconstitute African American studies, Latino studies, and others into a unified ethnic studies Ph.D. program. The Jewish studies faculty there, we have been told, seem to be implacably opposed, presumably because they believe that they and the scholarly tradition they represent have much to lose if their work is cast into a framework that is comparative above all.

Jewish cultural studies addresses this anxiety from several standpoints: that of the professional scholar of Jewish studies; that of the Jewish academic exploring a new interest in things Jewish; that of the young scholar who happens to find questions of Jewishness a productive field for exploring more general issues relating to the politics of difference. Although each cultural situation has its own dynamics and special epistemological problems, they have much in common as well. Thus questions of women's history and women's culture are common to all such enterprises, because in virtually all cultures the recorded history has been the history of men. Whatever methods, techniques, problems, and issues have been developed in one field of women's history will have supreme relevance for all others. Similarly, basic theoretical questions about the history of sexuality will be central to any endeavor in Jewish cultural history. A question as central to contemporary cultural studies most broadly conceived as whether "homosexuality" has always existed or is a specific historical cultural phenomenon will take its place as a central issue for Jewish cultural studies as well. For reasons such as these, despite the continuing need for linguistic expertise and the continued (although always and appropriately interrogated) validity of the demanding research methodologies of various disciplines, the lifeblood of the new paradigm is not isolation. Its trademark will not be the scholar poring over dusty manuscripts. The life of current discourse and the clamor of contention and contentiousness will drive the undertaking.

Research and critique of Jewish culture has much to offer to the cultural studies community as well, much that is specific enough to Jewish cultural history to be most richly articulated there but nevertheless applicable and useful in other cultural studies as well. Let us take, for example, the issue of diaspora (see Boyarin and Boyarin 1993). This has lately become a pivotal concept in certain parts of cultural studies, especially those involved in the study of postcoloniality. Cultures of peoples in diaspora, their cultural preservation, and the doubled consciousness of such peoples — as well as the ways that diaspora becomes paradigmatic of a certain cultural condition in the postcolonial era *tout court* — are increasingly vivid areas of thought within the paradigm. The Jewish diaspora, for which the term was invented, provides the longest history of diasporic cultural survival and production. Thus both its details and its theorization have much to offer to scholar-critics whose primary areas of focus are the black Atlantic or the Indian diaspora, for example.

And this brings us back to another critical juncture. Precisely because the cultural studies paradigm opens up to other groups doing cultural studies, it will have political and social effects. Specifically, one of our main goals in promoting the rubric of Jewish cultural studies is to move toward the recognition of Jewish culture as part of the world of differences to be valued and enhanced by research in the university, together with the differences of other groups hanging onto cultural resources similarly at risk of being consumed by a liberal universalist ethos. Cultural studies, as well as offering a disciplinary base for area studies, also provides a base from which the fundamental questions of difference and solidarity, of particular identity and universal concern, can be both explored theoretically and practiced.

Since questions of Jewish culture and identity are often raised in a sudden and confrontational way on many campuses, scholars of Jewish background may find themselves unprepared to respond in a flexible and responsible way. When scholars who are Jews have agreed to "pass" — not so much to pretend to Protestant backgrounds as to desist from being "too Jewish" — the repressions attendant on this agreement contribute to their pain, defensiveness, and confusion when African Americans accuse them both of white racism and of Jewish clannishness.

The construction of racial categories is in fact a key topic driving research in cultural studies in general. Likewise, it is one of the current themes in cultural politics inspiring research in Jewish cultural studies. Through research being done now (such as Dan Itzkovitz's essay in this volume), the tortured question of whether Jews are "white" is shown to have a complex history — and that history in turn sheds light on the politics of identity and exclusion in American life. The articulation of this legacy can reveal how much the persistence of racism has enabled Jews in the United States to be and become safely "white." Paradoxically, it can also reveal how such an indirect exploitation of racism curtails significantly the sphere in which we are free to continue being and to become Jewish, and suggest in turn unexpected insights into the constraints and creative potentials of other group identities in the United States.

One of our most ambitious goals is thus to shape a space of common discourse between Jews and others who share a critical approach to the politics of culture. By a "critical approach," we mean an understanding of history and identity that fully respects the powerful ways that they inform each other, yet also understands that in exploring and articulating our various identities we are simultaneously remaking history. This approach is vital to our contention that difference can be enriching and nonexclusive rather than constraining and competitive. Indeed, difference can heal. Thus, for example, through serious work done in this spirit it may become more possible for African Americans to understand the sources of Jewish pain, and for Jews to understand and acknowledge their debt to the African American experience. Jews, who as a group have clearly achieved enormous economic success in the United States as well as accumulating cultural capital, whether in Hollywood or in Harvard Square, have done so by and large at the cost of deculturation. That deculturation is itself a source of pain and loss, vague and anecdotal at times, overwhelming at others.

The discipline of cultural anthropology offers an acute example of one of the areas of silence this volume is intended to help overcome. On one hand, a disproportionate number of North American ethnographers, both in the "founding" generations at the turn of this century and more recently, have come from Jewish backgrounds. On the other hand, Jews as an ethnographic specialty have long been marginalized. Even in the 1990s, when there is much broader professional recognition of the potential and actual contribution the study of Jews can make to the liveliest debates in the discipline, younger ethnographers who work on Jewish materials seldom find a place among the lingering areal divisions and the newer "diversity" categories that dictate academic hiring choices. Much work in Jewish ethnography is therefore done by scholars who have established themselves through research on non-Jews and later turned to Jewish ethnography. Ben Orlove's essay grows out of and reflects on this context. He begins by describing the creation of a very specific, deliberate, and new space for the creation and expression of Jewish identity: a panel of professional anthropologists—the kind who "just happen" to be Jewish, as the saying goes—choosing to gather their own individual thoughts, and then gather together to begin articulating how Jewishness has shaped and been shaped by their experiences with non-Jews in the field.

In an essay sharing concerns with Walter Benjamin's groundbreaking study of the relation between originality and the simulacrum in photography (Benjamin 1969), Jack Kugelmass examines how mainstream American Jews utilize photographs of the Hasidic Other in helping to establish and stabilize their own Jewish identity. Kugelmass focuses on the *production of internal difference* within an ethnic group. The photography books analyzed by Kugelmass are, as he points out, not quite analogous to family albums, which serve to reinforce a preexisting sense of common identity. Rather, Kugelmass suggests that they sell themselves as a means by which self-styled "modern, acculturated" Jews can recognize the visibly different Hasidim as the Other within. In at least one of the books, Kugelmass says, "the author writes as if there existed some very great chasm between his subjects and his anticipated audience and that this project existed for the sole purpose of creating a bridge between two radically different sets of humanity where none had previously existed." Like the classic ethnographies analyzed by Johannes Fabian in his groundbreaking *Time and the Other* (1983), one of these books presents the contemporary Hasidic community of Williamsburg, Brooklyn, "as if it were located entirely in some kind of time warp." Like Pomo Indian baskets trapped in museum display cases, these icons may be articulated with the living world from which they are drawn (Sarris 1993), but only through a critical understanding of the many contexts in which our engagement with them takes place.

Kugelmass suggests that photographs are a particularly important part of the "portable homeland" of late-twentieth-century Jews, partly because "the physical tie to the Old World was fundamentally destroyed during the Holocaust." "Ties"—as both connections and constraints—to the Nazi genocide, through museum representations and the discursive space created by the term *Holocaust* itself, are the concern of Vivian Patraka's contribution. Patraka brings to the foreground the *uses* of "the Holocaust," most notably its crystallization as a major public component of Jewish identity. As necessary and imperious as the demands of commemoration may be, the fetishization of disaster—"Holocaust studies" as an academic subject, the very meal ticket of many Jewish studies programs—has given new life to the lachrymose conception of Jewish history as *primarily* a tale of endemic exclusion and suffering among compact majoritarian populations. Patraka documents what many of us could corroborate through personal memory: what is now called the Holocaust was once simply "the war." Far from simply "unmasking" or denouncing what has become the commonly accepted term, however, Patraka, like Kugelmass, suggests how we can engage cultural forms with a greater sense of responsibility for our place in the production of those forms. Without limiting the specificity of Jewish experience, Patraka wants to open up the comparative field of considerations that the Nazi genocide as an event of specieswide import seems to demand: "not just the violent elimination of a whole people, but all that goes into it: the beginning of terror, of the circulating discourses of oppression and exclusion, the constructing of a kind of state apparatus of oppression and the disinformation it produces, the incarcerations, and the wipeout and then the revolting denials and cleanups." Patraka thus refuses to leave the "Holocaust" as a cleaned-up icon.

Johannes von Moltke's "Identities on Display" further elaborates the connections between representations of identity and the politics of memory explored in different contexts by Kugelmass and Patraka. Von Moltke offers a "critical" reading of the contents and contexts of a major museum display on Jewish culture held in Berlin in 1992. He contends against the view that museums are but pale reflections of a lost plenitude, fragments shored up against a ruin, bulwarks against the overwhelming oblivion attendant upon "modernization." He is well aware that such an exhibit serves certain needs with regard to both German and Jewish collective identity. He knows that it is not innocent of the tendency, especially pernicious in the context of Germany's *present* difficulties with the cultural accommodation of "foreigners," to reinscribe the dichotomy between "Jews" and "Germans" that was so disastrously effective in Nazi ideology. And he cites the sardonic remark that the exhibit served to display Germany's "good intentions" in the best way, "by an intensive interest in Jews. But careful: not in living Jews..." Nevertheless, in what might be identified as resistance to the critical erasure of the possibility of *any* creative public recuperation and recirculation of lost frames of cultural meaning, he insists that debates occasioned by the exhibit went "a long way toward proliferating" the spaces available for the assertion and invention of Jewish difference in Germany today.

Contemporary Jewish difference and its relations to other differences are the themes of two essays in the volume: Maria Damon and Ann Pellegrini both explore the motives of Jews and African Americans, but not in the antagonistic frame within which they usually have been addressed in recent years. The two essays approach the issue from very different angles. Pellegrini begins by associating her work with a body of Jewish cultural studies that has investigated the construction of Jewish men as women within the "anti-Semitic imaginary of late-nineteenth- and early-twentieth-century Austria and Germany" and then asks: "What room does the intense, anti-Semitic identification of male Jews with 'woman' leave for Jewish women?" When she writes, moreover, "in the implicit equation of Jews and women, the Jewish female body goes missing," it is not only the anti-Semitic imaginary that she is critiquing but also the work of critics—including one of the contributors to this volume—who have not paid sufficient attention to this occultation. Through readings of the "racialized" female Jewish bodies of Freud's Dora, Sarah Bernhardt, and Sandra Bernhard, Pellegrini provides a highly nuanced understanding of the imbrications of race and gender, of the race/gender system, in the production and especially the performance of Jewish difference. The fact that Jews were so clearly marked as racially different and associated with blacks in the German-speaking cultural world, and the further fact that Sandra Bernhard performs her own identity as "African American" in her performance art, lead Pellegrini to some subtle and fascinating reflections of the interanimations of racial and gender categories and on the sociopolitical relations of Jews and African Americans in the United States. One highly significant consequence of her essay is to emphasize the inseparability of the European context of racism (i.e., anti-Semitism) from the American histories of racism, a separation that Paul Gilroy has taken pains to dissect as well (Gilroy 1993). Her essay is a contribution (and shows that Sandra Bernhard's work is also a contribution) to a rereading of the tense set of identifications and disses that mark Jewish and African American interaction in the contemporary United States.

Maria Damon takes a somewhat different tack in addressing the same set of issues. Where Pellegrini's own identifications and desires are ambiguously inscribed across her text, Damon adopts the frank autobiography that marks much of contemporary cultural criticism— cultural studies as bildungsroman. In a particularly rich moment, after describing her father's—largely successful—attempts at what she critically calls "assimilation" into a certain stratum of American culture, Damon describes how Yiddish jokes told by his "less crypto-

Jewish friends" would change her father's personality momentarily, and "the meek and decorous Anglophile scientist became for a moment a rowdy little boy—he was responding to real language." Damon makes clear, of course, that it is not that Yiddish per se is "real," but rather that "different vernaculars come to signify complicatedly in social self-constructions and social alliances." For many American Jews growing up when Damon's father was, social alliances with "Negroes" and indeed self-construction as black was not parodic, as it is for Sandra Bernhard—who in part riffs on precisely this tradition—but was crucial in personal and political critiques of American society. Her paper discusses three textual examples of Jewish men in the world of jazz and popular music who gravitated toward African American culture and wanted to associate themselves with it. Without romanticizing the strategy or ignoring its appropriative aspects and its misogynist overtones, Damon argues that "in different ways for each of the men I write about, blackness—and especially an appropriation of a black-identified language—becomes a way to be 'more Jewish' by providing a New World context for social critique, community, and an understanding of suffering and the 'human condition' both social and metaphysical." These two complex analyses, through the intensive reading of cultural materials, may help provide a somewhat different perspective (not a fix) on the problem of Jewish and African American relations in the United States today.

Daniel Itzkovitz focuses not on the charged relations between Jewishness and blackness, but rather on the work done in the broader culture by discussions of whether Jews are in fact "white." He begins by noting insistent, and only apparently confident, recent assertions by American Jewish writers such as Leslie Fiedler that by the middle of the twentieth century "the Jew has become...the symbol in which the American projects his own fate"—an assertion that would seem to corroborate the suggestion that, by now, Jews in America are unproblematically "white." Next, drawing on materials from the United States in the earliest decades of this century, Itzkovitz makes it abundantly clear that the racial identity of Jews was not just unsettled, but hotly debated; Kipling could refer to "a young Jew trying to appear white" at the same time that a Jewish apologist could insist that the anti-Jewish prejudice he opposed was by no means founded on racial grounds. Itzkovitz documents the complex of fears with which nativist Americans viewed Jews at that time, tracing out "the rhetorical slippage from murderer to Jew to millionaire to hostile foreigner to sodomite pervert." Bringing to light the racialist U.S. discourse on Jews, Itzkovitz reminds us not to be fooled into thinking that the important question is whether or not Jews *are* white. What is important is rather that this question is *taken to be important,* and its political charge reveals once again the covertly powerful link between nationality and race in the twentieth-century United States.

Ultimately there is no boundary line between images and displacements of Jewishness in "popular" culture and the Jewishness of high intellectual theory, between the marks of ethnicity imposed on or revealed by the body and the tropes of intertextuality deployed in the negotiation of different authoritative traditions. Where recent studies of Walter Benjamin's memory-work have emphasized the visual faculty, Jay Geller pushes the Benjaminian examination of the relationship among memory, sensation, and redemption in a new direction, sniffing out a covert olfactory thematics central to understanding how Benjamin's childhood Jewish milieu informed his adult writings. In Geller's analysis, even though the semicovert importance of the olfactory in Benjamin is indeed related to the traditional anti-Jewish trope of the "stinking Jew," its deployment in Benjamin's work far transcends the neurotic obsession with tainted origins. Geller's essay substantially advances what will no doubt continue to be a defining concern of Jewish cultural studies, the productive but troubled situation of Jewishness (or *Yiddishkeit*) in the origins of critical theory more generally.

The next four essays thematize in quite different ways the politics of language as a vital aspect of cultural studies. Chana Kronfeld interrogates the status of the "minor languages" within the theorizing of minor literature in modernism and especially in the Deleuze and Guattari essay "What Is a Minor Literature?" She argues that

> all too often the selective modeling of minor literature — as of "international modernism" — on a Euro-American geopolitics and linguistics effectively leaves all that is not English, French, or German (or "deterritorialized" versions thereof) outside our purview. This exclusion is not merely a result of a bad choice of examples but is logically entailed by the explicitly articulated principles of the most detailed theories of minor writing available to date. Only if we construct the major through the minor, not — as current wisdom has it — the minor though the major, can we begin to discern the regionalism, contextual diversity, and interdependence of even the most highly canonical forms of modernism.

Although she states explicitly that Hebrew and Yiddish modernism "do not fit into the postcolonial models now in vogue," it is, paradoxically, perhaps her essay that most directly intersects with theories of postcolonial literatures and their language politics. The choice of Yiddish and Hebrew writers of those languages — not even necessarily their "mother tongues" — to write in minor languages and not in German or Russian, is a response not entirely unlike that of those African and other writers who decline to write in English or French, as well as those Irish writers who write in Gaelic. In all these cases the connection between literary productions and practices on one hand, and nativism, nationalism, and diasporic and hybrid cultural identities on the other hand, is among the central questions of postcolonial theory. Kronfeld's central example, Avraham Ben-Yitzhak, close associate of Joyce, Schoenberg, Musil, Schnitzler, and especially Canetti, wrote several of his poems in German first and then in Hebrew — and did not publish the German versions. Yet, as Kronfeld shows, this was not a nativist impulse but precisely the deterritorializing critical move of the "minor." Kronfeld's essay, moreover, is the one that most explicitly represents its affiliations with Raymond Williams's work.

Daniel Boyarin's essay seeks to return diaspora to the Jews, not as their sole and privileged possession, but precisely to see how what has been learned about culture and hegemony in other situations of diaspora and colonization can teach us about the responses of Jews in antiquity and modernity to this situation. He considers several narratives of post-Temple Judaism, among which those from the Babylonian Talmud offer the instructive case of a group in diaspora constructing itself through reflections on the predicament of its own ancestors in their "own" land of Palestine under Roman colonial rule. By contrast, Hellenic-influenced texts such as the Book of Tobit or Roman-influenced ones such as Josephus's *History* are marked by the attempt to escape the colonial predicament through casting the colonized in the colors of the colonizer. At the broadest level, by studying shifts in paradigms of resistance and accommodation between earlier and later moments in Jewish cultural history, the author hopes to shed some light on the intersections between the politics of survival and of gender within diasporic communities in general.

Where Kronfeld's work considers the language politics of Yiddish and Hebrew together in the context of German and Russian modernisms, Naomi Seidman reckons the inner-Jewish differential political meanings of these two languages, especially insofar as they relate to gender — indeed, constitute a sort of gender imaginary within Ashkenazi Jewish society. Yiddish is *mame-loshn,* gendered female, while Hebrew is the "father's awesome, learned Holy Tongue" (Harshav), and thus gendered male. Taking this metaphor very seriously indeed, for its implications vis-à-vis the practices of gender within the East European Jewish cultural orbit (including Palestine) of the late nineteenth and early twentieth centuries, Seidman demystifies basic mythic and ideological structures of the "revival" of modern Hebrew. She argues that "the story of the revival of the Hebrew vernacular has been transmitted as a story about the conflicting claims of Jewish paternity and maternity, about the establishment of masculine control over areas of Jewish life traditionally in the hands of women, and about domesticity and guilt."

Ammiel Alcalay's work intervenes in two discourses that are intimately related to each other. The first is Europe's story of itself as the story of Christendom with the Jewish and Muslim presence on European soil neatly excised, and the second is the dominant Israeli cultural autogenealogy of itself as "European," effacing the cultural difference and cultural vitality of Arab Jews (and Christians and Muslims). Alcalay writes of the "deeper implications of the common fate of European Muslims and Jews faced with consecutive edicts of expulsion from Spain," namely, the ways that those extractions and exclusions "forced more than eight hundred years of 'Euro-Semitic' culture underground, forever marking Europe's own self-conception by excising itself of references to its tainted, impure past." Even more to the point, perhaps, "this suppressed chapter in European history returned with a vengeance in what has come to be our own legacy, during the Enlightenment and colonial periods when an imperial curriculum successfully managed to ethnically cleanse any references to Semites — Jews or Muslims — *that might indicate them to be both possessors of an autonomous history and inextricable partners in the creation of 'European' civilization*" (emphasis added). As significant as these considerations are, however (and "Western civilization" is all too much still with us), the most striking part of Alcalay's analysis is the way that he shows, paradoxically, that the construction of Europe as normatively Christian, non-Semitic, has powerful implications for the ways that the discipline of Jewish studies has been carried out in both the United States and Israel. Alcalay's querying of the excision of Jews and especially Sephardic Jews from the hegemonic narratives of Europe—and the ways that Hebrew scholarship has complied with this exclusion for its own cultural political purposes—can now be buttressed by referring to the work of two other critics, Marc Shell (1991) and Geoffrey Galt Harpham (1994).

Two radically divergent approaches to the cultural study of circumcision are exemplified in the essays by Gil Anidjar and Marc Shell. Utilizing a favorite strategy of recent work on medieval and early modern European culture, Shell focuses on a piquant point that calls into question both our spiritualized modern stereotypes of Christianity and our commonsense notions of the boundaries between Christian and Jewish identity. That point is the circumcision of Christ and the traditional relic that is his foreskin—"the only unambiguous trace of Jesus' actual flesh still on earth." Shell begins by documenting the medieval status of objects supposed to be the Holy Foreskin, which involved debates about both their authenticity and their ontological situation vis-à-vis other relics and the Eucharist. Building on this, he sketches out an analogous complex he believes is present in *The Merchant of Venice* and other texts. This other complex of relations ties together the association between circumcision and castration, and that between the "multiplication" of the phallus through the removal of the foreskin and the illegitimate "multiplication" of money by lending at interest. For Shell, then, the medieval *fetishization* of Christ's foreskin—as a precious *materialization* of a god who has become for the most part ungraspable, painfully unavailable spirit—is tied to the *demonization* of living, circumcised Jews.

In his consideration of circumcision as simultaneously the inscription of gender and the erasure of gender indeterminacy, Gil Anidjar follows the Derridean strictures of analytic writing, constantly attempting to evade the establishment of a fixed argument by pointing out the arbitrary presumptions inherent in each of the key points he articulates. Anidjar's investigation revolves around the twin polarities of memory and forgetting and of male and female. It attempts that which it acknowledges is impossible—a reading of circumcision that allows for the founding role of woman in the transmission of Jewish identity, for the possibility of reading "Jew" as "woman," while avoiding the twin traps of erasing the actual silencing of women's place in Jewishness and of reinforcing, once again, the assumption that the binary distinction between male and female is constituted within a given

Nature. This demand is addressed both to Anidjar's own procedure and to several recent studies that focus on circumcision as a *male* Jewish practice. Indeed, the intellectual aesthetic represented in this essay entails constant vigilance — a constant and often exasperating questioning of the "given" — as the only way in which an ethnic formation can be reimagined without at the same time reinventing repression. The essay exemplifies in turn the claim that "strong identities" can and should be the basis for the most sustained questioning — which is ultimately what this volume is about.

So . . . read, and question.

Bibliography

Asad, Talal, ed. 1973. *Anthropology and the Colonial Encounter.* London and Atlantic Highlands, N.J.: Ithaca Press/Humanities Press.

Benjamin, Walter. 1969. The Work of Art in the Age of Mechanical Reproduction. In *Illuminations,* 217–51. New York: Schocken.

Boyarin, Daniel, and Jonathan Boyarin. 1993. Generation: Diaspora and the Ground of Jewish Identity. *Critical Inquiry* 19(4):693–725.

Dominguez, Virginia. 1990. *People as Subject, People as Object: Selfhood and Peoplehood in Contemporary Israel.* Madison: University of Wisconsin Press.

Eilberg-Schwartz, Howard. 1990. *The Savage in Judaism: An Authropology of Israelite Religion and Ancient Judaism.* Bloomington: Indiana University Press.

Eilberg-Schwartz, Howard, ed. 1992. *People of the Body: Jews and Judaism from an Embodied Perspective.* Albany: State University of New York Press.

El-Or, Tamar. 1994. *Educated and Ignorant: Ultraorthodox Jewish Women and Their World.* Boulder, Colo., and London: Lynn Rienner.

Fabian, Johannes. 1983. *Time and the Other.* New York: Columbia University Press.

Fackenheim, Emil. 1978. *The Jewish Return into History: Reflections in the Age of Auschwitz and a New Jerusalem.* New York: Schocken.

Friedlander, Judith. 1990. *Vilna on the Seine.* New Haven, Conn.: Yale University Press.

Gilman, Sander. 1986. *Jewish Self-Hatred: Anti-Semitism and the Hidden Language of the Jews.* Baltimore: Johns Hopkins University Press.

Gilroy, Paul. 1993. *The Black Atlantic.* Cambridge, Mass.: Harvard University Press.

Goldberg, David Theo, and Michael Krausz, eds. 1993. *Jewish Identity.* Philadelphia: Temple University Press.

Goldberg, Sylvie Anne. 1989. *Les deux rives du Yabbok: La maladie et la mort dans le judaisme ashkenaze.* Paris: Le Cerf.

———. 1993. Les Études juives, héritage scientifique ou legs mémorial? In *Milieux et mémoire,* ed. Frank Alvarez-Pereire, 327–45. Jerusalem: Cahiers du CFRJ.

Grossberg, Lawrence, Cary Nelson, Paula A. Treichler, et al., eds. 1992. *Cultural Studies.* New York: Routledge.

Harpham, Geoffrey Galt. 1994. So . . . What *Is* Enlightenment? An Inquisition into Modernity. *Critical Inquiry* 20(3):524–56.

Hymes, Dell, ed. 1972. *Reinventing Anthropology.* New York: Pantheon.

Lambropoulos, Vassilis. 1992. *The Rise of Eurocentrism: Anatomy of Interpretation.* Princeton, N.J.: Princeton University Press.

Marcus, George, and Michael Fischer, eds. 1986. *Anthropology as Cultural Critique: An Experimental Moment in the Human Sciences*. Chicago: University of Chicago Press.

Marks, Elaine, and Isabelle de Courtivron, eds. 1980. *New French Feminisms: An Anthology*. Amherst: University of Massachusetts Press.

Neusner, Jacob, and Ernest Frerichs, eds. 1985. *"To See Ourselves as Others See Us": Christians, Jews, and "Others" in Late Antiquity*. Chico, Calif.: Scholars Press.

Sarris, Greg. 1993. *Keeping Slug Woman Alive: A Holistic Approach to American Indian Texts*. Berkeley and Los Angeles: University of California Press.

Shell, Marc. 1991. Marranos (Pigs), or from Coexistence to Toleration. *Critical Inquiry* 17:306–35.

Silberstein, Laurence, and Robert Cohn, eds. 1994. *The Other in Jewish Thought and Civilization*. New York: New York University Press.

Williams, Raymond. 1973. *The Country and the City*. New York: Oxford University Press.

1 / Surfacings: Thoughts on Memory and the Ethnographer's Self

Benjamin Orlove

At the 1993 American Anthropological Association panel called "Twice Strangers: Jewish Fieldworkers in the Christian West," few people drifted in late, and few left before the end. The audience in the crowded room listened with great concentration to Jane Sugarman describe the differing stories that Slavs, Albanians, and Greeks in Macedonia told her about the Jews from the region, taken away by German armies; to Stanley Brandes tell how, while he was attending Catholic religious services in Spain, he recalled the melodies he heard as a child at Yom Kippur services in a small Orthodox synagogue in the Bronx; to Marc Edelman first recount his gradual unpacking of the multiple meanings of the word *polaco* (Pole) in rural Costa Rica — Jew, Pole, peddler, stingy — and then link this understanding to racial discourses during subsequent briefer periods of fieldwork in Moscow and in the Bronx (where many Puerto Ricans and some African Americans, in certain settings at least, distinguish "Jewman" from whites); to Ruth Behar tell of her visit in 1992 to Turkey, the country from which her father's Ladino-speaking parents migrated to Cuba. The sense of involvement between panelists and audience continued through these papers, through the other presentations, and through the discussion as well.[1]

Two apparently opposed themes ran through this excited engagement between speakers and audience. The first was the novelty of a session centered on the experiences of Jewish researchers. Earlier examinations of Jewish themes had occasionally created some room for self-reflexive accounts by Jewish researchers but remained subordinate to the primary purpose of describing and analyzing particular Jewish groups and populations (Kugelmass 1988). The "Twice Strangers" session, by contrast, brought together an interest in the examination of Jewishness as a form of identity with a self-reflexive concern about ethnography.

This novelty stands in apparent opposition to the second aspect of the panel: its familiarity. In the oral versions of their papers, the panelists emphasized the similarities of their experiences through frequent spontaneous references to each others' papers. Many members of the audience were also eager to describe experiences of their own that paralleled the ones described in the papers. They did not have to return to files of field notes to check the details of their stories, or even to scrutinize their memories; instead, their descriptions of their recognition of their position as Jews in non-Jewish field settings were close to the surface, vividly recalled and vividly retold.

Many of the papers included stories that had been told before, but in other contexts: to one or two colleagues at coffee one afternoon, to relatives at a family gathering after returning from the field. It was the formal public nature of a professional meeting, rather than the stories themselves, that was new. The collective nature of the panel encouraged the presenters, who might have been less ready to tell intensely personal stories to a large audience if others had not similarly revealed themselves. Several people used the word *catharsis* to describe the effect of hearing all the papers.

There were differences as well as commonalities in the group of field-workers in Europe, Latin America, and the United States. We included different types of U.S. and Canadian Jews: some with one, some with two Jewish parents, with differing numbers of generations that separated us from our Ashkenazic and Sephardic immigrant antecedents. Yet we represented a fairly narrow range of ages, from the late thirties to the early fifties, and we were predominantly from large metropolitan areas of the northeast United States and adjacent portions of Canada. Older Jews and Jews from small communities might have been more cautious about speaking out, but we had felt the influences of the 1960s—the civil rights movement and ethnic revivals, the general orientation toward self-expression. Moreover, we had been exposed not only to the major Jewish organizations and movements in North America, but also to newer Jewish cultural forms that stood in some kind of opposition to them: to the writings of Amos Oz, Cynthia Ozick, Marge Piercy, Philip Roth, and others, to the films of Woody Allen, to magazines such as *Lilith* and *Tikkun,* and to religious and political alternatives such as *chavurot,* egalitarian minyans, and Peace Now.

As the participants, the discussants, and the audience all noted, though the papers had been written independently, most or all of them contained certain themes: the dilemmas of Jewish ethnographers, faced either with the dangers of hindering their research if they reveal themselves as Jews or with a lingering sense of inauthenticity if they do not; the particular ways in which Jewish ethnographers encounter discrimination; the difficulties of fitting Jews into national histories and identities of the countries in which we conducted field research and of the United States. Perhaps a key element of the panel lay in the storytelling mode itself, some suggested. Was this mode distinctive to Jews, to minorities, to ethnographers, to sessions on little-discussed topics?

Much of the discussion remained on this level of specificity. Dissatisfied with the particularities of the comments, and concerned about the marginality of studies of Jews (now reworked as the study of ethnographer-Jews) within anthropology, several individuals looked for more general overarching themes. A line of analysis proposed by several people first noted the inner nature of the distinctively Jewish experiences presented in the papers, which the ethnographers had not revealed to their informants, and then suggested that the panel really was about the contrast between private and public aspects of fieldwork. This contrast, in turn, was developed by those who wished to retain both a sense of Jewish distinctiveness and a vision of anthropology as a scholarly field committed to objectivity and truth. Following a somewhat old-fashioned epistemology of science, these people suggested that private, subjective experiences could support public, objective research by expanding the array of possible hypotheses that can then be examined or by directing scholarly attention to little-studied phenomena. More simply, these private experiences could increase the commitment of researchers to the discipline, making them more willing to undergo the rigors of fieldwork.

I found this formulation dissatisfying. Though at first I could not fully articulate my objections to it, I have since come to see how this formulation arose. Not only did it fit in with the prior theoretical commitments of its proponents, it was already so much in the air. The public/private contrast is a small step from the panel's juxtaposition of familiarity and novelty, from the transportation of old stories to new audiences. Moreover, this distinction between public and private aspects of the self opened up the topic of the nature of the ethnographer's self in general.

This distinction between public and private aspects of the self corresponded to a neat division between the ethnographer and the Jew within each of the panelists. As a trained professional, the ethnographer operated in public realms, while the Jew—whether defined in ethnic or religious terms—was a private individual. The deficiencies of such alignments became a central topic of the conversations among the groups of panelists, discussants, and audience members who went out to dinner and then regrouped at the bar of the hotel in which the conference was held. We finally disbanded well past midnight, these issues unresolved—an unsurprising outcome, granted the centrality of matters of selfhood, identity, and the "Other" to debates within many academic fields and within American society at large.

There are clear parallels between examining the ethnographer's self and examining the Jew's self. Taken separately, each raises a notion that has been widely accepted for a long time—that the self is not a unitary subject, but rather a complex entity, since different aspects of the self, as ethnographer or as Jew, emerge in different contexts. Taken jointly, these aspects raise the issue of the overlaps and connections among the various elements of the self, and therefore call into question the notion of the fragmented self. The observation that individuals possess multiple identities—along lines of gender, nationality, race, class, and the like—is often taken to suggest that the self is a mosaiclike set of pieces. To link Jewishness and the practice of ethnography is to raise more complex forms of coexistence and interactions among multiple identities. The title of the session, "Twice Strangers," offered a useful initial account of these interactions that, on discussion and reflection, seemed inadequate. I want to renew the discussions left unfinished in the hotel by turning to the two core sections of my own paper at the panel, a set of fieldwork stories (drawn from my dissertation research in highland Peru in 1971–72 and from a more recent research project conducted in the Lake Titicaca region in highland Peru and Bolivia in 1979–81, 1983, 1984, and 1985), and an examination of some issues of selfhood.

Surfacings in the Field

Turks and Moors

During the seventeen months in the early 1970s that I lived in Sicuani, a market town in highland Peru seventy-five miles from the city of Cusco, I would often walk through the main square, on my way from the two rooms I rented to some spot on the other side of town — the market or the post office or the priests' residence or the wide place on the road where I could catch a truck out to a peasant village. On the times when I returned home early, I would sometimes stop in the store of Annette Miguel, a member of a trader family of Middle Eastern origin in Sicuani.[2] I found her an engaging person to talk with: nervous, thoughtful, witty, and a bit of an outsider like myself.

Annette Miguel's family, and two other families whose large stores were also on or near the main square in town, were called *turcos*. Yet they were not Turks at all, but the descendants of the Arabs who arrived in Peru from what is now Syria, Lebanon, Israel, and Palestine. Nor were they Muslims, as most Turks are, but instead Christians, whose Maronite beliefs and practices were virtually identical to those of the Roman Catholic Church; they participated, though to a more limited extent than the families of Peruvian origin, in local Catholic religious life. They attributed the term to the fact that their grandparents and great-grandparents, arriving from Ottoman provinces before World War I, carried Turkish passports. At one point, after I had revealed to Annette that I was Jewish, she told me that her daughters had sometimes been followed home from school by other children who would simply call out after them "turca, turca."

I do not know whether Annette was aware of the jokes about the *turcos* that circulated in town. One provided an explanation for her Uncle Fuad's name. His birth was a particularly long one. After many hours of labor in which he did not emerge from the womb, it occurred to someone to shake a bag of coins in front of his mother's vagina. Upon hearing them jingle, he was in a hurry to grab them. "Fuad" was the sound that he made as he popped out. Another joke told how the patriarch of another *turco* family, lying on his deathbed, called to his children in turn. Each one replied, "Yes, father, here I am." The old man's final words were, "And who's minding the store?" The punch line was identical to that of the joke I had heard in the United States about Jewish storekeepers. Through such jokes, anecdotes, and gossip, the local people maintained an image of the *turcos* common to other trader minorities and, of course, to Jews: tightfisted, clannish, unsociable.

These highland Peruvians also had another label for an exotic people: *moros*, Moors, who appear in a variety of settings. They are one of the numerous types of people, animals, and mythological beings represented by masked dancers in festivals around Sicuani and in nearby provinces;[3] they are linked to the figure of Santiago Matamoros, a saint whose image appears in many churches. He is widely believed to have appeared in 1535 during the Spanish Conquest on a battlefield outside the city of Cusco, where he killed many Indians and assured the Spanish victory, much as he appeared in 718 on the battlefield of Covadonga in Asturias to kill many Moors and to begin the *reconquista*, the reconquest of the Iberian Peninsula, a process that lasted until 1492, the year not only of Columbus's landfall but also of the expulsion of the last Muslims and Jews from Spain. Local people use the expression *hay moros en la costa* — there are Moors coming to the coast — to mean that someone nearby might be eavesdropping on a conversation, or that an uninvited person might be about to drop in on a gathering. I never heard people connect the terms *turco* and *moro*, nor do I recall hearing the terms *árabe* (Arab) and *musulmán* (Muslim) in everyday conversation.

With such categories as the exotic *turcos* and the virtually mythological *moros*, where did I fit in? Certainly I was a *gringo*. This word, I discovered, included not only North Americans, but also many others who resented the term even more than I did: most Europeans, any fair-skinned or blond person, and even some Europeanized Peruvians from Lima. Gringos, like *turcos*, were an exotic people who came from a distant place. And Jews were more like *moros*: figures from tales and dances more than from everyday life. Jews were mentioned in the sermons and the readings from the Gospels that accompany masses, and figures representing Jews might appear in folk dramas, the passion plays that accompany some Catholic festivals, though they are not as directly manifest in the Andes as the masked figures of *judios*, Jews, who scamper, tricksterlike, in the plaza of the central

Mexican village where one of the participants in the "Twice Strangers" session conducted her field research (Friedlander 1975:143).

A New Name

To the mestizo shopkeepers, artisans, and officials of the market town of Sicuani, and to the Indian peasants in the surrounding villages, I was not Ben or Benjamín. They knew me by my middle name, Sebastian, a name that had been so unusual in the neighborhood in Brooklyn in which I grew up that I had revealed it only to a few close friends. Though Benjamín was not unknown in Peru, it was less common than Sebastián, and I wanted to fit in as much as possible. Moreover, I felt an impulse to break from my former life and transform myself into a new person in the field: not so much going native as going away.

Reflection affords a few instances in which I became aware, consciously or nearly so, that I chose not merely the somewhat more Peruvian, but also the definitively less Jewish, of my two given names. In a joking tone, I told several people that I'd had numerous inoculations before traveling to South America to imitate San Sebastián, martyred by arrows. When Peruvians, on seeing a document or meeting me in the company of other Americans, would find out that my other name was Benjamin, they would often ask me whether I was the youngest child in my family, since, Joseph-like, Peruvians often do bestow this name on a final child. These moments would raise the possibility of alerting others to the fact that I was Jewish. More often, though, I would either simply reply affirmatively or, alternatively, state that I was named for my grandfather. I rarely reflected, though, on the name Sebastián. I simply took it on, as I took on having sugar in my coffee, wearing socks to bed, pointing with my lips rather than my fingers, and the other new habits and rhythms — done sometimes alone, sometimes in view of others — that reduced the difference between me and the locals while making Sebastián more distinct from Ben.

And who was this Sebastián, who had hidden his hiding of a Jewish name even from himself? Whatever my name, I was inescapably a gringo, defined by the passport and identity papers without which residence in Sicuani would have been difficult, and marked by my strong accent. If I needed to be distinguished from the few other gringos in the area — the American priests and nuns, a few Peace Corps volunteers, the tourists who might get off the train en route between Cusco and Lake Titicaca — it would be as the gringo who spoke Quechua, a

Quechua with certain gaps in vocabulary but nonetheless passable, and certainly more fluent than the halting phrases of the other gringos in the area who attempted the language.

When local people mentioned physical differences between me and them, they invariably pointed to my great height rather than the skin color or hairiness that many North Americans presume would distinguish them from highland Peruvian Indians. Here, too, I would attempt an awkward joke, explaining that, having been born and raised near sea level, I had to grow particularly tall to come close to the sky, unlike the fortunate mountain dwellers, who needed no special effort to achieve this end. Only to a few would I say — and it seemed very frank to me at the time — that I grew up in a rich country where even working people like my parents could afford plenty of meat. This disclosure opened up a series of truths: I sought to find injustices in many realms of life, I had a strong identification with political economy orientations in anthropology, I was eager to study the workings of capitalism in the Latin American periphery and to link them to the North American core. My dissertation (1975) and the monograph (1977) that resulted from it traced the ways in which the international economy (in the specific form of wool exports) had shaped regional society in the remote highland interior of Peru. The privileges of powerful North Americans such as myself, I believed, included research grants as well as protein, but I could readdress these injustices by forming part of a global community of scholars committed to change. When I joined a protest march to challenge a visiting government minister, I quite sincerely felt that I had every right to take part in chanting "Obreros, campesinos, estudiantes, unidos venceremos" (Workers, peasants, students, united we will triumph).

On the few occasions when my presence was questioned, usually by peasant leaders or high school teachers, it was as a gringo, more specifically as a suspected CIA agent. Once I felt real fear, when the head of a peasant union demanded a detailed account of my reasons for living in Sicuani. I congratulated my accuser for his advanced political awareness and warned him about genuine CIA agents. I told him, "All that I have of the CIA is the 'I,' the intelligence." At this point I was able to move the conversation in the direction of international solidarity through a discussion of left-wing movements in the United States.

So clearly a gringo, could Sebastián have been a Jew? A circumcised penis, the sign by which Jewish men are known in many Christian settings, was not a point of disclosure. Men and women in highland Peru, generally modest, tend to avoid uncovering much of their bodies in public, or looking at those of others. Moreover, unlike North American men, who usually place their thumbs above their penises when they urinate, their other four fingers below, Peruvian men follow the obverse, more concealing, pattern—another one of the local habits that I adopted.

Most people assumed that I, like everyone they knew, was nominally a Catholic. Some of the more sophisticated townspeople, or the peasants more exposed to the evangelical Christianity then just beginning to make inroads, might ask me if I were a Catholic or a Protestant. If I did not wish to begin an extended conversation, I could cut off discussion with evasive but technically honest replies such as, "I rarely went to church when I was a child" or "My parents were not very religious." Quite often, though, I would simply say that I was a Jew. This response was almost always taken as a joke. I soon discovered how to evoke further laughter. "No, no," I would continue. "I *am* a Jew, my two parents are both Jews, and all four of my grandparents were Jews." The matter was sealed; the more I insisted on my status as a Jew, the more my listeners would laugh. There were only a few people whom I thought I had succeeded in convincing that I was Jewish. But even these individuals, when I raised the subject weeks or months later, would claim no knowledge of my being Jewish. Had they forgotten, I wondered, were they hinting that I should not bring up this uncomfortable topic again, or had they simply been unable to hold in their minds two contradictory images, the one of the Sebastián they knew and understood to be a gringo, the other of the semimythological Jew?

Aside from Annette and the other *turcos,* there were a few people whom I was able to tell that I was a Jew. The majority of these people, I believe, were the priests and nuns, a category that totaled a dozen or so, two Americans, two Irish, a Spaniard, a Colombian, and the rest Peruvian, split more or less evenly between people of coastal and highland origin. We developed a specific and enduring reciprocal fascination, since most of the Peruvian clergy, and one of the Irishmen, claimed to be members of a category of which I had heard since child-

hood but whose existence had never been confirmed to me: the peo-
ple-who-had-never-met-a-Jew-before. I was as intrigued by their questions as they were by my answers: Did I believe in God? Did other
Jews? What was a Jewish church like? After the first few weeks, these
questions abated, but they never entirely ceased, since some religious
holiday or new event in Middle Eastern politics could bring the topic
up once again. Yet my association with the clergy, if anything, would
have led local people to assume first that I was not a Protestant mis-
sionary of any sort and second that I was most likely a Catholic.

It was through the clergy that I met the one peasant family who
knew me as a Jew. Lizzie, a progressive American nun, spent a good
deal of time in the village of Hercca, about fifteen kilometers outside
Sicuani, where she set up discussion groups of health care issues and
engaged in several sorts of community development and conscious-
ness-raising activities. In Hercca she stayed in the home of Anselma,
a single woman with two small children. Anselma raised crops in her
few small fields, tended a flock of sheep, and received some wages
for her work in fields belonging to more prosperous peasants. When
other clergy traveled out to the villages, they tended to stay with the
richer families, most often older married couples. Anselma offered
Lizzie a contact with the humble poor to whom her religious and political convictions, including a nascent feminism, directed her; in turn,
Lizzie offered Anselma not only a route to more respectability and
the possibility of urban connections and employment, but also some
balance to her domineering mother and stepfather, who sought to in-
tervene frequently in her life. The two women had developed a close
friendship by the time that I met them, despite the poor Spanish they
both spoke. Lizzie did not invite other gringos to Hercca often, but
she did ask me to come, for, I believe, a wide range of reasons: curiosity about my anthropological insights and my proffered services
as an interpreter, fascination with me as a specimen of the counterculture, attraction to the range of ecumenical possibilities I offered,
and, finally, our shared pleasure in the intense personal conversations
we began soon after we met.

I spent several days in Hercca early on in my fieldwork, visiting
peasant families during the day and talking about politics, religion,
and personal matters with Lizzie in the evenings. Lizzie told Anselma
that I was Jewish soon after I arrived there. Once I completed my
brief explanation of Jewish religion and identity, we did not return to

the subject. I spoke with Anselma primarily about agriculture, markets, and village politics, and joined her and her children once to help a relative weed a large onion patch. Anselma seemed concerned that Lizzie be present when I was in the house, in part to allay any suspicions her parents might have about her ties with men. My Jewishness surfaced only once, one evening when Lizzie, Anselma and her children, and I were finishing dinner. Lizzie asked me to help her gather up the dishes and wash them. Anselma's younger child, a boy, was picking some bits of food from his soup bowl with his fingers when Anselma, perhaps self-conscious in front of an outsider such as myself, began to scold him for his lack of table manners: eat with a spoon, she told him, the way one should eat, not like an animal, not like a jungle Indian who hasn't even been baptized. She suddenly cut herself off in midsentence, turned, and ran out of the room, in embarrassment, I believe, in realizing that I, too, had not been baptized and that I could have been insulted by the comparison to animals and to *chunchos,* the term she had used for the Amazonian Indians.[4] Lizzie picked up the little boy, who was puzzled by his mother's abrupt departure. Anselma came back in the room later and seemed quite awkward with me for the rest of the evening. We never discussed that moment, or mentioned the fact of my being a Jew. Anselma struck me as reserved on the few occasions when I saw her later on in the course of my fieldwork, once at a wedding in Hercca, a few times in Sicuani when she came to visit Lizzie. Was this reserve mere embarrassment, or something stronger — horror, perhaps, at recognizing me as an unbaptized person? The local people, reluctant to take an unbaptized baby out of the home in which it is born, certain of the existence of the limbo to which the souls of babies go if they die unbaptized, clearly took baptism seriously. But my unbaptized status rarely surfaced in their minds, since gringos existed in the everyday world, Jews in the realm of tales.

One family with whom I spent a good deal of time knew me as a Jew. Francisco and Yolanda owned the corner store on the block on which I lived in Sicuani. A middle-aged couple with one daughter, they became my surrogate parents. They were the ones I would drop in on when I wanted to take a break from typing up field notes, the ones I told of my trips out to the Indian peasant villages, the ones to whom I passed on bits of news from letters from my parents, the ones who asked for me with genuine concern if I returned from a trip to an outlying village later than I had planned. Theirs was the one family whose parties I regularly attended, and in turn it was in their house that I organized a celebration after receiving a letter from my parents announcing that my one remaining single aunt had gotten married. Jewish themes surfaced in a few of our conversations about each others' families. My stories of the immigration of my father and of my mother's parents from Eastern Europe formed a counterpart to Francisco's parents' migration to Sicuani from the Peruvian city of Arequipa, halfway between the coast and the highlands. My openness about being Jewish was, I believe, a key step in our gradual process of establishing a deep frankness and confidence.

The Shaky Crown

One day I had stepped out from my rooms into the street and saw Francisco and Yolanda in the crowd that gathered at a mass held in a chapel in the small plaza in Sicuani near their store. It occurred to someone who was present to propose that I join the other men who were about to bear an image of the Virgin Mary on their shoulders in procession around the town. Though we formed the standard group of six, three on each side, the crowd found the spectacle amusing. Nearly a head taller than all the other men, I had to walk in a half-crouch so that my shoulders would be on the same level as theirs. Had I been in the front or back, the man at the opposite end could have lowered himself a bit to compensate for my height, but, positioned as I was in the middle of the three men on the Virgin's right, I had to take great care not to raise the image. People shouted out remarks to me in Spanish and Quechua, and took my grunted replies as very humorous. As I walked, with each step my legs extending far forward because of my bent knees, a popular image from underground comics drawn by Robert Crumb came to mind: Mr. Natural, whose exhortation to "Keep on truckin'" I was following at that very moment.

Several blocks down the street from the chapel, the entire group halted. The silver crown on the Virgin's head had begun to shake a bit and looked as if it might fall off altogether. The other five bearers and I stood as still as we could, and the crown settled itself down. A soft murmur of relief passed through the crowd, and we continued our procession. Whether it was the greater care that the other men and I took not to rock the image or the fact that our route took us from streets paved with cobblestones to newer, smoother concrete surfaces, the crown remained steady, and the festive atmosphere resumed.

Francisco and Yolanda made no mention of the teetering crown, and I, concerned that I might be faulted for causing a near-disaster, did not bring it up with them. I did talk it over with one of the Peruvian priests most interested in what he termed "traditional Catholicism." He thought that any blame for causing the crown to fall would have been laid on the people who lived in the house in front of which the event had occurred. Only much later did I begin to think through an alternative series of events: what if the crown had fallen, what if it had struck and injured or even killed someone? What, then, if the crowd had learned that I was a Jew? Would I have been to blame, would Francisco and Yolanda have been criticized as well, or the priest who had performed the mass? I thought of a story that I had heard several times in which another local Virgin had punished (*castigado*) a possibly non-Christian individual. The story was the explanation for the mysterious drowning, over twenty years before the time of my fieldwork, in a nearby lake of several members of a family of storekeepers. This family, the Miguels, close relatives of Annette's, were *turcos*. According to the version I heard, a lovely young woman entered the family store one Sunday in the middle of the afternoon, when the streets were nearly empty because everyone was having their dinner. She asked for credit to buy a bolt of blue cloth. The storekeeper refused, and she turned and left without speaking. At that moment the storekeeper realized that he had never seen this beautiful woman before. Wanting to talk to her, he ran out after her, but she had disappeared. The following Saturday, the storekeeper and his wife took their children to a nearby lake for an excursion. On a calm, cloudless afternoon, their boat capsized, and they all drowned. The people of Sicuani soon hit upon an explanation: the young woman was the image of the Virgin contained in the largest church on the lake, an image that is never taken out on procession. Wanting to replace her worn blue robes with new ones, this image took on human form and came to the richest store in town to request the cloth. She then returned to her church, and soon afterwards punished the *turco* who refused to give her credit. The people in the small town on the lake did provide her new robes soon after the drowning.

It was fortunate that this story of the Virgin's punishment did not occur to me as I stood while the crown of another Virgin trembled, since I would have found the thought extremely unsettling. I do not think that it occurred to the Peruvian priest with whom I spoke, or (though I am less certain of this) to Francisco and Yolanda. As I myself did, they kept the knowledge of my status as a Jew separate from their other thoughts. I was Sebastián, the gringo. What might have happened if they, or others, had realized that I was unbaptized, a Jew, a worse demon than a CIA agent?

Punch Lines

Before one of my return visits to the Lake Titicaca region, I received a call from a sociologist who worked for a small government agency, the Inter-American Foundation. He wanted me to travel to Bolivia and evaluate a small-scale agricultural development project that was attempting to process and sell quinoa, a drought-tolerant Andean grain. Sympathetic to the project's effort to develop markets for local crops, I accepted the offer. The week in a remote arid region of southern Bolivia proved interesting. The local people seemed pleased with this gringo whose Spanish was quite good, and whose Quechua was intelligible. Riding from village to village in a project jeep, sitting at the project headquarters waiting for an agronomist to arrive, I had many opportunities to chat with the Indian peasants. They asked me many questions about the United States and a few about Peru, and I indulged my curiosity about topics unconnected with marketing grain but of great interest to me: the villagers' obligation to serve government officials as unpaid porters, the local peasants' labor migration to Chile, the strange square stone altars located in the corners of some villages.

On one occasion, sitting in the sun in front of one of the project buildings, we began telling jokes. After telling a few jokes entirely in Spanish, one of the men began another joke in Spanish and then switched to Quechua. I held my breath, concentrating as hard as I could to catch every word, and then laughed all the harder at the humorous punch lines from the relief at having understood the Quechua ... and from something else, something that I sensed but could not specify. It took a few moments for this additional reason to surface: I heard the voices of my father and my uncles, at a family gathering, telling jokes in English with Yiddish punch lines, most of which I could understand. Suddenly wrested from the Andes back to New York, I was pulled back to the Andes again. The villagers had recognized the joke as an example of a genre, and began telling other jokes in Spanish with Quechua punch lines. I listened as they continued until we were interrupted by a secretary who called us in for a meeting to plan the next day's schedule. Throughout the next day, English jokes with Yiddish punch lines kept popping into my mind.[5]

I do not wish to rush to a point of anthropological comparison of dual identities, subordinate languages, code-switching and humor, nor to a point of methodological discussion about the ways that Jewish responses to hegemonic national identities prepared me to understand similar responses by indigenous groups. I want, rather, to stress my sense of surprise at the parallel. What was it that made this specific instance of connections between Bolivia and Brooklyn so unexpected, that made the general possibility of such instances so familiar?

The Fugue Aloft

On another of my return visits to the Lake Titicaca area, my flight out of Miami was delayed several hours because of mechanical problems. Rather than taking off soon after lunch, it was not until well into the afternoon that the few passengers were allowed to board. The plane spent some time on the ground, while the flight attendants served free drinks, and took off quite late. I read for a bit and then, relieved to be finally on my way, I looked out of the window. An enormous dark green shape lay below me: Cuba, already in shadow. Off in the distance were vast thunderheads, their bottoms dark gray, their tops a soft pastel in the last light of the sun. How lush the Caribbean looked even from this perspective, so unlike the Central Valley of California from which I had come, so unlike the remote high mountains to which I was headed.

Half dozing off, I kept looking at the clouds, and suddenly a thought hit me: the Incas are their David and Solomon, and the remote mountain villages their *shtetlach*. And more, I realized, both we and they face an uncertain world in which our memories may become untellable, in which our distinctiveness is invisible. How tenacious we both are, I thought, and settled down, this time falling asleep.

Idle notions on airplanes rarely remain in my mind, but this one had a force that engraved it more permanently, this identification of a "we" and a "they" that I had not known I was thinking of. It has since become easier for me to understand the force of this notion. In writing a memoir, *In My Father's Study*, about growing up as the son of an immigrant, I gained new understanding of the impulses that led me to conduct fieldwork in the Andes. There were professional and intellectual concerns that I had long acknowledged, and political ones as well; though I am no longer a student antiwar activist, I still believe that anthropologists can take part in public debates on broad questions. I have been aware, as well, of the draw of adventure, of the aesthetic appeal of mountain landscapes. But the key insight that the memoir gave me has been the discovery that, by living for years in the Andes, I could relive, face, and accept my double sense of loss: that I would no longer live within the extended family and the neighborhood in Brooklyn in which being Jewish was taken for granted, and that I would never see the prewar Eastern Europe of which my relatives spoke so often. I would be hard-pressed to think of a place that could satisfy, more than the Andes could, this impulse to attempt a return. The world to which I have been drawn for my anthropological work, like the world of my grandparents and the world of my childhood, lies on the fringes of Christendom.

The Question in the Anteroom

My final story takes place in 1990 in Quito, Ecuador, where I joined a number of scholars from Latin America, Europe, the United States, and Canada and a few Andean Indian activists at a conference on the theme of power and violence in the Andes.[6] At this conference I presented a paper on the Indian and mestizo narratives of political violence that drew on archival sources—newspaper articles, telegrams, and notarial documents—as well as conversations I had held in the field (Orlove 1991). Since I had written about some of the violent events from a more conventional political economy perspective (1980), the paper at the conference was a particularly clear step in my intellectual path from studying history alone to studying history and memory jointly, from an exclusively materialist perspective to one that also took ideology and culture into account.

One evening, a number of participants stood in the anteroom of a large meeting room in the hotel, where a formal presentation of a new book would begin in fifteen minutes or so. I was chatting with another participant, a Spanish woman, Teresa, whose conference paper focused on witchcraft accusations by officials of the Inquisition during the colonial period. At one point she asked me if I was Catholic or Protestant. When I told her that I was Jewish, she smiled broadly.

She shifted her weight from one foot to the other and back, rocking in delighted silence for a few seconds before telling me yes, how perfect. I recall the rest of our conversation well enough to recount it (she met very few Jews in her life, and never knew any of them well; she had some simple questions about Judaism; she was thrilled with imagining my sense of kinship with Indians, as I was thrilled to construct my own imagined version of the struggles involved in her academic feminist work as Spain was making a transition away from Franco's rule). In considering what led her to ask me her question, I can look both at my presentation itself (my possibly unusual depiction of Christian imagery; my possibly unusual degree of detail in considering divisions within the pre-Christian period of the history of the Andes, unlike the more conventional use of the Spanish Conquest as the one major divide in Andean history) and at the discussion after the presentation of papers and at meals—in which a major theme was the banter between Protestants and Catholics (including some priests, members of orders that had been active in the evangelization of Peru). The Latin Americans, to my knowledge, were all Catholic, though there were other divisions of gender, race, class, and nationality. The entire tenor of the conference, then, might have led Teresa to be attuned to issues of difference among Christians, and these issues might have reinforced the assumptions that North Americans, Europeans, and Latin Americans shared a common Christianity.

My conversation with Teresa did lead me to revise my paper for publication in slightly different directions than I might otherwise have taken; in particular, I addressed themes of savagery in greater detail. It is not the effects of the conversation on my scholarly writings that I wish to address, however, but the possibility of the conversation itself. First, it strikes me that David Gilmore, the organizer of the "Twice Strangers" session, chose well in restricting the panelists to Jewish ethnographers who had worked in Christian countries. Other panels may fruitfully address Jewish ethnographers in Muslim, Buddhist, Hindu, and fully secular countries. Had I chosen a different area of the world in which to specialize as an anthropologist, and had the conference been held not in Quito but in Rabat or Bangkok or Kathmandu, how different the dynamic between me and the other possible Teresas would have been.[7] Second, and more importantly, the space of Jewishness in academic anthropology is not just in the field or in published text pages, but in many intermediate spaces like the anteroom, the room in the former mansion where many different sorts of people can mingle and ask each other questions that are both personal and academic.

And finally, what had led me to reveal myself so willingly and thoroughly to Teresa? In earlier years, had I missed opportunities for such lengthy conversations? Had it not been for my openness in Sicuani with Lizzie, Annette, Francisco and Yolanda, I might not have moved on to the fugue on the plane. I might have diverted Teresa with a different answer: "Oh, I didn't get much of a Christian education," I could have said, a remark that I could have repeated to some relatives and friends. But the path that I began in Sicuani has continued through the anteroom, the "Twice Strangers" panel, and into this volume.

Reflections

Of the many aspects of selfhood that these stories raise, there are three that I would like to emphasize. The first is the issue of vulnerability: the sudden recognition that my Jewishness could place me at risk of harm from the non-Jews among whom I lived. After the Indian peasant woman Anselma, chastising her child for his uncivilized way of eating, was reminded of my own uncivilized condition, she treated me with much greater reserve. Though this withdrawal itself was in many ways an impediment to my fieldwork, an obstacle to the development of my relations with other people in the same village, I also realized that such exclusions could place me at far greater levels of danger. Had the Virgin's crown not merely shaken but also fallen and struck someone, the implications could have been severe indeed.

Balancing this vulnerability is the second aspect, the sense of intimacy that I felt: the sudden recognition that my Jewishness led me to share some experiences of the non-Jews I had come to know. On some occasions, I did not overtly express this intimacy, either because I was alone at the time or because I did not want to disrupt the flow of interaction. On other occasions, though, I did reveal my sense of connection. With Annette Miguel, the *turca* storekeeper, a commonality as outsiders provided the link; with my neighbors Francisco and Yolanda, exchanging stories of parents' migrations, of tangled dynamics of extended families, gave a kinlike bond in which many personal details were shared. Had I been careful to prevent these feelings from surfacing in conversations, they probably would not have surfaced as easily in my moments of solitary reflection and thought.

The third aspect is what I call the availability of memory. Many images from the past seem to inhabit some zone close to my consciousness: someone tells a joke and I remember other jokes that I heard from relatives and friends; I have a drink on an airplane, fall off into a reverie, and find myself thinking not only of the recent past and immediate future, but also of the grandmother I knew and the other grandparents and great-grandparents who died before I was born; chatting with a colleague at a conference, I find myself recounting stories of my childhood in Brooklyn. These various Jewish pasts are not simply an ethnic identity, concentrated in one piece of my self and absent from others, nor are they a cultural heritage, stored in a chest and removed ceremoniously on holidays and other occasions. Neither of these terms suggests the paradoxical qualities of these memories: the ease with which they can rise to the surface, their capacity for remaining below the threshold of visibility as well.

The long history of the Jews as a diasporic people connects these three different aspects (Boyarin 1994:242–60). The conditions of being dispersed among other peoples, of frequently living in close communities but never constituting the majority population, create both the sense of vulnerability and the feeling of intimacy. The availability of memory comes on the one hand from the absence of the undiluted attachments to homelands, sovereigns, and national histories that often characterize majority populations and on the other hand from the corresponding importance of retaining the multiple and disparate pasts (Anderson 1991).

At a few points, I felt something close to the "double consciousness" that W. E. B. Du Bois described (1968), of being simultaneously an American and a specific other, with Jewishness substituting for blackness. At other points, I experienced directly the familiar image of the Jew as the universal other; as the prototypical outsider, I could identify with Indians and with *turcos*. However, these aspects of Jewishness did not line up so neatly with a precise bounded identity. Instead, they had a looser and more local dimension—of humor and of a familial coziness captured by the Yiddish word *heimishkait,* homeyness, a charged word for diasporic peoples who lack homelands. These different associations, though, are too intermingled to allow me to disentangle them—to place on one side Jewishness as an instance of multicultural diversity, on another Jewishness as an instance of diasporic identity, on a third Jewishness as a piece of my personal biography.

Indeed, these feelings of vulnerability and intimacy and this availability of memory are familiar to virtually all ethnographers. Some manuals on fieldwork emphasize these fluctuations between poles of feeling: at times unprotected and defenseless against outsiders, at other times accepted and welcomed into their close confidence (Freilich 1977).

Memoirs of fieldwork also bring forward the third element, the theme of sudden recollections of the past, a connection that leads some to propose a similarity of fieldwork to psychotherapy or psychoanalysis. My reflections take me in a different direction, to note the diasporic nature of anthropology itself. When I was first in the field, I thought often of my fellow graduate students and went to some effort to correspond with them and to arrange visits to each other's field sites. The student cooperative houses, the seminar rooms, the bookstores, and the coffeehouses of Berkeley figured in our conversations as our distant homeland. This aspect of fieldwork heightens the diasporic sense of anthropologists, who share with most academics a dispersion in multiple centers (of university departments, museums, and the like) across the country, and who gather periodically for conferences. Even the intellectual activity of ethnography itself often takes the form of the availability of memory. Ideas do not enter an ethnographer's mind only as abstract entities, confined to the period of the writing and reading of field notes; they can appear as snatches of concrete conversations with concrete individuals, remembered in unexpected moments. Ethnographers are not just highly trained researchers who have internalized the professional and scholarly parameters of a field; they are also human beings whose work life includes many sorts of enduring social relations, many kinds of memory.

The term *surfacing* that I have been using throughout this essay seems appropriate for these three different elements of the stories and of my experiences. I prefer it to the notion of a "fragmented" identity. Objects that surface seem more dynamic and flexible than the static and rigid qualities of fragmented ones. To my ear at least, fragments sound as if they have firm, sharp edges, whereas things that surface have softer edges, sloughing off some small pieces and accreting others. Fragments, one might imagine, could be glued back together in a somewhat weakened and cracked version of a former whole; things that surface keep changing in appearance, and an entirely new side can swim into view. *Surfacing* also draws attention to the medium through which objects move. The images of Jewishness have surfaced in a reverie on an airplane, in a relaxed moment in an Indian peasant woman's house, during an exchange of jokes outside a development project building—taking form more slowly or more suddenly, leaving many ripples or few.

The Ethnographer's Self

The examination of selfhood can lead to an examination of some recent critiques of ethnography. Reduced to their simplest form, these critiques claim that ethnography can become a subtle and textual form of domination (Marcus and Fischer 1986; Clifford and Marcus 1986). Even when ethnographers claim to present directly the people they study by including direct quotations from these people, they are still controlling and shaping the text, and thus the image of the people about whom the text is written. By speaking for others while claiming to be allowing them to speak, the ethnographer engages in a kind of authorial duplicity. This troubling dilemma becomes especially acute because of its association with other forms of domination; the ethnographers, inevitably educated, usually from wealthy nations, often white and male, reinforce hierarchical orders through their insidious silencing. The apparently simple solution—to have the ethnographized become the ethnographers—cannot eliminate this difficulty, as recent studies of feminist and indigenous ethnography suggest (Stacey 1988; Abu-Lughod 1991; di Leonardo 1991; Limón 1991; Narayan 1993; Visweswaran 1994). The critiques have often centered on negative consequences for the represented objects of ethnographic inquiry, though they have also suggested the highly contingent self-representation of the ethnographer; these two pieces, at any rate, are inseparable, since they form essential elements of the challenges to objectivity.

Many ethnographers, eager to restore to ethnography the possibilities of truthful representation or of genuine political engagement, have questioned such postmodernist critiques on a variety of grounds (Gudeman and Rivera 1990). The "Twice Strangers" session, and my own reflections that preceded and followed it, lead me to raise certain issues with the presentation of the ethnographer's self in this postmodernist critique.

First, it is a gross oversimplification to bifurcate the many sites in which anthropologists engage with other people into two categories, the public sphere of producing texts and the private sphere of field-work. Ethnographic textual production is heavily dialogic, not only in its use of intratextual dialogues in the forms of direct quotation and reference, but also in the social production of texts themselves. The examples I have given here are not wholly idiosyncratic. The con-versations with particularly observant local people and nonanthro-pological outsiders, the development of early versions of texts as lec-tures, the circulation of presubmission drafts, the peer review process and other such mechanisms do not merely heighten the rhetorical ap-peal to truth; unlike literary genres and conventions, with their prior existence, these direct interventions place limits on the ability of authors to invent themselves. It is the absence of the social person of Carlos Castaneda, as well as qualities internal to his texts, that have limited the acceptance of his writings as ethnographies. The effec-tiveness of Clifford's destabilizing (1988) of such early foundational ethnographies as *Argonauts of the Western Pacific* and *The Nuer* rests in part on the record of the social presence of Malinowski and Evans-Pritchard, rather than on close readings of their texts alone.

This multiplicity of sites in which ethnographers engage as ethnog-raphers leads me to a second questioning of the postmodernist cri-tique, which presumes that ethnography follows certain spatial and temporal patterns. It contrasts the "there" where fieldwork is con-ducted with the "here" where ethnographic texts are produced and circulated, paralleling the contrast between the "then" of fieldwork, a time of openness when people speak and act in the presence of ethnographers, and the "now" of writing, a time of closure when ethnographers select and rework. As Gupta and Ferguson (1992) have shown, the growing importance of migrants, refugees, and other such populations have eroded this spatial separation. In these "global ethnoscapes" (Appadurai 1991), ethnographic texts are often read, and challenged, by the people about whom they are written.

As I have presented it, there is little that is wholly new in this chal-lenge to a postmodern view of the ethnographer's self. It is the route to this challenge that may constitute the element of newness in the "Twice Strangers" panel, and in this essay. Some feminist anthropol-ogists, for example, have arrived at this challenge from their cer-tainty of their subordinate position within patriarchal cultures and from their sense of commitment to political change (Mascia-Lees, Sharpe, and Cohen 1989; di Leonardo 1991). Others have proposed a critical cosmopolitanism (Rabinow 1986). Still other ethnographers may find nothing startling in the commingling of different aspects of their selves in fieldwork, in writing, and in other sites as well.

What might be somewhat newer in this challenge is the route that I have taken to arrive at it: the expansion of the notion of diaspora, linked both to Jewish and to ethnographic selves. The diasporic elements of the ethnographer's self heighten the sense of vulnerability on the one hand, the possibility of surprising discoveries of affinities and connections on the other. Moreover, the issue of memory is central to the ethnographic self as to the Jewish self. In majority populations in nation-states, the past, though often selective, can be well structured and heavily represented (Anderson 1991; Bhabha 1990); for members of diasporas, the past is fragile. There is no single principal path, always open to lead one to the diasporic past. Instead, there are a series of smaller tracks, each of them susceptible to obliteration if they are not frequented (Boyarin 1992:52–76). For anthropologists, too, the multiple aspects of selfhood lead to a kind of diasporic identity that places a great reliance on memory. This urgency of diasporic memory presents itself in particular forms in the case of ethnography, where past and present always intermingle in a complex and fluid manner. As other writers have noted, ethnographic research creates an availability of multiple pasts, and a corresponding unboundedness of the field itself (Stacey 1988). Memory does not begin when the ethnographer crosses the divide between "then" and "now" in leaving the field, since ethnographers engage actively with memory in the field. The memories of the field, moreover, are not permanently fixed by writing. They remain open to the ethnographer for further reexamination and to others who can respond to them.

Is There a Jewish Closet?

In a recent article, Dominguez raises a "complicated dynamic" that she "strategically dub[s] the epistemology of the Jewish closet" (1993: 622), borrowing on Sedgwick's notion of the epistemology of the closet (1990).[8] Dominguez writes:

> Closeted identities, [Sedgwick] argues, have particular epistemologies, and ghettoizing strategies, I would add, have particular histories. Some closets and ghettoes are externally imposed; others are strategic or self-

imposed.... Both closets and ghettoes entail confinement and disability, but they also sometimes produce space of one's own or room in which self-acknowledgment, assertiveness, and experimentation can take place safely. Those affected may feel resigned, indignant, relieved, or fearful, but never unaware.... Those in both closets and ghettoes often feel a desire for choice that can feed a complicated illusion of freedom. There is, after all, rarely a let-up in the need to manage and strategize one's encounters in accordance with one's choice. To be or not to be openly gay? To be or not to be assertively Jewish? (1993:622)

A variant of the Jewish closet appeared in the "Twice Strangers" panel. The presenters were in some sense engaged in a public coming out, as were the discussants, both of whom mentioned their own Jewishness early in their remarks (Sedgwick 1990:75–82). The sense of excitement at the session came in part from this saying publicly what had already been known. There was another dimension of the closet. The participants all understood that we would not engage in any outing (Gross 1994). We named as Jews only the long-dead pre-decessors (Durkheim, Mauss, Boas) and very senior scholars (Lévi-Strauss) whose Jewishness was well known. We remained silent on others: the senior scholars, a decade or two older than us, who had not spoken broadly about being Jewish; the anthropologists of our generation who had declined invitations to participate in the panel; the Jewish ethnographers who conducted fieldwork in non-Christian settings (and therefore were not invited). There was no discussion beforehand how to handle this topic. Nor did we reflect on the question of how we came to know whom to invite in the first place: like gays, Jews believe that they have the ability to recognize others like themselves.

There are many further directions that this comparison could take. Does the legal protection of religious freedom and the prohibition of certain sorts of discrimination offer Jews in America a kind of security lacking to gays? Does the debate over whether American Jews more resemble European Americans, whose ethnicity is partly a matter of choice, or people of color, whose race is determined, correspond to the debate over whether homosexuality is a preference or an orientation? Does anti-Semitism correspond to homophobia, and is there an equivalent to compulsive heterosexuality for Jews — normalized Christianity, perhaps, or a Protestant civic culture? However, I would like to return to the issue of surfacings, to an anterior and more individual-centered account of the moments of recognition.

Dominguez, focusing on the issue of management, points primarily toward the interpersonal and relational domains of concealment and revelation, of "openness" and "assertiveness"; I have sought to complement these with the intrapersonal domains of thought, reflection, and self-awareness. I have discussed the multiplicity of selves and the availability of these different selves—raising, as it were, the epistemology of the anteroom as well as of the closet. In particular, I have examined how my Jewish self interacts with my other selves, American and anthropological. The link to Dominguez's account, then, would begin with a comparison of the communalisms of the ghetto and the closet—and how the communalism of the ghetto surfaces outside the ghetto, in the forms of intimacy and of memory as well in the form of vulnerability. Dominguez provides another useful suggestion in her remark about the historical nature of ghettoizing strategies. Much as "closet" and "outing" are recent forms of talk, so too the "Twice Strangers" session reflected, if it does not seem immodest to suggest it, a particular point in American Jewish history and, moreover, an intersection with an especially self-reflexive moment in the history of anthropology.

Complex Selves and the Public Sphere

Do these stories and reflections lead to any conclusions? They point, I think, to notions of the self that, though certainly not new, stand in opposition to other widely held positions: on the one hand, a distrust of narrative so strong that it leads to indeterminacy, to the impossibility of anchoring any accounts of experience in historical processes or systems of power; on the other hand, a certainty about axes of categorizations that place individuals in well-defined boxes of gender, nation, race, and class. The former might propose a fragmented self, at most the product of certain forms of representation; the latter would map selves out onto already-established subject-positions. My stories and reflections suggest a complex self, with many countervailing trends and tendencies—but a self nonetheless capable of listening and speaking, of many forms of inner reflection and of conversation. This view echoes with notions of hybridity and with the more general potential for a public sphere of discourse: a view of difference that suggests not a precise and rigid geometry of identity and opposition, but rather shifting fields of encounters and exchanges (Gates 1993; Robbins 1993; Baker 1994).

The Jewish elements in my stories and reflections heighten certain attributes of these fields. They indicate the great vulnerability of individuals within these fields, a point increasingly apparent in a world of nationalist violence, warfare, and massacre. They note the precious possibility of the creation of moments and spaces of homey intimacy. Above all, they show the capacity of the past to resist being forgotten, to reappear with surprising freshness. Voices from the past, it turns out, are not engraved in memory, nor do they echo or reverberate; they are still speaking.

Many of the pasts that I have described are Jewish pasts, but not exclusively so. Nor do I wish to suggest that they are the only types of Jewish pasts; as I have suggested, the "Twice Strangers" session took place in a particular historical moment and drew on the experiences of a specific cohort of Jews. I refer instead to certain modes of witnessing and retelling. I am struck by the affinities between these modes and some current trends in anthropology that have occurred after the collective incorporation of postmodernist and self-reflexive critiques. Some of these stress the ties between anthropologists and the people with whom fieldwork is conducted; Gudeman and Rivera, for example, propose that conversation is as crucial a verbal mode of fieldwork as the writing of field notes or the composition of ethnographic texts, as they demonstrate in their own jointly written works on Colombia (1990; see also Brush and Orlove 1995). Others emphasize the links between anthropologists and the readers of anthropological texts; Scheper-Hughes calls for anthropologists to serve as moral witnesses (1992:26–30), carrying tales of the hard lives of the poor and the weak to wider audiences, as she has done in her own work on Ireland, Brazil, and South Africa.

Cultural difference and the public sphere: these themes are of great urgency in the world in which this book appears, a world less than a decade past the threat of a nuclear apocalypse, a world less than a decade away from the new century whose arrival we await with hope and fear. In this world, the notion of citizenship faces many threats. To suggest that citizenship is compatible with cultural differences, I have told you my stories and my reflections on them: tales of the unexpected ways in which my acceptance of my own particularities, as an anthropologist and as a Jew, have led me to find many moments of openness, to enter into new forms of conversation and exchange.

Notes

I would like to thank the Program in Jewish Studies at the University of California at Davis for the opportunity to present this paper. I am grateful to the friends and colleagues who offered thoughtful suggestions and comments on previous drafts: Ruth Behar, Jonathan Boyarin, Virginia Dominguez, Yosef Meyerowitz, Harriet Murav, and Bruce Rosenstock.

1. Not wishing to extend an already-long first paragraph any further, I have given an incomplete listing of the participants. In the panel, organized by David Gilmore, seven people presented papers (Marc Edelman, Jane Sugarman, Judith Friedlander, Jack Kugelmass, Ruth Behar, Stanley Brandes, and me), and two served as discussants (David Kertzer, Michael Herzfeld).

2. In this chapter, I often use pseudonyms for individuals, though not for places.

3. Although I do not recall seeing people wearing *moro* masks right in the provinces of the Sicuani region, they certainly were common in festivals in nearby provinces, figuring prominently in the patron saint festival, the Virgen de Carmen, of Paucartambo in the department of Cusco, and in festival dances in valley towns of the province of Chivay in the department of Arequipa.

4. The *chunchos* are another example of semimythological beings. The highland Quechua- and Aymara-speaking Indians know of the Amazonian Indians through the plume-wearing dancers who appear in festivals (Portugal Catacora 1981:92–97; van Kessel 1981:158–201) and through the headdresslike motif in textiles (Wilson 1991).

5. In an earlier version of this essay, delivered at the "Twice Strangers" session, I included some examples of the jokes. One Yiddish speaker expressed his offense at the vulgarity in the jokes—which included scatological terms—with such vehemence that I thought it better to drop the jokes; I recalled as well the time that a Peruvian anthropologist, raised in a bilingual household in a small highland town, chastised me for including a similar Quechua joke in another article. The two felt the same impulse—to protect their subordinate nonstate languages from the charge of being coarse and uncultured. In respect for that impulse (which I share only partially), I omit the jokes, available in any case in collections of folk humor.

6. This conference had been organized by the Working Group on Andean Anthropology and History, a subgroup of the Latin American Council on Social Sciences.

7. One colleague commented that certain unstated presumptions were at work in selecting among Christian nations, because countries such as South Korea and Malawi—both with large Christian populations—were excluded. I agreed with him; we had in fact restricted ourselves to Europe and Latin America, without offering an explicit justification for this decision.

8. In his comments on the "Twice Strangers" panel, David Kertzer made reference to Dominguez's article and examined some of the issues I discuss in this section.

Bibliography

Abu-Lughod, Lila. 1991. Writing against Culture. In *Recapturing Anthropology: Working in the Present,* ed. Richard Fox, 137–62. Santa Fe: School of American Research Press.

Anderson, Benedict. 1991. *Imagined Communities: Reflections on the Origin and Spread of Nationalism.* 2d ed. London: Verso.

Appadurai, Argon. 1991. Global Ethnoscapes: Notes and Queries for a Transnational Anthropology. In *Recapturing Anthropology: Working in the Present*, ed. Richard Fox, 191–210. Santa Fe: School of American Research Press.

Baker, Houston A. Jr. 1994. Critical Memory and the Black Public Sphere. *Public Culture* 7(1):3–33.

Bhabha, Homi K., ed. 1990. *Nation and Narration*. London: Routledge.

Boyarin, Daniel. 1994. *A Radical Jew: Paul and the Politics of Identity*. Berkeley: University of California Press.

Boyarin, Jonathan. 1992. *Storm from Paradise: The Politics of Jewish Memory*. Minneapolis: University of Minnesota Press.

Brush, Stephen, and Benjamin Orlove. 1995. A Conversation on Conversations. *American Ethnologist*. In press.

Clifford, James. 1988. *The Predicament of Culture: Twentieth-Century Ethnography, Literature, and Art*. Cambridge, Mass.: Harvard University Press.

Clifford, James, and George Marcus, eds. 1986. *Writing Culture: The Poetics and Politics of Ethnography*. Berkeley: University of California Press.

Di Leonardo, Micaela, ed. 1991. *Gender at the Crossroads of Knowledge: Feminist Anthropology in the Postmodern Era*. Berkeley: University of California Press.

Dominguez, Virginia. 1993. Questioning Jews. *American Ethnologist* 20(3):618–24.

Du Bois, W. E. B. 1968 [1903]. *The Souls of Black Folk: Essays and Sketches*. New York: Johnson Reprint.

Fox-Genovese, Elizabeth. 1993. From Separate Spheres to Dangerous Streets: Postmodern Feminism and the Problem of Order. *Social Research* 60(2):235–54.

Freilich, Morris, ed. 1977. *Marginal Natives at Work: Anthropologists in the Field*. Cambridge, Mass.: Schenkman.

Friedlander, Judith. 1975. *Being Indian in Hueyapan: A Study of Forced Identity in Contemporary Mexico*. New York: St. Martin's.

Friedman, Jonathan. 1992. Narcissism, Roots, and Post-Modernity: The Constitution of Self-Hood in the Global Crisis. In *Modernity and Identity*, ed. Scott Lash and Jonathan Friedman, 331–66. Oxford: Blackwell.

Gates, Henry Louis Jr. 1993. Beyond the Culture Wars: Identities in Dialogue. *Profession* 93:6–11.

Gross, Larry. 1994. *Contested Closets: The Politics and Ethics of Outing*. Minneapolis: University of Minnesota Press.

Gudeman, Stephen, and Alberto Rivera. 1990. *Conversations in Colombia: The Domestic Economy in Life and Text*. Cambridge: Cambridge University Press.

Gupta, Exhale, and James Ferguson. 1992. Beyond Culture: Space, Identity, and the Politics of Difference. *Cultural Anthropology* 7(1):6–23.

Kugelmass, Jack, ed. 1988. *Between Two Worlds: Ethnographic Essays on American Jewry*. Ithaca, N.Y.: Cornell University Press.

Limón, Jose E. 1991. Representation, Ethnicity, and the Precursory Ethnography: Notes of a Native Anthropologist. In *Recapturing Anthropology: Working in the Present*, ed. Richard Fox, 115–35. Santa Fe: School of American Research Press.

Marcus, George, and Michael Fischer. 1986. *Anthropology as Cultural Critique: An Experimental Moment in the Human Sciences*. Chicago: University of Chicago Press.

Mascia-Lees, Frances E., Patricia Sharpe, and Colleen Ballerino Cohen. 1989. The Postmodernist Turn in Anthropology: Cautions from a Feminist Perspective. *Signs: Journal of Women in Culture and Society* 15(1):7–33.

Narayan, Kirin. 1993. How Native is a Native Anthropologist? *American Anthropologist* 95(3):671–86.

Orlove, Benjamin. 1975. *Alpacas, Sheep and Men: The Wool Export Economy and Regional Society in Southern Peru.* Ph.D. dissertation, Department of Anthropology, University of California, Berkeley.

———. 1977. *Alpacas, Sheep and Men: The Wool Export Economy and Regional Society in Southern Peru.* New York: Academic Press.

———. 1980. Molloccahua 1931: Un levantamiento campesino en el sur del Perú. In *Rebeliones indígenas quechuas y aymaras: Homenaje al bicentenario de la rebelión campesina de Thupa Amaro 1780–1980,* ed. Jorge Flores and Abraham Valencia, 133–54. Cusco: Centro de Estudios Andinos Cusco.

———. 1991. La violencia vista desde arriba y desde abajo: Narrativas oficiales y campesinas de encuentros conflictivos en la sierra sur del Perú. In *Poder y violencia en los andes,* ed. Henrique Urbano, 237–59. Cusco: Centro de Estudios Regionales Andinos.

———. 1995. *In My Father's Study.* Singular Lives: The Iowa Series of North American Autobiographies, ed. Albert Stone. Iowa City: University of Iowa Press.

Portugal Catacora, Jose. 1981. *Danzas y bailes del altiplano.* Lima: Editorial Universo.

Rabinow, Paul. 1986. Representations Are Social Facts: Modernity and Post-Modernity in Anthropology. In *Writing Culture: The Poetics and Politics of Ethnography,* ed. James Clifford and George E. Marcus, 235–61. Berkeley: University of California Press.

Robbins, Bruce. 1993. *The Phantom Public Sphere.* Minneapolis: University of Minnesota Press.

Scheper-Hughes, Nancy. 1992. *Death without Weeping: The Violence of Everyday Life in Brazil.* Berkeley: University of California Press.

Sedgwick, Eve Kosofsky. 1990. *Epistemology of the Closet.* Berkeley: University of California Press.

Stacey, Judith. 1988. Can There Be a Feminist Ethnography? *Women's Studies International Forum* 11(1):21–27.

Taylor, Charles. 1989. *Sources of the Self: The Making of the Modern Identity.* Cambridge, Mass.: Harvard University Press.

van Kessel, Juan. 1981. *Danzas y estructuras sociales de los andes.* Cusco: Editorial Bartolomé de las Casas.

Visweswaran, Kamala. 1994. *Fictions of Feminist Ethnography.* Minneapolis: University of Minnesota Press.

Wilson, Lee Anne. 1991. Nature versus Culture: The Image of the Uncivilized Wild-Man in Textiles from the Department of Cuzco, Peru. In *Textile Traditions of Mesoamerica and the Andes: An Anthology,* ed. Margo Schevill, Janet Berlo, and Edward Dwyer, 205–20. New York: Garland.

2 / Jewish Icons: Envisioning the Self in Images of the Other

Jack Kugelmass

As social life becomes more fragmented and anonymous, we
express ourselves in a photograph. The more fragile our identity,
the more we need to reinforce it. To show that we exist.
                    HALLA BELOFF, *Camera Culture*

Photography and its social impact are subjects for continuing intellectual rumination. Scholars and critics such as Walter Benjamin (1980), Pierre Bourdieu (1990), Susan Sontag (1977), John Berger (1982), and Roland Barthes (1981) have suggested ways either to interpret photographs or to understand their impact on a world that increasingly knows itself through the mechanically reproduced image (Goldberg 1991). While most of these authors are concerned with the history of photography as a phenomenon that emerges from and has a peculiar impact on industrial society and, during the latter part of the nineteenth century, on the bourgeois conception of the self (Sekula 1981), others increasingly are examining specific photographic subgenres, particularly the snapshot (Coe and Gates 1977; Chalfen 1987; King 1978) and the posed photograph (Alloula 1986; Geary 1988; Trachtenberg 1989). For folklorists and anthropologists, both genres are of interest because they figure prominently in family productions. Indeed, the invention of photography in the first half of the nineteenth century coincided with the social transformation of Western society that ultimately affected the family. Photography became important because it alone could endow ruptured social units such as families "with visible histories and genealogies" (Goldberg 1991:105).

Although most observers have considered photographs not as collections but as autonomous objects unrelated to one another, recent studies have begun to look at collections (Alloula 1986; Edwards 1992; Geary 1988; Lutz and Collins 1993; Trachtenberg 1989), and a particularly interesting development from the standpoint of photoethnography has been the increasing attention paid to family albums (Chalfen 1991; Lesy 1980; Walker and Kimball Moulton 1989). Walker and Kimball Moulton include in this category the family album designed to document an evolving set of relationships; the event album (weddings, retirement parties, trips); autobiographical albums featuring "images of the people places and things that were important to the maker"; and albums documenting special interests such as hobbies, avocations, vocations, and objects of adoration (1989:172–74).

Walker and Kimball Moulton's assertion of the intimate nature and private art form of photo albums (ibid.:166) is correct only if the genre is restricted to the personal document. But clearly there are photo albums that serve the needs of collectivities much greater than the individual and the nuclear or extended family (Chalfen 1983:83). High school yearbooks are a case in point, as are the coffee-table albums that manage to make the most mundane city appear glamorous and cosmopolitan. Nor can picture magazines be left out of our consideration. Through what it chose to represent, *Life* naturalized the consumer, family, and domestic patterns of a single class within America (Kozol 1994:183). In like manner, by reproducing the world photographically, *National Geographic* miniaturizes it and helps to frame the American national purview—particularly the purview of its dominant class (Lutz and Collins 1993). And there are a variety of other albums intended for sale to groups, defined according to gender, interest, occupation, and particularly ethnicity.[1]

In this essay, I intend to argue that certain types of commercially created photo albums may play a role for large collectivities such as ethnic groups much like the role played by family albums for extended families. They celebrate group unity in the face of widespread dislocation, they provoke group memory, and they may even contribute to a collective dialogue on the nature of group patrimony and the perceived problem of cultural attenuation and social fragmentation.

This essay grows out of a larger study on the public culture of American Jewry. Thus far, I have looked at Jewish food and restaurants (Kugelmass 1990), living history museums, and the recent popularity of pilgrimages to Poland (Kugelmass 1992, 1994). I intend to include in the study a broad range of phenomena including popular literature and the iconography of the Jewish home. Here I present another part of this project—the image of the Hasid in the vernacular culture of American Jewry.

The five books I shall examine here are probably not a complete collection of photo books on this subject, yet I doubt that their number is much greater than the ones I have seen. They form part of a larger body of images of Hasidim that continually appear in magazines and other forms of graphic and plastic arts. Moreover, as I shall argue, their significance has more to do with their place within a broader genre that I shall call Jewish folk ethnography. But more about that later.

The books I examine are Frederic Brenner, *Jérusalem: Instants d'éternité* (1984); Leonard Freed, *La danse des fidèles* (1984); Philip Garvin, photographs, and Arthur Cohen, text, *A People Apart* (1970); George Kranzler, with photographs by Irving I. Herzberg, *The Face of Faith: An American Hassidic Community* (1972); and Mal Warshaw, *Tradition: Orthodox Jewish Life in America* (1976).

The opening section of Kranzler and Herzberg's *The Face of Faith* contains a series of images of religious institutions, synagogues, and other buildings in the Williamsburg section of Brooklyn. There is a section titled "The Men of Williamsburg" with shots of individuals either walking in the street or posing at home or in study halls, sections on women and children, on weddings, on livelihood, and on holidaying in the Catskills. Although the format suggests an ethnographic approach and the author of the accompanying text is familiar with this community, the book reads as a eulogy, less analytical than apologetic. The author writes as if a great chasm existed between subject and audience and his project existed solely as a bridge between two radically different sets of humanity where none had previously existed:

> The photographs of Williamsburg do not hide the drab setting of a low-income community, nor the wrinkles and creases in the faces of its people. They show the Old-World garb—Kaftan, velvet and fur hats, beards and Peyes [side locks] and various familiar and strange tokens

of otherness. If viewed in the proper frame of reference, the photographs reveal what is behind the extrinsic features. They communicate the inner dignity, the warmth, the boundless faith and inspiration that make Hassidic Williamsburg unique in the variety of American ethnic and religious communities.(5)

Consider this passage from the epilogue:

> Williamsburg is a testimony to the ethos of a tortured and persecuted but proud people that dwells in a realm of eternal values, regardless of the temporary setting and conditions that affect their individual, social, and communal lives. This Hassidic spirit of Williamsburg infuses the drab, dreary brownstone ghetto of the low-income neighborhood in Brooklyn, N.Y., with warmth, love, and inspiration. The ecological, economic, and social features recede. They merely serve to heighten the joy of communal living, of life itself, of survival and of confirmation of a faith that overcame concentration camps and gas chambers, as it had survived the tortures of Roman arena, auto-da-fes [*sic*] of the Inquisition, and the pogroms of Cossacks in the past. (111)

The panchronism apparent in the last statement is not a rhetorical flourish. It pervades the book. Hasidim are represented here as timeless manifestations of an authentic Jewish spirituality. Take, for example, the text that accompanies an image of a man in his fifties with divided white beard and carrying a *talis* (prayer shawl) bag looking downward as he walks: "Serenity: Inner concentration—reflecting the afterthoughts of the morning prayers and study. Meticulous, stately, self assured, he is the Elder of a value-directed community." Or an image of a man of about the same age photographed walking past a large brick wall: "Seriousness-distrust: Cast against the wall, he evokes memories of bitter experiences, of walls, of suffering and persecution—yet, he rises above it in mystic transcendence." Or one of the last images in the book, a portrait of a young Hasidic male somewhere in the Catskills: "Introspection: Long, deep thoughts in the wilderness, atop the mountains, inspire the serious young scholar as he ponders problems of his talmudic research."

Face of Faith is less an anthropological photo book than a kind of family album—a compilation of snapshots of people and places from the distant past. If it is reminiscent of the *kunstbaylage,* the weekend art magazine supplement of the *Jewish Daily Forward,* which reproduced during the 1920s and in 1930s rotogravure images of Eastern Europe, it is only vaguely so in that it represents by its existence the curiosity Jews have about other Jews removed from them by time and space. Yet *Face of Faith* lacks the sardonic tone and the deep familiarity the *Forward* generally used to picture traditional Jewish life. Indeed, the impression one gets both from the images and from the text is of Williamsburg not as the Old World—for that would imply something familiar—but as something much more ancient, as if it were located in a time warp. Upon entering it, we are linked, if not to biblical space and time, then to something very close to it. For example, the caption that accompanies a portrait of a middle-aged man with flowing beard and hair alludes to the resemblance between him and contemporary counterculture figures:

> "Channeled inspiration: It is more than the Yarmulkeh [skull cap] that differentiates him from the guru. His is not a rebellious flouting of conventionality, nor a turning to mystic sources for exotic inspiration and wisdom. His kind, joyous face speaks of the beauty of tradition and the infinite wisdom that has guided and inspired Jews through treacherous waters of physical exile for many centuries. His spiritual existence has never left the banks of the river that flows from heaven to earth and back. (24)

Williamsburg represents not so much the Old World as a very ancient world. Although the book attempts to bridge the gulf between that world and ours by stressing the kindliness of its inhabitants and showing us smiling faces, festivity, and considerable sociality, nowhere do we engage these people directly. Apparently the gulf is too large, or perhaps we are unworthy. Rather than dialogue, the book presents us with a series of timeless images—mementos from another time and another place. Our task, then, is to look, to admire, perhaps to emulate, but not to question.

Garvin's *A People Apart*, published in 1970, two years before *Face of Faith*, offers a similar sense of respectful distance. The cover image of a group of Hasidic men in black cloaks and hats with their backs to us is reminiscent of the closing image of *The Face of Faith*. But where *Face* shows us a benign representation of two older men strolling and chatting, the image in *A People Apart* is slightly menacing—a stationary group with smoke in front of them; they are performing the annual ceremony of burning leavened foodstuffs before Passover. The photographs in this book are overwhelmingly of study, prayer, and ritual. They are deeply black images—partly the result of poor mechanical reproduction, but partly also a matter of choice—of masses or groups of men in dark clothes engaged in religious activity. Individuals rarely appear. There are only a few photographs of women and children. There are no portraits of family life or of quotidian leisure; the few images of work all illustrate the centrality and ubiquity of the religious infrastructure of booksellers, scribes, kosher food vendors, wig sellers. Only the images of relaxing at summer retreats permit some variation: children doing calisthenics or riding bicycles, a boy opening a melon, women playing Scrabble, a posed image of a man about to toss a football. But these are very much the exceptions. This is a book about a religious idea, about Hasidism, not about a people or a community, and what we see is a world of intense devotion. It may hold some attraction for us, but it is much too foreign ever to be our own. In the words of Arthur Cohen, the author of the text, "the difference between them and us is that they are certain of their goal and their work," while "we are very much confused about the goal and the work" (32). Here there are encounters with Hasidim but a muteness nonetheless. They do not speak to us directly, and when they do it is largely unintelligible. Cohen describes a meeting arranged by a fellow student with the Lubavitcher rebbe, the leader of the largest Hasidic group and the one most committed to proselytizing among nonobservant Jews:

A Sunday night in winter. It was 1951. February or March, I think. Cold, wet, blustery, and the hour of eleven o'clock at night when the Lubavitcher Rebbe received petitioners, a fact which seemed to me somewhat mysterious. In my world, people were less than likely to be at their best near midnight. But this was not the case on Eastern Parkway. The vestibule where we sat . . . was crowded with people going back and forth, some waiting simply to speak with those who came out from the rebbe's study, to hear anything the rebbe might have said that could be of meaning to them.

We waited nearly two hours. It was almost one o'clock when we entered; a desk, books, and a line of simple chairs on which visitors were to sit. We remained standing until the rebbe asked us to be seated. Dov Slotnik [a fellow student at the Jewish Theological Seminary] spoke for us. The rebbe offered to speak in English, but he said he preferred to talk in Yiddish. He talked in Yiddish and I understood scarcely anything. The few words I spoke to him, in reply to questions, I phrased in halting Hebrew. I don't remember anything that was said. It was a simple theological argument, with simple rhetoric, uncomplicated analogies, benign exemplifications from science and secular learning which the rebbe seemed pleased to have at his command (he had studied engineering some years before at the Sorbonne). None of the rebbe's words impressed me." (15)

The muteness here stems from a difference in language, history, and commitment. But Hasidim do not remain as we first encounter them — with their backs to us — as they do in *The Face of Faith*. The final image is of three men, almost faceless, deeply engaged in study. Each has a visible hand supporting a head bent over a large book. It may not be an overtly welcoming image, but it is not a hostile one either. They are a people apart, but we may join the circle of study if we so wish. Still, theirs is a world separate from ours. And because it is an autonomous Jewish world — a world whose intellectual and spiritual foundations are remote from those of the world that we inhabit — it beckons, may initially repel, but leaves us ultimately with a sense well below marvel. Cohen writes:

> I could not understand enough to be impressed, and what was related to me by my companions after the audience concluded at about three in the morning was not up to my excessively rigid and uncharitable theological standards. In those days God and theology were a revenge.
>
> But what remains? That example of openness and willingness and care is retained. It was foolish to expect more, to anticipate revelations and mysteries, miracles and conversions. The rebbe might well have had the power to plant the seed, but I was not the ground to receive it.
>
> Nearly twenty years later, many theologies later, many books read and written later, I am still moved by the undertaking of their life. (16)

Published in 1976, Mal Warshaw's *Tradition: Orthodox Jewish Life in America* demonstrates a more complex use of the camera than Garvin's or Herzberg's by continually shifting between long and tight shots; and the images themselves are intimate, sometimes humorous, giving us less a sense of encountering an Old World tribe or a peculiar religious devotion than a sense of the strangeness of juxtaposing old ways and new. Indeed, as the title suggests, this book is not about a particular community as much as it is about a way of life among observant Jews. And perhaps because his subject matter is largely Lubavitcher Hasidim, who take pride in their worldliness and commitment to dialogue with other Jewish denominations, Warshaw felt less distanced, less the outsider, than many of the other photographers whose work is under consideration here. Whereas Cohen's text suggests an ultimately penetrable though nondialogical boundary between us and them, Warshaw tells us that "what had begun as a flirtation with the exotic became a transforming experience." Warshaw's ease in entering the world of his subjects creates a contagious intimacy. We see the daily routines of both work and celebration. Various sections deal with belief, ritual, holidays, childhood, daily life, and the life cycle; each is subdivided into minute details of ritual observance. The section titled "The Rituals That Sanctify Life" contains the following subsections: "Tefillin" (phylacteries), "Tallit and Tzitzit" (prayer shawl and ritual fringes), "Mezuzah" (door post amulet), "Tzedakah" (charity), "Handwashing," "Haircut," "Mikveh" (ritual bath), "Kashrut," "Shabbos"—a virtual catalog of ritual observance. Overall, the book suggests a very different kind of encounter than the other two books portray. We seem to be moving with each of these books increasingly from the abstract to the concrete, from the impenetrable to the penetrable, from the radical separation of self and other to the possibility of self as other. The detailing in Warshaw's vision suggests an exploratory, even experimental, curiosity, an expansion of the threshold of the self (Mullaney 1985). Warshaw invites the reader to enter terra incognita, to feel what it is like to be someone else.

One can sense a progressive development in these books (in the 1960s and early 1970s Hasidim clearly were much more marginal to American Jewish life than they have become since that time), but the primary factor here is not time. Nor for that matter does professional training play a role. Frederic Brenner is the only one of the photographers who has training in anthropology. Yet there is very little ethnographic vision shaping the work *Jérusalem: Instants d'éternité* aside from its focus on a particular neighborhood—Mea Shearim in Jerusalem. It is a remarkable book in large measure because of the proximity of the camera to its subject, which could only have been achieved through the cooperation of a very reclusive community. Here we see Hasidim in their *shtiblekh* (small study houses), with their *rebbeim* (spiritual leaders), at play, conversing, and in celebration. Missing are the everyday practices that extend a line of continuity from us to them. This portraiture presents us with a noble people. We are shown numerous images of men climbing iron staircases that suggest elevation in ways that are more spiritual than physical. The photographs of trudging through snow, bent-over Hasidim, and fleeting masqueraders is almost direct quotation from the work of Roman Vishniac (the same case could be made for the images of children in Herzberg's work), suggesting a "romantic atemporality," to use Marek Halter's description from the introduction. Other scenes of public and domestic life suggest the paintings of Rembrandt and van Eyck. Brenner's vision is more painterly than ethnographic. Its lyricism gives us proximity without deep understanding, contact without intimacy. There are no captions here. The book resolves the dilemma of self and other by envisioning Hasidim in much the same way that Herzberg does: as people from some other time, some other place.

The most striking and artistically original of these books is Leonard Freed's *La danse des fidèles*. Freed virtually spans the globe to give us images of Hasidim in America, England, and Israel. Here we have at least a few portrayals of work, and a rather intimate portrait of family and domestic life. Freed is associated with Magnum and, like Brenner, he is a photographer's photographer, able to present masterful images. Unlike Brenner's work, Freed's is complex and even contradictory, shifting between understanding and incomprehension, the familiar and the unfamiliar, the serious and the seemingly frivolous. Brenner's images of ascending Hasidim is a lyricism devoid of humor. Freed shows us a group of young men in an American *besmedresh* (synagogue study house) extending double file up the vertical rows of wooden benches piled along a wall. At its pinnacle is a boy engaging in what seems like light banter with an older dark-clad youth just below him. The image suggests the coexistence of intense, elevated discussion and jocularity, of boyhood and manhood, of the wild and the tamed. Freed's work has narrative captions, giving his subjects a voice—albeit a limited one—in his project. The caption for the image of the students in the *besmedresh* reads as follows:

> My mother came from a shtetl, a Jewish village [*sic*] in Eastern Europe. She had the habit of saying: "One can take the Jew out of the shtetl, but one cannot take the shtetl out of the Jew." Out of the shtetl, the Jews prospered and with comfort came sartorial decorum, while the men continued to wear black as a sign of humility. I asked why so few men wore ties. They informed me that there's no need if one has a beard. "But the majority of students are virtually beardless." — "Oh," they said, "but of course they will come!" (35)

If Brenner's work gives the impression of entering terra incognita, Freed's straddles the line: self and other are complexly interwoven here as if a third voice were emerging—something that never could have come about without the two separate selves interacting within an ethnographic encounter (Myerhoff 1988); we come away from this book feeling a degree of intimacy with his subjects. For example, the second image in the book is of a young Israeli couple in their kitchen with a child standing on the table. The boy points toward the father and the father waves his hat back at him. The mother watches, laughing. Next to her stands a daughter with a pacifier in her mouth. The caption reads as follows:

> They live in Mea Shearim, close to the walls of Jerusalem. They are poor, pious workers. In a whisper they asked if I would photograph their son. They have money they said, and they would pay — that is, if it wasn't too expensive. I told them I do not take pictures in order to sell them, but they really didn't seem to understand. Why otherwise would someone want to photograph their son? When I left them, they repeated that they had put some money aside and they could pay me.

Clearly, for Hasidim the creation of these photographs is for their sake only to the degree that the iconographic referent is limited to the idiom of the family album. For us, the photographs have two meanings — one aesthetic, the other social. The former conveys meaning by framing the photograph as artistic production; the latter, as I shall argue, draws its meaning from the construction of an ethnic rather than a family album.

Envisioning the Self: Folk Ethnography

What is the significance of these books? Why do they exist? My answer focuses on the role of folk ethnography in the construction of collective selfhood and the relationship between collectible objects and ethnic patrimony. Aside from Freed's, these books are clearly intended for sale to Jews, few of whom would buy the books because of their intrinsic artistic value. Then why buy them? It seems to me that if we add this literature to other kinds of coffee-table books, including photo books about Jewish immigration, about Jews in various lands, then we have available to us a corpus of material revealing the quests of American Jewry for self-understanding. I use the term *folk ethnography* for this literature because it needs to be distinguished from tourist photography, which it resembles. Albers and James (1988) distinguish three ways that tourism's media makers use cultural motifs to obscure the lived reality of their subjects: homogenization, whereby one group is used to represent a region, or a site is chosen and constructed for local groups to perform their culture; decontextualization, in which local culture is understood entirely through craft, costume, and performance (154); and mystification, through which the decontextualized subject is scripted as friendly, happy, and freely bestowing gifts on his or her tourist guests (155). Photo books on Hasidim differ largely with respect to where the self is presumed to be located vis-à-vis the subject.

Tourist photographs assume a guest/host relationship through which the otherwise radical separation of self and other is mediated, albeit temporarily, by the sojourn. I do not wish to claim that the coimagined connectedness between self and other in such folk ethnography eliminates the problematical nature of that relationship, or even that the guest/host relationship is absent. These books suggest otherwise. Moreover, they need to be distinguished from family albums, even from collective family albums in which no separation exists beween self and other. In a sense, folk ethnography photo books exist as an intermediary genre between tourist photographs and family albums. The latter, of course, are true collective representations: rarely the work of one person, they are a family's way of telling its own tale. Photo books are usually one person's tale about a collectivity either marginally connected to or entirely disconnected from that collectivity. Photo books vary with the talent of the photographer, the depth of his or her effort, the cooperation of the subject, and the conscious or unconscious thought patterns — the tropes or metaphors that themselves contain a variety of rhetorical strategies — that affect the gathering and processing of information, particularly in regard to the subjects chosen and the nature of the posing. Such tropes risk entrapment in the very hermeneutic circle that tourists undertake: it "begins with the photographic appearances that advertise and anticipate a trip, moves on to a search for these pictures in the experience of travel itself, and ends up with travelers certifying and sealing the very same images in their own photographic productions" (Albers and James 1988:136). In short, photographing Hasidim readily lends itself to recreating well-worn images. Moreover, none of these images approaches the level of serious reportage associated with photojournalism. The best of them are shaped by aesthetic considerations rather than by those of critical inquiry, and at least some are intended to satisfy the needs of patrons eager to add to their collections. Magazine and tourist photographs do not reflect back upon the self and cannot, therefore, threaten their consumers' construction of selfhood. But if they do not threaten, they still can open a window onto the world and, as Stephen Greenblatt argues in the case of *National Ge-*

ographic, offer "a safe and reassuring place to wonder," thereby "establishing a frame that at least a few readers every month will be driven to push beyond; inviting the beginning of moral awareness; creating a representation that makes it possible to begin to situate oneself in a vastly larger world" (1993:120). It is my contention that much of the material under discussion here offers such a place to wonder and, more importantly, an ability to disturb stemming from certain ideas about cultural authenticity and the genealogical progression of American Jewry.

These books employ only two basic tropes, reflecting at their base very opposite notions of continuity and discontinuity in Jewish life. The first trope, like so much of ethnographic writing, represents its subjects as authentic representatives of a time past, an Eden from which we are fallen (Clifford 1986). But unlike much of ethnographic understanding or the exoticizing eye of travel photography (Albers and James 1988:137), this reportage is not a search for the extraordinary or for cultural novelty. Hasidim here are less the surviving remnant of a sad, fragile species that must be protected than a representation of the essential Jewish self uncorrupted by the compromises of the many. Indeed, they are more like enactments of folkloric types; like *lamedvovniks*—the saints whose presence according to Jewish lore guarantees the preservation of the world—their existence betokens continuity. So the photographic investigator is loath to peer beneath the surface, to probe in order to discover the human frailties that ultimately make them like rather than unlike us. And, because the trope implies an underlying discontinuity between us and them, every action on their part exudes an authentic spirituality of which we are no longer capable. The rhetoric employed here is eulogaic and apologetic. Taken to its extreme, the trope becomes almost a never-never land representation devoid of any trace of mundane existence. Only one of the books would fall into this category; photographic representation is generally not as freewheeling as other graphic or plastic arts and, although images are frequently posed, the conventions fall squarely within the realistic tradition (which is not to say that they are, indeed, realistic but rather that they claim to be so). Nonetheless, the trope undoubtedly reflects many of the representations of Hasidim in popular Jewish culture. And its temporal and spatial orientation is very similar to how all of East European Jewish history and culture is understood by American Jews. The typical rhetoric employed here is a lyrical romanticism.

The second trope is the journey into the past. Although it resembles the first trope and is to some degree a subcategory of it—because there is at least an attempt at dialogue here—the result has a different feel. Here there is a distance bridgeable by the individual's spiritual journey. This trope envisions Hasidim as powerful defenders of a conquering faith and potential donors of spiritual gifts. Those who undertake the journey see themselves as reborn or changed in fundamental ways. The rhetorical modalities associated with this trope include the dialogical (Leonard Freed) and the folkloristic (Mal Warshaw). Although the two are frequently closely linked, the principal difference between them is that the former permits the subject a high degree of autonomy so that captions, through the use of subjects' voices, may disrupt rather than confirm conventional wisdom; the latter documents the minutiae of everyday life, the photographer acting as a "fly on the wall." The dialogical modality underlies an encounter between two others who share, at least in the mind of the photographer/ethnographer, a sufficient sense of common humanity, so that dialogue is possible (although not necessarily mutually intelligble). The folkloristic modality assumes that the locus of cultural authenticity resides with the other; it does not seek to engage in dialogue with the other but to salvage and collect for the benefit of the self, deracinated and therefore needing an infusion of rescued traditions.

Folk ethnography is different from the purely intellectual pursuits and speculations of academic ethnography. It exists not to advance human knowledge but to focus group understanding of the self and thereby reinforce the cohesiveness of the population that sponsors and consumes it. American Jewish folk ethnography takes several distinct forms: the first is tourism; the second, which is closely related to the first, is the creation—and more typically, vicariously, the ownership—of these and similar coffee-table books; a third is humorous writing and stand-up comedy.

A visit, whether actual or vicarious, through magazine or photo book becomes an allegory of a culture on the wane.[2] The message is a clear warning: Jewish survival requires a vigorous effort to ensure the loyalty of succeeding generations. The second form of folk ethnography, coffee-table books, is an attempted antidote to the problem of survival. Designed to be given as gifts, these books, through exchange within familial and ethnic webs of reciprocity, constitute statements about the nature and meaning of Jewishness for, and often by, people who are largely unable to articulate it themselves. Joke books may serve the same purpose, but their ephemeral nature (they are largely inexpensive paperbacks sold at checkout counters and card and gift shops) as well as the genre's conventions give joke books considerable transgressive license. Nor do they claim to function as bulwarks against cultural attenuation.

Coffee-table books are different. They depend on patrons who intend them—either for themselves or for others to whom they will give them—to have some prominence in the home and thereby act as icons of identity. How, then, do these books focus group understanding and reinforce cohesiveness? In what way are they an antidote to the perceived problem of ethnic loyalty among succeeding generations? I argue that the photo books I have examined do so by a discursive process of appropriation that promotes a sense of connection to ethnic subgroups from which the greater collectivity has significantly diverged. Moreover, such discursive appropriation has an important role to play in the reformulation of ethnic memory culture.

Constructing a Collective Self

Acquisition

"A photograph," Susan Sontag writes, "is not only like its subject.... It is part of, an extension of that subject; and a potent means of acquiring it, of gaining control over it" (1977:155). It does so as a surrogate of a person or thing; by giving us a consumer's relation to events whether or not we actually experience them; and by transforming things into information. Sontag continues: "The photographic exploration and duplication of the world fragments continuities and feeds the pieces into an interminable dossier, thereby providing possibilities of control that could not even be dreamed of under the earlier system of recording information: writing" (156). Through such books and related iconographic representations, the Hasid other is transformed into a broader ethnic panoply. Nor is such acquisition limited to Hasidim. An interesting case in point is Franz Hubmann's *The Jewish Family Album*, which begins its story with images of the shtetl, then makes its way through the great cities of Europe, the New World, and Israel, interspersing the great men of Jewish letters and philanthropy with images of Jewish types and street scenes.

Discursive Strategies

This ethnic panopticism, its controlling gaze, does more than review a particular group's history; it constitutes that history as a pageant, foregrounding the central places and characters as a dramatic sequence, building from destitution to social elevation, destruction to redemption. The latter theme underlies the books reviewed in this essay. The photo books I examined offer a way to use the past or what seems to represent the past to reconstitute group unity in the face of an overabundance of heterogeneity. As Pierre Bourdieu argues in the case of family albums:

> The images of the past arranged in chronological order, the logical order of social memory, evoke and communicate the memory of events which deserve to be preserved because the group sees a factor of unification in the monuments of its past unity or—which amounts to the same thing—because it draws confirmation of its present unity from its past: this is why there is nothing more decent, reassuring and edifying than a family album; all the unique experiences that give the individual memory the particularity of a secret are banished from it, and the common past, or, perhaps, the highest common denominator of the past, has all the clarity of a faithfully visited gravestone. (1990:31)

Constructing Ethnic Patrimony

Something in these books speaks to an underlying insecurity in contemporary Jewish life that has to do with collective identity. In a sense, this very insecurity is closely intertwined with the history of photography and the crucial role played by family photography, which according to Julia Hirsch "arises in an age which like the Renaissance is intensely curious about the self, its share in history, its place in time" (1981:11). But unlike Renaissance paintings, photographs are as much a reminder of loss as they are of something gained. Photography arose at the very moment when industrialization wreaked havoc on broad ties of kinship, favoring the nuclear over the extended family. And as Susan Sontag writes, they "supply the token presence of the dispersed relatives. A family's photograph album is generally about the extended family—and, often, is all that remains of it" (1977:9).

Photographs are like monuments—they are iconic representations of other times and other places—but with a peculiar transportability. American Jews' physical tie to the Old World was fundamentally destroyed during the Holocaust, and even in America, economically mobile Jews repeatedly establish, then abandon, settlements. The architecture of the past rarely figures positively in the daily life of American Jewry. On the contrary, monumental buildings are a burden readily dispensed with once the critical mass to maintain them is gone.

Collective Memory

The photo album is a trace of the past that assures us of an enduring identity, a sense of continuity in the face of change (Lowenthal 1975:9–10). Photographs are taken with that very fact in mind. Photographs act, therefore, as a vehicle for establishing collective memory out of individual experience (Boerdam and Oosterbaan Martinius 1980:115) and a way to integrate new members into family history and genealogy (ibid.:116). "The people who come together to be 'in' a photograph," writes Richard Chalfen, "shall stay together in a symbolic sense, in a symbolic form, for future viewing and exhibition events" (1981:110). These functions—collective memory and family history—have particular significance for the corpus of photographs discussed here.

Accessible to all, these photo books are destined for any home library. A blurb on the back cover of Mal Warshaw's *Tradition* says that "if there were such a thing as a coffee table Chanukah book, this would be it." Moreover, as part of a general iconization of Hasidim, these images form a part of a vernacular American Jewish domestic collection.

In their study of domestic symbols and the self, Mihaly Csikszentmihalyi and Eugene Rochberg-Halton report that "more than any other object in the home, photos serve the purpose of preserving the memory of personal ties." Moreover, because they bear the actual image of a person, they can impart "a tenuous immortality to beloved persons" as well as provide "an identity, a context of belongingness, to one's descendants" (1989:60). Perhaps this is why snapshots have, according to Richard Chalfen "tremendous 'staying power'—they survive in comparison to other valued and common items of material culture" (1981:107). Although photo books are mass produced, still they are *books,* and "are special to people because they serve to embody ideas and to express religious and professional values" (Csikszentmihalyi and Rochberg-Halton 1989:71). The things with which we choose to surround ourselves "constitute a symbolic ecology structuring our attention and reflecting our intentions and thus serve to cultivate the individuality of the owner" (ibid.:94).

But for American Jews, a symbolic ecology of books constitutes not so much the individuality of the owner but a sense of membership in a collectivity, a vital link increasingly significant given the absence, or at least the fragmentation, of other communal institutions. Indeed, like the meaning of things for adults generally, such objects "expand the boundaries of the self to include relationships with other people" (ibid.:112). Collections represent a search for continuity, an attempt to undo the discontinuity of past and present. As vessels for memories they "serve to integrate the various patterns around which the self is organized at different points in time" (ibid.). How else do we explain the sheer size of family photo collections consisting frequently of two thousand or three thousand images with individual albums of three hundred to four hundred photographs (Chalfen 1981:107)? These collections represent neighborhoods that have disappeared, people who have been exterminated, objects that have either been destroyed through neglect, war, or genocide or simply abandoned, as in the case of synagogues in old neighborhoods. In the case of families, they are a way for the members of one generation to communicate to the members of succeeding generations, to socialize the young in the customs of their elders (Chalfen 1991:212). Little wonder then that picture collections have particular significance for immigrant families whose members, according to Richard Chalfen, "demonstrate a need to construct an integrated account — one that maintains a sense of continuity by retaining pieces of the past and simultaneously illustrates a process of on-going personal, social, and cultural change" (ibid.:214). Collections are a past reorganized and scripted via memory.

Self as Other

It would not be entirely correct, however, to accept these books simply as a resolution of discrepancies felt within the life of American Jewry. I would like to suggest the possibility that their existence poses at least subliminally a disruptive dimension to the American Jewish psyche by deconstructing the peaceful coexistence of self and other through which American Jews have integrated themselves within

America's cultural mainstream. This reimagining of self as other may in fact be an implicit dimension of seeing oneself through photographs. Indeed, the emergence of photography was, according to Roland Barthes, a "disturbance" to civilization that forced the viewers to see themselves through strangers' eyes:

> To see oneself (differently from in a mirror): on the scale of History, this action is recent, the painted, drawn, or miniaturized portrait having been, until the spread of Photography, a limited possession, intended moreover to advertise a social and financial status—and in any case, a painted portrait, however close the resemblance (this is what I am trying to prove) is not a photograph. Odd that no one has thought of the *disturbance* (to civilization) which this new action causes. I want a History of looking. For the Photograph is the advent of myself as other: a cunning dissociation of consciousness from identity. Even odder: it was *before* Photography that men had the most to say about the vision of the double. Heautoscopy was compared with an hallucinosis; for centuries this was a great mythic theme. But today it is as if we repressed the profound madness of photography: it reminds us of its mythic heritage only by that faint uneasiness which seizes me when I look at "myself" on a piece of paper. (Barthes 1981:12–13)

Though they have a more social scientific point of view than Barthes's, two Dutch sociologists also argue against the purely integrative role of photography. They particularly dispute Bourdieu's rigid association of family photographs and traditional solemn family festivities, arguing that it is much too particular to traditional rural communities and overly grounded in Durkheimian notions of festivals as collective representations (Boerdam and Oosterbaan Martinius 1980:96–97). Photography is practiced on a much larger scale within modern communities despite "the gradual disappearance of solemn and ceremonial moments from family life" (ibid.:98). Indeed, Bourdieu's notion of photography as a "celebration of family unity" does not alone account for the meaning of photographs. It is simply much too functionalist a view to argue on behalf of photography's integrative function. As a tool for memory, it may also disturb and disrupt, suggesting through eruption into the present other ways of organizing reality. Do these books evoke the past for the sake of dispelling or laying to rest Jewish alterity, or to challenge the neatly ordered way in which Jews see their evolution from primitive to civilized? Folk ethnography might be looked at as a genealogically guided history, which, according to Foucault, "is not to discover the roots of our identity, but to commit itself to its dissipation. It does not seek to define our unique threshold of emergence, the homeland to which metaphysicians promise a return; it seeks to make available all of those discontinuities that cross us" (Rabinow 1984:95).

There *are* books that do the very opposite of folk ethnogaphy. Such texts posit a notion of American Jewry as a seamless entity whose history contains none of the might have beens that make historical and ethnographic awareness challenging intellectual exercises. A case in point is the recently released photo book *The Jews in America* (Cohen 1989), produced by the publisher of the "A Day in the Life" series. The book has much of the glitziness of those volumes: high-caliber portraiture with a conservative point of view now eschewed by even the most venerable of national photo magazines. The images offer a view of American Jews without the slightest hint of doubt about the community's well-being: suburban though not deracinated, prosperous though committed to tradition, American Jewish culture is a straight line of continuity from past to present, from Old World to New, from Orchard Street to Beverly Hills with nothing lost through a century and the climb from working to middle class. The book contains not a hint of the price Jews have paid for social mobility and no sense of disruptions in Jewish family life as neighborhoods change and the young and upwardly mobile move miles and sometimes thousands of miles away. Nor is there evidence of the decline in Jewish literacy, the demise in language-based ethnicity through the abandonment of Yiddish and the struggle to maintain or even constitute ethnicity within the idiom of the dominant language and culture. Although Chaim Potok's introduction describes the book as "in essence a discerning essay on the current condition of America's Jews: their triumphant and unprecedented integration into the host culture since their mass beginning on these shores in the 1880s and the sobering problems this success has brought about," it is hard to find any indication that the creator of this book was in the least bit interested in revealing sobering problems. Indeed, Potok quickly glosses over such disturbing aspects of American Jewish life:

> Long threads bind these images to the past. The young men who hold *Torah* scrolls and read from them; the scribe and his family gathered around a large scroll of parchment; the child with a *Simhat Torah* flag; the men who joyously carry their new *Torah* beneath a *hupah*—all have their origins in the Jewish people's passion for the Covenant. Em-

bodied by the sacred scrolls, this Covenant is the central concept that has propelled the Jewish people through history. It is the indissoluble contract with God or destiny, that still profoundly awesome and mysterious relationship between the Jew and the world. (11)

Potok proceeds along these same lines of evident continuity between past and present by remarking on the images of Jewish observance, taking particular note of a young man donning phylacteries in a dorm room surrounded by pop culture images and posters that bring to mind Jacob Riis's photograph of an older immigrant Jew celebrating the Sabbath in a tenement cellar. For Potok the two images betoken the links between God and man, while the numerous multigenerational images in the book

> depict another covenant: links between man and man. The family has always been the sacred unit of the Jewish people, its building block. Preserve that unit and you preserve the people. A cluster of families forms a community; and a dedicated community, one that respects and cares for all life, from youth to advanced age, is the goal and the gift of the Covenant people. Hence, the images in these pages of the young and the old in various communal activities. (11)

This is a book whose vision is so completely rooted in the present as the best of all possible worlds that nothing looms disturbingly on the horizon, certainly not an image of the irretrievable past or of other ways of constructing the present. By comparison the books on Hasidim are disturbing mirrors that reflect the self as a distorted image.

Conclusions

The acceptance of the Hasid into the popular iconography of American Jewry is striking primarily because it is so different from lived reality. As an iconic representation it is very much what the French social theorist Pierre Nora refers to as a *lieu de mémoire*, a site of memory, in the face of an age in which a lived sense of history is disappearing, along with the traces of distinctive cultures, languages, and ways of life.

Lieu de mémoire suggests the iconization of the Hasid, and a movement that one might call metaphorization. But metaphor of what? Perhaps we need to distinguish two opposite processes that may be at work here, each related to the separate terms of metonymy and metaphor. Metonymy acts as *pars pro toto* — one part stands for the whole. Metaphor joins together two otherwise discrete domains of experience. Through metonymy the Hasid simply stands for one highly visible aspect of the American Jew. The commercial photo book *The Jews in America* treats Hasidim in precisely this way, joining them to the larger ethnic panoply much the way *The Family of Man* joined human cultural diversity into a common thread of humanity. As metonymy, then, the Hasid stands for the Jew and in so doing disappears within a broader sense of pseudoethnic distinctiveness.

But if this iconization works as metaphor, the Hasid represents not one facet of the family of American Jewry but a differentness that for most of us has passed and is therefore no longer part of lived reality. Here, the metaphor works to remind us of disruption. Indeed, for many American Jews, the image of the Hasid represents a collective projection of an autonomous self—a self as radical other vis-à-vis the dominant culture—and a bulwark against the seemingly relentless process of assimilation and cultural attenuation. For most American Jews, interest in Hasidim does not negate other constructions of Jewish selfhood. Rather, it adds another layer of complexity in a never ending discussion on what it means to be a Jew.

Notes

This essay is a revision of an essay originally published as "The Imaging of Self and Other: Photo Books on Hasidim" (*Visual Anthropology* 6[1993]:303–22). Research on this project was made possible by generous grants from the National Endowment for the Humanities, the Lucius N. Littauer Foundation, and the Wisconsin Alumni Research Foundation of the University of Wisconsin-Madison.

1. In the case of American Jewry, in addition to a number of literary compilations, encyclopedias, and other sourcebooks, a growing number of photo albums (see, for example, Suhl 1972; Shulman 1974; Hubmann, Kochan, and Kochan 1975; Salamander 1991).

2. See Dershowitz's (1991:186) description of his reasons for visiting synagogues abroad.

Bibliography

Alba, Richard. 1990. *Ethnic Identity: The Transformation of White America*. New Haven, Conn.: Yale University Press.

Albers, Patricia C., and William R. James. 1988. Travel Photography: A Methodological Approach. *Annals of Tourism Research* 15:134–58.

Alloula, Malek. 1986. *The Colonial Harem*. Minneapolis: University of Minnesota Press.

Barthes, Roland. 1981. *Camera Lucida: Reflections on Photography*. New York: Hill and Wang.

Beloff, Halla. 1985. *Camera Culture*. New York and London: Basil Blackwell.

Benjamin, Walter. 1980. A Short History of Photography. In *Classic Essays on Photography*, ed. Alan Trachtenberg, 199–216. New Haven, Conn.: Leete's Island Books.

Berger, John (text), and Jean Mohr (photographs). 1982. *Another Way of Telling*. New York: Pantheon.

Boerdam, Jaap, and Warna Oosterbaan Martinius. 1980. *Netherlands' Journal of Sociology* 16:95–119.

Bourdieu, Pierre. 1990. *Photography: A Middle-Brow Art*. Stanford, Calif.: Stanford University Press.

Brenner, Frederic. 1984. *Jérusalem: Instants d'éternité*. Paris: Denoel.

Chalfen, Richard. 1981. Redundant Imagery: Some Observations on the Use of Snapshots in American Culture. *Journal of American Culture* 4:106–13.

———. 1983. Exploiting the Vernacular: Studies of Snapshot Photography. *Studies in Visual Communication* 9(3):70–84.

———. 1987. *Snapshot Versions of Life*. Bowling Green, Ohio: Bowling Green University Popular Press.

———. 1991. *Turning Leaves: The Photograph Collections of Two Japanese American Families*. Albuquerque: University of New Mexico Press.

Clifford, James. 1986. On Ethnographic Allegory. In *Writing Culture: The Poetics and Politics of Ethnography*, ed. James Clifford and George Marcus, 98–121. Berkeley: University of California Press.

Coe, Brian, and Paul Gates. 1977. *The Snapshot Photograph: The Rise of Popular Photography, 1888–1939*. London: Asch and Grant.

Cohen, David, ed. 1989. *The Jews in America*. New York: Collins.

Csikszentmihalyi, Mihaly, and Eugene Rochberg-Halton. 1989. *The Meaning of Things: Domestic Symbols and the Self*. New York: Cambridge University Press.

Dershowitz, Alan. 1991. *Chutzpah*. Boston: Little, Brown.

Edwards, Elizabeth. 1992. *Anthropology and Photography, 1860–1920*. New Haven, Conn.: Yale University Press.

Freed, Leonard. 1984. *La danse des fidèles*. Paris: Chene.

Garvin, Philip (photographs), and Arthur Cohen (text). 1970. *A People Apart*. New York: Dutton.

Geary, Christaud M. 1988. *Images from Bamum: German Colonial Photography at the Court of King Njoya, Cameroon, West Africa, 1902–1915*. Washington, D.C.: Smithsonian Institution Press.

Goldberg, Vicki. 1991. *The Power of Photography: How Photographs Changed Our Lives*. New York: Abbeville.

Greenblatt, Stephen. 1993. Kindly Visions. *New Yorker*, October 11, 112–20.

Gross, Larry. 1985. Life vs. Art: The Interpretation of Visual Narratives. *Visual Communication* 11(4):2–11.

Hirsch, Julia. 1981. *Family Photographs: Content, Meaning and Effect*. New York: Oxford University Press.

Hubmann, Franz, Miriam Kochan, and Lionel Kochan. 1975. *The Jewish Family Album: The Life of a People in Photographs*. New York: Routledge and Kegan Paul.

Katz, Molly. 1991. *Jewish as a Second Language*. New York: Workman.

King, Graham. 1978. *Say "Cheese!": Looking at Snapshots in a New Way*. New York: Dodd, Mead.

Kozol, Wendy. 1994. *Life's America*. Philadelphia: Temple University Press.

Kranzler, George (text), and Irving I. Herzberg (photographs). 1972. *The Face of Faith: An American Hassidic Community.* Baltimore: Baltimore Hebrew College Press.

Kugelmass, Jack. 1990. Green Bagels: An Essay on Food, Ethnicity and the Carnivalesque. *YIVO Annual* 19.

———. 1992. The Rites of the Tribe: American Jewish Tourism in Poland. In *Museums and Communities: The Politics of Public Culture,* ed. Ivan Karp, Christine Mullen Kreamer, and Steven D. Lavine, 382–427. Washington, D.C.: Smithsonian Institution Press.

———, ed. 1994. *Going Home: How Jews Invent Their Old Countries.* YIVO *Annual* 21.

Lesy, Michael. 1980. *Time Frames: The Meaning of Family Pictures.* New York: Random House.

Lifton, Robert J. 1993. *The Protean Self: Human Resilience in an Age of Fragmentation.* New York: Basic Books.

Loeb, Laurence. 1977. Creating Antiques for Fun and Profit: Encounters between Iranian Jewish Merchants and Touring Coreligionists. In *Hosts and Guests: The Anthropology of Tourism,* ed. Valene L. Smith, 185–92. Philadelphia: University of Pennsylvania Press.

Lowenthal, David. 1975. Past Time, Present Place: Landscape and Memory. *Geographical Review* 65(1):1–36.

Lutz, Catherine A., and Jane L. Collins. 1993. *Reading National Geographic.* Chicago: University of Chicago Press.

Mosse, George. 1991. *The Nationalization of the Masses: Political Symbolism and Mass Movements in Germany from the Napoleonic Wars through the Third Reich* Ithaca, N.Y.: Cornell University Press.

Mullaney, Steven. 1985. Brothers and Others, or the Art of Alienation. In *Cannibals, Witches, and Divorce: Estranging the Renaissance,* ed. Marjorie Garber. Selected Papers from the English Institute, New Series (11), 67–89. Baltimore: Johns Hopkins University Press.

Myerhoff, Barbara. 1988. Surviving Stories: Reflections on *Number Our Days.* In *Between Two Worlds: Ethnographic Essays on American Jews,* ed. Jack Kugelmass, 265–94. Ithaca, N.Y.: Cornell University Press.

Nora, Pierre. 1989. Between Memory and History: Les Lieux de Mémoire. *Representations* 26:7–25.

Pearl, Jonathan, and Judith Pearl. 1993. Television Grapples with Jewish Identity. *Moment,* October, 39–45.

Rabinow, Paul, ed. 1984. *The Foucault Reader.* New York: Pantheon.

Rosen, Jay. 1989. thirtysomething. *Tikkun* 4(4):29–33.

Salamander, Rachel, ed. 1991. *The Jewish World of Yesterday, 1860–1938.* New York: Rizzoli.

Sekula, Allan. 1981. The Traffic in Photographs. *Art Journal,* Spring, 15–25.

Shulman, Abraham. 1974. *The Old Country: The Lost World of East European Jews.* New York: Scribner.

Slesin, Suzanne. 1991. Family Photos: X-Rays of the Heart. *New York Times,* December 19, C1, C6.

Sontag, Susan. 1977. *On Photography.* New York: Dell.

Suhl, Yuri. 1972. *An Album of the Jews in America.* New York: Franklin Watts.

Tagg, John. 1988. *The Burden of Representation: Essays on Photographies and Histories.* Minneapolis: University of Minnesota Press.

Trachtenberg, Alan. 1989. *Reading American Photographs: Images as History Mathew Brady to Walker Evans.* New York: Hill and Wang.

Walker, Andrew L., and Rosalind Kimball Moulton. 1989. Photo Albums: Images of Time and Reflections of Self. *Qualitative Sociology* 12(2):155–82.

Warshaw, Mal. 1976. *Tradition: Orthodox Jewish Life in America.* New York: Schocken.

3 / Situating History and Difference: The Performance of the Term *Holocaust* in Public Discourse

Vivian M. Patraka

No term is fixed forever in its meaning (unless it has become invisible through disuse), but constitutes a set of practices and cultural negotiations in the present. The search for the best term to designate the Jewish genocide outlines an attempt to mark both its historical specificity and its uniqueness. This uniqueness has been linked to the extent of the perpetrator's intentionality, the degree to which the state apparatus legalized the devastation, the measure of its use of "technological weapons of destruction" (Stannard 1992:151), and the number of people killed. But every genocide, in the particularities of its specific history, is unique. And while each genocide is known by this distinct history, it also is understood in the context of other genocides and attempted annihilations, even though these relationships are not ones of simple analogy or equivalence. Thus the narrative of making meaning out of the term *Holocaust* continues.[1] The public performance of the term among Jews is multiple, varying in different cultural sites and used for differing political agendas and pedagogical purposes. Moreover, however proprietary the claims on the use of this term have been in some quarters, the evocative power of the term *Holocaust* has begun to extend its use tropologically to contemporary considerations of the destruction of groups other than Jews. Perhaps this is precisely because the term *genocide* functions as a delimiting generic, while *Holocaust* brings with it all the protocols of the unspeakable, the incommensurate, and a sense of unlimited scope to the pain and injustice. Or perhaps *Holocaust* connotes not just the violent moment of elimination of a whole people, but all that goes into it: the beginning of terror and circulating discourses of oppression and exclusion, the construction of a state apparatus of oppression and the disinformation it produces, the incarcerations, the annihilation, and then the revolting denials and cleanups. The entire array of cultural, social, and political forces amassed to effect genocide may be historically embedded in the term *Holocaust*.

Actually, the terms used to signify the attempted extermination of European Jewry constitute a varied history. Yehuda Bauer defines *Holocaust* as the English name "customarily used ... for the planned total annihilation of the Jewish people, and the actual murder of six million of them at the hands of the Nazis and their auxiliaries" (1989: 16). The word *Holocaust* derives from "the Greek word for whole-burnt" and is meant, presumably, to suggest the extent and the "manner of the death of the Jews of Europe" (Ezrahi 1980:2). Yet, as Sidra DeKoven Ezrahi points out, the notion of "burnt offering" to which the term is connected "raises problems through the sacrificial connotation that it attaches to the death of the Jews of Europe which is consistent with a prevailing Christian reading of Jewish history" (ibid.:2). By contrast, she suggests that neither *hurbn*, the Yiddish word for the Nazi genocide that connotes the violation of the continuity of life within the community, nor *shoah*, the Hebrew word that connotes "widespread, even cosmic disaster," waste and desolation, associates the victims with ritual sacrifice (ibid.:221). But, while English-speaking scholars critique the term *Holocaust* with its connotations of sacrifice for a purpose, of placating God with the mysteries of our suffering, they have generally agreed to use the term to refer to the Jewish genocide because of its function as a stable, recognizable historical referent.

During my own Brooklyn childhood in the 1950s, "the war" often designated the Jewish genocide, and "refugees" commonly signified those whom we now call Holocaust survivors. Jim Young notes that "because there was no 'ready-made' name in English [like *hurbn* or *shoah*] ... writers and historians [in the 1950s] who perceived these events separately from their World War II context were moved to adopt a name by which events could be known in their particularity" (1988:86–87). Only in the 1960s, as G. F. Goekjian notes, did the term *Holocaust* "gradually displace 'genocide' as the proper name of the Nazi destruction of the Jews" (1991:213–14). He uses the term *proper name* to suggest a proprietariness against which he will argue for applying the term *genocide* (and not *massacre*) to the history of the Armenians at the beginning of the twentieth century; but in doing so he also clarifies how the term *genocide* itself "was coined by Raphael Lemkin [in 1943 to serve as] a signifier for what was described as the 'unspeakable' fate of the Jews" (ibid.:213).

Bauer points out that Lemkin originally had two notions of genocide: (1) "the total 'extermination' of a people," and (2) the "extreme deprivation, destruction of educational institutions, interference in religious life, general denationalization and even moral poisoning" of a group (1989:20). The first notion emphasized the end product of annihilation, that is, destruction of the group, while the second emphasized the process, that is, persecution, that often leads to this end and could occur over a short or long time period. By the time of Lemkin's 1944 book *Axis Rule in Occupied Europe,* these two aspects of genocide had come together, so that Frank Chalk and Kurt Jonassohn could summarize Lemkin's definition of genocide as "the coordinated and planned annihilation of a national, religious or racial group by a variety of actions aimed at undermining the foundations essential to the survival of the group as a group" (Stannard 1992:279), a formulation, by the way, currently being contested for its omission of the political, social, and sexual from what constitutes an imperiled group.[2] Thus, while both the terms *Holocaust* and *genocide* were originally conceived to respond to the events in Europe against the Jews, *genocide* quickly took on the status of a generic, both describing the persecutions of other groups during this period and providing a means for defining actions against groups that would constitute genocidal destruction. And if this reiteration of the term *group* begins to suggest an essential or reified group identity, it must be noted that it is the perpetrators of a genocide who construct this distorted, malignant group identity against the multiple and divergent ways members of a particular community define themselves.

One way of contextualizing the current movement of the term *Holocaust* is by using Michel de Certeau's distinction between a place and a space in his application of spatial terms to narrative. For de Certeau, the opposition between "place" and "space" refers to "two sorts of stories" or narratives about how meaning is made. Place refers to those operations that make its object ultimately reducible to a fixed location, "to the *being there* of something dead, [and to] the law of a place" where the stable and "the law of the 'proper'" rules. Place "excludes the possibility of two things being in the same location.... Space occurs as the effect produced by the operations that orient it, situate it, temporalize it, and make it function in a polyvalent way." Thus space is created "by the actions of historical *subjects*." These actions multiply spaces and what can be positioned within them. Finally, the relationship between place and space is a process whereby "stories thus carry out a labor that constantly transforms places into spaces or spaces into places" (1984:117–18). De Certeau's distinction between a place and a space is crucial to my argument in the way it clarifies the differing strategies of attempting to move people through a landscape whose meanings are uniquely determined in contrast to providing an opportunity for contestation and multiplicity of association.

Though the domain of the Holocaust is mass death, the narrative(s) created about it need not make it an immobile, tomblike place nor create an inert body of knowledge intended only to conserve and preserve. Producers of public discourse on the Holocaust can actively engage in redefining this space so that, as I will presently show, even the seemingly standard definition of the Holocaust as relating solely to Jews is under interrogation at sites as formal as Holocaust museums and their fund-raising materials. And while I do not mean to be facile about the terrible stakes involved in memorializing these events, a narrative space for producing knowledge of the Holocaust — one that would construct its consumers as actively engaged in producing meanings — might be a powerful means to prolonging remembrance. Even if some contemporary groups do deliberately use the term *Holocaust* in a way designed to compete with or even erase the original referent, if we assert an exclusive, propriety claim over the term in response, we run the risk of magnifying one current perception: that the discourse of Jewish Holocaust functions as a kind of controlling or hegemonic discourse of suffering that operates at the expense of the sufferings of other groups. Instead, the notion of space, rather than mutually exclusive places, could signify a discourse on the Holocaust in which genocide stories of different groups could occupy the same locale without necessarily ejecting or evacuating the original referent of Jewish history and suffering. Even so, I wonder whether so much of the history of the Jewish genocide, the meanings attached to it, even the ethical, cultural, and linguistic protocols of where to look for meaning about such events, is so deeply embedded in the word *Holocaust* as to make the Jewish genocide a paradigmatic frame for other genocides located with the term.

Given all of these risks, it is worth considering how the referent of the Holocaust is configured by contemporary American Jews. As Jim Young notes in his 1993 book *The Texture of Memory:*

> Over time, the only "common" experience uniting an otherwise diverse, often fractious, community of Jewish Americans has been the vicarious memory of the Holocaust. Left-wing and right-wing Jewish groups, religious and secular, Zionist and non-Zionist may all draw different conclusions from the Holocaust. But all agree that it must be remembered, if to entirely disparate ideological ends. (348)

And despite the very palpable differences among us, both culturally and politically, it is still the case that many of our responses to the images, objects, and words connected to the Holocaust are "hard-wired," provoking automatic emotional meanings and an attitude of reverence. This makes it hard to get beyond a consensus on the agony, the loss, and the mindful viciousness that produced them so we can discern the actual discourse generated about the Holocaust and how it functions. Some of the strategies of this discourse are manipulative; they solicit our anguish, horror, and fear as the grounds for asserting larger meanings to which we may not wish to assent. But neither avoidance of the places in which these "fixed" narratives reside nor simple dismissal is, I think, useful. For this would risk separating us from our own emotions about the Holocaust, entombing them in these monumental stories so that they are no longer available for either examination or change. Instead, we have to create spaces for critique within and among those seemingly inevitable emotional hard-wirings and the places to which they get connected. I offer the discussion that follows as a step in that direction. I explore how the referent of the Holocaust is currently being configured at sites in the United States where a cultural performance of Holocaust history is being staged for public consumption—the U.S. Holocaust Memorial Museum in Washington, D.C., and the Beit Hashoah Museum of Tolerance in Los Angeles. I also want to put each of the museums against the background of their mass-mailed fund-raising letters to explore some of their ideological underpinnings.

Rhetorical Performance: Fund-Raising and U.S. Holocaust Museums

The fund-raising letters of both museums claim the term *Holocaust* in its Jewish specificity by enlarging its applications to include or relate to other oppressed groups. Both articulate the United States to genocide, but in contrasting ways: the D.C. letters locate the United States as a site of release from genocide; the Los Angeles letters configure the United States as a potential site for genocide. Finally, the announcements of both museums reveal how each museum, perhaps inevitably, given the desire to memorialize, oscillates between space and place—between the desire to provide spaces where museumgoers can perform acts of reinterpretation as historical subjects and the need to insist on the more public modality of inscribing over and over on a more passive audience the logic of a place conveying the monumental meaning of the Holocaust.

For each museum, the rhetorical performance of the term *Holocaust* expressed in the promises of the fund-raising letters can be linked to performance aspects of the actual museums that fulfill or contradict them. Of course, museums are ostensibly nonperformance sites: any museum that presents history is, to some extent, a place of death, and, in one way, this might actually enhance the ability of museums to represent genocide. But insofar as the museum attempts to portray the "liveness" (the usual hallmark of performance) of the now vanished bodies and what was done to them, it must use such performance technologies as archival footage via video monitors, as the D.C. museum does. To display this footage means that the once live bodies are now captured by the museum back into the reproductive economy: the museum must endlessly reproduce (in all its suffering and humiliation) what it asserts should not have happened to live bodies in the first place. And it must do so because its ideological underpinnings include the assumption (or is it the hope?) that displaying the violence of the Holocaust and its material, bodily effects (in as dignified a manner as possible) is a way of refuting the denial of this history, asserting its injustice, and preventing it from happening again.[3]

But there is a less mediated way to implement the "live" in relation to the history of the Holocaust. In a museum of the dead, the critical actors are gone and it is up to us, the spectators, to perform acts of engagement that make meaning and memory in and out of their absence. By using the word *meaning*, I do not intend to suggest that one can make sense, or value, or import out of the Holocaust; I use the word to signify a deeply informed engagement that enables a viewer to stand witness to these historical events. As Brecht notes in his play *Galileo,* "gawking isn't seeing" (879) and will not produce the engagement necessary for witness. Thus the "place" of the gawking bystander has to be turned into the "space" of ethically engaged witnessing. But, perhaps, more so than the distanciation solicited by Brechtian parable, even "seeing" enmeshed with empathy can be historically informed, engaged with the task of making larger connections despite the reality that no matter how perceptive or theoretically informed, those connections (including the Brechtian paradigm of materialist analysis itself) can never contain or manage this history.

So it is the museumgoers (along with the guards) who constitute the live, performing bodies in these museums. They are the focus of a variety of performance strategies deployed by the two museums for the sake of "the production of knowledge taken in and taken home" (Bal 1992:56). Some of these strategies produce the passivity and fascination of "gawking"; some induce a confirming sense of "seeing" by covering over what cannot be "seen" in the very act of offering us valuable information; and some position us to struggle *to see* at the same time we are conscious of our own difficult engagement in "seeing." Within the context of the promises in the fund-raising materials, I want to discuss some of the performance strategies of the D.C. Holocaust museum that involve the spectator's body spatially in the performance of making meaning. I will also examine the use of artifacts that disrupt, or at least complicate, the larger ways in which the museum locates the Holocaust in relation to American democracy. For the Beit Hashoah museum in Los Angeles, I want to investigate how its claim to create relationships between the Holocaust and other oppressions under the rubric of intolerance functions in practice, especially with regard to its inclusion of a film on the civil rights movement as the only path to reaching its Holocaust wing. Then I will speculate briefly about both these Holocaust museums in relation to the representation of genocide.

The U.S. Holocaust Memorial Museum and Its Fund-Raising Materials

We had downstairs [in the museum] waiting in line a lady being asked by [her] little child, what is the difference between freedom and liberated? . . . I couldn't butt into the middle, couldn't give that child the difference. But when you say liberated, you have to be enslaved first in order to be liberated, but freedom doesn't matter, wherever you are you can be free.

MR. HAROLD ZISSMAN, member of the Jewish resistance and survivor of the Holocaust, spoken to the author at the United States Holocaust Memorial Museum, 1993

The fund-raising materials for the United States Holocaust Memorial Museum in Washington, D.C., indicate what the museum promises to accomplish in order to elicit donations—a self-presentation that represents the main thrust of this institution (Bal 1992:558), prefiguring many of the strategies designed for the museum itself. I believe the target audience for these fund-raising letters is, primarily, the American Jewish community,[4] while the letters identify the target spectatorship for the museum as the public at large.[5] A captioned photograph locates the museum by its proximity to the Washington Monument as a means of validating it spatially as a national project. Quotations by Presidents Carter, Reagan, and Bush about the Holocaust further authenticate this undertaking, along with a 1945 statement by Eisenhower—not as president, but as general and liberator—asserting that he could give "firsthand evidence" of the horrors he saw "if ever there develops a tendency to charge these allegations merely to 'propaganda.'" Also included on the flyer is an official-looking image of the 1980 Public Law to create an independent federal establishment that will house "a permanent living memorial museum to the victims of the Holocaust" ("a short walk from our great national memorials" and hence, implicitly, connected to them). The effect of this is to deliberately blur the boundaries between the privately sponsored and the governmentally mandated.[6]

Of course, any Holocaust museum must enter into a dialogue with the country in which it is located and its positioning in these events, but the D.C. museum's emphasis on its geographies of announcement is insistent. A clear anxiety about denials of both the events of the Holocaust and its moral significance for Americans is embedded in these recurrent claims for legitimacy, even if some of the hyperbolic language can be chalked up to the discourse of fund-raising, which in itself constitutes a kind of melodrama of persuasion. Inevitably, an American Holocaust museum is caught on the cusp of happened here/ happened there, a conundrum, as Jim Young put it in a 1992 paper, over whether American history means events happening here or the histories Americans carry with them.

Presumably, then, learning about the events of the Holocaust, *precisely* because they didn't happen here, creates what one newsletter calls a "meaningful testament" to the values and ideals of democracy, thereby inscribing it within the history of American democracy, if not American history per se. It could be argued, then, that in this museum the Constitution is to be viewed through the prism of Jewish history as much as Jewish history is to be viewed through the prism of the Constitution. Thus one of the central strategies of the museum is to assert the way in which American mechanisms of liberal democratic government would prevent such a genocidal action from occurring in the United States, as well as to partially overlap, for the U.S. viewer, the perspective of the victims of genocide with that of the victors of World War II. This latter aspect would enhance what Philip Gourevitch describes as the museum's project to reinforce "the ethical ideals of American political culture by presenting the negation of those ideals" as well as our historical response to them (1993:55). In fact, images of American troops liberating the concentration camps constitute part of the final exhibit of the museum as well as the opening tactic of the Holocaust exhibit proper, where all that is seen and heard is presented through the eyes and ears of the liberating soldiers. Even the survivor testimony played for us in an amphitheater at the end of the exhibit prominently includes one narrative by a Holocaust survivor who eventually married the soldier who liberated her. Indeed, this marriage emplotment seems to embody a crucial strategy of the whole museum, with Jews and Jewish history (the feminized victim) married to American democracy (the masculinized liberator). Recalling that the American liberator in this survivor testimony is Jewish as well, I must note another, more implicit enactment in the museum, that of consolidating an American Jewish identity by marrying the positions of liberator and victim.

If what is critical for the museum's project is to extend our fictions of nationhood by the premise that a democratic state comes to the aid of those peoples outside its borders subjected to genocide, then the conferring of liberation becomes the story of American democracy. To assert this story entails backgrounding the masses of people who died before liberation (as opposed to the pitiful remnant left). It entails foregrounding the assumption that waging war can actually accomplish something and, more precisely, that saving Jews, Gypsies, leftists, Catholic dissenters, homosexuals, and Polish forced labor from the Nazis was one of the goals of World War II, rather than a by-product of winning the war by invading the enemies' territory. I could simply dismiss the museum's overall strategy as a simplistic appeal to hegemonic structures of governance. But to do so would be to deny that the museum *must engage* United States viewers with an ethical narrative of national identity in direct relation to the Holocaust. The alternative is to risk becoming a site for viewing the travails of the exoticized Other from elsewhere ("once upon a time") or, even worse, "a museum of natural history for an endangered species" (Bal 1992: 560). When didn't the "transnationality" of diasporic peoples have to be relocated within the narrative borders of the local nation in which they reside?

Moreover, the museum does not produce this idea of liberation from genocide as a completely unproblematic and unquestioned historical reality. Within the physical and conceptual envelope of its democratic discourse, the museum offers viewers a display of documents that echo and summarize parts of David Wyman's examination of *The Abandonment of the Jews* by the United States government. The museum displays the actual telegrams that communicate how, as late as February of 1943, with the Final Solution fully operational in European death camps, the State Department tried to shut down the channel through which it would have received information about what was happening to European Jews (information also designated for delivery via the State Department to the Jewish American community). The rationale was that such information would compromise our relations with the neutral countries from which these secret communications were emanating (Berenbaum 1993:161–62). This policy of suppression of information about and denial of aid to European Jews was challenged only by the intense labor of several men in the Treasury Department who had secretly gotten wind of the State Department's policy. Their efforts finally culminated in Randolph Paul's January 1944 "Report to the Secretary [of the Treasury] on the Acquiescence of This Government in the Murder of the Jews." To make a long, painful story short, in January 1944, Secretary of the Treasury Henry Morgenthau Jr. took this information to President Roosevelt, persuading him to establish the War Refugee Board by threatening (in a presidential election year) to release documents pertaining to the government's suppression of information and assistance (ibid.:163–64).

Despite the references to its proximity to national memorials in the fund-raising materials, the museum is actually closest physically to four mundane-looking government buildings, including the Treasury Building diagonally across the street. Much has been made of the way the museum copies the blocky functionality of these buildings in its initial entranceway, because this entrance is a false one, without a roof, while the actual doors to the museum are located several feet behind it. Thus the facade of the building recreates the solemn, neoclassical, and universalizing style of the government buildings around it, but marks its relationship to them as architecturally false. The documents that issued from the Treasury Building during the 1940s, however, manifest another relationship, one based in precise historical detail, previously suppressed. This creates a chronotopic connection, that is, a scene of interaction produced simultaneously out of temporal and spatial relationships, between the two buildings and the histories they contain. This puts into question the bland, monumental face of the Treasury Building (and its enabling circuits for commodification) by documenting what a group of people within this building at a particular historical moment "treasured." In offering this information, the museum constructs a localized historical contradiction to its own ideological claims about how democracies respond to genocides, thereby complicating the narrative of our national identity and, in so doing, turning an ostensible narrative place into a space for negotiating meanings. Caren Kaplan asserts that in a politics of location, "any exclusive recourse to space, place, or position becomes utterly abstract and universalizing without historical specificity" (1994:138). Because material history is used to make visible the private, invisible means within government deployed both to suppress and make known information about genocide, it can create a "productive tension between the temporal and spatial" (ibid.:119) and between the symbolic geography of governmental Washington and a geography of Washington constituted by site-specific locales—ones that situate the D.C. museum as well. Ideally, this scene of interaction opens a space of possibility for the spectator to consider how representative democracy operates in the present with regard to genocides elsewhere, rather than entirely soliciting a sense of disillusion, betrayal, and despair about the past. Finally, information about the Treasury Building also suggests that the museum's fund-raising letters function to some degree as a structural facade for an actual material space (i.e., the museum itself) that is more complex in its implications than the letters would suggest.

The fund-raising materials promise us another context for making meaning out of the exhibits as well. They describe the museum's Identity Card Project, a kind of interactive theater of identification. Each museum visitor is to receive a passport-sized ID card similar to the one a victim of the Holocaust was "forced to carry in Nazi Germany." At first the card is only to show the photograph of an actual person, with a brief background; then the card can be "updated" at "regular computer stations" for a fuller account. Most interesting is the actual list of victims from which these identity cards are drawn: they include Jews, Gypsies, homosexuals, Jehovah's Witnesses, and the handicapped, as well as others the Nazis labeled "undesirables." Thus, while still emphasizing the specific reference to Jews, the canon of the Holocaust victims has been reinterpreted and expanded, most pertinently to include homosexuals, whose desire for institutionalized recognition in the past had often been met with silence or resistance. This could offer us one means of considering the relationship of Jews to Other(ed) differences. Moreover, if the actual colored badges of these groups were to become part of the representation, they could convey the way the Nazis visually constructed categories of color upon religious, ethnic, sexual, political, and physical differences, thereby creating a racialized spectacle of visible difference where none existed. Such color coding could also complicate the monolith of European "whiteness" by exemplifying the ease with which that racial strategy was and continues to be manipulated for ideological and economic gain. The goal would be not to instill a passive "white terror" in white spectators, but to demonstrate the constructedness of "whiteness," its instability as a category, and the undesirability of relying on it for either self-knowledge or protection.

In actuality, the number of computers was inadequate to allow the enormous number of museumgoers to update their identity cards periodically, so we are simply given an identity card printed with the full individual narrative as we wait on line for the elevators to go up to the main exhibit.[7] And while the museum does exhibit multimedia materials on the persecution of Gypsies, homosexuals, and the handicapped, its documentation on the treatment of the German left by the Nazis turns out to be most critical to complicating its narrative of the Holocaust for the following reason: most conventional "how did it happen" histories of the Holocaust portray an escalating narrative of obsession with and restrictions and violence against Jews that culminates in the Final Solution. By contrast, the D.C. museum fills in some of the vacuum surrounding that history by documenting the ruthless suppression (including incarceration and murder) of socialists and communists from the start of the Nazi era (and early on in the exhibit, while museumgoers are still trying to read everything). This inclusion creates a fuller sense of Nazi ideology by offering the additional insight that this violence was constitutive of Nazism itself. It also challenges the simple binary emplotment of democracy versus fascism with a third term from the left.

However, while my readings of the actual museum emphasize sites for constructing multiple meanings and relationships, the fund-raising materials recall the larger ways in which the exhibits are to function. One flyer promises that the museum will orchestrate our emotions in the mode of a spectacle designed to command attention, transfix spectators, and narrativize in advance the experience of those who approach it: "You will watch, horrified" and "you will weep" over this "heroic and tragic story." One solicited emotional response to one monolithic, totalizing narrative. But there is also an overpowering sense of desire in all these descriptions, a need to create an utterly convincing spectacle that will say it all, stop time and space, prevent denial and make the suffering known. Of course, no representation can do that even if we hear the "actual voices of death camp survivors tell of unspeakable horror and pain." How could the unspeakable of genocide be spoken? How could the interiority of individual suffering on a massive scale be turned inside out into an exterior, if respectful, spectacle? Perhaps the consuming desire for the real in representation, for the convincing spectacular, is inversely proportionate to the process of genocide itself, which is not spectacularized, but silent, dispersed, and concealed. Perhaps this desire responds to the fear that whatever little is left to mark it afterwards will be forgotten. Or responds to the intense anxiety created by the growing trend Deborah Lipstadt documents in her 1993 book *Denying the Holocaust: The Growing Assault on Truth and Memory* operating in tandem with the temporal reality that many Holocaust survivors are very old or have died, so that the live, embodied narrative that functions as a bulwark against denial is being extinguished. But the personal artifacts that the letters claim will be collected in one of the museum's rooms—the suitcases, hairbrushes, razors, photographs, diaries, dolls, toys, shoes, eyeglasses, and wedding rings—despite their vivid materiality, are finally only the small detritus of annihilation that point to the inevitable absence of complete representation.

And yet, in practice, the museum's choice to include a roomful of nothing but piles of shoes is quite effective, in part because shoes are malleable enough to retain the shape of their individual owners and, even, here and there, an impractical bow or a tassel. So each shoe provides a small, intimate remnant of survival in the loss that, collected in piles, conveys the magnitude of that loss without becoming abstracted or aestheticized. The piles of shoes metonymically represent the huge body of shoes collected by the Nazis, which, in turn, metonymically represent the murdered people who wore them. So in their very materiality the shoes represent at once both absence and presence. Moreover, despite constantly blowing fans, the shoes smell (from their own disintegration) and thus involve our bodies in making memory. Other artifacts in the museum also call for physical activity in combination with our hermeneutic and emotional activity. Several times within the exhibit, we must cross via walkways through a tower of pictures that is taller than the exhibit's three stories. The photographs convey the quality of Jewish life and culture that was extinguished in the Polish town of Ejszyszki. One good thing about these pictures is that they represent how these people wanted to be seen, rather than how the Nazis made them look or how they looked when the liberators found them. But while the photographs' arrangement in the structure of a tower keeps directing us to look up, the top photos of this tower are so high they recede into invisibility. So we rehearse with our bodies not only the immeasurability of the loss, but also the imperfect structure of memory itself.

Even the sites of artifacts whose meaning is intended to be self-evident can become spaces, instead of places, changed by the paths visitors themselves create as historical subjects. The museum went to great pains, including revising its architectural plans, to exhibit a fifteen-ton freight car used to deport Jews. Walking through it offers us a physical trace of the frightening darkness and claustrophobic agony of the one hundred people crushed into this and other such cars. But as I moved toward this train car on the second day of my visit to the museum, I was approached by a married couple, Mrs. Sonya Zissman and Mr. Harold Zissman, who noticed I was speaking into a tape recorder and came to talk to me. Both had been involved in resistance in rural Poland. I reproduce part of our conversation at the site of this freight car:

VP: You're survivors?

SZ: I can't look at it [the freight car], I'm sick already. My husband, he was the head of a ghetto uprising... it's sickening to look at. You live day and night with that, day and night, as a matter of fact we were in the underground, we [both] escaped to the underground.

VP: Were you in a particular organization, is that what made you join the underground?

SZ: Organization? Nah. We were in the ghettos.... We were in the Eastern part of Poland and we knew what was going on.... Small towns, they had wooded areas, thousands and thousands of miles with wooded areas. We ran to these areas when the killing [of Jews in the ghettos started] and this was how we survived.

HZ: I escaped the ghetto. She ran away after the massacre was taking place in her town while she was in hiding. I escaped before it started in our ghetto — and I have very bad emotions between my family who dared why I should escape [and felt betrayed and who were subsequently killed]. [He weeps.]

SZ: And then the men were forming a fighting squadron... and the young ones were fighting.

VP: Did you get to be part of the fighting squad?

SZ: I was. My husband was. Down there in the underground.

VP: What's it like to be in the museum today?

SZ: Horrible. I got a headache already.... *But we gave them hell too,* don't worry.

VP: What does that mean?

SZ: Hell. The Germans.

VP: You gave them hell? How?

SZ: We used to mine the trains that were going to the front... so the soldiers were going on ten, twenty — that's how long the cars, you know, and they had ammunition going there with the train and [we would] tear them apart [by planting bombs under them]. We had the Russians [helping us], in the later years, '43, I think. They used to send us down sugar and salt and what we needed for [the fighting squadron] to live on.... My [previous] husband, my two brothers, my mother, got killed in the ghetto. [She weeps.]

VP: How many years were you in the underground?

SZ: For three years, because as soon as the ghetto started we had an underground.

VP: You mean you two were invisible and in hiding for three years?

SZ: Of course. We had to. You had no choice.

The live performance of survivor testimony by the Zissmans, "unmanaged" as it was by the museum proper, powerfully produced me as an engaged witness to their history, forcing me to negotiate their "unofficial" story with the "official" one surrounding it. What this conversation especially marked for me was how the museum's larger project of locating itself within a narrative of democracy displaced representations of acts of resistance by Jews in order to embed its narrative in the frame of American liberation. In other words, ideologically speaking, liberation requires a victim; there don't have to be resisters. Mr. Zissman put it more trenchantly when I asked him what he thought about the exhibits:

HZ: It's not so much important what I think because we have been through that [history]. We've been through the ghetto part [of the museum]. Only very few stories of our part [in this history] is being told. I wrote a scholar of the Holocaust...because very little is shown about our part [i.e., the Jewish resistance] for reasons beyond my understanding in fortysome years.... My own feeling is too much commercializing became the Holocaust here, the telling about the resistance and the participation of the Jews throughout Europe in resisting the enemy does not bring money, evidently.

VP: Victims do?

HZ: Exactly. Victims do.

The Beit Hashoah Museum of Tolerance and Its Fund-Raising Materials

In the process of evaluating aspects of the U.S. Holocaust Memorial Museum, I've asked myself "Just what would *you* have such a museum do? Position spectators as complicitous bystanders? As potential perpetrators of genocide? Who would come to such a museum?" But the answers to these questions are not self-evident. Locale and funding sources play a part in shaping what a Holocaust museum shows and who sees it. That the United States Holocaust Memorial Museum identifies itself as a national project imbricates the Holocaust into our national narratives and keeps a tight focus on the history of the Holocaust suits its Washington, D.C., locale and its federal grant of highly scarce land. Although it is privately funded, its quasi-governmental status helps produce what is and is not displayed within its walls.

The Beit Hashoah Museum of Tolerance is located in Los Angeles, adjacent to the Simon Wiesenthal Center (to which it is organizationally connected). It was built on private land, but received considerable funding from the State of California. As a result, this museum has a more insistent emphasis on pedagogy and is more explicitly targeted for schoolchildren and adolescents (i.e., an involuntary audience), although adjacent claims for extremely current technologies of representation are clearly intended to lure the public at large and attract funding from private donors. Under the rubric of teaching tolerance by providing examples of intolerance, it can display injustice in the United States and include a multiracial awareness of past and current American events. It also responds to its more immediate locale, Los Angeles, as a site of racial and ethnic tensions and includes those tensions (e.g., its speedy creation of an exhibit on the Los Angeles uprising of 1992) in its exhibits. While responding to the local, the museum also locates itself as an international project (like the Wiesenthal Center itself) that globally documents past and present violations of human rights.

In accordance with these projects, the fund-raising letters sent to private donors prior to the museum's opening employ a primary strategy opposite to that of the U.S. Holocaust Memorial Museum: the Beit Hashoah Museum of Tolerance will represent the United States as a site of "bigotry and intolerance," that is, as a potential place of genocide, with the Holocaust as the most horrific illustration of where intolerance could lead. While the D.C. museum quoted U.S. presidents to authenticate its project, the Beit Hashoah's charter member fund-raising flyer quotes Martin Luther King Jr: "Like life, racial understanding is not something that we find, but something that we must create." Thus the Beit Hashoah articulates the history of the Holocaust to an American landscape of prejudice and racism, a more liberal narrative that, to some degree, troubles our sense of national identity if not, as will be noted later, our fictions of nationhood. Moreover, given its claim to respond to and represent the international, the national, and the local, the focus of the museum is as diffuse (despite the presence of Holocaust exhibits that take up a fair share, but by no means most, of the museum's space and much, but not all, of the fund-raising descriptions) as the U.S. Holocaust Memorial Museum's focus was specific. This diverse range of arenas configured under the rubric of intolerance is represented in the fund-raising descriptions, which describe the path of this museum as follows:

First, visitors are confronted by ethnic and minority stereotypes as a means to challenge their current attitudes and perceptions. Second, they enter a Tolerance Workshop where they are given an "authentic social dilemma" and asked to choose and motivate others to moral actions (actually a large area resembling a video arcade where multiple interactive "games" about prejudice can be played). Third, visitors view "stereotypical ethnic and racial depictions from early movies," hear demagogues vilifying minorities, and "meet" via video "individuals who have made a difference," including Martin Luther King Jr., Robert Kennedy, and Raoul Wallenberg. Fourth, "in a series of illuminated computer-synchronized tableaux" that are "amazingly lifelike," visitors "go back in time" to experience "the events of the Holocaust" (actually, what is described are moments in the development of fascism and a genocidal mentality in Nazi Germany). Fifth, and finally, visitors stand before a replica of the gates of Auschwitz and hear the voices of Holocaust victims speak of "suffering and heroism."

While I can appreciate the goals of a Holocaust museum that seeks not only to serve as a place to memorialize victims of persecution, but also to create a laboratory for devising strategies to combat hate, violence, and prejudice in the present, I note several problems in the proposed strategies to achieve this. The continued insistence of the fund-raising letters that the museum presents "real life" to viewers obscures the way it is adjusting the parameters of a discourse. Moreover, while "persecution and devastation" have been the results of both anti-Semitism and racism, the museum risks creating an abstract equivalence between the two by configuring both as "an internalized matter of prejudice" (Bourne 1987:14). When tolerance becomes a personal matter, it cannot, for example, take into account the way racism functions as "a structural and institutional issue" within a system of power "hierarchically structured to get the maximum benefit from differentiation" (ibid.). Showing this system of exploitative differentiation is especially critical for a museum about genocide, since it is just this system that would profit most from the construction of competing narratives about the suffering of various groups, creating the divisiveness of what Michael Berenbaum called "a calculus of calamity" (1990:34). I recognize that this is exactly what the Beit Hashoah Museum of Tolerance is trying to avoid, but I don't think it takes its goals far enough. And missing from the museum's landscape of intolerance are the violent outbreaks of homophobia now occurring in the United States, nor is there much mention of sexism: in practice the museum privileges racism as the site of intolerance, not surprising if its purpose is to forge links with other genocidal situations using the more traditional notions of "group" that govern definitions of genocide. Finally, the threat of genocide and even actions deemed potentially genocidal may not be the best measure for evaluating the everyday oppressions to which people and groups are subject, and such a treatment may even serve to minimize the importance of daily oppressions, especially when they are not in line with a teleological narrative of escalating violence.

And, despite its emphasis on the interactive, by ending with the gates of Auschwitz the museum takes the space it tries to open up for a consideration of the interconnections among oppressions and re-contains it into a (computer-synchronized) place. Auschwitz becomes a monumental metonymy for the Holocaust, for all anti-Semitism(s), and for the consequences of intolerance. Using Auschwitz as an emblem of all anti-Semitism(s) may actually obscure the current mechanisms by which they function. Using Auschwitz as a metonymy for the consequences of intolerance is partly facilitated by the museum's Eurocentric gesture of locating its history of genocide only in the twentieth century. In so doing, the museum erases the historical reality that not only could genocide happen here, it *has* happened here, if not with the same obsessive deliberateness associated with the Final Solution. A museum with the goals of this one must take into account the massive genocidal annihilations in the Americas, and in particular in this country, committed against indigenous peoples and against Africans during slavery.

Why doesn't it? Is showing genocide within our borders "going too far" for such a museum? More generally, should we assume that if the Jewish genocide in Europe were backgrounded in a site dedicated to showing intolerance, other genocides, indigenous to the United States, would inevitably become foregrounded, historically more visible? There are African American and Native American museums slated for the Smithsonian Mall, but, as Philip Gourevitch has noted (1993: 62), no Museum of Slavery or Trail of Tears museum. Perhaps recognizing the contributions of specific ethnicities, emphasizing what their continuing presence and vitality offers us as a nation, constitutes a celebratory means of covering over what was done to them and who and what has been permanently lost. Our democratic discourse must repress highly visible representations of any genocide that occurred within our own national borders. In order to sustain its fictions of nationhood and its imagined community, it must produce yet another set of highly visible representations of what it marks as a genocide occurring "elsewhere," outside of its enlightened democracy. Indeed, the genocide film shown at the Beit Hashoah pertains to South American indigenous peoples, to Armenians, and to Cambodians. Curiously, then, at the Beit Hashoah, the perspective of the global with which it enhances its scope is in itself a tactful drawing of attention away from the full excess of "intolerance" in this country. From this perspective, it is the very performance of hegemonic democratic discourse, more pertinently our own "hardwired" fictions of nationhood, that we would need to interrogate and revise in order to make genocide "at home" visible.[8]

But that still does not fully account for what *is* shown at the Beit Hashoah as the last big exhibit before the Holocaust wing and how it is situated: the multiscreen feature on the civil rights struggle directed by Orlando Bagwell, director of the series *Eyes on the Prize*. Between the civil rights film viewing area and the Holocaust wing, there is a peculiar little film displaying the lives of the rich in the 1920s. It's like a sorbet, a palette cleanser between two gourmet courses. Why this rupture? Perhaps because historically, the directional signals are different: the call for African American civil rights is the call for removing the last vestiges of genocidal slavery (when is massive slavery not genocidal?); the elimination of civil rights for Jews in Germany is the beginning of the escalation toward genocide (a teleological narrative that would not suit the African American example) although it is also a grotesque and disorienting action in itself. The introduction to *Nationalisms and Sexualities* notes a convergence between the "persistence of nationalism explained as a passionate 'need' " and "the rights of sexual minorities legitimated through a discourse of civil liberties" (Parker et al. 1992:2), suggesting our deep ideological and political investment in the arguments of legal personhood. Moreover, the call for extending democracy to everyone fits with our "imagined communities of nationalism" even if this assimilative model, drawing as it does on the experience of white ethnic immigrants to the United States, fails to describe the circumstances of those brought here forcibly *to* genocidal conditions or those here before us submitted to them. The historical reality of slavery existing legally within democracy does not fit our national ideological fictions and is therefore always already in danger of being suppressed. To some degree, then, the model of civil rights and tolerance used by the museum, though certainly useful, glosses over very different histories and obscures the ideological interconnections of genocidal events that "happened here" and "happened there."

Perhaps it isn't such a bad thing that the Beit Hashoah does not try to visibly construct a relationship between the two since it was likely to be more analogizing and less historical than desired, and it does leave room for a network of meanings to be constructed by and among spectators. In April 1994, Black Entertainment Television broadcast a tour of the Los Angeles museum's major exhibits, narrated by African American and European American professional basketball players. The African American athletes testified to the museum's educational worth in challenging prejudice and intolerance and recommended that people come and bring their children. This televised tour reveals the cultural work this museum is now doing, that of turning itself into an object of discursive penetration and movement. But for me the stakes of what that television show might mean are even higher — that this museum, though flawed, is at least an ambitious first step toward putting the mechanisms of oppression (and not simply diversity) into public discourse. Admittedly it is problematic to assume that because of the history of the Holocaust Jews can function as the best guides to the larger landscape of intolerance in this country; such an assumption imparts an overarching symbolic significance to the events of the Holocaust. But, to the degree that this museum and this ethnicity assume the responsibilities of representing oppressions beyond their own, they make a gesture more unparalleled in the United States than dismissals of this museum as a Disneyesque theme park would acknowledge.

In his book *Storm from Paradise*, Jonathan Boyarin speculates that "the greater invisibility of genocide in America may be related to the general devaluation of history here compared to Europe" (30). Perhaps both the U.S. Holocaust Memorial Museum and the Beit Hashoah Museum of Tolerance enhance our appreciation for history in general. And both museums, by presenting the history of the Holocaust in relation to either ideals of democracy or negations of them articulate their function as guides: to the Holocaust, to paradigms of democracy and ethical behavior, and to constructions of Jewish memory and identity in relation to U.S. democracy. But both also call into question what constitutes representation in a representative democracy. And both—either explicitly at the Beit Hashoah or implicitly at the U.S. Holocaust Memorial Museum—interrogate the notion of the United States as safe haven. Finally, both museums, however imperfect, essay the impossible task of putting the Holocaust into representation and remembrance.

Notes

I would like to thank the following people for their editorial advice and encouragement: Elin Diamond, Jonathan Boyarin, Jill Dolan, Peg Lourie, Vida Penezic, and David Anderson. I also acknowledge the invaluable assistance of both Mary Callahan Boone, my researcher in the earlier stages of this work, and Annette Wannamaker, my 1994 researcher. Their work was funded by Graduate Research Assistant Awards from Bowling Green State University. This essay was initially a paper given at the 1992 Modern Language Association convention within a series of three "Performance in Cultural Studies" panels organized by Elin Diamond for the MLA Drama Division.

1. On April 19, 1993, three days before the United States Holocaust Memorial Museum actually opened, front-page news for the Bowling Green *Sentinel-Tribune* (and I'm sure many other local newspapers) included an article entitled "Survey: One in 5 Doubt Holocaust Happened." A Holocaust survey, done by the Roper Organization in the United States in November of 1992 and provided by the American Jewish Committee, sampled 992 adults. They were asked the question "Does it seem possible or does it seem impossible to you that the Nazi extermination of the Jews never happened?" This yielded the information that 22 percent of those asked said "It seems possible" it never happened, 65 percent said "It seems impossible" it never happened, and 12 percent replied with "Don't know/No answer." These statistics were framed in a box next to the article. If one actually reads the full article, one learns that the Roper survey found "that thirty eight percent of adults and fifty three per cent of high school students did not know the meaning of the term the Holocaust." Given my project in this essay, I am curious about what those executing the Roper survey deemed "the meaning" of the Holocaust. The information the survey presented, as well as its placement in time, constitutes a kind of self-evident rationale for a Holocaust museum (though the museum is never directly mentioned) or for a Holocaust pedagogy in the schools. This information also serves as a reminder that no historical referent is stable, transparent in its meaning, agreed upon in its usage, or even engaged with in the same way by any large group of people.

2. See, for example, Helen Fein, "Teaching about Genocide in an Age of Genocides," in *Teaching about Genocide: A Guide Book for College and University Teachers: Critical Essays, Syllabi and Assignments,* ed. Joyce Freedman-Apsel and Helen Fein (Ottawa: Human Rights Internet), 1992.

3. On the April 18, 1993, op-ed page of the *New York Times,* Jonathan Rosen, editor of *The Forward,* quotes Michael Berenbaum, who was the director of the projected museum, as saying, "What we are about is the Americanization of the Holocaust." In response, Rosen critiqued the soon to open museum as "building a shrine to Jewish victimization" and so inscribing this (Christian-created) role of suffering onto Jews within an American context. What interests me is the underlying debate this exchange represents: Will publicizing and creating a pedagogy for conveying the historical sufferings and injustices imposed upon a particular group result in better treatment for that group in the present? Or will it reinscribe their position as sufferers, possibly rationalizing or setting a precedent for further suffering? Neither assumption per se suggests fitting the historical events of the Holocaust into a discourse emphasizing the larger structures that produce atrocity and oppression, although Holocaust educational groups like the Facing History Project do try to include this in their pedagogy. Nor does either of the two link this "Americanized" Jewish narrative of suffering and oppression to the production of other discourses of historical suffering and oppression currently circulating—"founding" narratives crucial (however "essentialized") to the struggle against injustice, especially when these narratives are configured under the rubric of identity politics. It is at the Beit Hashoah Museum of Tolerance, in Los Angeles, that museum designers have tried to place, however imperfectly, this history of Jewish suffering in relation to that of other groups, most notably African Americans.

4. It is also the case that different language was used in fund-raising letters for different target groups within the Jewish community. One of my letters promised that in helping to fund the museum "you will make possible profound experiences of human emotion that will remain with visitors for the rest of their lives. No one who visits the Museum will be untouched." By contrast, the language of the flyer received by my parents, who live in a predominantly Jewish retirement community, was more personal and less restrained. It also focused more on what they, as visitors, would experience: "You will weep with entire families," and "when breaking hearts can bear it no longer, visitors will emerge into the light." Despite the differing vocabularies, both letters conceive guarantees of emotional identification or deep empathy with the victims of the Holocaust as an essential fund-raising strategy.

5. According to a 1991 description, it even hopes to attract what it refers to as "accidental tourists" in the Washington, D.C., area—interesting in retrospect since from its official opening on April 22, 1993, the museum has become such a deliberate tourist attraction they have had to ask people to stay away, and the space of "accident" has become the place of advance tickets and long lines.

6. Actually, the Washington Monument, by which the museum locates itself within a national landscape, was also privately sponsored on government land, see Kirk Savage, "The Self-Made Monument: George Washington and the Fight to Erect a National Memorial," in *Critical Issues in Public Art: Content, Context, and Controversy,* ed. Harriet F. Senie and Sally Webster (New York: Harper Collins), 1992.

7. More interesting in terms of the use of computers in relation to the Holocaust is the display, within the exhibit, of the Hollerith, a very early data-processing device. This device enabled the Nazis to assert in 1934 that "we are recording the individual characteristics of every single member of the nation onto a little card," here using technology as a means to impose and process the essentialized "characteristics" used to constitute people into groups. While these data were used to persecute Jews and other groups, the reference to "every single member of the nation" recollects the way in which persecution is interrelated with the regulation and containment of the popu-

lation as a whole. This reduction of the population to life-affirming or life-denying data ought to clarify the stakes for "normative" groups in resisting genocidal actions.

8. For such an exploration and reconfiguring of American democracy, see, for example, *Democracy: A Project by Group Material* edited by Brian Wallis, number 5 in the Discussions in Contemporary Culture series sponsored by the Dia Art Foundation, published in 1990 in Seattle by Bay Press. Also see Chantal Mouffe's "Radical Democracy: Modern or Postmodern?" (translated by Paul Holdengraber) in *Universal Abandon? The Politics of Postmodernism,* ed. Andrew Ross (Minneapolis: University of Minnesota Press).

Bibliography

Bal, Mieke. 1992. "Telling, Showing, Showing Off." *Critical Inquiry* 18 (Spring): 556–94.

Bauer, Yehuda. 1989. "The Place of the Holocaust in Contemporary History." In *Holocaust: Religious and Philosophical Implications,* ed. John Roth and Michael Berenbaum. New York: Paragon House.

Beit Hashoah Museum of Tolerance. Fund-raising letters to author, especially between 1991 and 1992.

Berenbaum, Michael. 1990. "The Uniqueness and Universality of the Holocaust." In *A Mosaic of Victims: Non-Jews Persecuted and Murdered by the Nazis.* New York: New York University Press.

———. 1993. *The World Must Know: The History of the Holocaust as Told in the United States Holocaust Memorial Museum.* Boston: Little, Brown.

Bourne, Jenny. 1987. "Homelands of the Mind: Jewish Feminism and Identity Politics." *Race and Class: A Journal for Black and Third World Liberation* 29, no. 1 (Summer):1–24.

Boyarin, Jonathan. 1992. *Storm from Paradise: The Politics of Jewish Memory.* Minneapolis: University of Minnesota Press.

Brecht, Bertolt. *Galileo.* 1993. In *The Bedford Introduction to Drama,* ed. Lee A. Jacobus. 2d ed. Boston: St. Martin's.

Certeau, Michel de. 1984. *The Practice of Everyday Life.* Translated by Steven Rendall. Berkeley: University of California Press.

Ezrahi, Sidra DeKoven. 1980. *By Words Alone: The Holocaust in Literature.* London: University of Chicago Press.

Goekjian, Gregory F. 1991. "Genocide and Historical Desire." *Semiotica: Journal of the International Association for Semiotic Studies* 83, no. 3/4:211–25.

Gourevitch, Philip. 1993. "Behold Now Behemoth: The Holocaust Memorial Museum: One More American Theme Park." *Harper's* 287, no. 1718 (July):55–62.

Kaplan, Caren. 1994. "The Politics of Location as Transnational Feminist Critical Practice." In *Scattered Hegemonies: Postmodernity and Transnational Feminist Practices,* ed. Inderpal Grewal and Caren Kaplan, 137–52. Minneapolis: University of Minnesota Press.

Lipstadt, Deborah. 1993. *Denying the Holocaust: The Growing Assault on Truth and Memory.* New York: Free Press.

Parker, Andrew, et al. 1992. *Nationalisms and Sexualities.* New York: Routledge.

Phelan, Peggy. 1993. *Unmarked: The Politics of Performance.* New York: Routledge.

Rosen, Jonathan. "The Misguided Holocaust Museum." *New York Times,* April 18, 1993, op-ed section.

Stannard, David E. 1992. *American Holocaust: Columbus and the Conquest of the New World.* New York: Oxford University Press.

"Survey: One in 5 Doubt Holocaust Happened." 1993. *Sentinel-Tribune,* Bowling Green, Ohio, April 19, 1.

United States Holocaust Memorial Museum. Fund-raising letters to author, especially from 1991 through 1992, including its "Charter Supporter Acceptance Form."

Wyman, David S. 1984. *The Abandonment of the Jews: America and the Holocaust 1941–1945.* New York: Pantheon.

Young, James E. 1988. *Writing and Rewriting the Holocaust: Narrative and the Consequences of Interpretation.* Bloomington: Indiana University Press.

———. 1992. "America's Holocaust: Memory and the Politics of Identity." Paper presented for the panel "The Holocaust and the American Jewish Imagination: Memory, Text, and Myth." Modern Language Association December conference.

———. 1993. *The Texture of Memory: Holocaust Memorials and Meaning.* New Haven, Conn.: Yale University Press.

4 / Identities on Display: Jewishness and the Representational Politics of the Museum

Johannes von Moltke

January 20, 1992. Fifty years have gone by since the Wannsee conference, at which a group of high-ranking Nazi officials gathered for breakfast and cognac to formalize what came to be known as the Final Solution. The return of this date and others associated with the Holocaust and the Second World War has begun to produce a "memorial culture" of its own; Claudia Koonz speaks of a "veritable culture of commemoration" that has arisen in Germany since the late 1970s and 1980s, when the fortieth and fiftieth anniversaries of these dates began to be observed with a certain degree of public and international visibility.[1] In the meantime, even in Germany where such commemorative acts continue to be especially charged, the political speeches on such occasions are becoming more or less predictable (though perhaps not quite "routine," as Koonz suggests).[2] On this particular day, however, these discursive forms of marking an anniversary were supplemented by the commemorative intervention of another cultural form: in Berlin, two museums provided an alternative to the predictable speeches by opening their doors to the public on January 20, 1992. In the Wannsee suburb, the villa where the notorious conference took place was inaugurated on this date as Germany's first and only Holocaust Memorial Museum.[3] While the exhibit is still in need of improvement, and the overall conception of the museum pales by comparison to the more recent Holocaust Museum on the Mall in

Washington, D.C., this was certainly a significant step in the right direction. The decision to finally establish this museum as a memorial institution acts on the insight that "by themselves, the sites of destruction lack what Pierre Nora has called 'the will to remember.' "[4]

On the same day, however, another exhibit opened in Berlin. By contrast to the exhibit in Wannsee, this one was centrally located right next to the Potsdamer Platz in the prestigious Martin-Gropius-Bau. Boasting a budget of approximately $7 million, this was clearly going to be the year's biggest exhibit in a city full of museum events. Furthermore, as part of the annual Berlin Festspiele, the exhibit was accompanied by a massive cultural program that included innumerable concerts, readings, films and videos, plays, symposia, lectures, book publications, and nationwide television programs, all of which contributed to proliferating the exhibit's discursive implications.[5] Consequently, when the doors opened on January 20 for an event that for weeks in advance had been hailed by the press as a cultural landmark, the crowd of some ten thousand visitors on the first weekend alone exceeded the capacities of the Martin-Gropius-Bau, forcing it to shut down temporarily. Those who did make it to the exhibition space on the second floor were rewarded with room after room filled with two thousand precious objects and texts, all of which combined to display something called "Jewish lifeworlds."[6]

Despite the obvious differences in magnitude and in the way they invoke the memory of January 20, both of these exhibits participate in the general "museum boom" of recent years. As one of the key sites of cultural politics today, the museum has rapidly been gaining ground as an ever more popular cultural medium. No longer just a bastion of high culture, "museum culture," as a recent book calls it, has taken its place alongside other media in shaping the changing contours of everyday life.[7] For even if we don't actually go to the museum fairly regularly (though, statistically, most of us do), we encounter forms of "musealization" at every turn—in reconstructed urban environments, in historical theme parks, in retro fashions and flea markets, in debates about the politics of popular exhibits and about the architecture of vast new museums such as the United States Holocaust Memorial Museum in Washington.

But there is more to this museum culture than simply its emerging status as a mass medium with popular appeal. For while such a boom itself may not be unprecedented (the first massive expansion of museum culture dates back to the early nineteenth century), the contemporary museum intervenes in a specifically postmodern dynamics of memory and amnesia. Along with the other institutions and sites that organize our social memory, the museum plays a pivotal role in the postmodern predicament of memorial culture. The mnemonic role of the museum may appear to be almost self-evident when the connection between the museum and memory is spelled out as clearly as in the two examples I have mentioned. I think, however, that this connection can plausibly be generalized as an aspect that relates in one form or another to all forms of musealization.

If there is a specifically postmodern articulation of the convergence between memory and the museum, it turns on the absolute crisis of modernity that is the Holocaust. As "the litmus test for any contemporary reading of the history of modernity," the Holocaust challenges us to find sites and forms that help us to remember, while simultaneously threatening us with a loss or impossibility of memory that has far-reaching consequences for the negotiation of cultural identity and difference:

> The issue of remembrance and forgetting touches the core of a multifaceted and diverse Western identity. . . . Without memory, without reading the traces of the past, there can be no recognition of difference, . . . no tolerance for the rich complexities and instabilities of personal and cultural, political and national identities.[8]

In this case, the specific role and the importance of the museum must be sought in the various ways in which it engages with this need for memory. But if the postmodern museum connects to the intractable questions of memory generated by modernity, the question remains of how to theorize that particular link: given the amnesiac tendencies that characterize the postmodern in Jean-François Lyotard's definition, for example, how do we explain the run on the museums in the 1980s and 1990s?[9] Doesn't the growth of a "memorial, or *museal* sensibility" that Andreas Huyssen finds manifest in everyday culture and experience suggest a spontaneous commitment to history and memory? Or is any such popular interest in the past perhaps brought about by some enlightening or pedagogical function of the museum as an institution? Huyssen's own suggestion is that we value the return to museal memory and to the monument as a "way of slowing down the speed of modernization" —not to bring it to a grinding halt, but to counteract the amnesia that it produces in the first place. The postmodern culture of memory, in this account, acts on the omissions of modernity itself, dragging the repressed and forgotten back into the public light of the museum in the form of material objects. This is why, in tracing the transformation of memory along the divide between modernism and postmodernism, Huyssen has suggested that we consider the museum "as the key paradigm in contemporary postmodern culture."[10]

Now, as Huyssen is clearly aware, this argumentation skirts along a culturally conservative vision of modernity, where modernization is understood as a relatively autonomous and basically disastrous course of events, in the face of which culture remains essentially powerless. One version of cultural theory that has articulated this view quite explicitly is organized around the notion of culture as compensation (*Kompensationstheorie*). In the opinion of critics like Hermann Lübbe and Wolfgang Zacharias, for example, culture and the museum function broadly to compensate for the corrosive processes of modernization that range from a loss of experience (*Erfahrung*) to an accelerated temporality where the past and the future encroach upon a present that is constantly on the retreat.[11] Pierre Nora describes this "acceleration of history" as "an increasingly rapid slippage of the present into a historical past that is gone for good, a general perception that anything and everything may disappear."[12] The function of culture and memory—which converge in the museum—then becomes to compensate for our lost experiences, to gloss over the instability of the temporal moment that ever so briefly becomes our present.[13] In his introduction to a volume of essays dedicated to the "Zeitphänomen Musealisierung" (musealization as a contemporary phenomenon), Zacharias consequently postulates "the necessity of the interpretive museum in the face of a need for stable meanings deriving from familiar origins."[14]

The glaring problem with such a position is that it leaves no space for the museum to do any work other than merely glossing over the deficiencies of modernization and creating the illusion of a sustained and fairly stable dynamics of history. As Wolfgang Fliedl points out in his critique of Lübbe's position, the implicit cultural and historical pessimism underpinning this concept of an inherently destructive modernization has serious consequences for the interpretation of culture generally and of the function of the museum in particular, for the compensation theory of culture "takes leave of the notion of cultural modernization. In order to make technological and scientific innovations bearable, culture is given the role of a counterbalance while barred from creating any pressures for innovation or developing a critical potential of its own."[15] In this view, the mnemonic role played by the museum becomes negligible, a mere appendix to a cultural sphere that is always already a matter of simulation anyhow.

I think we can and should take the museum more seriously than that. I therefore strongly concur with Huyssen's view that our contemporary museum culture acts on the omissions of modernism rather than compensating for them; in other words, rather than conceiving the museum as extrinsic to the generation of our modern and postmodern lifeworlds (which allegedly takes place elsewhere, not in culture), I take it to be centrally involved in that process. Where the compensation theorists see the museum in terms of diversion, as a spectacle that eases the pressures exerted by modernization in domains that, by extension, are the effective underside of a culture without agency (e.g., science, technology, economy), I want to emphasize the ways in which the museum participates in these struggles and thereby becomes a pivotal site for the negotiation of cultural identity. Moreover, while that negotiation depends crucially on the configuration of cultural memory, it is important to note that the museum constructs memories and identities only when and if its audience brings its cultural present to bear on the representational politics of the museums and their exhibits. That is, the link between museum and memory described by Huyssen should not divert us from the fact that the museum functions within a dialogic framework, that it is always embedded in different public spheres that contest and rearticulate the museum's function. By extension, the museum itself becomes an active participant in the articulation not only of cultural memory, but also of cultural identity—constituted both through memory and through museal discourse at large.

Nowhere do these two central aspects of musealization converge more forcefully than when it comes to the various forms in which museums exhibit Jewishness. Because of the ineradicable role of the Holocaust in Jewish history, and also because of the general importance of memory to the construction of Jewish identity, Jewishness as an object of museal representation meshes distinctly with the mnemonics and identity politics of the museum.[16] This connection is perhaps self-evident when the topic of a given exhibit is as explicitly concerned with questions of memory and memorialization as James Young's recent project on the politics and aesthetics of Holocaust memorials.[17] But I would argue that the same politics of memory and Jewish identity are at work in all the various forms of musealization that exhibit Jewishness, including the Judaica collections of prominent Jewish museums throughout the world; art exhibits emphasizing the role and fate of Jewish artists (such as the recent, highly acclaimed *"Degenerate Art,"* which showed in Los Angeles and Washington before traveling to the Altes Museum in Berlin, where the Nazis first exhibited the same famous artworks without the quotation marks in 1938); exhibitions of diasporic "Jewish lifeworlds" (as in the Berlin exhibit of 1992); and also museum architecture itself, as in the case of James Ingo Freed's Holocaust Museum in Washington, or Daniel Libeskind's design for the Jewish Museum currently under construction in Berlin.[18]

The following extended "visit" to the more extensive exhibit of the two Berlin openings of January 20, 1992, takes up the issue of Jewish diasporic identity after the Holocaust in an effort to show how the museum enters the fray of a particularly charged "memorial culture" — not in order to "compensate" for anything, but to engage with the possibilities and impossibilities of Jewish identity on the terrain of cultural (and political) representation. The essay traces the identity politics of the museum in relation to Jewishness, suggesting that the cultural form of the museum has become a crucial site for the articulation of Jewish identity. What I want to be asking, then, is this: What happens to Jewish ethnicity when it is put on display? What kinds of narratives can a (German) exhibit or museum construct around Jewish identity, and are there voices in those narratives that are reduced to silence? What are the political and representational stakes, the opportunities and the dangers involved in making Jewishness the object of a museal discourse in Germany today?[19]

Exhibiting Jewish Lifeworlds (A Guided Tour)

Like any other title, *Jewish Lifeworlds (Jüdische Lebenswelten)* causes the visitor to have certain expectations, to come to the exhibit with certain hypotheses about what its objects might add up to. Thus, the very concept of "Jewish lifeworlds" immediately raises crucial questions about the aesthetics and politics of the exhibit that it names: what makes up a "lifeworld," and how will particular lifeworlds be objectified for the purposes of exhibition? We might turn for help to the exhibit's subtitle, which read, somewhat tortuously: "Jewish Thought and Faith, Life and Work in the Cultures of the World." But rather than anchoring the potential meanings of the overall title (e.g., by supplying a geographical or temporal focus for the lifeworlds on display), this catalog merely repeats the fuzzy notion of "life" rather than somehow shoring up the possibilities contained in the term *lifeworld*. In other words, the task of filling that term with specifiable meanings would obviously have to be performed by the exhibit itself. However, given the broad and almost presumptuous range of possibilities initially suggested by the title, it should come as no surprise that the term became a site of intense struggle over its referent(s); the way in which the exhibit ultimately presented what its organizers took to be "Jewish lifeworlds" in the "cultures of the world" was thus measured against other ways of reading the concept of the "lifeworld" and became the subject of much debate. My own aim in taking up these debates along with a more "textual" description of the exhibit will be to provide one reading of the notion of lifeworlds in terms of *ethnicity;* while this connection was rarely, if ever, spelled out explicitly in the context of the exhibit, I want to suggest that it productively focuses the identificatory struggles waged around the exhibit's politics.

This still leaves us with further questions deriving from the central term of the title, also repeated tautologically in the ostensibly explanatory subtitle: even if we can agree on what a "lifeworld" may be, what is it that makes lifeworlds *Jewish* in the "cultures of the world"? And here, too, the question arises of just how the organizers were going to objectify Jewishness for the purposes of musealization. In particular, how would they address this issue in Germany and for a largely non-Jewish German audience, where both the social and the discursive positions of Jewishness remain particularly precarious and complex? (This involves the important issues of both the contexts and the mode of address of the exhibit, to which I will return at length). A visitor entering the Martin-Gropius-Bau on January 20, 1992, might therefore have had any number of expectations with respect to the exhibit's articulation of Jewishness. At worst, she might have had to fear an exoticizing display of the "scenes from Jewish life" type, staged behind glass with the help of life-size wax figures — the kind of colonial ethnology-cum-natural-history approach that still characterizes far too many museums of natural history. Visitors familiar with the Jewish Diaspora Museum in Tel Aviv, on the other hand, might have expected something in the line of Ariella Azoulay's description of its permanent exhibit, where "the most advanced technological means such as computers, videos, and holograms are used to construct the most banal and stereotypical and supposedly authentic images that visually signify groups of people as 'Jewish.' "[20] Then again German visitors, who, as recent events have shown, remain deplorably impervious to the very notion of diasporic Jewishness, might have been quick to expect to learn mainly about *Israeli* lifeworlds;[21] whereas those who had visited the Jewish Department of the Berlin Museum before it closed temporarily in 1988 would have been likely to base their expectations on some notion of Judaica, or Jewish ceremonial art, as an object of exhibition. In sum, the notion of "Jewish lifeworlds" announced by the title is significant not simply for the lack of any fixed referent, but also for the way in which this openness calls for the exhibit (and the visitor) to fill the term with meaning.

Upon entering the exhibit, visitors were soon to become aware that one of its defining features was obviously its wholehearted commitment to the open nature of its title. Rather than anchoring the term "Jewish lifeworlds" in a narrow selection of objects, in readily available clichés, or in privileged national traditions, the museum generated a view of diasporic Jewish identity as a mosaic of different facets with hardly an underlying essence. As a quick tour of the exhibit will show, the representation of diasporic lifeworlds in this particular museum was highly productive in the way it gestured toward Jewish identity as a hybrid, "disaggregated" form of ethnicity.[22]

On one level, this effect turned on a matter of bulk: the sheer magnitude of the lavishly displayed exhibit suggested a variety of Jewish lifeworlds in what one critic justifiably called "a truly unique encyclopedic effort."[23] If an encyclopedia is generally a nonnarrative form organized around the arbitrary order of the alphabet, however, this museological encyclopedia opened by generating at least the beginnings of a chronological narrative: the visit led off quite conventionally with "History of the Jewish People in Antiquity." I should add immediately that while the objects clearly signified "antiquity" to even the most distracted viewer (presenting ancient clay objects, stone capitals, and murals in the fragmented and decayed forms familiar from archaeological and paleontological disciplines), the reconstruction of their Jewish meanings was established contextually and demanded an additional effort—if only reading the labels or catalog descriptions that placed the archaeological items in a Jewish tradition.

This construction of a relationship between a contextual or "secondary" Jewish meaning and the more immediate connotations of age, archaeological value, and so on was then reversed in the following rooms, which focused almost didactically on the construction of Jewishness by displaying various aspects of Jewish houses, synagogues, and community. Thwarting the expectations that it had just raised with regard to a chronologically coherent narrative, the exhibit suddenly appeared to remember its claims to encyclopedic representation. Spice boxes, Sabbath lamps and cups, mezuzahs and Torah scrolls, even models of different Eastern European and Chinese synagogues—here was a collection of objects that conveyed a notion of Jewishness rather directly, if only in terms of Jewish ceremony and ritual.[24]

From this dual starting point, suggesting both a narrative of Jewish identity and a nonnarrative, taxonomic approach to its subject, the exhibit went on to offer a plethora of "Jewish lifeworlds" in the Rhinelands of the Middle Ages, in Eastern Europe, in late-nineteenth-century Berlin, in Yemen, Morocco, and Toledo, in Saloniki and Amsterdam, in America, in Palestine, and in Israel. As this list suggests, the overall form never quite settled for either of the two possibilities that the opening had established. If this was to be understood as a topographical map of Jewish lifeworlds, then how were the seemingly arbitrary historical epochs motivated (the Middle Ages instead of the Renaissance, the turn of the nineteenth century rather than the Enlightenment)? On the other hand, if the succession of individual rooms was to be understood as a chronological narrative (from antiquity through the Middle Ages to the founding of Israel or, in Henryk Broder's disingenuous phrase, "from Plato to NATO"),[25] then how did it account for and unify the geographical leaps? Thus, rooms like the one entitled "Ashkenazy: The Middle Ages in the Rhineland" hovered between the claim to represent a historical moment in some general evolution of Jewish lifeworlds, a geographical space that was home to a specific Jewish lifeworld, and a definitional entry into the encyclopedia of Jewish lifeworlds under the letter *A* for Ashkenazy. Now, I am aware that these are not necessarily mutually exclusive enterprises; yet, in retrospect, it seems that their coexistence should probably be understood as part of the exhibit's overall strategy, and that it was precisely the proliferation of (non)narrative representations of Jewishness that accounted for a certain sense of confusion as to the actual object of the exhibit. I will return to this impression momentarily to suggest how it might be read as highly productive in generating a notion of Jewish ethnicity that challenges prevailing discourses on Jewish identity, especially in the Federal Republic of Germany. Before doing so, however, I want to dwell on the way in which the exhibit proliferated and reinforced that sense of confusion.

On one level, the undecided nature of the exhibit's approach corresponded (in my own experience, at least) to a very tangible sense of disorientation—both physical and temporal—of a visitor wandering through the different rooms. This was certainly not a result of the architectural structure of the exhibit, which was laid out according to a clearly defined floor plan of contiguous rooms arranged in a square around a central atrium that was accessible from various points of the outer rooms. Rather, it was the contents of the rooms that continuously raised questions as to the mode of their successive connection. Thus, a trajectory that led from Jewish life in Eastern Europe (rooms 7 and 8) to Berlin (room 9) to Yemen (room 10) asked the visitor to establish connections between different lifeworlds that were contiguous only in the Martin-Gropius-Bau. Whereas the connection between rooms 8 and 9 could be read in terms of a historical narrative of Jewish (e)migration—Berlin as an often prolonged stopover for Jews from Eastern Europe on their way to America—the following rooms on Yemen, Morocco, and Sephardic Jews in medieval Spain again evoked the "encyclopedic" dimension of the exhibit, suggesting connections less in terms of a historical continuity of cause and effect than on the level of possible similarities (and differences) in Jewish life in the diaspora. Thus, though the more restricted causal connection between two contiguous rooms did occur occasionally (as in the example of rooms 7 through 9), I would argue that overall the construction of the exhibit might be related to a notion of montage, a form that film theory traditionally opposes to the narrative construction of fictional closure. Rather than narrating a continuous history of the development of Jewish identity, the disjunctive organization of different rooms worked more on the model of a series of jump cuts, which yield only fragmentary meanings.

Some of the exhibit's early critics would certainly have disagreed with the reading that I am proposing here, arguing instead that the totality of the objects collected in the exhibit amounted to a universalizing image of Jewishness. In their view, the sweeping range of geographical and historical spaces as well as the centerpiece of the exhibit—the large and representative atrium dedicated to the pivotal role of the written word in Jewish life—suggested a presumptuous approach that smoothed over the particularities of individual Jewish lifeworlds. Consequently, the "gigantomania" of this "megashow" was criticized not only for stretching the capabilities of exhibition as a cultural form; more precisely, it was held that the scope of the undertaking belied its dedication to the everyday "lifeworld."[26] Instead of the mundane particularities of everyday life, there remained nothing but the universal narrative of "Jews through the ages."

My point, then, is that quite the contrary is true, and that we read the massiveness of the exhibit not in terms of a universal narrative (which, as I have been suggesting, would be rather difficult, if not impossible, to construe either in theory or in the actual exhibit); instead, the overwhelming plethora of objects suggests a much more local version of Jewishness precisely *because of* the exhibit's spectacular excess. Not only did individual objects, photographs, and texts repeatedly particularize competing versions of Jewish lifeworlds and thus resist any universalizing frame; in addition, the geographical and historical leaps, as well as the multiple discursive reorientations that were demanded of visitors as they passed through contiguous rooms, vitiated both a universal history of "the Jew" and a reductive reading of essential Jewishness.

Such a fragmentary and discontinuous approach to the lifeworlds to be represented was further reflected in the quite disparate representational modes employed in the various rooms of the exhibit. Thus, the archaeological-paleontological mode of room 1 and the Judaica approach were by no means the only representational approaches chosen by the organizers to represent Jewish lifeworlds; instead these early rooms were followed by installations emphasizing aesthetic representation (the fine arts), while others focused on industrial and fashion design or on objects of everyday life (an old Singer sewing machine or mechanical parts manufactured by AEG, one of the leading electrical companies in Germany since 1883; clothing, tools, jewelry). Still others (particularly the central atrium dedicated to the role of the written word in Jewish life) worked within the discursive formations of the literary exhibit, displaying first editions of books by Jewish writers, opened to a given page beneath a framed portrait of the author. The presentation of such objects from the realms of aesthetics and culture, industry, ceremony, and everyday life is hardly surprising, given the exhibit's claim to represent "Jewish thought and faith, life and work in the cultures of the world"; and yet, there was a curious incongruity as to the representational status of these different exhibits.[27] For example, the exhibition contained three rooms that worked mainly with various modes of aesthetic representation: Eastern Europe was represented through numerous prints by Moritz Oppenheim and paintings by Marc Chagall and Issachar Ryback; one of the two rooms devoted to Israel (room 18) worked mainly with photographs; and the adjoining room (19) was entirely devoted to Larry Rivers's triptych entitled *The History of the Mazzah*. Clearly, these rooms all functioned within a representational mode generally associated with the art exhibit, but the inclusion of these particular pieces of art in an exhibit on Jewish lifeworlds also mandated that they speak to the topic at hand. How, then, was the visitor to read these paintings and photographs in the context of the three different rooms?

On one level the answer presumably needs to confront the role of authorship. It is hard to discount the hypothesis that these objects were included in the exhibit simply because the painters and photographers who produced them were Jewish. But this still does not answer the question of the sense in which the different paintings and photographs can be understood to represent Jewish lifeworlds in "Eastern Europe" or "Israel." At this point, a number of possibilities arise. In one reading they are mere stand-ins for some notion of "cultural production" in the diaspora and in Israel, respectively: here is an example, in other words, of Jewish creativity in "the cultures of the world." What I am calling the representational status of these artworks would then be equivalent to that of any other crafted or fabricated object displayed in the exhibit, such as the lanterns manufactured by AEG in Berlin around the turn of the nineteenth century, or the fragments of ancient clay receptacles in room 1. But that would mean to discount the mimetic function of these artworks, for clearly the prints by Oppenheim, as well as Ryback's representations of the Vilna synagogue or the shtetl, were meant to document not only the activity of Jewish artists, but also the sites and forms of Jewish life that their paintings represented. However, while this function is rather obvious when it comes to photography, whose authenticating function we habitually accept in the daily news, the mimetic function of cubist painting is certainly far more complicated. For what does Ryback's cubist rendering of a synagogue really tell us about the synagogue itself, rather than about the development of art in the early twentieth century, or about the precarious status of representation *tout court*? If we turn to Larry Rivers and his late-twentieth-century representation of the four thousand–year history of Jewish life, the terms of the question shift again. For here, in the final room of the exhibit (leaving aside the atrium), we return to the dualism of its overall conception: Rivers uses a decidedly nonnarrative form—collage—to represent a historical narrative. Again, this says as much about the Jewish history that it represents as about the possibilites of contemporary art; within the context of this exhibit, though, it becomes one representation of Jewishness (Rivers's) in the service of another representation of Jewishness (the exhibit's).

Why, then, am I insisting on pursuing the multifarious functions and connotations of individual objects in an exhibit that could just as well be described simply as a multimedia presentation of Jewish lifeworlds? Clearly, one of the aspects that I find most compelling about this exhibit is the way it combined and complicated the possibilities of narrative (if only that of the individual visit that follows the string of twenty rooms consecutively from the beginning, all the way around and into the atrium, which constitutes the largest and final room) with various decidedly nonnarrative devices that I have described in terms of encyclopedic representation, of montage and of collage. That representational ambivalence is further proliferated, I would suggest, by the way in which the exhibit constructs a hybrid representational discourse both within a single type of exhibit and among the different exhibition modes (aesthetic, archaeological, Judaica, etc.).

The deconstructive function of the exhibit with respect to the narrative-nonnarrative dichotomy should not be misunderstood as a mere poststructural "play" with representational strategies and categories. Instead, I want to suggest that we read the multiple layerings of the exhibit's representational modes on a symptomatic level, where they function as a rather precise diagnosis of Jewish diasporic identity. In other words, the very undecidedness built into the exhibit's approach to Jewishness as an object of representation refers to a fundamental characteristic of that object itself, for if the organizing principle was hardly a unifying one, then Jewishness ultimately emerged as a positively "scattered" notion, suggesting a diasporic ethnicity that negotiates identity between sameness and difference, coherence and fragmentation in the cultures of the world. Like each individual object, such ethnic identifications never quite line up with the representational categories that make competing claims on the ultimate "meaning" of the object or the ultimate identity of the Jew, respectively. To take only the example of national identification, to which I will be returning: if the exhibit made any one point especially clear, it was the fact that Jewish diasporic identity can function only as an ethnic signifier that always invokes the idea of national belonging (hence the topographical divisions of the exhibit according to different national cultures) while simultaneously insisting on a counternarrative to the nation. In that counternarrative, meanings refuse to line up neatly and begin to "wander" in and out of different referential regimes. In this sense, the signifying practices of the exhibit began to construct a museal analogue to the kinds of diasporic identifications that Daniel and Jonathan Boyarin describe in terms of a Mosaic tradition of wandering. In their reading, the biblical story

> is one of always already coming from somewhere else....Diaspora, in historical Judaism, can be interpreted then as the later analogue to nomadism in the earlier set of material conditions and thus as a continuation of the sociological experiment that the Davidic monarchy symbolically overturns.[28]

The stakes for Jewish identity, in this case, turn on a question that is by now familiar to theories of gender, but has received somewhat less attention when it comes to understanding ethnicity: the question of essentialism. The relevance of that question when it comes to locating Jewish identity in contemporary Germany becomes immediately evident when we consider the way in which the ethnic signifier functions with respect to German identity generally; here *ethnicity* as a term is certainly in disrepute but continues to lead a discursive life that creates strict boundaries between sameness and difference. In this context, we do well to remember that the ideological "legitimation" of the *Shoah* by the Nazis rests precisely on the racializing construction of the Jews as *essentially different*. Ideologically, the anti-

Semitism of the Third Reich, and the genocide in particular, relied at least in part on the essentialization of difference and the simultaneous aggressive establishment of the "Aryan" as a standard of "sameness." This is indeed an ideological aspect of fascism that extends beyond the specificity of national socialism and of the *Shoah,* motivating the racism of (not only) white supremacist movements and resurfacing in the nationalist explosions of ethnic conflict in Eastern Europe. The recurring aspect of this ideologeme rests with its essentializing gestures: where sameness and difference become essential norms, identities are no longer subject to negotiation.

Consequently, one reason for avoiding the concept of ethnicity in Germany today (other than in critical descriptions of the racism of skinhead ideologies), certainly lies in the inherently racist connotations of its German translations: both the word *ethnisch* and especially the term *völkisch* evoke the distinctly fascist legacy that it is still impossible to ignore. More generally, the notion of ethnicity resonates with a tradition that leads from the early nationalisms of the nineteenth century to the chauvinistic ideologies of an ethnically homogeneous nation before it reaches its peak, of course, in the explicitly racial construction of the German as Aryan. In an essay that is concerned with the ideological underpinnings of the radical right's renewed virulence in Germany, Ian Buruma has spelled out the historical inception of this trajectory:

> It was precisely because Germany was such a mixture of regions, of ethnic groups, religions, nationalities, and because German-speakers were never contained within the nation's shifting borders, that nineteenth-century nationalists made such a cult of blood and roots and *Kultur.*[29]

One might call this invocation of ethnicity its "hegemonic" form, for the ways in which it is responsible, as Buruma shows, for policing who will be admitted to the *Volksgemeinschaft,* and who, by birth, will always remain "outsiders" on the margins. Undoubtedly, this function of the ethnic signifier remains particularly evident today in the persistence of the *ius sanguinis* or "blood right" on which it is based (rather than the much more common *ius soli,* which allots citizenship according to place of birth, as in the United States, for example): a legal notion of hereditary Germanness that polices the construction of nationality by refusing German citizenship to the German-born children of Turkish immigrants while continuing to grant citizenship by default to generations of so-called *Volksdeutsche* in Poland, Russia, and elsewhere.

Now, while Jewishness after the Holocaust is clearly no longer defined in the racist terms of fascist ideology, it has nonetheless remained locked in a number of essentialized positions; in Germany Jews have been either monumentalized through a reigning philo-Semitic discourse (often quite literally, as the German examples in the recent exhibit on Holocaust memorials suggests) or they have been exoticized as German society's essential "other."[30] In fact, both of these positions amount to the same thing: there is no widespread understanding in Germany of Jewish identity in terms of diaspora—that is, as a form of ethnic difference that constantly negotiates its similarity and difference with regard to national identifications.[31] In this respect, the *ius sanguinis* is merely the legal expression for a cultural understanding of identity still tied to what Boyarin and Boyarin, following Jean-Luc Nancy, have described as the "myth of autochthony": it transports a notion of identity that assumes the necessity of a national belonging to a land and cannot conceive of the experience of diaspora "that has constrained Jews to create forms of community [and, I would add, identity] that do not rely on one of the most potent and dangerous myths—the myth of autochthony." They go on to suggest that the story closest to "the readings of the Judaism lived for two thousand years begins with a people forever unconnected with a particular land, a people that calls into question the idea that a people must have a land in order to be a people."[32]

As Daniel and Jonathan Boyarin's valorization of a Mosaic nomadism would imply, the "myth of autochthony" constitutes precisely the point where it becomes important to disarticulate the concept of ethnicity from its hegemonic logic—a project that Stuart Hall has also been pursuing in terms of a theory of "new ethnicities." Though it is engaged in the rather different context of black cultural politics in Britain, Hall's outline of a "new politics of representation [that] also sets in motion an ideological contestation around the term 'ethnicity'" is, I think, congenial to a reading of the Berlin exhibit in terms of the musealization of Jewish diasporic identity—particularly in the postwar (and now postunification) German situation. For in attempting to visualize that "new politics," Hall, too, is obliged to confront and displace a different notion of ethnicity that, from the point of view of the postcolonial subject-position he wants to articulate, is firmly entrenched, coercively regulating access to representation in all senses of the word. This hegemonic ethnicity appears "in the form of a culturally-constructed sense of Englishness and a particularly closed, exclusive and regressive form of English national identity, [and it] is one of the core characteristics of British racism today." As Hall makes clear, we can never entirely disregard these hegemonic constructions of the ethnic altogether, for this would be a proposition that is as impossible for the postcolonial subject in England as for a Jew living in, or even visiting, Germany today.[33]

What is at stake for Hall is a "decoupling" of ethnicity from those cultural constructions of an "embattled, hegemonic conception of 'Englishness.' " Since that decoupling itself cannot move around the hegemonic constructions that it contests, it must move through them, "splitting . . . the notion of ethnicity between, on the one hand, the dominant notion which connects it to nation and 'race' and on the other hand what I think is the beginning of a positive conception of the ethnicity of the margins, of the periphery."[34] This ethnicity of the margins is by no means positive in the sense that it somehow avoids conflict; rather, its liminality is subversive precisely to the extent to which it contests unifying definitions of the nation and of the ethnic by insisting on an agonistic culture of difference.[35] A cultural politics that could draw on this new construction of ethnic identities (what Hall calls "the politics of ethnicity predicated on difference and diversity") would then itself be able to "engage rather than suppress difference."

My reasons for engaging Hall's concept of a "new ethnicity" are decidedly *not* to draw any historical parallels between either British imperialism or the Thatcherite regulation of Englishness on the one hand and the ideology of an Aryan ethnicity in Nazi Germany on the other. I do want to suggest, though, that Hall's notion of an internal splitting of the very notion of ethnicity may usefully contribute to a description of Jewish ethnicity in Germany that would at once acknowledge the irreversible inscription of hegemonic Germanness that reached its devastating peak under Hitler, *as well as* the possibility of exploding that eth(n)os of German "blood and roots and *Kultur*"; it would allow, in other words, for the exploration of the role of marginalized ethnicities relative to the historically powerful appropriation of ethnicity for the homogenizing myth of the German.

Jüdische Lebenswelten, as I read the exhibit, refuses to privilege any individual narrative—national or otherwise. Or rather, if there is any one aspect that can be construed as the exhibit's dominant line on Jewish identity, it is simply the assertion that Jewishness is, first and foremost, a cultural construct. Represented through objects from various cultural realms, Jewishness emerges, moreover, as a distinctly relational category that slips in and out of different narratives, allowing visitors to get a fix on a given "encyclopedic" definition of Jewishness only to confront them with the instability of that definition's representational foundations. For instance, the nonlinear intersection of geography and history was employed for the purpose of *exploding* rather than "essentializing" the question of what it might mean to be Jewish. Like the careful selection of objects, the arrangement of the rooms put into play relational meanings of Jewishness that could not be integrated into one (master) narrative. As Julius Schoeps, one of the organizers, suggested in an interview, there was no "unifying thread.... The only possibility available to us was to present individual elements, to show Jewish life in different cultures."[36]

Thus, as the exhibit gradually constructed Jewish identity in terms of different historical and cultural positionings, visitors were led to recognize the contours of an ethnicity whose relational identifications (relative to, say, given national identities) always subvert all terms of the relation. On the one hand, to understand the display of a Moroccan dress or the model of a Beijing synagogue in terms of specifically *Jewish* lifeworlds is to understand Jewishness itself as a culturally and historically specific practice—as an ethnicity that continuously renegotiates its space between difference and sameness, between a claim to a given heritage and the question of assimilation. On the other hand, however, in the identification of all the exhibit's objects as *Jewish,* the ethnic signifier fundamentally unsettles the apparently stable signifying value of the nation-state, for there is no formula by which we can return from the same Chinese Jewish synagogue or the Moroccan Jewish dress to a stable notion of what it must then mean to be Chinese or Moroccan. Nor should we be concerned with any such return to stability; what the unsettling effect of these relational constructions suggests is that the negotiation between ethnicity and nation needs to remain bound up in a politics of representation built *not* on apparently stable reassertions of identity but on the persistent articulation of difference.

Identity Politics versus the Museum?

At this point, then, it is time to abandon the purely "textual" reading of the exhibit and to return to my introductory claim that any museum works to construct memories and identities only when and if it encounters a given audience that brings its cultural present to bear on the representational politics of museums and their exhibits. For as James Young suggests in the introduction to his own exhibit on Holocaust memorials, in attempting to assess the public function of any given exhibit, we always need to keep in mind "the fundamentally dialogical, interactive nature of all memorials and exhibitions."[37] To be sure, this is always a dialogue among unequal partners, which should not be theorized too quickly in terms of verbal communication. Perhaps it is better understood in terms of textuality and a textual mode of address. In this view, the museum constitutes both a text (possibly quite polysemous, as I have been arguing in the case of *Jüdische Lebenswelten*) and certain identifiable forms of addressing its "readership"—that is, the public, which then responds by visiting the exhibit, reading and debating, and in some cases writing and complaining about it.[38]

I therefore want to look at the discourses that were generated in the public reception of *Jüdische Lebenswelten* in order to suggest how this "dialogue" ultimately revolved around the political articulation of "new ethnicities." While the often critical tenor of these discourses may have called into question some of the aesthetic choices of the organizers, I would emphasize that the vociferous articulation of different subject-positions within the debate ultimately validates the exhibit's politics of representation while it opens up a space for the negotiation of Jewish identity in terms of ethnicity.

I realize, of course, that such a claim will seem paradoxical considering the fact that one of the major criticisms, which was voiced most strongly by the oppositional Jewish community in Berlin, concerned precisely the failures of the exhibit's representational politics.[39] If the exhibit can indeed be considered to describe Jewish identity in terms of culturally and historically specific processes of "negotiation," this seems to have struck a sensitive nerve in parts of the (Jewish) public. Inveighing against what they perceive to be a simplified representation of the relation between Jewish identity in the diaspora and the cultures in which Jews have attempted to carve out, or negotiate, their own spaces, these critics accused the organizers of misrepresenting the process of "negotiation" in terms that were too unencumbered by the very real and all too often mortal pressures of both assimilation and anti-Semitism.

As the outspoken groups who are gathered around Berlin's Jewish Round Table made clear, *Jüdische Lebenswelten* "exhibits" a number of strongly felt lacunae, particularly with regard to both the museum's and this exhibition's memorial strategies. The most obvious of these gaps consisted in the tendential invisibility of the Holocaust, whose presence was, it would seem, hidden away in wall texts and appeared only in mediated form in the images of the refugees arriving in Palestine, for instance.[40] If, as James Young, Julius Schoeps, and others have argued, "the Holocaust now functions worldwide as a new, fundamental mnemonic space (*Erinnerungsort*) for contemporary Jewish identity,"[41] then how could the museum bracket that space to such an extent? Moreover, by the token of this omission, did the exhibit participate in its own form of revisionism, constructing Jewishness as a wealth of bygone cultural life while erasing the memory of the genocidal erasure itself?

On one level, the criticism seems justified, especially if it is seen as motivated by the various forms of forgetting that have characterized the relations between Germans and Jews since the war. Yet it should be pointed out that this criticism is directed against an informed and, to my mind, convincing decision by the organizers not to "have the documents of the perpetrators in the same house as those of the victims": the exhibit was explicitly designed not to monumentalize the Nazis, but to celebrate instead the multiplicity of Jewish lifeworlds, and thus to counteract a general tendency to displace the memory of those lifeworlds by the memory of the event that intended their annihilation.[42] In itself, the (perhaps somewhat defensive) recourse to the informed nature of this decision need not be persuasive, however. After all, the potential legitimacy of the organizers' decision would appear to rest on the assumption that each visitor will not only notice the gaps in the first place, but also read them in terms of a substitutional logic that replaces the absence of the Holocaust with the plenitude of Jewish lifeworlds. Yet if we turn from the intrinsic aesthetic and conceptual choices to the broader context of the exhibit, other aspects that can serve to relativize the concerns of the critics move to the foreground. The organizers' motivations become fully justifiable, I think, when one considers the location of the Martin-Gropius-Bau: it was in fact all but impossible to enter the exhibit without noticing the adjacent bungalow on the ruins of the Gestapo headquarters, which houses *Topographie des Terrors,* a sparse but effective permanent exhibition of the scale of Nazi terror in the Third Reich. Without this exhibit, and without the program of plays, television series, and discussions that supplemented the self-conscious omission by commemorating the genocide, the claims that "what's missing is the blood"[43] would have had to be considered legitimate. Given that context, however, the absence of "blood" (which in any case was "missing" only in a very superficial sense) performed an important function in the representation of Jewish identity for a German audience: it supplemented the image of the victim, which Germans have been able to accept at best by a form of repressive monumentalization, with that of the Jews as the bearers of cultural lifeworlds. As the exhibit made abundantly clear, these lifeworlds are, moreover, far more complex than the heritage of the Enlightenment and Weimar culture — a heritage whose irretrievable loss a certain philo-Semitic discourse would lament. In this sense, Nachama makes an important point:

> The notion of "the Jew" has become all but identical with the mountains of corpses at Auschwitz. We were of the opinion that it was now time to move away from what is sufficiently well-known. We therefore wanted to show the multiplicity of cultures which were supposed to be annihilated, and thereby demonstrate that no genocide can ever hope for success. It is not possible simply to exterminate a people, a culture, especially if it has developed such varied life forms and strategies of survival as ours. I believe that for all those who visit the exhibit, the Holocaust will become still more inconceivable and unspeakable.[44]

While usefully resituating the exhibit in terms of its function within an evolving German-Jewish discourse of coming to terms with the past (*Vergangenheitsbewältigung*), Nachama's remarks expose themselves to another recurring critique that was launched against the conception of *Jüdische Lebenswelten.* This again concerns the question of what the exhibit as a whole, its objects as well as its critics, its objectives as well as its failures, had to say about the actual status of Jewish ethnicity in contemporary Germany. For the "multiplicity of cultures" that Nachama wanted to hold up against the threat, and the reality, of annihilation did, in fact, have to be excavated from the museums and archives. Whether as a result of national socialism or of the Inquisition, or because of some more abstract form of "historical progress," the different lifeworlds collected in the Gropius-Bau were largely historical worlds devoid of life. On one level it would almost seem, then, as though the only contribution of the exhibit to the history of Jewish life in postwar Germany is to be sought in its renewed erasure of Jews, for, as the members of the Jewish Round Table reminded us, Jewish lifeworlds *since* 1945 conveniently fell outside of the exhibit's purview. In this sense, the exhibit would not have contributed to a *shift* in the representation of Jews in postwar Germany, but instead consolidated their monumentalization. It is impossible to dismiss the angry voices that questioned the exhibit's commitment to the *lived* nature of the lifeworlds it promised. Michael Wolfssohn sarcastically unpacked this aspect of the show's logic:

> How can one prove good intentions? Above all by an intensive interest in Jews. But careful: not in living Jews. The risk of putting your foot in your mouth or getting your fingers burned is too high. Here, interest in dead Jews is less dangerous (and hence so popular).[45]

Similarly, Fritz Teppich of the Jüdische Gruppe Berlin argued that the exhibit actually suggested that the only remaining Jews live in the United States and in Israel (the two countries for which the exhibit's chronology extended into the present).[46] Whatever the nonlinear structure of its historical narrative, as a popular historical exhibit *Jüdische Lebenswelten* did conclude that narrative prematurely, and on this level it slighted those who are personally invested in the stakes of Jewish identity in contemporary German culture. One might hope that their protest will be taken up in the near future and turned into an alternative exhibit on aspects of Jewish life in Germany.

While these criticisms of the exhibit's monumentalizing approach to "dead Jews" were therefore important, it is at least equally important to note the way in which those angry voices performed precisely the kind of negotiation that I have been describing. In orchestrating an oppositional discourse, the critics countered the focus on "dead Jews" with the living articulation of difference.[47] I would further argue that such opposition is by no means incidental to this particular exhibit; for if a museum exhibition is more than merely an isolated aesthetic narrative—in other words, if it is always also a public form of display, answerable to more than just one imputed audience—then the contestatory claims that it spurs among specific groups need to be figured into the reading of the exhibition from the start. In a discussion of hegemonic and counterhegemonic exhibition practices in Israel, Ariella Azoulay puts this in terms of a supplementary subject-position that completes any exhibit's structure of address:

> In general, four main subjects may be discerned in the act of display: the exhibiting subject, the exhibited subject, the person to whom the exhibition is addressed, and an additional subject, the other who has been excluded from the exhibition.... When the exhibition takes place in a context of national or ethnic struggle,... [this] other subject is involved, the other who has been exluded from the arena of exhibition and whose status as either source or object of knowledge (or both) has been denied.[48]

Now to claim this position of the excluded other as a site of negotiation in which Jewish identity is able to represent itself in Germany is, of course, to run the risk of consigning any expression of such an identity to an essentially reactive mode: only when there is occasion to claim one's underrepresentation does there arise the opportunity for claiming a space of one's own, a space of difference. Yet the debates about the exhibit did indeed go a long way toward proliferating difference, turning the reactive mode to productive ends in what Homi Bhabha calls the "struggle of identifications."[49] For in articulating their critique, the oppositional groups at the Jewish Round Table not only had to situate themselves in relation to a mainstream German public that had celebrated the exhibit by the sheer numbers of people who appeared. In addition, the Round Table made a name for itself as "oppositional" *within* the Jewish community: to attack the exhibit was necessarily also to attack the Central Council of Jews in Germany (Zentralrat der Juden in Deutschland), which viewed the exhibit in an entirely favorable light.[50] In a country that at times almost did not seem to know that it was still home to other Jews besides Heinz Galinski (the president of the Zentralrat), this generational and ideological split *within* the Jewish community arguably constituted a significant event in the politics of representation. The heated debates carried out both at a public forum on the exhibit and in the press marked an important proliferation of Jewish subject-positions within the space of the German nation. Such a proliferation, then, was bound to perform at least as important a function in the deexoticization of Jewishness as the discourses intentionally orchestrated by the exhibit itself. In this sense, the fight over the exhibit's representational choices was simultaneously a fight over the representation of competing versions of Jewish ethnicity in contemporary cultural and political life. It was a struggle in which the myth of "the Jew"—itself a subtle legacy of the fascist past—broke up into Jews of different personal and historical investments, different institutional affiliations, different generational assumptions; and, clearly, these different Jews will also enter into different relationships with whatever it then means to be "German."

This suggests that there is at least the chance, opened up in part by this particular exhibit, for Jews and Germans to leave the postwar discourse that locks their relationship into frozen memorial postures. This does not mean leaving the memories and commemorations behind; they remain binding, even if in different forms, no matter how a German society might become ethnically reconfigured. Nor do I think that any mere redescription of the actual social, political, and cultural (self-)representations of Germans and Jews in terms of such "new ethnicities" could accomplish anything in the absence of continued efforts to negotiate those representations in practice. As Hall has pointed out, such negotiation includes the insistence "that rights of citizenship and the incommensurabilities of cultural difference are respected and that *the one is not made a condition of the other.*"[51]

Indeed, there is much to suggest that for the moment, the essentializing opposition of Germans and Jews, whose logic would seem to provide no space for either the German Jew or the Jewish German, remains. Yet if by sharpening our focus on a "positive conception of the ethnicity of the margins, of the periphery" it becomes possible to read the signs of Jewishness as representations that also disrupt the apparent security of what it means to be German, the configuration of the relationship between Germans and Jews must change. While I certainly do not pretend, nor wish, to resolve that salient opposition between German and Jewish identities, which has very real historical grounds, the effort to deconstruct this oppositional logic by rereading its cultural representations in the museum is an attempt to multiply and scrutinize the implicit assumptions that govern the persistent articulation of that logic.

Notes

This is a completely revised and rewritten version of an essay published earlier as "Exhibiting Jewish Lifeworlds: Notes on German-Jewish Identity Politics" in *Found Object* no. 3 (Spring 1994), pp. 11–31. Thanks again to Kerstin Barndt, Marianne Hirsch, Madeleine Kurtz, and Florian Miedel; thanks also to Michael Rothberg for motivating me to revisit this article in the first place, and to Heike Stange for her comments during one of numerous revisions.

1. Claudia Koonz, "Germany's Buchenwald: Whose Shrine? Whose Memory?" in *The Art of Memory: Holocaust Memorials in History,* ed. James Young (Munich and New York: Prestel, 1994), 112.

2. Ibid., 113. The fiasco that Philipp Jenninger suffered on one such occasion, when he outraged the public both in Germany and abroad with the tone of his speech on the fiftieth anniversary of *Kristallnacht* in 1988, now appears to be the exception that proves the rule. This is not to suggest, of course, that we cease watching very closely for other such "exceptions," both in Germany and elsewhere.

3. Memorials have been constructed on the sites of former concentration camps, and monuments abound, as *The Art of Memory* amply illustrates; yet the meager exhibit on display in the Wannsee villa is the only attempt to actually construct a *museum* around the events of the Holocaust.

4. James E. Young, "The Art of Memory: Holocaust Memorials in History," in Young, *The Art of Memory,* 23. Cf. also Pierre Nora, "Between Memory and History: *Les lieux de mémoire,*" *Representations* 26 (1989).

5. See in particular the voluminous catalog and the accompanying collection of essays (both entitled *Jüdische Lebenswelten, Katalog* and *Essays,* respectively), edited by Andreas Nachama et al. Both volumes were among the first publications of the newly relocated Jüdischer Verlag at Suhrkamp, for which the exhibit, in turn, was a prime advertiser.

6. The full title of the exhibit: *Jüdische Lebenswelten: Jüdisches Denken und Glauben, Leben und Arbeiten in den Kulturen der Welt* (Jewish lifeworlds: Jewish thought and faith, life and work in the cultures of the world).

7. Cf. Daniel J. Sherman and Irit Rogoff, eds., *Museum Culture: Histories, Discourses, Spectacles* (Minneapolis: University of Minnesota Press 1994). In their introduction to this volume, the editors go so far as to suggest that we are already witnessing the "coming of age of museum studies as a discipline in its own right [as] only another example of the rapidly expanding influence of the institution." (xviii–xix). Cf. also Wolfgang Zacharias, ed., *Zeitphänomen Musalisierung: Das Verschwinden der Gegenwart und die Konstruktion der Erinnerung* (Essen: Klartext, 1990), 168. Gottfried Fliedl's contribution, "Testamentskultur: Musalisierung und Kompensation," lists a whole catalog of phenomena pertaining to and illustrating the advances of "musealization," only one of which is "the increasing number of visitors, particularly in connection with the success of exhibitions as *the* foremost medium of cultural politics." Other examples include the rising number of new museums, as well as the cultural prestige accorded to their ever more lavish architectural status; the increased efforts and budgets spent not only on restoring but also on fully reconstructing old buildings (Berlin's Stadtschloß and Dresden's Frauenkirche are the two most prominent and — to my mind — outrageous German projects of this sort); the musealization of nature in parks and protected reserves; and also the dissolving boundaries of the very concept of the museum, which has begun to attach itself to various cultural activities such as guided cultural tours of cities or landscapes, history theme parks, etc.

8. Andreas Huyssen, "Monument and Memory in a Postmodern Age," in James Young, *The Art of Memory*, 10.

9. Cf. ibid.

10. Ibid., 11.

11. Cf. Huyssen's critique of Lübbe and Zacharias in "Monument and Memory in a Postmodern Age."

12. Nora, "Between Memory and History," 21.

13. Cf. Hermann Lübbe, "Zeit-Verhältnisse. Über die veränderte Gegenwart von Zukunft und Vergangenheit" in Zacharias, *Zeitphänomen Musalisierung*, 40–49.

14. Wolfgang Zacharias, "Zur Einführung: Zeitphänomen Musealisierung," in Zacharias, *Zeitphänomen Musalisierung*, 11.

15. Fliedl, "Testamentskultur," 175.

16. Cf. James E. Young, "Erinnern und Gedenken. Die Shoa und die jüdische Identität," in *Jüdische Lebenswelten: Essays*, ed. Andreas Nachama et al. (Berlin: Berliner Festspiele/Jüdischer Verlag, 1992).

17. Cf. Young, *The Art of Memory*; the exhibit this catalog accompanies was shown first in the New York Jewish Museum and is showing in Berlin as I write (October 1994). From here, it will travel to Munich.

18. On the debates about Libeskind's project, see my "Architecture Between the Lines: Daniel Libeskind's Design for the Berlin Jewish Museum," *Found Object*, no. 5 (Spring 1995): 78–101.

19. For a related discussion of the multifarious uses and abuses of monuments in Germany—i.e., of museums with a more specific function—for remembering (not only) Jewish suffering in the Holocaust, see Claudia Koonz's account in Young, *The Art of Memory*.

20. Ariella Azoulay, "With Open Doors: Museums and Historical Narratives in Israel's Public Space," in Sherman and Rogoff, *Museum Culture*, 104. Her examples include the fur hats of Eastern European Hasidim, Yemenite embroideries, pioneer scythes, and brick ovens for baking pita. At least one of these exhibits—the embroideries from Yemen—appeared also in the Berlin exhibit (though not as part of the kind of multimedia presentation described by Azoulay), and the organizers of this event were certainly familiar with the Jewish Diaspora Museum in Tel Aviv. I myself am not, and I can therefore not be certain whether my different interpretation of this and similar pieces in the Berlin exhibit can be attributed at least partly to a difference between the two exhibits or merely between their two "readers." Part of my argument, however, is intended to suggest precisely that even if the Berlin exhibit had been a duplicate of the permanent exhibit in Israel, the difference in national contexts clearly would have sufficed to change the meaning of even the minutest stitch in one and the same Yemenite dress.

21. For two particularly glaring examples (one of them patently anti-Semitic) of the German tendency to simply equate Jewishness with Israeli national identity, see my introduction to this article in its previous version: "Exhibiting Jewish Lifeworlds: Notes on German-Jewish Identity Politics," *Found Object*, no. 3 (Spring 1994), esp. 11–14.

22. I take the notion of "disaggregated" identities from Daniel and Jonathan Boyarin, who use it to suggest that "Jewishness disrupts the very categories of identity because it is not national, not genealogical, not religious, but all these in dialectical tension with one another." Boyarin and Boyarin, "Diaspora: Generation and the Ground of Jewish Identity," *Critical Inquiry*, no. 19 (Summer 1993): 721.

23. Gabriele Riedle, "Die Sehnsucht, gut zu sein. Zur Berliner Ausstellung *Jüdische Lebenswelten,*" *Freitag,* January 17, 1992. Interestingly, a more literal "encyclopedic effort" at defining Jewish identity culminated in that same year in the publication of a dictionary of Judaism edited by Julius Schoeps, who, predictably, was involved also in the organization of the exhibit. Julius Schoeps, ed., *Neues Lexikon des Judentums* (Gütersloh and Munich: Bertelsmann, 1992).

24. Closer inspection of the labels in this series of rooms confirmed the general sense of a museological shift from archaeology to a Judaica exhibit: the primary lenders here were the New York Jewish Museum, the Joods Historisch Museum in Amsterdam, the Israel Museum in Jerusalem, Prague's State Jewish Museum, and the Jewish Museum Department of the local Berlin Museum. Although these museums reappeared on labels throughout the remainder of the exhibit, their function here clearly had been to supply objects from their Judaica collections.

25. Henryk M. Broder, "Leiden an Deutschland. Deutsche Juden und Deutsche," in *Juden und Deutsche (Spiegel Spezial),* August 1992, 26.

26. See, for example, an article in *Neue Zeit* of January 11, 1992, entitled "Erschlagen"; or the interview with Barbara Hahn in *tageszeitung* of January 23, 1992 (Gabriele Mittag, "Da haben wir kein Definitionsmonopol. Interview mit der Berliner Literaturwissenschaftlerin Barbara Hahn über die Ausstellung jüdischer Lebenswelten").

27. I use the term *exhibit* here in both senses of the word, for as different *objects* drawn from different representational discourses, these exhibits exploded the unifying sense of a singular "exhibition," turning it into a number of different exhibits under one roof.

28. Boyarin and Boyarin, "Diaspora," 715–717.

29. Ian Buruma, "Outsiders," *New York Review of Books* 39, no. 7: 18.

30. For a more extensive illustration of these two complementary tendencies, see my "Exhibiting Jewish Lifeworlds," pp. 14–17.

31. It is quite significant, in this respect, that after Auschwitz, both Germans and Jews are suddenly at a loss for words in naming the Jews who now live in Germany. To be sure, not all of them are indeed German; yet for those who are, there is a revealing uncertainty about their identification as German Jews. Thus, while Heinz Galinski, the recently deceased chair of the central council of Jews in Germany, insisted on the somewhat laborious epithet "German citizen of Jewish faith" (which his successor, Ignatz Bubis, wholeheartedly adopted), others took embattled positions both for and against their characterization as "jüdische Mitbürger" (Jewish co-citizens). Meanwhile, official terminologies continued to proliferate: whereas in East Germany, one agreed on the term "Bürger jüdischen Glaubens" (citizens of Jewish faith), the West German Zentralrat insisted on retaining a measure of distance in its formula "Juden in Deutschland." In a book-length monograph entitled "Jews in Germany after 1945" (the first of its kind), Erica Burgauer thus concludes, fittingly: "German Jews? Jewish Germans? Jews in Germany? German citizens of Jewish faith? None of these 'shoes' quite seem to fit." Erica Burgauer, *Zwischen Erinnerung und Verdrängung: Juden in Deutschland nach 1945* (Reinbeck: Rowohlt, 1993), 13.

32. Boyarin and Boyarin, "Diaspora," 699–718.

33. Art Spiegelman's visit to Germany after the events in Rostock yielded another short cartoon of mice and cats in front of the typical East German *Plattenbauten;* the text and drawings, published almost simultaneously in the *New Yorker* and in the German weekly *Die Zeit,* quite literally "illustrate" the unease that the *Volksgemeinschaft* continues to inspire in the Jewish visitor.

34. Stuart Hall, "New Ethnicities," in *Black Film, British Cinema*, ICA Documents no. 7 (London: Institute of Contemporary Arts, 1988), 29.

35. The distinction here is basically that, described by Homi Bhabha, between diversity and difference. Bhabha's notion of hybridity, his insistence on the way in which "the cultural emerges only at the significatory boundaries of cultures, where meanings and values are (mis)read or signs are misappropriated," is crucial to my understanding of ethnic difference as a negotiation of such boundaries. Homi Bhabha, "The Commitment to Theory," *New Formations*, no. 5 (Summer 1988), 19; see also "The Third Space: Interview with Homi Bhabha," in *Identity*, ed. Jonathan Rutherford (London: Verso, 1990), 207ff.

36. "Jüdische Lebenswelten," *Semit* 4, no. 1 (February/March 1992), 1.

37. Young, "The Art of Memory," 21.

38. I would emphasize, however, that all such responses, including the "mere" act of visiting the museum, need to be understood as active interventions rather than as mere knee-jerk reactions in a manner always already prefigured in the exhibit's own mode of address.

39. This community, which includes the orthodox Adass Jisroel, the Jüdische Gruppe Berlin (Berlin Jewish Group), and the Jüdischer Kulturverein (Jewish Cultural Organization), is grouped around the Jüdischer Runder Tisch (Jewish Round Table). Their self-definition is oppositional in relation to the Jüdische Einheitsgemeinde (Jewish Unitary Community) and the overarching Zentralrat der Juden in Deutschland (Central Council of Jews in Germany), which, they feel, has monopolized representation of Jews in Germany since the days of its founding soon after the war. The Zentralrat, and more specifically its president, Heinz Galinski, who was one of the keynote speakers for the exhibit's opening ceremonies at the Berlin Hebbel-Theater, clearly endorsed the exhibit. Accordingly, the official publication of the Zentralrat, the *Allgemeine Jüdische Wochenzeitschrift*, published generally favorable reviews, which were in turn contested by articles published in the *Monatsblatt des jüdischen Kulturvereins Berlin e.V.* and in *Semit* (which at one point accused the *Allgemeine Jüdische Wochenzeitschrift* of stylistic transgressions ["germanisch-stabreimlerisch"] that would better behoove Wagner's German).

40. See, for example, Fritz Teppich: "Bitternis angesichts des vergoldeten Trubels," *Neues Deutschland*, January 13, 1992.

41. Young, "Erinnern und Gedenken," 151. Cf. Young, "The Art of Memory," 19.

42. Interview with museum director Andreas Nachama, "Den Nazis kein Denkmal setzen," *tageszeitung*, January 31, 1992.

43. Fritz Teppich, quoted in Marc Fisher, "In the Trap of History: Berlin Jews Decry Lifeless Exhibit," *Washington Post*, March 5, 1992.

44. Interview in *Frankfurter Allgemeine Magazin*, February 7, 1992.

45. Michael Wolfssohn, "Ein Ritual für gute Menschen. Die zweifelhaften Rollenspiele deutsch-jüdischer Erinnerung," *Der Tagesspiegel*, February 10, 1992.

46. "Wider das Bild vom schöngeistigen Juden. Kritische Stimmen zur Ausstellung 'Jüdische Lebenswelten' im Gropius-Bau," *Neue Zeit*, February 7, 1992.

47. Furthermore, it is important to remember that Wolfssohn's sarcasm only functions as long as we disregard the fact that the group of organizers that orchestrated this ostensible interest in "dead Jews" is itself predominantly Jewish. Their commitment to this project as something they considered an adequate representation of Jewishness for a contemporary Germany should mitigate Wolfssohn's cynicism.

48. Azoulay, "With Open Doors," 100.

49. Bhabha, "The Commitment to Theory," 14.

50. In fact, the council's president at the time had contributed to the exhibit's publications, and he had been one of the keynote speakers at the opening ceremony. Obviously, this opposition against the representational powers of the Zentralrat is not unprecedented. But whereas generational struggles were generally carried out internally in the Jewish communities (cf. Burgauer's documentation in *Zwischen Erinnerung und Verdrängung*), the arguments here are carried into the light of the public sphere generated by the exhibit.

51. Stuart Hall, "Culture, Community, Nation," *Cultural Studies*, October 1993, 360–61; emphasis in the original.

5 / Whiteface Performances: "Race," Gender, and Jewish Bodies

Ann Pellegrini

Throughout history people have knocked their heads against the
riddle of femininity.   SIGMUND FREUD, "Femininity"

Our investigation may perhaps have thrown a little light on the
question of how the Jewish people have acquired the
characteristics which distinguish them. Less light has been thrown
on the problem of how it is that they have been able to retain their
individuality till the present day. But exhaustive answers to such
riddles cannot in fairness be either demanded or expected.
          SIGMUND FREUD, *Moses and Monotheism*

As a historically contested identity, Jewishness offers a critical opening
for exploring the "interarticulation" of gender and race.[1] For Jewish
male bodies, marked for an anti-Semitic imaginary by overlapping
layers of blackness, effeminacy, and queerness, the sexualization of
"race" and the racialization of "sex" are constitutive features. The
intersection of race and gender at and *as* the site of Jewishness can
be seen in much of the popular and "scientific" literature of nine-
teenth- and early-twentieth-century Germany and Austria, where the
Jewish male was ubiquitously assimilated to the category "woman."
Indeed, the feminization of the Jewish male body was so frequent a
theme in this period that Jewishness — more precisely, the Jewishness
of Jewish *men* — became as much a category of gender as of race.[2]

108

Daniel Boyarin has proposed a novel reworking of Gayle Rubin's famous—and nearly canonical—feminist formulation, the "sex/gender system" (Rubin 1975). In his work in progress, he calls for thinking Jewishness in terms of a "race/gender system."[3]

Within the Western—and Christian—imagination Jewish difference has been pursued through overlapping and sometimes contradictory appeals to race, gender, religion, and nation. In fin de siècle Europe, for example, arguments for the "racial" difference of the Jews were informed by the props of sexual difference. Accordingly, the Jewish male's supposed effeminacy became one of the essential signposts of the Jewish people's racial difference (Gilman 1991, 1993a; Boyarin 1995; Geller 1992c; Garber 1992; Briggs 1985). The cross-stitching of racial and sexual difference was also apparent within scientific discourse. Many of the medical conditions for which Jews were held to be at higher risk as a "race" were the very same disorders to which women as a "sex" were considered more prone: "The Jews, as is well known to every physician, are notorious sufferers of the functional disorders of the nervous system. Their nervous organization is constantly under strain, and the least injury will disturb its smooth workings" (Maurice Fishberg [1911], quoted in Gilman 1991:63). Hysteria is one of the signal instances of the elision between the Jewish and female body (Boyarin 1995).

But what room does the intense, anti-Semitic identification of male Jews with "woman" leave for Jewish women? In the collapse of Jewish masculinity into an abject femininity, the Jewish female seems to disappear. Yet the Jewish female, no less than the Jewish male, is articulated through discourses of race and gender. One of the ambitions of this study is to bring the status of the Jewish female more directly into analysis, though it is not my aim to emphasize sexual difference over and against racial difference in order to make the Jewish female body appear.

Significantly, in the implicit equation of Jews and women, the Jewish female body goes missing.[4] All Jews are womanly, but no women are Jews. This, at any rate, is one of the consequences of Otto Weininger's famous "scientific" study, *Sex and Character*. For Weininger, Jew clearly means *male* Jew; in only one passage in his lengthy chapter on Judaism does he explicitly mention the "Jewess" (1906:319–20). The displacement of Jewish women from the scene of Jewishness is also one of the unfortunate side effects of Sander Gilman's path-breaking studies of race, gender, and Jewishness. Gilman has framed his arguments through and around the Jewish male. For the most part, the Jewish female enters the frame of analysis only to exit as a man in female drag.[5]

Ironically, during the very period in which Weininger was writing, which is also the historical period Gilman examines, Jewish women—far from disappearing from the scene—prominently figured in the literary and aesthetic imagination of fin de siècle Europe. In the novels of Eliot, James, and Proust, for example, Jewish women are exotic and erotic spectacles. The French stage was dominated and dazzled by Rachel in the first half of the nineteenth century and then, in the latter half of the nineteenth and into the early decades of the twentieth century, by Sarah Bernhardt. Both women were also international stars, their exploits on stage and off the subject of newspaper profiles and of popular and "high society" gossip. Jewishness—as performatively constituted and publicly performed—clearly needs to be thought through the female Jewish body, no less than through the male.

In what follows I want to restage some representative performances of the Jewish female body. I revisit Freud's Dora, laying especial stress upon the status of the name. My interest in this section is to show how Freud's transcription of the signs of male Jewishness into the enigma of woman and femininity does not finally succeed in erasing either the male or *female* Jewish body. These claims will be fleshed out more directly entr'acte, when the image of another Dora takes the stage. Next I move to a recent and contradictory occasion of Jewish "female" performativity, Sandra Bernhard's 1990 film, *Without You I'm Nothing*. My reading of Sandra Bernhard's queer (and queerly Jewish) enactments is an analogy extended: I trace theatrical tropes of performance quite nearly to their source and make Sandra Bernhard perform for me.

To introduce "race" into the domain of psychoanalysis is also a retrieval. Psychoanalysis, after all, dates to a historical period when the medical and natural sciences were deeply concerned with and, to some degree, even determined by biological theories of "race." In the historical context of psychoanalysis, "race" means "Jewishness." Nor is this only because of the historical fact that the founders and leading practitioners of psychoanalysis were Jewish.[6] Within the "thought-collective" of late-nineteenth-century Austro-German medical science, race called up the opposition "Jew/Aryan."[7] In the increasingly secular, urban landscape of nineteenth-century Europe, categories of religious difference, Christian/Jew, were transformed into categories of racial science, Aryan/Jew (Gilman 1991:202).

Nonetheless, the transformation was not total. The opposition Jew/Aryan vacillates among boundaries based on religion and culture, "race," and language.[8] This vacillation is itself instructive, indicating as it does the competing discourses that mapped late-nineteenth- and early-twentieth-century imagination of Jewishness variously into religion, nation, and race. Thinking *das Wesen des Judentums* through racial difference did not replace thinking the essence of Judaism through religious or cultural difference.[9] Rather, the rhetoric of "race" secularized the difference of the Jewish body from the Christian body (ibid.:38).

But it is important not to lay too much stress on this rhetorical shift from the language of theology to the language of scientific reason, especially given the epistemological links between these two worldviews (Keller 1985). Moreover, Eve Kosofsky Sedgwick has criticized attempts by historians of sexuality to locate a great paradigm shift in the definitional understanding of homosexuality. Such efforts, she argues, have the effect of flattening out "a space of overlapping, contradictory, and conflictual definitional forces" into a unidirectional, coherent narrative field (Sedgwick 1990:44–48). This insight applies also to contemporary efforts to understand the historical meanings of Jewishness and anti-Semitism. Gavin Langmuir argues that the transhistorical application of the term *anti-Semitism* unwittingly replays the racist stereotype of Jews as "unchangeable," "eternal," a people outside history (1990). Naming every incidence of hostility against Jews "anti-Semitism" suggests that the forms and meanings of hatred of the Jews are themselves historically continuous and identical.

The historical forms taken by anti-Semitic discourse in the nineteenth century were informed not only by emerging "racial sciences," but also by developments in anthropology and ethnology. Jewish difference was charted across a geography of race. "Black" Africa was one region to which the "racial" difference of the Jew was frequently traced back. The putative blackness of the Jew was a sign of racial mixing and, so, racial degeneration. The English anti-Semite Houston Stewart Chamberlain attributed Jews' "mongrel" nature to their indiscriminate race mixing; during the period of their Alexandrian exile, Jews had "interbred" with black Africans (quoted in Gilman 1993a: 21). In 1935, W. W. Kopp could warn of the dangers Jewish blood posed to Aryan stock; race mixing with Jews was liable to produce offspring with notably "Jewish-Negroid" features (ibid.:22).

Fascinatingly, at the same time (and often by the same people) that Jews were accused of too much crossing "racial" lines, they were also held to exemplify the perils of *in*breeding.[10] In her study of eighteenth- and nineteenth-century British animal husbandry, Harriet Ritvo points to the stress set on maintaining just the right balance between going outside and staying within "family" lines (1994). Ritvo suggests that the anxious attention taxonomists and animal breeders gave to the question of demarcating, managing, and naming "variety" may represent the displacement of broader cultural concerns over (and fascination with) differences within the "races of man." The parallels Ritvo identifies may provide some interpretive leverage for understanding how it is that Jews could be held to represent, at once, the dangers of too much and too little "race mixing." At both poles — hybridization (exogamy) and conservation (endogamy) — Jews were conceptualized as exceeding the norm. They were a "people" too much of extremes.

The anxiety-inducing problematics of racialized Jewishness provide the subtext for much of Freud's case studies. Freud the Jewish scientist was crucially implicated in medical narratives that placed the Jew, particularly the male Jew, at special risk for such diseases as syphilis and hysteria.[11] As Jay Geller has noted, the new biopolitics of anti-Semitism were shaped by — and adapted to — the changing economic, political, and social landscapes of nineteenth-century central Europe. The emergence of political anti-Semitism with its often biologistic frame, Geller explains, coincided with the rapid development and advancement of syphilogical discourses (1992a:22–23). Syphilology was harnessed to a political program whose aim was as much the management and containment of socially marginal(ized) populations — among them prostitutes, the first bourgeois feminists, and Jews (24) — as it was the management and containment of a contagious disease.

In order to put off these debilitating associations, Freud transformed a medical discourse about masculinity and race into a discourse about femininity and gender (Gilman 1991:81; 1993a:44).[12] Crucial to this project was removing the Jewish male from the scene of femininity.

This required concealing the Jewish male's hypervisible body, for his womanliness was written on and through that body. The caricatured signs of his effeminacy were visible in his stumbling gait and effete mannerisms, audible in his singsong voice, and detectable in his "peculiar" sexual tastes.[13]

This association between the Jewish male body and womanliness has a long history in European thought. In Freud's own day, the myth of Jewish male menstruation underwent a revival. Magnus Hirschfeld, an early leader in the German homosexual rights movement and proponent of the "third sex" view of homosexuality, cited male menstruation as one of the "proofs" of a continuum between male and female sexuality (Gilman 1987:303). For Hirschfeld, himself both Jewish and homosexual, the dangerously proximate body of the Jewish male could not be the exemplary site of male menstruation. Thus, Hirschfeld was concerned to document and analyze the "neutral" case studies of menstruating hermaphrodites.

Even Freud was disposed to a version of male periodicity, Fliess's.[14] In his letters to Fliess, Freud discusses his own monthly cycle. In a letter dated October 15, 1897, Freud tells his friend about the physical sensation that interrupted his (Freud's) self-analysis:

> I had the feeling of being tied up inside . . . and I was really disconsolate until I found that these same three days (twenty-eight days ago) were the bearers of identical somatic phenomena. Actually only two bad days with a remission in between. From this one should draw the conclusion that the female period is not conducive to work. (1985:270)[15]

The site of Freud's discharge was his nose, and in this may perhaps be detected a displacement upward, from genitals to face.[16] Moreover, as in other instances where Freud attempts to universalize a condition strongly, even uniquely, identified with the Jewish (male) body, Freud attempts to transform male menstruation from a sign of difference into a universal condition. Accordingly, the universal law of male periodicity became part of Freud's evidence for the universal condition of bisexuality (Gilman 1987:304).

The feminization of the Jewish male body took on especial significance for the health of the body politic, which was identified with masculine vigor. Otto Rank, a prominent and Jewish member of Freud's Viennese circle, called Jews "women among the people," who must "above all join themselves to the masculine life-source if they are to become 'productive'" (reprinted in Klein 1981:171). For another Otto

(Weininger), himself a baptized Jew and a repressed homosexual (Gilman 1991:133), Jewish male effeminacy had profound psychological and political meaning for the entire age.

Sex and Character was a best-seller and something of an international success, garnering praise from such unexpected quarters as American feminist Charlotte Perkins Gilman. Freud read the book in draft form *before* Weininger had added his concluding chapter, on the Jewish character. Yet, Freud was sufficiently familiar with the arguments of the published version to "feature" Weininger in a 1909 footnote, in the case history of "Little Hans," concerning the origins of anti-Semitism:

> The castration complex is the deepest unconscious root of anti-semitism; for even in the nursery little boys hear that a Jew has something cut off his penis—a piece of his penis, they think—and this gives them a right to despise Jews. And there is no stronger unconscious root for the origins of anti-semitism. Weininger (the young philosopher who, highly gifted but sexually deranged, committed suicide after producing his remarkable book, *Geschlecht und Charakter*), in a chapter that attracted much attention, treated Jews and women with equal hostility and overwhelmed them with the same insults. Being a neurotic, Weininger was completely under the sway of his infantile complexes; and from that standpoint what is common to the Jews and women is their relation to the castration complex. (1909b:36n1)

Daniel Boyarin has suggested that, first appearances to the contrary, in this passage Freud actually ends up identifying with Weininger's position (1994). What Freud has obscured in this picture is not only the Jewishness—and so the circumcision—of Little Hans, but Freud's own. In this footnote, Freud narrates the seen of Jewish difference as if it is the non-Jewish ("intact"?) boy gazing at, or imagining himself as gazing at, the circumcised penis. Yet, Boyarin argues, neither Little Hans nor Freud need look anywhere else. Boyarin concludes that Freud ends up putting Weininger forward *not* as an example of the neurotic roots of anti-Semitism, but as an example of a neurotic response *to* anti-Semitism. For Weininger, the end result was, quite literally, self-destruction.[17]

Freud, of course, pursued a different course. Both in his psychoanalytic theories and in his "life," Freud devoted himself to overcoming the pathological "femininity" of the male Jew (Boyarin 1994). One of the ways he accomplished this (or sought to) was to shift the burden of signifying castration and lack wholly onto women's bodies.

The Jewish male's body and the anxieties his difference provoked—for *Freud*—are admitted into the scene of psychoanalysis only when the putative focus is the unknowing Gentile male or a "proven" neurotic, like Weininger.

It is against this volatile background that Freud's *Fragment of a Case of Hysteria,* the case of "Dora," must be reevaluated. The case study was published in 1905, more than four years after Dora broke off her analysis on the last day of 1900. Freud prefaces the case study with an apologia for having gone public with the details of his patient's analysis (8). In an attempt to balance his public responsibilities as a scientist against his patient's privacy, Freud gives the principals in the psychoanalytic drama he is about to unfold stage names: "Needless to say, I have allowed no name to stand which could put a non-medical reader upon the scent [*die Spur*]" (23).

A defensive tone returns throughout the case study—especially on the topic of names and naming. In one instance, Freud is defending himself (again) against the anticipated "horror" or "astonishment" of his readers that he should have dared to broach such "delicate and unpleasant subjects [what he coyly calls "sexual gratification *per os*"] to a young girl" (48). Freud declares that the best way to speak about such things is "to be dry and direct." He prefers to "call bodily organs and processes by their technical names, and . . . [to] tell these to the patient if they—the names, I mean—happen to be unknown to her." To make clear his meaning, Freud gives an example of what it is to name with "technical" precision: "*J'appelle un chat un chat*" (48; emphasis in original). Yet this cunning double entendre could not—or so it seems to me—be further from Freud's stated aim, which is to be "dry," "direct," and "technical." Just after calling a pussy a pussy, Freud turns to French—again—to stress the "right attitude" for a physician to strike in undertaking treatment of a hysteric: "*pour faire une omelette il faut casser des œufs*" (49; emphasis in original).[18] In other words: just say it.

Freud himself does not, or at least not in so many words. Rather, he conceals the identity of his analysand, Ida Bauer, by renaming her "Dora." Yet Freud reveals—by putting off—the Jewish associations of Ida Bauer's hysteria. In *The Psychopathology of Everyday Life* (1901), Freud describes the thought processes that consciously and unconsciously determined Ida's renaming as Dora. He situates his recollection in the midst of a discussion concerning the extent to which mental ideas are determined. He is attempting to demonstrate that "certain seemingly unintentional performances prove, if psycho-analytic methods of investigation are applied to them, to have valid motives and to be determined by motives unknown to consciousness" (1901:239).

Applying the methods of psychoanalysis to himself, Freud traces a chain of associations from the only apparently arbitrary choice of the name Dora back to his sister Rosa's nursemaid, also called Dora. As it happens, "the girl [Freud] knew as Dora was really called Rosa, but had had to give up her real name when she took up employment in the house," to prevent any confusion with Rosa Freud (1901:241). Freud solves the riddle: when "looking for a name for someone *who could not keep her own,*" namely the analysand Ida Bauer, he settled upon Dora, a name that already signaled lost identity.

Feminist critics have discerned displaced aggression in Freud's renaming Ida Bauer after a nursemaid. To get even with her for stopping analysis, Freud reduces the middle-class Bauer to the level of a household employee. He also fills out his characterization of her as having acted "just like a governess" at the moment when she served him notice that she was discontinuing analysis (Freud 1905a:107). In so renaming Dora, Freud has also, inadvertently, put himself into the role of Herr K., who—Freud suggests—had aroused Dora's wrath by "[daring] to treat [her] like a governess, like a servant." Thus, the transference of aggression from patient to analyst, which Freud diagnoses in the case study, is actually an example of *counter*transference (ibid.:116–22).

Freud's paternalism and misogyny are among the factors that regulate the transaction whereby Ida Bauer becomes Dora. However, the unsettling proximity of femininity to Jewishness also exerts unconscious force. In this respect, both Freud's self-analysis and those feminist analyses of the case that focus exclusively on gender do not recognize the relay between gender and race in Freud's "seemingly unintentional performances." Freud indicates that there were three classes of names from which he could not choose a pseudonym for his woman patient: "the real name in the first place, then the names of members of [his] own family, to which [Freud] should object, and perhaps some other women's names with *an especially peculiar sound*" (1901:240; emphasis added). Within fin de siècle Austria, "an especially peculiar sound" broadly invokes the stigmatizing "hidden language" of the Eastern Jew, *Mauscheln* (Gilman 1991:10–37; 1993a:140, 190). Was the deflection of Jewishness from the site of Ida Bauer's analysis also one of the "seemingly unintentional performances" enacted in her renaming by Freud? And what connection might be established between Ida Bauer's new name and that of another person who could not keep *his* own, Freud himself?

Perhaps the "especially peculiar sound" that Freud does not or cannot further specify is the foreign sound of Freud's given name, Sigismund. Freud formally changed his own name on the records of his gymnasium from Sigismund to its German variation, Sigmund, in 1869 or 1870.[19] Jakob Freud had named his son Sigismund after a sixteenth-century Polish monarch, whom the elder Freud admired for his policy of toleration of the Jews (Klein 1981:46). From midcentury, the name Sigismund featured prominently in anti-Semitic jokes and comic literature (Gilman 1993a:70; Klein 1981:46). In his rejection out of hand of the names of family members, Freud also rejects his own name — again — and puts personal distance between Jewishness and his analysis of a case of hysteria.

Freud locates the developmental seat of Ida Bauer's hysteria not in her Jewishness, which disappears from the case study along with her name, but in the requirements of femininity. In his *Three Essays on the Theory of Sexuality,* published in the same year as "Dora," he views hysteria as intimately related to the achievement of femininity:

> The fact that women change their leading erotogenic zone in this way [from clitoris to vagina], together with the wave of repression at puberty, which, as it were, puts aside their childish masculinity, are the chief determinants of the greater proneness of women to neuroses and especially to hysteria. These determinants, therefore, are intimately related to the essence of femininity. (1905b:221)

It is during puberty, Freud hastens to remind us, that "the sharp distinction is established between the masculine and feminine characters"; prior to the onset of puberty, "the sexuality of little girls is of a wholly masculine character" (219). But the achievement of feminine sexuality is by no means a foregone conclusion. Indeed, the double burden Freud identifies as the switchpoints in a young girl's sexual maturation — namely, changing erotogenic zones and undergoing repression — is also responsible for the "greater proneness of women to neurosis and especially hysteria." In this respect, hysteria, far from being a deviation from normal femininity, is actually part of the "essence of femininity."

In sharp contrast to the insistence with which contemporary medical discourse linked the Jewish male to the feminine and from there to "womanly" diseases like hysteria and narcissism, Freud has represented femininity as a cultural and psychic project that puts *women* at heightened risk for hysteria. By emphasizing the distinction between masculinity and femininity as the signal difference in the etiology of hysteria, Freud effectively displaces the mise-en-scène of hysteria from race *and* gender wholly to gender. Ida Bauer's Jewish female body has faded into the figure of a deracinated femininity. From this figure, femininity emerges as a form of racial passing. The Jewish woman passes for — is posed as — the feminine *tout court*. Thus Jewish men are relocated on the side of the universal term: the masculine.[20]

Gilman's analysis of Dora's case (1991:81–96), as well as his overarching interpretation of Freud's transmutation of "race" into gender, falters on the question of Jewish female difference. Gilman demonstrates, with sometimes astonishing virtuosity, how Freud sought to set the hypervisible Jewish male body — including Freud's own — outside the scope of psychoanalysis. But, at times, not only does Gilman imply that masculinity has no gender and femininity, no race, but he treats race and gender as discrete, rather than mutually informing, structures. One consequence of this separation of masculinity and race, on the one side, and femininity and gender, on the other, is that the Jewish woman cannot appear in Gilman's analysis except in drag: as a Jewish man *or* as a "whitened" and presumptively Gentile woman.[21] *All Jews are womanly, but no women are Jews.*

But Jewish women are more than screens through whom might be detected the hidden figures of threatened and threatening Jewish masculinity. Freud continually links hysteria to puberty, the period of a young woman's life when she must leave behind "her childish masculinity" and embrace femininity. Freud's third essay in *Three Essays,* "The Transformations of Puberty," pivots on the transformation from masculine to feminine. This transformation is the *telos* of female sexual development. It is also the linchpin in masculinity's presumption to universality. However, by representing femininity as a derivative of masculinity, Freud also reveals "being" a woman as a passing performance. In his "General Remarks on Hysterical Attacks," for example, Freud implies that "Woman" is a performative accomplishment, not a brute fact: "In a whole series of cases the hysterical neurosis is nothing but an excessive over-accentuation of the typical wave of repression through which the masculine type of sexuality is removed and the woman emerges" (1909a:234). *The woman emerges.* Freud oddly anticipates Simone de Beauvoir's "One is not born, but becomes a woman."

Men too are made (and remade), not born. Gilman offers a stunning piece of evidence on this point: Freud's identification of the clitoris — the "girl's piece" — with the masculine. In Viennese slang of the time, the clitoris was called the *Jud,* or "Jew" (1993a:39). Female masturbation was known as "playing with the Jew." Gilman argues that the nickname *Jud* pejoratively synthesizes the bodies of Jewish men and all women and reflects "the fin de siècle Viennese definition of the essential male as the antithesis of the female and the Jewish male" (ibid.:38–39). Both the clitoris and the circumcised penis of the Jewish male, then, were "lesser" organs, truncated versions of the "real" thing.

Gilman convincingly demonstrates how the masculinization of the clitoris recuperates the Jewish male's "defective" part. Within the homologics of Freud's analysis, then, the girl's passage from boyish activity to "properly" passive femininity — though by no means a foregone conclusion — may tip off the recomposition or redirection of Jewish manhood. But this is not, or so it seems to me, the only redirection. The girl's passage from active, preadolescent masculinity to passive, mature femininity — which Freud presents as the normative and normalizing path of female development — recalls the historical movement of Jews from Eastern Europe into the urban centers of Western Europe and the United States. Is it possible to see in Freud's insistence on the transition from active masculinity to passive femininity not only his own ambivalence about Eastern Jewry, but also the ambivalent position occupied by Jewish women as they and their families moved from east to west? In this context, it is important to note that the anti-Semitic imagination often paired the "womanly" male Jew off with a "manly Jewess" (Geller 1992a:30). I suggest a structural analogy between the more dominant household role played by Jewish women in Eastern Europe (as compared to the "angel in the house" model of Victorian, Christian womanhood) on the one hand, and the masculinization of early childhood femininity on the other. The achievement of properly passive and vaginal female sexuality would then be structurally analogous to the "westernization" of Jewish household dynamics, in which the male publicly assumes the normative role of head of household and the female recedes to the background.[22]

In Freud's subterranean geography of Jewishness, gender, and race, East is to West as phallic women are to angels in the house; as the young girl's childish masculinity is to the woman's mature and passive femininity; as a woman's fully achieved femininity is to a man's overachieving masculinity. In Freud's own "case history," East was to West as his Galician mother, Amalie Nathansohn Freud, was to his German wife, Martha Bernays Freud.

Interpreting the achievement of stable femininity in relation to patterns of Jewish immigration from East to West has especial significance for Jewish women. In the closing decades of the nineteenth century, the period of the greatest migration of Eastern Jews into Germany, Jews comprised just over 1 percent of the German population (Kaplan 1991:5). The embourgeoisement of German Jewry was one of the cornerstones of Jewish assimilation; it was also the central task and responsibility of Jewish women. Like their Gentile counterparts, German Jewish women were expected to ensure and direct the smooth operation of domestic culture. Their highest task was marriage and family. Yet Eastern European Jewish women also comprised a share of the Jewish female workforce in Germany greater than their proportion of the Jewish population more generally. Their occupational profile also differed from that of German-Jewish women; at a time when German-Jewish women were entering what Marion Kaplan calls the "New Woman" careers (secretary, stenotypist, salesclerk), the Eastern immigrants were more likely to be concentrated in industry (ibid.: 160). Many immigrant women also found employ as family helpers or domestic servants in the homes of German Jews (ibid.:161).

Because newly arrived Eastern Jews were generally poorer than their German Jewish counterparts, they could not so easily emulate the sharp sexual division of labor that characterized the new middle-class ideal. Nonetheless, even, or perhaps especially, for the Eastern Jew, the project of assimilation was importantly, if impossibly, linked to embourgeoisement. The sexual division of labor, first point of entry into middle-class respectability, was probably of greater consequence for Jewish women and men than for Gentiles (Mosse 1985:12; Kaplan 1991:168).

When Freud describes the difficult and risky passage whose final destination is femininity, he is describing a developmental trajectory that demands of its subject *assimilation* to both gendered and racialized norms. As socially and psychically regulated identities, "gender" and "race" are always approximations; neither is ever fully or perfectly achieved, but is always impossibly realizable. Thus, "having" gender and "having" race are always to some degree marked out as the failure of identification.

For Jewish women — especially Eastern Jewish women — in the historical period in which Freud wrote the *Three Essays* and prepared Dora's case study for publication, the project of femininity might seem bound on all sides by the spectre of imminent failure. The shared ideal of womanhood was white, Christian, reproductive, and hidden from view. To supplement or redirect Gilman's account: Freud's description of the difficult passage from girlhood into womanhood is never fully deracinated. Where Gilman sees only the spectral presence of the Jewish male, I mark also the trace of Jewish female difference.

The female body and its truncated penis are charged switchpoints for managing what Freud elsewhere designates as the narcissism of minor differences.[23] The first occasion for Freud's discussion of the narcissism of minor differences is his essay "The Taboo of Virginity." He introduces the concept as a way to explain the role men's fear of women plays in the taboo of [female] virginity (1918:198–99). The taboo of virginity, Freud argues, is "part of a large totality which embraces the whole of sexual life" (198). At its core is a "generalized dread of women." Indeed, "one might almost say," with Freud, "that women are altogether taboo" (198). Perhaps, suggests Freud:

> This dread is based on the fact that woman is different from man, for ever incomprehensible and mysterious, strange therefore apparently hostile. The man is afraid of being weakened by the woman, infected with her femininity and of showing himself incapable. (198–99)

Woman's difference provokes man's performance anxieties. Yet in the context of Freud's larger argument here, where he is first trying out and trying on for size the narcissism of minor differences, things are really the other way round. Male performance anxieties require an outlet onto which to shift the burden of blame and responsibility: "the practice of the taboos we have described testifies to the existence of a force which opposes love by rejecting women as strange and hostile" (199). This "force" is the narcissism of *minor* differences!

Freud's exposition of this force and its operations crucially hinges on E. Crawley's 1902 anthropological study of "primitive" marriage.

In *The Mystic Rose: A Study in Primitive Marriage,* Crawley postu-lated that each person is separated from each and every other person by a "'taboo of personal isolation'" (1902; quoted in Freud 1918:199). Freud takes Crawley to mean that "it is precisely the minor differ-ences in people who are otherwise alike that form the basis of feelings of strangeness and hostility between them" (199). It is at this textual passage that Freud first identifies the narcissism of minor differences:

> It would be tempting to pursue [Crawley's] idea and to derive from this "narcissism of minor differences" the hostility which in every human relation we see fighting against feelings of fellowship and overpowering the commandment that all men should love one another. Psycho-analy-sis believes that it has uncovered a large part of what underlies the nar-cissistic rejection of women by men, which is so mixed up with despising them, in drawing attention to the castration complex and its influence on the opinion in which women are held. (199)

The clear implication is that men are making mountains out of mole-hills when they seek so sharply to differentiate themselves from "strange and hostile" women.

Yet Freud ultimately resists the temptation to pursue the narcis-sism of minor differences into the gap between man and woman. For, in the very next breath, he apologizes for having ranged so far afield: "the general taboo of women throws no light on the particular rules concerning the first sexual act with a virgin" (199)—which was the ostensible subject of his essay.

Just prior to this apology, Freud has universalized male dread of female difference: "In all this there is nothing obsolete, nothing which is not still alive among ourselves" (199). Freud's analysis of men's fear of women thus appears neither culturally nor historically specific. Or does it? After all, the diagnosis he offers of a masculinity contaminated by feminine difference was one in which male Jews, within Freud's own historical experience, were dangerously implicated. To the extent that the alleged atavism of the Jews made them Europe's interior rep-resentatives of those he one sentence later calls "primitive races liv-ing to-day" (199), once again Freud's diagnosis is too close to where *he* lives. Perhaps, then, it is this possibility, that femininity's debilitating effects are too much "alive among our [Jewish] selves," that inflamed Freud's own sense of dread and led him not into temptation.

My invocation of Christian language here is deliberate. I am pick-ing up the theme sounded by Freud when he describes the narcissism of minor differences as interfering with "the commandment that all men should love one another." The sudden and unexpected eruption of Christianity's Golden Rule into Freud's discussion here may even tip off whom or what Freud is responding to in his second and final attempts, in 1921 and 1930, to explain and clarify what he intends under the narcissism of minor differences. This is an interpretation Sander Gilman also offers. Citing this 1918 passage, Gilman suggests that Freud appeals to the Christian maxim of universal brotherly love in order to erase "the differences between himself, his body, and the body of the Aryan" (1991:176). The "Taboo on Virginity," an essay ostensibly concerned with the management of sexual difference, is really all about the boundary crises Aryan/Semite or Christian/Jew.

Freud's fullest description of the narcissism of minor differences appears in his 1930 essay *Civilization and Its Discontents.* There, he notes that "it is precisely communities with adjoining territories, and related to each other in other ways as well, who are engaged in constant feuds and in ridiculing each other.... It is a convenient and relatively harmless satisfaction of the inclination to aggression, by means of which cohesion between the members of the community is made easier" (1930:114). The examples he marshals to make this point are the very ones he has earlier cited in *Group Psychology:* tensions between Spaniards and Portuguese, South Germans and North Germans, Britons and Scots. The suggestion, in each case, is that the differences between these neighboring peoples are more imagined than real; they may also be, for this very reason, all the more intractable. In both essays, it is only *after* citing the social and psychical utility of producing difference where there is, in reality, nothing to choose between that Freud introduces the difference of the Jew.

The work Freud makes Jewish difference do in these two essays does, however, differ in important respects. In *Group Psychology,* Freud does not speak of "Jews" or the "Jewish people," as he does in *Civilization and Its Discontents,* but of the "Semite." In line with this difference is another: the "cultural group" that defines itself against the Jewish people is "their Christian fellows" (1930:114), whereas the Semite's antagonist is the "Aryan" (1921:101). Moreover, in *Group Psychology,* the division Aryan/Semite is classed among other insider/outsider, us/them distinctions whose "greater differences... lead to an almost insuperable repugnance, such as the Gallic people feel for the German, the Aryan for the Semite, and the white races for the colored." In *Civilization and Its Discontents,* by contrast, Freud nowhere suggests that Jews and Christians are separated by "greater" differences than distinguish any other traditional antagonists.

Yet even Freud's admission of the "greater differences" of the Jew into his *Group Psychology*—an admission that might seem to give comfort to Freud's own enemies—is ultimately made, I believe, in the service of minimizing those differences. First appearance to the contrary, viewed in the context of Freud's framing discussion, these "greater differences" end up being cut down to a far more manageable size. Just as the "minor differences" between, for example, South German and North German have been exaggerated and embellished to satisfy the narcissism of each, so too, Freud implies, have the allegedly "greater differences" of the Aryan and the Semite been blown out of all proportion to their actual relations.

What especially fascinates me in all this is the way that Freud's ability to minimize difference or rather *some* differences (of "race" and Jewishness, for example) is itself dependent upon his reproduction and maximization of other differences. In other words, his analysis of the narcissism of minor differences is caught (up) in the act of recapitulating it. The cultural and psychical tasks Freud ascribes to the narcissism of minor differences—displacing the burden of difference onto another individual or group of individuals, thereby channeling fear and aggressiveness into safer and culturally recognized territories—seems to me to describe the work Freud does in the course of developing and delimiting the rage and object of this theory. Between "The Taboo of Virginity" and *Civilization and Its Discontents,* Freud's attention has shifted from one category of exemplary difference to another. He resolves the problem of Jewish male difference by pointing to narcissism's tendencies to inflate and exaggerate the space between. To shore up the *in*difference of his own body in relation to the Aryan's or Christian's, however, Freud clings to and ambivalently promotes the difference between man and woman. He thus maximizes one relatively minor difference ("sex"), so as to minimize another ("race"). The anxieties provoked by Freud's own experiences of difference haunt and distort his account of sexual (in)difference. For me, at any rate, this best explains and modulates Freud's ultimate failure to extend to sexual difference (and "woman") the same clear-eyed recognition of the way that narcissism, compounded of anxiety and fear, so often makes something out of nothing.

I have never seen a funnier figure than Sarah Bernhardt in Scene II, where she appears in a simple dress, I am really not exaggerating. And yet one was compelled to stop laughing, for every inch of this little figure was alive and bewitching. As for her caressing and pleading and embracing, the postures she assumes, the way she wraps herself round a man, the way she acts with every limb, every joint — it's incredible.

SIGMUND FREUD, *letter to Martha Bernays, November 8, 1885*[24]

Between one apparatus and the other I prefer a wooden leg.

SARAH BERNHARDT, *letter to Dr. Samuel Pozzi*[25]

Am *I* making something out of nothing if I spy, behind the scenes of Ida Bauer's renaming, the figure of another woman? Or if I read between the lines of Freud's exculpatory French declamations — *J'appelle un chat un chat* or *pour faire une omelette il faut casser des œufs* — to uncover *le portrait d'une autre Dora*?

In a November 8, 1885, letter to his then-fiancée Martha Bernays, Freud begins by apologizing for not having written to her "for ages" (1960:178), explaining, "Yesterday my failure to write had another cause. My head was reeling; I had been to the Porte St. Martin theater to see Sarah Bernhardt" (179). Freud gazes at and is bewitched by Bernhardt's bodily acts. The "way she acts with every limb, every joint," her body so "alive and bewitching," her serpentine ability to "wrap[ ] herself round a man" captivate and hold Freud's rapt attention. Her staged gestures lead him to the woman "herself." Collapsing the distance between staged representation and "real" life, Freud calls Bernhardt "a remarkable creature" and imagines that "she is no different in life from what she is on the stage" (181).

The eroticized spectacle of Sarah Bernhardt anticipates another specular object: the hystericized female body, whose vocal cues (as in the "talking cure") and surface signs (as in "somatic compliance") are the privileged mechanisms and symptomatic center of psychoanalysis. The women (and men) who people Freud's case histories are, as it were, characters in search of an author/auteur. It is Freud who makes their inner life available to directed view. In all this, Bernhardt plays actress-heroine for the psychoanalyst turned dramaturge. "Esperance," the actress-heroine of Bernhardt's autobiographical 1922 novel, *The Idol of Paris,* and a thinly disguised figure for La Divine Sarah *elle-même,* represents acting as a form of self-defense. If she does not act, "neurasthenia and madness await her" (quoted in Shattuck 1991:34).

Act or go mad: performance is the enabling condition of Esperance's (Bernhardt's) life. In turn, decoding and deciphering the other's bodily performances is the self-authorizing gesture of psychoanalysis.

In her day (and to mark the end of it), Bernhardt's dramatics on the boards and off were critically praised and appraised for what they might reveal of the woman behind the mask. In a *London Times* obituary dated March 28, 1923, and evocatively captioned "The Idol-Woman and the Other," the obituary's unnamed author says of Bernhardt:

> The actress did create, with Sardou's help, a new type—the embodiment of Oriental exoticism: the strange, chimaeric idol-woman: something not in nature, a nightmarish exaggeration, the supreme of artifice. This type and Sarah became one. She wandered all over the world with it, and no wonder that it became in the end somewhat travel-stained.

As in Freud's collapse of Bernhardt's onstage and offstage personae ("she is no different in life from what she is on the stage"), the *London Times* obituary maintains no distance between the unnatural, Oriental "type" Bernhardt portrayed and Bernhardt herself. Ultimately, this type does not travel well, because it travels too much.

"Sardou's help" elliptically nominates the scene of Bernhardt's greatest success, as the Empress Théodora in Sardou's play of the same name. Indeed, the *London Times*'s description of Bernhardt as "strange, chimaeric idol-woman" echoes an appreciative 1885 review of her performance in this role. At that time, the critic Jules Lemaître called Bernhardt's Théodora "a Salomé, a Salammbô: a distant chimerical creature, sacred and serpentine with a fascination both mystical and sensual" (quoted in Gold and Fizdale 1991:215).

So, Bernhardt's "Oriental exoticism" points eastward to Istanbul and beyond—to Judaea, Herod's court, and the figure of Salome. Salome: she of the seven veils and John the Baptist's severed head. Salome: the role set aside for Bernhardt in the London premiere that wasn't of Oscar Wilde's *Salome*.[26] If Salome was the greatest role Bernhardt never played, she did not have to. It was a role Bernhardt was always already (imagined as) playing.

If "Oriental exoticism" stops off in Judaea, it also circles back to include an "East" closer to home, bringing into view the "atavistic" landscapes of Eastern Europe and Eastern Jewry. Eastern Europe was even the explicit locale of Bernhardt's first collaboration with Sardou, *Fédora*. Sardou's description of the play's titular heroine, a part explicitly written for Bernhardt, conjures a figure capable of making one's head reel: "A combination of masculine mind and childish superstition. Eyes so deep they make one dizzy. A voice that stirs unknown vibrations in us; the languor of the oriental linked indissolubly with the grace of the Parisian" (quoted in Gold and Fizdale 1991: 201). East and West, infantilism and masculinity, converge in Sarah Bernhardt.

Bernhardt's Jewishness forms a critical backdrop to her public reception. The image of the wandering Jew surfaces in the obituary's stage directions: *she wandered all over the world.* Bernhardt had attracted this stereotype before. An 1880 biography, which was explicitly intended to introduce Bernhardt to an American audience on the eve of her first American tour, resourcefully turned the stereotype of the wandering Jew into a myth of origins, Bernhardt's:

> Of Jewish origin and Dutch nationality, she was one out of the eleven children of a wandering beauty of Israel. The future tragedienne was born in Holland about thirty years since, on the road, her mother being at the moment of Sarah's nativity in the act of moving her Lares and Penates to fresh fields and pastures new. Possibly the nomadic conditions under which, as a puling infant, this strange woman drew her first breath, had an all-powerful influence on her after life. (Griffith and Marrin 1880:8)

Bernhardt's Jewishness somehow "explains" her dazzling theatrical success. Yet in a period when the Jew was noted and feared for his (and, in Bernhardt's case, decidedly *her*) mimetic talent to represent or pass himself off as someone or something else (Geller 1992a:30), attributing Bernhardt's acting abilities to her putative birthright reiterates dangerous associations between Jewishness and artifice.[27]

In an intriguing passage in her autobiography, Bernhardt herself suggests that her chosen profession and Jewish lineage are inextricably linked. She recalls the decision upon which her entire destiny hinged: should she be an actress (Jewish) or a nun (not-Jewish)? She claims initially to have inclined toward the latter vocation and remembers an occasion when the other great figure from the nineteenth-century French stage, Rachel, visited the convent at which the girl Bernhardt was being educated:

> She went all over the convent and into the garden, and she had to sit down because she could not get her breath. They fetched her something to bring her round, and she was so pale, oh, so pale. I was very sorry

for her, and Sister St. Appoline told me what she did was killing her, for she was an actress; and so I won't be an actress—I won't. (Bernhardt 1907:53)

Additionally, Bernhardt remembered that "when Rachel had gone out of the garden, looking very pale, and holding a lady's arm for support, a little girl had put her tongue out at her. I did not want people to put out their tongues at me when I was grown up" (ibid.). In this anecdote, Rachel is represented as Bernhardt's negative image, that which she would least like to become.

Bernhardt did not want to become another Rachel, a woman whose tuberculosis—a disease to which Jews were thought to be more susceptible—Sister St. Appoline officially put down to her immoral life as an actress. Of course, if it is true—as Gold and Fizdale (1991:38) assert—that Bernhardt *l'actresse* always kept a portrait of Rachel with her backstage to inspire her performances, then it seems that Rachel would continue, for better or worse, to be a point of identification for Bernhardt.

Although Bernhardt's autobiographical emphases on her girlhood conversion to Christianity and the vocational path—nun—quite nearly chosen were themes repeated in newspaper accounts of her life, she never finally succeeded in redefining her Jewishness as a strictly religious identity, which she could take on or put off at will. In the newspaper accounts that appeared at the time of Bernhardt's death in March 1923, the articles citing her baptism in the next sentence speak of her as the "Jewess." As in the 1880 biography, then, Jewishness as irreducible "essence" in the final analysis explained, conditioned, and delimited Bernhardt's theatrical appeal.

Nor could Bernhardt escape anti-Semitic characterizations. Marie Colombier's thinly disguised *Memoirs of Sarah Barnum* portrayed Bernhardt as greedy, sexually promiscuous, and talentless. Among other slurs, Colombier said that "Madame Barnum possessed to the full the characteristics of her race—the love of money, but without the skill to obtain it" (1884:29).

Similar accusations—of "Jewish" avarice and sexual promiscuity—were also made against Rachel (Gold and Fizdale 1991:36–38). Even in a sympathetic 1911 biography, "race," business acumen, and stagecraft come together: "Rachel was of the race that was businesslike as well as artistic" (Gribble 1911:105). Consequently, the comparison to Rachel both favorably measured Bernhardt's talents against

Rachel's and placed Bernhardt in an extended "family" relationship: the family of "race."

Anti-Semitic slurs followed Bernhardt on her Russian tour. Moreover, around the time Colombier's pamphlet was circulating in France, there appeared in Germany a collection written by the Viennese playwright Ottokar Franz Ebersberg, but purporting to be the "authentic" correspondence of Bernhardt and her admirers (see Gilman 1993b: 203–4). In one letter, written by "Bernhardt" to "Benjamin Disraeli," she happily compares "herself" to "the Misses Esther and Herodias 'of the Persian and Jewish ballet,'" and she asks, rhetorically, "Was it not Jewesses who accomplished everything and forced themselves into the tent of the enemy, and if flattery did not succeed, killed them as Judith did the stupid Holofernes?" (quoted in Gilman 1993b:204).

On two of the very infrequent occasions when Freud mentions a stage play in his psychoanalytic works proper, he names Hebbel's tragedy *Judith und Holofernes*.[28] In these rare passages where the female character and her name are identifiably Jewish, Freud cites not a "real" woman but a mythic figure whose exploits in defense of her "people" were taken up into the anti-Semitic sterotype of the Jewess as deadly seductress.

Certainly, this stereotype surfaced in connection with Bernhardt's "notorious" sexual life. Doubtless, rumors of her sexual exploits were overdetermined by her occupation; actresses were popularly thought to be little more than prostitutes. But, even more than that, the gossip was powered by the stereotype of the *belle juive*, a stock figure in the nineteenth-century imagination of Jewish femininity (Gilman 1993b:203–5). The *belle juive* was a deceptively feminine figure, "deceptive" because her beauty concealed her powers of destruction. She was, as Gilman also notes, the ultimate femme fatale, drawing Gentile men in to their doom. Her stereotypically dark hair and black eyes not only recall the "blackness" of the Jew (ibid.:202) but also anticipate Freud's later description of femininity *tout court* as the "dark continent" (Freud 1926:212). The hyperbolic femininity of the *belle juive* conceals her perverse masculinity.

Bernhardt's private life became a matter of very public speculation. Not only were her "countless" affairs with men known and much discussed, but rumors of affairs with women, most prominently the painter Louise Abbéma, were also widely circulated. Fictionalized accounts of Bernhardt's alleged affairs with women appeared in such pulp novels as Félicien Champsaur's undated *Dinah Samuel* and Jean Lorrain's 1906 *Le Tréteau* (Gold and Fizdale 1991:134). In their recent biography of Bernhardt, Gold and Fizdale are at pains to describe her bisexuality as the expression of a mixed nature.

In saying that Bernhardt "liked to play the man off-stage and on," Gold and Fizdale — like Freud before them — vacate any and all space between performance and performer. Yet the claim that there was finally no difference between Bernhardt on stage and Bernhardt *in the flesh* is true only in the limited sense that the anti-Semitic spectacle of Jewish femininity was always already staged and unnatural. This is no less true of Freud's spellbound attentions to her than of the anti-Semitic insinuations of Colombier and Chekhov against her.

"In life" Bernhardt's image followed Freud. For years, a portrait of her greeted Freud's patients as they arrived at his Viennese office. I like to imagine that the portrait adorning Freud's waiting room depicted Bernhardt in the celebrated role in which Freud had seen her, Sardou's Théodora. I like to imagine also that the Jewish woman Freud would famously rename Dora confronted the image of this other Jewish woman, Sarah Bernhardt, playing this other Dora (Théo-Dora), whenever she (Ida Bauer) entered Freud's office for analysis. The fantasy of this uncanny meeting need have no reality outside *this* text, however, even if the phantom of Sarah Bernhardt — Freud's "remarkable creature" and the *belle juive* of her generation — may well haunt the scene of Ida Bauer's renaming.[29]

> A particularly favourable occasion for tendentious jokes is
> presented when the intended rebellious criticism is directed against
> the subject himself or, to put it more cautiously, against someone
> in whom the subject has a share — a collective person, that is (the
> subject's own nation, for instance). The occurrence of self-criticism
> as a determinant may explain how it is that a number of the most
> apt jokes have grown up on the soil of Jewish popular life....
> Incidentally, I do not know whether there are many other instances
> of a people making fun to such a degree of its own character.
> SIGMUND FREUD, *Jokes and Their Relation to the Unconscious*

Without You *I'm Nothing*, the cinematic conversion of Sandra Bernhard's "smash hit one-woman show" (as she so frequently reminds us), represents a fascinating and offbeat interpretation of the Jewish female body as "performative accomplishment."[30] The film restages Bernhard's successful 1989 off-Broadway show of the same name in predominantly black supper clubs in Los Angeles. Despite the fact that in the stage show within the film Bernhard repeats much of the "original" material, the film is not a literal record of the stage show. However, the film does employ some of the conventions of the concert film and documentary, intercutting Bernhard's onstage performances with interviews with "real people" — except all the "real people" are played by actors.

The operative conceit of the film is that Bernhard has gotten too big for her own good. The smashing success of her New York play has spoiled her; she is "way out of hand." Bernhard needs to return to her roots, to her *black* roots as it turns out, in order to rediscover and recenter herself. So, she goes "home," back to where it all began, back to Los Angeles and the Parisian Room. In moving from East Coast to West Coast, the play has also shifted audiences: from white to black and, perhaps, from Jew to Gentile. The reactions of the black audience to Bernhard's onstage antics vary from bewilderment to boredom to hostility.

Without You *I'm Nothing* functions as a parodic send-up of the conditions of spectatorship and spectatorial (dis)identification by signaling them so brazenly. By explicitly representing what Laura Mulvey has termed the "unpleasure" of the audience within the film (1989: 21), as it watches Bernhard's performances, the film, by accident or intent, interrogates the terms of spectatorial pleasure and identification. The film may also interrogate and challenge the terms through which Mulvey advanced her interpretation of the male gaze, visual pleasure, and narrative cinema. The "unpleasure," to borrow Mulvey's term, of Bernhard's audience should not be understood as operating through the framework of sexual difference alone. To the extent that Bernhard may be seen to pose a threat to her audience's pleasure, that threat must be conceptualized as the anxious site/sighting of sexual *and* racial difference. Moreover, contra Mulvey and bell hooks (I will discuss this later), *Without* You *I'm Nothing* is not finally readable through a male gaze.

Without You *I'm Nothing* simultaneously teases and frustrates identifications.[31] The film forecloses an identification between its represented and "real" audience. It is the cinematic spectators — the audience "outside" the film — catching the audience within the film in the act of watching Bernhard who have the opportunity for recognition, self-recognition as it turns out. True to its name, then, *Without*

You *I'm Nothing* plays on the dialectic of within and without, self and other, present and absent. In its movement within and without, the film seems to evacuate any possibility of deciding, once and for all, on which side "realness" lies: hetero/homo, white/black, male/female, Christian/Jew, culture/camp.

Who is the *you* without whom Bernhard would be nothing? The film stages a number of possibilities. First, and most visibly, *you* is a collective person; it refers to the predominantly black audience, whom the film depicts disinterestedly watching Bernhard perform at the Parisian Room. At the film's close, Bernhard, draped in an American flag, apologizes to her audience for lying to them. The critics were right, she admits, she is "a petty, bilious girl." She wishes she could refund the price of admission to each and every one of them, because "without me—without *you*, I'm nothing." If the verbal slip is "just" a joke, the joke is on Bernhard. It reveals her narcissistic self-involvement. "Without *me,* you're nothing," she nearly said. Yet the indifference of the depicted black audience has made clear that Bernhard means nothing to them. As Bernhard bumps and grinds her way through Prince's "Little Red Corvette," stripping away the Stars and Stripes to reveal patriotic pasties and G-string, the audience gets up and—one by one—takes leave of Bernhard. Only one woman, a black woman whose spectral presence haunts and even frames the length of the film, remains. This lone black woman, then, is also an overdetermined site and citational point of reference for Bernhard's directed address, *you*.

In their contribution to the anthology *Fear of a Queer Planet*, Lauren Berlant and Elizabeth Freeman have interpreted Bernhard's American striptease thus: "Bernhard flags her body to mark a fantasy of erotic identification with someone present, in the intimate room: it is a national fantasy, displayed as a spectacle of desire, and a fantasy, *apparently* external to the official national frame, of communion with a black-woman-as-audience whose appearance personifies 'authenticity'" (1993:194; emphasis added). Although I agree with much of their analysis, I want to unsettle the presumption of Bernhard's "whiteness"—an identification that seems, after a fashion, to ground their critique.

Bernhard's hyperbolic attempts to be black, as she impersonates Nina Simone, Diana Ross, Cardilla DeMarlo (in a wickedly lesbotic reinterpretation of "Me and Mrs. Jones"), Prince, and Sylvester, constitute an ambivalent acknowledgment of the conditions under which minority cultures become visible to "mainstream"—which is to say "white"—America. A leading condition for the subaltern's visibility is reauthorization, via a commodifying exchange, by hegemonic culture. Expropriating the cultural products and even the identities of subaltern communities, majority culture transforms the historical particularities of racial, ethnic, or sexual identity/ies into the universal ground of "America" (hooks 1992:31).

The issue here is not to assign "ownership," but to ask on whose terms and to what effects subcultural capital gets exchanged. The multiple fortunes of hybridization are, of course, implicated in a postmodern (read "late capitalist") public-sphere-turned-shopping-mall. Nor is blackness the only term charged to and in this new consumer economy. For if recent mass market (and even high theory) trends are to be taken seriously, queerness too has a certain exchange value. Madonna herself may be only the most celebrated instance of the "straight queer," the heterosexual who self-consciously takes on the signifiers of high-fashion queerness. The aestheticization of queerness, its reduction to a look and a manner of dress one can take on or put off at will, picks up the popular cant of homosexuality as a "lifestyle" choice and thereby contains the threatening difference of queerness. In this respect, then, the "straight" answer to Bernhard-as-Sylvester's question—*Do you wanna funk with me?*—is yes.[32]

On one level, Bernhard repeats a history of "white" appropriation of "blackness." Not only does she perform songs popularized by and even identified with black divas, but a woman playing Bernhard's manager claims that "Ross, Nina Simone, Whoopi Goldberg—they've all stolen from her."[33] Moreover, Bernhard seeks to produce her body as black. The first song she performs in *Without You I'm Nothing* is Nina Simone's "Four Women." Costumed in Africa, in a dashiki, Bernhard sings: "My skin is black, my arms are long, my hair is woolly, my back is strong.... What do they call me? They call me Aunt Sarah.... My skin is tan, my hair is fine (whichever way I fix it), my hips invite you, Daddy, my mouth, like wine.... What do they call me? They call me sweet thing."

As the second woman, "sweet thing," Bernhard invites both comparison and contradiction between her "black" body and the "truly" black bodies of her band. In a visual citation of earlier close-ups of her male band members' lips, the camera closes in on Bernhard's mouth at the very moment she sings "my mouth, like wine." Has she displaced the sexual difference of her "feminine" lips upward and into an apparent "racial" similarity? Bernhard herself notes the "racialized" terms of her synecdochical identification with her (upper) lips: "They used to call me nigger-lips in high school" (quoted in "Funny Face" 1992:44).[34]

Bernhard is all mouth as she ventriloquizes the black. Bernhard's ventriloquism should not, I suggest, be understood as her attempt to speak *for* blacks. Rather, she represents herself as trying—and flamboyantly failing—to speak *to* blacks from the place of blackness. Bernhard's inability to translate and communicate herself denaturalizes "black-Jewish solidarity," an alliance that has never been inevitable or finally achieved.

How might the contested history and meanings of black-Jewish solidarity be thought through blackface? Michael Rogin has argued that one Jewish response to nativist sentiments in early-twentieth-century America was to see Jewishness in relation to other "monstrously alien" minority identities (1992:438). He suggests that Jewish blackface in the Jazz Age may be viewed as a mechanism of assimilation. Blackness as masquerade had exchange value; it was a switchpoint through which Jewish identity could be made to appear someplace else. Rogin argues that Jewishness passes through blackness into whiteness only by "wiping out all difference *except* black and white" (447; emphasis added). Jewishness, on Rogin's reading, does not transcend or unravel the fundamental binary opposition between black and white, but assimilates itself to the latter term.

Bernhard's blackface performances bear a different relation to the opposition black/white. She parodically reiterates white appropriations of blackness in order to destabilize the binary operations of exclusion and denial whereby whiteness presumes to speak for blackness. Bernhard's blackface is thus a kind of whiteface; she impersonates and parodies whites impersonating blacks. Seeking to deconstruct and reflexively critique white appropriations of blackness, Bernhard must perform that appropriation. As hooks observes, Bernhard "walks a critical tightrope" between criticizing cultural theft and repeat performance (1992:38). Ultimately, the shifting positions occupied by the black audience in *Without You I'm Nothing* indicate the ambivalent fortunes of (re)appropriation and subversion. Simultaneously the screen against which Bernhard projects herself as transgressive spectacle and the silent register of her inability to translate herself across racial boundaries, the black audience within the film remains the voiceless measure of Bernhard's grand success (or still more grand failure). In this regard, *Without* You *I'm Nothing* seems to present its critique of white appropriation from the standpoint of whiteness—a whiteness masquerading, unsuccessfully as it turns out, as blackness.

However, what prevents Bernhard's black performativity from being a "simple" act of appropriation is its open failure to forge an identification between her black audience of address and herself. The audience withholds its belief, refusing to authorize Bernhard's vision of herself. Moreover, Bernhard sets herself up as an object of ridicule for that audience, conspicuously dramatizing the distance between her audience's and her own self-understandings. The audience does not "get" Bernhard; Bernhard does not "get" her audience. But the very misrecognition is to some degree what compels the performance.

Bernhard's failure may also disrupt the pleasure the cinematic audience takes in watching *Without* You *I'm Nothing*. Bernhard's theatricalization of herself as black is the occasion of extreme displeasure for the black audience within the film.[35] The visible displeasure of the textual audience renders explicit the identificatory fictions that produce and sustain whatever pleasure the cinematic audience takes. In this way, the film potentially challenges the illusions of self-identity that not only determine the pleasure of narrative film, but also condition subjectivity. By showcasing the misidentifications between Bernhard and her audience, the film permits the cinematic spectators to gain some distance on themselves.

Nonetheless, the self-critique the film enables may also return to business as usual, reconstituting the self/other dichotomy. For the spectatorial pleasure of the "white" spectators, who comprise the vast majority of Bernhard's following, is founded in part on the represented discomfort or unpleasure of the "black" audience within the film. So obnoxious is much of Bernhard's performance, so arcane many of her jokes, that the film ultimately frustrates any lasting identification between even its (phantasmatically) white audience and Bernhard, thereby leaving no permanent site through which to constitute stable identity within or through the film.[36]

Throughout the film, it is Bernhard who is the preeminent site of mis-, dis-, and *dissed* identification. Twice the emcee at the supper club where she is performing introduces her as "Sarah Bernhardt," installing Bernhard within a theatrical tradition whose lineage begins with the Divine Sarah, arguably the first truly international star.[37] The name Sarah Bernhardt has also come to be identified with histrionics and over-the-top self-theatricalization. As a latter-day Sarah Bernhardt, Sandra Bernhard can point to the Jewishness, considerable talent for self-invention, and notorious sexual life of her predecessor with an assumed family resemblance.

If the emcee twice confuses Bernhard with her much more celebrated soundalike, neither can Bernhard herself seem to get her own identity straight. She refers to "me and my Jewish piano player," saying "we people get along so well." Despite the resistance of her black audience within the film, who are not in on the joke, Bernhard persists in identifying herself as black, even to the point of intercutting scenes of her onstage performances with the figure of a young black woman, never named by the film, but identified in the closing credits as "Roxanne" (Cynthia Bailey). Roxanne: most famously, the name of another object of ventriloquized desire, Cyrano's.

It is not always clear whether the black woman appears as counterpoint to or confirmation of Bernhard's blackness. Is she Bernhard's mirror image or her mirror opposite? Bernhard's explicit response to this question is that "Roxanne" represents a reality check on her film persona's presumption to blackness:

> We just thought it was really funny to have this deluded white performer, who thought she was a black diva, perform for a black audience. It was like letting her know that she not only was *not* a black diva, but she had no idea what it was like to suffer, you know in that skin. And of course, at the end, the black woman—the *beautiful* black woman— has the final word, which is "Fuck you, bitch. You may *think* you're black, but I'm the one who's paid the dues." (quoted in "Sandra's Blackness" 1992:116; emphases in original)

But, who are "we" and why the emphasis on the black woman's beauty, as if—in the end—(only) the black female's body really matters? As Berlant and Freeman suggest, the symbolic function Bernhard assigns to the black woman "perpetuates the historic burden black women in cinema have borne to represent embodiment, desire, and the dignity of suffering on behalf of white women" (1993:218). The black woman signifies, but will not, does not, or cannot speak for herself. Is this the only way to see the black woman's symbolic role in the film or, to put my question another way, is this the only way to understand Bernhard's relationship to her?

In *Black Looks,* bell hooks asks whether the black woman is "the fantasy Other Bernhard desires to become...or the fantasy Other Bernhard desires?" (1992:38). Answering the former, hooks claims that the black woman functions as a critical "yardstick Bernhard uses to measure herself" (38). But are identification and desire only thinkable as mutually exclusive possibilities? What if identification is one of the ruses through and by which transgressive desires are rerouted?[38]

Identification *and* desire link Bernhard to the black woman throughout the film. The first time we see Bernhard, she is sitting in front of a makeup mirror, concentrating all her attention on a strand of hair she is fussily trimming. As Bernhard comes into focus, the background music shifts from high European culture, signaled by Bach's first *Partita,* to the uniquely "American" sounds of jazz. This scene will later be cited, mirrored, by the black woman. The black woman stands before a bathroom mirror, listening to Ice Cube, and carefully cuts a strand of hair. Later, in a scene that registers the unstable border between identification and desire, we see Bernhard, on the bottom, having sex with her boyfriend Joe, who is black. Bernhard seems to have usurped the black woman's position in a heterosexual economy of exchange, which posits sexual difference and racial "sameness" as normative criteria. What if, however, it is the black man who has taken the black woman's place? Perhaps, as Elspeth Probyn suggests, Joe substitutes for Bernhard's "real" object of desire and identification, the black woman (1993:156).

However, it is not just Bernhard who crosses over into the black woman's territory by becoming, or seeking to become, black. In one scene, the black woman puts herself, or is put, in Bernhard's "place." The black woman is seen leaning against what appears to be a kosher butcher shop. As Jean Walton notes in her terrifically lucid reading of this film, Bernhard's black stand-in holds a copy of Harold Bloom's *The Kabbalah and Criticism* in her hand (Walton 1994:255). This scene signals the possibility (or wish) that Bernhard's identification with blackness and the black woman might, as it were, go both ways. The book title, which passes fleetingly into and out of the viewer's gaze, may also represent a teasing challenge to the filmic audience to subject the film and Bernhard to critical scrutiny.

The film's final, critical words belong to the black woman. As Bernhard stands before the now-empty supper club, gazing plaintively into the space her audience used to occupy, the camera's gaze and Bernhard's become identified, focusing intently on her last best hope, the black woman, who has materialized as if from nowhere. The black woman wears a flowing evening dress, her hair piled high on her head. She seems to return Bernhard's gaze, but with contempt (is this halfway to desire?), going so far as to mark that contempt in lipstick, femininity's signature. "Fuck Sandra Bernhard," she scrawls.[39] As the camera lingers over the black woman's parting statement, it also foregrounds a full glass of Rémy Martin, the liquor to which Bernhard — in the persona of a black lounge singer — has earlier pledged her fealty. In high culture contrast to Bernhard's bump and grind version of Prince's "Little Red Corvette," the black woman fairly floats out of the scene to the reprise of Bach's first *Partita*. The black woman is consumed by whiteness, as both she and the screen literally fade into white (Probyn 1993:151).

In her analysis of the film, hooks argues that "all the white women [in the film] strip, flaunt their sexuality, and appear to be directing their attention to a black male gaze" (1992:38). But who are *all* these white women? There are only three "white" women in the film: Bernhard; her cigar-smoking manager; and Shoshana, an obvious parody of Madonna. Now, Bernhard's "butch" manager hardly seems the type to be flaunting her sexuality and performing for *any* male gaze — at least not in the straightforwardly heterosexualized manner hooks ushers into (our) view. By "all the white women," then, hooks must mean "Shoshana" and *multiple* "Bernhards." Evidently, performance and cinematic spectacle only go so far. Hooks allows that Bernhard may be fragmented into pieces, but seems to rule out the possibility that any of these performing "pieces" might be other than white.

Hooks also insists that all the white women perform for a black male gaze. Yet who or where is the agency of that gaze? The black male gaze within the film — if that is what it is — is textual, and it is *not* unified with the extratextual gaze of *Without You I'm Nothing*'s cinematic audience.

Hooks introduces, but quickly drops, the possibility that Bernhard might be performing for a black female gaze (1992:38). Black women are Bernhard's "yardstick," not her objects of desire. Hooks chooses to read the interracial trajectory of Bernhard's desire heterosexually. This is, in my view, a telling misreading. The closing scene of the film, in which Bernhard strips for the sole remaining audience member, suggests that it is black womanhood Bernhard desires and black women whose gaze she seeks to meet. Recoding lesbian desire through racial difference, rather than through the terms of sexual difference, stages the nonidentity of "same-sex" love. The "same" is restaged as and in the difference "between" white and black. All the same, this does not answer to the concern that it is the black female body that bears the burden of signifying the "white" woman's difference — a point also made by Probyn (1993:158) and Berlant and Freeman (1993:218). It does, however, queerly complicate the relations between "racial" and sexual difference, identification and desire.

Blackness is not the only performative term the film tries to make visible. Does the black woman's disappearance into a screen of white light at the film's close represent only the territorialization of blackness by whiteness or/and does it destabilize the claims of either side — "whiteness" or "blackness" — to represent or incorporate "realness"? I want to suggest that this destabilization occurs through the introduction of an excluded middle term, which resembles both sides, but is identical to neither: Jewishness. This is a point hooks, Probyn, and Berlant and Freeman all miss. Although hooks and Probyn at least cite Bernhard's Jewishness, neither fully addresses what the historical associations between blackness and Jewishness might mean in the context of Bernhard's "will" to blackness.[40]

For hooks, Bernhard's "Jewish heritage as well as her sexually ambiguous erotic practices are experiences that place her outside of the mainstream" (1992:37). But what does Bernhard's Jewish heritage have to do with her queer erotic practices? Has hooks inadvertently defined that heritage in erotic terms? The representations of Jewish women, not unlike the representations of (other?) black women, have themselves been overburdened *as well as* overidentified with "sexually ambiguous erotic practices." Hooks insinuates, but does not finally clarify, connections between Bernhard's assumed blackness, on the one side, and her Jewishness and queerness, on the other. She locates Bernhard's "outside" in an "alternative white culture" whose "standpoint" and "impetus" the film traces to black culture (37). Yet in Bernhard's pulsating tributes to (and as) Sylvester, "You Make Me Feel (Mighty Real)" and "Do You Wanna Funk," as well as in her eulogy for Andy Warhol, she makes it clear that *queer* cultures, black and white, are also among the resources and expropriated sites of American (sub)cultural capital.

Similarly, when Probyn refers to Bernhard as a "white Jewish woman" (1993:156), it is not obvious to me what work "Jewish" is doing here. On this, the first and last occasion Probyn will cite Bernhard's Jewishness, she anxiously qualifies it as "white." However, isn't the relation of Jewishness and "race" one of the things *Without You I'm Nothing* contests? Berlant and Freeman too seem to lose sight of Bernhard's "racial" specificity. They (mis)identify the film's and Bernhard's "aesthetic distance" as working through the "straightness of the *generic* white woman-identified-woman" (1993:218; emphasis added).

Bernhard does not self-identify herself as white. Asked in a 1992 interview whether she "[related] to the world as a white person," Bernhard responded, "I never relate myself as a white person because I'm not a gentile; I'm a Jew. I feel like, culturally, I've gleaned from other cultures, but I also have a very rich one myself" (quoted in "Sandra's Blackness" 1992:116). In a 1993 interview (the too perfectly captioned "Egos and Ids"), Bernhard signals also the comparative *insignificance* of her sexualized and gendered differences — as a woman-loving-woman — when they are measured against the historical meanings of the Jew's "racial" difference:

> I feel more concerned about being a Jew than I do about equating myself with being gay. I feel like there's more anti-Semitism than there is anti-homosexual feelings. It's like if the Nazis come marching through, they'll come after me as a Jew before they do as a chic lesbian. (Bernhard 1993:4)

Pressed on the same point in another interview, Bernhard speaks even more directly of the inescapability of her Jewishness:

> If I am going to defend any minority part of myself, it is going to be Judaism. It's something that has formed my personality much more than my sexuality has.... You are born Jewish. It is not something you can deny or run away from. You can pretend you're not. You can get your nose fixed and play all kinds of games, but... (quoted in Sessums 1994:126)

Bernhard's Jewishness is not a "chosen" identity — even if accepting it or rejecting it is her choice. In contrast, she says, "you develop your sexuality" (127).

What interests me here is the way Bernhard conceptualizes her Jewishness, on the one side, and her sexual "identity," on the other. In representing herself as *born* Jewish, but *become* queer, she aligns Jewishness with nature and sexuality with nurture. Another way to express this division would be "essentialism" versus "constructionism."

In posing herself *as* the question of race, Bernhard appears to align herself with blackness not so much over and against whiteness as conceived through it. Her passage from blackness to Jewishness takes place through a caricatured whiteness. This transmutation through whiteness is dramatized in one of the film's early sequences. First, a "black" Bernhard performs Simone's "Four Women." After she completes the song, the black emcee encourages an incredulous audience: "Sarah Bernhardt, ladies and gentlemen. The lady came here all the way from New York City, so let's give her our support." Following Bernhard to the stage is "our very own lucky, lucky, lucky star, the original Sho-shanaaaaaa," the Jewish name Shoshana rhymingly replacing the Catholic Madonna. As Shoshana wriggles her way through a performance whose bad taste is exceeded only by its poor execution, the camera cuts away from Shoshana's dancing fool to the anonymous black woman walking in front of the Watts Tower, then cuts back to Shoshana. Finally, Bernhard, performing "Bernhard," returns to the stage, where she attempts, unsuccessfully, to lead the audience in a round of Israeli folk songs. She talks about the joys of growing up in "a liberal, intellectual Jewish household," but also confesses to a Gentile family romance: "I'd fantasize that I had an older brother named Chip and a little sister named Sally, and my name would either be Happy or Buffy or Babe." In fact, it is the white imitation-Madonna and the buxom "Babe" who appear the most obviously "false" of any impersonation in the film. "Whiteness," then, is recast as always already an imitation — variously of blackness, of itself, of nothing. It is also represented as Christian. Bernhard even concludes her rhapsodic "testimonial" to the joys of Gentile family values with this wish: "May all your Christmases be white."

It may be, as Mary Ann Doane has suggested, that "to espouse a white racial identity at this particular historical moment is to align oneself with white supremacists" (1991:246). Moreover, as Doane also argues, "both whiteness and blackness cover and conceal a host of ethnicities, of cultural backgrounds whose differences are leveled by the very concepts of white and black. Whiteness and blackness are historically *real* categories only in their lengthy and problematic collision with each other in the context of systems of colonialism and slavery" (246). This, on my viewing, is one of the things *Without* You *I'm Nothing* achieves, or comes close to achieving: namely, the disruption of the totalizing logic either/or, white/black. Ultimately, however, it also seems to me that the film and Bernhard can only disrupt monolithic whiteness by reconsolidating blackness.

Nonetheless, Bernhard's *whiteface* performances, through which she mimes and parodies whiteness as the historical agent of expropriation, complicate the relations Rogin traces in *The Jazz Singer.* Bernhard's blackface is *not* the mechanism whereby Jewishness transcends blackness and becomes white; her insistent equation of whiteness with Christianity blocks such a movement. Arguably, Bernhard's impersonation of whites impersonating blacks allows her to leave behind not blackness, but white guilt. In parodying the bald-faced failures of whiteness to speak for or even to blackness, Bernhard may be exculpating herself from any wrongdoings committed in the name of whiteness. This is a paradigmatically liberal gesture of disavowal and/as transcendence. It may also represent the reappearance of a political fantasy, black-Jewish solidarity.

Just as the gender performatives of a *Paris Is Burning* are not only about gender, the race performatives of *Without* You *I'm Nothing* are not only about "race."[41] I believe Bernhard works "race," which she represents as blackness, as a way to situate and resituate also her Jewishness, queerness, and womanliness. That Bernhard thematizes whiteness as "being," among its other attributions, a relation to Christianity acts to denaturalize the claims of "race." At the same time it indicates how Jewishness is articulated through multiple discourses: religion, race, gender, nationality, sexuality.

Blackness, arguably the constitutive elsewhere of American national identity, becomes a way of visibly re-marking and exteriorizing Bernhard's differences. Articulating her "otherness" through blackness reinscribes and potentially upends the historical terms of American racial definition. Perhaps blackness is the performative term most often seen, or recognized, in *Without You I'm Nothing* because it "appears" to be the one identity category on display in the film that Bernhard does not "really" embody, because Jewishness or queerness or womanliness are somehow facts about Bernhard. She just is those things, right? This is appearance as ontology.

In sum: Bernhard's open avowal of the coimplicating structure of identity categories illuminates what so often seems just a theoretical abstraction: gender or race performatives. Moreover, we are able more clearly to recognize and identify (with) those processes that constitute and are performed as subjectivity when Bernhard is acting up and acting them out than when "we" are "ourselves" becoming subject(s) through them. Meanwhile, if I take pleasure from Bernhard's performances at (and as?) the crossroads gender, "race," and sexuality, that pleasure is itself conditioned by the glimmer of recognition — I mean, self-recognition — provided in this occasion of spectatorship. It is prompted also by the prick of my desire, as if I were the phantasmatic *you* for whom Bernhard performs and without whom *her* "I" would be nothing.

Put otherwise: the *I* — whether mine, hers, or yours — is the intersubjective site, or citation, of the differentiating marks of desire and identification. Bernhard's self-referential performances succeed, in some small measure, in calling up and relocating something of the Jewish female subjects displaced by Freud's (and Gilman's) terms. To the extent that she articulates the specificities of her body by speaking through another other's terms, however, Bernhard is yet caught up in the endlessly repeating and repeated logic of identifications found, lost, and found again at someone else's address.

Notes

Earlier versions of this essay were read by Daniel Boyarin, Jonathan Boyarin, Judith Butler, Linda S. Garber, Marjorie Garber, Jay Geller, Naomi R. Goldenberg, Alice Jardine, Margaret R. Miles, and D. A. Miller. *This* version is the better for their generous attentions and critical challenges. The Bernhard section of this essay has also benefited from conversations with Paul B. Franklin, Thomas A. King, Paul Morrison, and Jean Walton.

1. Judith Butler describes identity categories, such as gender and "race," as "vectors of power" that "require and deploy each other for the purpose of their own articulation" (1993:18). For more on the interarticulations of power and identities, see Butler 1993, esp. 17–20 and 167–85.

2. This is a point most fully developed in Gilman 1993a.

3. Private communication with Boyarin.

4. Analogously, Elizabeth V. Spelman has pointed out how such commonly heard locutions as "women and blacks" either vacate any position for black women to occupy or suggest that their position is a composite of white women's and black men's experiences (1988:14–15, 193n32).

5. For a study in which Gilman does try, though with mixed results, to center the Jewish female body, see 1993b.

6. The relation of Freud's Jewishness to the history and development of psychoanalysis has been amply documented. The stigmatization of psychoanalysis as the "Jewish science" and Freud's own concern that the psychoanalytic movement not be

perceived as a "Jewish national affair" have also been much commented upon (Klein 1981; Yerushalmi 1991; Gilman 1991, and 1993a; Bakan 1990; Geller 1992b, 1992c; Gay 1987). For "Jewish national affair," see Freud's letter of May 3, 1908, to Karl Abraham (quoted in Yerushalmi 1991:42).

7. The term *thought-collective* is Ludwick Fleck's (quoted in Gilman 1991).

8. For a detailed historical study of the relationship between linguistics and the biology of race, see Olender 1992.

9. For one representative study of the Jewish "essence," see Otto Rank, "Das Wesen des Judentums." An English translation of this 1905 manuscript appears as Appendix C in Klein 1981:170–73.

10. Conversations with Daniel Boyarin concerning this paradox have been very helpful.

11. Charcot, the pioneering French theorist of hysteria and an early mentor to Freud, identified the "especially marked predisposition of the Jewish race for hysteria," citing inbreeding as the likely cause of Jews' heightened risk (quoted in Garber 1992:225). Syphilis too was strongly associated with Jews.

12. Gilman's analysis of Jewish masculinity and its fraught interstructuration through the discourses of race and gender is brilliant. But his analysis of femininity and the construction of the Jewish female leaves much to be desired.

13. Garber (1992) offers a useful summary of some of these stereotypes. See also Gilman on the Jewish foot (1991) and voice (1991, 1993a).

14. If Freud was for a time enamored of Fliess's theory, this is because he was — again, for a time — enamored of Fliess himself. For a discussion of their homoerotically charged relationship, see Garber 1995.

15. Cf. Freud 1985:61, 181.

16. Geller details the course of this upward displacement in 1992b and 1992c. For Freud's description of his own "nasal secretions," see 1985:63, 130, 181, 285.

17. Weininger commited suicide six months after the German publication of *Sex and Character.*

18. For other turns into French phrasing in *Fragment of a Case of Hysteria,* see, for example, 1905a:40, 41. For other readings of this turn, see Marcus 1985 and Gallop 1985.

19. In a close reading of the Hebrew and German inscriptions Jakob Freud entered in the Freud family bible, Yosef Hayim Yerushalmi has shown that it was Jakob Freud, and not Sigmund, who first used the German variation of "Sigismund" (1991:132n19).

20. Freud's realignment of the Jewish male body with the universal term is most clearly represented in *Moses and Monotheism,* his longest sustained meditation on the character of Jewishness. This point has also been made, though with different emphases, by Van Herik (1982), Gilman (1993a), and Eilberg-Schwartz (1994).

21. In his essay "Salome, Syphilis, Sarah Bernhardt and the Modern 'Jewess,' " Gilman describes the problem of identifying the Jewish woman's difference thus: "When Jewish women are represented in the culture of the turn of the century, the qualities ascribed to the Jew and to the woman seem to exist simultaneously and yet seem mutually exclusive.... When we focus on the one, the other seems to vanish" (1993b:195). Perhaps Gilman's own representations of Jewishness, "race," and gender are one such case in point?

22. The pivotal and dominant figure here would be Freud's own mother, Amalie Nathansohn Freud. One grandchild called her "shrill and domineering" (Appignanesi and Forrester 1992:14). In the memoirs of another grandchild, Martin Freud, Amalie

Freud's "eastern" origins are prominently mentioned. She was typically Galician, he says, "not what we would call a 'lady,' had a lively temper and was impatient, self-willed, sharp-witted, and highly intelligent" (ibid.).

23. For Freud on the narcissism of minor differences, see "The Taboo of Virginity" (1918:199); *Group Psychology* (1921:101); and *Civilization and Its Discontents* (1930:114–15).

24. Letter 84 of Freud 1960:181.

25. February 4, 1915, quoted in Gold and Fizdale 1991:316.

26. For another, and related, perspective on the Bernhardt-Wilde-Salome connection, see Garber 1992. See also Gilman's fascinating reading of this triangle (1993b).

27. Is it possible to catch in Alfred Rosenberg's vitriolic 1925 rantings against the degradations inflicted on German and, indeed, all European theater by "pseudo-French tragedy" and "Jewish commercial management... [with its] pursuit of the 'star'" (Rosenberg 1970:166–67) an allusion to Bernhardt, whose 1923 death did not put an end to her influence? Bernhardt, after all, not only was the most celebrated star of her era, she had cut her theatrical teeth on Racine—a synecdoche for the Greek-inspired French (pseudo-)tragedies that so earned Rosenberg's scorn. Moreover, Bernhardt herself even qualified as "Jewish management." She owned and operated several theaters during her career, beginning with the Théâtre de la Renaisance and culminating in her establishment of—what else—the Théâtre Sarah Bernhardt (Gold and Fizdale 1991).

28. I have already mentioned the first occasion, "The Taboo of Virginity" (1918:207–8); the second citation occurs in the midst of Freud's discussion of the army in *Group Psychology* (1921:97).

29. I am not alone in entertaining a fantasy whose prime players are Freud, Dora, and Sarah Bernhardt. George Dimock proposes Bernhardt as an iconic substitute for, or antidote to, the hysterical female patient (1994:243).

30. The term *performative accomplishment* is Butler's (1990b:271).

31. For another reading of Bernhard's "tease" and "refusal," see Berlant and Freeman 1993:193–229.

32. See, in this regard, the spate of 1993 articles on "straight" passing as "queer" in the *Village Voice* (Powers), *GQ* (Kamp), and *Esquire* ("Viva Straight Camp!").

33. The stage name Whoopi Goldberg indicates that blackness may also name itself through Jewishness. It also names a group this essay occludes: African American Jews.

34. Bernhard's "inflated" lips are a point of frequent and sometimes even anxious discussion (Green 1992:42; cf. "Look at Me" 1992:14 and "Hips, Lips, Tits, POWER" 1992:8). Her mouth is cited as her most distinguishing feature. An extreme close-up of her mouth is even the full-page subject of a Herb Ritts photo in his 1992 "photo album" of the "stars," *Notorious*.

35. In a 1992 interview with *Vibe* magazine, in which the flattering representation of "Sandra's blackness" is in sharp contrast to the companion piece dissing "whites who think they're black," Bernhard was asked how black audiences respond to her black characters. "The black audiences love me. It's kind of amazing. They really get it. They're very receptive to me, it's the highest honor, because if black people dig you, you must be doing something right" ("Sandra's Blackness," 1992:116). The displeasure recorded by the camera is a staged displeasure, then. According to Bernhard, "real" black audiences "really" do "dig" her act. It is an open question whether Bernhard has here accurately represented—or spoken for—her impossibly unified "black audiences."

36. I do not want to oversimplify the reception of this film. I am not claiming that all white people or all Jewish people like, or must like, this film. Nor do I mean to suggest that all black spectators are put off by Bernhard's bodily impostures. In neither case would this be "true" to the anecdotal evidence offered me by Jewish and African-American friends and colleagues whose reactions to *Without You I'm Nothing* do not so easily fall into "racial" or ethnocultural line. Rather, I am trying to offer a schematic of the spectatorial positions idealized and produced by the film. At minimum, it seems to me that the very divergent reactions this film has prompted make amply clear how the scene of (dis)identification is mediated through "race," gender, sexuality, and class positions.

37. Jesse Green's 1992 *Mirabella* article on Bernhard is even knowingly titled "The Divine Sandra."

38. Diana Fuss explores how identification simultaneously opens up and defends against the possibility of lesbian desire in the context of contemporary fashion photography (1992).

39. Berlant and Freeman make a similar point (1993:217).

40. See Gilman 1991 and 1993a on the Jew as "black."

41. For an analysis of the links between "race" and gender performatives in *Paris Is Burning,* see Butler 1993:121–40. Compare hooks 1992:145–56 and Phelan 1993:93–111. See also Harper 1994.

Bibliography

Appignanesi, Lisa, and John Forrester. 1992. *Freud's Women.* New York: Basic Books.

Bakan, David. 1990. *Sigmund Freud and the Jewish Mystical Tradition.* London: Free Association Books.

Berlant, Lauren, and Elizabeth Freeman. 1993. "Queer Nationality." In *Fear of a Queer Planet: Queer Politics and Social Theory,* ed. Michael Warner, 193–229. Minneapolis: University of Minnesota Press.

Bernhard, Sandra. 1993. Egos and Ids: Goodbye to All That Cool Stuff. Interview by Degen Pener. *New York Times,* August 8, sec. 9: 4.

Bernhardt, Sarah. 1907. *My Double Life: Memoirs of Sarah Bernhardt.* London: Heinemann.

Boyarin, Daniel. Forthcoming. "What Does a Jew Want?: The Phallus as White Mask."

———. 1995. "Freud's Baby, Fliess' Maybe: Homophobia, Antisemitism, and the Invention of Oedipus." *GLQ: A Journal of Lesbian and Gay Studies* (special issue: *Pink Freud,* ed. Diana Fuss) 2(1): 1–33.

Briggs, Sheila. 1985. "Images of Women and Jews in Nineteenth- and Twentieth-Century German Theology." In *Immaculate and Powerful: The Female in Sacred Image and Reality,* ed. Clarissa W. Atkinson, Constance H. Buchanan, and Margaret R. Miles, 226–59. Boston: Beacon.

Butler, Judith. 1990a. *Gender Trouble: Feminism and the Subversion of Identity.* New York: Routledge.

———. 1990b. "Performative Acts and Gender Constitution: An Essay in Phenomenology and Feminist Theory." In *Performing Feminisms: Feminist Critical Theory and Theatre,* ed. Sue-Ellen Case, 270–82. Baltimore: Johns Hopkins University Press.

———. 1993. *Bodies That Matter: On the Discursive Limits of "Sex."* New York: Routledge.

Colombier, Marie. 1884. *The Memoirs of Sarah Barnum.* Trans. Ferdinand C. Valentine and Leigh H. Hunt. New York.

Dimock, George. 1994. "The Pictures over Freud's Couch." In *The Point of Theory: Practices of Cultural Analysis,* ed. Mieke Bal and Inge E. Boer, 239–50. New York: Continuum; Amsterdam University Press.

Doane, Mary Ann. 1991. *Femmes Fatales: Feminism, Film Theory, Psychoanalysis.* New York: Routledge.

Eilberg-Schwartz, Howard. 1994. *God's Phallus and Other Problems for Men and Monotheism.* Boston: Beacon.

Freud, Sigmund. 1955. *The Standard Edition of the Complete Psychological Works of Sigmund Freud.* Ed. James Strachey. Trans. James Strachey et al. 24 vols. London: Hogarth Press and the Institute of Psycho-Analysis.

[1901]. *The Psychopathology of Everyday Life.* 6.

[1905a]. *Fragment of an Analysis of a Case of Hysteria.* 7: 7–122.

[1905b]. *Three Essays on the Theory of Sexuality.* 7: 130–243.

[1905c]. *Jokes and Their Relation to the Unconscious.* 8: 9–236.

[1909a]. "Some General Remarks on Hysterical Attacks." 10: 229–34.

[1909b]. *Analysis of a Phobia in a Five-Year-Old Boy.* 10: 5–149.

[1918]. "The Taboo of Virginity." 11: 193–208.

[1921]. *Group Psychology and the Analysis of the Ego.* 18: 69–143.

[1926]. *The Question of Lay Analysis: Conversations with an Impartial Person.* 20: 183–258.

[1930]. *Civilization and Its Discontents.* 21: 64–145.

[1931]. "Female Sexuality." 21: 225–43.

[1933]. "Femininity." *New Introductory Lectures on Psychoanalysis* (Lecture 33). 22: 112–35.

[1939]. *Moses and Monotheism.* 23: 7–137.

———. 1960. *Letters of Sigmund Freud.* Ed. Ernst L. Freud. Trans. Tania and James Stern. New York: Basic Books.

———. 1985. *The Complete Letters of Sigmund Freud to Wilhelm Fliess, 1887–1904.* Ed. and trans. Jeffrey Moussaieff Masson. Cambridge, Mass.: Harvard University Press.

"Funny Face." 1992. *The Face,* September, 40–46.

Fuss, Diana. 1992. "Fashion and the Homospectatorial Look." *Critical Inquiry* 18: 713–37.

Gallop, Jane. 1985. "Keys to Dora." In *In Dora's Case: Freud, Hysteria, Feminism,* ed. Charles Bernheimer and Claire Kahane, 200–220. New York: Columbia University Press. 200–20.

Garber, Marjorie. 1992. *Vested Interests: Cross-Dressing and Cultural Anxiety.* New York: Routledge.

———. 1995. *Vice Versa: Bisexuality and the Eroticism of Everyday Life.* New York: Simon and Schuster.

Gay, Peter. 1987. *A Godless Jew: Freud, Atheism, and the Making of Psychoanalysis.* New Haven, Conn.: Yale University Press.

Geller, Jay. 1992a. "Blood Sin: Syphilis and the Construction of Jewish Identity." *Faultline* 1: 21–48.

———. 1992b. "(G)nos(e)ology: The Cultural Construction of the Other." In *People of the Body: Jews and Judaism from an Embodied Perspective,* ed. Howard Eilberg-Schwartz, 243–82. Albany: State University of New York Press.

————. 1992c. " 'A Glance at the Nose': Freud's Inscription of Jewish Difference."
    American Imago 49: 427–44.
Gilman, Sander L. 1987. "The Struggle of Psychiatry with Psychoanalysis: Who
    Won?" *Critical Inquiry* 13: 293–313.
————. 1991. *The Jew's Body.* New York: Routledge.
————. 1993a. *Freud, Race, and Gender.* New York: Routledge.
————. 1993b. "Salome, Syphilis, Sarah Bernhardt, and the 'Modern Jewess.' "
    German Quarterly 66 (Spring): 195–211.
Gold, Arthur, and Robert Fizdale. 1991. *The Divine Sarah: A Life of Sarah
    Bernhardt.* New York: Vintage.
Green, Jesse. 1992. The Divine Sandra. *Mirabella,* August, 38–40, 42, 44.
Gribble, Francis. 1911. *Rachel: Her Stage Life and Her Real Life.* London: Chapman
    and Hall.
Griffith, F. Ridgway, and A. J. Marrin. 1880. *Authorised Edition of the Life of Sarah
    Bernhardt.* New York.
Harper, Phillip Brian. 1994. " 'The Subversive Edge': *Paris Is Burning,* Social Critique,
    and the Limits of Subjective Agency." *Diacritics* (special issue: *Critical Crossings,*
    ed. Judith Butler and Biddy Martin) 24.2–3 (Summer–Fall): 90–103.
"Hips, Lips, Tits, POWER!" ("Sandra Bernhard — Read My Lips!"). 1992. *The List:
    Glasgow and Edinburgh Events Guide,* August 21–27, 8–9.
Hooks, Bell. 1992. *Black Looks: Race and Representation.* Boston: South End
    Press.
Idol-Woman and the Other. 1885. *London Times* March 28.
Kamp, David. 1993. "The Queening of America." *GQ,* July, 94–99.
Kaplan, Marion A. 1991. *The Making of the Jewish Middle Class: Women, Family,
    and Identity in Imperial Germany.* New York: Oxford University Press.
Keller, Evelyn Fox. 1985. *Reflections on Gender and Science.* New Haven, Conn.:
    Yale University Press.
Klein, Dennis B. 1981. *Jewish Origins of the Psychoanalytic Movement.* New York:
    Praeger.
Langmuir, Gavin I. 1990. *Toward a Definition of Antisemitism.* Berkeley: University
    of California Press.
"Look at Me, I'm Sandra B." 1992. *Elle* (British), June, 12–16.
Marcus, Steven. 1985. "Freud and Dora: Story, History, Case History." In *In Dora's
    Case: Freud, Hysteria, Feminism,* ed. Charles Bernheimer and Claire Kahane
    56–91. New York: Columbia University Press.
Mosse, George L. 1985. "Jewish Emancipation: Between *Bildung* and
    Respectability." In *The Jewish Response to German Culture: From the
    Enlightenment to the Second World War,* ed. Jehuda Reinharz and Walter
    Schatzberg, 1–16. Hanover, N.H.: University Press of New England.
Mulvey, Laura. 1989. "Visual Pleasure and Narrative Cinema." In *Visual and Other
    Pleasures,* 14–28. Bloomington: Indiana University Press.
Olender, Maurice. 1992. *The Languages of Paradise.* Trans. Arthus Goldhammer.
    Cambridge, Mass.: Harvard University Press.
Phelan, Peggy. 1993. *Unmarked: The Politics of Performance.* London: Routledge.
Powers, Ann. 1993. "Queer in the Streets, Straight in the Sheets." *Village Voice* 29
    (June): 24, 30–32.
Probyn, Elspeth. 1993. *Sexing the Self: Gendered Positions in Cultural Studies.* New
    York: Routledge.

Ritvo, Harriet. 1994. "Barring the Cross: Hybridization and Purity in Eighteenth- and Nineteenth-Century Britain." Humane Societies. English Institute. Cambridge, Massachusetts, September 2.

Rogin, Michael. 1992. "Blackface, White Noise: The Jewish Jazz Singer Finds His Voice." *Critical Inquiry* 18: 417–53.

Roith, Estelle. 1987. *The Riddle of Freud.* New York and London: Tavistock.

Rosenberg, Alfred. 1970. *Race and Race History and Other Essays by Alfred Rosenberg.* Ed. Robert Pois. New York: Harper and Row.

Rubin, Gayle. 1975. "The Traffic in Women: Notes on the 'Political Economy' of Sex." In *Towards an Anthropology of Women,* ed. Rayna R. Reiter, 157–210. New York: Monthly Review Press.

———. 1993. "Thinking Sex: Notes for a Radical Theory of the Politics of Sexuality." *The Lesbian and Gay Studies Reader,* ed. Henry Abelove, Michèle Aina Barale, and David M. Halperin, 3–44. New York: Routledge.

"Sandra's Blackness." 1992. *Vibe* 1: 116.

Sedgwick, Eve Kosofsky. 1990. *Epistemology of the Closet.* Berkeley: University of California Press.

Sessums, Kevin. 1994. "Simply Sandra." ("Sandra in Wonderland: Bernhard Gets Bigger.") *Out,* September, 68–73, 124–27.

Shattuck, Roger. 1991. "Sacred Monster." Review of *The Divine Sarah: A Life of Sarah Bernhardt* by Arthur Gold and Robert Fizdale. *New Republic* October 14, 34–38.

Spelman, Elizabeth V. 1988. *Inessential Woman: Problems of Exclusion in Feminist Thought.* Boston: Beacon.

Trachtenberg, Joshua. 1943. *The Devil and the Jews: The Medieval Conception of the Jews and Its Relation to Modern Anti-Semitism.* New York: Harper and Row.

Van Herik, Judith. 1982. *Freud on Femininity and Faith.* Berkeley: University of California Press.

"Viva Straight Camp!" 1993. *Esquire,* June, 92–95.

Walton, Jean. 1994. "Sandra Bernhard: Lesbian Postmodern or Modern Postlesbian?" In *The Lesbian Postmodern,* ed. Laura Doan, 244–61. New York: Columbia University Press.

Weininger, Otto. 1906 [1903]. *Sex and Character.* Translation of the 6th German edition. London: Heinemann. New York: Putnam.

Yerushalmi, Yosef Hayim. 1991. *Freud's Moses: Judaism Terminable and Interminable.* New Haven, Conn.: Yale University Press.

6 / Jazz-Jews, Jive, and Gender: The Ethnic Politics of Jazz Argot

Maria Damon

I. Poetic Prelude

Shadow people, projected on coffee-shop walls
Memory formed echoes of a generation past
Beating into now.

Nightfall creatures, eating each other
Over a noisy cup of coffee.

Mulberry-eyed girls in black stockings
Smelling vaguely of mint jelly and last night's bongo drummer,
Making profound remarks on the shapes of navels,
Wondering how the short Sunset week
Became the long Grant Avenue night,
Love tinted, beat angels,
Doomed to see their coffee dreams
Crushed on the floors of time,
As they fling their arrow legs
To the heavens,
Losing their doubts in the beat.

Turtle-neck angel guys, black-haired dungaree guys,
Caesar-jawed, with synagogue eyes,
World travelers on the forty-one bus,
Mixing jazz with paint talk,
High rent, Bartok, classical murders,
The pot shortage and last night's bust.

Lost in a dream world,
Where time is told with a beat.

Coffee-faced Ivy Leaguers, in Cambridge jackets,
Whose personal Harvard was a Fillmore district step,
Weighted down with conga drums,
The ancestral cross, the Othello-laden curse,
Talking of Diz and Bird and Miles,
The secret terrible hurts,
Wrapped in cool hipster smiles,
Telling themselves, under the talk,
This shot must be the end,
Hoping the beat is really the truth.

The guilty police arrive.

Brief, beautiful shadows, burned on walls of night.
                    BOB KAUFMAN, "Bagel Shop Jazz"

In Bob Kaufman's poem, which serves as a kind of demographics of the shadowland of Hip, the nameless women, Jewish men, and black men he eulogizes (*lacrimae rerum sunt* in the culture wars) may appear to constitute a unified, triangular front in opposition to the "guilty police." Their outsiderhood and marginal, always already to-be-memorialized existence ("brief, beautiful shadows burned on walls of night") puts them in conspiratorial league (breathing together, unified by the beat) with each other against the stultifying forces of convention. Jazz culture in the tellingly named Coexistence Bagel Shop of San Francisco's North Beach area offered a liminal shelter made of dreams and shadows where these shadow people could mediate the straight world for each other. Yet these alliances were love-hate triangles, fraught with unease, ambiguous identifications and repudiations, affiliations and disaffiliations, instrumentalism and mutual objectifications ("smelling vaguely of mint jelly and last night's bongo player") as well as friendship, productive and reproductive collaboration, and genuine bonds based on shared (counter)cultural and social concerns, similar worldviews, and mutual respect. Though structurally each grouping is given a stanza apiece of approximately equal length, the tensions underlying Kaufman's brief profiles in coolness contrast the (nonethnicized) women's and Jewish men's "dreams" with the African American men's "secret terrible hurts" and fatalistic addictions ("this shot must be the end"). In Kaufman's vision, the women's lives are organized around sex, the Jews' around high modernism, high rent, and the relatively innocuous marijuana high, and the African Americans' around historical pain, bebop heroes (Diz, Miles, and Bird rather than Bartók or last night's anonymous bongo drummer) and the high stakes involved in believing in jazz. Moreover, the African American men are endowed with a serious interiority not accorded the other two; though all three groups have misgivings about their lives on the edge, the women dispel their doubts in the rhythm of sex, and the Jews are "lost in a dream world." For black men the creative possibilities offered by the jazz world can provide a respite from the trauma of social pain (of which they are fully conscious), while for the women and the Jews, jazz life *is* the risk they take rather than a balm. The vague anxiety of the first two points of the triangle becomes a tragic self-consciousness in the third.

And all of them talk talk talk, about navels, classical music, or bebop. The names they drop and, especially, the language that they use place them in relation to each other. Those relations are indeterminate, shifting as shadows do, rising, drifting, and receding as smoke does, as talk does, as the steam from a coffee on a cold San Francisco night does. Their talk mediates those relations, creates the texture, the noisy cups of coffee, the "idiomatic fog that veils the user" that provides the text for my inquiry.[1]

Kaufman was an African American Beat poet whose "Jewish" surname gave rise to many different accounts of his genealogy and his ethnic and religious affiliations, and who drew his greatest inspiration for his verbal creations from jazz. The vibrant and dynamic language of the African American music world, this linguistic realm of belonging, functioned as an object of desire for nonblack counterculturals. I focus here on the phenomenon of the Jewish hipster, Norman Mailer's "white Negro," in order to generate a thick description of Jewish men entering communities comprised primarily of non-Jews of color—sometimes to the extent of wanting to or actually adopting another ethnic designation. I examine how they negotiate race, class, and gender; how they use the women and the black culture available to them in their negotiations; and how they use language in turn to negotiate their relations to those black men and black, white, and Jewish women: how and why they talk. I believe attention to this paradigm of cross-cultural mimetic desire can further an analysis of the ethnic, class, and gender anxieties that seem to characterize American ethnic groups, particularly those undergoing a dramatic shift in social status. The particular people under discussion here will be, on the one hand, Mezz Mezzrow and Lenny Bruce as counterculturals; and on the other, Phil Spector and to a lesser extent Benny Goodman as examples of what Michael Rogin has eloquently demonstrated to be the strange and theatrical mimesis of black Americans by wannabe white Americans in the service of the latters' upward (whiteward) social mobility.[2]

Among Kaufman's most memorable lines is "Way out people know the way out." This essay is dedicated to people who find their way out, and to people who don't.

Contexts I: (Some) Jews and Their Fathers — No Way Out?

My father, who died in 1973, made his living measuring the body parts of living, primarily dark-skinned people around the world. Mostly other men. As a second-generation Jewish American man-child growing up in Boston, he was searching for his place in the social continuum of races as it was played and fought out in the streets of his childhood where Irish, Jews, and blacks battled each other with unequal resources for the living spaces left over by the Mayflower contingent. As an adult physical anthropologist at a prestigious research university, he channeled this obsessive self-searching into a discipline established by the nineteenth-century scientizing of the metaphysics of the great chain of being — a discipline (in all senses) that took him far from himself, desensitizing him to the *felt* pain of social difference (his own and others') as it legitimated his inquiry through words as dubious as they are Greco-Roman: *epidemiology, somatotyping, anthropometry, medical anthropology.* The use of these words placed him in the position of overseer, managing and interpreting the physical continuum of races imagined by this science. His attempt to master his ethnic and gender anxiety through intellectual discipline reinscribed him in that very intersection he found so problematic: a Jewish man — at least a Bostonian Jew from Eastern Europe growing up and living in the period spanning World War I through the Israeli nationalist experiment — was supposed both by Jews and by others to win battles not through physical prowess of the street but through verbal, scholarly performance.[3] What was he as a "man"? What was he as a "Jew"? He attempted to resolve some of these perceived contradictions through marriage with a Scandinavian Gentile woman. Together, they gave their three daughters unequivocally Christian names, sent us to aristocratic private day schools, and joined the Unitarian Church, which in Boston has the cachet of history, social-register prestige, and old money. Although I resist the nakedly judgmental connotation that the term has come to carry in contemporary cultural politics, I have been urged by friendly critics to use the blunt language of ethnic commentary: his goal, they point out, was *assimilation*. I am uneasy with the word. It collapses complicated motives and means into a word that appears to mean something—one thing, one currently-tinged-with-negativity thing. But what?

And sure enough, "Tell us what this means," writes JB in the margins of my first draft, with an arrow pointing toward the final, now-italicized word of the earlier sentence: "Assimilation?" Good question. (Who did my father ever really fool, other than one of my girls'-school classmates who, on learning after his death that he had been Jewish, remarked in astonishment: "Dr. Damon? Jewish? But—he wasn't vulgar!" And is that what assimilation—whatever it is—is about anyway? Fooling people?) My dictionary offers a definition of "assimilate" tailored to the occasion. "*v.i.* 1. to become like or alike. 2. to be absorbed and incorporated: as, minority groups often *assimilate* by intermarriage." The two are distinctly different, to be *like*, or to be *devoured by*. The intransitivity of the verb in the second instance renders power invisible: Absorbed by what? Incorporated into what? To be absorbed, intransitive, means to be engrossed, fascinated, preoccupied (example: my father was completely absorbed in his studies).[4] That is not what is meant in the "minority group" example. To be incorporated, intransitive, means to adopt a legal status as a corporation, or to be united. Again, this is not what is meant by the example given for "assimilate." Obviously, we know the present absence signified here: to be absorbed or incorporated *into the dominant, majority group*. (My father wanted to be incorporated, devoured and digested, by the dominant Gentile mainstream.)[5] If this parenthetical example is so, he picked an unwitting mediator, a stranger in a strange land: my mother, immigrated from postwar Denmark at age thirty, was the "foreigner" in our family, the one who spoke with an amusing accent, the one whose peasant roots (her family are pig farmers, no less) resonate with the nostalgia I hear from other Jews (never my own Jewish relatives) for shtetl cooking and customs. She is much more Tevye-like than my urbane father, who taught us how to eat artichokes, read us Greek myths from Bulfinch at bedtime, and celebrated Mozart's birthday. He was the polished cosmopolitan who had read everything, she the bumpkin with the love of nature and earthy humor, who joked that she too had read a book once: Shakespeare in the original Danish. He couldn't change a lightbulb; she was the omnipotent Earth Mother (or her 1950s incarnation, Supermom) who did all the cooking, yard work, child care, and housework and held a skilled professional — but low-prestige enough to not threaten my father — job. But Tevye-ishness notwithstanding, she wasn't Jewish, and he was.

At certain jokes in Marx Brothers movies, however, at certain puns or Yiddishisms unexpectedly uttered by his less crypto-Jewish friends, my father's personality changed dramatically. He shed the cool and unassuming sophistication modeled after what he had seen of British manners in his year as a Marshall Scholar. Tears of laughter (or were they tears of pain and longing?) rolled down his cheeks as he jiggled with helpless mirth. The meek and decorous Anglophile scientist became for a moment a rowdy little boy — he was responding to real language. Sometimes, afterward, with a mixture of glee and shame, he would explain the jokes to us, sometimes not. These linguistically saturated moments have clued me in to the power of vernacular. Because of my removal from living traditions in Judaism and Jewishness, and because, nonetheless, their cultural forms ruled unacknowledged from the depths of my family's psyche, I sometimes fear that I inhabit the unconscious of an earlier generation of American Jews and am still working out their complexes.

The alliances I want to examine here are not the ones my father made, but ones he could have made — ones I would like to make. Unlike him, many Jewish men of his generation resolved their anxieties about ethnicity and community by bonding with non-Jews of color. It was not shame about their outcast status as Jews that prompted these alliances but rather the sense that Jewish American culture, by assimilating upward, was abdicating the special role of critique available to social outsiders.

But first, another contextual digression: a word from our noncorporate (unincorporable, unassimilable) but corporeal sponsors in outrageousness about what words mean to them.[6]

Contexts II: Words, Words as if All Worlds Were There: A Way Out?

Most bebop language came about because some guy said
something and it stuck.... Before you knew it, we had a whole
language.... We didn't have to try; as Black people we just
naturally spoke that way. People who wished to communicate with
us had to consider our manner of speech, and sometimes they
adopted it.   DIZZY GILLESPIE, *To Be or Not to Bop*

Down to the Jewish ghetto on Maxwell Street I went, to look
around in the second-hand stores. I came to one store where an old
Jewish man with a long beard and a little yomelkeh stood in the
doorway, and I heard something that knocked me out. An old-
fashioned victrola setting out on the curb was playing a record,
Blind Lemon Jefferson's "Black Snake Moan," and the old Jewish
man kept shaking his head sadly, like he knew that evil black
snake personally:
  Oh-oh, some black snake's been
  suckin' my rider's tongue.
                         MEZZ MEZZROW, *Really the Blues*

Quincy Troupe and Miles Davis's collaborative autobiography of Miles
concludes with a brief statement by Troupe about Miles's language. It
anticipates critics who may be offended by the vulgarity of the text,
and functions not so much as an apology as it does as a manifesto:

> Had we sanitized the language in the book, the voice of *Miles* wouldn't
> sound authentic.... Miles speaks in a tonal language ... the same word
> can take on different meanings according to the pitch and tone, the
> way the word is spoken. For example, Miles can use motherfucker to
> compliment someone or simply as punctuation.... Besides, when I hear
> Miles speak, I hear my father and many other African-American men
> of his generation. I grew up listening to him on streetcorners, in barber-
> shops, ballparks and gymnasiums, and bucket-of-blood bars. It's a speak-
> ing style that I'm proud and grateful to have documented.[7]

The language in which the story of *Miles* is told (the improvisational,
tonal, and rhythmic quality) is at least as much the story as what we
might call "narrative content" (melody). Language and music are co-
extensive, and verbal fluency in the jazz idiom is as crucial a talent as
musical ability. As Ben Sidran has pointed out, "the musician *is* the
document,"[8] and this text includes not only musicianship but also
clothing, physical style, and verbal virtuosity. For example, when Duke

Ellington invited Sonny Greer into his orchestra, there was much scrutiny of the flashy drummer, even after his successful audition: "He used a lot of tricks. . . . Maybe, we thought, he wasn't all that he was cracked up to be." The litmus test was verbal: "We stood on the street corner and waited for him. . . . 'Watcha say?' we ask him. . . . Sonny comes back with a line of jive that lays us low. We decide he's okay."[9] Similarly, even after his playing had been accepted by the other band members, Louis Armstrong was put off by what he perceived as the uptightness of Fletcher Henderson's band, for which he had left Chicago and come to New York, until the trombonist and the tuba player got into a fight and cussed each other out with imaginative and outraged invective. At that point, Armstrong says, "I commenced to relax — you know — feeling at home."[10]

While Michael Rogin has persuasively argued that Al Jolson used blackface in order to negotiate his assimilation away from Jewishness into the American mainstream, I argue that, in different ways for each of the men I write about, blackness becomes a way to be "more Jewish" by providing a New World context for social critique, community, and an understanding of suffering and the "human condition" both social and metaphysical.[11] Many European-descended Jews as well as non-Jewish performers used blackface as part of their acts — along with a host of other ethnic stereotypes: the "wop number" and the "sheeny number" had their moments in the spotlight along with the "coon number." But observing the ubiquity of blackface, and indicating its function as enabling Americanization, cannot be elided into a generalization about Jewish Euro-American[12]/African American relations, or about Jewish desires to assimilate — that is, to shed or camouflage their "Jewishness" in favor of a less socially opprobrious, nebulous "whiteness" purchased at the expense of the caricatured black man or woman. While Rogin points out the mechanisms whereby Jolson's blackface performance enabled his move *toward* American power centers — marriage with an Anglo woman, mainstream success with regard to public recognition and the acquisition of wealth — a number of Jews found in African American culture the resources for resisting absorption into a dominant culture they found stultifying, hierarchic, unjust, unaesthetic, and un-Jewish.

In each case, attention to the particulars of individuals' rapports with their own and others' cultures reveals a rich texture of motive, response, and artistic/cultural production that merits specific regard.

I have chosen examples of Jews whose enamorment of African American culture is motivated not by the impulse to assimilate but by the impulse to resist. The impulse is not unproblematic, and this essay is neither an apologia for these Jews' means of identification nor a condemnation, but an investigation of that move. Each of the three people I discuss here sought to associate himself with African American music culture differently: Mezz Mezzrow by realizing his childhood conviction that he would grow up to become a "colored musician"; Lenny Bruce by adopting the language of the jazz milieu and by his outspokenness about civil rights issues and racism; Phil Spector by producing black music and by trying on occasion to "act black" in ways that inadvertently come close to the caricatures of an earlier generation of white performers.

As for the role of music in this phenomenon, musicianship was one of the few pursuits in this country and in the Eastern European cultures these men descended from that provided both social and geographic mobility for members of traditional underclasses. Though klezmorim (Jewish male professional folk musicians) were of a special, not-quite-respectable class with their own argot, they were allowed to wander from town to town with minimal difficulty and were credited with the ability to represent and draw forth the human soul as no other artist could. On immigrating, many of these klezmer musicians became participants in New World forms of popular music.[13] In the past several decades' revival of interest in klezmer, which blends elements of Eastern and Western European folk music, Middle Eastern and North African music, and now American jazz, it is often referred to as "Jewish jazz."

But while the musical forms of jazz and the visual forms of performance are fully worthy of investigation, I focus on language as an index of cultural kinship and mimesis. Why language, and why these two ethnic groups? The first point is simply the obvious: language is culture. Language use is a primary element in self-constitution and self-representation for any group, ethnic as well as nonethnic. The second is that, though the foregoing is virtually a truism, it is also something of a truism (and here all standard caveats about stereotypy apply) that African American and Jewish traditions share a love of verbal display and value language performance far beyond its strictly utilitarian, signifier-equals-signified status as a "tool" for communication. Jews and African Americans also share, as historic underclasses of Europe and the United States respectively, a need for strategies of exclusion through language; codes, double entendres, and alternate languages protected emotional and political meanings from a series of overlords. Though he cautions against reading his work as an essentialistic demonstration of certain tropes as "black," Henry Louis Gates Jr. has amply documented the dynamics of wordplay, the importance of mastering circumlocution, and the centrality of "signifyin(g)" practices in African American culture.[14] The Armstrong and Ellington examples offered earlier, as well as the enormous body of scholarship on the practice of signifying, demonstrate a cultural appreciation for the well-turned phrase, the spontaneous and devastating repartee, the one-upmanship involved in games of utterance. There are Jewish works analogous to Gates's; Sigmund Freud's, Benjamin Harshav's, and Max Weinreich's loving analyses of Yiddish styles of communication walk, like Gates's *The Signifying Monkey,* the shaky, challenging line of argument between cultural essentialism and historicocultural investigation of "language skills" characteristic of Jewish practice.[15] But though these studies are far less well known to the general academic audience than Gates's endearingly subversive semiotic simian, the clichés about Jewish culture that signal a perception of Jews (by Jews) as loving smart talk are myriad at the colloquial level: "Three Jews, four opinions." "A Jew always answers a question with another question." Or the joke about the Jew stranded on a desert island who built two synagogues (when he was rescued and questioned about this he responded, waving his hand in the direction of one of them, "That's the shul I *don't* go to!")[16] indicate a high valuing of debate, expression, and difference of opinion and open-ended critique. ("Expressing opinions is one of the greatest human pleasures," a friend's father insisted when his wife asked him why he had to do it all the time.)

"Talking back" to the movie screen shares something with asking the Torah to reveal itself again and again for the purpose of questioning, response, interpretation—a sense of personal relationship with a narrative or textual authority, a relationship that more than permits challenge and interaction: it mandates them. A shared excitement over the possibilities of verbal invention and a recognition of the protean, nonstatic richness of language suggests an insight common to (though again, not exclusive to) both cultures that language is embodied, that it "speaks us," and at the level of popular culture the degree to which one participates in this medium indicates one as a mensch or as a hip cat.

Texts: Finally

The following three examples offer windows onto different permutations of a Jewish desire for verbal participation in African Americanness, and particularly the ways in which African American language comes to have (for these Jewish men) a physical dimension, a *body*—specifically a woman's body—that is likewise an object of desire. The first two are from Mezz Mezzrow's *Really the Blues,* a jazz autobiography, and Ronnie Spector's *Be My Baby.* In both cases the woman figures become emblematic occasions for their ethnic transitions, embodying their desire and/or discomfort; they are vehicles, in terms of the mimetic triangle, for these Jews' desire for black masculinity. The third text is supplied by Lenny Bruce, the man who made Jewishness hip, and who I believe occupies a special place on this continuum of mimesis and appropriation.

First, here's Mezz:

> I was put in a trance by Bessie's moanful stories and the patterns of true harmony in the piano background, full of little runs that crawled up and down my spine like mice. Every note that woman wailed vibrated on the tight strings of my nervous system; every word she sang answered a question I was asking. You couldn't drag me away from that victrola, not even to eat.
>
> What knocked me out most on those records was the slurring and division of words to fit the musical pattern, the way the words were put to work for the music. I tried to write them down because I figured the only way to dig Bessie's unique phrasing was to get the words down exactly as she sang them. It was something I had to do; there was a great secret buried in that woman's genius that I had to get. After every few words I'd stop the record to write the lyrics down, so my dad made a suggestion. Why didn't I ask my sister Helen to take down the words in shorthand? She was doing secretarial work and he figured it would be a cinch for her.
>
> If my sister had made a table-pad out of my best record or used my old horn for a garbage can she couldn't have made me madder than she did that day. I've never been so steamed up, before or since. She was in a very proper and dicty mood, so she kept "correcting" Bessie's grammar, straightening out her words and putting them in "good" English until they sounded like some stuck-up jive from McGuffy's Reader instead of the real down-to-earth language of the blues. That girl was schooled so good, she wouldn't admit there was such a word as "ain't" in the English language, even if a hundred million Americans yelled it in her face every hour of the day. I've never felt friendly towards her to

this day, on account of how she laid her fancy high-school airs on the immortal Bessie Smith.

Inspiration's old lady gave birth to a new brainchild one afternoon at a Rhythm Kings rehearsal.... My head began to buzz while I played. I had to cut loose some way, to turn my back once and for all on that hincty, killjoy world of my sister's and move over to Bessie Smith's world body and soul. My fingers itched for a horn, so I could sit around and blow with my real friends for the rest of my life. I was so hyped up I couldn't sit still....

Finally, without knowing for sure what I was going to do, I ran home. I sneaked into the house and stole my sister's Hudson-seal fur coat out of the closet, then I beat it down to a whorehouse and sold it to the madam for $150. With the dough I made for the Conn Music Company and bought an alto sax for cash. Then I began to breathe easier—my sister had paid for her fine-lady act and put me in a business where they said "ain't" all day long and far into the night. Great deal.

The Rhythm Kings were rehearsing all afternoon.... Every note I blew that day was a blast at my sister and her book-learning. I couldn't go home after that, naturally, so the same day I moved into a room across from the poolroom. Come to think of it, I *ain't* been home since.[17]

In this brilliantly telling anecdote, Mezz (advertised on the cover of his autobiography as "the first white negro") relates the final straw that sent him irrevocably into African American culture. The incident revolves around language use: in particular, the contrast between the way two women use language. In Mezz's eyes, his sister's "ethnic cleansing" of Bessie's soulful and sensual language, rendering it prissy and inauthentic, constitutes a cardinal violation against the profound spirit of the blues. Both his sister's preferred idiom and the fur coat he steals epitomize the upward mobility he scorns (the narrative, dictated to a more sympathetic—male—amanuensis more than twenty years later, still quivers with vital righteous wrath). In what he sees as a punishment fitting to the crime of Helen's privilege, he uses the theft to buy his first alto sax and move out of the family home forever. That is, he uses his sister's accessory to the crime of upward assimilation to facilitate his own downward assimilation, prostituting his sister's coat to a prostitute in a gleeful act of what he considers Helen's degradation, not realizing that she may have as much in common with Bessie Smith as he does—and that his anecdote implicates him in her familial oppression.

Another early turning point for Mezz in his romance with African American culture is when he overhears the male partner of a dancing black couple cry out to the woman "Perculate, you filthy bitch!" which inspires the name of his first band, the Perculatin' Fools. What Mezz perceives (rightly) as verbal inventiveness and uninhibited, "picturesque" language is also a misogynistic display; along with the participants in the forum on the "white Negro" (Norman Mailer, Ned Polsky, et al.), Mezz shares a distorted understanding that the freedom of expression he envies in black culture also, implicitly, confers permission to be overtly misogynistic. Although his language is respectful and reverent when he speaks of Bessie Smith, the women in his immediate life—his sister and the mother he only mentions once, early in the memoir—were domesticating and hence negative forces in his psychic life. Many Jewish men and women of the period found that pressure to assimilate and resistance to assimilation led to conflict between the genders.[18] Far from Rogin's description of Jolson's Oedipal scene, what Mezz offers is an anti-Oedipal desire to undermine the goodness—the purity—of his family of origin in favor of the earth goddess Bessie Smith and the social milieu her songs inhabit. This meeting of ethnic, class, and gender anxiety—represented by the two women Mezz constructs as opposites—plays out the conflict between the standard English to which his social group of origin aspired and the jazz argot Mezz loved and prided himself on mastering to the point of being able to pass as African American.

At one point much later in Mezz's career, during a prison sentence he is serving for selling drugs, he arranges to have himself put in the black section of the segregated prison by insisting that, appearances notwithstanding, he is actually black. At Christmastime, the Christian whites organize a carol choir, and the Jews, not to be outdone, counterorganize a Chanuka choir. Mezz remarks with amusement that "they ask me, a colored guy, wouldn't I care to lead it. I find out once more how music of different oppressed peoples blends together. . . . I don't know the Hebrew chants, but I give it a weepy blues inflection and the guys are all happy about it. They can't understand how a colored guy digs the spirit of their music so good."[19] Mezz has so deeply identified with African American culture that he greets the Jewish music as exotic but appealingly resonant with blues feeling, something he can identify with because of a common understanding of suffering. It is not clear to me whether he is being tongue-in-cheek or straight here; it doesn't appear to cross his mind that the Jewish prisoners have divined his ethnicity of origin.

My second example is drawn from Ronnie Spector's *Be My Baby,* an account of her abusive marriage to Phil Spector, boy-genius of rock and roll musical production. Throughout the book, Ronnie identifies herself usually as a "half-breed" (of black and white parentage), and occasionally as black, as in the following passage, in which, after sending Ronnie and her unambiguously black mother to Watts to buy him some Afro wigs (Spector was very sensitive about his thinning hair), he takes them to a gospel sermon at a church in Watts. Bearing in mind that this is not Spector in his own words but a portrait drawn by his abused ex-wife, I think there is much to be learned from the woman who has been the object of mediation between this Jew and the African American culture he loves:

> Phil loved his Afro wig. I guess it made him feel like he had soul or something, because after he got it, he wanted us all to go back down to Watts to hear some real gospel music at the Reverend James Cleveland's church. I wanted no part of it. I never liked straight gospel music because I could never understand what they were singing.
>
> Of course, Phil had his heart set on it. So we all piled into the back of his limousine — me, my mother and Phil. He also brought along a pair of bodyguards. Afro wig or no Afro wig, Phil wasn't taking any chances going down to Watts. He even brought one of his pistols, which he tucked into his jacket pocket.
>
> My mother just shook her head. "Phil!" she said. "Why you want to bring a gun into a church?"
>
> "This?" he said, patting his gun like he was in the Old West. "This is my peacemaker. I brought it along in case there's any trouble." Thank God he at least had the sense to have the bodyguards wait in the car when we went into the church.
>
> We found seats in the back just as Reverend James Cleveland's choir started singing. They were wailing and moaning and singing out in that way that gospel people do, and Phil was moaning and wailing right along with them. He was rolling his shoulders and shaking his arms, and pretty soon he was sweating and shouting out "Amen" like he was at a Baptist revival meeting. It was funny, really. Here I was, this black girl, bored out of her mind at a gospel concert, sitting with a Jewish man in an Afro who looked like he was about to speak in tongues.
>
> After the singing, Phil kept on shouting "Amen" all through Reverend Cleveland's sermon. When the Reverend held out the collection plate, Phil jumped to his feet with a hundred-dollar bill in his hand. "Oh, no!" my mom gasped under her breath. But it was already too late to stop him.

> We bit our lips and watched Phil jog all the way up the aisle of that crowded black church, an Afro wig on his head and a hundred-dollar bill in his hand. When I saw the handle of his .38 bobbing up and down in his jacket pocket, I actually started praying. "Please God," I whispered. "Don't let it fall out."
>
> After the service people were still staring at Phil as we worked our way through the crowd to the limousine that was waiting at the curb. My mother and I were embarrassed for him, but Phil actually looked proud as he smiled and wiped the sweat from his forehead.
>
> "I guess I showed them I'm not just *any* white guy," he bragged.
>
> "That you did, Phil," my mother agreed. "That you surely did."[20]

Obviously, this scene is not complimentary. Spector tries to pass as an insider, a belonger, in an environment in which he feels he must carefully juggle his concern for personal safety (and the simultaneous perceived need to *hide* this concern), his display of wealth, which sets him apart from the majority of the congregation, and his performance of at-homeness and appreciation, which he hopes will affirm his presence and make him welcome. Yet Spector's gaucheries appear to have their origins in a desire to reconnect with a soulful quality of faith that has gone out of the respectability of secular, assimilated Jewish American life. And this involves a move *down* the scale of social prestige.

Ronnie Spector, née Bennett, wears her own ethnicity lightly; her autobiography introduces her as the daughter of a black mother and a white failed-musician father who deserts the family (another ethnic stereotype challenged), who learned makeup tricks ("big hair" and exaggeratedly elongated eyeliner) from the Hispanic and Asian kids in the neighborhood in which she and her co-Ronettes — her sister and cousin — grew up. At one point she recounts witnessing from her dressing room a fight between black and Hispanic youths over whether the Ronettes were a black or a Hispanic girl group; she comments with amusement that they were both, since she and her sister are black and their cousin is Hispanic. ("Do you think we can pass for black?" she asks her sister, who responds, "We *are* black. *And* Spanish. And probably a whole lot of other things too that we don't know about.... We've got enough kinds of blood to keep everybody happy.")[21] Similarly, in the wig episode, she is amused and embarrassed, rather than offended, by her husband's behavior. Unlike her husband, Ronnie Spector is not fixated on ethnic identity as a social marker; her sense of identity is more nuanced, less insistent and less threatened than his. Like Kaufman's "Caesar-jawed" Jews with "synagogue eyes," Spector is "lost in a dream" that can arouse a tolerant, albeit exasperated, compassion.

As a Jew, Phil Spector is indeed not just any white guy. He has specific historical reasons for identifying with African American history. At the same time, his controlling and abusive treatment of his wife, his role as producer of black talent, and his class status in comparison to many of the singers he helped to midwife into stardom all implicate him in the parasitism of which whites and white Jews have often been accused by black Americans.

Mezz's distaste for his sister and passion for Bessie's soulful earthiness, as well as Spector's need to dominate his black wife and his welcoming of Ronnie's mother into his own family life (as well as his extreme disgust with his own mother, "a tiny woman. A real Jewish-mother type," says Ronnie, and particularly with her unannounced appearances at the recording studio to bring him — it's hard to believe Ronnie isn't exaggerating here — chicken soup!)[22] express these men's desire to align themselves with or appropriate what they perceive as the tastes, distastes, and desires of black men. Although sexual politics play a crucial role in this nexus of identity formation, I am not making the crude argument for sexual envy that Mailer delineates in his analysis of the white hipster (which has it that white men covet the mythic sexual prowess of the "Negro"); what is at stake is, rather, a far more poignant and complicated desire to maintain outsiderhood in a living, viable artistic and social community.

Because of the traditionally in-between nature of Jewish American ethnicity, these conflicts and resolutions proliferate among the Jewish men I am examining here. Mezz, a member of a wealthy family that owned a chain of drugstores in Chicago, reacted vehemently against Jewish solidarity among other popular musicians, including Al Jolson and Sophie Tucker: "I didn't go for that jive at all; being a Jew didn't mean a thing to me. Around the poolroom I defended the guys I felt were my real brothers, the colored musicians who made music that sent me. . . . I could never dig the phony idea of a race — if we were a 'race' — sticking together all the way."[23] Phil Spector was a millionaire whose mother infuriated him by bringing chicken soup to the recording studio. Both turned to a kind of essentialized African Americanness to salvage their integrity. In the mostly male world of jazz, the appeal of skilled and challenging music and musicianship and the attractiveness of African American race pride acted as magnets, drawing non–African American men into the musical idiom, the culture, and the language of jazz.

Perhaps the most interestingly ambiguous formulation of this complex mimesis of/and alterity is to be found in my third "case," Lenny Bruce's signature *shpritz,* in which he reverses the terms. Instead of Jewish men being honorary blacks, black people, especially black musicians, become honorary Jews in his famous antiessentialist routine:

> I neologize Jewish and goyish. Dig: I'm Jewish. Count Basie's Jewish. Ray Charles is Jewish. Eddie Cantor's goyish. B'nai Brith is goyish; Haddassah, Jewish. Marine Corps—heavy goyim, dangerous.... Koolaid is goyish. All Drake's Cakes are goyish. Pumpenickel is Jewish, and, as you know, white bread is very goyish. Instant potatoes—goyish. Black cherry soda's very Jewish.... Trailer parks are so goyish that Jews won't go near them. Balls are goyish. Titties are Jewish. Mouths are Jewish. All Italians are Jewish. Negroes are all Jews. Irishmen who have rejected their religion are Jews.... Baton-twirling is very goyish.[24]

What Bruce does here is load Jewishness with connotations of (ethnic) soulfulness, femininity, earthiness, and hipness. Refusing genetic, religious, or even cultural essentialism, he nonetheless incurs a different danger: that of self-allegorizing a "Jewishness" so grandiose and all-pervasive that it is, as it were, *preessentialistic* in its claims to a transcendent, inchoate *prima materia*—soul substance—that is nonetheless localized in the minutiae of daily life: food, consumer products, living arrangements, pastimes, and body parts. Most Jewish hipsters identified African American culture as the stable alternative, the nostalgic embodiment of the earthiness and vitality that threatened to get bleached out of secular and assimilated Jewish culture in the New World. They turned to it in part to provide themselves with a fixed reference point for their own changing identities: blackness and soul were unambiguously synonymous for them, and the closer they could associate themselves with black culture, the more soulful they were. Lenny Bruce pulls the switch: it is Jewishness that stands as the reference point for all that is spontaneously creative, earthy, and Other. Like Mezzrow and Spector, Bruce also undertakes his ethnic self-creation in the realm of language and utterance, freely mixing "the jargon of the hipster, the argot of the underworld [or more properly, show business], and Yiddish."[25] Lenny Bruce was a vaudeville kid with intellectual aspirations who managed to both displace and assert himself in every milieu he moved in: the show-biz world, the ethnic Jewish world, the world of the intellectual hipster. What Bruce the ultimate Jewish hipster does, in this instance of positing Jewish identity as primarily hybrid by moving through all other identities, is to hippify Yiddish by mixing it in with the already identifiably hip idiom of jive. Like Mezz, Bruce married within his professional milieu—but he married "white." Like Jolson and Goodman, he married a "shikse goddess"—but this one was a stripper of lowly pedigree. Hot Honey Harlow, in terms of class if not caste, was arguably as far from Vanderbilthood (Benny Goodman, for example, married a Vanderbilt) as Bessie Smith. Honey's divinity lay in her beauty rather than in her social status. Though his perspective does not offer much in the way of emancipatory gender politics per se, Bruce is perceptive enough to satirize his own "looksism": in the skit "A Black Black Woman and a White White Woman," he challenges his assumed male audience to choose between a "black black woman and a white white woman"—who turn out to be, respectively, Lena Horne and Kate Smith; then he adds, having made that point, "so now we're discriminating against ugly people."[26]

Like my father, these three men married outside their Jewish culture. On the Jewish side of my family, it is assumed that my father's choice of life partner was symptomatic of his distaste for all things Jewish, most especially his family members. But exogamy does not always reflect self-hatred; it can be an attempt to achieve the fulfillment of a "truer" sense of oneself, to correspond more fully to what one feels one ought to be or in some sense already is. If Mezz feels that Jews have abdicated their special status as outsiders under social pressure to assimilate upward, he would feel that the status of blacks in the United States offers a truer reflection of the ideal position of Jews— and that it makes him more of a "mensch" to move into a black idiom. "African American" is a historical category into which as Jewish Americans these men do not fit. But one generation previously, not at all far back in memory, their European Jewish forebears did occupy a position structurally analogous—as national underclass, as mythic Other, as sequestered populations.[27] There is an element of nostalgia and mourning, and a perceived opportunity for self-regeneration for Jews as creative nonparticipants in mainstream culture, in this identification with another oppressed ethnic group. "They" are more "us" than "we" have become. This is a convoluted form of projection, yearning, essentialism that actually corresponds more closely to Lenny Bruce's model ("Jewishness" as the signifier for soulfulness) than is initially apparent.

At the same time, it does not quite correspond to the paradigm suggested by Toni Morrison: that blacks and black culture serve as vehicles, catalysts, for white self-recognition. In her model, blackness appears either as a moment of extreme otherness that allows a breakthrough or challenge to an original but problematic white self-concept—or as an oppositional background against which the white individual constructs his or her identity.[28] Mezz is no Jolson—speaks of him, in fact, with contempt—precisely for trying to force a "phony" Jewish solidarity within the entertainment world. African Americans do not figure as Other in Mezz's aspirations, as they clearly did for both Jolson and Benny Goodman, both of whom married "up" into the Anglo socialite world. The problem of essentialism is not Mezz's, perhaps, but mine. Who am I to say that he did not, after all, "become a colored musician" when he grew up? To insist that Mezz was "really Jewish" but "thought he became black" would reinforce an arbitrary racialization. Being "gemisht" makes me sensitive to this arbitrariness: Jewish law says I'm not Jewish because my mother isn't; under the Third Reich, on the other hand, I would have qualified as genetically Jewish; I define myself as culturally Jewish, unlike my siblings, who do not identify as Jewish at all. Why not extend the same leeway to Mezz?

In a period in which many Jewish Americans believed that they were faced with a choice between continued loyalty to working-class anonymity and immigrant "greenhornism" on the one hand, and upward social mobility-cum-assimilation on the other, Jewish men perceived in the jazz world an alternative community in which "difference" was affirmed as a virtue. And so was "individualism." Jazz offered a perfect community of individuals. Nonconformism to traditional family (and racial) relations and the cultural sophistication of the jazz world made it, moreover, a site for an alternative construction of masculinity that eschewed, on the one hand, the Jewish image of the boorish and insensitive Anglo "jock" and, on the other hand, the emerging stereotype of the passive, scholarly but ineffectual Jewish man. It was an arena in which one could succeed, and in fact attract considerable attention to oneself, but not in ways that appeared to spell compromise and assimilation. The jazz world offered a model of masculinity for Jewish men, in other words, that enabled difference without weakness. In contrast to Fanon's "black skin, white mask" paradigm of mimesis and alterity, in which the white mask, assumed to camouflage alterity, corrodes the psychic health of its wearer and must be wrenched off, this is a mimesis that flaunts otherness and permits solidarity between people recently emerging from a context of oppression and people whose oppression is ongoing in the American context.

Nonetheless, these gestures at solidarity were fraught with problematic contradictions. Black musicians did not necessarily perceive their relationship to Jewish music people as one of fraternal understanding. Although the integrity of people like impresario Norman Granz, booking agent Ben Bart, and musicians Artie Shaw and Red Rodney is acknowledged, others are taken to task for their exploitive association with black musicians. Duke Ellington's autobiography signifies heavily on the subject of Louis Armstrong's producer Joe Glaser (Armstrong was "a living monument to the magnificent career of Joe Glaser"),[29] as well as his own early producer Irving Mills ("In spite of how much he made on me, I still respected the way he operated").[30] Likewise, Diz's characterization of Granz as encouraging competition in an entrepreneurial way varies in spirit if not factually from Granz's own portrait of himself as someone deeply dedicated to breaking the race barrier.[31] James Brown chronicles his stormy association with Syd Nathan of King Records, who tried to bury "Please Please Please" — Brown's first million-seller — and who initially gave him "half a cent a side for writer's royalties and maybe another half a cent for performance."[32] Benny Goodman was sporadically insensitive to matters of racial prejudice, using the line "You know, I have problems too. I can't belong to this or that club because I'm Jewish" to avoid the responsibility of sticking up for his black sidemen when they encountered discrimination on the road.[33] In all of the accounts by black musicians I have read, when these musicians do speak of being exploited they do not attribute this exploitation to the Jewishness of their managers but seem to see it as a labor/management or black/white dynamic.

Goodman used black music — and musicians — to get what he wanted: music of a high quality, prestige, material comfort, and upward social mobility. Mezz didn't need or respect blackface—he *was* black. His search for a position of critique that was simultaneously located within a community led this upper-class Jewish Chicagoan to identify wholesale as a black musician. And Lenny never pretended to be other than what he was—a renegade Euro-American Jew with an attitude. Lenny used whatever verbal and cultural ammunition lay at hand for his relentless exposé of social hypocrisy and human weaknesses; the most trenchant and effective tool he could wrap his tongue around and let fly was the current jazz argot. It held everything he valued—subversiveness, speed, wit, artistry, originality, flexibility and room for improvisation, flamboyance, social critique without party lines or platforms.

How might Italian, Irish, and black people respond to Bruce's call to the soul of Jewishness? Would Count Basie, Ray Charles (to whose "Aramaic cantillations" Allen Ginsberg owes partial inspiration for the rhythms of his poem "Kaddish"),[34] and Dylan Thomas (a Welshman who makes it into Bruce's catalog) claim this honorary tribal status with as much zest as Mezz adopted blackness? Billy Eckstine's (white) managers wanted to sign his name X-stine "(for fear someone might think he was Jewish?)."[35] Likewise, Billie Holiday's autobiography stresses the fact that her lover John Levy was black rather than Jewish (as one might assume from his name) and that the papers ran pictures of him after their arrest to prove the point.[36]

Bruce himself was acutely aware of the fact that he *wasn't* black: in his routine "How to Relax Your Colored Friends at Parties," the drunken white Christian guest clumsily tries to bond with the black guest by mumbling anti-Semitic slurs against their mutual hosts and attempts to compliment the black guest by saying, "You look like a white Jew to me," signifying on the designation of Jews as "white Negroes." Bruce's complex routines undermine the stability of identity perhaps more than Mezz, who was quick to deny his Jewishness, or Spector, whose undignified antics reveal a shallow understanding of the concept of identity even though his musical exploits indicate a sensitivity to the special ethnicity of the sound he wanted to capture. Bruce wasn't trying to pass for other than he was; he didn't engage in Goodman's disingenuous me-tooism as a way of exculpating himself, and he certainly wasn't a booster of conventional Judaism. At no point, however, does Bruce deny his Jewishness; rather, he adds to it textured layers of argotic richness and performative personae. For these reasons, as well as his talent, his jazzlike use of improvisation, and his verbal ability to create abstract *"extensions* of realism, as opposed to realism in a representational form," Bruce was widely respected among black jazz musicians.[37] It has been argued, also, that Bruce's shticks correspond to traditional Jewish jeremiads and his "message" to Jewish ethics;[38] he sprinkled his monologues with Jewish words like *rachmones* (compassion) and punctuated his punch lines with *Emmes* (truth), as well as *cool* and *dig*—jive terms. So Bruce fits most closely the argument I have tried to weave loosely around these gems of texts: that attraction to African American culture among Jewish men emblematizes and helps actualize some kind of positive nostalgia for the meaningful aspects of traditional Jewish life. He is without doubt the most interesting of the Jewish artists I have discussed here, the most self-conscious and self-critical, the most "synagogue-eyed."

It is not surprising to find an enthusiasm for the richness, immediacy, and hermeticism of African American speech acts among disaffected Jews. Jive functions in the States as Yiddish functioned in Europe but had ceased to function in America—that is, as an infinitely inventive and renewable medium for cultural survival. Mezz, for instance, uses jive as a code of initiation. The Citadel edition of his book opens with a passage in jive—which Mezz exuberantly defines as "a polyglot patois [that is] not only a strange linguistic mixture of dream and deed...it's a whole new attitude toward life"—accompanied by an endnote: "See pages 354–360 for a translation of this jive." One of the proudest moments of his life is finding his name, "Mezz," in a jive dictionary, defined as the finest marijuana available. Phil Spector believes that *amen* is the signal word that will confirm his status as a black churchgoer or at least as "not just any white guy." Note the difference between these two perceptions of African American language. Although Mezz turns to the African American idiom as the wellspring of spontaneous authenticity, he knows that its power lies in its infinite mutability and nuanced subtlety—its un-pin-downability, and thus its ability to undermine its own cachet of authenticity. Deciding in his early teens that he "was going to be a colored musician" when he grew up, Mezz did not so much appropriate the idiom as apprentice himself to it, with a full understanding of the poetry, dynamism, and social importance of this "four-dimensional surrealist patter."[39] The transformation took years. Spector, on the other hand, believed that a quick gimmicky disguise and the ejaculation of a few stereotyped phrases—balanced by the gun and the bodyguards—would safeguard his passage and even impress the congregated African Americans.

Way Out: Mad Cops

When Mezz was arrested for dealing, the police questioned his living situation with his wife, Johnnie Mae, and their son, Milton. "Was I colored. No, Russian Jew, American-born. How in hell did I come to be living with a 'spade'? Well I had this screwy idea that when you loved a girl you married her without consulting a color chart."[40] Though the last few paragraphs of Mezz's opus insist that "I only hope they spell my name right in *Who's Who*, and get the dates of my prison record straight, and don't forget to say 'Race, Negro,' "[41] he is not above reverting to his ethnicity of origin—if it'll make the cops mad.

Notes

1. The phrase is Lenny Bruce's (1984:63), and so brilliant that I feel compelled to use it at least once in every paper.

2. Rogin focuses on Al Jolson, who was the frequent butt of Bruce's and Mezzrow's irritated disavowal.

3. Recent work by, among others, Ella Shohat and Ammiel Alcalay has done much to break down monolithic and essentialist conflations of "Jew" with "European" or "Euro-American Jew." However, my personal investment as well as the biographies of the persons under consideration specify Euro-America as my context.

4. A line delivered by a colleague at his memorial service: " 'I love to measure,' Al would say almost guiltily."

5. See David Biale's study of eroticism in Jewish (male) history, in which he discusses the late-nineteenth-century Jewish literary phenomenon of novels featuring tortured intellectual Jewish men who become involved with devouring, castrating-type Gentile women (1992:173–75).

6. "Words as if all worlds were there," Creeley 1982:221.

7. Davis and Troupe 1989:414–15.

8. Sidran 1981:xi.

9. Shapiro and Hentoff 1955:227.

10. Armstrong 1954:205.

11. Rogin 1992:417–53.

12. For two equally incoherent examples of the confusion over collective designations of Jews, see San Juan 1991 and Lerner 1993.

13. See Slobin 1982. My grandmother used to tell of a man appearing at her home when she was a young girl and announcing to her mother, "Liebe, don't you remember me? I was Itche Moishe and I played at your wedding in Smargón. Now I'm Irving Morris and I'm with the Boston Opera. Here are some tickets to *Aïda*." There are

many works of literature that attest to the importance of music in secular Jewish life, its portability and peripatetic nature, and hence its significance in mediating the shift from Old World to New. For a postmodern "talk-poem" version of such a tale (in which a violin that passes from hand to hand through generations appears as a recurrent trope) see Antin 1984.

14. Gates 1988. Since Mezz Mezzrow was so explicit and theoretical about his love of "jive," Gates quotes him fairly extensively in his descriptions and definitions of "signifying" intended to educate a non-African American readership (69–70).

15. Freud's *Jokes and Their Relation to the Unconscious* is sometimes, but not sufficiently or regularly, recognized as a kind of ethnic manifesto; Harshav 1990; Weinreich 1980. Weinreich points out an astonishing phenomenon that speaks directly to a love of wordplay he characterizes as specifically Ashkenazi: in several places in Germany and Eastern Europe, Jews celebrated holidays by eating food whose names in Yiddish were puns for the name of the prayer or holiday in Hebrew. The day featuring a prayer beginning *kol mevaser* ("the Voice of the Messenger"), for example, was observed by eating cabbage soup, *kohl mit vasser*! Only in Yiddish, he says, would language be so literally a binding agent between cultures, and cross-cultural puns be so literally actualized in material practice (4–5). Right away a similar African diaspora example comes to mind: the accommodation of the identities of Christian saints to West African deities based on details of appearance etc. Not linguistic puns, but visual puns operated in this cultural cross-referencing.

16. Kugelmass 1986:81.

17. Mezzrow and Wolfe 1990:53–54.

18. See Prell forthcoming.

19. Mezzrow and Wolfe 1990:316.

20. Spector and Waldron 1990:171–72.

21. Ibid., 57–59.

22. Ibid., 97.

23. Mezzrow and Wolfe 1990:49.

24. Bruce 1967:41–42, 1972:6.

25. Bruce 1972:6.

26. Bruce, "A White White Woman and a Black Black Woman," *What I Was Arrested For* (Fantasy Records, 1966).

27. For this reason I find misplaced E. San Juan's tone of outrage that Jews (and Irish) should be considered oppressed. San Juan speaks of Jewishness and Irishness as if they were simply ethnicities that have been occasionally and mistakenly racialized, rather than acknowledging that "race" is itself a construct, and that these particular ethnicities have (very much within modern memory) been racialized and economically othered.

28. The opening, and powerful, example of Toni Morrison's major thesis in *Playing in the Dark: Whiteness and the Literary Imagination* (1992) is a passage in which Marie Cardenal's attendance at a Louis Armstrong performance catalyzes an ultimately healing, but excruciating and harrowing, breakdown. Morrison speculates usefully on whether a performance of a European piece of music by a European musician would have had the same (de)familiarizing and shocking effect.

29. Ellington 1973:36.

30. Ibid.:89.

31. Gillespie 1979:405–7. Gillespie suggests that Granz was trying to set the musicians against one another: "[Jazz at the Philharmonic] wasn't much musically because Norman Granz got his nuts off by sending two or three trumpet players out there to

battle each other's brains out on the stage. And he'd just sit back and laugh. . . . Norman had a weird sense of competition. He thought that the battle would not only be on the stage, but that the guys would have a funny feeling toward one another afterward." Here's Granz on the same subject: "The whole basis for the [Jazz at the Philharmonic] was initially to fight discrimination . . . to break down segregation and discrimination, present good jazz and make bread for myself and for the musicians as well. I felt that it made no kind of sense to treat a musician with any kind of respect and dignity onstage and then make him go around to the back door when he's offstage. . . . So wherever we went, we stayed in the best hotels. . . . [A great musician is] supposed to be treated as a great artist on and off the stage."

32. Brown 1990:94.
33. Crow 1990:137.
34. Allen Ginsberg, "Caw Caw," *Holy Soul Jelly Roll* (1994), liner notes.
35. Gillespie 1979:183.
36. Holiday 1973:170.
37. Bruce 1972:46.
38. Kofsky 1974:87–99. Kofsky analyzes (too schematically) Bruce's comedianship in terms of three Jewish religious roles—the rabbi, the *maggid,* and the *tzadik*—and then discusses Bruce's aesthetic and ideological debt to jazz musicians in how he structured his monologues.
39. Mezzrow and Wolfe 1990:226.
40. Ibid., 300–1.
41. Ibid. 331.

Bibliography

Alcalay, Ammiel. 1993. *After Jews and Arabs: Remaking Levantine Culture.* Minneapolis: University of Minnesota Press.

Antin, David. 1984. "Dialogue." In *tuning,* 219–68. New York: New Directions.

Armstrong, Louis. 1954. *Satchmo: My Life in New Orleans.* New York: Da Capo.

Biale, David. 1992. *Eros and the Jews.* New York: Basic Books.

Brown, James, with Dave Marsh. 1990. *James Brown, the Godfather of Soul.* New York: Thunders' Mouth Press.

Bruce, Lenny. 1967. *The Essential Lenny Bruce.* New York: Ballantine.

———. 1972. *How to Talk Dirty and Influence People.* Chicago: Playboy Press.

———. 1984. *The (Almost) Unpublished Lenny Bruce.* Philadelphia: Running Press.

Collier, John Lincoln. 1989. *Benny Goodman and the Swing Era.* New York: Oxford University Press.

Creeley, Robert. 1982. *The Collected Poems of Robert Creeley, 1945–75.* Berkeley: University of California Press.

Crow, Bill. 1990. *Jazz Anecdotes.* New York: Oxford University Press.

Davis, Miles, and Quincy Troupe. 1989. *Miles: The Autobiography.* New York: Simon and Schuster.

Ellington, Duke. 1973. *Music Is My Mistress.* New York: Da Capo.

Feather, Leonard, and Jack Tracy. 1979 (1963). *Laughter from the Hip.* New York: Da Capo.

Freud, Sigmund. 1960. *Jokes and Their Relation to the Unconscious.* Trans. James Strachey. New York: Norton.

Gates, Henry Louis Jr. 1988. *The Signifying Monkey: A Theory of African-American Literary Criticism.* New York: Oxford University Press.

Gillespie, John Birks, with Al Fraser. 1979. *To Be or Not to Bop: Memoirs of Dizzy Gillespie.* New York: Da Capo.

Harshav, Benjamin. 1990. *The Meaning of Yiddish.* Berkeley: University of California Press.

Holiday, Billie, with William Dufty. 1973. *Lady Sings the Blues.* London: Barrie and Jenkins.

Kaufman, Bob. 1965. *Solitudes Crowded with Loneliness.* New York: New Directions.

Kofsky, Frank. 1974. *Lenny Bruce: The Comedian as Social Critic and Secular Moralist.* New York: Monad.

Kugelmass, Jack. 1986. *The Miracle of Intervale Avenue.* New York: Schocken.

Lerner, Michael. 1993. "Jews Are Not White." *Village Voice* 38, no. 20 (May 18, 1993): special section: "White Like Who?" 33–34.

Mailer, Norman. 1968. "Hipsters." In *Advertisements for Myself,* 265–314. London: Panther.

Mezzrow, Mezz, and Bernard Wolfe. 1990 (1946). *Really the Blues.* New York: Citadel.

Morrison, Toni. 1991. *Playing in the Dark: Whiteness and the Literary Imagination.* Cambridge, Mass.: Harvard University Press.

Prell, Riv-Ellen. Forthcoming. *Fighting to Become Americans: Ethnicity and Gender in Jewish-American Culture.* New York: Basic Books.

Rogin, Michael. 1992. "Blackface, White Noise: The Jewish Jazz Singer Finds His Voice." *Critical Inquiry* 18, no. 3 (Spring): 417–53.

San Juan, E. 1991. "The Culture of Ethnicity and the Fetish of Pluralism." *Cultural Critique* 18 (Spring): 215–29.

Shapiro, Nat, and Nat Hentoff. 1955. *Hear Me Talkin' to Ya.* New York: Dover.

Shohat, Ella. 1989. *Israeli Cinema: East/West and the Politics of Representation.* Austin: University of Texas Press.

Sidran, Ben. 1981 (1971). *Black Talk.* New York: Da Capo.

Slobin, Mark. 1982. *Tenement Music.* Urbana: University of Illinois Press.

Spector, Ronnie, with Vince Waldron. 1990. *Be My Baby.* New York: HarperCollins.

Weinreich, Max. 1980. *The History of the Yiddish Language.* Chicago: University of Chicago Press.

7 / Secret Temples

Daniel Itzkovitz

They have sojourned in the midst of mankind and have wandered from land to land, stamped everywhere with the seal of mystery, looked upon by all not of their creed as a 'peculiar,' enigmatical, incomprehensible people.   *The Forum,* July 1914

To obtain control over public opinion it is first necessary to confuse it.   *Protocols of the Elders of Zion*

In a recent article Daniel and Jonathan Boyarin discuss the ways that some French theorists' use of "the jew" allegorizes, and thus erases, real Jews. The Boyarins claim that in allegorizing the Jews these philosophers are "complicit in perpetuating the cultural annihilation of the Jew."[1] In their most extended critique they take Jean-François Lyotard to task for using the term *jew* "to represent the outsiders, the nonconformists: the artists, anarchists, blacks, homeless, Arabs, etc.— and the Jews."[2] The uppercase Jew gets lost in the crowd, crammed into the lowercase, allegorical "jew." Appropriating the name "jew" to signify otherness, Lyotard forgets the "reality" of practicing Jews, and those "untheorized, unphilosophical, unspiritualized" people who call themselves "Jews," and "basically repeats Sartre's thesis about the production of the Jew by the anti-Semite."[3]

I want to begin this essay by rethinking the Boyarins' critique of Lyotard and the others in an American context. As opposed to Europe, where "the Jew" is constructed as an allegory for otherness, in twentieth-century America the Jews have often seemed a good metaphor for the notion of "American" itself—the "American," that is, was an identity whose imagined severed ties to the land and to tradition, and whose obsession with money, reminded many of the stereotypic Jew. This is true for a wide spectrum of commentators, whether they thought this allegorical connection was a negative or a positive thing. As Albert Lindemann has pointed out, while "European anti-Semites were nearly unanimous in seeing the United States as a 'jewified' land, without a sense of honor, of history, of aristocratic virtue," many, such as Justice Louis Brandeis, asserted that "the Jewish spirit . . . is essentially modern and essentially American."[4] By the fifties, when Jewish American writers such as Norman Mailer, J. D. Salinger, Allen Ginsberg, Grace Paley, Philip Roth, and Saul Bellow were "giving voice to the nation," Mailer was to proclaim "we are all Jews to a degree,"[5] and Leslie Fiedler to note matter-of-factly that "the Jew has become on all levels from *Marjorie Morningstar* and *For Two Cents Plain* to *Augie March* and *Goodbye, Columbus* the symbol in which the American projects his own fate."[6]

Do the other-as-Jew allegory and the nation-as-Jew allegory do the same work? While the former describes an ur-outsider's relation to an insider's community, the latter describes America's modern situation of rootlessness, disconnection from the past, and the sameness of difference. By this last I mean that the allegory works to create a fantasied space where (ethnic, historical, racial, class, gender, etc.) difference becomes (national) sameness—a sort of queer nationality.[7] And while the Boyarins criticize Lyotard for "basically repeat[ing] Sartre's thesis about the production of the Jew by the anti-Semite," the American-as-Jew allegory is produced most vociferously, within the borders of America, by Jewish writers.[8]

But this Jewish American autoallegorization, like the European Jewish allegory, is also part of a system of identity abnegation. Despite its universalist claims, the American allegorization of Jewish sameness is always bound up with a sense of, and anxiety about, Jewish difference. If Mailer's "we are all Jews to a degree" is a celebration of a culturally diverse America, where individual and group differences find shelter under the warm cloak of liberal tolerance, it also reveals a certain speechlessness as to just what the content of Jewish difference really is. The Jew in these universalizing accounts, as in the work of the French theorists the Boyarins challenge, loses all particularity. In these accounts, Jewishness explains difference, but Jewish difference is never explained.

This is not to say that attempts have not been made. The flip side of these universalizing accounts of the Jew is the mountain of essays, tracts, books, articles, songs, novels, and short stories produced in the first half of this century dedicated to the very mission of locating Jewish difference.[9] And while a stable location was never discovered, the difference that was most often settled upon was a difference that unsettled. Far from being the symbol of Americanness at these moments, Jewishness was thought to hover along the outskirts of an ever-unstable border of normativity. In particular, Jewish male identity was represented as both a disruption and a limit in the anxious construction of American notions of nationality, class, whiteness, masculinity, and culture.[10] Jewishness came to define the limits of these categories because, in its disarticulation, the Jew often also seemed to slip back and forth into white Americanness. In fact, the more "the same" the Jew was, the more there was to fear, and the more the Jew slipped across the line into otherness: the Jewish male was American but foreign; white but racially other; consuming but nonproductive. He was an inauthentic participant in heterosexuality, and inauthentically within the walls of high culture. In all of these cases the Jewish male was imagined to be a secret perversion of the genuine article.[11] And this ambiguous position set the stage for a series of national crises that helped delimit the terms of white Americanness, and in which popular notions of the Jew played a central role.

Two important and similar moments in Jewish American history perhaps best exemplify how the grasping for Jewish difference articulated a notion of Jewishness as the suspect embodiment of a series of perversions. While there are great differences between Leo Frank, the Atlanta pencil factory supervisor and B'nai B'rith president found guilty of the brutal murder of thirteen-year-old "little Mary Phagan" in 1913, and Richard Loeb and Nathan Leopold, the boy geniuses who murdered and mutilated thirteen-year-old Bobby Franks in Chicago in 1924, the similarities between the cases warrant a brief comparison. Both were highly sensational cases that brought wealthy Jewish defendants to trial for the sexually tainted murders of very young people, and while the "public" was a very different entity in each case (Southern populist in one case, Northern industrial in the other), public opinion in both trials was unified and catalyzed by the similar characterization of the defendants as perverts and sodomites. In both cases, the rhetorical slippage from murderer to Jew to millionaire to hostile foreigner to sodomite pervert was so smooth as to be rendered almost unnoticeable. Populist leader Tom Watson, writing shortly after Frank was kidnapped from his prison and lynched by an angry mob, captured these slippings succinctly: "In putting the Sodomite murderer to death the Vigilance Committee has done what the Sheriff would have done if [Georgia Governor] Slaton had not been the same mould as Benedict Arnold. Let Jew libertines take notice! Georgia is not for sale to rich criminals."[12] As Watson's diatribe makes clear, the sexual, racial, economic, and national paranoia that found its articulation in both the Frank and Leopold and Loeb cases had implications beyond the cases themselves. And while every account of Jewish difference does not bind together so neatly such a colorful array of identificatory limits, I want to argue that Watson makes explicit connections that are often present in twentieth-century American notions of Jewishness, even when they are not spoken.

The relationship between Jewishness and homosexuality will be crucial to this discussion. Not only were the terms *sodomite* and *homosexual* strategically attached to Jewish men in the popular imaginary, as becomes strikingly clear in diatribes such as Watson's, but there are several basic similarities in the ways anxieties concerning the sodomite and the Jew were popularly represented. The most prominent of these commonalities is the trope of secrecy, or hiddenness. The Jew, like the homosexual, was seen as having a hidden identity, and both were imagined to perform secret acts that substantiated their elusive identities. Even in the brief Watson excerpt, anxiety about a secret plot simultaneously to buy out and demoralize Georgia is bursting at its seams. For a number of decades anxieties concerning Jewish secrecies emerged in even the most unlikely places and reveal an elaborate web of associations embedded within them.

I will also argue that the definitional impasse presented by Jewishness reveals it as, ultimately, a "difference that has no content," to use the formulation Jonathan Goldberg applies to sodomy.[13] This can be opposed to early-twentieth-century cultural theorist Walter Lippmann's argument that Jews embody "a distinction [from other Americans] without a difference."[14] Lippmann posits a content to Jewishness, a "distinction," that, somehow, is not "different," while the model I would like to use claims that Jewish difference is a difference with no content, or, more exactly, with a fluid and ever-shifting content that cannot mark Jewishness as distinct. As exacting as early-twentieth-century American accounts of Jewish difference often become, they are most striking, taken as a whole, for their inability to arrive at a solid notion of "the Jew." Jewishness kept slipping within and among the categories of race, nation, religion, and culture, and the criteria for affiliation and disaffiliation (notwithstanding the religious law that defines as Jewish those individuals whose mother is Jewish) were very vulnerable to contestation. Who belonged? What were the qualifications? Were there certain exclusive beliefs or practices; a certain number of ancestors defined as Jewish; a certain size nose; a certain look in the eyes; a certain smell; a certain relation to language; dirt; morality; community; culture? Could one choose to be Jewish? Is a Jew white? If a Jew converted was she still a Jew? If a Jew became an American was he still a Jew?

What is further remarkable in the work that does claim to identify Jewish difference are the extremes that are said to mark it. Israel Wechsler outlined some of these in 1925:

> The Jew is said to adhere to a worn-out religion and to worship false gods; at the same time he clings to the ideal of the purest monotheism. He is a moral person who leads a clean home life, and has a low sense of honesty and morality in his dealings with his neighbors. He is the shining example of a continuous social group, closely knitted in his communal life; and he is a rebel, a revolutionist, an iconoclast, a breaker-up of society. He is *par excellence* the capitalist exploiter and the financial slave-driver of humanity; and he seeks to disrupt and subvert the capitalist social structure of centuries. He is a staunch socialist and Bolshevik, and at the same time a rabid individualist and anarchist. He is educated and polished and cultured, and he is low and vulgar and loud. He furnishes a large number of superior types and geniuses, and he has a greater number of mental and moral defectives. He is shy and meek and afraid, and he is bold and pushing and grasping. . . . He is of noble stock with a family tree which can be traced to whole princely forests, and is a mongrel among races. He is a coward and a brave man. He has the oldest conception of national unity, but does not know the meaning of patriotism. He is cunning and clever, and yet he concocts the inane plots of the "Elders of Zion." He is peaceful and harmless and moral, and kills Christian children for Passover feasts.[15]

In Wechsler's examples, Jewish difference is not marked by a containable, distinctively Jewish trait, but rather by the state of extremity itself.[16]

The elusive and ever-shifting location of Jewish difference functioned strategically. The confusion surrounding the definition of Jewishness merely produced more intense efforts to define and contain it, and its lack of solid content gave it a particular rhetorical energy that was crucial to the self-definition of the American culture into which it was always bleeding. As the chain of crimes Watson attaches to the Jew begins to reveal, the definitional slipperiness of Jewishness was mobilized to regulate and maintain a number of categories—particularly whiteness, Americanness, culture, masculinity, and heteronormativity—bound up with one another, while also defining the limits of socially sanctioned economic and sexual relations between men, between whites, and between members of certain classes. I will return later to the meanings imagined to be contained within the Jew's closet, but first will attempt to sort through some of the many ways that Jewish difference is disarticulated in the first half of this century.

White Jews: So Congenial, So Alien

What is the nature of Jewish difference? It would be difficult to distinguish what came to be the public fantasy of the Jews' hidden life from the public experience of the Jews' bodily presence. Jewish difference was all the more threatening because it was lurking somewhere behind an apparent bodily sameness, and anxieties concerning the troubled "whiteness" of the Jew inform all discussions of the possibilities and impossibilities of Jewish American assimilation.

Walter Benn Michaels has recently argued that the question of race in America lost its biological underpinnings in the 1920s, and that they were replaced in particular by a new, nationalist notion of "culture." As a result of this process, a new type of slippage between racial and national identities developed:

> Insofar as the question, Are you white? has been and continues to be successfully replaced by the question, Are you American?—insofar, that is, as a question supposedly about biology has been preserved as a question supposedly about national identity—one might say that the very idea of American citizenship is a racial and even racist idea, racist not because it embodies a (more or less concealed) preference for white skins but because it confers on national identity something like the ontology of race.[17]

That American ideologies of race, culture, and nation should be entwined is no surprise. Madison Grant made this claim quite clearly in a nativist, anti-Jewish essay in 1925: "Our institutions are Anglo-Saxon, and can only be maintained by Anglo-Saxons and by other Nordic peoples in sympathy with our culture."[18] But the slight difference that lies between Grant's "Anglo-Saxons" and Michaels's "white skins" reveals that the equivalencies being set up—of race, nation, and culture—are not as clear as they at first seem.

Michaels *is* interested in exploring the subtle exchanges between the cultural value, "whiteness," and the bodily marker, white skin. But although he utilizes representations of Jewishness to make his point, Michaels is less concerned with the question of the specific Jewish relation to the complications of American whiteness.[19] If he is correct that "American" and "white" identities became conflated in a new way in the early twentieth century, it is not immediately apparent how a Jew would answer the questions of race and nationality that Michaels maps onto one another.[20] Rather, the persistence of the questions "What race is the Jew?" and "What is the Jew's national allegiance?" reveals that the construction of twentieth-century American nationality can never be as simple as the articulation of the binaries of American and foreign, white and black.[21]

While there is clearly a "preference for white skins" in the negotiations of Americanness, Michaels himself points out that there is also a simultaneous vigilance that keeps an eye out for those who merely *look* white, or even those who merely *act* white. So while some confidently claimed that Jews are simply "a subdivision of the Caucasian race,"[22] many others were not so sure. This is why Kipling's quip, "like a young Jew trying to appear white," was circulating in popular American magazines, and why the caricature shown in Figure 7.1, which reads "Corbin's 'White Jew' and Whiter Jewess," was amusing.[23] Does a Jew who *is* able to appear white, and who does have a great deal of "sympathy for [Anglo-Saxon] culture" remain a Jew? Numerous theories attempted to remedy this problem marking the Jew physically, behaviorally, through skin color, nose size, accent, manners, and mannerisms, but there was always a chance that the Jew (again, I am speaking about Jews of European origin) would slip by—there was always the chance that the Jew *trying* to appear white really *does* appear white (and, by extension, American). This slippage was constantly undoing the self-containment of whiteness, troubling the borders of national, cultural, and racial belonging.

Figure 7.1

Randolph Bourne, writing in 1916, was struck by the peculiar relation Jewish people have to their "host nation," the Jews' simultaneous assimilation and maintenance of difference. While he does not
directly discuss the Jews' whiteness, it lies within the complicated interplay of his ideas of "assimilation," "race," "culture," and "nation":

> Has it not always been the anomaly of the Jew that he was at once the
> most self-conscious of beings — feels himself, that is, religiously, cultur-
> ally, racially, a being peculiar in his lot and signally blessed — and yet
> has proven himself perhaps the most assimilable of all races to other
> and quite alien cultures? Which is the cause and which is effect? Is he
> assimilable because he has had no national centre, no geographical and

political basis for his religion and his mode of life, or has he not had his Jewish nation because he has been so readily assimilated? Is it not just this in the Jewish personality that has piqued and irritated and attracted other peoples, that it is at once so congenial and so alien?[24]

Bourne implies here that "race" and "culture" are two separate things, that Jews, "the most assimilable of all races," can put on and take off cultures without losing their racial identity. That the Jewish race does not have the same relation to Jewish culture that the white race has to American culture has, vaguely, something to do with the physical geography and political "basis" of American nationhood. But these categories become more and more difficult to disentangle, their own "basis" difficult to discern. It is the Jew's performance of whiteness—the self-erasure of the Jew's Jewishness—that enables his or her smooth assimilation: to assimilate is to take on not only a new nation and culture, but also, following Michaels's logic, a race.[25] The very idea of being an "assimilable" "race" explodes the category of race itself. And if, as Bourne asserts, race, religion, and culture are what make Jews "peculiar," and the assimilated Jew is nonreligious, enmeshed in national culture, and passing as white, not only is "race" rendered incoherent, it is also no longer clear of what Jewish difference consists.

If the substance of Jewish difference was revealed to be inarticulable in Bourne's essay, this hardly means that so-called Jewish assimilation to American whiteness was a seamless transition. As Bourne remarks, it is the perceived double quality of Jewish identity—at once "culturally and racially...peculiar" and "the most assimilable of all races to other...cultures"—that made Jews "at once so congenial and so alien." This uncanny sameness of Jewish difference caused a great deal of unease during a time when America was obsessed with maintaining cultural, and especially procreative, boundaries between "races." And the possibilities presented by these simultaneous and incessant drives to mark Jewish difference and to render Jews the same, despite the clear inability to do either, were highly problematic to a racial schema that insisted on visibility as a primary (although not quite exclusive) criterion.

The early-twentieth-century confusion concerning the Jews' relationship to "race," "nation," and "culture" replicates itself in contemporary historical discussions of Jews in America. It is most apparent in discussions of the Jews' race and relation to whiteness. Eminent historian John Higham, for instance, discusses the problematic relation Jews have had to American nationality in his history of Jewish immigration and assimilation in America, but sees these problems as clearly nonracial:

> Except in the 1930's, American racists rarely singled out the Jew as the exclusive or even as the major object of attack. Traditional American racism manifested itself as the exclusion of dark-skinned people from any possibility of equal social status in white society. It simply did not apply to Jews, except as a basis of identification with other whites.[26]

Seeing race as a "skin color" problem that keeps people from "equal social status," Higham considers American Jews to be problematized white ethnics whose "otherness" is constructed situationally. Rather than seeing an overarching racist ideology behind this situation, Higham tracks particular, and generally unrelated, tropes that get played out to serve various social and political uses.

Writing in almost direct contradiction to Higham, Robert Singerman claims in a recent essay that American "nativist" anti-Semitism was theoretically rooted in biological racism, having "a clearly identifiable genetic component."[27] Whereas Higham classes Jews as white ethnics who recall a clear "identification with other whites," Singerman finds nativist racists everywhere stretching their non-Anglo race categories to accommodate Jews. Popular racialist T. Lothrop Stoddard, for instance, placed Jews in the most popular spot for them: as "Asiatic elements."[28]

Regardless of whether the Jew was ultimately seen as white or as a racial alien, the important point seems to be that the Jew, by virtue of the unconventional Jewish relation to race, nation, and culture, occupies a position of fundamental instability that could be mobilized to various, and particular, effects. Notwithstanding the absoluteness of Higham's claims, both he and Singerman are, in a sense, correct. It is exactly this definitional instability that marks the Jew's liminality. And this instability, which hid inside the seeming stability of the Jews' proximate whiteness, fed fantasies of dangerous secrets behind the eyes of the suspect Jew.

Substantially a Foreigner

Unlike fin de siècle European accounts of Jewish bodily difference, which, as Sander Gilman has recently claimed, revolved primarily around the moral, social, and medical differences thought to occur via the circumcision of Jewish males, by the turn of the American twentieth century circumcision was a generally accepted, routine medical hygienic practice across racial lines.[29] But there was still, in the United States, a remarkably common obsession with the Jew's body, which focused on locating an obviously inscribed otherness where there seemed to be none; if it could be located, the Jew could then be "known" by the same means other races were known. Like many American nativists, Stoddard imagined the Jew as not only genetically, but also *bodily* different; he described Jews as having "dwarfish stature, flat faces, high cheekbones, and other Mongoloid traits."[30] But because actual Jewish bodies often contradicted the varied descriptions ascribed to them by racialists, the common American conflation of race and visible difference was undone.

Predictably, those theorists who resort to nonbodily accounts of Jewish difference often become both hyperbolic and inarticulate: the Jew emerges from under the sameness of white skin as, in the words of racialist Burton J. Hendrick, "always and necessarily alien."[31] Hendrick speaks as if the description "alien" explains itself, and as if "always and necessarily" keeps clear the ever blurring lines between Jew and non-Jew. This retreat to the empty certainty of "always and necessarily" was not a move peculiar to racialist kooks like Hendrick; a quarter-century earlier Mark Twain had broadly proclaimed:

> By his make and ways ... [the Jew] is substantially a foreigner wherever he may be, and even the angels dislike a foreigner. I am using the word foreigner in the German sense — *stranger*. Nearly all of us have an antipathy to a stranger, even of our own nationality.... You will always be ... substantially strangers — foreigners — wherever you are.[32]

With all his certainty about "always" and "substance," Twain raises more questions than he settles about Jewish difference. By "make" Twain seems to mean the Jew's natural body, his biological race, and by "ways" he implies the Jew's cultural practices. But exactly what part of the Jew's "make" and "ways" gives "substance" to his foreignness?

While he has no doubts about the fact of the Jew's difference, not surprisingly the confidently proclaimed substance of this difference is more difficult to locate. Twain's essay walks a fine line between defining Jews by their historical and cultural determinants and defining them racially. Utilizing a pseudoevolutionary schema, ultimately the cultural and the natural blend indistinguishably:

In the hard conditions suggested, the Jew without brains could not survive, and the Jew with brains had to keep them in good training and
well sharpened up, or starve. Ages of restriction to the one tool which
the law was not able to take from him—his brain—have made that
tool singularly competent; ages of compulsory disuse of his hands have
atrophied them, and he never uses them now.[33]

By the logic of Twain's evolutionary fantasy, cultural adversity has
created in the Jew two biological developments: an immense increase
in brain capacity and a concurrent physical degeneracy and emptying
of bodily productivity. Discarding any consideration of a racialist argument, Twain manages to reassert, albeit somewhat mythically, Jewish bodily difference. Like Stoddard, the only "substantial" difference Twain can find is written in the Jew's body. But rather than relying
on the vicissitudes of racial science, Twain's evolutionary myth tells a
story in which Jewish bodily/gender identity derives from a problematic of Jewish productive practices. Jewish men, as New York police
commissioner Theodore Bingham claimed in explaining the supposed
disproportional prevalence of Jewish criminals, were "men not physically fit for hard labor."[34]

For many turn-of-the-century American writers, Jewish relations
to economic productivity became the primary means by which to understand Jewish male bodily difference. As one writer proclaimed,
"had the Jews scattered . . . and had they gone into the producing end
of business, they would have been treated just as any other group
from Europe."[35] The Jew, it was thought, was "congenitally a nonproducer."[36] "Even in direst poverty," another noted, "they contrive
to avoid hard muscular labor."[37] This belief plugged into an ideology
that connected Jewish-inflected anxieties of gender, nationalism, and
economics.

The meanings within the Jew's productivity-tied bodily difference
are intricately related to other contemporary discussions of productive bodies and nationality. As Mark Seltzer has recently discussed,
the imagined, healthy American national body at the turn of the century was mirrored by an imagined, healthy male body. Seltzer points
out that, as the first *Boy Scouts of America* handbook (1910) claimed,
"degeneracy is the word" that described what must be feared both
individually and nationally. American boys must develop their bodies
to provide "the physical regeneration so needful for continued national existence." And in a men's club speech the same year Twain's

essay was published, Teddy Roosevelt echoed this insistence on the conflation of a strong masculine body and a strong nation, celebrating "that vigorous manliness for the lack of which in a nation, as in an individual, the possession of no other qualities can possibly atone."[38]

America's massive influx of Jews at the turn of the century was perceived as a threat to the integrity of the "national body." And just as their "swarming" was imagined to threaten, in the words of Henry James, national "overflow," to "burst all bounds,"[39] the imagined Jewish body that is stateless, degenerating, and nonproductive — that is not "vigorously manly" — is a body that threatens the strong nation. And despite the efforts of Zionists in both the United States and Europe who attempted to combat this image of the Jew by calling for a "Judaism with muscles," in the popular imaginary "the Jew" was a weak, nonproductive man, with shriveled body and atrophied hands.[40]

There is a clear lineage from Twain's comments on the evolution of the Jew's body to Lewis P. Brown's defense of the Jew against accusations of being a malingerer:

Powers neglected tend to atrophy. Fish in subterranean streams will lose the sense of sight. Ducks out of water will lose the ability to swim. And so men unable to use physical force lose altogether the sense of fight. Their bodies wither.... Physical prowess could not avail him.[41]

Brown, however, takes the issue in a different direction than Twain, into the realm of Jewish ineptitude in socially sanctioned male physical exchange. Here we see how these issues revolving around the Jew's productive body begin not only to trouble gender lines, but also to reflect back onto relationships between men. Jewish men who lose their sense of fight do not merely drop safely away from the homosocial economy, no more than "nonproductive" Jews drop away from economy itself: the Jew's embodiment of a troubled masculinity *troubles* normative masculinity itself. As Edwin J. Kuh figured it in the *Atlantic Monthly*, "the suppression of physical development in Jewish children makes them a tempting butt for their neighbor."[42] The anxiety about the temptations conjured by the Jewish man's "tempting butt" need hardly be remarked; the temptation, it seems, is at once to beat and to fuck.[43]

It was a criminal impetus that was immediately reattributed to the Jew. In texts such as Kuh's the Jew often became an object not only of scorn, but also envy and fear, and his "unnatural" economic practice was imagined both to give him unfair advantage over, and to endanger, non-Jewish masculinity. If the Jewish male's ability to fight was questioned by writers such as Brown, the economic prowess widely attributed to the Jew was almost invariably invoked in the language of competition and fighting, which inferred that the Jew had unfair advantage over other men. Not only can "none beat the Hebrew at a bargain,"[44] but according to one author the prevailing non-Jewish sentiment conveys precisely an anxiety about being beaten: "They are beating us. They beat us in the schools, in the colleges, in business—everywhere, and we are not used to being beaten and don't like it." This is what makes them, in the eyes of another author, "all fair game for the Aryan who hates to be beaten."[45]

These intermingling economic and sexual anxieties—the fear of temptation, violation, and economic exploitation—begin to express some of the ways in which the production of the liminal, near-white, near-American, economically threatening and culturally indeterminate Jewish male's difference played a crucial role in policing turn-of-the-century borders of socially sanctioned relations between men. The Jewish male was imagined to embody a series of desires and fears from which capitalism had to protect itself.[46] Tom Watson, in no uncertain terms, imagined the dynamic between Jews and the white working people of America the day Leo Frank's death sentence was commuted to life imprisonment (Watson imagined that Jewish money bought Frank's respite):

> Like the Roman wife of old, we feel that something unclean, something unutterably loathsome has crept to bed with us, and befouled us during the night; and that while the morning has come again, it can never, *never* restore our self-respect. *We have been violated, AND WE ARE ASHAMED!*[47]

Passing; or, The Jew's Prosthesis

While he was in jail in 1964 for the murder of Lee Harvey Oswald, Jack Ruby became obsessed with the idea that, because of a public misunderstanding of what he had done, "all the Jews in America were being slaughtered." In addition to the massacre of "twenty five million innocent people," Ruby, the former Jacob Rubenstein, envisioned his brother Sam "tortured, horribly mutilated, castrated and burned in the street outside the jail."[48] Given the anti-Semitic treatment he received from his prosecutor (who called him "Jew-boy") and the Dallas press (who often called him by his legally changed birth name), it might be argued that Ruby's fantasies are not as far-fetched as they first seem. But putting all conspiracy theories aside for a moment, I want briefly to look at one of the reasons Ruby gave for his vengeful act. In the words of the police sergeant who first questioned Ruby: "Ruby had said he wanted to kill Oswald 'because he wanted the world to know that Jews do have guts.' "[49]

In one act Ruby was protecting the nation (by killing the president's assassin), protecting the Jews (by proving both their national loyalty and their virility), and, since guts are distinctively macho body parts, giving himself a macho body. Unfortunately, because the Jew has historically signaled a simultaneous rupture of race, nation, and masculinity, Ruby's feeling that his attempt to do these three things was a failure was probably an accurate assessment.[50] But his impulse to build up his "body image" and his inverse fear of (his brother's) castration make sense given the rhetoric of uneasy Jewish male embodiment.

By the turn of the century, there was already a public mechanism in effect to detect the Jewish male trying to be something he wasn't. If the imagined Jew was thought to have overdeveloped bankbooks and brains at the expense of an underdeveloped (or decaying) body, he was also imagined to be endlessly trying to compensate for his bodily lack. This is why *The Great Gatsby*'s Meyer Wolfsheim's favorite ornament is his cuff links, made of the "finest specimens of human molars."[51] And this is why it was such a credible rumor when Leopold and Loeb were accused of being "gland robbers." One press report claimed that "the color given to the belief that these two youths slew Tracey [a murder and gland-robbery victim] is by partial identification of the boys as gland robbers who had kidnapped Charles Read, a taxi driver, and after a crude operation, left him on the prairies."[52] The images of Ruby, Wolfsheim, and Leopold and Loeb's virtually Ozian display of lack (if I only had some guts . . . a tooth . . . a gland . . .) work because the Jew was always thought to be trying to get something he obviously didn't already have. This last bizarre accusation, in particular, resonated with the popular logic of the Jew's body. In the two criminals, known to be millionaires, geniuses, and lovers, the nonproductive and unmanly images of the Jewish financier and the Jewish intellectual converged. In them nationalist body politics met homophobic ideology, threatening America's national health by being at once nonproductive and nonreproductive. Performing the "crude operation" that made them "gland robbers" (which, it seems to me, can only mean testicle stealers) must have been understood to be a feeble and misguided way to compensate for their own nonphallic selves.[53]

This figure of the criminally nonphallic, endlessly overcompensating Jewish man is crucial to the construction of Jewish difference and its relationship to visibility within nationalist body politics. If Ruby, Wolfsheim, and Leopold and Loeb were all "known" criminals, they were inhabiting a space that had already been clearly mapped out for them—that of the suspect Jew. It was a space that Hannah Arendt pays much attention to when, in 1944, she describes Jewish pariah types in American popular culture:

> The type which [Charlie] Chaplin portrays is always fundamentally suspect. He may be at odds with the world in a thousand and one ways, and his conflicts with it may assume a manifold variety of forms, but always and everywhere he is under suspicion, so that it is no good arguing rights or wrongs.[54]

The Jewish male was, particularly in the first half of this century, always suspect, always on the verge of the criminal, and while Arendt does not say as much, this criminality rarely moved far from the taint of both the economic and the sexual.[55] These connections are more apparent in some of the numerous early-twentieth-century reports on the problem of crime and the Hebrews. Eugenicist Charles Davenport, for instance, claimed that:

> Statistics indicate that the crimes of Hebrews are chiefly 'gainful offenses,' especially thievery and receiving stolen goods, while they rarely commit offenses of personal violence. On the other hand, they show the greatest proportion of offenses against chastity and in connection with prostitution, the lowest of crimes.[56]

The separation here is, I think, only an apparent one. For the Jewish criminal, crimes against property had the power to slip, symbolically at least, into offenses against chastity. So one could heed Commissioner Bingham's warning to the public about Jewish criminals—

> The crimes committed by the Russian Hebrews are generally those against property. They are burglars, firebugs, pickpockets and highway robbers—when they have the courage; but, though all crime is in their province, pocket-picking is the one to which they seem to take most naturally.[57]

—and still not know what it is that the Jew finds "most natural" to pick out of pockets. The rhetoric of the criminal Jew depends on this point of condensation—that which blurs the distinction between one's wallet and one's glands. Pocket picking, that most intimate of "crimes against property" was not-so-distant kin to the "criminal intimacy" of which the Jew Leo Frank was accused by the Supreme Court in 1914.[58] And as I began to say in the preceding section, because the particular type of cultural value found in both the phallus and the wallet is coded as male and vulnerable, in particular, to the intimate encroachment of another male, the imagined Jewish male economic prowess was often experienced as a threat to (and theft of) manhood itself.[59]

In Willa Cather's violent short story "Scandal," a famous opera diva finds out that her look-alike is being paraded around the city by Siegmund Stein, a physically disgusting Jewish businessman. The "scandal" is, of course, the idea that she would be involved in a passionate romance with "one of the most hideous men in New York":

> He has one of those rigid, horse like faces that never tell anything; a long nose, flattened as if it had been tied down; a scornful chin; long, white teeth, flat cheeks, yellow as a Mongolian's; tiny, black eyes, with puffy lids and no lashes; dingy, dead-looking hair—looks as if it were glued on.[60]

Cather notes that Stein's ugliness is a permanent bodily feature, "not the common sort of ugliness that comes from overeating and automobiles." But Stein's ugliness is not complete without its attempted, and failed, performance of bodily completion: his prosthesis, his "glued on" hair.

The dead hair in itself does not seem as important as what it signals, an incomplete body and a Jew trying to pass for something he is not. And a Jew who is doing that is almost always also trying to place himself in a heterosexual economy. In "Scandal" the Jew's awkward heterosexuality is revealed to be merely a performed spectacle: "one of Stein's many ambitions," we are told, "was to be thought a success with women."[61] Not to *be* a success, but to be thought one. It is precisely the Jew's lack of determinate sexual identity, beyond being a transparently inadequate spectacle of normative desire, that is so terrifying about him. In Stein's case, the Jew's obvious prosthesis helps locate him in a crowd, but can only intimate what is behind the "face that never tells anything."

Inside the Jew's Closet: *Shvaygn = Toyt*

> Vibrantly resonant as the image of the closet is for many modern op-
> pressions, it is indicative for homophobia in a way it cannot be for
> other oppressions.... Ethnic/cultural/religious oppressions such as anti-
> Semitism are more analogous in that the stigmatized individual has at
> least notionally some discretion ... over other people's knowledge of her
> or his membership in the group.... A Jewish or Gypsy identity, and hence
> a Jewish or Gypsy secrecy or closet, would nonetheless differ again from
> the distinctive gay versions of these things in its clear ancestral linearity
> and answerability, in the roots (however tortuous and ambivalent) of
> cultural identification through each individual's originary culture of (at
> a minimum) the family.[62]

Eve Kosofsky Sedgwick's useful differentiation between homophobia
and anti-Semitism notwithstanding, and without claiming any absolute similarity in these two oppressions, there are many ways, as
this article has attempted, in part, to show, that American anxieties
concerning the secrecy of the homosexual closet have been mapped
onto popular perceptions of American Jews. In marking only the clear
separation (between "Jewish" secrecy and "distinctive gay" secrecy),
Sedgwick's analysis examines neither the popularly constructed contents of the Jew's closet nor the retroactive relation these cultural
fantasies have on the constitution of actual Jewish and queer identities. *Only* separating homophobia and anti-Semitism does not fully
account for the ways that anti-Semitism and homophobia are inflected
by one another, and the ways discourses of Jewishness and queerness
speak through one another. The language of anti-Semitism utilizes and
is bound up with the discourse of homophobia in particularly resonant ways.[63]

My point here is not to equate homosexuality and Jewishness (or
the fear of them), but to think about the ways both, as closet identities, begin to inform one another. This approach can be distinguished
from that of other writers who have recently considered Jewishness
and issues of sexuality and gender. In a number of provocative books,
for example, Sander Gilman examines the entangled histories of race,
medicine, and psychiatry in the work of Freud, Otto Weininger, and
other fin de siècle, mostly Western European, authors, unearthing
European anxieties, theories, and insinuations about Jewish relations
to normative gender categories.[64] This knowledge about the Jew's sexuality bears out in the United States as well. In a report to the New

York *Medical Record* on race and "mental defectives," for instance, M. G. Schlapp and Alice E. Paulson found nearly twice as many diagnoses of "sex instability, including homosexuality" among those labeled "Semitic" than any of the eight other racial categories included in the study.[65] And if the diagnostic concurrence of "sex instability" and Jewishness was given common play among psychologists at the time, it was equally common in nonmedical communities.[66] In celebrated legal cases such as the Leo Frank and the Leopold and Loeb trials it seemed to surprise no one that the deviance of Jewish defendants was a central aspect of the trials.

But Gilman roots this connection in ways that become problematic when they are mapped onto American fin de siècle notions of Jewishness. In his most recent work he locates two major terms for the location of Jewish difference: circumcision in the Jewish male body, and madness, particularly neurasthenia, in the Jewish psyche. Not only was the mark of Jewishness medically extracted from circumcision in the American context, but, as Gilman himself points out, neurasthenia was seen not only as a particularly Jewish mental disease, but as an American one as well: "Neurasthenia, the American disease... was also the disease of the Jews."[67] It is clear that different terms must be found to read American Jewish male difference. Given the central difficulty in locating Jewish difference, centering on the problematic of Jewish visibility, I would like, rather, to use Sedgwick's notion of the closet as the epistemological metaphor for discussing Jewish difference. Rather than discovering difference in one particular location, I want to claim that the central operative factors of Jewish American difference are the problematic terms of Jewish visibility itself. And the imagined contents of the Jew's closet were almost invariably inflected by the economic and the sexual.[68] The more commonly overt image of the secretive Jew, whose "pecuniary affairs," according to one post–Civil War observer, "are usually in the dark," was mirrored and magnified by what one turn-of-the-century American psychologist remarked was "the frequency with which we find hidden sexual complexes among Hebrews."[69]

As "Scandal" makes clear, Cather's troubled identification with the idea of the Jew is at least in part related to this dual aspect of the Jew's secrecy. In "Paul's Case," her construction of an exotic Jewish secrecy gives form to an articulation of queer desire:

It would be difficult to put it strongly enough how convincingly the stage entrance of that theatre was for Paul the actual portal of Romance.... It was very like the old stories that used to float about London of fabulously rich Jews, who had subterranean halls, with palms, and fountains, and soft lamps and richly appareled women who never saw the disenchanting light of London day. So, in the midst of that smoke-palled city, enamoured of figures and grimy toil, Paul had his secret temple, his wishing carpet, his bit of blue-and-white Mediterranean shore bathed in perpetual sunshine.[70]

In this early story we get a brief glimpse of the connection Cather makes between the stereotypic image of the hidden, corrupting deviance of the Jew and the hidden sexuality, the "secret temple" and "wishing carpet," of a closeted young boy. If we looked inside Paul's closet we would find a family of rich, exotic London Jews.

As these examples show, it is not merely (as Sedgwick implies) — or, rather, simply — one's Jewish identity that is closeted, but a whole series of identifications that are condensed within the secrecies of Jewishness. The Jewish closet can only be understood in terms of the imagined secrets of its contents. These are the intertwining secrets of the nonproductive, yet "fabulously rich," Jewish financier, and the nonreproductive Jewish pervert, both of whom insidiously jeopardize the national health. To "come out" as a Jew is to tell a story not only of ethnic, familial, or religious identity, but also of a popular imaginary that conflates dangerous sexual, racial, economic, and national secrets.

Notes

1. Daniel Boyarin and Jonathan Boyarin, "Diaspora: Generation and the Ground of Jewish Identity," *Critical Inquiry* 19 (Summer 1993): 699.

2. Jean-François Lyotard, *Heidegger and "the jews,"* trans. Andreas Michel and Mark S. Roberts (Minneapolis: University of Minnesota Press, 1990), 700.

3. Ibid.

4. Albert Lindemann, *The Jew Accused: Three Anti-Semitic Affairs, Dreyfus, Beilis, Frank, 1894–1915* (Cambridge: Cambridge University Press, 1991), 207. Lindemann points out that French anti-Semite Edouard Drumont "equated 'Americanism' and 'Semitism' " and German scholar Werner Sombart "made much of the similarity of the Jews and the Anglo-Americans" (206–8).

5. Norman Mailer, introduction to *After the Lost Generation* by John W. Aldridge (New York: Arbor House, 1985 [1951]), iii.

6. Leslie Fiedler, "Leopold and Loeb: A Perspective in Time" (1958), in *The Collected Essays of Leslie Fiedler* vol. 1 (New York: Stein and Day, 1971), 444.

7. The Boyarins, I think, are challenging a sense of the term *jew* that has been recently attached in the United States to the term *queer*, i.e., an allegorical term for the

nonnormative, the politically or culturally "twisted." And while I would not claim that Roth or Bellow allegorized the nation in the interest of queerness as it has been recently understood, because of the peculiar relationship Jewishness has to American normativity, the terms of queer difference are helpful in thinking about the drive to concretize a Jewish/American metonymy. On queer nationality, see Lauren Berlant and Elizabeth Freeman, "Queer Nationality," *Boundary 2* 19, no. 1 (1992):149–80. My discussion is also indebted to Eve Kosofsky Sedgwick's exploration, in *Epistemology of the Closet*, of the impasse between minoritizing and universalizing accounts of homosexual identity (Berkeley: University of Californina Press, 1990), esp. 82–90.

8. Not surprisingly, the 1950s Jewish celebration of the Jewish "conquest" of America was fearfully predicted by turn-of-the-century racist writers who had apocalyptic visions of America's racial future. So, in "The Conquest of America," Herman Scheffauer pictured the "alien Jew" fully conquering Nordic America (*Contemporary Review*, February 1914), and a decade later eugenicist Albert E. Wiggam speculated that "other races will be out-bred and supplanted by the Jew" (*The Next Age of Man* (1927), quoted in Robert Singerman, "The Jew as Racial Alien," *Anti-Semitism in American History*, ed. David Gerber [Urbana: University of Illinois Press, 1986], 113). In perhaps the clearest articulation of this anxiety, journalist Burton J. Hendrick opined that "unquestionably, we are face to face with one of the most remarkable phenomena of the time. New York, the headquarters of American wealth, intelligence and enterprise—the most complete physical expression, we have been told, of the American idea—seems destined to become overwhelmingly a Jewish town" ("The Great Jewish Invasion," *McClure's*, January 1907, 310).

9. This essay will focus mainly on writings from the period between 1880 and 1940—a period that spans from the beginning of the massive influx of Eastern European Jewish immigrants to America to the beginning of the Second World War—but the issues I bring up resonate into the present.

10. I say Jewish male here because the overwhelming majority of material that wrestles with Jewish difference clearly and importantly genders "the Jew" as a male. Jewish women are most often ignored in most representations of Jewishness through a mechanism that considered "the Jew" in highly gendered (as male) situations—primarily ones that revolve around commerce and sexuality. However, these exact issues do get played out in very interesting ways in relation to Jewish women in the voluminous discussions of Jewish prostitution and the Jewish white slavery menace. For a helpful summary of this literature, see Edward J. Bristow, *Prostitution and Prejudice: The Jewish Fight against White Slavery 1870–1939* (New York: Schocken, 1983).

11. It is common in discussions of American anti-Semitism to divide anti-Semitism according to the class of the anti-Semite. While I agree that this division is useful at times, I am trying here to attend to the meanings inside notions of Jewish difference that this division elides. Both patrician and populist versions of anti-Semitism are catalyzed by a certain anxiety regarding the instability of particular identity categories, and both utilize similar notions of "the Jew" to define and delimit these identity categories. See Michael N. Dobkowski, *The Tarnished Dream: The Basis of American Anti-Semitism* (Westport, Conn.: Greenwood, 1979).

12. Tom Watson, *The Jeffersonian*, August 21, 1915: 1.

13. Jonathan Goldberg, *Sodometries* (Stanford, Calif.: Stanford University Press, 1992), 10.

14. Walter Lippmann, "Public Opinion and the American Jew," *American Hebrew*, April 14, 1922: 575.

15. Israel S. Wechsler, "The Psychology of Anti-Semitism," *Menorah Journal* 11 (April 1925): 160.

16. Indeed, at least one commentator took this dynamic itself to be the marker of Jewish difference: "The Jews are chosen for this purpose... of intensifying life wherever they go.... Whatever the Jew is, he is intense" ("The Altruism of Louis Brandeis," *Current Literature*, March 1911: 273.

17. Walter Benn Michaels, "The Souls of White Folk," in *Literature and the Body: Essays on Populations and Persons,* ed. Elaine Scarry (Baltimore: Johns Hopkins University Press, 1988), 192. For other challenging discussions of whiteness and American cultural nationalism, see Walter Benn Michaels, "The Vanishing American," *American Literary History* 2 (Summer 1990), and "Race into Culture," *Critical Inquiry,* Summer 1992; David R. Roediger, *The Wages of Whiteness: Race and the Making of the American Working Class* (New York: Verso, 1991), and *Towards the Abolition of Whiteness* (New York: Verso, 1994); and Lauren Berlant, introduction to *The Anatomy of National Fantasy* (Chicago: University of Chicago Press, 1991).

18. Madison Grant, "America for the Americans," *Forum,* September 1925.

19. And Michaels sometimes simplifies the matter by broadly historicizing in a manner that seems to obfuscate difference even while reasserting it. See, for example, his discussion of the Progressive era, in which he claims that while "no black person could become an American citizen, any white person could. For whites, joining the American race required nothing more or less than learning to identify oneself as an American" ("The Vanishing American," 225). For an excellent and differently nuanced consideration of the problems of whiteness and ethnicity, see Roediger, "Whiteness and Ethnicity in the History of 'White Ethnics' in the United States," in *Towards the Abolition of Whiteness.*

20. I hope not to fall here into the same allegorizing trap as many whom I discuss. The self-conception of "the Jewish community" by many Jews who then claim to speak for it performs an elision of differences of origin, class, gender, sexual orientation, and culture among those individuals self-identified as Jewish. I am speaking in this paper largely about Ashkenazi, or German and European-descended, Jews because it is the group that those whom I read here are discussing, but it also seems crucial to challenge the notion that these are "the Jews," and to be aware of the challenges that otherwise racially marked Jews — Sephardic (Iberian, North African, and Middle Eastern), Ethiopian, Asian, African American, etc. — and nonwealthy or middle-class Jews pose to the hegemonic claims of the autoallegorized "Jewish community."

21. Bernard Drachman, in his essay "Anti-Jewish Prejudice in America," exemplifies the common appeal of these binaries to commentators on Jewishness. In his essay he attempts to substantiate his claims of Caucasian/Jewish oneness by appealing to these very binaries of race and national belonging: "That the European peoples do not look upon the Jew as alien in race is clearly manifest through their conduct in those portions of the world, such as the Southern and Western States of this country, South Africa, and Australia, where the white race is brought into close contact with the colored races and where their antipathy and opposition to these latter are very intense. Never, to my knowledge, has there been in those countries a suggestion of antagonism to the Jew on racial grounds. On the contrary, he is recognized there more fully and completely, perhaps, than anywhere else as *a true Caucasian* and his cooperation is sought in the struggle of the white peoples against the colored races, who are looked upon as the common enemy. We may, therefore, safely dismiss the theory that Jew-hatred is a matter of racial antipathy. The prejudice against the Jew is emphatically not 'race-prejudice'" (*The Forum,* July 1914: 34; emphasis added). This is, of

course, particularly remarkable, having been written at the height of the Leo Frank episode.

22. Ibid., 32.

23. Rudyard Kipling quoted by Sydney Reid, "Because You're a Jew," *Independent,* November 26, 1908: 1215. Illustration from *Puck,* July 30, 1879, copied from Michael Selzer, *Kike!* (World Publishing, 1972). These concerns were also circulating in the turn-of-the-century African American press as well; contemplating an African American–Jewish alliance, Robert Abbot, editor of the *Defender,* asked his audience, "Is the Jew a white man?" (January 2, 1915). See Greg Tate's "The Last Black Picture Show" (*Village Voice,* April 19, 1994: 22) for a contemporary consideration of the same question.

24. Randolph Bourne, "The Jew and Trans-National America" (1916), *War and the Intellectuals* (New York: Harper and Row, 1964), 128.

25. It might also be argued, and it has been, most prominently in an article by Michael Rogin, that it is the Jew's performance of blackness that ultimately set the stage for a successful assimilation ("Blackface, White Noise: The Jewish Jazz Singer Finds His Voice," *Critical Inquiry* 18 [Spring 1992]). That is, Rogin argues that the predominance of Jews in the early-twentieth-century blackface performance industry worked to help Jews reinscribe America's racial binary, while placing themselves (because of their demonstrated ability to wipe off, with the cork, all racial markers) firmly in the camp of white folk. While I agree that blackface carries a tremendous amount of meaning in Jewish American history, I would suggest an alternate approach, which looks at signs of cross-racial identifications, desires, etc. in Jewish blackface rather than simply finding in it a reinscription of a black/white racial binary (cf. Eric Lott, *Love and Theft: Blackface Minstrelsy and the American Working Class* [New York: Oxford University Press, 1993]). My current argument, I hope, complicates the idea of "successful assimilation" both by pressing the meanings of assimilation and by rethinking the terms of difference in the category of the Jew. Finally (and again), this whole line of thinking is troubled even more by the intraracial differences that constantly challenge the racial self-conception of Jews themselves.

26. John Higham, *Strangers in the Land: Immigrants in Urban America,* revised ed. (Baltimore: Johns Hopkins University Press, 1984), 149.

27. Singerman, "Jew as Racial Alien," 103.

28. Lothrop Stoddard, *Racial Realities in Europe* (1924), quoted in Singerman, "Jew as Racial Alien," 115. Singerman cites a startling number of race theorists and popular writers who subscribed to the Jew-as-Asian theory. These movements often used the Jewish/Asian identity to map the fear of the great "yellow peril" onto "the Jewish peril." Journalist Kenneth L. Roberts, in a popular *Saturday Evening Post* series, was one of many to use this tactic: "It must not be forgotten, moreover, that the Jews from Russia, Poland and nearly all of Southeastern Europe are not Europeans: they are Asiatics and in part, at least, Mongoloids. California long ago realized the importance of barring Mongoloids from white territory; but while they are barred in the West, they pour in by millions in the East" (Singerman, "Jew as Alien," 116–17).

29. Sander Gilman, *Freud, Race and Gender* (Princeton, N.J.: Princeton University Press, 1993), 49–92. For other recent and important discussions of the cultural meanings of circumcision, see James Boon, "Circumscribing Circumcision/Uncircumcision: An Essay Amidst the History of Difficult Description," in *Implicit Ethnographies,* ed. Stuart Schwartz (New York: Cambridge University Press, 1994), and Daniel Boyarin and Jonathan Boyarin, "Self-Exposure as Theory: The Double Mark of the Male Jew,"

in *Rhetorics of Self-Making,* ed. Debbora Battaglia (Berkeley: University of California Press, 1995).

30. Stoddard, *Racial Realities in Europe.*

31. Burton J. Hendrick, *The Jews in America* (1923), quoted in Singerman, "Jew as Racial Alien," 117.

32. Mark Twain, "Concerning the Jews" (1899), in *Mark Twain on the Damned Human Race,* ed. Janet Smith (New York: Noonday, 1962), 175. For a helpful discussion of Twain and Jews, see Sander Gilman, "Mark Twain and the Disease of the Jews," *American Literature* 65, no. 1 (March 1993).

33. Ibid., 168.

34. Police commissioner Theodore A. Bingham, "Foreign Criminals in New York," *North American Review,* September 1908: 383. Short on guts, the Jewish criminal, according to Bingham, was much more inclined toward the "receiving of stolen goods rather than to the more daring crimes of robbery and burglary" (384). This common trope of the Jewish criminal, which signaled the hidden and unnatural economic practices of the Jews, will come into play again shortly.

As even Bingham's discussion makes clear, the representation of the Jewish nonproducer goes hand in hand with the image of the Jew who makes money unnaturally, that is, without "producing" it. The Jewish usurer during the Middle Ages and the Renaissance, and later the Jewish banker, were the most common forms this representation took. On the Jew as usurer, and the usurer as Jew, see Benjamin N. Nelson, *The Idea of Usury: From Tribal Brotherhood to Universal Otherhood* (Princeton, N.J.: Princeton University Press, 1949); R. I. Moore, *The Formation of a Persecuting Society* (Cambridge, Mass.: Basil Blackwell, 1987); and Jacques Le Goff, *Your Money or Your Life: Economy and Religion in the Middle Ages,* trans. Patricia Ranum (New York: Zone Books, 1988).

35. Herbert Adams Gibbons, "The Jewish Problem: Its Relation to American Ideals and Interests," *The Century,* September 1921: 789.

36. Paul Scott Mowrer, "The Assimilation of Israel," *Atlantic Monthly,* July 1921: 105.

37. Edward Alsworth Ross, "The Hebrews of Eastern Europe in America," *Century,* September 1914: 786.

38. Mark Seltzer, *Bodies and Machines* (New York: Routledge, 1992), 149.

39. Henry James, *The American Scene* (New York: Scribner's, 1946 [1907]), 131–32.

40. Max Nordau, cited in David Biale, "Zionism as an Erotic Revolution," in *People of the Body: Jews and Judaism from an Embodied Perspective,* ed. Howard Eilberg-Schwartz (Albany: State University of New York Press, 1992), 285. Frank Norris's *McTeague* offers a typical literary example of a shriveled and grasping Jew, Zerkow, "a dry, shriveled old man [who] had ... eyes that had grown keen as those of a lynx from long searching amidst muck and debris; and claw-like, prehensile fingers" (New York: Penguin, 1982 [1899]), 43.

41. Lewis P. Brown, "The Jew Is Not a Slacker," *North American Review,* June 1918: 858.

42. Edwin J. Kuh, "The Social Disability of the Jew," *Atlantic Monthly,* April 1908: 438.

43. Brown has a similarly interesting take on the reformulation of Jew-as-bottom via their unproductive bodies. "Since it availed him not to whet his sword," Brown narrates, "he filled his coffers instead" ("The Jew Is Not a Slacker," 860).

44. Ross, "The Hebrews of Eastern Europe in America," 787.

45. Reid, "Because You're a Jew," 1215; Abram Lipsky, "Prejudice against Jews," *Independent,* December 17, 1908. For a fascinating illustrated account of a Jew who challenges his goyishe wife's ideas about weak Jews ("I clung to the tradition, or whatever it is, that Jews are rather cowardly") by fighting to protect her honor, see "The Experiences of a Jew's Wife," *American Magazine,* December 1914. In this article by an anonymous author, Jewish noncombativeness is chalked up to restraint rather than weakness. See also the somewhat bizarre assertions concerning Jewish men dominating boxing ("a majority of the prize-fighters in New York are really Jews who operate under Irish names") in the vastly paranoid article by Burton J. Hendrick, "The Jewish Invasion of America," *McClure's,* March 1913, and, of course, Robert Cohn, the boxing Jew in Hemingway's *The Sun Also Rises* (New York: Collier, 1986 [1926]).

46. One way these dynamics might be understood in relation to a more extended history is suggested by recent work by Marc Shell and Jody Greene, who have both traced the historic interplay between theories of unnatural sexual and economic practices from Aristotle and the Old Testament to the Renaissance. But while Shell does analyze *The Merchant of Venice,* neither he nor Greene addresses the implications of the conflation of sodomy and usury on Jewish identity. Neither, that is, addresses the fact that *usury* was a term whose meanings were fully imbedded in the thinking of Jewishness for centuries. If, as Jonathan Goldberg claims, sodomy retained a certain independent force of meaning when the medicalization of homosexuality occurred in the mid-nineteenth century, the Jew, via usury and the new concerns about the gold standard, bankers, and the late-nineteenth-century capitalist boom, seems to have retained his connections with (and as) the sodomite. Jody Greene, " 'You Must Eat Men': The Sodomitic Economy of Renaissance Patronage," *GLQ* 1, no. 2 (1994): 163–97. Marc Shell, *Money, Language and Thought* (Berkeley: University of California Press, 1982), and *The Economy of Literature* (Baltimore: Johns Hopkins University Press, 1978), 89–113.

47. Tom Watson, *Jeffersonian,* June 24, 1915: 1. For many observers of the Frank case, Frank's alleged sexual perversion *became* his visibility: "If you have seen any good pictures of him," one observer noted, "you will understand what I mean when I say that he looks like a pervert. It is a slightly significant fact, I think, that I sized him up as one the first time I saw him, before a whisper of the perversion testimony came out.... Others have told me they were impressed the same way" ("Old Police Reporter," quoted in Leonard Dinnerstein, *The Leo Frank Case* [New York: Columbia University Press, 1968], appendix D, 174). One of those others may have been Georgia governor Nathaniel Harris, who visited Frank in his prison cell: "Frank laughed—a queer sort of laugh—a laugh that showed, at least to me, a hard, careless heart, and the doubt, which I had about his guilt, was lessened greatly, as I heard the laugh, and looked into his face" (*Autobiography* [Macon, Georgia, 1925] 367). Watson states it most graphically: "[Frank] is a lascivious pervert, guilty of the crime that caused the Almighty to blast the Cities of the plain....[One need only see] those bulging, satyr eyes...the protruding fearfully sensual lips; and also the animal jaw" (quoted in C. Vann Woodward, *Tom Watson: Agrarian Rebel* [New York: Rinehart, 1938], 438). While none of these commentators overtly connects Frank's supposedly visible perversion to his Jewishness, the connection was unmistakably there (as Dinnerstein points out, "jewpervert" was even condensed into one word by one commentator on the case [98]). For an excellent discussion of the economic and sexual politics of the Frank case, see Nancy MacLean, "The Leo Frank Case Reconsidered: Gender and Sexual Politics in the Making of Reactionary Populism," *Journal of American History,* December 1991.

48. John Kaplan and Jon R. Waltz, *The Trial of Jack Ruby* (New York: Macmillan, 1965), 344.

49. Melvin M. Belli, *Dallas Justice: The Real Story of Jack Ruby and His Trial* (New York: David McKay, 1964), 167.

50. Although he also had a sense of his own triumph: "I'm a guy geared to fight... a little Heb being a big guy. One fellow, Mac, he said I was the toughest Jew he ever knew" (Elmer Gertz, *Moment of Madness: The People vs. Jack Ruby* [Chicago: Follett, 1968], 471).

51. F. Scott Fitzgerald, *The Great Gatsby* (New York: Collier, 1992 [1925]), 77.

52. "Chicago Boys Are Accused of New Crimes: Murder and Gland Robbery Traced to Them," *Chicago Tribune* (Paris ed.), June 3, 1924: 1.

53. Given the chains of associations I have begun to unravel, it is perhaps unsurprising that Ruby was "diagnosed" by court psychiatrists, "despite his heated denials, [as] latently homosexual." Kaplan and Waltz, *Trial of Jack Ruby*, 273. See also Belli, *Dallas Justice*, 95.

54. Hannah Arendt, "The Jew as Pariah: A Hidden Tradition," in *The Jew as Pariah: Jewish Identity and Politics in the Modern Age* (New York: Grove, 1978), 79. For Arendt, Chaplin need not be a Jew in order to be a "jew": "Chaplin has recently declared that he is of Irish and Gypsy descent, but he has been selected for discussion because, even if not himself a Jew, he has epitomized in an artistic form a character born of the Jewish pariah mentality" (69).

55. For a discussion of paranoia, sexuality, and relations between men, see Eve Kosofsky Sedgwick, *Between Men: English Literature and Male Homosocial Desire* (New York: Columbia University Press, 1985), esp. chapters 5 and 6.

56. Davenport quoted in Dobkowski, *Tarnished Dream*, 67.

57. Bingham, "Foreign Criminals in New York."

58. Dinnerstein, *Leo Frank Case*, 82.

59. Note also the ambiguity as to how the contents of the picked pocket *function* for the Jewish criminal, how the testicles function for Leopold and Loeb. Their imagined theft seems to have two intermingling meanings at once: an attempt to symbolically refurbish an always-inadequate Jewish relationship to masculinity, and an expression toward their victim of perverse Jewish sexual desire. In other words, the theft defines the Jew's relation to both masculinity and desire.

60. Willa Cather, "Scandal," in *Collected Stories* (New York: Vintage, 1992), 162.

61. Ibid., 163.

62. Eve Kosofsky Sedgwick, *Epistemology of the Closet* (Berkeley: University of California Press, 1990), 75.

63. For a recent consideration of rhetorical similarities between homophobia and anti-Semitism, see Alisa Solomon, "The Eternal Queer: In the Symbolic Landscape of Homophobia, We Are the Jews," *Village Voice*, April 27, 1993.

64. Gilman's writings on the subject include *The Jew's Body* (New York: Routledge, 1991), *The Case of Sigmund Freud: Medicine and Identity at the Fin de Siècle* (Baltimore: Johns Hopkins University Press, 1993), and *Freud, Race and Gender*. Other recent work that has tried to think about Jewishness and sexuality or gender includes Jay Geller, "A Glance at the Nose: Freud's Inscription of Jewish Difference," *American Imago*, Winter 1992, "The Unmanning of the Wandering Jew," *American Imago*, Summer 1992, and "(G)nos(e)ology: The Cultural Construction of the Other," in Eilberg-Schwartz, ed., *People of the Body*; David Biale, *Eros and the Jews: From Biblical Israel to Contemporary America* (New York: Basic Books, 1992); Paul Breines, *Tough*

Jews (New York: Basic Books, 1990); and Harry Brod, ed., *A Mensch among Men: Explorations in Jewish Masculinity* (Freedom, Calif.: Crossing Press, 1988).

65. Schlapp, M. G., M.D., and Alice E. Paulson, M.A., "Report on 10,000 Cases from the Clearing House for Mental Defectives," *Medical Record,* February 16, 1918. While there are 239 cases among Semites in a pool of seven thousand "mental defectives," the next highest category is Celtics, of whom 122 qualify.

66. For other examples in the American psychology literature, see, for example, Thomas Salmon, "Immigration and the Mixture of Races in Relation to the Mental Health of the Nation," in *Modern Treatment of Nervous and Mental Diseases,* ed. William White and Smith Ely Jelliffe, vol. 1; and A. Meyerson, M.D., "The 'Nervousness' of the Jew," *Mental Hygiene* 4 (1920).

67. Gilman, *Freud, Race and Gender,* 106. Discussing psychologist Richard von Krafft-Ebbing (130), Gilman discusses the European connection made between American and Jew with which I began this essay. On the meanings and permutations of neurasthenia as *the* American mental illness, see Tom Lutz's study *American Nervousness, 1903* (Ithaca, N.Y.: Cornell University Press, 1991). Lutz unfortunately does not consider the exchanges between "Americanness" and "Jewishness" that occurred via neurasthenia.

68. For an alternate consideration of Jewish hiddenness that focuses the terms of its discussion on Jewish linguistic practice, see Sander Gilman, *Jewish Self-Hatred: Anti-Semitism and the Hidden Language of the Jews* (Baltimore: Johns Hopkins University Press, 1986).

69. David Gerber, "Elite Anti-Semitism in the Marketplace," in Gerber, ed., *Anti-Semitism in American History,* 216; Salmon, "Immigration and the Mixture of Races," 258.

70. Cather, "Paul's Case" (1905), in *Collected Stories,* 179. For helpful discussions of queerness and Cather's story, see Eve Kosofsky Sedgwick, "Across Gender, Across Sexuality: Willa Cather and Others," in *Displacing Homophobia: Gay Male Perspectives in Literature and Culture,* ed. Ronald R. Butters, John M. Clum, and Michael Moon (Durham, N.C.: Duke University Press, 1988); and Judith Butler, "Dangerous Crossing: Willa Cather's Masculine Names," in *Bodies That Matter: On the Discursive Limits of "Sex"* (New York: Routledge, 1993).

8 / The Aromatics of Jewish Difference; or, Benjamin's Allegory of Aura

Jay Geller

"Das Jüdische war vielleicht oft nur ein fremdländisches, südliches (schlimmer: sentimales) Aroma, in unserer Produktion und in unserm Leben" [Jewishness was perhaps often only a foreign, southern (worse: sentimental) aroma, in our productive work and in our life]
  Walter Benjamin writing to Ludwig Strauss, September 11, 1912

How does one characterize the Jewish physiognomy of that perhaps last great physiognomist of our times, Walter Benjamin? Based on the purported content of his work, debates have raged between its so-called theological or Jewish and materialist or non-Jewish extremes: should his life be periodized or dialecticized or constellated about these poles?[1] Motifs and allusions are weighed; intents and iterations are divined. What qualifies him as Jewish: Zionism, messianism, exegetical ingenuity, concern with the ethical or the kabalistic, marginality, exile, the networks of parents and friends, his status as a "prophet" of modernity? His Jewishness, however, is not delimited by the matrix of psychobiography: the contradictions of being raised in an upper-class, assimilated Jewish household whose existence was repudiated by the dominant anti-Semitic culture. Neither is it confined to the schemata of intellectual history: his interaction with Jewish friends, thinkers, and writings.

This assay into Benjamin's Jewish physiognomy follows that strange, almost queasy aroma that Benjamin associates with Jewishness in his letter to the poet and Zionist Ludwig Strauss. But the smells exuded by Benjamin's corpus leave by definition an elusive trail. According to Benjamin, smell preserves but is not preserved in memory; it is amorphous and formless, indefinite and weighty (Benjamin 1969d:214). Moreover, while olfaction can evoke the collective experiences that in part constitute prehistory or *temps perdu,* smelling per se is an apparently nontransmissible individual experience. Consequently, Benjamin's aroma of Jewishness should not be able to contribute to a physiognomic portrait—and yet in his letter to Strauss Benjamin refers to "our productive work and our life." Jewish smelling had a collective component as well in the nineteenth and early twentieth centuries. Jewish difference in the figure of the stinking Jew—"hatred for the physical nature of the one who is hated [i.e., the Jew]" (letter to Gershom Scholem, October 22, 1917; Benjamin 1966:153; 1994:99)[2]—was a part of that period's collective experience. This essay examines how the atmosphere of Jewishness—the emissions (and omissions) of Jews and non-Jews alike—often bypassed consciousness, but left the trace of trauma upon Benjamin's corpus; and these traumatizing Jewish representations at times shaped the corpus in their image.

Benjamin's past, his Jewish prehistory, is, as he quotes Proust, "unmistakably present in some material object" (Benjamin 1969c:158). The object in question is Benjamin's corpus and its production of sentences and use of names. His sentences are the "entire muscular activity of the intelligible body" (Benjamin 1969d:214). They bear names, the archives of "nonsensuous [i.e., abstract] similarities, nonsensuous correspondences" (Benjamin 1978e:335), between words and worlds; and hence "what the name preserves but also predesignates [is] the habitus of a lived life" (Benjamin 1982b:1038). This study of Benjamin's Jewish physiognomy focuses upon two of his key terms that frequently intersect with one another as well as with the olfactory: *aura,* "the associations which...tend to cluster around the object of perception," (Benjamin 1969c:186), and *mimesis,* "the powerful compulsion...to become and behave like something else." (Benjamin 1978d:333) They both entail relations with otherness—as distant as the sacred or the ideal, as near as the woman or the Jew—and are particularly conditioned by the emanations of his anti-Semitic era.

Just as the terms *aura* and *mimesis* are interwoven in Benjamin's work, so this essay conjoins them with a number of other phenomena that fill the landscape that German Jews traveled in the nineteenth and early twentieth centuries: the traumas of anti-Semitism, including popular and scientific identifications of Jewish difference with stench and with the mimetic; the contradictory demands of bourgeois assimilation; a Jewish redemptive tradition correlated with scent. Benjamin's language is found to be frequently suffused with the social discourse of smells. Further, his work is juxtaposed with to-him-familiar contemporary writings, including those of Freud and Klages, which render these connections both more explicit and more explicitly. Finally, reading Horkheimer and Adorno's olfactory analysis of anti-Semitism as a triangulation of Freud's theory of the repression of smell and Benjamin's discussion of mimesis brings the correspondences between Benjamin's terminology and his situation as a German Jew more to the fore.

In his life Benjamin recognized that he could not repress either extreme of the dialectic, the duality, of German Jewishness: "German and Jew stand opposite one another like related extremes" (letter to Gershom Scholem, October 22 1917; 1994:98); he realized that this self-characterized "last European" (cf. Arendt 1969:17–18) could not escape "my Jewish self" (letter to Florens Christian Rang, November 18, 1923; Benjamin 1994:215). And in his work, social discourse about the stinking Jewish mimic, like the aromas of anti-Semitism and piety, seeped past his conscious intention and left mimetic traces there that shaped his historian's task and his Jewish physiognomy. "And since similarity is the organ of experience, this means: the name can only be recognized in contexts of experience. Only there is its essence, that is, its linguistic essence, knowable" (Benjamin 1982b:1038). With the smell-laden, Jewish-tainted names *aura* and *mimesis,* Benjamin's writings emit a symptomatic scent of his times as well as seek to rescue smell and mimesis from their anti-Semitic identifications and release their redemptive possibilities. Perhaps because scent is less implicated in the domination of vision than is the more frequent trope of "image," following both smell and Benjamin's discussion of it may aid us in recovering the "generative and inconspicuous experiences" lying "closed in the hard shell of incommunicability" (Benjamin 1972g: 275). Further, through such a historical reconstruction of Benjamin's Jewish physiognomy, "the lifework is preserved in this work and at the same time canceled; in the lifework, the era" (Benjamin 1969f: 263 [Thesis xvii]).

An Ideal Reading of Smell

As can be seen in the title of Susan Buck-Morss's recent study of the *Passagenwerk*, or "Arcades" project, *The Dialectics of Seeing*, the visual rather than the olfactory dimension is perceived to have primacy in the work of Walter Benjamin. After all, seeing, seeing resemblances, is something the bespectacled Benjamin claimed to be very good at (cf. Benjamin 1972h:261; Stoessel 1983:178). This privileging of the optical is coeval with the reception of Benjamin in the United States; the first two collections of his essays bear the titles *Illuminations* and *Reflections*. Even a cursory glance at the critical literature shows a plethora of ocular images employed about and in his work. That literature is rife with references to dialectical images, the flash, phantasmagoria, and the optical unconscious. Cultural materialist analyses focus upon Benjamin's late work on the visual media of photography and film. In discussions of Benjamin's notion of "aura," attention is directed at its visual aspect. For example, Benjamin glosses an image from Baudelaire's poem "Correspondances" — "Man wends his way through forests of symbols / Which look at him with their familiar glances" (cit. Benjamin 1969c:181, 189) — with the remark that "to perceive the aura of an object we look at means to invest it with the ability to look at us in return" (Benjamin 1969c:188). On another occasion Benjamin himself defines aura as "the unique appearance of a distance, however close it may be" (Benjamin 1969e:222). Due, albeit passing, mention is made of the synesthetic component of (auratic) experience — for example, the smell of colors — and an occasional commentary upon Benjamin's discussion of the modern sensorium locates a dialectical relationship between vision and touch that generates a transgressive knowing (cf. Taussig 1993; Frisby 1986). Yet vision remains paramount. Images as both captivating and, potentially, liberating are seen to make up both the object — whether of nineteenth-century Paris or of Berlin in 1900 — and the subject of his critical practice. These snapshots that Benjamin has passed down to us have an aura of their own, even as we hold them in our smudgy hands. They seem to confirm our own ocular view of the catastrophic history of capitalist society: from the modernist panopticon to the postmodernist circulation of simulacra.

"The sense of sight," Susan Buck-Morss (1992:24) writes, "was privileged in this phantasmagoric sensorium of modernity," but Benjamin's images also tell us another history, one that his commentators and perhaps he too were unconscious of.[3] Marleen Stoessel (1983: 11) begins her analysis of Benjamin's notion of aura thus: "In Greek and Latin [aura] signifies *air* and *breath*." *Aura* begins with smell. According to the first definition in *Webster's New World Dictionary* (1984), an aura is "an invisible emanation or vapor, as the aroma of flowers." More to the point, when Benjamin (1969c:185) first introduces *aura* to his argument in "On Some Motifs in Baudelaire," the term is appositively defined as a "breath of prehistory [that] surrounds" a thing. An aura envelops the object with a perceptible — smellable — air of mystery; the verb *umwittert*, translated as "surrounds," conveys the sense of something mysterious or uncanny that is tacitly sensed, and it stems from the verb *wittern*, "to scent." Despite the primacy afforded vision in discussions of aura, odors play more than an etymological role as the heterogeneous residue of scent wafts its way through Benjamin's analysis of aura and the *mémoire involontaire*, experience (*Erfahrung*) and art, Baudelaire and Proust. Is Benjamin's discussion of smell just the accident of Baudelaire and Proust's sensory predilections or the facticity of olfactory phenomenology (cf. Howes 1987)? Conversely, does the play of scents that perfume his argument have a clear-cut intent such as the elaboration of an osmics, a science of smell? Benjamin always fought and thought against the merely contingent and the purely intentional. Olfaction offers a necessary interpretive key to the utopian elements of Baudelaire and Proust, contributes to Benjamin's critique of Kant's aesthetic and bourgeois culture, and gives intimations of redemption. The aroma secreted by Benjamin's notion of aura evokes both what is prehistoric and what is outside of history. Because olfactory emanations from the aura elicit the really disgusting and the disgustingly real, attending to them would redeem a material dimension that had been shrouded by a phantasmagoria of perfumes, evacuated by the urban renewal instituted by the likes of a Parent-Duchatelet or a Haussmann, or rendered indifferent to a subject subjected by a "complex kind of training" (Benjamin 1969c:175) into anosmia. But more, the telltale smells that hover about these sites are the textual effects of the trauma of Benjamin's German-Jewish prehistory; they are transmogrifications of the smell of the Jew: the "foreign . . . sentimental aroma" of Jewishness and the *foetor Judaicus*, the Jewish stench.

Smell makes up a significant portion of the data of the *mémoire in-volontaire* that Benjamin arrays. In the Proust essay Benjamin (1969d: 214) comments that the "bottommost" stratum of the *mémoire in-volontaire* is

> one in which the materials of memory no longer appear singly, as images, but tell us about a whole, amorphously and formlessly, indefinitely and weightily, in the same way as the weight of his net tells a fisherman about his catch. Smell [*Der Geruch*] — that is the sense of weight of someone who casts his nets into the sea of the *temps perdu*.

Years later the smells of Proust would return in his discussion of Baudelaire's lyric chronicle of shock, the loss of experience, and the decline of aura in the modern world: "The scent [*Der Geruch*] is the inaccessible refuge of the *mémoire involontaire*" (Benjamin 1969c: 184). This inaccessibility recalls the unapproachable aspect of the auratic and thereby confirms his comment that the data of the *mé-moire involontaire* corresponds to auratic experience. Smell, tradition-ally considered one of the proximate senses, seems polar opposite to an experience described as a certain pathos of distance.[4] Even the Kantian description of smell as "taste at a distance" (Kant 1974:36 [§19]) is insufficient mediation. Smell's solicitation of the *mémoire involontaire* provides aura with a temporal dimension, a distance, such that it promises redemptive possibilities beyond mere nostalgia for a "certain hour in one's life" (*Erlebnis*; Benjamin 1969c:163). In his discussion of the interconnected correspondences elicited in Baude-laire by fragrance, Benjamin (1969c:184) describes how smell effects on the individual level of memory what he elsewhere ascribes to vi-sion on the collective level of history: a scent "will ally itself only with the same.... [It] deeply drugs the sense of time [*Zeitverlaufs*]. A scent [*Duft*] may drown years in the odor [*Dufte*] it recalls." In this passage Benjamin describes how smell anesthetizes homogeneous se-rial time, the rationalized temporality of modernity; this enables the individual to recognize "a memory as it flashes up" (Benjamin 1969f: 255 [Thesis vi]) and leap across the years to salvage the past.

As his depiction of olfactory workings indicates, not only does the *mémoire involontaire* provide the closest analog to the critical histo-rian's experience of the *Jetztzeit,* the messianic "time of the now" (Benjamin 1969f:261, 263 [Theses xiv, A]), but this discussion of re-membered smells provides a mirror of, if not a model for, his determination of the form of the historical object as a dialectical image. Like the recollection of an odor, the historian "rescues" the image by blasting it out of the "homogeneous course of history" (*Verlauf der Geschichte*; Benjamin 1969f:263 [Thesis xvii]; cf. Benjamin 1982a:1: 592 [N9, 7; 9a, 3]). Such apperceptions take place in a "moment of danger" (Benjamin 1969f:255 [Thesis vi])⁵ by someone who is, in a Baudelairean passage cited by Benjamin (1969c:164), "in all the corners sniffing [*flairant*] out the dangers or dodges."

Yet such appropriations are called forth by the object: smell solicits smell, and the mimetic character of "the monadological structure" of the image demands its recognition (cf. N10, 3; Benjamin 1983–84: 23). The objective character of such olfactory and visual cognitions extends beyond such solicitation; each apperception opens up a realm of objectivity. The scent of a woman or of a cookie simmering in tea opens upon another scene: an objective realm. Thus we cannot, like a Kantian subjectivity armed with its schemata, its infusions of meaning, possess the smell, but it can like Valéry's fragrant flower possess us (cf. Benjamin 1969c:186–87). The smell is embedded in an experiential continuum (*Erfahrung*) of contiguous relations with memory traces that may never have been registered by individual consciousness as well as with the repetitions of ritualized collective life like the cliché, common sense, and the seasonal festival. The objective character of the image is different. Unlike olfaction, vision is tied to a notion of intention: "Vision does not enter into the form of existence . . . which is devoid of all intention and certainly does not itself appear as intention" (Benjamin 1977:35). But Benjamin eventually reconfigures the historian's purview such that the constellated ruins of a culture dispersed seemingly haphazardly across the historical landscape crystallize to form the monadic image.

In the "Arcades" project, Benjamin's reconstruction of nineteenth-century Paris, images of images far exceed references to smells. Smell and vision were opposed in a series of antinomies that, at least with regard to these senses, were more deductive than dialectical: prehistory versus the modern, use value versus commodity, *Erfahrung* versus *Erlebnis,* nostalgia versus history, individual versus collective, and so on. Benjamin sketches the contours of the opposition between smell and vision in a chiasmic series of notes written during his earliest efforts on the project (Benjamin 1982b:1033–34 [O° 75–77]):

The arcade as temple of Aesclepius. Spahall. Taking a constitutional. Arcades (as spa halls) in ravines. At Schuls-Tarasp, at Ragaz. The 'gorge' as landscape ideal during our parents' time. How the sense of smell awakens when striking upon far-reaching 'memories.' As I stood before a shop window in St. Moritz and saw mother-of-pearl [aus Perlmutt] pocket knives as 'memories,' it seemed to me as if I could now smell them.

What is sold in the arcades are souvenirs. The 'souvenir' is the form of the commodity in the arcade. One always only buys souvenirs in this and that arcade. Rise of the souvenir industry. How the manufacturer knows it. The customs official of industry.

How after many years visual memories surface changed. The pocket knife that came to mind, as I happened upon one (decorated) with the place name between mother-of-pearl [perlmutternem] Edelweiss in the shop window at St. Moritz, tasted and smelled.

In this sequence Benjamin opposes past memories and present souvenirs, accidental recollections and manufactured (intentional) mementos, the personal and the impersonal, landscapes and arcades, ideals and industries, experiences and commodities, unchanging odors and transformed sights. Smell is associated with imbibing, not buying; with familial relations—"the time of our *parents*," "*mother*-of-pearl"—not relations of production like the manufacturer and the customs official. Benjamin (1978b:15–16) took pride in his own writing because he never employed the first-person pronoun except in letters. Such a personal sensory faculty as smell hence had no place in a critical analysis of the Parisian arcades.

After this moment, smell largely fades from his attention. In more than nine hundred published pages of notes and quotes that followed these first notebook jottings, smell is mentioned only once, as an urban problem, and then only to be displaced onto the visual register. Benjamin cites from an 1823 history of the shawl (Rey 1823:201–2; cit. Benjamin 1982a:1:630 [O8a, 2]):

It is by the mental faculty, called reminiscence, that the wishes of the man condemned to the brilliant captivity of the cities repair to a rural abode, his primitive habitation, or at least to the possession of a simple and tranquil garden. His eyes yearn to rest upon the green sward (away) from the weariness of the counter or the burning clarity of the salon lamp. His sense of smell [Son odorat], wounded by the emanations of a pestilential mire, seeks out the perfume [le parfum] exhaled by flowers. A border of humble and sweet violets carry him off to ecstasy.

In this passage the urban dweller, the bourgeois proper, manufactures apotropaic images, floral designs whose imagined scents serve to counter the poisonous odors of the city and restore the viewer to heights of nostalgic ecstasy. Pleasant smells do not exist as part of the urban landscape. Such odors are only a part of the bourgeoisie's prehistory, its family romance; the exhalations of the pictured violets transform the founding fantasies of the cultured bourgeoisie—the male bourgeois individual imagining himself as a moral aristocrat leisurely enjoying his country garden amid a scene of domestic bliss—into idyllic memories (see Schlegel 1962:61–63). This singular reference to the stench of the nineteenth century, indeed one that delimits the stink to an appositive clause that is overcome by the urban dweller's *vision* of smell, suggests that Benjamin succumbed to the bourgeoisie's own olfactory division of the world: the deodorized public sphere and the perfumed nostalgia of the private.[6]

The utopian vision of a scent-free public space, that is, of a space free of the stinking masses—the crowd—who threatened to inundate that space, was already projected by the philosopher who propounded the ideal of a public sphere emptied of all obstacles to interaction, Kant. Kant considered stench as emblematic both of crowds and of the olfactory sense itself: "disgusting odors [*Gegenstände des Ekels*] (especially in crowded places) always outnumber pleasant ones" (1974: 36, 37 [§19, §20]; also see Stallybrass and White 1986:139–40). Consequently, Kant considered smell an expendable sense. Benjamin, like Kant before him, found the smell of crowds unbearable. Recalling in "A Berlin Chronicle" the hated stairways of his old school, Benjamin (1978b:52) described experiencing the invasion of odors emitted by the "herd" of fellow schoolmates: "defenselessly exposed to the bad odors emanating from all the bodies [*den schlechten Ausdünstungen*] pressing so closely against mine." Through the linkage of pleasant smells to prehistory—whether this configuration is understood as aura or as nostalgia—and the virtual avoidance of unpleasant ones, Benjamin is not just recuperating bourgeois fantasy, he is acting out the memory of his specifically German Jewish bourgeois upbringing. Yet after examining the shocking contradictions intrinsic to that origin and the trauma they generate, the seemingly one-sided determination of smell will become more complicated.

The Shock of the Jew

Benjamin was raised a German Jew in an anti-Semitic Germany. Political anti-Semitism may have been in abeyance as he was reaching maturity, but not the Jewish Question.[7] In Germany the everyday anti-Semitic attitudes of the non-Jewish population met the self-deluding nonrecognition of liberal assimilationist Jewry; where the former held for Jewish difference, a belief founded upon a panoply of particular character and physical traits, the latter publicized Jewish sameness, a notion based upon Enlightenment ideas and economic self-confidence. Benjamin, like other German Jewish intellectuals of his generation, rejected both their elders' self-delusions and their nostalgic, inconspicuous religiosity that passed for Judaism (cf. Kafka 1953:74–85; Scholem 1980); Benjamin and his peers also knowingly maintained a rarely requited love affair with German culture (Goldstein 1912:192; cf. Arendt 1969:30–31; Scholem 1976b:88–89).

As early as 1912, Benjamin, playing both historical object and subject, began to discern within himself the monadological structure created by the tension between these dialectical extremes, the "duality" of the German and the Jewish. This recognition arose during Benjamin's profound intellectual involvement in the 1911–12 controversies over the nature of Jewish identity and the possibility of a German-Jewish symbiosis (cf. Smith 1991; Rabinbach 1985). At this time the historical economist Werner Sombart followed up his massive indictment of Jewish character and participation in the development of capitalism *The Jews and Modern Capitalism* with an even more controversial discursus entitled *The Future of the Jews*. There he offered his solution to the "greatest problem for humanity... the Jewish problem" (Sombart 1912:6; cit. Smith 1991:321). Because the Jews by nature are not suitable to enter the higher ranks of society, he suggested a separate but equal coexistence between Western Jews and Germans. Numerous Jewish and non-Jewish intellectuals responded to Sombart's authoritative pronouncements, many of which were collected in Arthur Landesberger's *Baptizing Jews* (1912).

Soon thereafter came another round of debate with the appearance of Moritz Goldstein's "German-Jewish Parnassus." In the distinguished non-Jewish nationalist journal *Der Kunstwart*, Goldstein offered a Zionist response to the Jewish Question and hectored his readers to recognize the reality of anti-Semitism and repudiate all forms of assimilationist self-denial. But just as Sombart had asserted that the Jews dominated the economic and the political, so Goldstein asserted that they monopolized the intellectual life of Germany. And his solution was not dissimilar: the Jews should abandon illusory hopes for integration, renounce what they cannot properly do—to write in German as Germans—and instead (re)turn to Jewish identities, Jewish sources, and, eventually, Jewish languages. While Benjamin did not participate in the series of responses that soon ensued, he did report to Ludwig Strauss that he had been following the controversy and read all of the articles. In that letter of September 11, 1912, Benjamin goes on to write: "If we are two-sided, Jewish and German, then we were until now totally and affirmatively focused upon the German; Jewishness was perhaps often only a foreign, southern (worse: sentimental) aroma, in our productive work and in our life" (cit. Smith 1991:329). Until these debates forced him to begin thinking through what it meant to be a German Jew and thus to make "Judaism important and problematic to me" (letter to Ludwig Strauss, October 10, 1912; cit. Benjamin 1972-:2.3:836), the Jewish extreme of this child of assimilated parents was just an atmosphere, an aroma.

Smell is the code word here for Benjamin's "Jewish" childhood. In *Berlin Chronicle* he records an odor-laden reminiscence of reading *New Companion of German Youth,* a gift he received one Christmas. That scene typified the hybrid existence of assimilated German Jews: they marked their Germanness by sharing the festivity, if not the piety, of their Gentile neighbors (Scholem 1980:28–29; cf. 1981:35: "even his grandparents celebrated Christmas as a 'national festivity'"). Such celebrations also emphasized the largely negative character of their Jewishness: their Judaism was defined by its distinction from that of their "coreligionists" in Poland and Russia. The smells (*Düfte*) and aromas (*Aromata*) that exuded from young Walter's book also were indicative of German-Jewish identity. They emanate from adventures in a Mediterranean past and suggest an "ancestral portrait." When assimilated German Jews like Benjamin's parents traced their ancestry, they tended to turn their noses toward the southern climes of the aristocratic Sephardim,[8] and certainly away from the east of the stinking *Urjuden* (primitive Jews; see Aschheim 1982:chap. 3; and later in the present essay). And these odors intermix with the smells of bourgeois holidaymaking.

In a recollection adjacent to this one, more sentimental scents come to the fore. Fragrance, the "sweet lavender scent" of sachets hanging in a linen cupboard, signals the "paradise" of the bourgeois home (Benjamin 1978b:53–55; 1972h:278–80).[9] But this nostalgic idyll is divided against itself. The clearly detailed image of the sweetly scented home is contiguously opposed by a dark, inaccessible space in which his mother's dressing gowns were hung.

Benjamin then evokes the uncanny breath of his own prehistory that surrounds this reminiscence of the bourgeois phantasmagoria of possessions and sensations. He recalls how the young Walter dreams of a ghost who arises from the dark reaches of that inaccessible corner of the home in order to steal the paradise of goods. The ghost takes these possessions without removing them; he compares this to a spirits' banquet in which all is consumed by the dead but nothing seems to be eaten or drunk. The well-lit warehouse of domestic tranquility and goods is possessed; the silks and the sweet-smelling sachets are doubled.

This doubling suggests that it may be more accurate to describe the aroma from his youth as two scents, one noisome and one more salubrious. As he later wrote to Strauss, until this new problematizing of the Jew in himself, what he knew of Jewishness consisted "only of antisemitism and an indefinite piety" (letter to Ludwig Strauss, October 10, 1912; cit. Benjamin 1972-:2.3:836). During the next several years, and to different degrees throughout the remainder of his life, Benjamin endeavored to discover the positive content of Jewish life and spirit rather than simply inhale the negative and evanescent aromas that surrounded him in his youth. Yet, while the odor of piety might have evaporated, the stench of anti-Semitism would trail after him—first contributing to his 1915 decision to sever ties to the youth movement with which he was so involved at the time of the *Kunstwart* controversy and ultimately poisoning him at the French-Spanish border in 1940. Where Benjamin the critical historian sought out the messianic sparks, the now-times of the past, in the present he continually encountered the mythic repetitions of an unredemptive anti-Semitism.

Anti-Semitism inhabited the life of the assimilated German Jew. Yet its everydayness had a doubly deodorizing effect. On the one hand, the routinization of anti-Semitic attitudes and expressions reduced them to background noise all but beyond conscious recognition. On the other hand, because the persistence of anti-Semitism did not harmonize with the belief of the Jews of Benjamin's parents' generation that they were—or at least were on the verge of being—fully accepted by their Gentile neighbors, they generated rationalizations to silence the dissonance. That generation represented anti-Semitism either as a class-determined atavism that was breathing its last, as a reflex that once rationally reflected upon would be overcome, or as a pretext or disguise for other problems and concerns such as political mobilization and class conflict.[10] Hence they endeavored to fend off with excuses or a forced, seemingly overindulgent smile—with what Benjamin (1969c: 176) would call "mimetic shock absorber[s]"—the recognition that anti-Semitism was intrinsic to Jewish/non-Jewish relations as well as to any particular manifestation of anti-Jewish sentiment.

These responses by German Jewry to their anti-Semitic surroundings were much like those of individuals to an urban crowd as described by Poe in "The Man of the Crowd." Benjamin (1969c:171) cites Poe to illustrate the experience of shock:

> By far the greater number of those who went by had a satisfied business-like demeanor, and seemed to be thinking only of making their way through the press. Their brows were knit, and their eyes rolled quickly; when pushed against by fellow-wayfarers they evinced no symptom of impatience, but adjusted their clothes and hurried on. Others, still a numerous class, were restless in their movements, had flushed faces, and talked and gesticulated to themselves, as if feeling in solitude on account of the very denseness of the company around. When impeded in their progress, these people suddenly ceased muttering, but redoubled their gesticulations, and awaited, with an absent and overdone smile upon the lips, the course of the persons impeding them. If jostled, they bowed profusely to the jostlers, and appeared overwhelmed with confusion.

Moreover, although neither Poe nor Benjamin notes it here, the crowd, as perceived from Kant to Benjamin to Horkheimer and Adorno, stinks. "The shock experience which the passer-by has in the crowd" (Benjamin 1969c:176) is a smell.

Consciousness could attempt to fend off shocks. As Benjamin (1969c: 160–62), drawing upon the work of Freud and other psychoanalysts, points out, such defense against external stimuli is a primary purpose for consciousness—that is, for the Enlightenment ego in which German Jewry placed such faith. But ego defenses such as denial or fright do not always succeed. Sometimes such shocks are traumatic, immobilizing the individual until they are repeatedly worked through and laid to rest. More often these repeated shocks served to discipline their victims by eliciting mimetic responses. To illuminate how the seemingly chaotic plethora of modern stimuli serve to train the individual, Benjamin resituates Poe's characters in the factories described by Marx.

Poe's "pedestrians act as if they had adapted themselves to the machines and could express themselves only automatically. Their behavior is a reaction to shocks." Benjamin then repeats the line from "The Man of the Crowd": "If jostled, they bowed profusely to the jostlers" (1969c:176).

If not intended as allegory for the Jewish condition, Benjamin's citation of Poe does evoke a number of Jewish associations.[11] For instance, such jostling had been an everyday occurrence for Jews in Poe's time.[12] Like all shock, anti-Semitism threatens to overcome the individual (ego): it both denies self-determined existence to the Jews and seeks to impose its own determinations of Jewish identity upon them. In an oppressive society, filled with legal, administrative, and social—as well as physical—obstacles to self-determination that constantly remind the oppressed of their status, victimizing shocks become a form of discipline and servility a trained response. They become the image their oppressors seek to impose upon them. In the wake of emancipation the legal conditions and the forms of jostling may have changed, but anti-Semitism remained an ongoing experience of shock. If they were now acting the self-righteous German rather than the passive "Jew," the shock of anti-Semitism still shaped the behavior, experience, and identities of these German Jews.

Rare Shock Tests

The shock discipline of one generation became the trauma of the next. Benjamin was of the generation that sought to disavow the self-delusions of liberal, bourgeois Jewry (cf. Ash 1989:11–13). Nonetheless, Benjamin's appropriation of the work of Carl Jung, Ludwig Klages, and other politically retrograde, frequently anti-Semitic writers has presented a problem for Benjamin's many readers.[13] For example, one of Benjamin's biographers, Julian Roberts (1982:218), serves up apologies in the face of Benjamin's failure to explicitly repudiate their anti-Semitic positions if not their work: "He knew perfectly well that Klages was an anti-Semite and near Fascist, and, what is more important, he wove Klages's ideas brilliantly into his own critique of that position."

Apologetic also seems to be Benjamin's mode; unlike Roberts, however, Benjamin offers his apologies with an ironic edge. With regard to the leader of L'Action française, Léon Daudet, who sought to liberate France from the twin perils of syphilis-induced degeneration and of judaization, but who also wrote "Baudelaire. La malaise et l'aura," an essay extensively extracted in the "Arcades" project (see 1982a: 1:318, 340 [J10, 1–5; J20, 8]),[14] Benjamin (1969d:206) comments that his "political folly is too gross and too obtuse to do much harm to his admirable talent."[15] In one of the rare mentions of anti-Semitism in the "Arcades" project, Benjamin (1982a:2:781 [W8a, 6], 795 [W16, 2]) notes without comment the "filiation of antisemitism with Fourierism" with reference to Fourier's "hate" for the Jews and his successor Toussenel's 1845 *The Jews: Kings of the Era.*

An anti-Semitic utterance of Baudelaire also appears in the J folder. There Benjamin (1982a:1:380 [J40,1]) seems to dismiss Baudelaire's anti-Semitism as a peculiarly French form of humor, *une gauloisserie:* "Baudelaire's gallic joke: 'Beautiful conspiracy to organize for the extermination of the Jewish race. / The Jewish *librarians* and witnesses of the *redemption.*' Ch[arles] B[audelaire]: Oeuvres II p 666 (Mon coeur mis à nu) Céline has carried on the tradition (jocular murderer and thief)." And yet Baudelaire's "joke" could not have been more pointedly directed at Benjamin, collector of books, virtual resident of the Bibliothèque Nationale, messianic thinker, and exile from Nazi Germany. When Benjamin refers to Baudelaire's joke and its appropriation by Céline in "The Paris of the Second Empire in Baudelaire," he subsumes its call for the extermination of the Jews under the category of fascism. He apposes the remark and its reception to the insight that the "cult of the joke...became an inalienable component of fascist propaganda" (1972a:516).

A conversation between Scholem and Benjamin during their last meeting, in February 1938, also suggests that there may be another ironic tinge to this designation of "gauloisserie" as well. Scholem (1981:212–13) reports:

> [Benjamin] told me that those of Céline's admirers who were influential on the literary scene got around taking a clear stand on [his anti-Semitic polemic *Bagatelles for a Massacre*] with this explanation: 'Ce n'est qu'un blague' — meaning that it really was nothing but a joke. I tried to show him how frivolous such a recourse to an irresponsible phrase was. Benjamin said his own experience had convinced him that latent anti-Semitism was very widespread even among the leftist intelligentsia and that only very few non-Jews... were, so to speak, constitutionally free from it.

Benjamin did not trust even those French writers like Gide who adopted the moralistic high ground and suggested that *Bagatelles* perhaps ought to be seen as "anything other than a game"; even if they will not excuse Céline's apparent intentions—the desire "for stirring up banal passions"—Benjamin wonders whether or not they oppose the possible consequences of the book (letter to Max Horkheimer, April 16, 1938, Benjamin 1994:558). The reaction to Céline indicates an endemic anti-Semitism that may not be able to be subsumed under a theory of fascism. Baudelaire's comment then *may be* merely a joke, a cliché, *banal,* a part of the collective experience and hence employed unconsciously. Indeed, Benjamin's relative lack of commentary on the anti-Semitic excrescences of these exemplary nineteenth- and early-twentieth-century figures highlights the ordinariness of their comments.[16] Commenting upon them might suggest, in the manner of his parents' generation, that they are shockingly exceptional. The danger of such anti-Semitic utterances lay in the fact that they do not appear to shock.

Yet Benjamin's insight into Gide's reaction to Céline—that recognizing anti-Semitism is not the same as foreclosing its effects—also applied to Benjamin himself, except that the antecedent of *its* shifted from anti-Semitism to recognition of it. The traumatic prehistories of anti-Semitism and Jewish response as well as the persistence of anti-Jewish attitudes mediated Benjamin's own situation and left their mark. They inflected his writing in and as a German.[17] His letters, autobiographical works, and critical practice are neither inured to nor manifestly injured by anti-Semitism, but they do exhibit or enact the attempt to work through trauma: repetitions with and without transformation, anxious anticipations that arise from a prehistory of shock, construction of monumental notions that like fetishes implicate but do not designate some traumatic cognition.

At times Benjamin appears to repeat the faults of the fathers—at the mercy of events and of German identifications. In the wake of Rathenau's assassination in 1922, the Berlin pogrom of November 5, 1923, and Hitler's beer-hall putsch several days later (November 18), Benjamin writes to his friend Florenz Christian Rang about the "most terrible moments" of the German people. Benjamin expresses his deep hesitation about letting his "Jewish self" be counted among those endorsing Rang's repudiation of anti-Jewish attitudes and actions. He feels muted because these violent anti-Semitic outbursts are a German matter about which a German and not a German-identifying Jew like himself is called upon to speak out, to write a public response like the one Rang solicited from him. Wondering whether he can even speak in concert with non-Jewish Germans about the situation in Germany, he concludes:

> [The] core of the current [i.e., November 1923] Jewish question [is that] Jews today endanger even the best German cause ["true Germanness"] for which they stand up *publicly,* because their public German expression is necessarily [perceived as] venal (in the deeper sense). It cannot produce a certificate of authenticity.... Everything having to do with German-Jewish relationships that has a visible impact does so to their detriment; furthermore, nowadays a salutary complicity obligates those individuals of noble character among both people to be silent about their ties." (1994:215)

Anti-Semitism from this perspective inconveniences the Jew — sometimes unto death — but basically it is a German problem, an aberration, that the Germans are obligated to correct for their own sake. Is this conclusion the self-delusion on the part of a thinker who conceded in this letter to Rang that emigration to Palestine was out of the question since he could not *not write* in German and who later, when exile was not a matter of choice, imagined he would be exhibited in America as "the last European"? Perhaps, but by placing emphasis on this speech about the cessation of public speech and by overcoming his usual reticence to discuss current events in letters (cf. Scholem 1981: 23), this communication from Benjamin (unlike the "communication" that he eventually submits to Rang for publication, which eschews the Jewish Question)[18] evidences, rather, that this time the shock of pervasive anti-Semitism and negative Jewish identifications could not be parried.

More often Benjamin's autobiographical writings, such as the fragments of "A Berlin Chronicle," composed in Ibiza in 1932, signal how the experience of growing up Jewish in an anti-Semitic culture left a lingering anxiety in his interactions. He breaks off these reminiscences after speculating about the "shock" of a *pas encore vu* experience and extrapolating the consequences of such a call from the future. To illustrate his speculation he describes his recollection of a "forgotten" fact. One night Benjamin's father had informed the young Walter in great detail about a relative's death, but the reminiscing narrator only now realizes what was left out of that conversation: the cause of his cousin's death, syphilis. *Après coup* this particular detail gives the conversation meaning. Its particularity also explains the elder Benjamin's failure to mention it; because of its venereal associations the label "syphilis" was replaced by his generation with either silence or euphemism (Benjamin 1978b:59–60).

This forgotten detail from a time prior to sexual maturity insinuates an anxious prehistory to the account. It shapes both the entire reminiscence — in the "Berlin Chronicle" a walk through Berlin serves up a montage of chronotopes of Benjamin's developing sexual desires and his encounters with, by definition, diseased prostitutes — and his later life. The fear of contracting syphilis surrounded any anticipated sexual encounter with an aura of anxiety, thereby conditioning any number of social relationships. The forgotten fact of syphilis is also a trope of Jewish diasporic history: by the turn of the century syphilis began to assume a Jewish aura as Jews increasingly shared associations with diseased sexuality and reproduction (both biological and artificial) that threatened to erode identities and foreclose a future (Geller 1992a; also Gilman 1993). The uncontrolled mimesis of the "Great Imitator" syphilis and of the assimilating Jew augured the demise of the bourgeois order. And with August Wassermann's development of the reagent test, syphilis would assume a Jewish name; a "positive Wassermann" became synonymous with the disease. For Benjamin, who within a year of recalling this nighttime conversation would be composing his essays on language, similarity, and the mimetic faculty, the forgotten detail may have had particular pertinence; the constellation of syphilis with two key foci of Benjamin's work, names and mimesis, as well as with the Jews suggests an even greater resonance to this "call from the future."

The tacit relationship between the forgotten fact and Jewishness is rendered more explicit in the chronicle itself during another moment of anxious anticipation. Benjamin describes wandering the streets of Berlin on Rosh Hashanah in search of the reform synagogue: "an immense pleasure filled me with blasphemous indifference toward the service [Gottesdienst], but exalted the street in which I stood as if it had already intimated to me the services of procurement [Kupplerdienste] it was later to render to my awakened drive" (Benjamin 1978b: 53). "Dienst" performs a metonymic service of conjoining sect and sexuality.

Benjamin preserves both scenes, unlike most of "A Berlin Chronicle," when he reworks it into Berlin Childhood around 1900. The recollections, now given the headings "Sexual Awakening" and "News of a Death," immediately follow one another near the beginning of the altered version as if the awakening of sexuality was to be complemented with its demise (1972h:251–52).[19] Although in "A Berlin Chronicle," these scenes are but two of a series of discontinuous moments and places by which sexuality comes to represent Benjamin's self-identity, that he later makes them representative of sexuality suggests they are emblematic of the narrative trajectory implicit in the "Chronicle." Scholem's reservations about the retention of "Sexual Awakening" in *Berlin Childhood* appear to confirm that the other focus generating this trajectory is Jewishness: "I urgently advised [Benjamin] to delete this section because it was the only one in the whole book in which Jewish matters were explicitly mentioned, thus creating the worst possible associations" (Benjamin 1994:401n3). Such associations together with the forgotten fact of syphilis transform this chronicled life into an allegory in which sexuality is a screen for or displaces his Jewishness.

A year later, after his flight from Germany in the wake of Hitler's seizure of power, Benjamin returns to Ibiza, where he imagines another shock from the future. He begins the second version of his brief composition "Agesilaus Santander" with a recollection of parental prophecy (cit. Scholem 1976c:206):

> When I was born the thought came to my parents that I might perhaps become a writer. Then it would be good if not everybody noticed at once that I was a Jew. That is why besides the name I was called they added two further, exceptional ones, from which one could [not] see... that a Jew bore them.... Forty years ago no parental couple could prove itself more far-seeing. What it held to be only a remote possibility has come true.... Instead of making [this pseudonym] public by the writings he [i.e., Benjamin as writer] produced, he proceeded with regard to it as did the Jews with the additional name of their children, which remains secret. Indeed they only communicate it to them when they reach maturity.

In this piece the secret, unsaid names shape any anticipated ethnic encounter. Their hidden presence explicitly intends to screen the Jew. Jewish identification no longer evokes, as it once did in Wilhelmine Berlin, sentimental aromas; rather, in Nazi Germany it portends the stench of death.

With this tale of a lifesaving, if not people-redeeming, bestowal of a pseudonym Benjamin perversely mirrors a practice common to assimilated Western Jews. At his circumcision every Jewish boy receives his Hebrew name; in Benjamin's Berlin this name is in addition to the secular ones, albeit ones that are nonetheless often stigmatized as peculiarly Jewish, that he receives at birth (Scholem 1976c:216–17). These two "exceptional names," which sever any Jewish connection, both invert and substitute for the two names—circumcision[20] and the Hebrew name—that incorporate the Jewish boy into the covenantal community as well as indelibly mark him as Jewish. The writer's inaudible names recall Benjamin's earlier "call" from the future. Like that "forgotten fact," the secret name has an *après coup* structure; it only becomes significant, revealed, with the attainment of (a religious, sexual, or "new") maturity. But his parents' naming and syphilis have something else in common: the telltale name is inscribed on the body, specifically on the penis. In the case of the "exceptional" names, the mark is not a chancre but an absence—the lost foreskin. Benjamin's two shocks lead to the conclusion that being a Jew in post-Emancipation Germany is the lost origin, the trace that precedes consciousness but nonetheless leaves its mark. The *mémoire involontaire* of this "forgotten" Jewish life—the "aroma...of Jewishness," that is, "of antisemitism and an indefinite piety"—became activated in the smell-laden discussions of aura and mimesis.

A Noisome Gnosis

The vision these aromas invoke is not just that of a virile sexuality that screens Benjamin's recollection or the flowering meadows of bourgeois fantasy, but one of the repulsive, feminized, and often sexualized "odor" that pervaded the popular and scientific imagination of post-Emancipation Europeans: the innate stench of the Jew, the *foetor Judaicus*. The tradition of an odor peculiar to the Jews goes back at least to Marcus Aurelius (Jaeger 1884:113; cf. Sombart 1911:356). Perhaps the most respectable modern disseminator of the *foetor Judaicus* was the philosopher Arthur Schopenhauer, who talks repeatedly of being overcome by it (e.g., 1958:2:375, 645). The attempts to develop racial sciences routinely exhale the reputed stench of the Jews, whether in the racial biochemistry and olfactory metaphysics of Gustav Jaeger (1884), the racial psychology of Edgar Berillon (1908–9), or the racial anthropology of Hans Günther (1934). And even in denying any inherent cause of Jewish noisomeness other than dietary predilections and the "uncleanness...that since ancient times has often clung to the Jews," the prominent nineteenth-century German ethnographer

Richard Andree attests that the "bad smell of the Jewish quarters in North Africa and the Orient, in Poland, Hungary, and Prague's Josephstadt is well known" (1881:68). It was known, for example, to Nietzsche, who in the *Anti-Christ* betrays his shock at the smell of the East European Jew: "One would no more choose to associate with 'first Christians' than one would with Polish Jews.... Neither of them smell very pleasant" (1968:161).

The smelly Jew was also a common figure in German literature. For instance, in Oskar Panizza's 1893 "Der operirte Jude," the "terrible smell" of the protagonist Itzig Faitel Stern signals that the attempt to transform this Jew into a German has come undone (Panizza 1980:79–80).[21] Heine too draws upon the image of the stinking Jew; he concludes his last *Hebrew Melody*, "The Disputation," with a line that seems to have found its echo in Nietzsche. Donna Bianca intones: "I don't know which one is right— / But I'll tell you what I think / Of the rabbi and the friar: Both of them alike, they stink" (Heine 1982: 688). Heine was not the only Jewish writer who appropriated this stereotype. Lacking Heine's irony, several generations of German Jewry also promulgated this characterization; however, they displaced it onto the East European Jews from whom they distinguished themselves (Aschheim 1982).

The stereotyping of the Jews in terms of the Jewish stench coincided in the nineteenth century with a more general olfactory heuristic. Smell figures all that is opposed to the bourgeoisie's public persona. For the European bourgeoisie smell is the "sign of the lower social strata, lesser races, base animals," and of sexuality: the *odor di feminina* and the *aura seminalis* (Horkheimer and Adorno 1972:182; cf., inter alia, Corbin 1986; Stallybrass and White 1986; Rosario 1991; Rindisbacher 1992; Le Guérer 1992; Gray 1993). Because from a phenomenological perspective, a smell and its perceiver become united (Howes 1987), odor symbolized what imperils the clearly delineated distinctions such as those between races, genders, classes, species, and the public and the private upon which bourgeois identity seem to depend. Smell's association with the feared loss of clearcut identities was reinforced linguistically; in German (as in English) *riechen* (to smell) signifies both the emission and the perception of an odor.

This semantic ambiguity also connected smell to the primitive since for some nineteenth-century language theorists the failure to distinguish between objective and subjective perspectives was a sign of primitiveness (cf. Jaeger 1884:108). Olfaction, like its object, was tied to animality. Whereas smell is highly developed in animals, it has become almost rudimentary in the human, a biological fact that nineteenth-century comparative brain anatomy proved—at least for the European. According to G. Eliot Smith, "sometimes, especially in some of the non-European races, the whole of the posterior rhinal fissure is retained in that typical form which we find in the anthropoid apes" (cit. Ellis 1928:46). Smell lies in a "most ancient...a remote and almost disused storehouse of our minds" (Ellis 1928:55). The bourgeoisie's repression of smell differentiated them from both their primitive ancestors and the atavistic survivals who are indigenous to the colonies, the proletarian precincts, Poland, and the Pale. Consequently, discourse on the primitiveness of olfaction helped maintain the evolutionary superiority the European bourgeoisie claimed for themselves on their Darwinist ascent to world hegemony.

Upright and Stuffed Up

One work, written contemporaneously with Benjamin's early formulations of the aura, manifests a configuration of elements—sex and sight, memory and shock, the primitive and the bourgeoisie's self-identification with civilization—that overlaps with both the social representation of smell and Benjamin's analysis of the nineteenth century. This most symptomatic discussion is secreted in a pair of footnotes to Freud's discussion in *Civilization and Its Discontents* of the correlation between the civilizing process and the renunciation of (sexual) instinct. There he situates the repression of smell at the crux of phylo- and ontogenetic development. On the species level, the "devaluation of olfactory stimuli" is coeval with crossing the threshold between animal and human. This repression of smell "is the organic defense of the new form of life achieved with man's erect gait [*aufrechten Gang*] against his earlier animal existence," of which the smell of a female in heat was emblematic. Yet as vision now comes to dominate sexual life (and by implication civilization itself), this defense against smell is almost too effective: it threatens to render the "whole of [genital] sexuality" utterly repugnant. Indeed, Freud speculates that the repression of smell is "the deepest root of the sexual repression which advances along with civilization" (Freud 1961d:99n, 106nn). Although Freud laments the loss of sexual satisfaction in the development of human culture, his discussion of smell and repression of it manifests the bourgeois moralism of which Benjamin accused psychoanalysis when he was reviewing another speculator about sexuality and the origin of human culture, Eduard Fuchs.[22] Both Freud and Benjamin consider the assumption of an upright gait (*aufrechten Gang*) or erect posture (*Aufrichtung*) as a, if not the, threshold of human development, but Freud's insistent repetition of *aufrecht* and its cognate *Aufrichtung* goes beyond marking an evolutionary juncture and appears to superimpose a moralistic perspective. The terms' connotations suggest that with the raising of the bent-over human posture came the ascendancy of the manly, bourgeois values of honesty, sincerity, uprightness.

The moralistic bourgeois dimension of the repression of smell comes explicitly to the fore in Freud's discussion of smell and individual development. Because of the primordial depreciation of the sense of smell, olfactory stimuli are usually not noticed by consciousness. Hence when smells go unperceived, they fill the reservoir of the *mémoire involontaire*, often bringing all contiguous stimuli with them. But when they are perceived — and for Freud the stench of excreta is the primal odor — the individual undergoes a shock experience that both arouses feelings of disgust and begins a process of shock discipline. With the aid of such phylogenetic supplementation a proper upbringing teaches children that their strong-smelling excreta are "worthless, disgusting, abhorrent and abominable" and inculcates in them the cultural virtue of cleanliness. Civilized people know to hide their own stinking excreta; they repress the aromas of their youth. Were it not for the organic repression of smell the necessary reversal of a child's values from narcissistic to moral, from animalistic to social, would "scarcely be possible" (Freud 1961d:100n).

For Freud, the significance and the experience of olfaction are depreciated both phylo- and ontogenetically; smell signifies what is rejected — animality and sexuality — as well as what was never consciously perceived: the memory of that prehistory. As a consequence of organic repression and the cultural values they help to develop, smell and smell-related terms signify the gravest offenses to the social contract. Those persons who smell like "substances that are expelled from the body" (Freud 1961d:100n) are themselves expelled from the social body. Conversely, a civilized society consists of individuals who have adopted the values of uprightness and anosmic cleanliness. No dirty, stinking, crooked Jews need apply.

Not surprisingly, these last implications are not expressly argued by Freud. Whether motivated by ambivalence, identification, or disciplinary demands—especially the fear that his work would be dismissed as particular Jewish predilections rather than universal science—Freud rarely directly engaged anti-Semitism, yet his arguments were often deformed about unacknowledged racial representations. In his work he endeavored to undercut the presuppositions of anti-Semitic discourse (see Geller 1993a), to appropriate and transform its negative valuations (see Geller 1992b), or, when necessary, to repress its conclusions (see Geller 1993b). Freud's analysis does not explain the particularities of Benjamin's discussions of odor; rather, it complements them. Freud displays the offal he does not or cannot say; he releases the threatening odors that the nineteenth-century bourgeoisie did not deign to sniff. And Horkheimer and Adorno would eventually constellate this discussion of smell with Benjamin's notions of both the ritual dimension of aura and mimesis in order to develop a hermeneutic of anti-Semitism. They thereby elicit the implicit concern of both Freud and Benjamin with Jewish identification and its olfactory dimension.

The Trace of an Aura

The *foetor Judaicus* left its trace upon Benjamin's discussion of aura as well. At the conclusion of "Some Motifs," Benjamin (1969c:194) writes: Baudelaire "paid dearly for consenting to this disintegration [of the aura in the experience of shock]—but it is the law of his poetry, which shines in the sky of the Second Empire as 'a star without atmosphere.'" The trail left by the smell of the Jew begins at the source of Benjamin's concluding citation. It is from a passage in Nietzsche's "History in the Service and Disservice of Life" that anticipates a number of the characteristic traits of Benjamin's notion of aura: "If this shroud is removed, if a religion, an art, a genius is condemned to move like a star without atmosphere, no wonder they soon harden up, dry up, and cease to bear." The "shroud" or "atmosphere" to which Nietzsche refers draws upon aura's etymological origins in air, breath, vapor: "Every living thing needs a surrounding atmosphere, a shrouding aura of mystery" (*geheimnisvollen Dunstkreis*; literally, "mysterious circle of vapor"; Nietzsche 1990:121). The immediate context is a discussion of how contemporary historiographic practices contribute to the disintegration of the "aura" that (should) surround religious events: "their cold, pragmatic curiosity" if applied to the birth of Christianity or the Reformation "would be just enough to render every spiritual *actio in distans* quite impossible." Nietzsche's conclusion clearly extends beyond the religious—or, rather, it suggests the religious aspect as well as the import of distance to all auratic phenomena.

By capping off his discussion of Baudelaire with a reference to Nietzsche, Benjamin is doing more than evoking a fellow analyst of the loss of aura; he is also calling upon a writer who shared Baudelaire's preoccupation with olfaction. The poet's predilection for odors is described in the "Arcades" project as a "strong fixation" and as probably a "fetishism" (Benjamin 1982a:1:440 [J67a, 3]); and while smell per se is not treated as a distinctive motif in "Some Motifs," it is amply represented.

Where Baudelaire overvalues smell erotically, Nietzsche transvalues it philosophically.[23] Smell, for Nietzsche (1968:36), is a foremost diagnostic tool: "The nose...is nonetheless the most delicate tool we have at our command: it can detect minimal differences in movement which even the spectroscope cannot detect." In *Ecce Homo,* he credits the nose as the source for his analysis of the nineteenth century: "I was the first to discover the truth...to experience lies as lies—smelling them out.—My genius is in my nostrils" (Nietzsche 1969: 326). He describes the results:

> My instinct for cleanliness is characterized by a perfectly uncanny sensitivity so that the proximity of—what am I saying?—the inmost parts, the 'entrails' of every soul are physiologically perceived by me—*smelled.*
> This sensitivity furnishes me with psychological antennae [*Fühlhörner*] with which I feel and get a hold of every secret: the abundant *hidden* dirt at the bottom of many a character...enters my consciousness almost at the first contact. (Nietzsche 1969:233)

Nietzsche is able to "scent from a distance." Testifying to this claim was his apparent ability to smell Polish Jews from his residence in Sils-Maria (compare Nietzsche 1968:161).

Other researchers have found traces of another influence upon Benjamin's discussion of aura that is even more suffused with the *foetor Judaicus.* The controversial psychologist, philosopher, and anti-Semite Ludwig Klages has been credited by some for contributing to Benjamin's thinking about aura. The extent of Klages's influence is contested but sufficiently visible for Adorno to excoriate Benjamin for his insufficiently critical appropriation of Klages's mythic mentality in the first version of the Baudelaire essay.[24] More recently, Julian Roberts (1982:178) claims that Klages's theory of the image is a primary source for Benjamin's discussion of aura: "Benjamin's theory of 'aura' was taken directly from Klages." Other genealogies of Benjamin's notion of aura by Werner Fuld (1979) and Marianne Stoessel (1983:11 and n), also concede certain affinities. For their part, however, Fuld gives more credit to Klages's elder colleague and mentor Alfred Schuler, whose lectures on Roman antiquity continuously invoke both the auratic glow that transformed things into artworks and the eventual loss of that aura,[25] and Stoessel (1983) locates the beginnings of Benjamin's understanding of aura—if not his use of the particular term—a number of years prior to Klages's work on the archaic image. Both Klages's theory of the image (and later of the symbol) and Benjamin's notion of the aura downplay the role of the intellect and critique the Kantian subjective origin of meaning. Further, both relate the appearance of the object/image in terms of a synesthetic epiphany and a mythic world of natural correspondences, as well as ascribe an eros or pathos of distance to that experience. Like the auratic objects of the *mémoire involontaire*, Klages's archaic images are, he claims, real, material events recovered through ecstatic, hence nondeliberate and momentary, anamnesis. In addition, Klages describes a "nimbus" about the object of insight (cf. Roberts 1982:104–9).

But the effect of Klages upon Benjamin's work is less problematic as an intellectual historical matter, a genealogy of ideas, than it is an ethicohistorical one, an accounting for the impact of social actions and attitudes. That is, Klages was a notorious anti-Semite. Although his most execrable work, a rabidly anti-Jewish introduction to Schuler's *Nachlaß*, first appeared in 1940, Klages had aired his sentiments toward the Jews many years earlier in the graphological articles and treatises that first attracted Benjamin to him.

Odor played a very prominent role in the works of both Schuler and Klages—just as it had in those of an earlier anti-Semitic pair, Fourier and Toussenel, whose olfactory cosmology is excerpted in the "Arcades" project (Benjamin 1982a:2:767, 780, 787 [W 2, 2; 8, 6; 11a, 9]; also see Le Guérer 1992:196–97). In a mythicizing variant of Benjamin's own critical discussion of allegorical ruins and the dialectical appropriation of images of the past, Klages describes how Schuler used to visit archaeological sites where he would perceive "an indescribable odor... emanating from the ruins just as they break through the surface" (Klages 1940:8–9). The incense-loving Schuler spoke of how this intoxicating aura (*Hauch*) about the preserved soul of the past immediately dissipates while unleashing in him visions of lives long ago reduced to shards. Throughout his introduction to Schuler, Klages emphasizes the aromas of both dead and living souls as auratic indicators of soul-ful mimesis. He describes how in *Green Heinrich* Keller's depiction of a pubescent working-class girl embodied "the *aroma* of the Munich soul" and his setting Heinrich and Anna's kiss in the cemetery signified that "the breath [*Anhauch*] of the already 'glorified' ancestors had inspired the embryonic love in the still half-childlike souls to the risk of uncertainly groping tenderness" (Klages 1940:20–21). Schuler and Klages's suffusion with scent was even mocked by their critics; Friedrich Wolters wrote that they were "*drunk with foreign scents and poisons, where they believed to breathe the air of a landscape that felt like home*" (1929:138; cit. Klages 1940:83).[26] Similarly, in the one quasi-explicit reference to Klages's views on Jews, Benjamin once again smells the aroma of anti-Semitism and employs the language of olfaction: "These important scholars [Klages and also Bachofen] *scent* [*wittern*] the archenemy and not without cause" in Jewish theology (letter to Scholem, January 14, 1926; Benjamin 1994:288; emphasis added).[27]

The history of fulminations against the Jewish stench culminated in a scene in *Mein Kampf*. Hitler (1943:57) writes: "The cleanliness of [the Jews], moral and otherwise, I must say, is a point in itself. By their very exterior you could tell that these were no lovers of water, and, to your distress, you often knew it with your eyes closed. Later I often grew sick to my stomach from the smell of these caftan wearers." This passage is a key moment in Hitler's self-described "transformation into an anti-Semite." The failed painter conjoins Kant's antiaesthetic of smell (see my discussion later in this essay) with Wagner's antiaesthetic of the Jew—the "outward appearance [of the Jew] has something disagreeably foreign to [whoever observes him and hence] can never be thinkable as a subject for the art of re-presentment" (Wagner 1897:83)—to initiate his own critique of judgment. Arousing instinctive revulsion toward the Jew smell allows Hitler to bridge the phenomenal and the noumenal. He smells and judges.

Hitler's olfactory antiepiphany perversely evokes the depiction of the Davidic Messiah in B. Shabbat 93b:

And further it is written, *And He will let him have delight in* [*hariho*, literally, "will let him scent"] *the fear of the Lord* [Isa. 11:3]. R. Alexandri said: 'This teaches us that they burdened him with commandments and sufferings like millstones' [assuming *hariho* derives from *rehayim*, millstones]. Rava said: '[This teaches us that] he will scent [the truth] and will adjudicate, as it is written, *and he shall not judge after the sight of his eyes, neither reprove after the hearing of his ears, yet with righteousness shall he judge the poor* [Isa. 11:3–4].' (cit. Patai 1979:28–29)[28]

This talmudic passage is part of a tradition that ties smell to judgment and redemption. The smell of the sacrifice bound God to humanity, and incense was perpetually burned at the Temple (cf. Exod. 30:7–8). Such aromatic offerings were a sign of a redemptive covenant. After the flood waters subsided Noah left the ark and "built an altar to the Lord . . . and offered burnt offerings on the altar. And when the Lord smelled the pleasing odor, the Lord said in his heart, 'I will never again curse the ground because of man' " (Gen. 8:20–21). Conversely, the censers of incense that Korah and his fellow rebels wrongfully carried set them apart from the remainder of the Israelites and distinguished them alone for God's punishment (Num. 16:16–35); whether these censer-bearers would ever be redeemed remained a matter of much rabbinic debate (Patai 1979:198). This scene also shaped Benjamin's understanding of messianism. In his "Critique of Violence" Benjamin (1978d:297–300) sees an image of the messianic end of human history (as well as of revolutionary change) in God's expiating annihilation of the odorous company of Korah.

Benjamin ties another smell-related scene to the narrative of exile and redemption. In "Franz Kafka: On the Tenth Anniversary of His Death" Benjamin (1969b:126) depicts the village at the foot of Kafka's Castle with its pigsty, cigar-strewn, stuffy back rooms, and "air [that] is not free of all the abortive and overripe elements that form such a putrid mixture." He recognizes in Kafka's creation another village from talmudic legend. This talmudic turned Kafkan village is the locus of exile and a figure for the body. Kafka and his contemporaries live and languish in this village while awaiting the Messiah about whose imminent arrival we have been informed. They are not choked up from sweet-smelling sentimentality; rather, they are choking on the noisome foulness that suffuses this site of endlessly deferred redemption.

With the release of certain Jewish-associated scents into Benjamin's work, the air-freshening breath of nostalgia that suffused his discussion of smell begins to turn. In the olfactory metaphysics of a Nietzsche, a Klages, or a Hitler the stench of the Jew serves as a paradigm of the bad. Their image of the *foetor Judaicus* as a negative aura provides definition to the aromas of Jewishness that Benjamin had inhaled. Because it transforms the subjective genitive into the objective, because it is negative, and because it is an object of social discourse, the representation of the smell of the Jew as the *foetor Judaicus* contrasts with the sentimental aromas of Benjamin's personal remembrance.[29] This noisome extreme of the olfactory imagination is anything but sentimental, and if foreign, it nonetheless would be ascribed to him by the likes of a Klages or a Hitler. The aura of the Jewish stench that surrounds Benjamin's perception of aura implicates a more critical, less utopian, function for smell in Benjamin's texts. This "collection of associations"—the memory fragments mediating Benjamin's German-Jewish duality together with the social history of the *foetor Judaicus*—disrupts the self-determining idealities of remembrance and allows the critical reader to sniff a splenetic reading of smell despite Benjamin's efforts at deodorization. Obversely, the relationship between odor and redemption in the Jewish tradition no less redounds upon Benjamin's smell-suffused notion of aura.

Toward a Splenetic Reading of Smell

As has been noted, Benjamin all but excludes nineteenth-century olfactory experience from the "Arcades" project. In the one reference to smell in his early notes to the project he appears to oppose diametrically the nostalgic, personal character of smell to the (potentially) redemptive, collective one of vision. Yet in "Some Motifs" the relationship between these senses realizes the chiasmic structure his project notes had suggested but apparently never developed. Although the olfactory and the visual are distinctive, they are not isolated from one another. Benjamin places them in a series of interconnections and dialectical tensions. Such sites include childhood recollections and the synesthetic *correspondances* in which "a woman's smell, for instance, in the fragrance of her hair or breasts" yields Baudelaire lines like "the azure of the vast vaulted sky" or "a harbor full of flames and masts" (Benjamin 1969c:183). The appropriation of such positive *correspondances* sets up a contrast that allowed Baudelaire "to fathom the full meaning of the breakdown which he, a modern man, was witnessing" (Benjamin 1969c:181).

This last disjunctive effect of smell suggests that in addition to an ideal aspect, odor also assumes a splenetic one in Benjamin's work. He takes the title of the first section of *Fleurs du Mal*, "Spleen and Ideal," to reflect the dialectic of extremes that characterizes Baudelaire's experience of modernity: "The *idéal* supplies the power of remembrance; the *spleen* musters the multitude of the seconds against it" (Benjamin 1969c:183). Emblematic of the latter, notes Benjamin, is a line from Baudelaire's poem "Craving for Oblivion": "The beloved spring has lost its scent" (cit. Benjamin 1969c:183). The loss of scent indicates the "present state of collapse" (Benjamin 1969c:184) of the ideal; its aura dissipated, the world has become a one-dimensional or anesthetized phantasmagoria. In these splenetic times the poet no longer "wends his way through forests of symbols"; rather, he is the fencer of "The Sun." Benjamin focuses upon the lonely poet trying to parry the shocks of modern life: "I go, alone, to practice my curious fencing." He cites without comment the line that follows: "In every corner smelling out [*flairant; aufzuspüren* (cf. Benjamin 1972i:25)] the dodges of rhyme" (1969c:164). With this splenetic poet nosing out the spoils of modernity, however, Benjamin counters another scene of elagiac sniffing in *A Berlin Chronicle*, one that is a mournful complement of the nostalgic idylls that in his work fragrantly evoke the prehistories of the bourgeoisie. In discussing the composition of that work, he describes it as consisting of reminiscences of people long gone, now "shadowy [and] wraithlike [they] sniff [*wittern*] at thresholds like a genius loci" (1979b:28). In modernity the sense of smell has not been lost; it just assumes new forms. Through the evocation of smell Benjamin sets these extremes of *spleen* and *ideal* in ironic tension.

Benjamin also rubs his nose into another reading of smell: the critical perception of smell as stench. He collects his data for his "Arcades" project under the sign of stench. In the N folder he describes "the method of this work": "I have nothing to say. Only to show.... The rags [*Lumpen*], the refuse [*Abfall*]."[30] With this statement Benjamin the collector (*Sammler*) becomes Benjamin the ragpicker (*Lumpensammler*)[31] Baudelaire depicts the ragpicker in a poem translated by Benjamin, "Ragpicker's Wine." The ragpicker, "poking with his stick at the ragged ends of speeches and scraps of language... in the gray dawn of the day of revolution," had already been rendered emblematic of the politicized intellectual by Benjamin at the conclusion of his 1930 commentary on Siegfried Kracauer's *White Collar Workers* (Benjamin 1972f:225; cf. Witte 1991:118). This figure later resurfaced in "The Paris of the Second Empire in Baudelaire" to highlight the "commerce in garbage" and to epitomize the (lumpen)proletariat.[32] But in the nineteenth century the ragpicker was also "the archetype of stench" (Corbin 1986:146). According to an 1831 report by the sanitary commission of the Jardin des Plantes, the ragpickers walk the streets "laden with different products plucked from the capital's refuse, its fetid odor seeming to be so much identified with their persons that they themselves resemble veritable walking dunghills. Can it be otherwise in view of the nature of their activity in the streets, their noses continually in dunghills?" (cit. Corbin 1986:141).

Baudelaire (1982:114) too draws upon the olfactory register. He describes the ragpicker as "reeking of sour wine" and "staggering under enormous sacks of junk / — the vomit of surfeited Paris." But with the exception of a paraphrase of Baudelaire, in which the ragpicker seeking numbness is "surrounded by the aroma of wine casks" (Benjamin 1972a:522) the emanations—the aura—of this "refuse" do not make their way into either Benjamin's Baudelaire essays or the "Arcades" project's folders.[33] Similarly, the prostitute, who functions as an allegory of objectification and modernity for Benjamin and whose smell pervades Baudelaire's poetry, remains deodorized (cf. Corbin 1986:146, 178, 185–86, 205–6). Neither Hugo nor Lamartine nor Musset can compare to Baudelaire in comprehending "the odor of misery and despair," according to Léon Daudet in "Baudelaire: The Malaise and the Aura," a work excerpted by Benjamin in the J folder. Daudet later concludes that "in his Parisian poems, Baudelaire extracts the quintessence, toxic and salubrious, of that immense laboratory of stone, where the worst instincts smoke, where lofty aspirations blaze.... He made its scent breathe out hot and doleful" (1929: 213, 254–55).

Yet throughout the "Arcades" project Benjamin betrays a remarkable anosmia, olfactory blindness. While Benjamin oversees an archaeology of the visible and touches upon the recovery of the tactile in nineteenth-century Paris, he apparently is not attuned to the "other dialogues [that] were taking place ... ; heavy animal scents and fleeting perfumes [that] spoke of repulsion and disgust, sympathy and seduction" (Corbin 1986:229). Corbin concludes his masterly study of odor and the French social imagination lamenting that "discourse on odors was interdicted" and previous historians had "neglected these documents of the senses" (1986:229). While Benjamin notes the import of hygiene in several of the preliminary sketches of the "Arcades" project, there is no folder to indicate any plan of research. In contrast to the emphasis upon the biopolitical understanding of nineteenth-century Europe that conditions contemporary historiography, Benjamin's historical materialist stress upon capitalist modernity (see Benjamin 1983–84) leads him to focus upon a Hausmann who plotted the boulevards and to ignore totally the locus of much contemporary historiography, the Parent-Duchatelet who toured the sewers (cf. Harsin 1985; Bernheimer 1989; Corbin 1990). Smell is not completely ignored, but, as my analysis of the rare olfactory reference attests, it does not escape the parameters of certain bourgeois pseudoaristocratic nostalgia.

Yet Benjamin's own ragpicker description of his method — to show rather than say — together with his identification with that ragpicker people,[34] the Jews who allegedly bear a scent that pejoratively codes them as marginal, may allow us to sniff or interpolate the stench of a splenetic reading of smell. Benjamin diagnosed "the decline or disintegration of the aura" as a major symptom of the breakdown of experience that marked the modern. Yet, he noted a corresponding apotheosis of an auratic aesthetic, the Kantian "l'art pour l'art" movement. Fragrance is synonymous with the auratic work of art. Benjamin (1969c:186–87) cites Paul Valéry:

> We recognize a work of art by the fact that no idea it inspires in us, no mode of behavior that it suggests we adopt could exhaust it or dispose of it. We may inhale the smell of a flower whose fragrance is agreeable to us for as long as we like; it is impossible for us to rid ourselves of the fragrance by which our senses have been aroused, and no recollection, no thought, no mode of behavior can obliterate its effect or release us from the hold it has on us.

The insistence of this fragrant flower, however, ironizes Valéry's in other respects rather Kantian reverie. By exhaling its aura, the work of art undercuts its claim to be art. That is, for Kant smell characterizes what cannot be art. In contrast to the universal communicability of beauty, smell exemplifies the form of pleasure that is incommunicable (cf. Kant 1952:48–49 [§39]). Moreover, smell is associated with disgust (Ekel). In his Anthropology from a Pragmatic Point of View,

Kant asserts that "filth seems to awaken nausea [*Ekel*] less through what is repulsive to eye and tongue than through the stench associated with it." He goes on to describe smell as the "sense with a specific organ [that] is the most thankless and also, it seems, the most expendable" (Kant 1974:36, 37 [§19, §20]; also see Stallybrass and White 1986: 139–40). Even agreeable fragrances such as that of Valéry's flower arouse disgust because, forced upon the perceiver, they interfere with the freedom necessary for aesthetic pleasure. All smells are in effect disgusting, and the disgusting is the "one kind of ugliness [that] is incapable of being represented conformably to nature without destroying all aesthetic delight, and consequently aesthetic beauty [because] the artificial representation of the [disgusting] object is no longer distinguishable from the nature of the object in our sensation" (Kant 1952:173–74 [§48]). The disgusting is too real, too close; it both has an aura — in the dictionary sense (i.e., it reeks) — and has no aura — in the conventional Benjaminian reading (i.e., it is not art).

Yet the disgusting smell does not so much call into question Benjamin's analyses of aura as it evokes other dimensions of experience and analysis.[35] The distance that characterizes the aromatic aura of the disgusting is not the spatiotemporal separation between the audience and the work of art; it is the negated space between the perceiver and what lies behind and outside of that work. The secret(ed) scent of Valéry's flower, of auratic art amid the disintegration of aura, arises from other dialectical extremes Benjamin analyzes in "The Work of Art in the Age of Mechanical Reproduction." With the increase in the cult value of art came a corresponding development in its opposite, in its exhibition value. "The cult value would seem to demand that the work of art remain hidden," but instead it is open to the public. And in another dialectical reversal the public exhibition of the work of art first wrenched it out of the "fabric of tradition" and everyday life and then resituated it in temples to the cult of beauty — museums and exhibition halls — as the authentic work of the creative individual (Benjamin 1969e:225, 223). Such exhibited art is defined by its aura, but this aura is artificially induced and institutionally sustained (cf. 1969e:224 on the cult of beauty). On the one hand, the work of art became a fetishized commodity; its exhibition value was built upon the sweat-producing labor of others. On the other hand, fetid odors threatened to seep through the doorways of these temples. The dis-

tance generated by these ritual sites was the distance of exclusion—
what the sanitized bourgeois sensibility must be spared: "the refuse
of the physical world" (Adorno 1977:128), "the pestilential mire"
(Benjamin 1982a:1:630 [O8a, 2]), the miasma of urban life, the barbaric stench of the oppressed, the noisomeness of the masses. Whereas
smell, the smell of incense and sacrifice, would reinforce the ritual
and transcendent elements normally associated with the concept of
aura, smell was also the trace of the silenced, the forgotten, and the
invisible—the victims of the deritualized human sacrifice inflicted by
the modern capitalist system. The splenetic olfactory critic can sniff
out these simulacra of aura that are suffused in the stench of modernity just as a Proust or a Benjamin inhales the scent of prehistory from
the aura surrounding a flower or a mother-of-pearl pocket knife.

A Coeval Pair

Benjamin intertwines aura with another notion that evokes—and, in
its influences and inheritors, renders explicit—Jewish representations
of the often odorous and frequently odious kind.[36] That notion in its
natural- or prehistorical form is called "mimesis" and in its modern
form "reproduction." Benjamin posits the existence of a human mimetic faculty. More than the perception of similarities, it is "a rudi-
ment of the powerful compulsion in former times to become and behave like something else" (Benjamin 1978e:333). In his first self-
contained foray into mimesis, "Doctrine of the Similar," astrology,
presumably arising out of the imitation of celestial processes and assuming a natural correspondence between human life and cosmic
events, is his prime example. The image of stars looking down upon
us and returning our glance leads Benjamin to speculate in a fragment
from his Nachlaß that the experience of the aura and the development of the mimetic faculty are coeval:

> Do relations exist between the experiences of the aura and those of as-
> trology[?] Are there earthly creatures as well as things which look back
> from the stars? Which from the heavens actually return their gaze? Are
> the stars, with their gaze from afar, the prototype of the aura? May one
> assume that the look was the first mentor of the mimetic faculty? (Ben-
> jamin 1972-:2.3:958)

While Benjamin does not have his mimetic hermeneuts such as the
astrologer sniff out correspondences, smell does appear in his "Doc-

trine of the Similar." Smells are the essences to which language as mimetic and allegorical correspond:

> Language is the highest application of the mimetic faculty: a medium into which the earlier perceptive capabilities for recognizing the similar had entered without residue, so that it is now language which represents the medium in which objects meet and enter into relationship with each other, no longer directly, as once in the mind of the augur or priest, but in their essences, in their most volatile and delicate substances, even in their aromata. (Benjamin 1979:68).

The formula for this connection between the mimetic character of language and aroma had emerged two years earlier at the site of a parallel transformation of religious experience: the hashish trance. While modernity had both disenchanted the world and offered in its stead a benumbing phantasmagoria, Benjamin (1978c:179) concluded that drug intoxication rather than necessarily contributing to this anesthesia could paradoxically offer an introduction to "profane illumination," a sudden insight into the mystery of the everyday. The hashish trance provided access to the experience of both the aura (Benjamin 1985c:588) and the mimetic: it "volatizes representations into verbal aromas [*Wortaromen*] in which the actual representation-substance in the word...is completely vaporized." During this particular drug experiment Benjamin acted out this profane illumination about the mimetic character of language with a word redolent with mimetic associations: "the root: ape" (*Affe*) generated "the ape apes" (*der Affe äfft*) and "to ape, mimic, be mimicked" (*äffen, nachäffen, voräffen*; Benjamin 1985c:598).

By speaking of the aromata of objects and words in these contexts of transformed religiosity Benjamin is not so much perfuming his language as suggesting a more worldly, yet still explicitly religious, mediation of aura and mimesis. Odors contour the ritual dimension characteristic of both the aura and the pre(linguistic) history of mimesis. The olfactory dominates the sensorium in the primary ritual performed by the augurs and priests: sacrifice. According to *Pirke Avoth* 5.5, the first of the ten wonders done for "our fathers in the Temple [was that a] woman never miscarried on account of the stench of the meat of Holy Things" (Neusner 1984:155). The scent of the offering not only goes directly to the gods but also is perceived immediately by the officiants. The eyes may be a window to the soul, but the nose was the gateway to the brain (cf. Gonzalez-Crussi 1991:73).

Cutting off One's Nose to Spite One's Faith

Although Benjamin associates aromata with essences, the scent is not the bearer of "images" in his discussions of the mimetic faculty. In the fragment in which he speculates about the common origin of aura and mimesis, Benjamin (1972-:2.3:958) explicitly excludes the nose as a center of the mimetic faculty: "In this context a polarity is produced in the center of the mimetic faculty of man. It shifts itself from the eyes to the lips, thereby taking a detour around the entire body." With this formulation, Benjamin has constructed his own rather curious constellation. The usual astrological representation would draw a line connecting the polarities, the extremes. The passage from eye to lip normally would traverse the nose, but according to Benjamin the mimetic faculty takes a detour. Its circumambulation would miss the nose. The eyes perceive similarities, and the lips produce them. By contrast, the nose neither generates signs nor recognizes them. Benjamin usually represents smells either as signs of themselves — "of all sensual impressions it will ally itself only with the same scent" (1969c:184) — or as symbols of Jewish bourgeois life. Although this analysis has uncovered both splenetic and redemptive aspects of Benjamin's discussion of smell and the olfactory emanations of aura, his smells do not engender critical similarities but rather remain, on the surface, ideal, nostalgic, and personal simulacra of dialectical images.

Benjamin's phylo- and ontogenetic history of the mimetic faculty suggests another reason for the omission of the nose. At its origin mimesis is the drive to become the other, yet Benjamin's discussion of the visual, the vocal, and their conjunction in the written leaves a residue of difference: the mimetically producing and comprehending self that smell threatens to overcome. The nose becomes the other; it becomes itself a sign.

The nose is a sign of the Jew that, until the development of rhinoplasty, no assimilation could remove. The Jewish nose was the visual correlate of the Jewish stench. In Moses Hess's *Rome and Jerusalem,* a work Benjamin read and respected (cf. Scholem 1981:36, 138; Benjamin 1972e:809), the Jewish nose blew the belief held by many Jewish reformers that the German perception of the Jewish religion as ritualistic and atavistic was the primary obstacle to emancipation.

Hess (1943:52) wrote that the German "objects less to the Jews' peculiar beliefs than to their peculiar noses.... Jewish noses cannot be reformed."

The traditionally comic character of such noses and other stereotypically Jewish physical features played a role in speculations about a physiological predisposition toward mimetic behavior that predated Benjamin's own. Freud's 1905 discussion of comedy focuses upon an "impulsion ... to imitation" (*Drang ... zur Nachahmung*) and an "ideational mimetics" (*Vorstellungsmimik*; 1961c:192, 191). Comedy arises from the recognition of the difference between another person's exaggerated or inexpedient movement and "the one that I should have carried out myself in his place" (191). This mimesis-based comedy of movement is the source of all other comedy such as that of "bodily shapes and facial features ... for they are regarded as though they were the outcome of an exaggerated or pointless movement" (Freud 1961c:190) that the audience imagines itself imitating. Freud's examples of such comedy — "staring eyes, a hooked nose hanging down to the mouth, ears sticking out, a hump-back" (190) — fill the repertoire of Jewish caricature. The compulsion to imitate hence results in the construction of the stereotypical Jew.

Imitation Is the Hebraist's Form of Falsity

The compulsion to imitate was itself a part of that construction. Some essential relationship between Jewishness and mimesis was disseminated not only in anti-Semitic discourse but also by the Zionist critique of assimilated Jewry (Geller 1994).[37] In the wake of political emancipation many Western European Jews sought social emancipation through acculturation and assimilation. The popular Gentile perception of their adoption of European manners, dress, language, and so on was mediated, however, by Darwin's discovery that imitation was a natural talent rather than a cultural practice (Norris 1980). Darwin described how adapting to one's surroundings — masking one's true identity — often ensured evolutionary survival. Writers like Klages concluded from this discussion of mimicry in nature that the Jews' ability to acculturate, to imitate European manners, was an animalistic talent evolutionarily hewn for their survival; Jews employed their innate gift for mimicry in order to live in a hostile world. Or put more sinisterly, Jews sought to secrete their presence in the world. When analogies were drawn between the adaptation of animals to their environment (as described by Darwin) and Jewish assimilation into European society, natural, value-free animal behavior was equated with typical Jewish deceit (cf. Norris 1980:1233–34).

When Klages (1904:60) described the Jews as "the apes of culture" he entered this tradition. Klages racially coded mimesis, just as he had odor. For Klages, the Jew, like the hysteric, is in his essence never at home with himself, always other than himself (cf. Klages 1940:81, citing Klages 1904:60–62; 1910:78–80 and nn). The Jew "partakes of the customs and practices of his hosts to awaken the appearance of essential likeness" (1940:81). Klages draws upon the image of the extremely adaptable feminized Jews popularized by Otto Weininger's notorious misogynistic and anti-Semitic 1903 *Sex and Character:* "Because they are nothing in themselves … [they] can become everything. … [The Jew] adapts himself to every circumstance and every race, becoming, like the parasite, a new creature in every different host" (1906:320). Klages concludes his diatribe by declaring that "an imitation humanity appears to arise, where the old inhabitant races fall on decay" (Klages 1940:81).

Yet it was on the basis of such graphological writings that Ludwig Klages has been credited for influencing Benjamin's thinking about mimesis as well as aura. Graphology, Benjamin (1978e:335) asserted, "has taught us to recognize in handwriting images that the unconscious of the writer conceals in it" and thus had led him to recognize script's mimetic dimension as "an archive of nonsensuous similarities, of nonsensuous correspondences." While Benjamin does not explicitly name Klages, commentators assume Benjamin had him in mind since his enthusiasm for Klages's handwriting work goes back at least to 1914; that year Benjamin appears to have solicited him for a lecture on graphology.

Through his characterization of the mimicking Jews, however, Klages called forth a different notion of mimesis than he would ascribe to handwriting. Lacking any profound connection with their own being and therefore unable mimetically to manifest their own souls, the rootless Jews, according to Klages, ape the appearance of others. In mirroring surfaces rather than depths, they embody a negative mimesis or antimimesis.

Dialectic (of Enlightenment) at a Standstill

Freud too seems to evoke the assimilating Jew who tries to pass for a Gentile—along with the figure of the miming Jew—when he (1961c:

192–93) explores the visible effects of the reactivated memory traces, which he calls "ideational mimetics":

> If...a member of *certain races,* narrates or describes something, it is easy to see that he...also represents its subject-matter in his expressive movements: he combines the mimetic and the verbal forms of representation....He may have broken himself of the habit of painting with his hands, yet for that reason he will do it with his voice; and if he exercises self-control in this too, it may be wagered that he will open his eyes wide when he describes something large and squeeze them shut when he comes to something small. (emphasis added)

Freud's examples of the mimetic response like Klages's aping Jew snare anti-Semitism into the signifying web of Benjamin's notion of mimesis: the Jew is the imitator, the imitated, and the difference between.

This conclusion becomes more explicit in Horkheimer and Adorno's *Dialectic of Enlightenment.* For Horkheimer and Adorno the Third Reich and its extermination of the mimetic Jews is the culmination of the twin histories of Europe: "a well-known, written history and an underground history. The latter consists in the fate of the human instincts and passions which are displaced and distorted by civilization....The relationship with the human body is maimed from the outset" (Horkheimer and Adorno 1972:231). These histories begin with the repression of smell as described by Freud:

> The compulsive urge to cruelty and destruction springs from the organic displacement of the relationship between mind and body; Freud expressed the facts of the matter with genius when he said that loathing [*Ekel*] first arose when men began to walk upright and were at a distance from the ground, so that the sense of smell which drew the male animal to the female in heat was relegated to a secondary position among the senses. (Horkheimer and Adorno 1972:232–33)[38]

Freud's speculations help to explain the contradictions, ambivalences, and distortions that shape (Western) civilization's relationship to nature in general. When Benjamin's onetime colleagues at the Institute of Social Research constellate Freud's discussion of smell with Benjamin's focus on mimesis,[39] they then are able to develop a construct for the analysis of anti-Semitism in particular. By this conjunction of extremes, Horkheimer and Adorno read the Jewish physiognomy that marks Benjamin's terms.

Benjamin opens his essay "On the Mimetic Faculty" thus: "Nature creates similarities. One need only think of mimicry" (1978e:333). But where Benjamin then jumpshifts to concerns of epistemology and linguistic philosophy, Horkheimer and Adorno's analysis begins with the natural substrate of mimesis in order to address domination and politics. Their focus is less upon the decay or transformation of the mimetic faculty than upon civilization's successful or failed attempts to repress it. With their examination of the role of mimesis in protection and defense—on how, for example, the mimetic body stiffens like "circumambient, motionless nature" (Horkheimer and Adorno 1972:180) before any threat to survival—they thereby emphasize, as Darwin does, how "imitation belongs to the realm of nature rather than culture, to the inhuman as well as the human, that its practice might be organic, unconscious, and involuntary, that its teleology might be political rather than aesthetic, and that it may serve as a pivot of historical change" (Norris 1980:1233).[40] This Darwinian understanding of mimesis as a natural phenomenon contributed to the belief in an inherent Jewish talent for mimicry. The language-focused notion of mimesis Benjamin presents is not opposed to the more corporeal one of his colleagues; rather, their notions provide complementary readings of the phenomenon: Benjamin from the perspective of messianic time, Horkheimer and Adorno from the perspective of the empirical history of modernity. Indeed, their shift to the political does not so much diverge from Benjamin's initial analyses of mimesis as it correlates with the contours of Benjamin's later developed notion of the "mimetic shock absorber" and the adaptation processes of the factory worker (cf. Benjamin 1969c:175–78).

Horkheimer and Adorno (1972:184) also shift the sensory register in their discussion of mimesis from the visual and aural to the olfactory. Smell, for them, provides the basis for the mimetic faculty:

> The multifarious nuances of the sense of smell embody the archetypal longing for the lower forms of existence, for direct unification with circumambient nature, with the earth and mud. Of all the senses, that of smell—which is attracted without objectifying—bears clearest witness to the urge to lose oneself in and become the 'other.' . . . When we see we remain what we are; but when we smell we are taken over by otherness.

Horkheimer and Adorno's analysis releases the olfactory dimension implicit in Benjamin's discussion of mimesis. By arguing from Freud's phylogenetic discussion of smell's repression that the olfactory sense betrays the "memory of prehistory" (Horkheimer and Adorno 1972:

71), they also implicate smell in the recovery of the lost world of experience—the aromata—that mimetic language mediates.

They also fill in the gap in Benjamin's topography of the mimetic body when they point out several "mimetic cyphers" including "the nose—the physiognomic *principium individuationis,* symbol of the specific character of an individual, described between the lines of his countenance" (Horkheimer and Adorno 1972:184). The context for their invocation of the nose indicates that Horkheimer and Adorno are, however, more concerned with the response to mimesis than to mimetic response. And it is one of many that tie the Jews to mimesis. Horkheimer and Adorno argue that "there is no anti-Semite who does not basically want to imitate his mental image of a Jew, which is composed of mimetic cyphers: the argumentative movement of a hand, the musical voice painting a vivid picture of things and feelings irrespective of the real content of what is said, and the nose" (185). Implicit in this characterization is the assumption that the Jews, perhaps more than any other people, bear the traces of insufficiently repressed mimesis: "Undisciplined mimicry is the brand of the old form of domination, engraved in the living substance of the dominated and passed down by a process of unconscious imitation in infancy from generation to generation, from the down-at-heel Jew to the rich banker" (182). The assumption of the mimetic Jew belongs to the anti-Semite: "This machinery [of using suppressed nature in the service of the domination that suppresses it] needs the Jews.... The gentile sees equality, humanity, in his difference from the Jew.... It matters little whether the Jews as individuals really do still have those mimetic features which awaken the dread malady, or whether such features are suppressed" (185). Like Benjamin, Horkheimer and Adorno discern that the anti-Semites justify their hatred of the Jews based on instinct and racially different physiology; they also concur with his speculation that the repudiation of the physical nature of the Jews is part of a general turning against nature.[41]

As part of this analysis of anti-Semitism, Horkheimer and Adorno examine how the rationalized body, disciplined against nature, reacts with disgust, embarrassment, and ultimately violence before any manifestation of mimetic behavior, be it a gesture or an odor. Benjamin's colleagues evoke the *foetor Judaicus* when they tie smell to the "disinfecting" intentionality of anti-Semitism that led to the Shoah:

The sense of smell is considered a disgrace in civilization.... As a despised and despising characteristic, the mimetic function is enjoyed craftily. Anyone who seeks out [wittert] 'bad' smells, in order to destroy them, may imitate sniffing to his heart's content, taking unrationalized pleasure in the experience. The civilized man 'disinfects' the forbidden impulse by his unconditional identification with the authority which prohibited it; in this way the action is made acceptable.... This is the schema of the anti-Semitic reaction. (Horkheimer and Adorno 1972:184)

They describe this schema as "deeply imprinted... a ritual of civilization" (171). Anti-Semitism and its image of the Jew as embodied mimesis are coeval with civilization. In an apparent reversal of Klages, Horkheimer and Adorno depict the relationship of anti-Semite and Jew as one of antitype and type. Anti-Semites mimic the mimics rather than nature; they endeavor not to become one with nature but to dominate it—above all, in themselves. Antedating this mimesis of mimesis is a "false projection":

It is the counterpart of true mimesis.... Mimesis imitates the environment, but false projection make the environment like itself. For mimesis the outside world is a model which the inner world must try to conform to: the alien must become familiar; but false projection confuses the inner and outer world and defines the most intimate experiences as hostile. (187)

Anti-Semitism transforms the Jew into the feared mimetic nature: "The mere fact that a person is called a Jew is an invitation forcibly to make him over into a physical semblance of that image of death and distortion" (186).

Horkheimer and Adorno's histories of mimesis and of smell are inextricably tied to the history of the Jew in Europe. As "civilization" developed through its ongoing struggle against humanity's mimetic nature, the Jews became the projection screen for the dominant culture's fears of uncontrolled mimesis. And with the advent of Emancipation, assimilating Jews recapitulated that same history:

But especially where a nation (the Jews, for example) was brought by its own destiny to change to a new form of social life, the time-honored customs, sacred activities, and objects of worship were magically transformed into heinous crimes and phantoms.... From the reflex of disgust [Ekel] at excrement or human flesh to the suspicion of fanaticism, laziness, and poverty, whether intellectual or material, there is a long line of modes of behavior which were metamorphosed from the adequate and necessary into abominations. (92)

Having abandoned their old world of *Erfahrungen* the stinking Jews became disgusting to themselves.

"To Read What Was Never Written"

Just as Benjamin had endeavored to reappropriate the notion of the commodity by blasting it out of the homogeneous course of events and then both resituating and revalorizing it within a new configuration (cf., inter alia, Taussig 1993; Stoessel 1983; Roberts 1982), so he also sought to rescue mimesis and aura-affiliated smell from their anti-Semitic associations, "to read what was never written" (Benjamin 1978e:336), and release their "image[s] of redemption." In writing about aura and mimesis Benjamin did not generate an analysis of the Jewish Question as such. But names, those archives of nonsensuous similarities, are always secreting ideas and experiences in Benjamin's work whether it be death as a syphilitic or birth as a Jew. And especially when they are constelled with other phenomena their monadological structure crystallizes and their aromata are released to provide an olfactory physiognomic portrait of Benjamin's Jewishness.

Did Benjamin simply ignore the anti-Semitic utterances, the social discourse of the stinking mimetic Jew, that traverses the work of Klages and others, and instead rescue what he could from them for his own critical configurations? Or was he traumatized by the catastrophic configuration of social representations of smell, mimesis, and anti-Semitism that those splenetic critics Horkheimer and Adorno would sniff out during that state of emergency for the Jewish people, the Shoah, such that this olfactory image did not so much "flit by" or dissipate as leave its mimetic (rather than semiotic) traces on his physiognomy? Or, finally, did he embrace these allegations and revalue them? Even as this essay has mapped out Benjamin's olfactory shock experiences and their consequences, even as it has recovered from his part ideological, part traumatic anosmia the seemingly "inconsequential and buried" (Benjamin 1982a:1:460 [J77, 1]) scents that configure his Jewish physiognomy, a case can be made for this last redemptive possibility. Just as aura was paired with mimesis, it was also opposed to "reproduction." Just as the development of language led to transformations in the disposition of the mimetic faculty, modern technological change has also had its effects. New forms of reproduction have facilitated the apparent triumph of a new objectivity in which the sensuous similarity of the reproducible fact has become truth and supplanted both the aura and mimesis. In "The Work of Art in the Age of Mechanical Reproduction" Benjamin examines the new forms of reproductive art photography and film. Such art contravenes the values of auratic art because it subverts the authority and authenticity of the original, erases distance, undermines tradition, and opens access. Rather than denigrating these arts he analyzes how through shock they offer access to regions that are elided in the auratic arts: they open upon the optical unconscious, revealing the phenomenological and the structural conditions for representation, and they generate a tactile appropriation of the world by which the spectator begins to embody—that is, to mime—the otherness of the world. Reproduction undercuts the authority of the simulacra, the unoriginal originals of commodified art, and reveals "entirely new structural formations of the subject" (Benjamin 1969e:236). Such reproduction presents the redemptive possibility of providing a countervailing force to the culminating appearance of the ersatz aura: fascism.

In writing about aura, Benjamin also sought to configure the idea of redemption in a profane age. Yet, for Benjamin, aura is absent from the modern world except in the intimate gaze of a (nature) lover or in the *mémoire involontaire* of a Proust, or rather aura is ever present in such grotesque simulacra of itself as the fetishized commodity and the Führer. The name *aura* in Benjamin's critical vocabulary does not so much describe what is as much as it embodies the difference between the modern and prehistory. And it is doubly emblematic of the great gulf between the noumenal and the phenomenal that characterizes the modern: in its utopian-nostalgic form, aura endeavors to satisfy our longings for a world before separation and difference, a world suffused with the noumenal, a world of unmediated mimetic interaction. Conversely, in its illusory form, aura severs all ties with the sacred even as it simulates the ritual relationships of distance and domination; moreover, it occludes its own unsaid conditions of production beneath the veil of the natural and the supernatural. Restoring the prehistoric aura and its noumenal effusions as the basis of material social life appears impossible, while redemption for this modern ersatz aura is death.

The ties to smell, however, indicate a different configuration within the name *aura* itself, and this configuration escapes the ideologically constrained intentionality of Benjamin's language. Since all language is, by definition, imbued with the noumenal "aromata" (cf. Benjamin

1978e; 1979) as well as with the historical unsaid (i.e., with the conditions for its production), every linguistic act has an objective—olfactory—character. Readers, by following their noses, may recover another dimension of experience, the other language emanating from *aura*. While fragrances recall the nostalgic idyll of childhood prehistory, the redemptive character of such sweet smells is compromised by its all too personal character and by its inner contradiction: childhood memory draws upon a phantasmagoria generated by bourgeois artifice, self-delusion, and expropriation. But the odorous remainder emitted by *aura* also suggests that Benjamin is revalorizing a derogatory Jewish identification—the stinking Jew—as well as rescuing a particular strand of Jewish messianic thinking. Contributing to the redemptive possibilities of the aura, then, is a transfiguration of Jewish otherness. And *aura,* in particular, represents a redemptive moment in which olfaction, as the sense of materiality and as the character of that which the dominant class fears and thus seeks to foreclose, escapes the optics of discipline and control. Adorno, who with Horkheimer had released the odorous dimension of mimesis in order to analyze anti-Semitism, concluded his introduction to the first edition (1955) of Benjamin's *Writings* by invoking an olfactory reverie of Nietzsche's Zarathustra to describe the redemptive power of Benjamin's thought: "And a new scent, one bringing salvation, already surrounds [the earth]—as does a new hope" (Nietzsche 1980:189; cit. Adorno 1988:16). This profane stench, as the trace of otherness in the everyday, seeps through the "strait gate" (Benjamin 1969f:264 [B]) of the redemption from the forces of totality and identity.

Notes

The "precious but tasteless seed" of this essay was produced as a response to a series of papers on Walter Benjamin for the Critical Theory and Discourses on Religion Consultation at the 1989 American Academy of Religion annual meeting. My thanks to Ned Lukacher for supporting that original dissemination, to Jonathan Boyarin for his contribution to its eventual germination, to James Rolleston for his aid during all of its stages, and to Hans-Jakob Werlen for his advice on translation.

1. These opposing interpretations of Benjamin, most prominently represented by Scholem and Adorno, respectively, are summarized by Jennings 1987:5–11.

2. Where a translation exists it is employed; otherwise the translations are the author's.

3. Buck-Morss does, however, acknowledge that "sight was not exclusively affected. Perfumeries burgeoned in the nineteenth century, their products overpowering the olfactory sense of a population already besieged by the smells of the city" (1992:

24). She then cites Benjamin on smell drugging the sense of time (cf. Benjamin 1969c: 184). While her comment on olfactory anesthesia is quite accurate, her illustrative quote from Benjamin moves in a contrary direction, as I will discuss later.

4. Indeed, this aspect of smell bears a similarity to the trace, which Benjamin opposes to the aura: "The trace is the appearance of proximity, however remote the object that left it behind. Aura is the appearance of distance, however close the object that evokes it." Yet overcoming the Proustian and the Kantian subject by smell is more characteristic of the effect of aura: "In the trace we take possession of the object; in aura it takes possession of us" (Benjamin 1982a:1:560 [M16a, 4]).

5. The German term for moment, *Augenblick*, literally means "eye glance"; this etymology suggests how the German language may constrain the understanding of epistemology to visual metaphors.

6. Benjamin had earlier yielded to such a bourgeois "nostalgic utopia" when he employed a vision of smell to mediate the romantic bourgeois opposition between city and nature. In his 1927 essay on Gottfried Keller, the nineteenth-century German-Swiss realist novelist whose work enshrined as well as olfactorily coded that opposition, Benjamin writes that Keller's "vision of the world" can be characterized by two odor-laced lines from the old Swiss national anthem: "Most beautiful rose, if all others have passed away from me / [You] still perfume [*Duftest*] my desolate shore" (Benjamin 1972b:292). On Benjamin's essay as a "nostalgic utopia," see Witte 1991:106. On the olfactory dimension of Keller, see Rindisbacher 1992:72–86 and my discussion of Klages.

7. As Pulzer (1964:189) notes: "The decline of the overtly anti-Semitic organizations after 1900 is deceptive. In Germany the various parties quarreled and vegetated; at the same time anti-Semitism was more openly accepted than before by several other parties, an increasing number of political and economic interest groups, and many nonpolitical bodies, such as students' corps . . . [hence] a decline in sectarian fanaticism and in the vehemence of anti-Semitic propaganda, combined with the widespread acceptance of mild, almost incidental anti-Semitic opinions."

8. Or western: Benjamin believed that he was related on his father's side to the Van Gelderns, a family of Dutch court Jews that included Heinrich Heine's mother and Salomon van Geldern, who was famous in the eighteenth century for his travels in North Africa; cf. Scholem 1981:18.

9. Benjamin stocks his memory with details from Schiller's nationalist ode to the German bourgeois household, "The Song of the Bell." Benjamin's family, like many assimilated Jews, may well have endeavored to prove their Germanness by mimetically reproducing the stock self-images of the German bourgeoisie offered up by their national poet.

10. Representative of these views is the discussion in Nordau 1884:2–3; cf. Arendt 1969:30–34; and Klein 1985:chap. 1.

11. Other evocative references include the depiction of the pedestrians' restlessness and gesticulation, which were a part of the standard inventory of Jewish caricature; the image of servility too was a frequent component. Buttressing the implicit analogy of the urban crowd with the Jews are Benjamin's qualifier about their social and employment positions and its renewed citation following this passage: "One might think [Poe] was speaking of half-drunken wretches. Actually they were 'high-class people, merchants, lawyers, and stock-jobbers' " (1969c:171; translation modified). These three professions were largely identified as Jewish.

12. One of the most famous accounts appears in *Interpretation of Dreams*, where Freud (1961b:197) recalls his father's being assaulted on the sidewalks of Freiberg.

13. Cf. Adorno's response to Benjamin's "Arcades" exposé; letter of Theodor W. Adorno to Benjamin, August 2, 1935; Benjamin 1994:494–503, esp. 497–98. Benjamin's relationship with Carl Schmitt has also been contentious; cf. Weber 1992.

14. However, Benjamin ignores Daudet's discussion of aura in "Baudelaire: The Malaise and the Aura" (1929:205–8, 212), which draws upon aura's connection with epilepsy and by extension with illness of the soul.

15. Some ten years later, he would describe Daudet's work, such as the 1922 anti-Jewish tract *Stupid 19th Century*, as "an especially bizarre and poisonous flower" that grows out of the "alliance between ignorance and baseness"; letter to Max Horkheimer, April 16, 1938; Benjamin 1994:558.

16. I would like to thank Professor James Boon for recalling to me the implications of my own presuppositions.

17. Cf. Kafka's letter to Max Brod, June 1921, on the impossibility of a German Jew (not) writing in German; Kafka 1977:288–89; also cf. Arendt 1969:31–32.

18. Almost immediately after sending Rang his "Communication" he writes him a follow-up letter in which he concedes that touching upon the Jewish Question would have been "to put it mildly... inappropriate" (letter of November 26, 1923; Benjamin 1994:219). He also expresses his concerns—which he claims to have set aside, if not overcome—about the negative effect his public expression of support for Rang would have on his (i.e., Benjamin's) efforts to attain a Habilitation (219).

19. While many sections of Benjamin's reminiscence appeared prior to the 1950 publication by Adorno of the entire collection, these two do not. Moreover, since we lack both Benjamin's earlier versions of the collection and his possible oral communications with the Adornos, whether this juxtaposition as it appears was in fact intended by Benjamin cannot be ultimately determined. Cf. Tillman Rexroth's editorial notes, Benjamin 1972-:4.2:968–69.

20. The Hebrew words for *name* and *circumcision* are homophones: *mila*. Further, in the kabalistic tradition circumcision inscribes on the penis a name: the name of God (Tanhuma Tsav 14; cit. Wolfson 1987:78).

21. Benjamin was quite familiar with the work of this now rather obscure writer. In 1930 Benjamin composed a radio talk in which he discussed Panizza's work along with E. T. A. Hoffmann's. Although Benjamin does not specifically refer to this story, he does refer to others from the collection in which it appeared (1972d:645, 647). Moreover, one of Benjamin's favorite authors, Mynona (Salomo Friedländer), had earlier written a parody of "The Operated Jew," "The Operated Goy."

22. Benjamin 1972c:495–500; in his discussion of upright gait in the "Arcades" project, Benjamin (1982a:1:131–32 [B10, 2 — B10a, 1]) shifts the terminology from the implicitly moral to the mechanical (i.e., vertical and horizontal) and also cites Wilhelm Lotze, who questions the significance usually placed upon the shift in orientation. Already in a 1920 fragment, "Perception and Body" (1985a:67), Benjamin had mused in a general way about the transformation in perception with the assumption of an upright gait.

23. On Nietzsche's privileging olfactory perception for his genealogy of culture, see Blondel 1991:113–24. Blondel writes, "Genealogy is properly speaking *Otorhinology*, a listening to an olfactory perception of the distant or profound body" (113), and then proceeds to cite an extensive selection of passages from Nietzsche's work that draw upon an olfactory hermeneutic.

24. Letter of Theodor W. Adorno to Benjamin, August 2, 1935; Benjamin 1994: 497–98. In response Benjamin argues for the retention of Klages as part of a critique of his and Jung's notions of the archaic image; cf. the editorial notes to "Charles Baude-

laire. A Lyric Poet in the Era of High Capitalism," which include Benjamin's correspondence with Adorno, Horkheimer, and Scholem on this matter, Benjamin 1972-:1.3: 1066–92, esp. Benjamin's letters to Adorno (April 23, 1937 [1067]; July 10, 1937 [1070]), to Scholem (August 5, 1937 [1070]), and to Horkheimer (September 28, 1938 [1091]).

25. Just as Robespierre looked to ancient Rome in a time of crisis (Benjamin 1969f: 261 [Thesis xiv]), so too Benjamin—to the Rome imagined by Alfred Schuler. Although they were delivered during World War I the lectures were not published until World War II (1940).

26. Klages apparently confirms the privilege of aroma if not the judgment about his discernment of the native and the foreign since he emphasizes this odorous—for him odious—passage. In the introduction Klages omits the author's name, claims the born-Protestant Wolters is Jewish (although under 1940 German law he could be so classified since he was the grandson of a Russian Jewish poet and translator), and changes the title to *Book of Vengeance*.

27. In a later letter to Scholem (August 15, 1930), Benjamin (1994:366) alludes to Klages's anti-Semitism while praising his new philosophic tract, *The Spirit as Adversary of the Soul*: "It is without doubt a great philosophical work, regardless of the context in which the author may be and remain suspect."

28. Luther's Bible more literally translates *hariho* and Isa. 11:3: "mein Riechen wird sein bei der Furcht des Herrn."

29. While Benjamin plays upon the typicality and kitschiness of the lavender sachets of his reminiscence, he personalizes the experience.

30. Benjamin 1982a:1:574 (N1a, 8). Cf. his description in "The Paris of the Second Empire in Baudelaire" (1972a:583) of the poet as the one who "every moment pauses on his way in order to pick up the refuse he bumps into."

31. Cf. Benjamin 1982a:1:441 (J68, 4), in which he quotes Baudelaire, "Of Wine and Hashish," describing the ragpicker as one who not only collects the refuse of the city but catalogs it as well. Benjamin claims that Baudelaire identifies with the ragpicker. Irving Wohlfahrt (1984) depicts Benjamin the historian as ragpicker.

32. Benjamin 1972a:521. Also cf. 1982a:1:441–42 (J68, 3—J68a, 6); Benjamin focuses on the ragpicker as proletarian, garbage as objects to be collected, and wine.

33. The one exception (1982a1:630 [O8a, 2]), the excerpt from Rey, *Manufacturer of Cashmere*, explaining the rationale for flower prints on shawls, is discussed earlier.

34. In "The Paris of the Second Empire in Baudelaire" Benjamin (1972a:523–24) connects the ragpicker to a racial discourse. First he identifies him with the "Race of Cain," which is opposed to the "Race of Abel" in Baudelaire's poem "Abel and Cain." Then he ties these descendants of Cain to the race of "peculiar commodity-owners" (citing Marx 1976:275), i.e., the proletariat whose only property is their own labor. In *The Jews and Modern Capitalism* Sombart (1911:177) suggests that the Jews "could be called the fathers of the refuse trade [*Abfallindustrie*]."

35. Because it indicates even as it repudiates the real, the material, the detritus left over from history's victorious swath through the past—in sum, the objective realm that Benjamin hopes to redeem, to have redeemed—the disgusting smell embodies the ambivalent value determinations that the word *Ekel* had long had for Benjamin. In his memoir of his friendship with Benjamin, Scholem (1981:55) recounts how "*Ekul*, which in contrast to *Ekel* was used in a highly positive sense," was a favorite pet name shared between Benjamin and his wife, Dora.

36. Among the other motifs that were coded Jewish and played significant roles in Benjamin's work are atavistic ritual, urbanism, and French culture; on the Jewishness of an interest in matters French, see, for example, Mehlman 1987:669–70.

37. And by Kafka as well. In his Kafka essay, Benjamin (1969b:122) remarks: "Do we possess the doctrine which is accompanied by Kafka's similes and explained in the gestures of K. and the mimicry [*Gebärden*] of his animals? It is not there; at most we can say that this and that alludes to it." Benjamin's focus upon three mimetic acts—similes, gestures, mimicry—that have "a similar relationship to doctrine as the Haggadah does to the Halakah" at the very least alludes to some relationship between Judaism and mimesis.

38. If the end began with the repression of smell—then the return of smell—like mimesis and aura—offers Horkheimer and Adorno, if not a whiff of redemption, then a pessimistic commentary on humanity's dialectical fate. The concluding note of their work "The Genesis of Stupidity" begins with an allusion to Goethe's *Faust I* (cf. "Walpurgisnacht," ll. 4067–68) and Nietzsche's *Ecce Homo* (1969:233): "The true symbol of intelligence is the snail's horn with which it feels [*Fühlhorn*] and (if Mephistopheles is to be believed) smells its way" (Horkheimer and Adorno 1972:256). If it scents any obstacle, it recoils, "becoming one with the whole" (256). This oscillation of progress and petrification continues both ontogenetically and phylogenetically with a crucial dialectical shift: if mimetic defense impedes intellectual progress, the defense against mimesis distorts it. In an earlier discussion of the myth of Odysseus and Circe, Horkheimer and Adorno (71 and n41) had already noted speculations about the relationship between smelling and reason: having determined with the aid of Freud's footnotes from *Civilization* that "in the image of the pig the pleasure of smell is already reduced to the unfree snuffling of one who has his nose to the ground and renounces his upright carriage," they cite a note from Wilamowitz-Moellendorff, *Odysseus's Return Home,* 191: "Schwyzer has quite convincingly related *noos* [autonomous reason] to snorting and snuffling" etymologically. Smell, the zero-degree sense of intelligence and of mimesis, comes to symbolize for Horkheimer and Adorno the horns of humanity's dilemma.

39. While Jay (1973:269–70) provides only the most incidental of genealogies for Horkheimer and Adorno's use of the term *mimesis,* Susan Buck-Morss (1977:87–88) at least mentions its long-playing role in the history of aesthetic speculation from Plato and Aristotle on. In invoking Horkheimer and Adorno's adoption of the term she discusses Benjamin's understanding of the notion; she does not relate it to their application of it to the analysis of anti-Semitism, nor in fact does she pay any but the most indirect attention to its use in that analysis.

40. These consequences of Darwin's study of animal imitation for later understandings of mimesis is clearly borne out by Horkheimer and Adorno (cf. 1972:180–82).

41. Cf. letter to Scholem, October 22, 1917: "A principal component of *vulgar* anti-Semitic as well as Zionist ideology is that the gentile's hatred of the Jew is physiologically substantiated on the basis of instinct and race, since it turns against the physis.... Whatever basis and grounds [this principal component] may have, in its most primitive and intensive forms it becomes hatred for the physical nature of the one who is hated" (Benjamin 1994:99).

Bibliography

Adorno, Theodor W. 1977. The Actuality of Philosophy. *Telos* 31.

———. 1988. Introduction to Benjamin's *Schriften.* In *On Walter Benjamin: Critical Essays and Recollections,* ed. Gary Smith. Cambridge, Mass.: MIT Press.

Andree, Richard. 1881. *Zur Volkskunde der Juden.* Bielefeld/Leipzig: Velhagen & Klasing.

Arendt, Hannah. 1969. Introduction: Walter Benjamin 1892–1940. In Benjamin, *Illuminations*.

Aschheim, Steven E. 1982. *Brothers and Strangers: The East European Jew in German and German Jewish Consciousness, 1800–1923*. Madison: University of Wisconsin Press.

Ash, Beth Sharon. 1989. Walter Benjamin: Ethnic Fears, Oedipal Anxieties, Political Consequences. *New German Critique* 48: 2–42.

Baudelaire, Charles. 1982. *Les Fleurs du Mal*. Tr. Richard Howard. Boston: Godine.

Benjamin, Walter. 1966. *Briefe*. Ed. Gershom Scholem and Theodor Adorno. 2 vols. Frankfurt: Suhrkamp.

———. 1969a. *Illuminations*. Ed. Hannah Arendt, tr. Harry Zohn. New York: Schocken.

———. 1969b. Franz Kafka. On the Tenth Anniversary of His Death. In *Illuminations*.

———. 1969c. On Some Motifs in Baudelaire. In *Illuminations*.

———. 1969d. The Image of Proust. In *Illuminations*.

———. 1969e. The Work of Art in the Age of Mechanical Reproduction. In *Illuminations*.

———. 1969f. Theses on the Philosophy of History. In *Illuminations*.

———. 1972-. *Gesammelten Schriften*. Ed. Rolf Tiedemann and Hermann Schweppenhäuser. 7+ vols. Frankfurt: Suhrkamp.

———. 1972a. Das Paris des Second Empire bei Baudelaire. *Gesammelten Schriften* 1.2.

———. 1972b. Gottfried Keller. *Gesammelten Schriften* 2.1.

———. 1972c. Eduard Fuchs, der Sammler und der Historiker. *Gesammelten Schriften* 2.2.

———. 1972d. E. T. A. Hoffmann und Oskar Panizza. *Gesammelten Schriften* 2.2.

———. 1972e. Juden in der deutschen Kultur. *Gesammelten Schriften* 2.2.

———. 1972f. Ein Aussenseiter macht sich Bemerkbar. *Gesammelten Schriften* 3.

———. 1972g. Theologische Kritik: Zu Willy Haas, *Gestalten der Zeit*. *Gesammelten Schriften* 3.

———. 1972h. Berliner Kindheit um Neunzehnhundert. *Gesammelten Schriften* 4.1.

———. 1972i. Translation of Charles Baudelaire, *Tableaux parisiens*. *Gesammelten Schriften* 4.1.

———. 1977. *The Origin of German Tragic Drama*. Tr. John Osborne. London: NLB.

———. 1978a. *Representations*. Ed. Peter Demetz, tr. Edmund Jephcott. New York: Harcourt Brace Jovanovich.

———. 1978b. A Berlin Chronicle. In *Representations*.

———. 1978c. Surrealism. In *Representations*.

———. 1978d. Critique of Violence. In *Representations*.

———. 1978e. On the Mimetic Faculty. In *Representations*.

———. 1979. Doctrine of the Similar. *New German Critique* 17: 65–69.

———. 1982a. *Das Passagen-Werk*. Ed. Rolf Tiedemann. 2 vols. Frankfurt: Suhrkamp. (Vol. 5 of *Gesammelten Schriften*)

———. 1982b. Pariser Passagen I. In *Das Passagen-Werk. Zweiter Band*. (Vol. 5.2 of *Gesammelten Schriften*)

———. 1983–84. N [Theoretics of Knowledge, Theory of Progress]. *Philosophical Forum* 15.1–2: 1–40.

———. 1985a. Wahrnehmung und Leib. In *Gesammelten Schriften* 6.

———. 1985b. Berliner Chronik. In *Gesammelten Schriften* 6.

———. 1985c. Protokolle zu Drogenversuchen. In *Gesammelten Schriften* 6.

———. 1994. *The Correspondence of Walter Benjamin.* Ed. Gershom Scholem and Theodor Adorno. Tr. Manfred R. Jacobson and Evelyn M. Jacobson. Chicago: University of Chicago Press.

Berillon, Edgar. 1908–9. Psychologie de l'olfaction: La fascination olfactive chez les animaux et chez l'homme. *Revue de l'hypnotisme et de la psychologie physiologique* 23: 98–103, 135–38, 167–69, 196–200, 235–39, 263–67, 303–7.

Bernheimer, Charles. 1989. *Figures of Ill Repute: Representing Prostitution in Nineteenth-Century France.* Cambridge, Mass.: Harvard University Press.

Blondel, Eric. 1991. *Nietzsche: The Body and Culture. Philosophy as a Philological Genealogy.* Tr. Seán Hand. Stanford, Calif.: Stanford University Press.

Buck-Morss, Susan. 1977. *The Origin of Negative Dialectics: Theodor W. Adorno, Walter Benjamin, and the Frankfurt Institute.* New York: Free Press.

———. 1989. *The Dialectics of Seeing: Walter Benjamin and the Arcades Project.* Cambridge, Mass.: MIT Press.

———. 1992. Aesthetics and Anaesthetics: Walter Benjamin's Artwork Essay Reconsidered. *October* 62.

Corbin, Alain. 1986. *The Foul and the Fragrant.* Cambridge, Mass.: Harvard University Press.

———. 1990. *Women for Hire: Prostitution and Sexuality in France after 1850.* Tr. Alan Sheridan. Cambridge, Mass.: Harvard University Press.

Cuddihy, John Murray. 1974. *The Ordeal of Civility: Freud, Marx, Lévi-Strauss, and the Jewish Struggle with Modernity.* New York: Basic Books.

Daudet, Léon. 1929. Baudelaire: Le Malaise et 'L'aura.' In *Flambeaux.* Paris: Bernard Grasset.

Ellis, Havelock. 1928. *Sexual Selection in Man.* Vol. 4 of *Studies in the Psychology of Sex.* Rev. and enl. ed. Philadelphia: Davis.

Freud, Sigmund. 1961a. *The Standard Edition of the Complete Psychological Works.* Ed. and tr. James Strachey. London: Hogarth.

———. 1961b. *The Interpretation of Dreams. S.E.* 4–5.

———. 1961c. *Jokes and Their Relationship to the Unconscious. S.E.* 8.

———. 1961d. *Civilization and Its Discontents. S.E.* 21.

Frisby, David. 1986. *Fragments of Modernity: Theories of Modernity in the Work of Simmel, Kracauer and Benjamin.* Cambridge, Mass.: MIT Press.

Fuld, Werner. 1979. Die Aura. Zur Geschichte eines Begriffes bei Benjamin. *Akzente* 26: 352–70.

Geller, Jay. 1992a. Blood Sin: Syphilis and the Construction of Jewish Identity. *Faultline* 1: 21–48.

———. 1992b. (G)nos(e)ology: The Cultural Construction of the Other. In *The People of the Body,* ed. Howard Eilberg-Schwartz. Albany: State University of New York Press.

———. 1993a. A Paleontological View of Freud's Study of Religion: Unearthing the *Leitfossil* Circumcision. *Modern Judaism* 13: 49–70.

———. 1993b. Freud v. Freud: Freud's Readings of the *Denkwürdigkeiten eines Nervenkranken.* In *Reading Freud's Reading,* ed. Jay Geller et al. New York: New York University Press.

———. 1994. Of Mice and Mensa: Antisemitism and the Jewish Genius. *Centennial Review* 38: 361–85.

Gilman, Sander. 1993. *Freud, Race, and Gender.* Princeton, N.J.: Princeton University Press.

Goldstein, Moritz. 1912. Deutsch-jüdischer Parnaß. *Der Kunstwart* 25.11: 281–94.

Gonzalez-Crussi, F. 1991. *The Five Senses*. New York: Vintage.

Gray, Richard T. 1993. The Dialectic of 'Enscentment': Patrick Süskind's *Das Parfum* as Critical History of Enlightenment Culture. *PMLA* 108: 489–505.

Günther, Hans. 1934. *Rassenkunde des jüdischen Volkes*. Munich: Lehmann.

Harsin, Jill. 1985. *Policing Prostitution in Nineteenth-Century Paris*. Princeton, N.J.: Princeton University Press.

Heine, Heinrich. 1982. *The Complete Poems of Heinrich Heine*. Tr. Hal Draper. N.p.: Suhrkamp/Insel.

Hess, Moses. 1943. *Rome and Jerusalem: A Study in Jewish Nationality*. Tr. Meyer Waxman. New York: Bloch.

Hitler, Adolf. 1943. *Mein Kampf*. Tr. R. Manheim. Boston: Houghton Mifflin.

Horkheimer, Max, and Theodor W. Adorno. 1969. *Dialektik der Aufklärung*. Frankfurt: Fischer.

———. 1972. *Dialectic of Enlightenment*. Tr. John Cumming. New York: Seabury.

Howes, David. 1987. "Olfaction and Transition: An Essay in Ritual Uses of Smell." *Canadian Review of Sociology and Anthropology* 24: 390–416.

Jaeger, Gustav. 1884. *Entdeckung der Seele*. Vol. 1, 3d ed. Leipzig: Kohlhammer.

Jay, Martin. 1973. *The Dialectical Imagination: A History of the Frankfurt School and the Institute of Social Research, 1923–1950*. Boston: Little, Brown.

Jennings, Michael. 1987. *Dialectical Images: Walter Benjamin's Theory of Literary Criticism*. Ithaca, N.Y.: Cornell University Press.

Kafka, Franz. 1953. *Letter to His Father/Brief an den Vater*. Tr. Ernst Kaiser and Eithne Wilkins. New York: Schocken.

———. 1977. *Letters to Friends, Family, and Editors*. Tr. Richard and Clara Winston. New York: Schocken.

Kant, Immanuel. 1952. *The Critique of Judgment*. Tr. James Creed Meredith. Oxford: Clarendon.

———. 1974. *Anthropology from a Pragmatic Point of View*. Tr. M. J. Gregor. The Hague: Martinus Nijhoff.

Klages, Ludwig. 1904. Typische Ausdrucksstörungen und das Wesen der Hysterie. *Graphologische Monatsheft* 7.

———. 1910. *Die Probleme der Graphologie. Entwurf einer Psychodiagnostik*. Leipzig: Johann Ambrosius Barth.

———. 1940. Einleitung. In Schuler, *Fragmente und Vorträge aus dem Nachlass*.

Klein, Dennis B. 1985. *Jewish Origins of the Psychoanalytic Movement*. Chicago: University of Chicago Press.

Landesberger, Arthur, ed. 1912. *Judentaufen*. Munich: Miller.

Le Guérer, Annick. 1992. *Scent: The Mysterious and Essential Powers of Smell*. Tr. Richard Miller. New York: Turtle Bay.

Marx, Karl. 1976. *Capital*. Tr. Ben Fowkes. Vol. 1. New York: Random House.

Mehlman, Jeffrey. 1987. Review of Sander L. Gilman, *Jewish Self-Hatred*. MLN. 102: 668–72.

Neusner, Jacob. 1984. *Torah from Our Sages*. *Pirke Avot*. Dallas: Rossel.

Nietzsche, Friedrich. 1968. *The Anti-Christ*. In *Twilight of the Idols/The Anti-Christ*. Tr. R. J. Hollingdale. Harmondsworth: Penguin.

———. 1969. *Ecce Homo*. In *On the Genealogy of Morals/Ecce Homo*, tr. W. Kaufmann. New York: Random House.

———. 1974. *The Gay Science*. Tr. Walter Kaufmann. New York: Vintage.

———. 1980. *Thus Spoke Zarathustra*. In *The Portable Nietzsche*, ed. Walter Kaufmann. New York: Viking.

———. 1990. History in the Service and Disservice of Life. In *Unmodern Observations,* ed. William Arrowsmith, tr. Gary Brown. New Haven, Conn.: Yale University Press.

Nordau, Max. 1884. *Die conventionellen Lügen der Kulturmenschheit.* Leipzig: Bernhard Schlicke.

Norris, Margot. 1980. Darwin, Nietzsche, Kafka, and the Problem of Mimesis. *MLN* 95: 1232–53.

Panizza, Oskar. 1980. The Operated Jew. *New German Critique* 21.

Patai, Raphael. 1979. *The Messiah Texts.* Detroit: Wayne State University Press.

Pulzer, Peter G. J. 1964. *The Rise of Political Anti-Semitism in Germany and Austria.* New York: Wiley.

Rabinbach, Anson. 1985. Between Enlightenment and Apocalypse: Benjamin, Bloch and Modern German Jewish Messianism. *New German Critique* 34: 78–124.

Rey, J. 1823. *Fabricant de cachemires: Etudes pour servir à l'histoire des châles.* Paris.

Rindisbacher, Hans J. 1992. *The Smell of Books: A Cultural-Historical Study of Olfactory Perception in Literature.* Ann Arbor: University of Michigan Press.

Roberts, Julian. 1982. *Walter Benjamin.* London: Macmillan.

Rosario, Vernon A. 1991. Erotic 'Non' Fictions and the Scent of the Perverse. Unpublished manuscript.

Schlegel, Friedrich. 1962. *Lucinde.* In *Dichtungen,* ed. Hans Eichner. Vol. 5 of *Kritische Friedrich-Schlegel-Ausgabe,* ed. Ernst Behler, with Jean-Jacques Anstett and Hans Eichner. Munich: Verlag Ferdinand Schöning.

Scholem, Gershom. 1976a. *On Jews and Judaism in Crisis: Selected Essays.* Ed. Werner J. Dannhauser. New York: Schocken.

———. 1976b. Jews and Germans. In *On Jews and Judaism in Crisis.*

———. 1976c. Walter Benjamin and His Angel. In *On Jews and Judaism in Crisis.*

———. 1980. *From Berlin to Jerusalem: Memories of My Youth.* New York: Schocken.

———. 1981. *Walter Benjamin: The Story of a Friendship.* Tr. Harry Zohn. Philadelphia: Jewish Publication Society.

Schopenhauer, Arthur. 1958. *World as Will and Representation.* Tr. E. F. J. Payne. 2 vols. Clinton, Mass.: Falcon's Wing.

Schuler, Alfred. 1940. *Fragmente und Vorträge aus dem Nachlass.* Ed. Ludwig Klages. Leipzig: Verlag Johann Ambrosius Barth.

Smith, Gary. 1991. 'Das Jüdische versteht sich von selbst': Walter Benjamins frühe Auseinandersetzung mit dem Judentum. *Deutsche Vierteljahrschrift für Literaturwissenschaft und Geistesgeschichte* 65: 318–34.

Sombart, Werner. 1911. *Die Juden und das Wirtschaftsleben.* Leipzig: Duncker and Humblot.

———. 1912. *Die Zukunft der Juden.* Leipzig: Duncker and Humblot.

Stallybrass, Peter, and Allon White. 1986. *The Politics and Poetics of Transgression.* Ithaca, N.Y.: Cornell University Press.

Stoessel, Marleen. 1983. *Aura. Das vergessene Menschliche: Zu Sprache und Erfahrung bei Walter Benjamin.* Munich: Carl Hanser.

Taussig, Michael. 1993. *Mimesis and Alterity: A Particular History of the Senses.* New York: Routledge, Chapman and Hall.

Wagner, Richard. 1897. *Judaism in Music.* In *Richard Wagner's Prose Works,* ed. W. A. Ellis. Vol. 3. London: Kegan Paul.

Weber, Samuel. 1992. Taking Exception to Decision: Walter Benjamin and Carl Schmitt. *Diacritics* 22.3–4: 5–18.

Weininger, Otto. 1906. *Sex and Character.* Tr. of 6th ed. New York: Putnam.

Witte, Bernd. 1991. *Walter Benjamin: An Intellectual Biography.* Tr. James Rolleston. Detroit: Wayne State University Press.

Wohlfahrt, Irving. 1984. Et cetera? Der Historiker als Lumpensammler. In *Passagen. Walter Benjamins Urgeschichte des neunzehnten Jahrhunderts,* ed. Norbert Bolz and Bernd Witte. Munich: Wilhelm Funk.

Wolfson, Elliot R. 1987. Circumcision and the Divine Name: A Study in the Transmission of Esoteric Doctrine. *Jewish Quarterly Review* 78 (July–October): 77–112.

Wolters, Friedrich. 1929. *Stefan George und die Blätter für die Kunst. Deutsche Geistesgeschichte seit 1890.* Munich: Bondi.

9 / Beyond Deleuze and Guattari: Hebrew and Yiddish Modernism in the Age of Privileged Difference

Chana Kronfeld

(First Century Jerusalem. A crowd of followers congregates outside the hovel where Brian, an anachronistic, parodic double for Christ, lives with his mother. The chanting mob arouses Brian from his first night with his lover, Judith, who is the sole female member of the Peoples' Front of Judea, an ineffectual splinter group fighting against the Roman occupation. Reluctantly, Brian opens the window and tries to get the noisy crowd to disperse.)

> Crowd: A blessing! A blessing!
> *(More pandemonium)*
> Brian: No, please. Please. Please listen.
> *(they quieten)*
>   I've got one or two things to say.
> Crowd: Tell us. Tell us both of them!!
> Brian: Look . . . you've got it all wrong. You don't need to follow me. You don't need to follow anybody. You've got to think for yourselves. You're all individuals.
> Crowd: Yes, we're all individuals.
> Brian: You're all different.
> Crowd: Yes, we *are* all different.
> Dennis: I'm not.
> Crowd: Sssshhh!
>
> MONTY PYTHON, The Life of Brian<a>[1]</a>

The 1979 movie *The Life of Brian* offers itself, in Monty Python's irreverent parodic logic, as parable or midrash on the place of Hebrew and Yiddish modernism in the age of privileged difference. Difference iterated and echoed in unison ("Yes, we *are* all different") is difference erased, a gesture that can be met only with resistance, with a refusal to be different in the manner prescribed by the consensus ("I'm not"). From its collective vantage point outside Brian's door, the crowd embraces otherness as a force that consolidates a majority. In the process, they turn Brian, that antiheroic mock-Christ, into a figure of absolute yet vacuous authority. But it is Dennis, the little bearded man in the left-hand corner of the frame, the one who mumbles "I'm not" and is never heard from again, on whom I wish to turn the spotlight.

What does it mean to be that writer, that reader on the margins of international modernism, in the corner of the picture yet part of it, when the crowd at the center clusters around a homogenized, privileged construction of difference? What does it mean for the visibility or audibility of that writer, that reader, when the center, in the process of championing difference, denies both that writer's modernism and his or her minor status?[2] Finally, what does it mean for the field if the very theoretical models that aim to uncover "the damage inflicted on minority cultures" participate in replicating its institutional structure (JanMohamed and Lloyd 1990:9)?

Modernism is famous for its affinity for the marginal, the exile, the "other." Yet the representative examples of this marginality typically are those writers who have become the most canonical high modernists. Their "narrative of unsettlement, homelessness, solitude and impoverished independence" (Williams 1989:34) may indeed have been cast in minor, discordant tones, but those tones were composed in the major key of the most commonly read European languages: English, French, German. While they sometimes acknowledge the multicultural, international nature of the movement, handbooks as well as theoretical debates on modernism and minor writing consistently focus on -isms and writers that are well within this major linguistic and geopolitical key. Consequently, even hugely influential trends within European modernism itself are sometimes made to sound like a casual codetta: Scandinavian modernism, by many accounts the overture to all later trends; or the two very different variations on futurism, the Italian and the Russian; or the still resonant din of Romanian dada (described by most critics as French).[3] These modernisms usually get the cursory nod, while the focus of discussion remains on the canon-ically privileged modalities of difference in Kafka and Pound, Proust and Joyce.

Very few of the discussions of international modernism available in English or French or German include Russian acmeism or Russian imaginism, although important poets who see themselves as affiliated with these trends can be found not only in Russia but also all the way over in the Palestine of the 1920s and 1930s. We may love to read the acmeists Anna Akhmatova and Osip Mandelstam, even the imaginist Sergey Yesenin, in translation, but this does not make our view of international modernism more inclusive.[4] This is perhaps only natural, since historical and theoretical discourse on literature is always tacitly based on what I call a selective modeling of literary production, a modeling that both constitutes and serves its own cultural prototypes. But the selective processes, their tendentiousness and utility, should be opened up for analysis and not simply accepted as inevitable, built-in blinders.

Raymond Williams exposes the link between consolidating a Euro-American modernist canon from what was once a marginal literary trend and erasing unprivileged formations of marginality. His words resonate with special poignancy because they may have been among his last. These are his notes for the first chapter of an unfinished book, brilliantly edited and introduced by Tony Pinkney in the posthumous volume *The Politics of Modernism:*

> After Modernism is canonized, however, by the post-war settlement and its accompanying, complicit academic endorsements, there is then the presumption that since Modernism is *here* in this specific phase or period, there is nothing beyond it. The [once] marginal or rejected artists become classics of organized teaching and of travelling exhibitions in the great galleries of the metropolitan cities. 'Modernism' is confined to this highly selective field and denied to everything else in an act of pure ideology, whose first, unconscious irony is that, absurdly, it stops history dead.
>
> ... We must search out and counterpose an alternative tradition taken from the neglected works left in the wide margins of the century. (Williams 1989:34–35)

Searching out and counterposing such alternative traditions on the margins of modernism is, indeed, my primary goal here, for the exclusion of minor modernisms from standard accounts of this international movement is most damaging outside the official borders of the unarticulated yet powerful cartographic paradigm: international modernism = Europe + United States. Let me offer just one example. Malcolm Bradbury and James McFarlane's excellent critical anthology *Modernism 1890–1930* ([1976] 1981) is much more sensitive than most traditional treatments of modernism to the movement's diversity and heterogeneity. It nevertheless adheres implicitly to the cartographic formula, never straying beyond the boundaries of Europe and the United States. Not coincidentally, this same anthology also systematically marginalizes the crucial role women writers and editors played in the dynamics of international modernism, minimizing even the contribution of those women who were active within the Euro-American frame.[5]

How to search out and counterpose an alternative tradition and alternative theory of marginal modernisms without universalizing them out of existence? How to account, within a theoretically rigorous model, both for the women and minorities traditionally marginalized within the Euro-American canon and for the diverse groups and individual female and male writers outside the cartographic and linguistic mainstream? Writers the world over have self-consciously participated in — not simply been "influenced by" — the great international experiment with the -isms of modernism. But, ironically, Arabic, Hebrew, Senegalese, Japanese, and Yiddish literatures (among many others) have been excluded from recent theories of minor writing by the theoretical premises of the very same recovery project that should have made their voices audible.

Nevertheless, current theories of the minor have had an important effect in a number of ways. They have refocused attention on the decentering, deterritorializing, indeed the revolutionary and innovative force of minor writing. At the same time they have also underscored the potential appropriation of the minor by the major canonical system; and they have pointed out ways in which a minor literature can replicate exclusionary practices in its attempt to model itself after the hegemonic literary canon. Recent discussions have also helped reinscribe the association between minor and modernist, charging the old alliance between the two concepts with a new political urgency. All these perspectives have proven exceedingly helpful to me in the articulation of the history and theory of marginal modernisms (Kronfeld 1996).

Yet coming as I do from the perspective of two literatures, Hebrew and Yiddish, whose (different) modernisms and modes of minor writing do not fit into the postcolonial models now in vogue, I am troubled by what I see as the exclusionary effect of current definitions of the minor. All too often the selective modeling of minor literature—as of "international modernism"—on a Euro-American geopolitics and linguistics effectively leaves all that is not English, French, or German (or "deterritorialized" versions thereof) outside our purview. This exclusion is not merely a result of a bad choice of examples but is logically entailed by the explicitly articulated principles of the most detailed theories of minor writing available to date.[6] Only if we construct the major through the minor, not—as current wisdom has it—the minor through the major, can we begin to discern the regionalism, contextual diversity, and interdependence of even the most highly canonical forms of modernism. Theories of modernism that are modeled on belated, decentered, or linguistically minor practices may provide some insight into the processes that have become automatized or that were rendered imperceptible in the canonical center. Through the multiple, broken prisms of the minor, the mystified notion of a unified canonical modernism is exploded, subjecting the very language of center and periphery itself to a critique that exposes its own historicity.[7]

Perhaps the best-known representatives of the current direction in theorizing about minor literature are Gilles Deleuze and Félix Guattari, whose intent is undoubtedly progressive but whose effect may be quite restrictive. Their famous essay "What Is a Minor Literature?" (chapter 3 of Deleuze and Guattari [1975] 1986),[8] elaborated somewhat critically by David Lloyd (1987 and 1990)[9] and somewhat less critically by others (compare Renza 1984), explicitly restricts minor, deterritorialized writing to "oppositional" writing in a major language:[10] "[a] minor literature doesn't come from a minor language; it is rather that which a minority constructs within a major language" (Deleuze and Guattari 1986:16). But, according to the same authors, minor literature (linguistically thus restricted) becomes the most, in fact the only, privileged category in the new theory and politics of culture: "there is nothing that is major or revolutionary except the minor" (1986:26). Furthermore, "the minor no longer designates specific literatures but the revolutionary conditions for every literature within the heart of what is called great (or established) literature" (1986:18).[11]

I believe this principle has highly restrictive theoretical and methodological consequences for a discussion of both modernist and minor writing. In a nutshell, Deleuze and Guattari's restriction of the minor to the language of the major culture precludes modeling an international trend such as modernism on its "nonmajor" linguistic practices. And, more generally, it implicitly rejects any historically, culturally, and linguistically specific formations of the minor. Deleuze and Guattari's highly influential essay and its offshoots in English and American postcolonial cultural criticism present a challenge I want to address in some detail. Anticipating the exclusionary potential of their critical project, Dana Polan, the translator of Deleuze and Guattari's *Kafka,* includes a rather strongly worded cautionary note in the introduction to the 1986 American edition: "Dangerously, despite all the efforts of Deleuze and Guattari to deconstruct hierarchies, American literary criticism may treat them . . . as aesthetes of a high-culture avant-garde closed in on its own fetishes of interiority. . . . One hopes that a translation of *Kafka* will be something that readers will question, as well as use" (xxvi).

More significantly for our purposes, Polan forewarns the readers that a "picking up of Deleuze and Guattari, then, would have to examine not only what they enable but also what they disenable, what they close off" (xxvi). It is precisely the consequences of this disenabling potential that I wish to argue against, with an eye to reinscribing those marginal modernisms that Deleuze and Guattari's model would write off as not "truly minor" and, by implication, as not fully capable of being agents of social and aesthetic change. Of greatest interest to me is the slippage between the concepts of the minor and the modernist, a slippage that is implicit in Deleuze and Guattari's account and becomes self-critically explicit in Lloyd's extended version.

Underlying both Deleuze and Guattari's three characteristics of minor literature and Lloyd's extended conditions for minor writing is the same fundamental principle: a minor literature is not written in a minor language. I will have more to say about this linguistic imperative later on. But, to begin, here are the defining features of the minor (within the language of the major), according to Deleuze and Guattari: "The three characteristics of minor literature are the deterritorialization of language, the connection of the individual to a political immediacy, and the collective assemblage of enunciation" (1986:18).

Lloyd provides a more nuanced and historicized interpretation of what he describes as Deleuze and Guattari's "impressionistic" and "mostly synchronic" account (1987:5). Yet his analysis reproduces the basic structure and methodolgical grid of their argument. As Gluzman astutely points out, both theories try to squeeze the highly diffuse and open-ended category of minor literature into a "checklist" of "necessary and sufficient conditions for membership in the category of minor writing."[12]

Lloyd's conditions for minor writing (as distinct from *minority* writing) expand and interpret each of Deleuze and Guattari's characteristics. Their first and second characteristics of the minor are further divided by Lloyd into two conditions each, and the third is interpreted as having three interrelated parts. Here are Lloyd's conditions for the minor: (1) "exclusion from the canon and, by extension, from the 'canonical form' of the state"; (2) sustained "oppositional relationship to the canon and the state" (3) "common perpetuating of non-identity"; and (4) refusal "to represent the attainment of autonomous subjectivity" (1987:21–22). Conditions (1) and (2) may be read as politicized, historicized extensions of Deleuze and Guattari's first characteristic, the deterritorialization of language. Conditions (3) and (4) may be seen as a more socially nuanced articulation of their second characteristic, the connection of the individual to political immediacy. Lloyd proposes further a triad of concrete stylistic strategies for minor writing that correlate roughly with Deleuze and Guattari's highly suggestive but unclear third characteristic, the "collective assemblage [*agencement*] of enunciation [*énonciation*]" (1986:18). These for Lloyd are three distinct but interrelated modes of intertextuality: parody, translation, and citation.

These criteria, and their attendant rhetorical devices, while much more coherent than Deleuze and Guattari's, preserve some of the original theory's methodological and historical difficulties. As Lloyd himself acknowledges, they fit not only minor writing but also — modernism!:

> A minor literature so defined overlaps in many respects with what has become known as modernism, and in most respects with post-modernism. . . . If minor literature belongs to the general field of modernism, it does so only as the negative critical aspect of modernism. In other words, wherever the writer continues to conceive the work as playing in some

sense a prefigurative and reconciling role, that work remains, whatever its stylistic features, assimilated to a canonical aesthetic. Hence modernists such as Eliot, Pound, and Yeats clearly belong within a major paradigm by right of the claims to transcending division and difference that constantly inform their works.

This ascription evidently initially has to ignore the difficulties these writers have in maintaining such claims in their historical moment, and to overlook the "minor" stylistic features to which they constantly have recourse. But these stylistic features...are symptomatic of a crisis of canonicity that is definitive of modernism itself. (1987:23-24)

The attempts at separating the notion of the minor and the modernist seem to create more difficulties than they resolve. Minor literatures are modernist only in that they take a critical or oppositional stance within the canon. But in order to take such a stance they have to be minor (by Lloyd's conditions 1 and 2). Since the same negative characteristics (or negations of "major" ones) define both critical modernism and minor writing, perhaps one way out of the impasse is to do away with the stylistic features or treat them as necessary but not sufficient conditions: if a writer possesses the stylistic features of a minor writer (parody, translation, citation) but turns out to serve some reconciling function in the canon (whichever way that is to be assessed), then that writer will not count as minor, despite those intertextual strategies. But in what sense are these stylistic features related to minor status and not simply typical of (major or minor) modernism? And if, as Lloyd acknowledges finally, "the crisis of canonicity...is definitive of modernism itself," how then can it be used to define only the oppositional (the minor) formations of modernism?

What I find far more troubling than this logical slippage is the implicit dehistoricization of both the minor and the modernist that accompanies it. Clearly, minor writing existed before modernism, even according to Deleuze and Guattari's linguistic principles, and it will continue to exist after modernism, but conflating the minor and the modernist without providing any historical criteria of contextualization blurs the temporality and cultural specificity of both: it entails that modernists be seen as major even if for the literary and political canon of the time their position was resistant and was only later assimilated to a canonical aesthetic. And cannot the process of canonization of a once minor poet historically turn her or his role into a "major" (canon preserving) one? As Raymond Williams pointedly observed in the passage I quoted earlier, "The marginal or rejected [modernist] artists become classics of organized teaching" (1989:34); or is Lloyd suggesting that some positions or stylistic strategies are "essentially," "eternally" critical? The reification of critical categories is no less a danger for progressive approaches than for conservative ones.

Let us consider for a brief moment an intriguingly analogous example taken from the opposite end of the literary-critical spectrum. Hugh Kenner is one of the modernist canon's most astute readers and an active participant in its formation and preservation. In his well-known article "The Making of the Modernist Canon" (1984) Kenner identifies "the supranational movement called International Modernism" exclusively, unabashedly with Irish and American "decentralized" English writing. To be a modernist is indeed to be an expatriate, a decentered writer, but it has to be in the one and only language of modernism: English. And not, God forbid, the English of African or African American or even Australian and Canadian modernisms. The deterritorialization that Kenner privileges is exclusively Amero-Irish, yet he gives this non-English English the name "International Modernism": "Though the language of International Modernism, like that of air control towers, proved to be English, none of its canonical works came either out of England or out of any mind formed there. International Modernism was the work of Irishmen and Americans. Its masterpieces include *Ulysses, The Waste Land,* the first thirty *Cantos*" (1984:367).

Kenner goes to some lengths to make his case by arguing, first, that French, German, Russian, and Italian models were important only in nonverbal modernisms and in (technological) modernity and, second, that none of the important English proponents of international modernism was in fact English. For that purpose he has to brutally de-canonize Virginia Woolf ("She is not part of International Modernism; she is an English novelist of manners, writing village gossip" [1984: 371]). He also needs to perform some acrobatics to deterritorialize those (male) "International Modernists" he does not wish to decanonize: "By contrast [with the expatriate American talent Pound, Eliot, H. D.] the native talent is apt to seem unimportant, or else proves not to be native: even Wyndham Lewis, who went to an English public school (Rugby), had been born near a dock at Amherst, Nova Scotia, on his American father's yacht" (1984:369).

This blatantly biased selective modeling of "international" modernism would be quite amusing if it were not so symptomatic. Although Deleuze and Guattari end up with a much more convincing illustration of modernist deterritorialization, their monolingual construction of the minor-within-the-major has a similarly exclusionary effect. This is the underlying premise of their famous reading of Franz Kafka as the prototypical example of minor writing. Let me stress that it is not the interpretive accuracy of their reading of Kafka that I am concerned with here, nor do I intend this as a critique of Kafka's own views about German, Yiddish, and Hebrew. What I focus on, instead, are the consequences of Deleuze and Guattari's use of Kafka as the paradigmatic example for their theory of minor writing. Their account of Kafka as a model for the minor runs into difficulties in three ways: the very choice of Kafka, the manner in which his minor status is constructed, and the modes of oppositional minority literature that such a construction excludes.

First, choosing one of the major writers of the international modernist canon as the example of minor literature immediately calls into question the usefulness of the category of minor writing itself. Nevertheless, one might argue, Kafka's major status within the canon was not part of the conditions under which his writing was shaped; furthermore, as Bluma Goldstein has observed, while Kafka is certainly highly canonical in the context of international modernism and as a contributor to that old category "world literature," his position in the German literary system is much more ambivalent.[13] Clearly, however, this choice pulls the category of the minor away from the senses of "marginalized," "suppressed," "excluded" — namely, away from a focus on the minor as a feature of the history and politics of a work's reception.

Second, in the process of constructing Kafka's minor position as a Jew writing in the hegemonic German within a Czech environment, Deleuze and Guattari in effect erase all the non-German dimensions of his literary affiliation — a remarkable feat since in the foreground of their narrative are pronouncements about multiculturalism, polylingualism, and in particular the "situation of the German language in Czechoslovakia, as a fluid language intermixed with Czech and Yiddish," which is what "will allow Kafka the possibility of invention" (1986:20). But upon closer examination it becomes clear that Deleuze and Guattari uncritically adopt the view (which Kafka himself may have held) that Yiddish is in principle just an oral, popular resource that a writer like Kafka can use only to deflate German, not a full-fledged language but a means to achieve that underlying goal of all minor writing, the deterritorialization of the major language, while rejecting Hebrew and Czech altogether:

> Kafka does not opt for a reterritorialization through the Czech language. Nor toward a hypercultural use of German with all sorts of oneiric or symbolic or mythic flights (even Hebrew-ifying ones), as was the case with the Prague school. Nor toward an oral, popular Yiddish. Instead, using the path that Yiddish opens up to him, he takes it in such a way as to convert it into a unique and solitary form of writing.... He will tear out of Prague German all the qualities of underdevelopment that it has tried to hide. (1986:25–26)

In order to reduce Kafka's project to that one "truly minor" goal of deterritorializing German, Deleuze and Guattari need to radically ignore Kafka's profound (yet resistant and therefore minor on their own account!) engagement with the intertextual echo chambers of Yiddish and Hebrew literary culture. Even if Kafka, like many of the Hebrew and Yiddish modernists of his time, did choose to resist the ornate allusive pastiche of biblical and liturgical phrases, to reject the "oneiric," symbolic mode of premodernist engagement with Jewish literary sources, this should not be mistaken for a total rejection of Hebrew as a literary-cultural affiliation. On the contrary, this move might be precisely what draws Kafka so much closer to the minimalist project in the Hebrew and Yiddish modernisms that emerge in the Vienna and Berlin (and also in the Moscow, Warsaw, Kiev, Tel Aviv, and New York) of Kafka's time.[14] Other critics have observed Kafka's resistant, abstracted thematization of the reading strategies and the interpretive models developed within Hebrew and Yiddish literatures (parable, midrash, Hasidic tale, textual commentary) in place of the customary citational style of premodernist Jewish textual traditions.[15] What remains to be studied, however, are the ways in which Kafka's metatextual practices may in fact point to partial affiliation (simultaneous with his other central European ones) with the liminal modernisms of the Hebrew *anti-nusach* (antiformulaic) modernists (Uri Nissan Genessin, Avraham Ben-Yitzhak, David Fogel, Dvora Baron, and Yosef Chaim Brenner).[16] What also needs to be explored is Kafka's possible alignment—not in terms of influence but as historicized intertextual affiliation—with the general project of Yiddish minimalist expressionism whose resistance to the citational model was articulated in the aesthetic principles of *nakete linyes,* naked lines, and *nakete lider,* naked poems (see Eric [1922] 1973).

Deleuze and Guattari's reduction of Kafka's literary cross-cultural project to an essentially monolingual tension between "good" and "poor" (that is, Jewish) German is therefore, at best, an instance of what I describe elsewhere as the single-lens construction of literary affiliation. My argument is that many of the exclusionary practices of literary theory and historiography can be traced back to an optical difficulty with stereoscopic and kaleidoscopic vision: the difficulty of seeing writers like Kafka, for example, as simultaneously maintaining multiple literary affiliations, and of viewing these multiple affiliations as partial, potentially contradictory, and ambivalent. But that is precisely the kind of critical vision I believe we need.

Deleuze and Guattari's narrative, slipping in and out of a suggestive but highly misleading *erlebte Rede* with the text of Kafka's diaries, his letters, and his lecture on Yiddish (1948–49; 1954) denies not only his work's links to the textual practices of Hebrew and Yiddish literature but also the very possibility of producing such oppositional literatures in the nonmajor languages. This third problem is to my mind the most critical one, for it is here that Deleuze and Guattari's model, and others based on its fundamental premises, come closest to Kenner's exclusion of the whole world except Ireland and the United States from international modernism: Kafka's modernism could only have been German and it could only have been oppositional (in the privileged sense) in German. Hebrew, on this account, cannot be the language of a minor literature during Kafka's period because it is associated with Zionism, mysticism, and a reterritorialization of language in the service of a nation building process—all ways in which a minority literature replicates the formations of a hegemonic, major culture. Yiddish fares even worse since it is considered to be not a language but a "graft"; it is denied minor status and access to independent literariness because it is nothing but impoverished German and therefore useful only for the purpose of a modernist dismantling of German from within (1986:25).

Interestingly, the denial of minor status to these (and, by their first principle, all other!) literatures in "indigenous" minority languages is correlated with the erasure of Hebrew and Yiddish modernisms. Deleuze and Guattari deny, or are simply ignorant of, the unparalleled creative explosion of Hebrew and Yiddish modernism, in fact of several very different modernisms, across the shifting centers of Jewish literature but also, significantly, in the cities where German was the dominant language of culture. Vibrant and oppositional, the project of these modernists needs to be understood both in its internal gesture of resisting and disrupting the whole structure of Jewish cultural/textual tradition; and, externally, in its self-conscious, ambivalent affiliations with the European modernist trends, whose margins these writers inhabited and whose borders they wished to stretch.

Both Hebrew and Yiddish early modernisms remained, above all, deterritorialized expressive systems and not only during the first quarter of this century, before the center of Hebrew literature moved to Palestine. Yiddish, which never had a territory, reveals all the linguistic marks of a deterritorialized language, marks that Deleuze and Guattari, following Vidal Sephiha, call "tensors" (1986:22). As the proverbial landless language (its writers joke bitterly about imaginary trips to "Yiddishland"), Yiddish became an ideal vehicle for international radical experimentation with modernism. This breathtaking project was halted only with the decimation of the Yiddish writers and readers in the Nazi genocide and the Stalinist purges. From about 1910 on, and especially during the years between the two world wars, Yiddish poets, writers, and dramaturgs created some of the most innovative modernist writing in Europe—impressionist, futurist, expressionist—in groups that clustered around literary magazines like *Albatros, Khalyastre* (The gang), *Ringen* (Rings), and *Milgroym* (Pomegranate). In the movement's perpetually shifting centers, Berlin and Warsaw, Kiev and Moscow, the Yiddish modernists participated in a critique of major European culture launched from the deterritorialized linguistic, cultural, and often political margins. In the period immediately after World War I, at least nineteen Yiddish-language journals and periodicals were published in Berlin alone (Alt 1987). It is perhaps not accidental that Deleuze and Guattari's model reveals the greatest anxiety (conveyed by them ventriloquistically through Kafka's [1986: 25]) about Yiddish, for Yiddish modernism is the ultimate counterexample to their exclusive association of deterritorialization with minor/modernist writing in a major language.

As far as Hebrew modernism is concerned, its many trends and (equally many) countertrends call into question the simple opposition of minor and major literature, and expose the fuzziness of the distinction between a deterritorialized and a reterritorialized language. These examples simply aim to suggest that theories of minor writing will continue to replicate the exclusionary practices of the major if they dismiss those forms of oppositionality that resist, quite literally, "the idiom of the hegemonic culture" (Gluzman 1993a): the ultimate refusal to obey the linguistic imperative to write in the language of the major modernisms of European culture. Let me offer a single glimpse, by way of closure, at one particularly intriguing form of resistance to the crowd's iteration/erasure of difference ("I'm not") with which I began this essay.

In Vienna, as early as 1908, the first modernist Hebrew poet, Avraham Ben-Yitzhak (known also as Sonne, 1883–1950), developed the initial forms of a radically new liminal modernism that was later to become the foundation for an alternative direction in Hebrew letters, a direction shaped to a large extent by an unprecedented number of women poets and by the non-Zionist male poet David Fogel. Marked, as Dan Miron has observed, by a minimalist aesthetic of "thinness" (1991:89–90) and obsessed with metartistic questions of perception and expression, Ben-Yitzhak's poetic project, like Fogel's later one, was lodged uneasily, critically, in the space between impressionism and expressionism, testing the limits of both. By the time he moved to Vienna from his native Galicia, Ben-Yitzhak already possessed remarkable erudition in European letters.[17] In Vienna he met Fogel, the Hebrew poet who would develop and refine the Viennese-Hebrew versions of marginal modernism that are now commonly described as *anti-nusach* (antiformulaic) poetics.[18]

During these years Ben-Yitzhak also met and befriended some of the central literary and artistic figures of the period — James Joyce, Arnold Schoenberg, Georg Brandes, Robert Musil, Hugo von Hofmannsthal, Arthur Schnitzler, and others — who would seek out his company because of his profound engagement in the literary questions of the time. Herman Broch maintained a lifelong literary correspondence with him and offered him a chair in philosophy and literature at a major American university (Hever 1992:98; see also Silberschlag 1985:39–40 and Ha-Ephrati 1976:162–66, 172–75). In his memoirs of the 1930s, Elias Canetti, Ben-Yitzhak's devoted friend, describes him as an admired figure and role model: "The greatest Viennese writers were attracted to him as if spellbound. . . . In many ways he was a model. Once I had known him no one else could become a model for me."[19] By the time Canetti met him, Ben-Yitzhak had already stopped writing (Hebrew) and had become instead a sort of oral vehicle for (one is tempted to say almost an embodiment of) a modernist poetics.

The language of Canetti's extraordinary memoirs underscores this unique role throughout, but let me quote here some particularly suggestive examples. Canetti characterizes his daily need to listen to "Dr. Sonne" speak as "an addiction, such as I had not experienced for any other intellectual." Listening to him one "forgot that the speaker was a human being.... [One] never regarded him as a character; he was the opposite of a character" (1986:133–35). At this point Canetti develops a detailed analogy between Ben-Yitzhak's "oral poetics" and a written—though unfinished—text that serves as Canetti's most prototypical example of the decentered formations of Viennese modernism to which he has apprenticed himself:

> But though I would not presume to reproduce his [Ben-Yitzhak/Sonne's] statements, there is a literary creation to which I believe he can be likened. In those years I read Musil. I could not get enough of *The Man without Qualities,* the first two volumes of which, some thousand pages, had been published. It seemed to me that there was nothing comparable in all of literature. And yet, wherever I chanced to open these books, the text seemed surprisingly familiar. This was a language I knew, a rhythm of thought that I had met with, and yet I knew for sure that there were no similar books in existence. It was some time before I saw the connection. Dr. Sonne *spoke* as Musil *wrote....* Day after day I was privileged to hear chapters from a second *Man without Qualities* that no one else ever heard of. For what he said to others—and he did speak to others, though not every day—was a *different* chapter. (ibid.:136; emphases in the original)

What the Hebrew critics have always referred to as Ben-Yitzhak's "silent period," from 1930 to his death in Israel twenty years later, is here recorded not as a turning away from a hopelessly marginal (Hebrew) modernism, but as a resort to an oral (German) modernism, an art that is all process: "It was always new, it had just come into being" (ibid.:135). The fact that in Vienna, in the early and mid 1930s, Ben-Yitzhak "foresaw the worst and said so" (ibid.:145) underlines how untenable the option to write in German had become for him by that time. In fact, we now know that Ben-Yitzhak actively tried out "the German option" earlier on. In an extraordinary piece of archival work that resulted in a two-volume annotated edition and monograph on Ben-Yitzhak's poetry and poetics, Hannan Hever (1992, 1993) discovered that six of the Hebrew poems in the *opus posthumous* also had German versions and that two were apparently written in German first and in Hebrew only later (1992:85).

Yet Hebrew was to remain the language in which Ben-Yitzhak conducted his low-key modernist experiment on Viennese soil. For a poet of Ben-Yitzhak's interests, sensibilities, and background the choice of Hebrew as the language of modernist minimalism was as far from self-evident as can be imagined. Not only was Hebrew not his native tongue, but it was not the first language of his readers, either, and in many cases not even the second. Hebrew had been the tongue of sacred intertextual study for the better part of its history, although it always maintained a minor, secular (and intertextually more pared down) strand. By the time Ben-Yitzhak started writing, Hebrew had already come a long way in the short span since its revival as a language of modern poetry in the 1890s in the work of Chaim Nachamn Bialik and Shaul Tschernichovski. But it was still, in the first decade of the twentieth century, a largely textual language, lacking severely not only in the registers of colloquial speech and slang but also in popular and subcanonical literature. The heritage of *melitsah,* the intertextual pastiche of fixed expressions borrowed from biblical, talmudic, and liturgical citations, was still very much there, now more as a stylistic memory, tempting with its rich metaphoricity and with the resonance of its intertextual echo chamber. As Bialik, the major canonical writer of premodernist Hebrew literature, had forewarned, the status of Hebew was not going to change until Hebrew "got a life" and became a vehicle for unmarked, normal discourse.[20]

The Hebrew that Ben-Yitzhak so stubbornly stuck to even though he had another, more mainstream medium open to him, must have seemed a very unlikely instrument for minimalist, pared down expression. Yet that was precisely the challenge that Ben-Yitzhak and others after him undertook, a challenge that — in that particular respect — is not unlike Kafka's attempt, in Deleuze and Guattari's construction, to deterritorialize German from within. Ben-Yitzhak's project, which Deleuze and Guattari's model would not recognize as minor, is the ultimate act of modernist oppositionality: to write from a position of dialogic tension with German impressionism and expressionism and with the forerunners and paragons of international modernism as a whole; to critique the modernist project and to try to explore it further but to do so in a language these major modernists cannot understand. By grafting a radically modern idiom onto an ironically biblical, strongly anti-rabbinic Hebrew, Ben-Yitzhak revived but thoroughly secularized the silences and gaps that mark biblical narrative as a new model for modernism, in the process forcing Hebrew to do what it had never done before.[21] But the price was enormous. Ben-Yitzhak published only twelve poems in his lifetime and went into total (written) silence after 1930. Yet he continues to be, perhaps because of his change-enabling, liminal position between cultural and linguistic categories, a revered, almost mythologized figure in the small world of Hebrew letters.

I believe that in making the choice to write in Hebrew, Ben-Yitzhak knew that he would be denied entry into the modernist canon, a canon that would nevertheless continue to describe itself as a truly minor, truly international modernism. He refused to constitute his minor modernist project as productive, in Lloyd's sense of the term. And yet, in abdicating a high modernist canonicity, in resisting reterritori-alization, identity, and income, Ben-Yitzhak both asserted and denied the possibility of his project's ever leaving a mark. The opening lines of the last poem published during his lifetime can be read as an ambiguous midrash on the success/failure of his — and Hebrew's — minor modernism: "Happy are the sowers that will not reap / for they will wander a long way off."[22]

אַשְׁרֵי הַזּוֹרְעִים וְלֹא יִקְצֹרוּ
כִּי יַרְחִיקוּ נְדוֹד.

Notes

I am grateful to Bluma Goldstein, Michael Gluzman, and Naomi Seidman for their invaluable feedback and most careful critical readings of this essay, and to Eliyah Arnon for his diligent bibliographic assistance. A somewhat modified version of this essay appears as the introduction to my book, *On the Margins of Modernism: Decentering Literary Dynamics* (1996).

1. Quoted from the script, published as *Monty Python's The Life of Brian (of Nazareth)*, written by and starring Graham Chapman, John Cleese, Terry Gilliam, Eric Idle, Terry Jones, and Michael Palin (London: Mandarin Paperbacks, 1992 [1979]), 46. Movie directed by Terry Jones, produced by John Goldstone (London: Handmade Films, 1979).

2. Beyond the parabolic reading, *The Life of Brian* may also participate quite literally in the discourse on the margins of modernism in thematizing the Eurocentric tendencies of modern "Judeo-Christian" appropriations of "indigenous" Middle Eastern cultures. Brian, a British-named half-Roman, is a deflated stand-in for the historical Jesus but nevertheless gets to be the lead character in the film. He is depicted as a de-Orientalized "Judeo-Roman," who is oddly unfamiliar with the cultural practices of his society. In a hilarious parody of the obligatory chase scene in action movies, Brian almost gets caught by Roman centurions because he is unable to haggle over prices in the marketplace. The "real" Jesus is only heard sermonizing from afar at the very beginning of the movie, never commanding the foreground of the frame, struc-

turally analogous in his insertion into the narrative to Dennis, the bearded man in the corner who mumbles "I'm not." The movie audience is restricted to the point of view of the group of bickering onlookers standing at a distance, calling one another "big nose." We can never hear the nonparodic, non-Westernized Jesus. He remains mere background, a completely marginal figure, an inauthentic double of a double.

3. Dada was launched by the expatriate Jewish Romanian poet Tristan Tzara (1896–1963), né Samuel Rosenstock (his assumed last name means "trouble" in Hebrew, and he indeed meant it). Other eponymic tales abound, both about Tzara's first and last name, and about the name of the movement. Tzara's famous manifestos of 1916–21 were collected and translated by Barbara Wright in Tzara, *Seven Dada Manifestoes and Lampisteries*, 1992 [1977]. The liminality and polylingualism of Romanian Jewish modernism (Marsel Janco, Dan Pagis, Paul Celan, in addition to Tzara) remain largely unexplored.

4. So how come the principles of Russian acmeism (such as "A = A") sound so much like the Anglo-American imagism we all canonized a long time ago?

5. Akhmatova is mentioned only once in the entire book and then only as a source reporting "the literary youth in [the Soviet Union] to be 'wild' about [Mandelstam's] prose"; see Donald Fanger, "The City of Russian Modernist Fiction" (476). Marina Tzvetayeva is nowhere to be found. Marianne Moore and H. D. are mentioned only in lists of poets but do not receive individual critical attention. Else Lasker-Schüler gets seven words, three of them her name. Virginia Woolf and Gertrude Stein are the only women modernists to be discussed in any detail. This marginalization of women modernists, I submit, is quite the norm in general discussions of modernism. It is avoided only in volumes devoted exclusively to women's literature or to corrective literary history, such as Bonnie Kime Scott's groundbreaking anthology *The Gender of Modernism* (1990).

6. My critical reading of these theoretical materials has greatly benefited from an ongoing research dialogue with Michael Gluzman. He discusses theories of marginality in the context of canon formation in the introduction and conclusion of his Ph.D dissertation, "Suppressed Modernisms: Marginality, Politics, Canon Formation" (1993b).

7. The dichotomy of center and periphery itself may be an example of the numerous cross-generic connections so common in modernism between literary affiliations on the one hand and critical/theoretical trends on the other. It is born of the ambivalent affair between the theories of Russian formalism and the practices of Russian futurist poetry.

8. Originally published in *Kafka: Pour une littérature mineure* (1975). An abbreviated version of their essay appears in Ferguson et al. 1990:59–69.

9. See Lloyd 1987, especially pp. 19–26; and Lloyd 1990:381–82.

10. The idea of the minor as oppositional is developed in JanMohamed and Lloyd 1990:369–93. This volume contains several essays on minority discourse that would be denied status as "truly minor" by the theoretical framework that the editors of this very book adopt from Deleuze and Guattari. This is just one illustration of the urgent need for the theory of the minor to catch up with critical practice.

11. In his 1990 interpretation of Deleuze and Guattari, Lloyd seeks to neutralize the exclusionary impact of their typology by distinguishing "minor" from "minority" writing. But note that he still implicitly correlates only minor writing (namely, in a major language) with the progressive anticanonical stance, whereas minority literature is associated only with the possibility of "fulfilling a major function," namely, replicating the conservative processes of the canon. The other (logical and empirical) possibility of a minority literature fulfilling a minor, oppositional function — in its own

"minority language" — is not addressed because it would refute Deleuze and Guattari's linguistic imperative: "Any definition of 'minor' writing is obliged to take into account its oppositional status *vis-à-vis* canonical or major literature thus described. For this reason, a too hasty identification of 'minority' with 'minor' literature will inevitably be inaccurate, and Deleuze and Guattari are thus far correct to remark in their study of Kafka that it is perfectly possible for a literature of minorities to 'fulfill a major function.' ... Deleuze and Guattari are equally correct to seek to differentiate a literature of minorities written in a 'minority' language from a minor literature which would be that of minorities composed in a major language. For 'minor literature' is so termed in relation to the major canon, and its characteristics are defined in opposition to those which define canonical writing" (JanMohamed and Lloyd 1990:381).

12. Michael Gluzman (1993a), unpublished manuscript. I discuss this criterial definition and the model of categorization it invokes in chapter 1 of Kronfeld 1996 in the context of the failed search for a definition of modernism. Let me just suggest here that an intensional definition of a politicized, historicized concept of minor writing — that is, a definition based (logically) on necessary and sufficient conditions or (linguistically) on a checklist of distinctive features — is probably the wrong way to go. It would be like trying to account for context-dependent metaphor by using transformational grammar. More important perhaps, this type of definition tends to replicate the same neoclassical Eurocentric classificatory drive that the privileging of the minor aims to undo. For two independent critiques of this classificatory drive, see Foucault ([1970]1973) and Lakoff (1987).

13. In conversation. For a discerning analysis of Kafka's radical readings of Jewish cultural tropes in their central European context, see Goldstein 1992:40–65.

14. On the role of Vienna and Berlin among the shifting centers of modern Hebrew literature, see Silberschlag (1985:29–43) and Nash (1985:44–58) in Abramson and Parfitt (1985).

15. See especially Robert Alter's essay "The Power of the Text" in Alter 1991: 67–92. On Kafka's resistant, modernist recasting of the Hasidic narrative model, see Goldstein's innovative essay (1968). On Kafka's numerous intertextual links with the bilingual Hebrew-Yiddish writer Y. L. Peretz, see Jofen 1984. Deleuze and Guattari do acknowledge Kafka's ties to the Yiddish theater, but they underscore the performative, not the literary, nature of that cultural link (1986:25). For an account that stresses Kafka's textual, almost exegetical preoccupation with the cultural function of the Yiddish theater, see Goldstein 1992:46–47; see also Torton Beck 1971.

16. Alter (1991:40) describes the haunting scene, related in a postcard from Kafka to Robert Klopstock (sent from Berlin on October 25, 1923), in which a terminally ill Kafka struggles through the unbelievably difficult Hebrew of Brenner's novel *Shkhol ve-khishalon* (*Breakdown and Bereavement*) ([1902] 1972), a page a day.

17. See Leah Goldberg's adoring memoir of Ben-Yitzhak, *Pgisha im meshorer* (Encounter with a poet) (1952). As a major poet of the dominant *moderna* group in Palestine, and as the founder and chair of the Department of Comparative Literature at the Hebrew University in Jerusalem, Goldberg, in her moving memoir-cum-literary criticism, went a long way toward establishing Ben-Yitzhak's minor-key modernism in a canon then shifting from the domination of a maximalist version of futurist/expressionist affiliation (Goldberg's own *moderna*) to a more minimalist/imagist one. Thus, Goldberg's recovery of Ben-Yitzhak for the Hebrew canon needs to be seen alongside Nathan Zach's and Dan Pagis's rediscovery of Fogel as a "proleptic paragon" for the late-modernist project of their own Statehood Generation. It is significant, however, to note the subversive aspect of Goldberg's role: by canonizing Ben-Yitzhak she helped

undermine the hegemony of her own (predominantly male) literary group and point in a direction of privileging the early minor modernisms that Zach and Pagis were to follow a few years later.

18. See Gluzman et al., *David Fogel (1891–1944) and the Emergence of Hebrew Modernism*.

19. This volume of Canetti's memoirs is aptly titled *Das Augenspiel* (1985), translated by Ralph Manheim as *The Play of the Eyes*. All quotations are from the English translation. See especially the chapter titled "Dr. Sonne," 89–162.

20. I am referring to Bialik's quite astonishing protomodernist essay "Chevley lashon," a punning title I translate as "Language Pangs." Benjamin Harshav has argued persuasively for a sustained and complex analogy between modernism, the revival of Hebrew, and what he has termed "the Jewish revolution" (in Harshav 1993). Let me stress that for Ben-Yitzhak, as for the other anti-*nusach* (antiformulaic) modernists, the choice to write in Hebrew cannot be explained simply as an extension of Zionist nationalism. Ben-Yitzhak's intensely critical association with institutional Zionism is described with vivid candor by Leah Goldberg ([1952] 1988:42–43).

21. For an account of Ben-Yitzhak's potential "exportation" of biblical gaps, biblical cadence, and "the *language* of the prohpets" into the mainstream modernist stylistic norm, see Canetti 1986:150 (italics in the original).

22. From "Ashrey ha-zor'im" (in Ben-Yitzhak 1992:20). The various versions we have of the poem date from 1925 to 1928. The second line in the Hebrew replaces the idiom designating productive accomplishment, *yarchiku lekhet* (will go far, will achieve a lot) with its nonidiomatic deflation, *yarchiku nedod* (literally, will wander far). These lines, as well as the rest of the poem, read as a parodic rejection of *shibbutz*, the premodernist Hebrew literary tradition of mosaic-like citations of sacred texts. At the same time it also rejects the authoritative plenitude of New Testament allegory, sermon, and parable. Note, for example, the iconoclastic conflation of Psalms (126 and 127) with the Sermon on the Mount and the Parable of the Sower. On the poem's intertextual engagement with Christian sources as well as its internal critique of Zionist politics, see Hever 1993:144–55. Dan Pagis's reading of the poem emphasizes metapoetic aspects such as the total renunciation of aesthetic ornament—a perspective that fits Pagis's own poetic project: to turn Ben-Yitzhak, posthumously, into a model for the minimalist poetics that he and the late modernists of the fifties and sixties (Amichai, Zach, Ravikovitch) were struggling to legitimize. See Pagis's entries on Ben-Yitzhak in *The Modern Hebrew Poem Itself* (Burnshaw et al. [1965] 1989:50–53).

Bibliography

Abramson, Glenda, and Tudor Parfitt, eds. 1985. *The Great Transition: The Recovery of the Lost Centers of Modern Hebrew Literature*. Totowa, N.J.: Rowman & Allanheld.

Alt, Arthur Tilo. 1987. "A Survey of Literary Contributions to the Post–World War I Yiddish Journals of Berlin." *Yiddish* 7(1): 42–52.

Alter, Robert. 1991. *Necessary Angels: Tradition and Modernity in Kafka, Benjamin, and Scholem*. Cambridge, Mass.: Harvard University Press.

Ben-Yitzhak, Avraham. 1992. *Kol ha-shirim* (Collected poems). Edited by Hanan Hever. Tel Aviv: Ha-Kibbutz Ha-Me'uchad.

Bialik, Chaim Nachman. [1953] 1964/65. "Chevley lashon" (Language pangs). In *Kol kitvey Ch. N. Bialik* (Collected works), 185–190. Tel Aviv: Dvir.

Bradbury, Malcolm, and James McFarlane, eds. [1976] 1991. *Modernism 1890–1930*. Harmondsworth: Penguin.

Brenner, Yosef Haim. 1971. *Breakdown and Bereavement*. Translated by Hillel Halkin. Ithaca, N.Y.: Cornell University Press.

———. [1902] 1972. *Shkhol ve-khishalon* (Breakdown and bereavement). Tel Aviv: Am Oved.

Canetti, Elias. 1986. *Das Augenspiel: Lebengeschichte, 1931–1937*. Munich: C. Hanser.

———. 1987. *The Play of the Eyes*. Translated from the German by Ralph Manheim. New York: Farrar, Straus & Giroux.

Chapman, Graham, et al. [1979] 1992. *Monty Python's The Life of Brian (of Nazareth)*. London: Mandarin Paperbacks.

Deleuze, Gilles, and Félix Guattari. 1975. *Kafka: Pour une littérature mineure*. Paris: Minuit.

———. 1986. *Kafka: Toward a Minor Literature*. Translated by Dana Polan. Minneapolis: University of Minnesota Press.

Eric, Max. [1922] 1973. "Leshon ha-ekspresiyonizm ha-yehudi" (The language of Jewish expressionism). In *Yorshey ha-simbolism ba-shira ha-eyropit ve-ha-yehudit* (Heirs of symbolism in Euopean and Jewish literature), ed. and tr. Benjamin Hrushovski (Harshav), 138–39. Jerusalem: Akademon.

Fanger, Donald. [1976] 1981. "The City of Russian Modernist Fiction." In *Modernism 1890–1930*, ed. Malcolm Bradbury and James McFarlane, 467–80. Harmondsworth: Penguin.

Ferguson, Russell, et al., eds. 1990. *Out There: Marginalization and Contemporary Cultures*. New York and Cambridge, Mass.: New Museum of Contemporary Art and MIT Press.

Fogel, David. 1923. *Lifney ha-sha'ar ha-afel* (Before the dark gate). Vienna: Machar.

———. 1975. *Kol ha-shirim* (Collected poems [1915–1941]). 3d rev. ed. Edited by Dan Pagis. Tel Aviv: Ha-Kibbutz Ha-Me'uchad.

———. 1983. *Le'ever ha-dmama* (Toward stillness). Edited by Aharon Komem. Tel Aviv: Ha-Kibbutz Ha-Me'uchad.

———. 1990. *Tachanot kavot* (Stories; Diary). Edited by Menachem Perry. Tel Aviv: Ha-Kibbutz Ha-Me'uchad.

Foucault, Michel. [1970] 1973. *The Order of Things*. New York: Random House.

Gluzman, Michael. 1993a. Unpublished manuscript.

———. 1993b. "Suppressed Modernisms: Marginality, Politics, Canon Formation." Ph.D. diss., University of California, Berkeley.

Gluzman, Michael, Chana Kronfeld, and Eric Zakim, eds. 1993. Special issue: *David Fogel (1891–1944) and the Emergence of Hebrew Modernism*. *Prooftexts* 13(1).

Goldberg, Leah. 1952. *Pgisha im meshorer: al-Avraham Ben-Yitzhak Sonne* (Meeting with a poet). Merchavya, Israel: Sifriat Ha-Po'alim.

Goldstein, Bluma. 1968. "Franz Kafka's 'Ein Landarzt': A Study in Failure." *Deutsche Vierteljahrsschrift für Literaturwissenschaft und Geistesgeschichte* 42: 745–59.

———. 1992. *Reinscribing Moses: Heine, Kafka, Freud, and Schoenberg in a European Wilderness*. Cambridge, Mass.: Harvard University Press.

Ha-Ephrati, Yoseph. 1976. *Ha-mar'ot ve-ha-lashon: le-toldot ha-te'ur ba-shira ha-ivrit ha-chadasha* (The presented world: Evolution of the poetic language of nature description in Hebrew poetry). Tel Aviv: Porter Institute for Poetics and Semiotics.

Harshav, Benjamin (Hrushovski). 1993. *Language in Time of Revolution*. Berkeley: University of California Press.

Hever, Hanan. 1992. "Postscript: On the Life and Work of Avaham Ben-Yitzhak." In *Kol ha-shirim* (Collected poems), by Avaham Ben-Yitzhak, ed. Hanan Hever. Tel Aviv: Ha-Kibbutz Ha-Me'uchad.

———. 1993. *Prichat ha-dumiya: Shirat Avraham Ben-Yitzhak* (The flowering of silence: The poetry of Avraham Ben-Yitzhak). Tel Aviv: Ha-Kibbutz Ha-Me'uchad.

JanMohamed, Abdul R., and David Lloyd, eds. 1990. *The Nature and Context of Minority Discourse*. Oxford: Oxford University Press.

Jofen, Jean. 1984. "The Jewish Element in the Work of Franz Kafka." *Modern Jewish Studies Annual V, Yiddish* 5(4):87–106.

Kafka, Franz. 1948–49. *The Diaries: 1910–1923*. 2 vols. Edited by Max Brod and translated by Joseph Kresh and Martin Greenberg. New York: Schocken.

———. 1954. "An Introductory Talk on the Yiddish Language." In *Dearest Father*, tr. Ernst Kaiser and Eithne Wilkins, 381–86. New York: Schocken.

Kenner, Hugh. 1984. "The Making of the Modernist Canon." In *Canons*, ed. Robert Von Hallberg, 363–75. Chicago: University of Chicago Press.

Kronfeld, Chana. 1996. *On the Margins of Modernism: Decentering Literary Dynamics*. Berkeley: University of California Press.

Lakoff, George. 1987. *Women, Fire, and Dangerous Things: What Categories Reveal about the Mind*. Chicago: University of Chicago Press.

Lloyd, David. 1987. *Nationalism and Minor Literature: James Clarence Mangan and the Emergence of Irish Cultural Nationalism*. Berkeley: University of California Press.

———. 1990. "Genet's Genealogy: European Minorities and the Ends of the Canon." In *The Nature and Context of Minority Discourse*, ed. Abdul R. JanMohamed and David Lloyd, 369–93. Oxford: Oxford University Press.

Miron, Dan. 1991. *Imahot meyasdot, achayot chorgot: al shtey hatchalot ba-shira ha-eretzyisre'elit ha-modernit* (Founding mothers, stepsisters: The emergence of the first Hebrew poetesses and other essays). Tel Aviv: Ha-Kibbutz Ha-Me'uchad.

Nash, Stanley. 1985. "The Hebraists of Berne and Berlin Circa 1905." In *The Great Transition: The Recovery of the Lost Centers of Modern Hebrew Literature*, ed. Glenda Abramson and Tudor Parfitt, 44–58. Totowa, N.J.: Rowman & Allanheld.

Pagis, Dan. [1965] 1989. "Avraham Ben-Yitshak." In *The Modern Hebrew Poem Itself*, ed. Stanley Burnshaw et al., 50–53. Cambridge, Mass.: Harvard University Press.

Renza, Louis. 1984. *"A White Heron" and the Question of Minor Literature*. Milwaukee: University of Wisconsin Press.

Scott, Bonnie Kime, ed. 1990. *The Gender of Modernism: A Critical Anthology*. Bloomington: Indiana University Press.

Sephia, H. Vidal. 1970. "Introduction à l'étude de l'intensif." *Langages* 18 (June): 104–20.

Silberschlag, Eisig. 1985. "Hebrew Literature in Vienna: 1782–1939." In *The Great Transition: The Recovery of the Lost Centers of Modern Hebrew Literature*, ed. Glenda Abramson and Tudor Parfitt, 29–43. Totowa, N.J.: Rowman & Allanheld.

Torton Beck, Evelyn. 1971. *Kafka and the Yiddish Theater*. Madison: University of Wisconsin Press.

Tzara, Tristan. [1977] 1992. *Seven Dada Manifestoes and Lampisteries*. Collected and translated by Barbara Wright. London: Calder Press.

Williams, Raymond. 1989. *The Politics of Modernism: Against the New Conformists*, ed. and introduced by Tony Pinkney. London: Verso.

10 / Lawless Attachments, One-Night Stands: The Sexual Politics of the Hebrew-Yiddish Language War

Naomi Seidman

Eros and language mesh at every point.... Together they construe
the grammar of being.   GEORGE STEINER, *After Babel*

The expression MAME-LOSHN ("mama-language") is a typical
Yiddish compound of Slavic and Hebrew roots, connoting the
warmth of the Jewish family, as symbolized by mama and her language, embracing and counteracting the father's awesome, learned
Holy Tongue.   BENJAMIN HARSHAV, *The Meaning of Yiddish*

In the past few decades, critics and historians have begun contesting
and reevaluating the centrality of Eliezer Ben-Yehuda's role in the revival of spoken Hebrew.[1] These critics argue, either explicitly or by implication, that the Hebrew revival actually occurred both much earlier
and much later than the 1890s, when Ben-Yehuda was attempting to
realize his project of raising a child to speak solely Hebrew. That is,
Hebrew or *Loshn-koydesh* was occasionally spoken in the centuries
before the revival, by Jews from different communities who shared no
other language, or by fervent Jews who wished to sanctify the Sabbath by speaking only the Holy Tongue. Moreover, the work of writers
like Sh. Y. Abramovitsh, whose Yiddish-inflected style infused written Hebrew with the idiomatic flexibility it had sorely lacked, had already set the stage for a full-blown vernacular revival years before
Ben-Yehuda's project was launched.

Nevertheless, neither the scattered episodes of Hebrew speech nor the fluency of Abramovitsh's Hebrew style directly produced a Hebrew-speaking environment, and Ben-Yehuda's experiment was no more successful. Hebrew finally did begin to become the vernacular of an entire society only during the Second Aliya (the wave of immigration that began in 1905 and lasted until 1914), under conditions very different from Ben-Yehuda's isolated work in Jerusalem of the 1880s. Benjamin Harshav is perhaps most responsible for the demystification of what has become an article of faith in Israel, Ben-Yehuda's "revival" of the Hebrew tongue. Harshav's revisionary linguistic history of the *yishuv* (which parallels recent historical approaches to many other aspects of *yishuv*, or pre-Statehood, history) insists that "in spite of his pathetic figure and life, Ben-Yehuda had no real influence on the revival itself, which began to strike roots about twenty five years after his arrival in Erets-Israel, in the milieu created by the Second Aliya" (1993:84). Whatever one makes of his actual function in the Hebrew revival, however, it would be impossible to deny that Ben-Yehuda's position vis-à-vis modern Hebrew has attained the status of popular national mythology.

The mythologizing of Ben-Yehuda's career begins with his own writings. In his autobiography, Ben-Yehuda describes the circumstances surrounding the birth of his son in the hushed tone of a witness to a miracle:

> On the fifteenth of Av, the first new settlement of the *yishuv* was founded, the settlement of *Rishon-letsiyon*. On that very day, in a dark corner of a small room close to the Temple Mount, the child was born with whom the first experiment of reviving Hebrew as a spoken tongue was supposed to commence.... Is it not one of the wondrous events of human history that the beginning of the revival of our land, if one can call it that, and the beginning of the revival of our language happened simultaneously, on the same day, virtually at the same hour? On the day that the first settlement of the nation that had decided to return to the soil of their fathers was founded in the land of the fathers, on that very day was born the son who was destined to be the first of the children of the nation who would return to speaking the language of the fathers. (9–10)

Ben-Yehuda's narrative employs the vocabulary of the miraculous most markedly in noting the coincidence of the birth of the first Hebrew-speaking child with the founding of the first Hebrew settlement. The magical quality of the birth is heightened in Ben-Yehuda's account by the child's appearance ex nihilo, as it were, an effect achieved partially by the mother's absence from the narrative. But the birth is translated from the biological not only to the supernatural sphere, but also to the realm of "human history," a history dominated here by fathers, the fatherland, and the language of the fathers. The word *fathers* (*avot*) is repeated three times in the last line cited above, in "land of the fathers" (*admat avot*), "country of the fathers" (*erets avot*) and "language of the fathers" (*leshon avot*); the passage utterly avoids the myriad feminine topoi and literary conventions for describing Zion and the Land of Israel. The word *avot*, of course, could also be translated as "ancestors," but there are other elements of Ben-Yehuda's narrative, as related by himself and others, that suggest the importance of paternity to his Hebraist-Zionist project.

In describing Ben-Yehuda's place in the pantheon of Zionist heroes, Harshav conveys his sense that the myth of the Hebrew revival is inextricably intertwined with Ben-Yehuda's role as father:

> Popular mythology feeds off of the image of a hero who personifies an idea, the individual who in his personal life, which is understood by all, and especially in his suffering and sacrifice, is a symbol of the exalted goal. Thus Herzl is constructed as a legendary king (although "*Hibat Zion*" preceded him); Bialik as the poet-prophet, who paid with his "blood and fat" for the blaze his verses struck in the people (although there were other first-rate poets among his peers, such as Tshernikhovsky and Steinberg); Trumpeldor as "the one-armed hero" (although he lost his hand defending Russia from the Japanese); Brenner as the personification of the "in-spite-of-it-all" (as if his assassination at the hands of Arab rioters justifies the despair in his writings); and Eliezer Ben-Yehuda as the father of the Hebrew revival, who sacrificed his family on its altar. (84)

Harshav intends his catalog to demonstrate the condensation and distortion by which the idiosyncrasies of individual life stories are remade in the broad shapes of national ideas and values. Thus, the single-mindedness of Ben-Yehuda's lonely endeavor, his planting linguistic seeds in what could not have been very fertile ground, is encoded in the phrase "father of the Hebrew revival."[2] And Ben-Yehuda's paternal role is not just a figure of speech. In account after account, the varied scope of Ben-Yehuda's linguistic experiment is primarily reduced to and expressed by his activities as father, rather than as editor, publisher, inventor of new words (or as his detractors would have it, manager of the Hebrew "word factory"), or founder of various language societies.

The condensation of Ben-Yehuda's story differs from Harshav's other examples, however, because his heroism is both derived from and qualified by his fatherhood: popular mythological reworkings of Ben-Yehuda's career demonstrate not only the centrality of the family drama to the Hebrew revival, but also the degree to which this drama is touched with the psychological and ethical ambiguities of patriarchal (self-)sacrifice. While other stories about national heroes often suppress the less attractive characteristics of their subjects, Ben-Yehuda's problematic fatherly behavior almost always has a major part in the cultural texts that transmit his story. Rather than eliding Ben-Yehuda's "sacrifice" of his family, popular biographies, children's books, critical histories, and so on cite his zealotry and its domestic effects as further proof of Ben-Yehuda's laudably unswerving commitment to Hebrew, an enhancement rather than a diminution of his heroic stature. What emerges in these narratives is a fable as morally complex as the binding of Isaac, an intertext to which Harshav's description of Ben-Yehuda's "sacrifice" of his family "on the altar" of the Hebrew revival indirectly refers.

My aim here, however, is not to judge either Ben-Yehuda's character or his role in the Hebrew "revival," nor to decide whether Ben-Yehuda's family troubles were the price he paid or exacted for the vernacularization of Hebrew. Rather, I will examine the insistence with which the story of the revival of the Hebrew vernacular has been transmitted as a story about the conflicting claims of Jewish paternity and maternity, about the establishment of masculine control over areas of Jewish life traditionally in the hands of women, and about domesticity and guilt. The stories that have arisen around the figure of Ben-Yehuda, I would argue, have the cultural power they have because they reflect and reinforce basic conflicts of Hebrew and Erets-Israeli society during the interwar period during which these myths began to circulate. Ben-Yehuda's family troubles and language obsession in fact encode and condense the overlapping territories of the language conflict and gender ideologies of his own and later times.

Let me draw the outlines of a few versions of what could be called the "primal scene" or the founding myth of the revival of Hebrew as a living tongue. In Ottoman Jerusalem of the 1880s, Eliezer Ben-Yehuda, by supreme linguistic and ideological determination, raised the first native Hebrew speaker in modern times, his son Ben-Tsiyon (later Itamar). The experiment involved creating a "pure" Hebrew environment, severely restricting the child's access to other languages while immersing him in Hebrew speech. Ben-Yehuda relates that he taught his wife Hebrew quickly, even though this task "was a little hard at first." Ben-Yehuda goes on to explain this difficulty: "As with virtually all Jewish women, and everyone except for a few *"maskilim"* and Hebrew writers of the day, even this daughter of the *maskil* Sh. N. Yonas knew no Hebrew, although she could read the Hebrew letters and write Yiddish" (83).

Most historians seem to agree that Dvora Ben-Yehuda learned Hebrew slowly, if at all. In one version of the story published as an educational pamphlet by the Hebrew Language Academy, Ben-Yehuda is said to have forbidden his first wife to speak to their firstborn until she could speak to him in Hebrew, a process that, according to this pamphlet, took Dvora Ben-Yehuda five years.[3] Ben-Yehuda, in having a willing wife, was luckier than at least one of the members of the Jerusalem group who had sworn allegiance to Ben-Yehuda's project. As Ben-Yehuda reports, "Arye Horwitz would argue with his wife incessantly because she didn't know Hebrew and didn't have time to learn" (26). Despite the lack of such obvious discord in the Ben-Yehuda household, the difficulties of raising a child in a language one parent could only speak haltingly and the other barely at all seem to have taken their toll. Amos Elon summarizes the domestic manifestations of Ben-Yehuda's project in these words:

> Ben-Yehuda's wife knew no Hebrew; while still on shipboard he told her that in Palestine they would speak nothing but Hebrew. He ruthlessly kept his vow. When his first son, Itamar, was born (by a curious coincidence on the same day the colony of Rishon le-Zion was founded) he became the first child in centuries to hear only Hebrew from both his parents and almost nothing from anyone else, for he was kept isolated from all human contact lest the purity of his Hebrew be spoiled by alien sounds....
>
> It was a risky undertaking. The language was still archaic. Many words indispensable in modern intercourse were missing. The child had no playmates; until his third year he remained almost mute and often refused to utter a word. (1971:97)

In a later passage, Elon recounts that "when Ben-Yehuda's aged mother, who spoke no Hebrew, arrived in Palestine shortly before her death, Ben-Yehuda, who had not seen her for years, refused to talk with her in a language she could understand" (1971:110).

In her biography of Eliezer Ben-Yehuda, Chemda Ben-Yehuda, who was Eliezer's second wife as well as Dvora Ben-Yehuda's younger sister, vividly describes Eliezer standing at the door to the birth chamber and giving the midwife and the female neighbors a Hebrew language exam before he would let them attend the birth; one barren woman, believing she could benefit through sympathetic magic from proximity with the new mother, was allowed to enter—but on the condition that she not call out the prescribed phrase "this is my child," since she could not manage it in Hebrew. Chemda describes Dvora's efforts to silence the excited witness to the birth:

> At every moment Sheyne-Malke wanted to say something loving to the new-born child in Zhargon. The mother, however, reminded her of the prohibition against speaking by putting her finger to her lips, and the woman remained silent. After that, we always called her the 'dumb aunt' (*hadodah ha'ilemet*). (1940:13)

While Ben-Yehuda writes little about his wife's Hebrew-speaking abilities, passages in his memoir bear traces of his guilt for having sacrificed his wife to the cause; despite Dvora's frail health, Ben-Yehuda writes, he did not allow her a servant girl for fear she would contaminate the pure Hebrew environment, an act of linguistic zealousness he later admitted had been unnecessary. In a long and apologetic passage, Ben-Yehuda defends his decision not to hire a maid servant to help the new mother:

> The new mother was naturally weak and sickly; poverty, pregnancy, and birth had weakened her further. But even so she willingly and good-naturedly agreed not to have a servant girl in the house, so that the child's ears would hear no sounds other than those of Hebrew. We were afraid of the walls of the house, afraid of the air in the room, lest it absorb the sounds of a foreign tongue emanating from the servant-girl, which would enter the child's ears and damage his Hebrew hearing and the Hebrew words would not be absorbed as they should be and the child would not speak Hebrew. . . . This holy soul, who was destined to be the first Hebrew mother of the revival era which would give the nation a Hebrew-speaking generation, lovingly took upon herself the suffering of raising a child without even a little help, although she herself was weak and sickly. (131)

Ben-Yehuda may have been making a reference to any one of these scenarios when he confessed that his determination to speak only Hebrew at times overrode ethical imperatives:

I speak Hebrew, only Hebrew, not only with the members of my household, but even with every man or woman whom I know to understand Hebrew to some degree, and I do not take care in this matter to abide by the laws of common respect or courtesy to women [*kibud nashim*]. I act in this with great rudeness, rudeness that has caused many people to hate me and has engendered much opposition to me in Erets-Israel. (57)

If Dvora's Hebrew was limited, her husband's was not much better. One witness to the experiment reported that when Eliezer, for example, wanted Dvora to pour him a cup of coffee with sugar,

he was at a loss to communicate words such as 'cup,' 'saucer,' 'pour,' 'spoon,' and so on, He would say to his wife, in effect: "Take such and such, and do like so, and bring me this and this, and I will drink" (*k'khi kakh, ve'asi kakh, vehavi'i li kakh, ve'eshteh*). (Fellman 1973:58)

Under the circumstances, it is not surprising that Itamar Ben-Avi did not speak until he was four, as he relates in his memoirs. According to Ben-Avi, he spoke his first sentence in the following circumstances: Yehiel Mikhal Pines, a family friend, fearing the child would grow up to be retarded or deaf and mute, advised Dvora to speak to her child in a language other than Hebrew. She began singing Russian lullabies to him and was caught one day when her husband returned home unexpectedly. Itamar relates that the argument that followed caused "a great shock to pass over me, when I saw my father in his anger and my mother in her grief and tears, and the muteness was removed from my lips and speech came to my mouth" (16).

Ben-Avi's "real" or imagined memory of the "primal scene" of the birth of Hebrew speech has disturbing similarities to the Freudian construction of the "primal scene," although in the case of Ben-Avi, the child's perception of the father's aggressive behavior toward his wife is anything but a misunderstanding. Itamar Ben-Avi, by connecting his first Hebrew words with both the rage of his father and the linguistic transgression of his mother, underlined the centrality of a parental and gender struggle in his own linguistic development. If we take all these accounts, including Ben-Yehuda's idealized one, as a collective myth of the Hebrew revival, it seems clear that the mother's silence, self-sacrifice, and absence (or, alternatively, her transgression) are built into the mythical structure.

I am not, it should be noted, arguing against the sincerity of Ben-Yehuda's perceived need for such radical measures as the linguistic quarantine of the first Hebrew-speaking child from his mother, the midwife, or a servant girl. But neither do I think that the silence, or silencing, of these women during the primal scene of the birth of modern Hebrew speech is trivial, secondary, or accidental, whether one reads the scenes I outlined above as literal truth or as myth. Given Ashkenazic educational patterns, in which boys and girls learned Yiddish in their mother's arms, while boys were later introduced to Hebrew by their father or a male teacher, there is a certain logic to Ben-Yehuda's diverting this historical trajectory by prohibiting the speech of the child's mother. Moreover, Ben-Yehuda attempted to raise a child to speak Hebrew within the confines of the traditional Jewish family and in the larger setting of the old *yishuv*, with its conservative religious and social mores. The Hebrew revival finally succeeded under very different social and family circumstances, and its primary setting was not the home but the settlement school or its urban counterpart. As Harshav puts it, an important aspect of the Hebrew revolution was "the establishment of *social cells in a 'social desert'* (in Eretz-Israel) by groups of young people and children who cut themselves off from the chain of generations" (113; emphasis in the original). In raising a Hebrew speaker within a traditional domestic Jewish environment, Ben-Yehuda may have had no choice but to substitute the paternal for the maternal role in the child's linguistic development.

Although Ben-Yehuda's experiment took place in an environment manifestly different from the ones in which the Hebrew revival eventually took hold (the Second Aliya, the labor movement, Tel Aviv, and the settlements), Ben-Yehuda became the symbol of the revival primarily during this later period. While it is not surprising that the Hebrew revival would choose a hero for itself from an earlier period, I would argue that the narratives of Ben-Yehuda's life and vision served a particular purpose for later Hebraists. For one thing, Ben-Yehuda's domestic difficulties may well have proved the importance of combining a domestic and social revolution with the linguistic one.

But Ben-Yehuda's experience also encoded some of the larger difficulties inherent in the Hebrew revival: what the Ben-Yehuda family drama exposes is that the Hebrew revival, and the Hebrew-Yiddish language war that ensued, was, on one level, the struggle between a "mother tongue" and a "father tongue." The revival of Hebrew as the living language of an entire population and the concomitant suppression of other languages (primarily Yiddish) that was so central to this project were accomplished without the aid of a state apparatus such as the one that succeeded in destroying the Soviet Hebrew literary scene. Instead, the revival of spoken Hebrew called into service an array of deeply rooted Jewish desires, prejudices, and anxieties, including, I will argue, psychosexual ones. The first attempts at Hebrew speech, as we have seen, both involved the Jewish woman in a more central role than other nationalist projects and reduced that role to its biological minimum. The Hebrew revival also implicated Jewish women because it commonly (though not universally) saw its task as the suppression of the Yiddish language, with all its feminine associations. The growing Hebrew-speaking culture generated psychic momentum from actively stigmatizing what it saw as the womanly tongue. The revival operated in part according to what could be called a "politics of revulsion"; the Yiddish critic Avraham Golomb once argued that the Hebrew revival was motivated more strongly by hatred of Yiddish than by love for Hebrew.[4] Even if we take into account Golomb's Yiddishist bitterness, it seems clear that Hebrew was revived at least partially by tapping into a strong distaste for the disempowered *galut* (diaspora) existence that was often consciously or unconsciously perceived as having emasculated or feminized the Jewish collective; this distaste reflected itself, above all, in the rejection of the *mameloshn* that both expressed and was the product of the objectionable Eastern European past.

The fight to acquire Hebrew was, of course, as much an individual and psychological struggle as it was a larger cultural one. In his memoirs, Itamar Ben-Avi relates the story of his having ranted feverishly in Yiddish during a severe illness, leading his father to impose a linguistic rather than medical quarantine on the small boy so that he not be exposed to any more "jargon" (18). The story is of interest for more than one reason: first is its suggestion that the First Hebrew Child, for all the "purity" of his Hebrew environment, must have been exposed to more Yiddish than the historiography admits. But it also encodes a phenomenon that would be repeated throughout the long process of reviving Hebrew as a vernacular. In the structure of Ben-Avi's linguistic transgression, Yiddish forms the suppressed or unconscious level that erupts into consciousness when psychic control weakens. Like the Yiddish "layer" that underlies the German of the assimilated Jew in Freud's jokes, Yiddish remained alive in the new Hebrew speaker, deviously pursuing the expression denied it.

As Ben-Avi's and other stories attest, the process of creating a new Jew, or a Hebrew-speaking Hebrew (*ivri*), could not have been an easy one. Yiddish was not just the property of women, it was also the mother tongue of a large portion of the men trying to revive Hebrew; Yiddish, by its primacy and emotional claims, was always threatening to encroach on the territory Hebrew had fought to stake out for itself. The gender associations of the languages were all the more potent, that is, for being less than absolute. Similarly, the historical embeddedness of Hebrew in Yiddish, which to a large extent made the Hebrew revival possible, also complicated the establishment of Hebrew as a self-sufficient language and turned the revival into a drama of disentanglement.

Ben-Yehuda's attempt to forge a new mother tongue in the new homeland required, according to this logic, both the erasure of the old language and the silencing of the women who were associated with it. While Ben-Yehuda's social and ideological isolation certainly contributed to the difficulties of his self-imposed task, domestic strife around the issue of Hebrew speech continued for many years after the Hebrew revival was well under way. In 1929, the Revisionist Zionist leader Zev Jabotinsky complained that "even the most fervent Zionist cannot guarantee that his wife is also a Zionist or that she takes his side with regard to the importance of Hebrew speech" (1972a: 369). There is some evidence that his own family could be included in this estimation. One pamphlet issued by the Hebrew Language Academy relates that Jabotinsky finally had to exempt his wife from the fine he exacted from anyone in his house who failed to speak Hebrew exclusively.[5] While Zionists continually stressed the necessity of female participation in the Hebrew revival, it was clear to them that the segment of the population least able to make the transition to Hebrew speech quickly were the women. Official concessions, mirroring Jabotinsky's private one, were made: the Yiddish writer Zrubavel reported that, in the 1930s, the Histadrut, the Zionist-Socialist Federation of Labor Unions, required Hebrew speech of all its members, with the exception of "women who had been in the country for less than two years" (17). The Histadrut were making allowances for women not because they were particularly chivalrous, of course, but because men could be expected to have some knowledge of Hebrew: a male pioneer who had acquired a rudimentary *yeshiva* education could, if pressed, assemble a simple sentence by cutting and pasting fragments of remembered religious Hebrew texts.

Hebraism went beyond the prescription of a language; it also involved a mindset often explicitly or implicitly marked as masculine. Jabotinsky, in a series of linguistic tracts that dovetailed with his Revisionist political programs, campaigned not only for the exclusive use of Hebrew, but also for a Hebrew devoid of Yiddishisms and Eastern European "ghetto" intonations. In a 1927 letter to Dr. Yevin, the well-known Hebrew teacher, he describes his disgust at hearing Jewish women trying to speak Hebrew: "The woman says, 'Thank God, I'm much better,' but she speaks in a whining, almost sobbing tone, as if she were relating some disaster" (1972b:50). Jabotinsky's misogynist revulsion far exceeds the purely linguistic character of his observation: Hebrew intonation must distance itself from an entire mindset, marked here as "feminine," which fuses complaint with euphemism (a typical Eastern European Yiddish speech act). What Jabotinsky insists on is not just a different accent or intonation, but also a new type of speech performance, the straight-talking, clipped, and unemotional mode of address that has since become increasingly identified with Hebrew and Israeli speech patterns.[6]

The debate over the proper pronunciation of Hebrew sometimes drew upon sexual polarities as well. Ben-Yehuda, for instance, characterized the Ashkenazic dialect (or accentual system) as "soft, weak, without the special strength the emphatic consonant gives to the word" (205). Harshav describes the prevailing preference of the Sephardic or Oriental accentual system over the Ashkenazic one as a shift from what was perceived as a weak and "whining" intonational pattern to a forceful accent as far removed from Yiddish-inflected Hebrew as possible. Harshav summarizes the typical attitude toward the Sephardic accent: "This is the perspective: our language is pioneering, coarse, strong, masculine—like the 'masculine' rhyme imposed by the Sephardi accent as opposed to the soft, 'feminine' rhyme dominant in Ashkenazi poetry" (163). Thus, not only was the language chosen by the Hebraist pioneers the one associated with Jewish masculinity, they also preferred an intonational system and an accentual pattern they perceived as masculine. The revival, in this way, reinforced and solidified Hebrew's masculine associations in its adoption of particular speech patterns as well as a regnant Hebrew accent.

The narratives of Ben-Yehuda's experiment dramatized and provided an exalted setting for the domestic and sexual conflicts that were to become ubiquitous in the struggle to revive Hebrew speech on a larger scale. The folklorist Alter Druyanov relates a riddle that circulated during the early years of the Hebrew revival: "Someone said that Erets-Israeli women are better than all other women in the world, since all other women talk without understanding, while the Erets-Israeli woman understands but does not speak" (joke 2663). Druyanov adds in a footnote that the joke refers to women's difficulty in learning to speak Hebrew. The joke, if it was ever funny, derives a certain sadistic-comic power from more than just the difficulties women were having in mastering a language for which their education did not prepare them; it also invokes the stereotypical views of women as foolishly garrulous, "talk[ing] without understanding."[7] Enforcing the language laws, as Ben-Yehuda was not the first husband to attempt, had the added "benefit" of finally shutting up the Jewish woman. And the quasi-talmudic form of the joke only reinforces the equation between men and proper Hebrew speech, which includes the mastery of rabbinical discourse.

Ben-Yehuda's bookishness, his "bourgeois" image (emblematized, perhaps, by his assumption that a "normal" household requires a maid), as well as his stubborn insistence on making the conservative city of Jerusalem the center of his pioneering linguistic efforts did not endear him either to his Orthodox neighbors or to later generations of Hebrew activists. Nevertheless, Ben-Yehuda's story acquired considerable cultural currency, and it continues to fascinate generations of Israelis.[8] There are many reasons why this should be so, but among these I would propose: for both Ben-Yehuda and the language pioneers that came later, Hebrew was not just a language, it was also a corrective to the no longer acceptable ways of Jewish women, a reorganization of traditional family structures, and a recovery program for wounded Jewish masculinity.

Even as successive waves of immigration ensured the continuing need for Hebraist activism, the work of the Hebraists began to bear fruit. Where the first revivers of spoken Hebrew told stories about the thin veneer of Hebrew speech breaking under the impact of fever or a husband's absence, later generations of Zionists increasingly had wondrous tales to recount, especially of the children who had been born in Palestine and educated in the new Hebrew schools of the *yishuv*. Anecdotal material about the new generation of Hebrew-speaking children reveals how deeply the linguistic transformation symbolically stood for a psychosexual one. While the Ben-Yehuda family drama had pitted male against female speech, the new psycholinguistic drama was taking place most primarily within the structure of Jewish masculinity. Itamar Even-Zohar, with barely concealed pride in the macho character of Hebrew, in the success of Zionism at "transforming the identity, the very nature of the people," relates the well-known story of the visit of two Yiddishists to pre–World War I Tel Aviv:

> The elder one says to the other: 'The Zionists boast that Hebrew is becoming the natural tongue for the children of Palestine. I will show you that they are lying. I will tweak one of the boy's ears, and I promise you that he will not cry out "Ima" but "mame" in Yiddish.'
> So saying, he approached one of the boys and tweaked his ear. The boy turned on him and shouted "hamor" ["donkey," in Hebrew]. The Yiddishist turned to his friend and said: I'm afraid the Zionists are right.
> (1986:131–32)

This anecdote is so similar to others that arose about different figures (usually connected in some way with Yiddish) that one can detect in it a "joke type." The success stories of the Hebrew revival, and this anecdote is of course an example, often involved children, as in the Yiddish poet Yehoash's awed report of the Tel Aviv street urchins playing ball "in Hebrew" (3). The awe of older Yiddish-speaking Jews visiting Palestine, either sincere or exaggerated by proud Hebraists, seems to apply equally to the two—presumably related—phenomena: children speaking Hebrew and *Jewish* children playing ball. The implications of the anecdote about the two Yiddishists, however, go further than the suggestion that the new generation has succeeded in acquiring a new mother tongue or even that it enjoys sports. Itamar Even-Zohar interprets this joke as suggesting that "a nation cannot be tweaked by the ear and cry 'mother,' that is, run for help to its mother. The 'Jewish mother' thus had become culturally incomprehensible" (132). Even-Zohar's analysis assumes that the little boy stands in for "the nation" that cannot "be tweaked on the ear." Underlying this interpretation is the idea that each new Hebrew speaker did, in fact, feel himself (or, more problematically, herself) to represent the entire Hebrew nation. In such a capacity, the child had become orphaned, just as the Hebrew nation had cut itself off from its feminized mother tongue. Implicit in all the anecdotes related here are not only the obsolescence of the "Jewish mother," but also the replacement of the despised diaspora "femininity" with a new model for Jewish masculine behavior. *Mame-loshn* is, literally, the language of "mama's boys," whereas Hebrew is the language of the ferocious, disrespectful young.

Yeshurun Keshet relates another anecdote that circulated somewhat later, after the refugees of Hitler's Europe began to arrive: a refugee child in one of the temporary camps that had been set up beside a kibbutz ran home crying to his mother, "Mame, di hebre'ishe shkotsim'lekh viln mikh shlogn" ("Mama, the little Hebrew Gentile-boys want to hit me") (120). Keshet's story captures the difference between the Yiddish-speaking diasporic Jewish male, clinging to his mother in fear and helplessness, and his fierce Hebrew counterpart, who is associated, in the mind of the Yiddish child, with the non-Jewish hoodlums of Europe. The new Hebrew male, this anecdote seems to be saying, is so different from his diasporic "other" that recognizing him as Jewish requires a major shift in the Jewish/non-Jewish paradigm. This last story, however, has a pathos lacking in the jokes I related earlier, since the young refugee boy is genuinely afraid, unlike the older Yiddishists. The unadulterated pride with which the earlier anecdotes were repeated is somewhat mixed, in this anecdote, with the bittersweet regret that overtook even the most hardened Hebraists in the wake of the genocide of European Jewry.

It is no coincidence, perhaps, that one of the most notorious of acts of hostility by the militant Brigade for the Defense of the Language was its struggle in the autumn of 1930 against the showing of the Yiddish film *Di yidishe mame,* a film Arye Pilovski describes as of "extremely limited aesthetic value" that was nonetheless the occasion of an international Jewish scandal.[9] Pilovski relates that the film was only shown after protests and threats under the protection of the British police, and even then the brigade succeeded in disrupting the event. When additional screenings were cancelled, the Yiddish press decried the "pogrom" against Yiddish in Palestine.[10] Yosef Klausner, in an article protesting the film when it was first scheduled, explained the Hebraist fervor as directed specifically against *this* Yiddish film, rather than merely using it as a convenient scapegoat for more general anti-Yiddish attacks. As Klausner put it, Yiddish was dangerous precisely because it was the language of "our mothers and the masses."[11]

The sentimental Yiddish film, with its clear call for loyalty to the Jewish mother and its appeal to a broad audience, represented more than just a linguistic danger to new Hebrew speakers. It also threatened to wear down the emotional barriers that the Hebrew pioneers shored against Yiddish and its symbolic attractions.

At least some of what is at stake in these stories transcends the Hebrew revival and the Hebrew-Yiddish conflict; the Zionist embrace of masculinism has derivations other than the Hebrew-Yiddish language conflict. The fin de siècle Central European cult of youth and athletic clubs (and, in the previous generation, dueling fraternities) certainly contributed to early Zionist culture. Max Nordau's influential speech on "Muskeljudentum" (Jewry of muscle) upon the opening of the Zionist sports organization Bar Kokhba is perhaps the clearest Zionist statement of the necessity of improving the physical prowess of feminized Jewish men. In a passionate appeal for global Jewish transformation, Nordau contrasts the stereotypical Jewish male with his vision for a new variety of Jewish masculinity—one that was once the rightful property of Jewish men:

> In the narrow Jewish street our poor limbs soon forgot their gay movements; in the dimness of sunless houses our eyes began to blink shyly.... Let us take up our oldest traditions; let us once more become deep-chested, sturdy, sharp-eyed men. (1980:435)

Early Zionist literature and art are replete with references to the ideal man. Herzl was described by one Zionist as "a magnificent man," an example of "the most aristocratic manliness" (54). The Zionist artist Lilien used Herzl's figure and face in his biblical portraits, even placing him naked in the Garden of Eden as Adam. Nevertheless, language became an important component in sexual identity, for Central as well as Eastern European Jews, combining with models of athletic masculinity to form a single linguistic-somatic structure.

Considering the degree to which Hebrew was intended as a program for the most fundamental self-transformation (including sexual self-transformation), it is not surprising that the first step in Hebraization often entailed a name change, with Hebrew being mined for masculine signifiers. Ben-Yehuda, in fact, may well have been the first to perform this more-than-symbolic act, which he ecstatically described in his memoirs: "I felt I had been reborn" (116). As Reuven Sivan relates, the militant Hebrew Language Brigade (*Gedud meginey hasafah*) considered it a public service to "help people Hebraize their names" (120). Amos Elon describes the practice of changing one's name (which appears in a number of biblical stories) as a "magic act," tracing the Hebraizing of diaspora names to

> the old Jewish custom of changing the name of a very sick man in the hope of cheating the angel of death. Thus, it may be more than accident that so many Jewish refugees from lands of persecution—even more often their sons—have shown a proclivity to redefine themselves with names that denote firmness, toughness, strength, courage, and vigor: *Yariv* ("antagonist"); *Oz* ("strength"); *Tamir* ("towering"); *Lahat* ("blaze"); *Kabiri* ("tremendous"); *Hod* ("splendor," "majesty"); *Barak* ("lightning"); *Tsur* ("rock"); *Nechushtan* ("bronze"); *Bar Adon* ("son of the master," or "masterful"); or even *Bar Shilton* ("fit to govern"). (1971:120)

Although the Hebraization of women's family names typically followed that of their husbands or fathers, some women took the opportunity of the widespread name changes to adopt their own Hebrew names; these names can reveal something to us about how self-transformation was viewed by women, who could be assumed to be outside the cult of Hebraic masculinism. Among the most prominent examples are writers like Rachel, who dropped her family name. Rachel's use of her first name alone, which is in keeping with her poetics of simplicity, might also signal a newfound freedom from both the European past and her own family history. The name also serves to present the poet as a neobiblical character, or as a woman with whom her reading public could feel itself on an intimate first-name basis. Yocheved Bat-Miriam's matronym, as Ilana Pardes calls it, signals the young Hebrew woman's adoption of her own foremother as a voluntary family affiliation: "Bat-Miriam's choice of a name," Pardes argues, "needs to be seen both as a concrete challenge to the patrilinear naming system and as a critique of culture in which literary tradition, like names, is passed down from father to son" (1992:42).

In feminine reworkings of Zionist/Hebraist practice such as Bat-Miriam's, the desire to forge a connection with the biblical past often turns out to contain an element of feminist subversion (just as the feminine use of the biblical topos "land = beloved woman" could produce a lesbian rather than a heteronormative love poem). In the case of Bat-Miriam's adoption of a name, the reversal of the biblical parent-child relationship—in the Bible Yocheved is the mother of Miriam—in the modern Hebrew name can also be seen in the light of the Zionist reversal of the parent-child hierarchy. Here, the biblical mother becomes the daughter's daughter or, alternatively, the biblical daughter becomes the mother's mother, so that biological affiliation and the respect and authority traditionally invested in the older generation give way to a fluid model of imaginative and voluntary affiliations.

Other women writers chose names from nature, as did many men. Malka Shechtman, for instance, called herself Bat-Chama, daughter of the sun. Again, in cases like these, the feminine version of the Zionist model often contained an additional revolutionary element, since the women were clearly setting up a personal rather than a dynastic or family model of name transmission. A brief perusal of a collection of articles by Zionist women workers published in 1930 suggests how widespread such name changes were among women: of forty-five contributors, ten use only their first names and three use a single initial. Among these ten, two names are of Yiddish origin while one is European; the others are Hebrew names (it is impossible to decide whether these names were adopted, although names like Carmela and Techiya have a distinctly Zionist ring). Of the family names, one, Bat-Rachel, is a matronym. One woman signs herself Dinah Bat-Chorin (Dinah the Free Woman, or Dinah the Daughter of a Free Person), while another one is called Nechama Bat-Tsiyon (Nechama the Daughter of Zion).[12] A woman taking a name like Bat-Chorin or Bat-Tsiyon was doing more than transforming a Yiddish family name into a Hebrew one; she was also rejecting the patriarchal transmission of family names. To adopt a family name with a clear feminine marker, even as a pen name, is to announce one's independence from husband and father and to suggest the possibility of other familial or quasi-familial structures.

In other cases, name changes revealed both the revolutionary discontinuities called for by Hebraism and the submerged continuities that managed to survive even the most extreme attempts at Zionist self-transformation. The Hebrew poet Avot Yeshurun, in a 1974 interview with the Israeli journalist Chayim Nagid, explained how and why he changed his name from Yechiel Perlmutter. The change was not only from a diasporic name to a Hebrew one, but also from a name with a recognizable Yiddish meaning ("pearl-mother," or "mother-of-pearl"), which includes a reference to "mother" rare in a family name, to a Hebrew name that means "Fathers are watching us" (Avot, "fathers"; Yeshurun, "are or will be watching us"). Yeshurun recounts that he chose the first name, Avot, on his entry into the army, immediately following the founding of the State of Israel. He had long wished to change his name, he explained, but felt particularly strongly that he should have a Hebrew name for his swearing-in ceremony. Yeshurun describes how he lay awake the night before the ceremony, trying to think of a name that would suit him:

> At dawn, I said to myself: remember your childhood. Maybe I could come up with something from my childhood. . . . I remembered my mother singing beautiful lullabies to my brothers in her beautiful voice. Once, she bent over the cradle and sang to the youngest one in Yiddish and Ukrainian. But the children wouldn't fall asleep, and my mother stopped singing and instead called out excitedly, "*tatelekh, tatelekh,*" [a common Yiddish term of endearment meaning "little fathers, little fathers"]. And then the children understood that she wasn't going to sing and he went to sleep by himself. From this I took the name "Avot" and was very satisfied with it. (Nagid 1974:11)

Yeshurun's story is emblematic in a number of ways. The first might be the poet's sense of the importance of finding himself a Hebrew name for the occasion of his induction into the new Israeli army. Any Hebrew name would signify a new masculinity, given the associations of the language with the proud biblical history of Jewish sovereignty; but Yeshurun was not simply translating his name from German or Russian into Hebrew, as some did, but also selecting a name that would confer a new identity befitting a Hebrew warrior. The name Avot Yeshurun either referred to "the fathers of Jerusalem" or formed a sentence meaning "the fathers will see" or even "foresee," since the kind of sight implied by the verb *yeshurun* is associated with powerful observation over space or time. And the modern Hebrew Avot, as a replacement of the traditional Hebrew (Yiddishized) Yechiel ("God lives or will live"), substitutes a human — albeit male — history for an affirmation of faith in the divine. In calling himself Avot, he not only chose a name that would signify his belief in a new and powerful connection with his patrilineage, he also erased the old name, with its associations of femininity and its recognizably Yiddish ring.

Nevertheless, the account Yeshurun gives of his self-transformation also indicates that his name expressed a strong sense of continuity with his past, in the form of his Yiddish-speaking mother. The name Avot, for all its patriarchal grandeur, is in fact a translation of the Yiddish term used for little boys, "little fathers." Translated back into Yiddish, the name means "little boys are watching us," as if Yeshurun were reversing the course of his own history or imagining his present circumstances from the amazed perspective of a little Eastern European child. The disappearance of the diminutive in the move to Hebrew might signal the process of replacing a Yiddish childhood with a Hebrew adulthood, but it might also be a clever concealment of the continuing existence of the Yiddish boy. Yeshurun's memorializing of his mother is also curiously ambiguous. By having her choose his name, as it were, he admits her continued importance to his new life. But the story of his choice and the name itself also signify her absence, erasure, or silence. The name comes, that is, at the moment when the mother breaks off her lullaby and moves away, just as the young man chose his name at the moment his youth would be ruptured by his shouldering of the adult burdens of a Zionist soldier. This account, in all its complexity, reveals something of the ways in which radical discontinuity and continuity combine with respectively masculine and feminine models of identity in the Zionist narrative.

The Hebrew writers of the Moderna perceived their greatest achievement as the creation of a monolingual, "natural" Hebrew, one that could express their new environment without undue self-consciousness or linguistic borrowing. It is the margins of modern Hebrew literature that attest to the strain of defending the borders of this monolingualism. Yiddish literature, by way of contrast, could afford to address directly the Hebrew it could also easily encompass in its own linguistic repertoire. Thus, the Hebrew-Yiddish language debate took place not at the margins of the Yiddishist canon, but at its very center.

Yiddishists confronted with the sexual politics of the Hebrew-Yiddish language war had two choices: on the one hand, they could resist the identification of Yiddish with women, instead drawing attention to its status as the language of the "masses." Yehoash's new Yiddish translation of the Bible, which was seen as a modern updating of the old Yiddish "women's Bible," certainly could be included in the efforts to rehabilitate Yiddish as a language for men as much as women.

Other Yiddishists took the other tack and found themselves defending women and Yiddish simultaneously. Yankev Glatshteyn, who published his first Yiddish poems under a female pseudonym, satirized the Zionist Hebrew program in his 1929 collection *Kredos,* in a response to the ill-treatment of Yiddish writers in Palestine. Significantly,

the silenced other of these poems is often embodied in female or matriarchal characters. One poem is entitled "Dort vu di tseder" (There
where the cedars), an ironic shorthand reference to the well-known
anthem "There Where the Cedars Bloom" sung by German-speaking
Zionists, which is itself reworked from a patriotic German song ("Die
Wacht am Rhein" [The watch on the Rhine]) popular at the turn of
the century. The German original is easily detectable behind the revised Zionist lyrics:

> There where the cedar kisses the sky,
> And where the Jordan quickly flows by,
> There where the ashes of my father lie,
> In that exalted Reich, on sea and sand,
> Is my beloved, true Fatherland.

While the father and "Fatherland" are prominent in the Zionist version
of the song, Glatshteyn's portrait of "where the cedars bloom" foregrounds the women who have been omitted in the other version, specifically presenting the matriarch Rachel as the victim of the Hebraists:

> There where the cedars bloom —
> They don't let you speak Yiddish.
> They don't let my language touch the lips.
> Mother Rachel, who cried her way through the entire *taytsh-chumesh*,
> Lies at the crossroad and waits, silent —
> She would cry for her children
> But she only knows Zhargon. (1929:72)

The power of Glatshteyn's Yiddishist message lies not only in its evocation of a sentimental rhetoric of maternity, but also in its appropriation of Zionist themes, beginning with the title (and Glatshteyn, later
in the poem, uses some Hebrew as well) and continuing with the
claim that the matriarch Rachel properly belongs not to the Hebrew
Bible or to the Holy Land, but to the Yiddish translation of the Bible
for women and to her diaspora children. Glatshteyn's ploy could work,
of course, not only because Rachel has been associated with the diaspora, but also because of the associations he could count on his audience to make between Yiddish and women, especially older women.

Glatshteyn's bitterness at the Zionist suppression of Yiddish long
outlasted the years of the outright "language war." In a poem first
published in 1961, "Ret tsu mir yidish" (Speak Yiddish/Jewish with
me), the poetic speaker calls Israel "my Yiddish (or Jewish) country"
and promises to answer in Hebrew if he is addressed in Yiddish. In

the earlier poem, Glatshteyn used the figure of Rachel to personify the silenced language. Here, however, it is the men who suffer the brunt of the repression, while the women are described as retaining some expressive freedom. Thus, the poetic speaker discovers a loophole in the masculinist Hebrew program, finding a conversational partner in the Jewish woman and sorrowfully acknowledging the silencing of the Jewish man. The different status of men and women in the Hebrew project is implied in the second stanza, where he spies his "grandparents," the patriarchs Abraham and Sarah (of course, Yankev is the Yiddish form of Jacob, the grandson of Abraham and Sarah):

> God help us, Grandpa-Grandma.
> Abraham is crossing the street in silence.
> Don't take it to heart, Yankele,
> Says Sarah, he understands every word.
>
> That's the way it goes here.
> A man has to stifle his Yiddish.
> But a Jewess from the *yidish-taytsh*
> Still has something to say. (1961:165)

Sarah comforts Yankele, the poetic persona, by reassuring him that although Avrom is silent, "Hu meyvin kol dibur" (He understands every word) a Hebrew code phrase inserted into Yiddish speech to warn the interlocutor that a nearby non-Jew can understand Yiddish.[13] Thus, the poem enacts a double dislocation of traditional Jewish values, one social and one linguistic: the patriarchs are imagined as Yiddish speakers, as generations of Ashkenazic domestication of biblical figures had rendered them; and as Yiddish speakers, they would be treated as outsiders in the Jewish state. In this context, the function of the Hebrew code phrase is completely reversed, working to reassure Yankele that Abraham is not an outsider rather than warning him that he is. Glatshteyn's clever demonstrations of the interconnectedness of Hebrew and Yiddish reinforce the poem's message that Hebrew speakers may not have changed as completely as the Zionists boast.

The discourse of linguistic maternity was so powerful that Hebraists could not completely cede the status of "mother tongue" to Yiddish. Arguing for the sole legitimacy of Hebrew as the Jewish national tongue, Achad Ha'am rhetorically asks whether an individual's proper language could be anything other than the one in which "they sang to him lullabies, that was rooted in his soul before he even knew who he was and which developed along with him" (1961:111). What is true for the individual, Achad Ha'am argues, is also true for the nation. But the move he makes in this passage is a contradictory one, since the metaphorical mother tongue of his audience (as a national collective) may have been Hebrew, but the one in which most of them were in fact lulled to sleep was almost certainly Yiddish.[14] At stake, of course, was not only the emotional power of this maternal rhetoric, but also the long-entrenched connections between nationality and the concept of "mother tongue."

The older generation of Hebrew writers in the *yishuv*, less compelled as they were by the revolutionary aspect of Hebraist rhetoric, tended to be have more moderate positions on the question of bilingualism than did the younger, modernist generation. When Chayim Nachman Bialik greeted the Yiddish writers Sholem Ash and Perets Hirshbein at a 1927 reception to mark their visit to Palestine, he made a speech in their honor, using traditional concepts of Hebrew-Yiddish complementarity and hierarchy to describe what he considered the proper relationship between Hebrew and Yiddish writers. Bialik began by noting the difference between his own hostile reception in New York and the pleasant reception accorded the Yiddish writers in Tel Aviv, since, "thank God," the Hebrew-Yiddish language war had already been settled in Palestine. A newspaper report the following day summarized the rest of his speech in the following words:

> Hebrew and Yiddish are a marriage made in heaven that can never be dissolved, just like Ruth and Naomi, but the very instant that Yiddish tries to cut herself off from Hebrew, she ceases to be ours....As of the present, the edict of Rabbenu Gershom [against bigamy] does not apply to languages. ("A Reception," 1)

Bialik's pleasantries are combined with an undercurrent of warning. The relationship between Hebrew and Yiddish, which he begins by describing through the presumably necessary institution of marriage, becomes a contingent homosocial friendship. In this friendship between a Jewish and originally non-Jewish partner, Yiddish is in the position of Ruth, that is, she is a visitor in Palestine on sufferance and liable to be evicted if she does not follow the rules. Bialik's slightly risqué allusion to the prohibition against bigamy places the bilingual writer in the scenario; the triangle reestablishes not the Hebrew language, but rather the powerful male in a position of dominance over the two women-languages.

The Socialist-Zionist organ of the Hebrew writers' union recorded the reactions of the younger Hebraist writers to the polite welcome Bialik, Ya'akov Fichman, and Berl Katznelson had accorded the visiting emissaries from the world of Yiddish. The writers who boycotted the reception were primarily of a younger generation—Greenberg is an obvious exception—and their responses generally had nothing of the goodwill the speeches at the reception had demonstrated. The younger Hebrew poet Avraham Shlonsky described the reception as a farce, a diplomatic ceremony designed to mask the need for a decisive position on the language question. In a direct and disdainful reference to Bialik's conciliatory position on Yiddish in Palestine, Shlonsky attacked those who signed the "marriage contract" without any power of attorney from the Hebrew camp:

> We never accepted the match between the languages, so we're not going to dance at the wedding. And we're not going to wait for any Rabenu Gershom to make a rabbinical decree against multilingualism.... We want our Erets-Israeli breath to be purely Hebrew. With both lungs! (1927:1)

Shlonsky's rhetorical stance in this passage recalls his earlier assaults on *melitsa,* the elevated allusive style of premodernist Hebrew poetry, as a kind of textual enslavement. In a 1922 manifesto, he compared the sublime *melitsa* style of the compulsory biblical allusions to a traditional marriage in which sexual relations have become habitual and automatic. As Shlonsky put it, the new modernist poetry rejected *all* traditions, but particularly sexual ones:

> Civil marriage, free love between words, without arranged matches of style, without family pedigrees and dowries of associations, and most importantly: without the bridal canopy and the marital blessings! Any combination of words—lawless attachments, one-night stands. (1922:154)

Zohar Shavit, in her study of *yishuv* literature and ideology, interprets Shlonsky's vehement attack on Bialik's stance on Yiddish as merely a pretext for his poetic revolution against the hegemony of Bialik's style.[15] But in an important sense, the internal poetic struggles of Hebrew literature and the larger linguistic conflict intersected. By the twenties and thirties, with the growth of spoken Hebrew in

Palestine, Hebrew was itself developing what could be called "internal diglossia"; the gap between the lofty quasi-biblical style that characterized the Hebrew poetry of Bialik's generation and the vernacular that could already be heard on the streets of Tel Aviv was increasingly apparent to the younger generation of writers. Thus, Shlonsky's explicit agenda of lowering the register of Hebrew poetry, one he only partially realized, demanded a double-pronged attack—first on the sublime style of Bialik and his epigones, and second on the threatened encroachment (and historical primacy) of Yiddish as the modern Jewish vernacular. And he could use similar rhetorical strategies in both battles, since the Hebrew high style and the Yiddish vernacular were part of the same traditional structure that was encoded in and exemplified by rigid and stultifying gender codes. The Hebrew sublime and denigrated Yiddish coarse speech, in Shlonsky's view, were two sides of the same obsolete coin. Shlonsky's radical refusal of bilingualism, and his couching of this refusal in a marital metaphor, recalls Ben-Yehuda's determination to create a "pure" Hebrew atmosphere for what Harshav refers to as the First Hebrew Child. Both projects link the creation of a monolingual environment with a refusal of female company, of feminine speech, and of dialogue with the "other."

Shlonsky's response to Bialik's pious blessing of the eternal linguistic union of Hebrew and Yiddish did not become a rallying cry because it shed any new light on the language question—after all, Shlonsky did no more than rephrase Bialik's remarks in the negative. Shlonsky's slogan, "We never accepted this match made in heaven," was echoed because he succeeded in fusing a revolutionary sexual ethic (though one not necessarily beneficial to women) with a call for an exclusive loyalty to Hebrew. Where Bialik projects the Hebraist disavowal of Yiddish onto the camp of the Yiddishists, Shlonsky takes full, conscious responsibility for the ideological repudiation of Yiddish and uses it to launch a generational war against the poetic norms of Bialik and his epigones. And while Bialik's words are no more than a mildly clever extension of an exhausted metaphor, as automatic as the *melitsa* allusiveness Shlonsky decried in his Futurist manifestos of the early twenties, Shlonsky's answer recharges the metaphor's dormant sexual dimension. At the same time, Shlonsky repudiates the tinge of sexual looseness in Bialik's comparison of monolingualism with bigamy by announcing that his own disinterest in "two women" was not because of any conformance with rabbinical law. In Shlonsky's formulation, the move to a revitalized Hebrew and away from Yiddish requires no apology or concession to tradition. Shlonsky takes Bialik's heterosexual metaphor and reworks it into a plea for the health of the solitary body who wishes to "breathe" Hebrew with both lungs. Hebraism, for Shlonsky, is a gesture of both literary and erotic freedom, an expression of (masculine) liberation from a conservative literary code, an atmosphere contaminated by the presence of women and stifled by its repressive sexual order.

The furious outbreak that followed the reception for Ash and Hirshbein in Tel Aviv may mark the end not only of traditional Jewish bilingualism, but also of the Hebrew-Yiddish sexual-linguistic system as a whole. It is curious, therefore, that perhaps the single most powerful phrase to describe this system can be found in the metaphor presented by Bialik and attacked by Shlonsky. Although the metaphor of Hebrew and Yiddish as husband and wife is implicit in the structure of Hebrew-Yiddish bilingualism, it seems to have broken through the surface of public discourse only at the moment when the relationship was reaching its ultimate dissolution.

Notes

1. See Fellman 1973:112 ff., Harshav 1993:83ff., and Wexler 1990:18ff. Alter does not explicitly discuss Ben-Yehuda's role in the revival of Hebrew as a spoken language; his *Invention of Hebrew Prose* presents various ways in which Hebrew prose discovered or invented Hebrew style, idiom, and vocabulary for their own purposes — before, during, and after Ben-Yehuda's work.

2. Of course, the phrase "the father of the Hebrew revival" is the English, rather than the Hebrew, term for Ben-Yehuda's role in reviving Hebrew. In Hebrew, he is called by the quasi-divine name of *mechaye hasafah*, the "'reviver' of the language." Nevertheless, references to Ben-Yehuda's paternal role are ubiquitous in his own and in other writings on his contribution to the revival.

3. "Eliezer Ben-Yehuda," *Papers of the Hebrew Language Academy* (Jerusalem: Hebrew Language Academy, 1970).

4. Avrom Golomb writes: "If we objectively analyze of all the new words that have been formed in 'New Hebrew' or 'Modern Hebrew,' it would be hard to decide what had a greater effect on them, the love of Hebrew or the hatred toward Yiddish and everything connected to Yiddish.... The young Hebrew speakers have no connection to the Jewish people and they want no connection with them" (1962:152).

5. In "Zev Jabotinsky" [Hebrew] (Jerusalem: Hebrew Language Academy, 1970), 7.

6. For an analysis of Hebrew speech patterns, see Katriel 1986.

7. A well-known rabbinical epigram states that "ten measures of talk came down into the world, [and] nine were taken by the women" (Kiddushin 49b). From this talmudic saying was derived the Yiddish proverb *a yidene hot nayn mos reyd* (a woman has nine measures of talk).

8. The popular song "Eliezer Ben-Yehuda," with lyrics by Yaron London and music by Matti Caspi, is one piece of evidence for continuing interest in Ben-Yehuda; see Matti Caspi and Yaron London, "Eliezer Ben-Yehuda," *Elef zemer ve'od zermer* [One Thousand and One Songs], ed. Rafi Pesakhzon and Talma Alyazon (Tel Aviv: Kineret Press, 1981), 100. Note the song's emphasis on Ben-Yehuda's fatherhood and its mention of Itamar as *gever kilvavi,* "a man after my own heart." A recent film entitled *The Word Maker* examines Ben-Yehuda's life largely from the perspective of his embittered son, who repeatedly resorts to the biblical story of the binding of Isaac in discussing his father's treatment of him.

9. This incident is discussed in Pilovski 1986:213–15.

10. Pilovski cites a letter written originally to the Hebrew daily *Do'ar hayom* and reprinted in the Yiddish journal *Literarishe bleter* in which L. Chayn-Shimoni described the incident as a "pogrom" and criticized "the 'cultural Hebraists' who think that they are against the rooting of Hebrew in Palestine through acts of violence, but then do nothing to stop these actions when they occur" (1986:214).

11. Cited in Pilovski 1986:213.

12. See the collection *Divre po'alot* [The words of working women], ed. Rachel Katznelson-Shazar (Tel Aviv: Mo'etset hapo'alot, 1930), i–iii.

13. On Glatshteyn's use of this phrase and for a broader explanation of the poem, see Hadda 1980:140–41.

14. Jonathan Culler (1982) associates the metaphorical impulse with particularly masculine anxieties. Men's "loose mammalian connection with children" may encourage an emphasis on symbolic connections: "One might predict an inclination to value what are generally termed metaphorical relations—relations of resemblance between separate items that can be substituted for one another, such as obtain between the father and the miniature replica with the same name, the child—over metonymical, maternal relationships based on contiguity" (60). While Culler's biologism is rather simplistic, it does provide us with the argument that Hebrew, as the metaphorical mother tongue, is thus a fatherly "mother tongue," while Yiddish is the metonymical mother tongue, and thus doubly feminine.

15. Shavit 1982:176–77.

Bibliography

Achad Ha'am [Asher Ginzburg]. "*Tkhiyat haru'ach*" [The revival of the spirit], *Al parashat derakhim* [At a crossroad]. Tel Aviv: Dvir Press, 1961 [1898].

Alter, Robert. 1988. *The Invention of Hebrew Prose*. Seattle: University of Washington Press.

Ben-Avi, Itamar. 1927. *Avi* [My father]. Jerusalem: Ben-Yehuda Press.

Ben-Yehuda, Chemda. 1940. *Ben-Yehuda: Chayav umif'alo* [Ben-Yehuda: His life and project]. Jerusalem: Ben-Yehuda Press.

Ben-Yehuda, Eliezer. 1978. *Hachalom veshivro* [The dream and its fulfillment]. Ed. Reuven Sivan. Jerusalem: Mosad Bialik.

Culler, Jonathan. 1982. "Reading as a Woman." *On Deconstruction*. Ithaca, N.Y.: Cornell University Press.

Druyanov, Alter. 1991. *Sefer habedicha vehachidud* [The book of jokes and witticisms]. Tel Aviv: Dvir.

Elon, Amos. 1971. *The Israelis: Founders and Sons*. Middlesex: Penguin.

Even-Zohar, Itamar. 1986. "Language Conflict and National Identity." In

Nationalism and Modernity: A Mediterranean Perspective, ed. Joseph Alpher. Haifa: University of Haifa Press.

Fellman, Jack. 1973. *The Revival of a Classical Tongue: Eliezer Ben-Yehuda and the Modern Hebrew Language.* The Hague: Mouton.

Glatshteyn, Yankev. 1929. *Kredos* [Credos]. New York: Farlag Yidish Leben.

———. 1961. *Di freyd fun yidishn vort* [The joy of the Yiddish word]. New York: Der Kval.

Golomb, Avrom. 1962. "People and Language: Jewish Nationality and Yiddish Language." *Yearbook of the New Jewish School in Mexico, I. L. Perets.*

Hadda, Janet. 1980. *Glatshteyn, Yankev.* Boston: Twayne.

Harshav, Benjamin. 1993. *Language in Time of Revolution.* Berkeley: University of California Press.

Hebrew Language Academy. 1970. *Papers of the Hebrew Language Academy.* Jerusalem.

Jabotinsky, Zev. 1972a. "Hebrew in Erets-Israel." In *Olamo shel Zhabotinski: mivchar dvarav ve'ikarey torato* [The world of Jabotinsky: A selection of his works and the essentials of his teaching], ed. Moshe Bella. Tel Aviv: Dfusim.

———. 1972b. *Mikhtavey Zhabotinski* [Jabotinsky's letters]. Tel Aviv: Merkaz.

Katriel, Tamar. 1986. *Talking Straight: Dugri Speech in Israeli Sabra Culture.* New York and Cambridge: Cambridge University Press.

Keshet, Yeshurun. 1974. "Dvora Baron." In *Dvora Baron: Miukhar al ma'amarey bikoret* [Dvora Baron: A selection of critical essays]. Tel Aviv: Am Oved.

Nagid, Chayim. 1974. "Interview with the Poet Avot Yeshurun." *Yidiot achronot,* October 11.

Nordau, Max. 1980. *"Muskeljudentum"* [Muscular Judaism]. Reprinted in *The Jew in the Modern World,* ed. Paul Mendes-Flohr. New York and Oxford: Oxford University Press.

Pardes, Ilana. 1992. "The Poetic Strength of a Matronym." In *Gender and Text in Modern Hebrew and Yiddish Literature,* ed. Naomi B. Sokoloff et al. New York: Jewish Theological Seminary Press.

Peretz, Yitchok Leyb. 1913. "Introductory Remarks." *Di ershte yidish shprakh-conferenz* [The first Yiddish language conference]. Vilna.

Pilovski, Arye Leib. 1986. *Tsvishn yo un neyn: yidish un yidish-literatur in erets-yisroel, 1907–1948* [Between yes and no: Yiddish and Yiddish literature in Erets-Israel, 1907–1948]. Tel Aviv: World Council for Yiddish and Jewish Culture.

Shavit, Zohar. 1982. *Hachayim hasifrutiyim berets israel: 1910–1933* [Literary life in Palestine: 1910–1933]. Tel Aviv: Hakibuts hame'uchad.

Shlonsky, Avraham. 1922. *"Melitsa"* [Poesy], *Chatoteret-olam* [Hump of the world] Reprinted in *Yorshey hasimbolism bashirah* [The successors of symbolism in poetry], ed. Benjamin Hrushovski. Jerusalem: Akademon, 1973.

———. 1927. *"Al hashalom"'* [On peace]. *Ketuvim,* May 18, 1.

Sivan, Reuven. 1990. "Havayot vechavayot beleshonenu hamitcha deshet" [Conditions and experiences in our reviving language]. Jerusalem: Rubenstin.

Wexler, Paul. 1990. *The Schizoid Nature of Modern Hebrew: A Slavic Language in Search of a Semitic Past.* Wiesbaden: Otto Harrassowitz.

Zrubavel, 1936. *"Mir bashuldikn un monen akhrayes"* [We accuse and demand responsibility]. *Yidish in erets-yisro'el* [Journal of the League for the Rights of Yiddish in the Land of Israel].

11 / Masada or Yavneh? Gender and the Arts of Jewish Resistance

Daniel Boyarin

Merneptah's epitaph for the Israelites was premature, for it was precisely the ability of the Jews to survive in a hostile imperial world that constituted their political genius.

DAVID BIALE, *Power and Powerlessness in Jewish History*

The genius of the Jewish people is diaspora.   (SIDNEY BOYARIN)

The Diaspora People as a Woman

Historically the Jewish male is, from the point of view of dominant European culture, a sort of woman. I should state early and often just what I mean by this term, in order to prevent misunderstanding of my intent. I am not claiming a set of characteristics, traits, behaviors that are essentially female but a set of performances that are culturally read as nonmale within a given historical culture. This culture can be very broadly described as Roman in its origins (Veyne 1985) and as European in its scope and later history. It is the culture of romance. As Jo Ann McNamara has written of the dominant men of twelfth-century Europe:

> They had fused personhood with manhood, and to defend their manhood they had to become ever more manly. They had to persecute with ever-increasing severity anyone who threatened the inner core of that image. Women were victimized by their exclusion and male victims—heretics, homosexuals, Jews, any rebels who didn't fit the mold—were

turned into women. This was a tragedy for women and for the not-men, half-men, effeminate men who were the objects of this relentless persecution. (1994:22)

A very recent writer—a psychoanalyst—continues to reflect this ideology of maleness by assuming confidently that "strength, assertiveness, activity, stoicism, courage, and so forth" are "gender syntonic" for men (Lane 1986:147). Within the context of a culture in which these are considered the essential characteristics of manliness, Jewish men (and certain classes of Christian men as well) appeared to be not-male, *fem(m)inized*. The odd spelling of this term is to signal, once more, that such "fem(m)inization" is not with respect to an essential femininity (e.g., Jungian *anima*)[1] but with respect to a cultural construction of the female as femme (not butch).

Rabbinic male subjectivity is *ideally* different from general European male ideals.[2] I claim that there is something correct—although seriously misvalued—in the persistent European (Roman and later Christian) representation of Jewish men as a sort of women, in a culture in which being a man was predicated on possessing the phallus, the symbolic marker of coherence, power, and sublimation from the body,[3] in short, of human completion. And Jewish men didn't have it. As John Hoberman has put it: "By the time Weininger absorbed it, this intuitive sense of the Jew's deficient masculinity had been germinating for centuries, dating from the Middle Ages" (1995:143). In the anti-Semitic imaginary of Europe (and perhaps Africa and Asia as well), Jews have been represented traditionally as female, but, as Sheila Briggs points out with reference to the latest forms of this representation, this obtained only with respect to "the negative sense of the feminine" (1985:256) There is, however, a positive possibility to "feminization" as well. I argue that traditionally Jewish men identified *themselves* as fem(m)inized—and I call attention once more to my definition—and understood that fem(m)inization as a positive aspect of their cultural identity.

Perhaps the most remarkable feature of the Book (or in Jewish parlance, Scroll) of Esther is that it is about a Jewish woman who has sexual intercourse with a Gentile, and not even quite under conditions that could be called rape, and yet survives as a Jew and as a Jewish heroine, as a model Jew, for whom pious Jews name their daughters until this day and who has a holiday in her honor. Through this strategy—and associated tactics of deceptiveness—she not only saves herself but also the entire Jewish people. She is to be compared to other Jewish heroines such as Ya'el (in fact not actually Jewish, but acting on behalf of the Jews) and Judith, both highly valorized within the Jewish hermeneutic tradition and, to the best of my knowledge, never condemned for their deviousness in achieving victory over stronger male adversaries. I would like to suggest that the Jews identified themselves as a people with these heroines and thus as female, with the appropriation of tactics of survival that belonged "by nature" to women. A nineteenth-century Danish theologian, Hans Lassen Martensen, made reference to this representation, writing that "women try to gain power through craft as well as dissimulation, intrigues, tricks, and lying. . . . Martensen illustrated this corruption of female nature with reference to powerful women of ancient Israel and Judaism" (Briggs 1985:236). For Jews, however, dissimulation, intrigues, tricks, and lying, when they served the purpose of survival, were valorized, as were the powerful women of ancient Israel who employed these practices.[4]

In a recent essay Amy-Jill Levine has advanced our understanding of the antecedents of rabbinic Judaism's feminized self-understanding. In the prerabbinic dystopic vision of the Book of Tobit, Levine writes, "In exile, dead bodies lie in the streets and those who inter them are punished; demons fall in love with women and kill their husbands; even righteousness is no guarantee of stability" (1992:105).[5] The text, according to Levine, has three strategies in order to provide a "clear solid ground for self-definition." Of these three, the one that holds the most interest for my project is "a series of boundary-breaking events—eating, defecating, inseminating, interring" that function "to institute, transgress, and then reinforce distinctions."[6] Readers familiar with Bakhtin will immediately perceive that we are in the realm of the grotesque body, the permeable, quintessentially female (birth-giving, lactating) body, interacting and intersecting with the world and not closed in on itself, as the body of autochthony, the classical (male) body would be. This body, of course, has both utopic and dystopic aspects. On the one hand, it is the vulnerable body, the body that is invaded, penetrated, and hurt. On the other hand, it is the fecund body, the body that interacts with the world and creates new life (Bakhtin 1984)—in short, a perfect representation of the dangers and the powers of diaspora. As Levine has remarked, "Woman is, in effect, in a perpetual diaspora; her location is never her own, but is contingent on that of her father, husband, or sons" (1992:110). No wonder, then, that the diasporic people imagine themselves as female. In Levine's Mary Douglas–inspired reading of Tobit's representations of the body as the corporate body of the Jews, only the negative side of this equation seems to be mobilized; the only products of the grotesque body are abjects (114). For the Hellenistic Book of Tobit, diaspora is wholly deleterious; as Levine writes:

> As a woman, as unaware, as unable to interact, as impeded from conceiving, Sarah cannot represent the covenant community. Instead, unless she is redeemed by the community's pure, male representatives, Sarah represents what could be its fate in the diaspora: ignorant, childless, and in the undesired embrace of idolatry represented by the demon. (112)

There is an enormous shift between the Judaism represented by the Book of Tobit and that of the Rabbis of late antiquity, precisely in the realm of the gendered representation of the social body of Israel. For the Hellenistic-Jewish novella, only a male figure can represent Israel (Levine 1992:113); the Rabbis can conceive of themselves, as of the People itself, as female. We might conceive of this as a move from a Douglassian world within which the primary concern is reestablishing the chaotic and threatened borders of purity to a Bakhtinian one in which it is precisely the breaching of borders of the social/ individual body that produces life; from one in which diaspora and fem(m)inization of the social body are seen only as a threat to one in which they are celebrated (however warily) for their ethical and creative possibilities.[7] Tobit is dreaming of an immediate end to diaspora; for the Rabbis it has become the condition of their lives as Jews. For the Rabbis, especially the Babylonian ones, the condition of diaspora held spiritual promise as well as danger, purity in the midst of impurity. To be sure, for the Rabbis as well, "[the woman's] identity only assumes meaning when she becomes a wife," but for the Rabbis, wifehood had very positive significance. Israel, after all, was God's wife. Needless to say by now, I hope, this did not necessarily cash out as a better life for human wives. Thus, all of their more positive sense of sexuality and wifehood did not necessarily change the fact that, as Levine so acutely concludes:

> By constraining women's roles, by using women as tokens of exchange to preserve kinship and economic ties, by depicting them as the cause as well as the locus of despair, and by removing them from direct contact with heaven, the Jewish male has brought order to his diaspora ex-

istence. In captivity, he can assert his freedom and his self-identity by depicting the other as in captivity to him. (117)

With this vitally important critique in mind constantly, we can go on to explore the ways that Jewish (and early Christian) maleness was, nevertheless, a form of resistance to Roman phallic masculinity.[8]

Rather than seeing the breakdown of the phallic imaginary as a product of trauma, as does Kaja Silverman in her *Male Subjectivity at the Margins,* earliest Christian (until Constantine) and Jewish texts present a culture of men who are resisting, renouncing, and disowning the phallus. This is entirely clear with respect to the early Christians. Since many of them were men of power and status in their pre-Christian lives, it is hard to argue that it was trauma that dislodged the dominant fiction for them. Ambrose was a provincial governor before his conversion, so, for him, becoming Christian was truly a renunciation of the phallus, as it was for his compatriot, Prudentius, and many others at the time. Their status in the church, while it had many attributes of power, had to be configured differently from their former status (Burrus 1994). If anything, it was their resistance to the dominant fiction that brought trauma upon them and not the opposite. It is clear that they renounced and resisted the "phallus" as a particular cultural product, one belonging to a culture they had rejected. The peculiar promise of the Jewish text, on the other hand, seems to be in its premise that such a renunciation does not imply an exit from male sexuality entirely. It was the condition of not being imperial, of being colonized, that presents this possibility to the Rabbis — a possibility not of a temporary disruption but of demystifying "the phallus" for what it is, a violent and destructive ideological construct. Instead of reading this alternative mode of constructing maleness as anomalous, thus accepting the terms of the dominant fiction as reality, I offer an antithetical reading of Jewish history in which the absence of the phallus is a positive product of cultural history and not a signifier of disease. In the text that we will be reading first, the intimate connections among sexuality, politics, and gender are directly thematized. Hundreds of years later than the Book of Tobit, the rabbinic texts of the Babylonian Talmud use the body also as a symbol for the diaspora people and through fantasies about Rabbis and Romans render much more complex and nuanced ways of considering the gendered social body of the Jewish people in diaspora. A "woman" is now not only she whose purity is threatened but also she who has powers and potentialities for survival.[9]

Cops and Rabbis

The text begins on a purely political note that seems hardly to have anything to do with gender:[10]

> Rabbi El'azar the son of Rabbi Shim'on found a certain officer of the king who used to catch thieves. He [the rabbi] asked him [the officer], "How do you prevail over them? Aren't they compared to animals, as it is written 'at night tramp all the animals of the forest' (Ps. 104:20)?" *There are those who say that he said it to him from the following verse: 'He will ambush from a hiding place like a lion in a thicket' (Ps.10:9).* Said he to him, "perhaps you are taking the innocent and leaving the guilty."
>
> He [the officer] said to him, "How shall I do it?"
>
> He [the rabbi] said to him, "Come, I will teach you how to do it. Go in the first four hours of the morning to the wine-bar. If you see someone drinking wine and falling asleep, ask of him what his profession is. If he is a rabbinical student, he has arisen early for study. If he is a day-laborer, he has arisen early to his labor. If he worked at night, [find out] perhaps it is metal smelting [a silent form of work], and if not, then he is a thief and seize him."
>
> The rumor reached the king's house, and he [the king] said, "Let him who read the proclamation be the one to execute it." They brought Rabbi El'azar the son of Rabbi Shim'on, and he began to catch thieves. He met Rabbi Yehoshu'a, the Bald, who said to him, "Vinegar son of Wine: how long will you persist in sending the people of our God to death?!"
>
> He [Rabbi El'azar] said to him, "I am removing thorns from the vineyard."
>
> He [Rabbi Yehoshu'a] said to him, "Let the Owner of the vineyard come and remove the thorns." (Baba Metsia' 83b)

This brief story is about resistance to and collaboration with "Roman" domination. It also thematizes blatant abuse of power. It is, therefore, a text that teaches us much about rabbinic ideologies of power and resistance. As we shall see presently, such ideologies are intimately involved with models of gender.

The story begins by assuming that thieves are necessarily stronger than those who seek to catch them. The rabbi cannot believe that the officer of the king is successfully catching thieves, since they are compared to animals, and on the physical plane it is understood that animals will always defeat human beings. A certain orientation toward physicality is already being projected here. Thieves are analogized to animals, and animals are associated with strength. The opposite of this proposition would be that humans—that is, being human, what later Judaism would call being a "mentsh"—are precisely defined by physical weakness. The rabbi assumes that if the officer is indeed catching somebody, it must (or might very well) be innocent people, since otherwise how could he, a weak mentsh, be successful against those who are bestial and strong? In other words, I suggest, the semiotics of this text at its very beginning sets up the paradigm of valorized weakness versus a denigrated physical strength.

In place of power, the rabbi proposes stealth as a tool to defeat crime. The rabbi is then recruited by the Roman authorities as a collaborator who turns over Jewish thieves to the Roman authorities. This behavior is roundly condemned by the narrative. Rabbi El'azar is called "Vinegar, son of Wine" (Wicked One, Son of a Saint) and asked, "How long will you persist in sending the people of our God to death?" The story thematizes, therefore, communal solidarity and resistance under conditions of domination. As long as the rabbi's "advice" to the Roman policeman consisted of modes of preventing the capture of innocents, then his behavior was satisfactory, but as soon as he himself began to engage in capturing thieves—guilty or innocent[11]—and turning them over to the Romans, he was condemned. The narrative goes on to further elaborate the consequences of collaboration, or rather of employment of physical political power altogether:

> One day a certain laundry man met him, and called him, "Vinegar son of Wine." He said, "Since he is so brazen, one can assume that he is wicked." He said, "Seize him." They seized him. After he had settled down, he went in to release him, but he could not. He applied to him the verse, 'One who guards his mouth and his tongue, guards himself from troubles' (Prov. 21:23). They hung him. He stood under the hanged man and cried. Someone said to him, "Be not troubled; he and his son both had intercourse with an engaged girl on *Yom Kippur.*" In that minute, he placed his hands on his guts, and said, "Be joyful, O my guts, be joyful! If it is thus when you are doubtful, when you are certain even more so. I am confident that rot and worms cannot prevail over you."
>
> But even so, he was not calmed. They gave him a sleeping potion and took him into a marble room and ripped open his stomach and were taking out baskets of fat and placing it in the July sun and it did not stink.... He applied to himself the verse, 'Even my flesh will remain preserved.' (Ps. 16:8–9)

The rabbi performs a bizarre test on himself for righteousness. In order to demonstrate that his actions with regard to the Jew that he sent to his death were blameless, he attempts to prove (to himself) that his body is indeed impermeable—that is, that he possesses the "classical" body, the body that, at least since Plato, has always been associated *by male culture* with the male, while the open, permeable, porous, embodied body is "female."

Our "hero," however, problematizes that understanding of masculinity paradoxically through his own attempts to substantiate it. He begins by making the claim that since he is so certain that he is righteous, he is equally sure that his body will be impervious to the depredations of worms after his death. That is, he experiences himself as the classic impermeable body, the body that is pristine and closed off from the outside world. Ironically, however, the test that the rabbi devises in order to prove his self-image is precisely one that undermines it. The integrity of his body is violated in the bizarre operation of removing basketfuls of fat from his stomach and placing them in the sun to see if they will, indeed, be immune from rotting. We have, then, an incredible moment of self-destruction of the very models of masculinity that are being both proposed and defeated at the same time.

As Mikhail Bakhtin has pointed out, the image of the body part grown out of all proportion is "actually a picture of dismemberment, of separate areas of the body enlarged to gigantic dimensions" (1984: 328). The rabbi is clearly grotesquely obese if several basketfuls of fat could be removed from his body. The topoi of exaggerated size, detachable organs, the emphasis on the orifices and stories of dismemberment are all representations of the body as interacting with the world, not self-enclosed like the classical body. Moreover, the association of the coherent, impermeable body with imperial power is thematized directly in the story as well. When the rabbi acted in consonance with imperial power, he was attacked by the text. However, when he allowed his body to be dismembered, to be made grotesque, in a process that is almost parodic of birth, as well as castration, then he was validated by the text.[12] The talmudic text bears out Bakhtin's remarkable insight by combining in one moment the monstrous belly that "hides the normal members of the body" and the actual dismemberment of that monstrous organ. Indeed, the image of what is done to the body of the rabbi is almost a mad cesarean section, a parodic appropriation of female fecundity.[13] This association makes perfect sense in the logic of the grotesque body, because it is precisely in the association of fertility and death that the grotesque draws its power (ibid.:238).

If we think through what it was that this rabbi was feeling guilty for—collaboration with the violence of the "Roman" authorities—then this particular response, grotesquifying and "feminizing" his body, makes perfect sense. If the violence of Rome was experienced as a peculiarly male imposition, then correction of having participated in this violence would require a self-feminization. This representation, that is, of the necessity to become female in order to renounce and repent for violence, will be doubled later in the text. This response, moreover, has "positive" meanings as well—not only corrective or reactive ones—just as and just because the grotesque body itself is suffused with creative power: "All these convexities and orifices have a common characteristic; it is within them that the confines between bodies and between the body and the world are overcome: there is an interchange and an interorientation" (ibid.:317). This body can be taken, then, as an ideal representation of Jewish culture in diaspora as a site where the confines between the body of Jewish culture and other social bodies are overcome,[14] not forgetting, of course, the frequently violent response from many of those other bodies. Paradoxically, however, this diasporization of the body is also a pursuit of purity, of a moral pristineness that engagement with power seemingly would preclude. This paradox of diaspora as the site of purity and cultural interchange is inherent in postbiblical Jewish culture. No wonder, then, that the rabbi's body is both purified and violated in the same operation, rendered classical through precisely that which marks it as grotesque.

The dismembered, "castrated" male body is also deterritorialized, as the text troubles to relate to us in its continuation. Another of the rabbis, put into precisely the same situation of either collaboration with Roman tyranny or probably dangerous resistance, is urged to simply run away:

> To Rabbi Ishma'el the son of Yose there also occurred a similar situation. Eliahu (the Prophet Elijah) met him and said to him, "how long will you persist in sending the people of our God to death?!" He said to him, "What can I do; it is the king's order?" He said to him, "Your father ran away to Asia-Minor; you run away to Lydia."

The appropriate form of resistance that the Talmud recommends for Jews in this place is evasion. The arts of colonized peoples of dissimulation and dodging are thematized here as actually running away, the very opposite of such "masculine" pursuits as "standing one's ground." Later I will treat the myth of the foundation of rabbinic Judaism in such an act of evasion and trickery, the escape of Rabbi Yoḥanan ben Zakkai from besieged Jerusalem in a coffin, which the Rabbis portray as the very antithesis of the military resistance of the Zealots (*sicarii*) who wanted to fight to the very last man and preserve their honor. Here we find the same political theory — "Get out of there!" — adumbrated in a much less direct way, though it is all the more rich in its overtones for that. The text designates "diaspora" modes of resistance, deterritorialization, the grotesque, dismembered, dephallicized male body; resistance not as the assumption of power and dominance but as resistance *to* the assumption of dominance: "Run away to Lydia," and this prescription is put into the mouth of one of the most authoritative oracles that rabbinic culture can produce, Elijah the Prophet. Nor is this recommendation unique in rabbinic texts. As the Palestinian Talmud recommends, "If they propose that you be a member of the *boule,* let the Jordan be your border" (Mo'ed Katan 2:3, 81b and Sanhedrin 8:2, 26b).[15] Even though a case can be made that the diaspora modes of ideal masculinity are more pronounced in Babylonia than in Palestine of the talmudic period, this distinction is only relative. In Palestine, as well, the Jews of this time were in diaspora. The tenacity that is valorized by these texts is the tenacity that enables continued Jewish existence, not the tenacity of defending sovereignty unto death. Masada is hardly a model for these men.[16] Rabbi Yoḥanan ben Zakkai is.

While I emphasize the syntonic aspects of the rabbinic self-representation as female or feminized and "wifely" behavior toward another male as an ideal and of the dephallicized male body, there can be no doubt that the Rabbis were sensitive to the dystonic aspects of this representation as well — or at least to some of them — as the talmudic narrative will expose. Not surprisingly for the ancient (and, for that matter, the modern) world, the political quickly shades into the sexual. This narrative, which seems to be almost as uncensored as a dream, sports unusually graphic and explicit representations of maleness and the question of maleness as figured through the body:

When Rabbi Ishma'el the son of Yose and Rabbi El'azar the son of Rabbi Shim'on used to meet each other, an ox could walk between them and not touch them. A certain matron said to them, "Your children are not yours." They said, "theirs are greater than ours." "If that is the case, even more so!" There are those who say that thus they said to her: "As the man, so is his virility." And there are those who say that thus did they say to her: "Love compresses the flesh." ...

Said Rabbi Yoḥanan, "Rabbi Ishma'el the son of Yose's member was like a wineskin of nine *kav*; Rabbi El'azar the son of Rabbi Shim'on's member was like a wineskin of seven *kav*." Rav Papa said, "Rabbi Yoḥanan's member was like a wineskin of three *kav*." And there are those who say: like a wineskin of five kav. Rav Papa himself had a member which was like the baskets of Hipparenum.[17]

I would like to suggest here that the connection between the first part of the story and this sequel, within which the "virility" of this same rabbi is impugned, is not accidental, not by any means. The solution that the rabbi has been offered to the problem of Roman domination and collaboration is a "feminizing" one. He is counseled not to "stand up and fight" but rather to run away.[18] From the point of view of Roman culture, such behavior would be heinously cowardly and feminizing (Barton 1995). This, plus their enormous abdomens, apparently signified impotence to that stereotypical figure of Roman culture in rabbinic literature, the *matrona,* who mocks our heroes in time-honored Mediterranean terms by impugning the legitmacy of their wives' children, in effect calling them cuckolds.

What follows next is a deliciously humorous bit of linguistic by-play. The rabbis, exhibiting for once the stereotypical male pride in the phallus, understand that the matron is obliquely "complimenting" them that they are so enormous that they could not possibly fit into their wives' vaginas. They accordingly answer her cryptically, "Theirs are bigger than ours." The matron, however, apparently was referring to their abdomens and not to any conjectures about the sizes of their penises. She, misunderstanding in turn their answer and thinking that they are claiming that their wives' abdomens are even larger than the husbands', retorts, "If your wives are even fatter than you are, then all the more so that you could not have intercourse." At this point the obese rabbis finally understand the matron's concern and answer — according to one tradition that the size of a man's genitals is in keeping with the size of the rest of his body and, according to another, that desire overcomes obesity.

It is at this moment of anxiety about paternity that the account of the gargantuan phalli of the rabbis is mustered, not altogether different from Roman sexual humor, in which, according to Amy Richlin, "the central persona or protagonist or narrator is a strong male of extreme virility, occasionally even ithyphallic (as in the Priapus poems)." The function of this figure is anxiety on his part "to defend himself by adducing his strength, virility, and (in general) all traits that are considered normal—and this is the appeal of the joke teller to his audience, as if both are confirming and checking with each other that they are all right" (Richlin 1992:58). Given the way that the situation of being dominated would insistently have been read (by the dominators) as feminizing with the inevitable leakage of such affect into the consciousnesses of the dominated males as well—there being no domination completely without hegemony—and the explicitly female modes of resistance that rabbinic culture developed, in opposition to the honored modes of resistance current among the Romans, it is no wonder that some rabbinic males felt it especially necessary to adduce their strength and virility in order to confirm and check with each other that they were all right and that indeed their children were theirs.[19] At the same time, the text represents that "female" mode of resistance as being a highly honored option, for after all, there is no greater voice of authority within these texts than the voice of Elijah the Prophet. In other words, I am postulating that within the culture the "weapons of the weak" were valued, not despised. While there is anxiety expressed within the text about the consequences of employment of the "feminine" arts of survival for the virility of the men, these anxieties perhaps have more to do with what the outside world will say than with inner-cultural gender patterning. After all, it is the voice of the Roman matron who is portrayed by the text as querying the potency of our heroes. On the other hand, the text clearly thematizes as well the negative moment in the response of oppressed men to their representation as not-male, machismo with all of its violent and repressive consequences toward the women of their own community. While this move seems to have been generally resisted within rabbinic Judaism, it is obviously not absent and clearly represented—satirized?—here.[20]

This is a very significant point, for it illustrates the enormous complexity of the plays of gender in cultural interactions and self-definition. On the one hand, it is clearly the case that the behaviors the

Rabbis portray as ideal for themselves are understood as proper male demeanor within their own systems of cultural values, particularly since gender dimorphism and separation of roles obviously was crucial to them. They therefore reject representations that would despise such practices as "effeminate." At the same time, they live within and are an integral part of a larger cultural world, within which those very valorized rabbinic practices are often stigmatized as "female," and the Rabbis seem sometimes to have been willing and able to take that representation in and transvalue it into a positive self-representation as female or feminized. For a Josephus, however, roughly contemporary with the author of the Book of Tobit, such a representation was as uncomfortable as it would be to a modern Zionist. In the next section of this analysis, I will contrast two Jewish paradigms of resistance to Roman domination, the first from Josephus and the second from the classic of rabbinic culture, the Babylonian Talmud. While the political aspects of the innovations in ethos that the Rabbi Yoḥanan ben Zakkai story opens up within rabbinic Judaism have been frequently remarked, their concatenation with a sexual or gendered set of representations and self-representations has not.

The events at Masada have become, (in)famously, paradigmatic for a certain modern Jewish consciousness. But it was not always so. Indeed, when the Jewish settlement of Palestine was founded in modern times, no one knew how to spell the name Masada in Hebrew, so an early kibbutz that took the name used the Greek version. As a recent critic noting that the Josephus text was preserved only by Christians has observed: "The story of the fall of Masada thus did not vanish from the records of Jewish history, but it disappeared from the Jews' collective memory" (Zerubavel 1994:75).[21] Masada, both in its early textualization and in its modern Zionist appropriations, has everything to do, I will argue, with manliness. It is accordingly very important in understanding the gendered politics of rabbinic Judaism to gain some insight into the rejection of Masada as a model for Jewish behavior, indeed as even a memory.

The best context for understanding the Josephan meanings of Masada is provided by an article that appears immediately before Zerubavel's in the same issue of the same journal. In her article, Carlin Barton talks about the dishonor of defeat within Roman culture and the modalities for the recovery of lost honor. One central paradigm involves "the redemption of honor through ferocious self-destruction" (Barton 1994:46). In recounting a moment in Lucan's epic *Bellum Civile,* Barton describes a nearly uncanny analogue to the "events" at Masada: "According to Lucan, a group of six hundred Caesarian soldiers under the commander Vulteius was crossing the Adriatic on a raft when it was surrounded and trapped by many thousands of Pompeians. Despite the overwhelming odds, the Casearians battled until darkness brought a truce." Vulteius makes a stirring speech, representing suicide as the greatest act of freedom that a man can make. Then:

> At dawn, the *devota inventus,* the devoted band of warriors, having re-jected the light of life, and consecrated to the gods of the underworld, ferocious and secure, commit singularly bloody and joyous mutual sui-cide, each man thrusting his breast against the steel of his neighbor. Lu-can concludes: no ship's company had ever earned comparable praise; yet even this glorious precedent has not taught cowardly nations how easy it is to escape self-immolation because, he says, when tyrants im-pose their will by terror liberty shrivels, until no one realizes *that the purpose of the sword is to save every man from slavery.* (ibid.:46–47; emphasis added)

The entire situation is exactly, precisely that of Josephus's Masada. The Jews have fought bravely for three years; the end is near and hope for victory is gone. Rather than submit to slavery, in the night the Jews kill all their women and children and then each soldier is killed by the sword of his fellows. The last alive kill themselves, and this "cowardly nation" has demonstrated to the Romans, à la Josephus, that they have indeed learned the purpose of the sword. The compar-ison is not, in fact, uncanny. Josephus was, I suggest, simply writing the Jews into a Roman value system. While scholars have long real-ized, of course, that the leader El'azar's speech reported by Josephus is a historiographical fiction, modeled on Roman exemplars and topoi, they have not emphasized how totally the situation and events, the very narrative, and, even more to the point, its values are entirely and thoroughly Roman. These *sicarii* (daggermen) are Jews who es-cape the domination of Rome by remaking themselves as Romans and whom the Rabbis, in turn, despised.

The Israeli general and archaeologist, excavator and producer of Masada, Yigael Yadin was thoroughly moved by what he took as Josephus's realistic account:

No one could have matched [Josephus's] gripping description of what took place on the summit of Masada on that fateful night in the spring of 73 A.D. Whatever the reasons, whether the pangs of conscience or some other cause we cannot know, the fact is that his account is so detailed and reads so faithfully, and his report of the words uttered by Elazar ben Yair is so compelling, that it seems evident that he had been genuinely overwhelmed by the record of heroism on the part of the people he had forsaken. (Yadin 1966:15)

The obvious and exact correspondence between Josephus's narrative and the Roman evidence cited suggests, however, another interpretation. Far from being a conscience-ridden return to and valorization of "his" people, the account of the honorable suicide to avoid surrender at Masada was another step in Josephus's self-Romanization and thus a further emphasis on his true *andreia,* manliness, just as its adoption by Yadin was a maneuver in the modern transformation of "sheep-like effeminate" Jews into real Israeli men. For both, I argue, their "resistance" was in fact submission (to cultural norms of masculinity), while the submission of their Jewish opponents was, in fact, resistance, through a maintenance of historical Jewish cultural norms.[22] I refer to no lesser authority for this judgment than Marek Edelman, the socialist co-commander of the Warsaw Revolt, who saw this very clearly: "This was a revolt!? The whole point was not to let them slaughter you when your turn came. The whole point was to choose your method of dying. All of humanity had already agreed that dying with a weapon in the hand is more beautiful than without a weapon. *So we surrendered to that consensus*" (quoted in Zertal 1994:38; emphasis added).

The Zionist leaders decided that Edelman was insane and silenced his voice. For evidence of how thoroughly the "Roman" ethos was internalized in modern Zionist culture, the following account by Yael Zerubavel will suffice:

A member of a [Palestinian Jewish Zionist] youth movement expressed his and his friends' reluctance to participate in the days of mourning in solidarity with European Jewry [while the genocide was taking place!], claiming that instead his movement's gathering at Masada was a sufficient expression of their solidarity with those Jews who did not choose servitude.[23]

Zerubavel notes that even during the 1960s in Israel, "the partisans and the Ghetto fighters" were honored "as 'Zionist' or 'Hebrew Youth,' " but the Israeli official discourse referred to "the other Holocaust victims as Jews" (Zerubavel 1994:80). In contrast to earlier Passover Haggadot within which the wicked son was nearly always some sort of soldier or military figure, in the Haggada published in the year of Israeli independence by the Haggana Shock Troops, the "heroes" are respectively a ghetto fighter, absurdly portrayed as a Hasid with a machine gun, and an Israeli guerrilla (see Figure 11.1).[24]

The exemplary rabbinic moment of truth was entirely opposite to Masada. Here is the tale as it is told in the Babylonian Talmud, Gittin 56a-b (following the text in Ms. Vatican 140), in which the opposition to Masada's heroes, here referred to as "hooligans" (בריוני) is thematized directly in the narrative:

Father of Lies,[25] the leader of the hooligans in Jerusalem, was the nephew of Rabbi Yoḥanan ben Zakkai. He [Yoḥanan] sent to him [Father of Lies]: "Come to me in secret!" He came. He [Yoḥanan] said: "How long will you continue to do thus [refuse to make peace, Rashi] and kill everyone with hunger?!" He [Father of Lies] said: "And what can I do? If I say anything to them [the hooligans], they will kill me?" He [Yoḥanan] said: "If you see a solution for me, I will go out. Perhaps there will be some measure of salvation." He [Father of Lies] said: "Proclaim yourself sick, and everyone will come to ask about you. Then take something stinking to place next to you and they will say that you have died. Then have your students [carry the bier], for they [the hooligans] know that the live are lighter than the dead."

He did so. Rabbi Eli'ezer on one side and Rabbi Yehoshu'a on the other went in [to carry the bier]. When they arrived at the door, they [the hooligans] wanted to pierce him. They [the students] said: "The Romans will say that you have pierced your Rabbi." They wished to push him. They said: "They will say that you pushed your Rabbi."

They opened the gate.

When they arrived there [at the Roman encampment], He [Yoḥanan] said: "Peace be upon you, O king!" He [Vespasian] said: "You are now liable to be put to death twice. First of all: I am not king [and you called me king],[26] and secondly, if indeed I am king, why did you not come to me until now?" He [Yoḥanan] said: "As for what you said that you are not king; indeed, you are a king" — for were he not a king, Jerusalem would not have been given over into his hands, as it says "The Lebanon[27] will fall before the mighty" [Isa. 10:34], and there is no mighty other than a king, as it says "His mighty one will be from him; [his ruler] will arise from his midst" [Jer. 30:21].

And as for what you said that if you are king, why have I not come until now; the hooligans that are here did not let me."

He [Vespasian] said to him: "If there is a barrel of honey and a snake is wrapped around it, would you not break the barrel, in order to get

Figure 11.1

rid of the dragon?"[28] [I.e., should you not have broken down the walls in order to destroy the hooligans? Rashi]

He [Yoḥanan] was silent.

Rabbi Akiva applied to him [Vespasian] the verse: "He overturns the wise and confuses their judgment" [Isa. 44:25]; "He should have said. We would take a tongs, remove the dragon, kill it, and leave the barrel sound" [i.e., we hoped to be able to defeat and kill the hooligans, make peace with you, and leave Jerusalem intact].

By and by, there came a messenger from the king saying: "Arise, for the king is dead, and the leaders of Rome [the Senate] have appointed you king!" He [Vespasian] put on one of his shoes and wanted to tie it and couldn't get it on; then he tried to take off the other one, and couldn't take it off [for his limbs had become moist from happiness; Rashi].

He [Yoḥanan] said to him: "Don't worry, for it says 'Good news moistens the bone'" [Prov. 16:30].

He said: "What is my cure?"

"Let him bring before him someone that he does not like, for it says 'a depressed spirit dries the bone' [Prov. 14:32]...

He [Vespasian] said: "Ask of me something, and I will give it to you."

He [Yoḥanan] said: "Give me Yavne and its sages, and the dynasty of Rabban Gamliel, and doctors to cure Rabbi Zadoq [who had been fasting in order to save Jerusalem].

Given the almost identical situation and the exactly opposite response, it would not be going too far to speculate that here we have the only possible allusion to Masada that there is in rabbinic literature — and that, of course, only via a suppression. The Rabbis of our talmudic text reveal their stance vis-à-vis the "Zealots," the defenders of Masada who are also those who are refusing any peace treaty with Rome in Jerusalem by dubbing the *sicarii* "hooligans." The very heroes of Josephus's narrative are called "hooligans" and seen as more of an enemy than Rome itself and its emperor, Vespasian. Whether or not, however, this is an actual reference to Josephus's narrative, the almost exact "reversal of values" that it encodes is highly significant. This is the founding moment of the rabbinic movement, for Rabbi Yoḥanan ben Zakkai and his students — Yavne and its sages — are the foundation of all of rabbinic literature. Thus we see at the foundation — symbolized by an inauguration — of the rabbinic value system the precise obverse of the "manly" Roman values encoded by Josephus in his narrative. Rabbi Yoḥanan prefers life and the possibility of serving God through the study of Torah over everything else. He is willing to abase himself, to pretend to be dead — a virtual parody of the Masada suicide? — to make peace with the Roman over against the Jewish zealots, even to sacrifice Jerusalem in order that Jewish life and Torah might continue. Where the Josephan zealots proved themselves "real men" by preferring death at their own hands to slavery, the rabbis prefer slavery to death. As Carlin Barton has remarked: "Seneca despises the caged, mutilated and degraded King Telesphorus of Rhodes for clinging to life at the price of his honor (*Epistulae* 70.6–7; cf. *De ira* 3.17.3–4), and brands his famous aphorism, 'Where there's life there's hope,' as 'effeminatissima'" (Barton 1993:30). "Where there's life there's hope," or "Where there's life there's Torah," could practically be the motto of the rabbinic movement from Rabbi Yoḥanan ben Zakkai onward, and it was, therefore, "effeminatissima." Zionist ideology completely introjected this Roman value system. Thus "a prominent Palestinian Zionist leader, Yitzhak Gruenbaum, stated that 'the trouble of the Diaspora Jews is that they preferred the life of a "beaten dog" over dignified death'. He continued by urging to prepare for a last stand that would allow the settlers at least to leave behind 'a Masada legend'" (Zerubavel 1994: 79). On the other hand, Schopenhauer seems certainly to have understood something about Judaic culture in his insistence that it is characterized by an "optimistic" will to live, which he, of course, despises, as he despises everything "effeminate" (Le Rider 1993:27–28).

Rabbinic literature adumbrates an entire — very particular — ethics of colonial survival. This ethics is, moreover, tightly imbricated with issues of gender and sexuality as well. And colonized people are frequently, therefore, stereotyped in gendered terms as not manly. Familiar to Jews and to many colonized peoples would be the following characterization of gypsies on the part of a fin-de-siècle Austrian: "All those who know them agree that they are a compound of vanity, vulgarity, coquetry, seriousness and indifference. *They have not a trace of manly intelligence, but this makes them all the more cunning and deceitful.* . . . Their cowardice, above all, seems to me an essential element" (Hans Gross [1902], cited Le Rider 1993:134). In other words, gypsies behave like women. James C. Scott has already paid attention to this factor in his account of Schopenhauer's and Weininger's descriptions of Jews and women as "naturally" mendacious:

> The logic of the argument is marvelously perverse. Patterns of speech that are adaptations to inequalities in power are depicted as natural characteristics of the subordinate groups, a move that has, in turn, the great advantage of underlining the innate inferiority of its members when

it comes to logic, truth, honesty, and reason and thereby justifying their continued domination by their betters. (Scott 1990:36)

I suggest that in such situations, colonized people may sometimes come to identify themselves *with* or even *as* women, and—without for a moment forgetting the dangerous aspects of this identification *for* women[29]—this identification can now and then be a source of ethical awareness.

Notes

1. I am uncomfortable with the cuteness of the graphemic manipulation but have not yet had any success in finding an alternative form that will reliably remind the reader that I am not referring to an essential or natural femininity. For the toxic effects of that ideology, see Connell 1995:12–15.

2. I emphasize *ideally* to make clear that I am not claiming that Jewish men necessarily behaved differently from other men but that there were different cultural ideals at work, which may even sometimes have had a referent in "reality." For the continuity between medieval and classical ideas about maleness, see Bullough 1994:31.

3. "Real men—that is, representative Arthurian heroes—don't have bodies" (Kinney 1994:49). For quite a different—but not entirely irreconcilable—reading of the same text, see Dinshaw 1994.

4. This point has frequently been missed in non-Jewish readings of the stories of Ya'el and Judith that take these as condemnations of the women. In a future work, I hope to undertake a full-length study of the Book of Esther and associated practices of the holiday of Purim, under the sign of the "hidden transcript."

5. Tobit is a fiction written in the Hellenistic period but dated back to the eighth century B.C.E. Levine makes the very elegant observation that it is no accident that the protagonists of the narrative are of the tribe of Naphtali, "which was geographically separated from the other Rachel tribes," and is accordingly always-already diasporized "even in Palestine" (Levine 1992:107): "Naphtali dwelt among the Canaanites, *the inhabitants of the land*" (Judg. 5:18; emphasis mine indeed).

6. The other two involve imaginary geographies and an emphasis on genealogical purity: endogamy. Neither of these, of course, is irrelevant for the present project. If I do not treat them here, it is because I haven't worked out how to deal with them together. For the moment, I would like only to cite George Nickelsburg's apt remark (as paraphrased by Levine) that the focus on endogamy is "less a matter of ethnic purity than it is an argument against any 'arrogant disdaining of one's own people,' which then could lead to the loss of self-identity," upon which she comments: "However, when in-group and out-group are problematic categories, ethnic purity would not be an unexpected agendum" (Levine 1992:108).

7. The contrast between Douglas's and Bakhtin's respective responses to the grotesque, then, would be related to the particular historical cultural formations that they focused on and not theoretically driven differences.

8. I am developing this critique at some length elsewhere. Here I may briefly state my initial conclusions from that analysis. As I have argued previously (Boyarin 1993), rabbinic culture is mischaracterized if it is understood to have been fundamentally misogynistic or sanctioning violent control of women by men. It was not and did not. This does not, however, render it on the whole "better" from a feminist perspective,

because it was nevertheless men who held all the symbolic and political power in the system; it was they who determined whether or not violence against women, for example, was or was not to be permitted. Women maintained a certain degree of economic autonomy vis-à-vis their husbands as well, but it was men and a male power structure that determined the degree and kind of that autonomy and could cancel it at any time as well. In this sense women were indeed "in captivity" to men.

9. I scrutinize the (negative) consequences of such self-representation for women more fully elsewhere.

10. This portion of my text is a rereading of a talmudic narrative that I have treated before (Boyarin 1992). My reading here partially overlaps with and partially corrects (or supplements) my earlier treatment.

11. It is important to note that according to Jewish law, thieves are never executed but only required to make restitution with a fine.

12. This pattern repeats itself in Babylonian rabbinic literature. It is not, therefore, a sport. See Boyarin 1994.

13. In other words, this operation is a form of what I have been calling couvade, a critique of male power through a mimesis of femaleness.

14. I am mobilizing Mary Douglas's (1978) formative insight here as to the homology between practices relating to the individual body and cultural and social problems relating to the body of the group. Whereas she, however, was primarily concerned with practices that defend the body, and thus the body politic, from impurity, I am finding here a set of symbolic representations that at least partially overcome the confines between the Jewish body and the world.

15. In other words, if you are called to serve as an official of the Roman government, leave town!

16. Samson is a figure of fun in rabbinic literature, the Maccabees are remembered only for their miraculous lighting of the candelabrum in the Temple, and Masada is not mentioned even once. Fifty years ago, the very Hebrew form of the name of the place was not part of the Jewish sociolect!

17. Rav Papa is also a legendary fat rabbi, as is known from several other Babylonian talmudic intertexts.

18. Note that this counsel provides almost a direct antithesis to the Greek (and Roman) ideal of *andreia,* manliness. The whole question of *andreia* (and its Roman equivalent, *virtus*) has to be thought through with reference to rabbinic texts. As Zeitlin has phrased it: "What is manliness, the quality the Greeks call *andreia,* a word that is synonymous with virile courage, as even we understand it, and requires a willingness to face danger, to risk one's life, and to maintain control over self and others? Continuing the epic values of heroic renown (*kleos*) and in pursuit of an everlasting name and glory in a city ruled by democratic principles as well as by protocols of honor and shame, the Athenian male in this competitive, agonistic society faces problems of collective identity and responsibility along with a growing sense of individual selfhood that will develop into a full-fledged concern in later antiquity." The question that I am addressing is: What about Jews and Christians in this picture of a manliness defined in these ways? How do the Jewish and Christian branches of Hellenistic-Roman culture accept, reject, modify, resist, and collaborate with such notions of manliness? Here it is apposite, however, to point out that the motif of "self-control" or "restraint" as determinative of *andreia* is not the same thing as renunciation or submissiveness, the more typical ideals of the early Christians and Jews. Such self-control is, indeed, one of the trappings of the powerful (Scott 1990:50–51).

19. Compare the moralizing interpretation of the מדידש״א, explaining why rabbinic penis size is religiously significant. It is very interesting to note that until the מדידש״א in the sixteenth century, the commentatorial tradition had been very anxious to interpret the "members" discussed here as anything but the *membrum virile*.

20. There is an enormous difference if we read this text as satirizing machismo or as asserting it. Go figure!

21. Zerubavel's harrowing account of the use of Masada in early Zionist praxis and ideology (1994:76–77) indicates how completely they are informed by European non-Jewish cultural norms.

22. This by itself, I hasten to add, is hardly a critique, since I am not defending any notion of an essential, forever-given Judaic essence. The point is to overturn the usual hierarchical description of authenticity and surrender in a situation in which I make my own value judgments about which stance I wish to assert as the content of my Jewishness.

23. There is, to be sure, something moving to me in the very self-contradiction in the statement by an Israeli that "thanks to [Masada], many Jews may have continued to *survive,* who acted like them . . . and *died* heroically" (quoted in Zerubavel 1994:85), just as there is something grand, majestic, and moving in the original Roman cult of honor — or a bullfight.

24. This illustration confirms beautifully Zerubavel's contention that "the partisans and the ghetto rebels were thus separated from the 'Holocaust' to serve as a symbolic bridge between Exile and modern Israel. Along with the defenders of Masada and Tel Hai, they became part of Israel's heroic past. Conversely, the rest of the Holocaust experience was relegated to the period of Exile and associated with the 'Other', namely the submissive Diaspora Jew" (1994:80; see also Zertal 1994).

25. "Father of Lies" is a wonderful joke. The two-centuries-later rabbinic rebel against the Romans, Bar Kochba, was punningly dubbed Bar Kozba, *Son of Lies!* The text is cunningly creating a genealogy here. However, it should be mentioned that other manuscripts read "Father Dagger," suggesting a somewhat less derisive attitude toward the figure. Indeed, the latter may simply be his name.

26. Supplied from editions.

27. Typically understood as referring to the Temple with reference to the verse: "This goodly mountain, the Lebanon" (Deut. 3:25), the goodly mountain being, of course, the Temple mount.

28. I wonder if the sudden shift into the Latin diction is for the "local color." I can see no other reason for it.

29. Tania Modleski reminds us of "how frequently male subjectivity works to appropriate 'femininity' while oppressing women" (1991:7). I explicitly treat the oppression of women by fem(m)inized rabbinic Jewish men elsewhere.

Bibliography

Bakhtin, Mikhail. 1984. *Rabelais and His World.* Trans. Hélène Iswolsky. Bloomington: Indiana University Press.

Barton, Carlin A. 1993. *The Sorrows of the Ancient Romans: The Gladiator and the Monster.* Princeton, N.J.: Princeton University Press.

———. 1994. Savage Miracles: The Redemption of Lost Honor in Roman Society and the Sacrament of the Gladiator and the Martyr. *Representations* 45 (Winter):41–71.

———. 1995. The "Moment of Truth" in Ancient Rome: Honor and Embodiment in a Contest Culture. Unpublished Essay. Berkeley.

Berkowitz, Michael. 1993. *Zionist Culture and West European Jewry Before the First World War.* Cambridge: Cambridge University Press.

Biale, David. 1986. *Power and Powerlessness in Jewish History.* New York: Schocken.

Boyarin, Daniel. 1992. The Great Fat Massacre: Sex, Death and the Grotesque Body in the Talmud. In *People of the Body: Jews and Judaism from an Embodied Perspective,* ed. Howard Eilberg-Schwartz, 69–102. Albany, N.Y.: State University of New York Press.

———. 1993. *Carnal Israel: Reading Sex in Talmudic Culture.* The New Historicism: studies in cultural poetics. Berkeley and Los Angeles: University of California Press.

———. 1994. Jewish Masochism: Couvade, Castration, and Rabbis in Pain. *American Imago* 51 (Spring):3–36.

———. Forthcoming. The Colonial Drag: Zionism, Gender, and Colonial Mimicry. In *Dimensions of (so-called) Postcolonial Studies,* ed. Kalpana Seshadri-Crooks and Fawzia Afzal-Kahn. Durham, N.C.: Duke University Press.

Briggs, Sheila. 1985. Images of Women and Jews in Nineteenth- and Twentieth-Century German Theology. In *Immaculate and Powerful: The Female in Sacred Image and Reality,* ed. Clarissa W. Atkinson, Constance H. Buchanan, and Margaret R. Miles, 226–59. Boston: Beacon.

Bullough, Vern L. 1994. On Being a Male in the Middle Ages. In *Medieval Masculinities,* ed. Clare A. Lees, 31–45. Minneapolis: University of Minnesota Press.

Burrus, Virginia. 1994. Fecund Fathers: Heresy, the Grotesque, and Male Generativity in Gregory of Nyssa's *Contra Eunomium.* Unpublished paper. Madison, N.J.

Connell, Robert W. 1995. *Masculinities.* Berkeley and Los Angeles: University of California Press.

Dinshaw, Carolyn. 1994. A Kiss Is Just a Kiss: Heterosexuality and Its Consolations in *Sir Gawain and the Green Knight. Diacritics* 24 (Summer–Fall):205–26.

Douglas, Mary. 1978 [1969]. *Purity and Danger: An Analysis of Concepts of Pollution and Taboo.* London: Routledge and Kegan Paul.

Hoberman, John M. 1995. Otto Weininger and the Critique of Jewish Masculinity. In *Jews and Gender: Responses to Otto Weininger,* ed. Nancy A. Harrowitz and Barbara Hyams, 141–53. Philadelphia: Temple University Press.

Kinney, Clare R. 1994. The (Dis)embodied Hero and the Signs of Manhood in *Sir Gawain and the Green Knight.* In *Medieval Masculinities,* ed. Clare A. Lees, 47–57. Minneapolis: University of Minnesota Press.

Lane, Frederick M. 1986. The Genital Envy Complex: A Case of a Man with a Fantasied Vulva. In *The Psychology of Men: New Psychoanalytic Perspectives,* ed. Gerald I. Fogel, Frederick M. Lane, and Robert S. Liebert, 131–51. New York: Basic Books.

Le Rider, Jacques. 1993. *Modernity and Crises of Identity: Culture and Society in Fin-de-siècle Vienna.* Trans. Rosemary Morris. New York: Continuum.

Levine, Amy-Jill. 1992. Diaspora as Metaphor: Bodies and Boundaries in the Book of Tobit. In *Diaspora Jews and Judaism: Essays in Honor of and in dialogue with A. Thomas Kraabel,* ed. J. Andrew Overman and Robert S. MacLennan, 105–18. Atlanta: Scholars Press.

McNamara, Jo Ann. 1994. The *Herrenfrage:* The Restructuring of the Gender System, 1050–1150. In *Medieval Masculinities,* ed. Clare A. Lees, 3–30. Minneapolis: University of Minnesota Press.

Modleski, Tania. 1991. *Feminism without Women: Culture and Criticism in a "Postfeminist" Age.* New York: Routledge.

Richlin, Amy. 1992. *The Garden of Priapus: Sexuality and Aggression in Roman Humor.* New York: Oxford University Press.

Scott, James C. 1990. *Domination and the Arts of Resistance: Hidden Transcripts.* New Haven, Conn.: Yale University Press.

Silverman, Kaja. 1992. *Male Subjectivity at the Margins.* New York: Routledge.

Veyne, Paul. 1985. Homosexuality in Ancient Rome. In *Western Sexuality: Practice and Precept in Past and Present Times,* ed. Philippe Ariès and André Béjin, 26–35. Oxford: Oxford University Press.

Yadin, Yigael. 1966. *Masada: Herod's Fortress and the Zealots' Last Stand.* London: Weidenfeld and Nicolson.

Zertal, Idith. 1994. The Sacrificed and the Sanctified: The Construction of a National Martyrology. *Zemanim* 12 (Spring):26–45.

Zerubavel, Yael. 1994. The Death of Memory and the Memory of Death: Masada and the Holocaust as Historical Metaphors. *Representations* 45 (Winter):72–100.

12 / Exploding Identities: Notes on Ethnicity and Literary History

Ammiel Alcalay

Every notion in vogue, including the retrieval of "roots" values, is necessarily exploited and recuperated. The invention of needs always goes hand in hand with the compulsion to help the needy, a noble and self-gratifying task that also renders the helper's service indispensable. The part of the savior has to be filled as long as the belief in the problem of "endangered species" lasts. To persuade you that your past and cultural heritage are doomed to eventual extinction and thereby keeping you occupied with the Savior's concern, inauthenticity is condemned as a loss of origins and a whitening (or faking) of non-Western values. Being easily offended in your elusive identity and reviving readily an old, racial charge, you immediately react when such guilt-instilling accusations are leveled at you and are thus led to stand in need of defending that very ethnic part of yourself that for years has made you and your ancestors the objects of execration. Today, planned authenticity is rife; as a product of hegemony and a remarkable counterpart of universal standardization, it constitutes an efficacious means of silencing the cry of racial oppression. We no longer wish to erase your difference, We demand, on the contrary, that you remember and assert it. At least, to a certain extent.

TRINH T. MINH-HA, *Woman, Native, Other*[1]

As 1992 came and went, with its proliferation of quincentennial Sephardic or Arab/Jewish conferences, festivals, publications, tours, exhibits, and commemorations, I felt some relief at not having been called in as a "native informant" until the very end of December. Throughout the year, I yearned for a transcendent moment of the kind described by Edmond Jabès as "a moment we do not manage to classify, whose consequences we do not manage to exhaust and whose effects we do not manage to neutralize."[2] Yet, with rare exceptions, it seemed a year of missed opportunities, a year when the deeper implications of the common fate of European Muslims and Jews faced with consecutive edicts of expulsion from Spain were obscured to the point of oblivion. For those edicts of expulsion affected not only the hundreds and thousands of Muslims and Jews forced into exile; they also forced more than eight hundred years of "Euro-Semitic" culture underground, forever marking Europe's own self-conception by excising references to its tainted, impure past. This suppressed chapter in European history returned with a vengeance in what has come to be our own legacy, during the enlightenment and colonial periods when an imperial curriculum successfully managed to ethnically cleanse any references to Semites — Jews or Muslims — that might indicate them to be both possessors of an autonomous history and inextricable partners in the creation of "European" civilization. It is this very legacy that continues to affect not only our discipline but also the way we think of ourselves and the world we inhabit.

In the context of Jewish studies, particular questions and issues that have already been debated in other fields remain largely unexamined and even unformulated as possibilities. The idea that Spanish culture might, for instance, be the *result* of an intense struggle for, between, and against the memory and reality of its Arabic and Hebrew past, rather than the "self-evident" "national" outgrowth of a particular ethnic group, is rarely taken as an initial assumption. Rather than hold conferences, for example, questioning the very term *European* or pondering just how many generations of nativity in a particular place is needed in order for "blood" and ethnicity to turn into accurate geographical description, the activities of 1992 only buttressed the impermeability of the categories themselves. Whichever myth one subscribes to — an idealized "multicultural" garden of coexistence or the precarious existence of a minority allowed its few moments of brilliance by the tyrannical rule of the majority, along with all the more or less subtle gradations in between — the terms of discussion have remained the same: Arab Muslim, Sephardic Jew, and Spanish Christian, with only the latter being granted the magical status of "European," despite the residence of the former on European soil for close to a millennium. The containers of identity remain fixed and iconic, regardless of the qualities their contents might possess.

The quincentennial also conveniently provided the finger in the proverbial dike that would shore up any leaks contaminating one arbitrarily constructed historical period from another. The construction of a "glorious" past (even when that "glory" is contested) is often, as in this case, more a concession dedicated to fending off the present and more recent past than a means of coming to terms with the continuing significance of the materials themselves. In this sense, the discourse of historical Jewish/Muslim relations in Spain has generally been constructed with certain assumptions or silences regarding present political realities. The very terms of debate (as seen, for example, in an exchange between the prominent Jewish historians Norman A. Stillman and Mark R. Cohen),[3] range over an extremely limited spectrum of possibilities. The very terms *Jew* and *Arab* remain mutually exclusive and are rarely problematized by particular historical, economic, political, or cultural circumstances.

Perhaps even more significantly, at least as far as Jewish studies (however it may be construed) is concerned, this discourse has almost categorically refused to take into account the present political, social, and cultural status of Sephardi, Arab, or *mizrahi* Jews in *historical* and nonideological or apologetic terms as a focal point through which different interpretations of the past can be filtered. One typical assumption is that since Arab Jews came from less "developed" countries, they could not compete with Ashkenazi Jews in the "open" market Israel presented; here, for example, is a statement from Jane Gerber's *The Jews of Spain* on the status of the *mizrahim* in the Israel of the 1960s: "Coming from Muslim countries with less advanced economies, their skills were often limited and their per-capita income and educational attainment were typically and strikingly inferior to Ashkenazi levels."[4]

The perpetuation of one narrative (or at least one set of constituent terms through which versions of that narrative are told), replete with experts armed with all the "required" data, only serves to police the borders of a policy of separate development. This move *away* from the multiply constructed contexts of textuality and more toward entrenchment into narrowly defined territories, small fiefdoms of power composed of self-serving and "self-evident" truths, obscures the ways we have come to accept the "infallibility" of those very "truths." Moreover, it preempts even the possibility of raising precisely the kinds of issues that not only need to be raised but that the very materials under scrutiny *demand* be raised. For example, one can look at the unquestioned canonical status of Golden Age Hebrew poetry in Spain as a way of detaching it from the incredibly varied and rich tradition of Levantine Jewish culture that follows it over the next millennium. Ghettoizing "accomplishment" in one discrete period, with only flashes of glory to follow, leaves little room for a cohesive narrative that can be presented as an alternative to the centrality of the "European" Jewish narrative.

This pattern is made all the more resilient by the fact that far too few texts are easily available outside of a highly specialized academic context. While many nations have standardized editions of premodern texts, this is not the case for Hebrew. As things stand now, only selections of some major writers (Ibn Gabirol, Shmuel HaNagid, Yehuda Ha-Levi, for example) are available, and many others simply have not entered the vocabulary. The classic rhymed verse narratives of Yehuda al-Harizi, for example, are out of print. From the tenth to the twentieth century, one can point to literally hundreds of writers whose influence on the present has hardly been felt because of the difficulty of gaining access to their work. While substantial "readings" exist, there is, for example, no radical *rereading* of the Hebrew poetic tradition, no text such as *Introduction to Arabic Poetics* by Adonis; one could make a good case that the *lack* of such an endeavor is the *result* of the contemporary unavailability of the tradition itself. Ironically, many of the writers in question—for a variety of reasons too complex to delineate here but having to do with place, spheres of influence, usage, and intent—could have a lot to say to younger Israeli writers who are again fully inhabiting a Levantine space but are still looking for a language to do it in. In addition to this, the aura of prerequisite expertise that keeps such texts in a highly sheltered but largely inaccessible domain makes them unavailable for translation. Thus, the gaps existing in Levantine Jewish texts available for use in teaching outside of Israel, for example, are truly enormous. The complex set of issues that such a situation presents should be of vital concern not only to Israeli writers, literary historians, educators, and the general public but also to scholars of medieval, Renaissance, post-Renaissance and modern Jewish life, in all its aspects.

Yet for reasons that are certainly as intriguing as those causing the problem in the first place, open debate over a topic as crucial as this never surfaces.

What can, for want of a better term, be called Zionist discourse (with its hybrid Enlightenment, romantic, revolutionary, and colonialist legacy, as well as its attendant assumptions regarding Jewish history and the diaspora), has permeated every aspect of modern Jewish culture. The earnest critique of this legacy and these assumptions has only begun. In some fields, such as history, revisionist work has gained a foothold. Other fields, such as sociology, anthropology, and literary studies, are still dominated by modes of discourse that can only be called paternalistic, ahistorical, and inadequate. In literary studies, the field that most concerns me here, we can see this expressed on all levels. On the one hand, completely vulgar and almost comical assertions not only abound, but go unquestioned in purportedly academic contexts. Two of my favorite instances of this are as follows; the first is from a preface to a book of interviews with contemporary Israeli writers:

> Equally remarkable, I am abashed to point out that every one of the 18 writers who appear in this collection is of Northern European or North American, *Ashkenazi* background. Not a one can point to roots in the *Sephardi* Jewish communities of Southern Europe or the Arab countries. And yet such is the literary culture of contemporary Israel that, though of course exceptions could be cited—novelists Amnon Shamosh and Sammy Michael, poet Ronnie Someck, a number of others—my claim to being representative can justly stand. To all intents and purposes, Israeli literary culture today is not only predominantly leftist but wholly dominated by *Ashkenazim*.[5]

After being "honest" about his quandary, this author goes on to exonerate himself of any culpable judgment; he has, after all, mentioned some Sephardi Jewish writers so he knows that they exist. However, since there are no others, his "claim to being representative can justly stand." Thus, Q.E.D., "Israeli literary culture today...is wholly dominated by Ashkenazim." The next example reaches much greater heights of absurdity, purely on logical grounds:

> Israel is geographically part of the Middle East—and indeed is a major factor in contemporary Middle Eastern consciousness. Yet as astute an Israeli intellectual as Shulamit Hareven defines literary Israel as a territory whose borders skirt present-day Manhattan and nineteenth-century

Odessa, with Czernowitz somewhere in between. She would prefer a more Mediterranean Israel, though she surely knows that such an Israel is, in literary as well as political terms, still very much within the realm of utopian fantasy. Yoram Bronowski, too, is clear on this point: that Israeli literature moves willy-nilly on paths determined by European literature. It does seem that, for literary purposes, the Israeli sensibility is incontrovertibly a Euro-American sensibility. Very little about Israeli belles lettres can be called Levantine, even though a sizable proportion of the Israeli population (a segment that includes such authors as A. B. Yehoshua, Nissim Aloni, and Erez Bitoun [*sic*]) has Levantine or Oriental antecedents. From a Middle Eastern perspective, then, all Israelis, even those of Moroccan or Persian or Yemenite origin, are European; their literature is European; their outlook is alien or external to the Middle East.[6]

This speaks for itself and, though the temptation is great, one does not, in the end, even feel compelled to add any typographical emphases. On the other hand, it is remarkable to observe just how deeply ingrained similar attitudes are, to varying degrees, in mainstream scholarship. These less blatant instances are often harder to contend with since they form the very building blocks of commonplace assumptions in practically all modern Hebrew literary criticism and literary history, whether written in Hebrew, English, or other languages. More insidious, embedded in gaps and silences, this discourse relies on exclusion or partial accommodation as a means of asserting truth and maintaining control. A few examples chosen from the work of Gershon Shaked, Benjamin Harshav, and Robert Alter, three dominant figures in modern Hebrew literary studies, can serve as an introduction to the problematic involved.

In the fourth and last volume of his *Hebrew Literature 1880–1980,* Gershon Shaked looks at writers (particularly Shimon Ballas and Sammy Michael) whom, as one of the primary arbiters of "taste" in the Israeli literary establishment, he had consistently chosen to ignore. He describes the work of these and other *mizrahi* writers as an expression of "socialist realism (though it is really more social than socialist)." In addition, Shaked describes their work simply as a reaction; writing about Ballas and Michael, he states: "Their immigration to Israel exposed them to social and ethnic humiliation. The Ashkenazi community turned them from a social elite into a second class. When they were able to express themselves in Hebrew, they set out to accuse those who had humiliated them."[7] Other writers he discusses (such as Amnon Shamosh and Yitzhaq Gormezano Goren), "prefer the folklore and customs that were to the Zionist lifestyle."[8] Shaked also takes pains to find "precedents" in mainstream Israeli writing to anything that might be construed as "innovative" in work by *mizrahim*. Again, writing about Ballas and Michael, he points out that "these two realistic writers 'dared' to raise the Jewish-Arab question — caustically, and while identifying to one degree or another with the Arab position — only after this issue had been raised in a complex, camouflaged and ambiguous way by the members of the new, modern-grotesque school as represented by A. B. Yehoshua."[9] In every instance, the judgmental language implies superiority and inferiority: the "Oriental" is barely capable of socialist realism, only "social" realism; the "Oriental" is incapable of independent agency, but can only express him or herself in reaction to dominance; the "Oriental" is only capable of folklore and customs, not an ideology or a lifestyle; the "Oriental" is incapable of innovation and can only crudely imitate more complex and ambiguous literary works through direct representation and identification.

In one of a series of exchanges following the appearance of excerpts from Shaked's book, Shimon Ballas stated:

> In other words, there is no reason to relate to me — as a writer or as a human being — as to someone having principles or a worldview. One should only see my political positions as a reaction to the humiliation that I supposedly suffered. But what about the pure Ashkenazis who also felt solidarity with the Arabs and fought along with me? They didn't struggle because of degradation but because they had principles. But I, at least according to Shaked, couldn't possibly develop any principles but only react as a result of my humiliation. Such a claim is not only perverse, but racist.[10]

In Benjamin Harshav's new book, *Language in Time of Revolution*, Shaked's more openly polemical assumptions are woven into the realm of scientific authority and historical objectivity. In his preface, "the Jews" remain unqualified; thus, when he speaks of the numbered immigrations to Israel (the First through Fifth), he can conveniently exclude the people who do not fit into Zionist historiography. If such people are excluded (the waves of Yemenites, brought in as a more "practical" alternative to Palestinian labor; the Bukharians and Moroccans who established early urban presences in Jerusalem, for example), then their linguistic influence can also be eliminated. In fact, outside of one mention of the educator Nissim Bechar, absolutely no role or presence is accorded to "non-European" Jews in the Hebrew revolution.

Harshav assumes the destiny of Jews to be universal: "In this sense, Jewish history is a staggered history: what happened to one Jewish group earlier happened to another group later."[11] This "universalization" of Jewish destiny, however, in addition to being completely ahistorical, cuts off areas of inquiry that demand attention, eliminating not only the need or the desire but even the possibility of beginning to think about modern Hebrew literature and its complex development in a *truly* comparative sense, alongside so many other cultures and literatures that underwent similar processes (Arabic, Persian, Turkish, Greek, Urdu, Japanese, or Bosnian, to mention only a few).

The revival of Hebrew and the creation of a new society, according to Harshav, "gave its users a vehicle for expressing a totality of twentieth-century experience in a language of their own."[12] The assumption here, of course, is that without such a vehicle, one could *not* express a totality of twentieth-century experience. Reading more carefully, one can build on the nature of Harshav's distinctions:

> But unlike other ancient civilizations that were modernized and gained independence at about the same time in their own traditional space, Hebrew came back to its ancestral land from a long absence, from the outside, and from the world of Europe and modernity. It was not an ancient language of a great ancient civilization, stagnant for hundreds of years (as Arabic or Indian cultures were), that is now gradually growing into the twentieth century, but rather a new language, recreated in the very heart of the transitions of modernity, in the context of the intellectual ferments in Russia, which itself underwent an earthquake, trying to embrace abstract, idealized forms of the culture of the modern West.[13]

In this passage there are subtle yet clearly identifiable judgments being made: other ancient civilizations "were modernized" — passively acted upon, they did not modernize themselves; the world of Europe and modernity presumably never fully touched the "traditional space" of these ancient civilizations; unlike Hebrew, at the very "heart" of modernity, the ancient civilizations only "gradually grew" into the twentieth century. Later on, these prejudices are made explicit in such journalistic clichés as "backward, Ottoman-ruled Palestine,"[14] "backward and despotic Ottoman Empire, in that desolate and hot land, amid the hostile Arabs,"[15] and "orderly British Mandatory rule that recognized Hebrew as one of the three official languages in Palestine."[16]

In "Ashkenazi or Sephardi Dialect?" Harshav accomplishes a re-markably erudite leap of faith. After he endows the Ashkenazi dialect with richness, subtleties of nuance, musicality, and flexibility (as op-posed to the artificiality of the "so-called" Sephardi stress, which, nevertheless, became the official pronunciation), we are told that vari-ations in "correct" pronunciation (where Ashkenazi overrules Sephardi stress positions) entail more than "just a phonetic issue." They give "a specific character to Israeli speech and its speakers. And beyond that, *this is the basic mode of the whole revival in Eretz-Israel*: an ideological decision and a drastic imposition of a new model of be-havior, radically different from the Diaspora past, is accompanied by *a subtext of old behavior,* which reemerges with time: the Jew comes out from under the Hebrew."[17] Thus we come full circle; since non-European Jews have been excluded from the narrative, this Jew (like "the Jews" mentioned in the preface), we are made to understand, is clearly an Ashkenazi Jew.

Finally, in Robert Alter's new collection, *Hebrew and Modernity,* we can see further manifestations of some of the problematic issues described here. Yet again we learn, inexplicably, that "Hebrew litera-ture, though now created preponderantly in the Middle East, resolutely remains a Western literature, looking to formal and even sometimes stylistic models in English, German, and, to a lesser degree, Russian, French, and Spanish."[18] The fact that novelists like Shimon Ballas and poets like Moshe Sartel might look to Lebanese, Iraqi, Palestinian, Egyptian, Turkish, or Greek models is a nonissue. While Alter remains resolutely sensitive to the nuances and resonances of Hebrew litera-ture in its Eastern and Western European contexts, his informed read-ings in the diversity of premodern Mediterranean and Levantine He-brew writing are tainted by his own qualifications. Modernity proper remains a European enterprise:

> That is to say, by the late eighteenth century, European Jewry was launch-ing the radical historical transformation we call modernization, and what was at issue now in the act of writing Hebrew was not just an aesthetic pursuit but a programmatic renegotiation of the terms of Jew-ish collective identity. . . . To write, let us say, a sonnet or a poetic epi-gram in Hebrew was an act of competitive cultural imitation, but one carried out within the confines of a highly conventionalized formal struc-ture, and as such chiefly an aesthetic exercise, however deep the feeling behind some of the individual poems.[19]

In slightly more elevated terms, we again encounter the crucial and truer difference of *European* agency; the novel becomes an idealized form representing consciousness itself while "premodern" poetry can only aspire to be an "aesthetic excercise."

In other words, there can be no "modernity" before "modernity" proper. The crisis facing Judaism during the Inquisition, for example, in the "age of discovery," when new parts of the self were interrogated, discovered, and charted, is not "modern" enough to fit such criteria. Within the domain of such exclusive terms, the fertile field of analogy and inquiry between *marrano* and nineteenth-century Jewish experience remains cordoned off. Yet, as Shmuel Trigano has written, "the Marrano Sephardic Jews served, paradoxically, as the prototypes and the anguished laboratory of modernity, the 'political animal' divided into the fantasizing private person, and the universal citizen, abstract and theoretical. The citizen is 'free' but subject to law and the coercion of power. The private individual is 'free,' but that liberty can only be exercised between the four walls of 'cellular' rooms."[20]

Alter's proprietary relationship to the past is accompanied by a good deal of mystification, about both the status of modern Israeli writers and the particularities of the Hebrew language itself (one might almost even say: *'al 'ijaz al'ibrani*/"the inimitability of Hebrew," to paraphrase the Arabic dictum *'al 'ijaz al'-quran*/"the inimitability of the Quran," such a central idea to both classical Arabic and Hebrew literature). Regarding contemporary Israeli writers, we are given to accept the fact that translation of more popular writers such as David Grossman, Amos Oz, and A. B. Yehoshua somehow already implies or guarantees the importance of their work. The idea that contemporary Israeli writing might be a highly contested field, a place where social and political struggles occur, is never even broached as a possibility. The "Israeli literature which has become abundantly available in English translation"[21] has become so, presumably, only because of its quality. There is no intimation that this availability might have something to do with the creation of a receptive space affected by the political and economic relationship that exists between the United States and Israel, and everything that goes along with that, including the politics of publishing. Why aren't Iranian, Lebanese, Turkish, or Moroccan novels available with such immediacy? And even more to the point, why are only some Israelis translated and published abroad?

While Alter links some Israeli writers with their Yiddish antecedents and apparent American or European contemporaries, these links are made to appear so seamless and natural that one finds it hard to even imagine that there might be parallel worlds, worlds where writers like Yitzhaq Gormezano Goren would find antecedents in Albert Cohen and Jacqueline Kahanof; where the work of Albert Memmi and Clarisse Nikoidski could exist alongside that of Albert Swissa and Amira Hess; where the work of Samir Naqqash and Shimon Ballas would find antecedents in Taha Hussein and contemporaries in Edwar el-Kharrat, Ghassan Kanafani, Yahya Taher Abdullah, and Hannan al-Shaykh. One could go on and on: while the abundance of Yiddish literature is assumed, we are never given, for example, even a cursory description of the massive production of literature in Judeo-Spanish and what *its* significance might be for the growth of another whole branch of modern Jewish writing as seen in the work of Haim Davico, Isak Samokovlija, Laura Bohoreta Papo, Elissa Rhais, Catulle Mendes, Ryvel, Albert Ades, Albert Josepovici, Mony de Boully, Veza Canetti, and so many others whose names are neither mentioned nor known in practically all studies purportedly meant to cover Jewish modernity.

Without belaboring a point that already seems belabored to the point of tediousness: my aim here is not to engage in accusations, to expose the "sins" of ignorance (no matter how egregious), or put the "blame" for the state of things as they are on this or that person. I am not writing as a victim, reaching, as Trinh Minh-ha puts it, to defend "that very ethnic part of" myself. Nor is it my aim to "struggle for my rightful share," to impose — along with the policy of separate development — a policy of *equally* separate development. The idea here is not to vie for a bigger slice of the pie but to redefine the nature of the pie itself. Other areas have seen remarkable achievements in the past decades, combining theoretical erudition with a true scholarly zeal to produce authoritative and easily available editions of both classical and noncanonical texts. On the American scene, for example, African American and women's studies have presented new paradigms, standards, and challenges.

The study of Hebrew literature and the writings of Jews in other languages stands at a crucial juncture. A combination of chauvinism, ideological blinders, political blindness, and the lack of a true comparative perspective has severely tested the abilities of students to emerge intact from most of the contexts now available in which such studies can be pursued. We can either expect more of the same or strive to open the field up to new directions and new definitions. Entire periods are waiting to be defined and examined. No intellectual history of nineteenth- and early-twentieth-century Jewry in the Levant, with its relationship to European thought, currently exists. Who, for example, has studied the correspondence between the great Orientalist A. S. Yahuda and Saul Tschernikovski, or Yahuda's remarkable critique on Freud's *Moses and Monotheism?* A literary scholar attuned to the complexities of contemporary Israeli and Jewish writing in other languages could open up the whole issue of writing in an acquired language, moving across different cultures and periods. These are only suggestions hinting at the enormous range of unexplored material available, material whose unveiling would unquestionably dislodge and make obsolete the kind of facile, unfounded generalizations that presently dictate what can and cannot be studied, known, or imagined. The amount of writing that remains "unread," in the largest sense of that term, is staggering. And the questions that this writing engenders, particularly when they are viewed through the lens of the complex amalgam of Israeli culture in *all* its aspects, are the questions that many literatures are or should be asking themselves.

The works of Ivo Andric, winner of the Nobel Prize in what was then Yugoslavia, have resurfaced lately as a source of anti-Muslim prejudice in Serbian cultural discourse. In particular, his thesis, *The Development of Spiritual Life in Bosnia under the Influence of Turkish Rule* (written in 1924 and published in English in 1990), has been cited in various texts on Bosnia. Andric, though adopted as part of the Serbian literary canon (often as an "antidote" or in direct opposition to the Croatian writer Miroslav Krleza), was himself a Croat. It is in this context, in an essay called "Ivo Andric's Place in Croatian Literature," that the Bosnian Croat novelist and critic Ivan Lovrenovic discusses the absolute resistance to even speaking of Croatia's three towering modern literary figures, Tin Ujevic, Ivo Andric, and Miroslav Krleza, in the same breath:

> What model does this phenomenon present for a culture's internal relationship? Just this, that such a culture has a serious problem with the *recognition* of its own contents and their worth, with the realization of its own creative energies; in other words, in the final analysis, it has a problem with *self-recognition.* Furthermore, it means that this culture

has a serious problem with the *integration of its own differences*. And this, in itself, contains within it a more burdensome and global diagnosis: such problems all derive from an *insecure identity*.[22]

Lovrenovic goes on to make an analogy between the way Croatian literary history and literary politics abandoned not just Ivo Andric but everything having to do with Bosnia:

> The essence of this relationship resulted from an optical illusion in which, *looking at everything from the center,* the Bosnian Croat problematic was always and in its entirety viewed as an *appendage,* and a *second-class* appendage at that.... And we are speaking here of a full body of work stretching over half a millenium; the literary and linguistic continuity and memory of a whole world that had always been a vital element of Croatian history and the Croatian people. What does the tenacity and continuity of this optical deformation tell us? It tells us that the only model given legitimacy, the *metropolitan paradigm* of center and periphery, is inadequate. Putting it simply, this culture, as well as its literature, have had a different historical formation, polycentric and polymorphous.[23]

One does not have to stretch the imagination far to see the remarkably fertile analogies present in this seemingly distant and highly localized example.

Lovrenovic also speaks of those forces that have the means at their disposal—in the form of a state, an army, and a police force—to exert and maintain control over a writer, a work, or an event. This bitter knowledge of defeat and subjugation, so long a Jewish instinct, can be contrasted with Harshav's almost chilling tone of triumphalism: "But in place of the Hebraized terms, new 'foreign words' and concepts were introduced, within the proportions of good taste allowed in a given genre. This was—and is—the *cosmopolitan openness* (as well as the Yiddish and Russian background) of modern Hebrew. It was this openness that constructed a modern State with universities, literature, and an air force."[24] This in turn can be contrasted to the wise irony of Isaac Bashevis Singer, who, when he was asked what the difference between Hebrew and Yiddish is, replied, "Hebrew is Yiddish with an army."

The very imprecisions I have pointed to are what Erica Hunt describes in her highly cogent essay "Notes Towards an Oppositional Poetics" as "codes and mediations that sustain the status quo" and "abbreviate the human in order to fit us into structures of production."[25] In this case, we are meant to fit into the structures that produce meaning and significance — as writers, scholars, critics, students, and consumers of cultural artifacts. But such structures and strictures contradict our experience, no matter how casual or urgent it might be. To be "abbreviated" in the multiplicity of our possible range of identities is a form of oppression. In a context of extreme violence, the contemporary Bosnian writer Nedzad Ibrisimovic was asked if he should be spoken to as a writer, as a fighter in the army of Bosnia-Herzegovina, or just as a plain Bosnian suffering with everyone else. He answered: "You can't talk to me as a writer because I can't talk while I'm writing and when I stop writing, I'm not a writer." This answer, ironic and playful as it might seem under the circumstances, embodies an insistence on the autonomous nature of plurality and a steadfast refusal to be pinned down into one category or another. It is the categorical assertion and acceptance of difference *beyond* "a certain extent." Without losing sight of the possibility of universal desires, claims, and responsibilities, what remains crucial is precisely this ability to maintain a diversity of selves and roles that can act locally in many places at once.

Notes

1. Trinh T. Minh-ha, *Woman, Native, Other* (Bloomington: Indiana University Press, 1989), 89.

2. Edmond Jabès, *From the Desert to the Book: Dialogues with Marcel Cohen,* trans. Pierre Joris (Tarrytown, N.Y: Station Hill, 1990), 40.

3. See Mark R. Cohen's "The Neo-Lachrymose Conception of Jewish-Arab History" followed by Norman A. Stillman's "Myth, Countermyth, and Distortion" in *Tikkun* 6, no. 3: 55–64. There is also an exchange of letters in the following issue, vol. 6, no. 4: 96–97, entitled "Revisionist Jewish-Arab History: An Exchange."

4. Jane S. Gerber, *The Jews of Spain* (New York: Free Press, 1992), 279.

5. Haim Chertok, *We Are All Close: Conversations with Israeli Writers* (New York: Fordham University Press, 1989), 4–5.

6. Warren Bargad and Stanley F. Chyet, *Israeli Poetry: A Contemporary Anthology* (Bloomington: Indiana University Press, 1986), 3.

7. Gershon Shaked, "Struggling against the Ashkenazi Establishment," in *Modern Hebrew Literature* 10, new series (Spring/Summer 1993): 4–5.

8. Ibid., 6.

9. Ibid., 7.

10. "Rehabilitation or Libel: A Conversation Between Ya'akov Besser and Shimon Ballas," *Davar,* October 23, 1992, 25. My translation.

11. Benjamin Harshav, *Language in Time of Revolution* (Berkeley: University of California Press, 1993), 15.

12. Ibid., 81.

13. Ibid., 82.

14. Ibid., 84.

15. Ibid., 110.

16. Ibid., 85.

17. Ibid., 166.

18. Robert Alter, *Hebrew and Modernity* (Bloomington: Indiana University Press, 1994), 7.

19. Ibid., 42–43.

20. Shmuel Trigano, *La nouvelle question juive* (Paris: Gallimard, 1979), 208. My translation.

21. Ibid., ix.

22. Ivan Lovrenovic, *Ex tenebris: sarajevski dnevnik* [Ex tenebris: A Sarajevo journal] (Zagreb: AGM, 1994), 43.

23. Ibid., 44.

24. See Harshav, *Language in Time of Revolution*, 129.

25. Erica Hunt, "Notes Towards an Oppositional Poetics," in *The Politics of Poetic Form: Poetry and Public Policy*, ed. Charles Bernstein (New York: Roof Books, 1990), 200.

13 / The Holy Foreskin; or, Money, Relics, and Judeo-Christianity

Marc Shell

My purse, my person, my extremest means,
Lie all unlock'd to your occasions.
                    SHAKESPEARE, *The Merchant of Venice*[1]

What was it about Christ's foreskin that made it the object of unique cult veneration?

Christians have a material God. But God's material *person* has all but disappeared since Jesus' Ascension to heaven on the fortieth day after his Resurrection.[2] All that one might have now, in the period before the Second Coming, is spiritual inscriptions, as it were, in material media — *spiritualia sub metaphoris corporalium* (corporeal metaphors of things spiritual).[3] Or so it would seem.

However, as John Calvin writes, "On ne pouvait laisser échapper le corps de Jésus-Christ sans en retenir quelque *lopin*" (they couldn't let Christ's body escape without retaining some piece of it).[4]

Many Christians wanted or needed a material relic *lopped off* from the divine *corpus*. Thus they discovered remnants of Jesus' body — relics of blood from various wounds (including those from the Circumcision and the Crucifixion) as well as sweat, tears, baby teeth, hair, umbilical cord, fingernails, urine, feces, and other bodily excrescences.[5] For other excrescences: Calvin in *A Treatise on Relics* hints at beliefs about relics of Christ's urine and feces (3:264). Each of these bodily leftovers is iconologically problematic in its own way. (Jesus' umbili-

345

cal cord, for example, is Mary's human flesh as well as Jesus' partly human flesh.) Since relics were perceived "as the living Saint"[6] while feces ordinarily were thought of as "dead" — even as "diabolic" — remains or leftovers, the adoration of Jesus' feces in some church treasuries is interesting, particularly in view of the psychoanalytic association of feces with money and gift giving.[7] The only unambiguous trace of Jesus' actual flesh still on earth, however, is the foreskin removed from his body eight days after his birth on our "New Year's Day."[8] That cut is the "Holy Foreskin."[9]

The relics of Jesus' flesh and blood are uniquely treasured in Catholic dogma and highly appraised in the treasuries of Catholic churches because they literalize the otherwise figurative Eucharist. "Eat me," Jesus is interpreted to have said at the Last Supper.[10] The Eucharist ceremony would live up to this commandment. It transforms the bread on the paten and the wine in the chalice more or less literally into Jesus' flesh and blood.

Just how literally we should understand this transformation — and just how literally we should understand the difference between figurative and literal meanings — has always been a matter for church debate. The Lateran Council of 1215 argued that in the Eucharist the wafer literally became flesh only when it reached the middle of the celebrant's throat, but agreement was not unanimous. What privileges the Holy Foreskin in this debate about transubstantiation is that the *praeputium* is already what the bread can only figure. Thanks to the Holy Foreskin, Jesus' commandment, "Eat me," could be followed to the letter.

The Holy Foreskin is privileged in Catholic dogma in much the same way as the Holy Grail and its contents. The Grail's literalization of the Eucharist blood helps to explain the special status of the Grail and its contents as Jesus' *sang real,* or real/royal blood. By the same token, the Holy Foreskin's literalization of the Eucharist flesh helps to explain the enduring popularity of the Foreskin as Jesus' *carne vera sancta,* or true and holy meat — as the Foreskin is called in Italy.[11] No fanciful argument involving transubstantiation needs to make the point that a cut of the Foreskin, if genuine, can provide the most valuable kind of spiritual and material fleshly nourishment, both *intellectus* and *res.* Saint Birgitta's description of the joy of eating Christ's Foreskin says that "so great was the sweetness at the swallowing of this membrane that she felt a sweet transformation in all her members and the muscles of her members."[12] "Of all things that Jesus Christ left on earth," writes Baillet in his history of the Holy Week, "nothing is more worthy of our veneration than the flesh that he distributed for us.... Thus nothing merits more that we carefully gather and preserve it."[13]

Christian travelers, projecting onto others the alimenatry characteristics they feared in themselves, sometimes told tales of "barbaric" and "cannibalistic" peoples who would eat human testicles and foreskins. According to Buffon, Persian women were said "to swallow the part of the foreskin which a child has lost in circumcision as an infallible remedy against sterility."[14]

Among commercial traders, of course, the genuineness of the treasured Foreskin was always subject to question, especially as the prices in the European relics market skyrocketed and tales of their theft along the major trade routes became so common that they came to form a medieval literary genre, replete with hints of financial corruption, much like that of twentieth-century journalists' articles about "priceless" artworks.[15] And so they developed various tests to determine the genuineness of any given foreskin. Tasting was the test of choice. A properly trained physician chosen by the local priest would taste the shriveled leather in order to determine whether it was wholly or partly human skin. Since tasting involves a little consumption — or so one school of *gastronomie* and the anthropology of taste would have it[16] — the surgeon who ate Jesus would be called *croque-prépuce*.[17]

The uniqueness or oneness of the treasured foreskin was subject to question as well as its genuineness, and this too led to analogies with the Eucharist. Many churches claimed to have the Foreskin.[18] Could it be that some of these churches had only a part of the Foreskin? The Protestant Calvin doubted that it was physically possible to divide the Foreskin into so many pieces. Calvin marveled similarly at the number of churches that had vials of the Virgin Mary's breast milk: "Had Mary been a cow all her life," wrote Calvin, "she could not have produced such a quantity."[19]

Perhaps, though, the Foreskin had multiplied into many Foreskins, each one of which miraculously kept the unique patina or aura of the original. The idea of the multiplication of the Foreskin led to comparisons with the Miracle of Loaves and Fishes. Nineteenth-century Calvinists would recognize the idea of this multiplication as a brunt of Nast's satire *Milk-Tickets... in Place of Milk* (Figure 13.1).[20]

Figure 13.1

Honorat Nicquet mentions the Holy Foreskin in this context when he "assimilate[s] the [apparent] multiplication of the wood of the True Cross [as suggested by its appearance in homes and churches throughout Europe] to the Body of Christ in the Eucharist."[21] Other writers, skeptical of a particular church's claim to have the authentic Foreskin, denigrated the relic the Holy Foreskin only in order to elevate the "relic of relics" that is the Eucharist. Guibert of Nogent, for example, in his *On the Relics of the Saints* (c. 1130), doubts the authenticity of the Holy Foreskin owned by the monks of Charroux—Charroux, literally "red flesh," from the French term *chair rouge*[22]—just as he promotes "the veneration of the Eucharist, which was the physical presence of the body of Christ, as superior to the veneration of ordinary... relics."[23]

"Be circumcided in the Lorde, and cut awaye the foreskynne of your hertes," says Saint Paul—depending as usual on the distinction between figure and letter—in Coverdale's version of the New Testament.[24] Christianity, in its attempt to "transcend" the purported materialism of Judaism, seeks to replace "literal" circumcision with "figural" circumcision of the heart. Paul's way of distinguishing between the literal and figural realms encouraged theologians to investigate whether the divine body into which the Eucharist wafer is transformed (in the celebrant's throat) is circumcised and also whether, in the interval between the Resurrection and the Ascension, Jesus' foreskin was resurrected along with his penis.[25] The Pauline call for absolute dematerialization thus encouraged willy-nilly an adoration of the Foreskin among some Christians that, along with the general adoration and handling of bodily leftovers, seems sometimes to border on social pathology. It is worth reporting here the striking claim that, of medical and psychiatric patients in contemporary America who are preoccupied with their absent foreskins to the point of seeking surgical reconstruction or "uncircumcision," all are Christian and none is Jewish.[26]

In considering the Holy Grail in its iconic and monetary aspect, we saw how Christ is thought of simultaneously as both container and contained thing—as both purse and purse. (The word *purse* means either "money-bag" or "the contents of a money-bag"—or "money-bag and contents taken together.")[27] And in considering the aurigenesis of Christ, we saw how the Virgin Mother is thought of as the purse (or container) of the purse that is the infant Christ, as expressed in the story about the iconoclast Steven. Another story about Christ and purses is told about the eighth century iconoclast Emperor Constantine V, who convened the council on image worship, or iconolatry, in 753 A.D.:

> Taking in his hand a purse full of gold and showing it to all, he asked, 'What is it worth?' They replied that it had great value. He then emptied out the gold and asked, 'What is it worth now?' They said, 'Nothing.' 'So,' said he, 'Mary' (for the atheist would not call her *theotokos*), 'while she carried Christ within herself was to be honored, but after she was delivered she differed in no way from other women.'[28]

Mary, whether as Danaë-like recipient of God's golden semen or as purselike bearer of Christ, is not of the same substance as the god (*théos*) she contains in the way that money is of the same substance as the interest (*tokos*) it generates. The divine Son, though he has a likeness (*homoiótés*) to Mother Mary, is not of the same substance (*homousios*).

The iconodule confusion of purse (as container) and person (as thing contained) informs a famous episode in Shakespeare's *The Merchant of Venice*. The Christian gentlemen Salario and Solanio tell a story about Shylock, who is a sort of Elizabethan Money Devil. Shylock, says Solanio, ran through the streets of Venice, crying out for his precious "stones":

> 'My daughter! — O my ducats! — O my daughter!
> Fled with a Christian! — O my Christian ducats! —
> Justice! the law! my ducats, and my daughter!
> A sealed bag, two sealed bags of ducats,
> Of double ducats, stol'n from me by my daughter!
> And jewels, — two stones, two rich and precious stones,
> Stol'n by my daughter! — Justice! find the girl!
> She hath the stones upon her, and the ducats!'[29]

Having lost the person of his own "flesh and blood" — namely, his supposedly consanguineous child Jessica — Shylock is concerned with the loss of his purse, or scrotum, by means of which he might generate another such child.[30]

And, like many a Money Devil in Christian ideology, Shylock cries out at the loss of the purse, or moneybag, by means of which he might generate other coins as interest.[31] (In the traditional Greek and

Christian understanding of usury, children and interest are compared and contrasted as *tokos,* or offspring.)[32]

The Christians' joy at Shylock's double loss of generative potency might be worth considering in terms of the reported practice in Christendom of lopping off the foreskins or testicles of enemies and hoarding them as monetary war "tribute" in such varied places as Montenegro and Sicily.[33] The existence of this practice was often projected by Christian missionaries or traders onto the "barbaric" peoples of Africa: travelogues of the 1590s thus depict African blacks assembling presentation baskets of their defeated enemies' testicles (Figure 13.2).[34]

In *The Merchant of Venice,* when Alcides redeems a virgin "tribute" and Bassanio gives Antonio the "tribute" that is Portia's ring,[35] the Christians' joy at Jessica's running off with Shylock's "stones" tells more about the white Venetian Christians than about either the alien Jew Shylock or the Moslem prince of African Morocco whom the Christians seek to stigmatize. The Christians' mockery of the Semite projects Jewish or Moslem circumcision (removal of the prepuce) as a Christian fear of castration (removal of the stones).[36] Here as elsewhere in Judeo-Christian ideology, the Jewish ritual circumcision stirs up Christian memories of their originary crucifixion's myth and becomes a motive spring for anti-Semitism.[37]

In *The Merchant of Venice* it is the Christian Antonio who embodies the literal castration that the joyful yet fearful Christians project onto Shylock. Antonio would have sacrificed his person as well as his purse for his friend in imitation of Christ's stigmatic sacrifice on the cross. (Certain Protestant theologians would count his attempt to imitate Christ as sinfully presumptuous.)[38] But Antonio turns out to be a penniless man with little to give. And in this play that conflates coins with testicles, Antonio comes to describe himself as a castrated ram — "a tainted wether of the flock."[39] This wether's opposite number is the Jew who supplied money to Shylock and who presumably remains even after Shylock disappears: Tubal. (*Tubal* was pronounced "two ball";[40] *Jew* may have been pronounced "ewe," a term that in *The Merchant of Venice* suggests the fertile person, the "fulsome ewe," that is, the wealthy Portia.)[41] Even as Shylock disappears from the action of this Christian comedy about the search for a golden fleece of love, Tubal's Fortunatus-like power of purse and person remains left over.[42]

The view that coin clipping and penis snipping amount to the same thing (at least for Jews) is the basis for the anti-Semitic mockery in

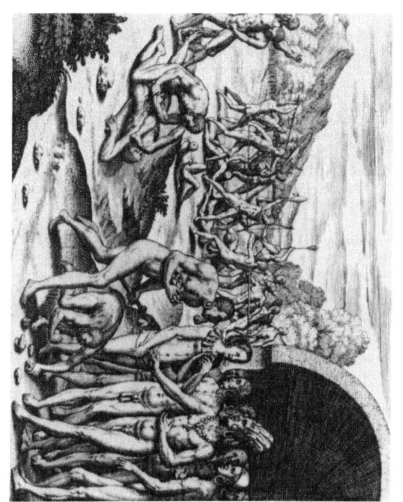

Figure 13.2

Figure 13.3

"The Circumcision," which appeared in an Austrian periodical just before the First World War (Figure 13.3).[43] This cartoon's assertion, that Jews practice circumcision because it is lucrative in much the same way that people snip ducats because it is profitable, suggests more about Christians than about Semites. For "The Circumcision" projects onto the Jewish practice the characteristic foreskin adoration that modern Christians repress, or fear to recognize, in Christianity itself. After all, they are Christians, not Jews, who have revered a foreskin as the moneylike relic of relics, seeing it as the quintessence of ideal realization and seeking at once both to preserve and to consume it.

And what became of Christ's Foreskin? Its history is shrouded in a mystery like that of the Holy Grail. We are told, however, that the Virgin Mary, who had carried the infant Jesus in her womb, or somatic "purse," kept the Foreskin with her all her life as a precious jewel. Saint Birgitta in her *De Praeputio Domini* tells us further that Mary entrusted this treasure to Saint John.[44] The Holy Foreskin was thereafter safeguarded for seven centuries in a shriveled phayactery-like leather pouch or purse. One day, however, someone carried the purse into the court of King Charlemagne at Aix-la-Chapelle.[45] There artists made for it a golden reliquary in the shape of the leather purse. This was the famous eighth-century *Purse Reliquary of the Circumcision*.[46] Gauthier, discussing "the traffic in relics and art investments," remarks that the shape of the purse that contained Christ's Foreskin was thereafter commemorated by adopting it as the fashionable shape (for purses and some pockets) in Christendom.[47] A historical study of the shape of purses in conjunction with their contents as coins or as Christ would constitute a telling contribution to the study of Judeo-Christian art as fashion.[48]

Notes

1. 1.1.137–38.
2. See Schapiro 1979, "Ascension."
3. Panofsky, *Netherlandish Painting,* 142.
4. J. Calvin, *Traité des Reliques* (Collin de Plancy, *Dictionnaire,* 3:46). See also MacCulloch and Smith, "Relics," 655, on "the extraordinary mystical ideas associated with this relic."
5. For blood: Calvin, in the *Traité* (Collin de Plancy, *Dictionnaire,* 3:264) discusses blood preserved with the prepuce. For tears: Thiers, *Dissertation,* tells how the Benedictines of Vendôme persuaded the local people that the tear that they guarded was so valuable as to make for a good deal of income. For teeth: Saintyves, *Reliques,* 192. For the umbilical cord and hair: Collin de Plancy, *Dictionnaire,* 2:45, 62.

6. Geary, *Furta Sacra.*

7. See Freud, "Character and Anal Eroticism," and my "Money Complex of Psychoanalysis," in *Money, Language, and Thought.*

8. Jesus' circumcision eight days after his birth is celebrated at the Feast of the Circumcision of Our Lord (Bentley, *Restless Bones,* 141). Jesus was probably circumcised as a Jew: "And when eight days were fulfilled for his circumcision, his name was called Jesus, the name given him by the angel before he was conceived in the womb" (Luke 2:21). Jesus is said to be the Son of God as well as the son of Joseph, so there is discussion among the Church Fathers as to whether Joseph circumcised Jesus, as would have been the case with regular Jewish fathers.

9. For this term, which translates the French *saint prépuce,* see Collin de Plancy, *Dictionnaire,* 47. The term was used in the Middle Ages to refer to the foreskin at Coulombs. There is said to have been a Saint Praeputius (Laurent and Nagour; cited by Bryk, *Circumcision,* 25).

10. "Take, eat: this is my body" (1 Cor. 11:24). "And he took bread...and gave unto them, saying, This is my body" (Luke 22:19). In "Down the Rabbit-Hole" Alice eats "a very small cake...on which the words 'EAT ME' were beautifully marked" (Carroll, *Alice in Wonderland,* 12).

11. The parish priest of Calcata, Italy, exposed the sacred *carne vera* as late as January 1, 1983 (Bentley, *Restless Bones,* 141).

12. Birgitta, *Reuelationes,* ch. 37, reads as follows: "Now she feels on her tongue a small membrane, like the membrane of an egg, full of superabundant sweetness, and she swallowed it down....And she did the same perhaps hundreds of times. When she touched it with her finger the membrane went down her throat of itself" (cited Bryk, *Circumcision,* 28).

13. "De tout ce que Jésus-Christ a laissé sur la terre, rien ne serait plus digne de notre vénération que le sang qu'il a répandu....Rien ne méritait donc d'être recueilli et conservé avec plus de soin" (Baillet, *Histoire de la Semaine sainte*). It is worth considering here one supposed difference between the blood of the Crucifixion and the flesh of the Circumcision: that the sacrifice of blood saved all humankind (it was done, as Baillet says, "pour le salut du genre humain") but that of flesh merely marked Jesus as a Jew.

14. Buffon, *Voyage* 2: 200; cited by Bryk, *Circumcision,* 31.

15. On the *translatio* of relics, see Geary (*Furta Sacra*). Christian medical doctors were especially interested in obtaining the Holy Foreskin. Eliade, *Encyclopedia,* 279, points out that the foreskin at Coulombs was "venerated by pregant women hoping for an easy childbirth."

16. I am grateful to M. Coscuella — the excellent chef at the Ripa Alta restaurant Plaissance-dans-Gers, France — for his explanation of the centuries-old debate among French *gastronomes* about whether there is any "true" taste without a little consumption. This was during a long disquisition on the traditional way to remark and enjoy the changing flavors and aromas of Armagnac.

17. "Au commencement du dernier siècle, pendant la régence, l'évêque Noailles [at Châlons-sur-Marne, in the Church of Notre-Dame en Vaux, where one of the Holy Foreskins or parts thereof was kept] considérant que ce prépuce était l'objet d'un culte souvent scandaleux, surtout de la part des femmes, et se doutant bien que c'était une fausse relique, voulut la faire examiner. Elle était dans un morceau de velours rouge; un chirurgien, après avoir ouvert le velours, n'y trouva qu'un peu de poudre; il la mit sur la langue, et déclara que le prétendu prépuce n'était qu'une poussière de sable. On appela depuis ce chirurgien *croque-prépuce*; mais il n'y eut plus de prépuce à Châlons-

sur-Marne" (Collin de Plancy, *Dictionnaire,* 2:47). Cf. the practice of *metzitzah* (Hebrew) — i.e., the oral sucking of the tip of the penis to staunch the blood after circumcision (*Enciclopedia Judaica Castellana*; cited Trachtenberg, "Circumcision," 467).

18. Examples would include churches at Charroux, Antwerp, Paris, Bruges, Boulougne, Besançon, Nancy, Metz, Le Puy, Conques, Hildesheim, and Calcata (Italy). See Müller, *Die "hochheilige Vorhaut,"* 24.

19. Calvin, *Traité*; cited by Eliade, *Encyclopedia,* 278.

20. For further details, see my *Art & Money,* ch. 3.

21. Nicquet, *Titulus sanctae crucis,* vol. 1, ch. 25; Hastings, *Encyclopedia,* 655.

22. Bentley, *Restless Bones,* 139.

23. *Dictionary of the Middle Ages.* See Guth, *Guibert.*

24. Coverdale, Jer. 4:4 Paul taught that "circumcision is a matter of the heart, spiritual and not literal" (Rom. 2:29) and that "in him [Christ] also you were circumcised with a circumcision made without hands by putting off the body of flesh in the circumcision of Christ" (Col. 2:11). Cf. Phil. 3:18; Gal. 5:6, 6:15.

25. For the theological investigation, see Müller, *Die "hochheilige Vorhaut."*

26. None of the patients studied by Mohl et al., "Prepuce Restoration Seekers," were Jewish. Cf. Greer et al., "Foreskin Reconstruction," and Waring, *Foreskin Restoration (Uncircumcision)*, which includes a chapter on "grief, depression, and resentment" as well as letters and statements from readers. For a history of circumcision written for medical students, see Remondino, *History of Circumcision.*

27. OED, s.v. "Purse."

28. *Vitae Nicetae,* in *Acta Sanctorum* Ap. I, app. 23, written 820/830; in Martin, *Iconoclastic Controversy,* 62.

29. Shakespeare, *Merchant of Venice,* 2.8.14–21.

30. "I say my daughter is my flesh and blood," says Shylock (*Merchant of Venice* 3.1.29). The Christian gentleman Solanio challenges Shylock's paternity of Jessica: "There is more difference between thy flesh and hers than between jet and ivory; more between your bloods than there is between red wine and rhenish" (3.1.31–33). For *purse* as "scrotum," see OED, s.v. "Purse," 8b; for the cognate French term *bourse* as "scrotum" as well as "bag" — and also as "place where bankers assemble" — see Bouchet, *Sérées,* 1:96 (cited Laqueur, *Making Sex,* 62–63).

31. For remarks on the Money Devil's moneybags, see Gaidoz, "Diable d'argent," col. 209.

32. In Plato, *Republic* (507) and Aristotle, *Politics* (1258), the product of monetary generation, or use, and the product of sexual generation, or a child, are compared as *tokos,* or offspring. Aristotle's insistence that making money breed is unnatural was an important influence on the Church fathers' thinking. On the identification of natural with economic offspring in Shakespeare's *Merchant of Venice,* see my "Verbal Usury." For analysis of the link between various Christian, Jewish, and Muslim doctrines of toleration and monetary interest, see my *Children of the Earth,* ch. 8.

33. For Montenegro, see Krauss, in *Münchener Medizinische Wochenschrift*; for Sicily, see Dulaure, *Die Zeugung,* 184 (cited by Bryk, *Circumcision,* 107–8). On the Holy Foreskin of Christianity in "*mystisch-erotische*" anthropology generally, see esp. Stoll, *Geschlechtsleben,* 683–87.

34. See Lindschotten, *Ander Theil;* in Stoll, *Geschlechtsleben,* 505.

35. Shakespeare, *Merchant of Venice,* 3.2.54–55; 4.1.419.

36. Cavell, *The Claim of Reason,* 480, remarks that the forfeit that is to be "cut off and taken / In which part of [Antonio's] body pleaseth [Shylock]" (1. 3. 146–47) suggests the foreskin that is cut during circumcision and also the testicles that are cut

off during castration (which many people interpret to be the significance of circumcision or fear of its result). Cf. Reik, *Fragments of a Great Confession,* esp. 336. Just as Shylock in act 1 once intended to circumcise the bodily part of Antonio (and hence turn him into a Jewish brother), so Antonio in act 4 intends to circumcise the spiritual part of Shylock (and hence turn him into a Christian man). For Paul, a Christian is a Jew whose heart is circumcised: "For he is not a real Jew who is one outwardly, nor is true circumcision something external and physical. He is a Jew who is one inwardly, and real circumcision is a matter of the heart, spiritual and not literal" (Rom. 2:28–29).

37. In 1939 Freud wrote that "among the customs by which the Jews made themselves separate, that of circumcision has made a disagreeable, uncanny impression, which is to be explained, no doubt, by its recalling the dreaded castration, and along with it a portion of the primeval past which is gladly forgotten" (*Moses and Monotheism,* 91). Already in 1909 Freud had written that "the castration complex is the deepest unconscious root of Anti-Semitism; for even in the nursery little boys hear that a Jew has something cut off his penis — a piece of his penis, they think — and this gives them a right to despise Jews" ("Five Year Old Boy," 36). For an elaboration of the psychoanalytic view here, see Trachtenberg, "Circumcision, Crucifixion, and Anti-Semitism."

38. Antonio's offering his own person as the surety on his friend's loan may be a presumptuous imitation of Jesus' sacrifice on the cross. Martin Luther writes that "there is a common error, which has become a widespread custom, not only among merchants but throughout the world, by which one man becomes the surety for another" (Luther, *Von Kaufshandlung und Wucher,* in *Werke* 25:298–305).

39. Shakespeare, *Merchant of Venice,* 4.1.114.

40. Cf. Kökeritz, *Shakespeare's Pronunciation,* 354–55.

41. See my *Money, Language, and Thought,* ch. 3.

42. On the topos of the inexhaustible purse and on the story of Fortunatus, see Grimm, *Teutonic Mythology,* 871 and 976.

43. "The Circumcision" is discussed briefly in Fuchs, *Die Juden in der Karikatur,* and Seiden, *Paradox of Hate.*

44. Birgitta, *Reuelationes,* ch. 37; and Bryk, *Circumcision,* 24–5. Other authorities say that Mary left the Holy Foreskin in the care of the Holy Mary Magdalene.

45. "In his temple was Charlemayne, when the aungell broght him the prepuce of oure Lord, when he was circumcised" (Maundeville, *Buke,* xi.42).

46. Discussed in *Treasures of French Churches*; C. de Linas, "Le Reliquaire;" Gauthier, "Le Tresor de Conques" and *Emaux*; and Taralon, *Tresors,* 293–94, 204–8.

47. Gauthier, *Highways,* 18.

48. One would also consider pouches, pockets, handbags, and pocketbooks as well as bodices and codpieces. The history of the shape of piggy banks might supplement this research. On these see Samhaber, *Das Geld,* 142; Breugel's various depictions of banks; Henkel and Schöne, eds. *Emblemata,* 1286; and the frontispiece to Veit's *Liebe Geld* (which shows one of the oldest piggy banks in the world).

Bibliography

Acta Sanctorum. 1863-. Editio novissima. Ed. and pub. Society of the Bollandists. 67 vols. Brussels.

Aristotle. 1984. *Politics.* Trans. Carnes Lord. Chicago.

Baillet, Adrien. 1703. *Histoires des festes mobiles dans l'Église, suivant l'ordre des dimanches et des féries de la semaine.* Paris.

Bentley, James. 1985. *Restless Bones: The Story of Relics*. London.

Birgitta. 1500. *Reuelationes*. Nuremberg.

Bolger, Doreen, et al. eds. 1992. *William M. Harnett*. Fort Worth and New York.

Bouchet, Guillaume. 1873–82. *Les sérées de Guillaume Bouchet*. Ed. C. E. Roybet. 6 vols. Paris.

Bryk, Felix. 1974. *Circumcision in Man and Woman: Its History, Psychology, and Ethnology*. Trans. David Berger. 1934. Reprint New York.

Buffon [Georges Louis Leclerc, comte de?]. 1719. *Voyage de Gemelli Careri*. Paris.

Calvin, John. 1854. *A Treatise on Relics*. In Collin de Plancy, *Dictionnaire*, vol. 3.

Carroll, Lewis. 1971. *Alice in Wonderland; Through the Looking Glass; The Hunting of the Snark; Backgrounds/Essays in Criticism*. Ed. Donald J. Gray. New York.

Cavell, Stanley. 1979. *The Claim of Reason*. Oxford.

Collin de Plancy, J. A. S. 1821–22. *Dictionnaire critique des reliqueset des images miraculeuses*. 3 vols. Paris.

Doverdale, Miles. 1538. *The Newe Testament both Latine and Englyshe*.

De Linas, C. 1887. "Le Reliquaire de Pépin à Conques." *Gazette Archéologique*, 37–49, 291–97.

Dictionary of the Middle Ages. 1933. Ed. Matthew Bunson. New York.

Dulaure, J. A. 1903. *Die Zeugung*. Trans. and expanded by S. Krauss u. K. Reiskel. In *Beiwerke zum Studium der Anthropophyteia*. Leipzig.

Eliade, Mircea, ed. 1987. *Encyclopedia of Religion*. 16 vols. New York.

Enciclopedia Judaica Castellana. 1947–51. Ed. Eduardo Weinfeld. 10 vols. Mexico City:

Freud, Sigmund. 1909. "Analysis of a Phobia in a Five Year Old Boy." In *Standard Edition* 10.

———. 1939. *Moses and Monotheism*. In *Standard Edition* 23.

Fuchs, Eduard. 1921. *Die Juden in der Karikatur*.

Gaidoz, H. 1892–93, 1894–95. "Le grand Diable d'argent: Patron de la finance." *Mélusine: Recueil de Mythologie — Littérature populaire, traditions et usages*, vols. 6 and 7.

Gauthier, Marie-Madeleine. 1986. *Highways of the Faith: Relics and Reliquaries from Jerusalem to Compostela*. Trans. J. A. Underwood. Secaucus, N.J.

———. 1963. "Le Trésor de Conques." *Rouerge roman*, Saint-Léger Vauban (La nuit des temps).

Geary, Patrick J. 1978. *Furta Sacra: Thefts of Relics in the Central Middle Ages*. Princeton, N.J.

Greer, Donald M., Paul C. Mohl, and Kathy A. Sheley. 1982. "A Technique for Foreskin Reconstruction and Some Preliminary Results." *Journal of Sex Research*, n.s. 18, no. 4: 324–30.

Grimm, Jakob, and Wilhelm Grimm. 1882–1888. *Teutonic Mythology*. Trans. James Steven Stallybrass. 4 vols. London.

Guth, Klaus. 1970. *Guibert von Nogent und die hochmittelalterliche*. Kritik an der Reliquienverehrung. Augsburg.

Henkel, Albert, and Albrecht Schöne, eds. 1976. *Emblemata: Handbuch zur Sinnbildkunst des XVI. und XVII Jahrhunderts*. Stuttgart.

Kökeritz, H. 1953. *Shakespeare's Pronunciation*. New Haven, Conn.

Krauss, H. 1980. "Der Suaheli Arzt." *Münchener Medizinische Wochenschrift* 55, no. 10: 517.

Laqueur, Thomas. 1990. *Making Sex: Body and Gender from the Greeks to Freud*. Cambridge, Mass.

Laurent, Emile, and Paul Nagour. 1934. *Magica Sexualis: Mystic Love Books of Black Arts and Secret Sciences.* Trans. Raymond Sabatier. New York.

Lindschotten, J. H. von. 1598. *Das Ander Theil der orientalischen Indien.* Frankfurt.

Luther, Martin. 1883-. *Von Kaufshandlung und Wucher* (1524). In Luther, *Werke, Kritische Gesamtausgabe,* ed. J. K. F. Knaake et al. Weimar.

MacCulloch, J. A., and Vincent A. Smith. "Relics." In Hastings, *Encyclopedia of Religion and Ethics,* vol. 10.

Martin, Edward James. 1930. *A History of the Iconoclastic Controversy.* New York.

Maundeville, Sir John. 1889. *The Buke of John Maundeuill* (ca. 1400). Roxburghe Club. London.

Müller, Alphons Victor. 1907. *Die "hochheilige Vorhaut Christi" im Kult und in der Theologie der Papstkirche.* Berlin.

Nicquet, Honorat. 1870. *Titulus sanctae crucis.* New ed. Antwerp.

Panofsky, Erwin. 1953. *Early Netherlandish Painting.* Cambridge, Mass.

Plato. 1968. *Republic.* Trans. Allan Bloom. New York.

Reik, Theodor. 1949. *Fragments of a Great Confession.* New York.

Remondino, Peter Charles. 1891. *History of Circumcision from the Earliest Times to the Present: Moral and Physical Reasons for Its Performance.* Philadelphia.

Saintyves, Yves. 1912. *Les Reliques et les images légendaires.* Paris.

Samhaber, Ernst. 1964. *Das Geld: Eine Kulturgeschichte.* Munich.

Schapiro, Meyer. 1979. *Late Antique, Early Christian, and Medieval Art.* New York.

Seiden, Mortin Irving. 1967. *The Paradox of Hate: A Study in Ritual Murder.* London.

Shakespeare, William. 1973. *The Merchant of Venice.* Ed. Brents Stirling. Baltimore.

Shell, Marc. 1979. "Verbal Usury in *The Merchant of Venice.*" *Kenyon Review,* new series 1 (4): 65–92.

———. 1993. *Children of the Earth.* Oxford:

———. 1993. *Money, Language, and Thought: Literary and Philosophical Economies from the Medieval to the Modern Era* (1982). Reprint Baltimore:

Stoll, Otto. 1908. *Das Geschlechtsleben in der Völkerpsychologie.* Leipzig.

Taralon, J. 1966. *Trésors.* Paris.

Thiers, J. B. 1669. *Dissertation sur la sainte larme de Vendôme.* Paris.

Trachtenberg, Moises. 1989. "Circumcision, Crucifixion, and Anti-Semitism: The Antithetical Character of Ideologies and Their Symbols Which Contain Crossed Lines." Trans. P. Slotkin. *International Review of Psycho-Analysis* 16, no. 4: 459–71.

Veit, Ludwig. 1969. *Das Liebe Geld: Zwei Jahrtausende Geld- und Münzgeschichte.* Munich.

Waring, Mark. n.d. *Foreskin Restoration (Uncircumcision).* Listed and described *Amok: Fourth Dispatch.*

14 / On the (Under)Cutting Edge: Does Jewish Memory Need Sharpening?

Gil Anidjar

That he not fantasize his sexuality around a faucet [*Qu'il ne fantasme pas sa sexualité autour d'un robinet*].
HÉLÈNE CIXOUS, *"La venue à l'écriture"*

Histoires de Femmes

It is probably not possible to write a history of man's body and its pleasures because the historical record was created in a cultural tradition where no such history was necessary.
THOMAS LAQUEUR, *Making Sex, Body and Gender from the Greeks to Freud*

CIR-CON-SI, imprints itself in the hypothesis of wax.
JACQUES DERRIDA, *"Circumfession"*

A famous *Jewish* mnemonic device if there is one, circumcision,[1] insofar as it is male circumcision, could be called and *named* "une histoire d'hommes," that is, both a story of men and a fragment in the history of male bodies. In Rachel Biale's words, it is one of "those *mitzvot* [commandments] which are linked to gender and apply only to men" (1984:10). Circumcision would have thus happened to Hebrew and Jewish men. This seems unproblematic enough. One could further claim that the meaning of circumcision reflects or participates in constructing the meaning of male identity. Julia Kristeva, for example, states that circumcision is a separation of (and by) the male from the female: "what the male separates himself from, this other whom circumcision carves upon the genitals, is the other sex" (Kristeva 1980: 119; see also Eilberg-Schwartz 1992:24).[2] One could, however, suggest that these formulations articulate a certain forgetting. *Naming* circumcision as being *about* men or males ("ce dont le mâle se sépare") could thus be, however unintentionally, something of an *oubli*.[3] An analogy:

> "Culture" is one of the many *names* that one bestows upon the trace of being othered from nature, and by so *naming*, effaces the trace. (Spivak 1992:775; emphasis added)

The targets—or perhaps more adequately the horizons—of this *oubli*, in its inscription in and around circumcision, may then be argued to be "women." Though by arguing so, it is possible that having named myself, I will also have opened the *possibility* of forgetting and effacing who or what was also just named: "women." I shall soon return to this mode and possibility of forgetting, and will only note for now that what Gayatri Chakravorty Spivak calls naming, insofar as it is *also* (if not only) forgetting, will concern me throughout.

In order to read this recurring inscription of a memory (that may or may not offer guarantees) upon a Jewish body,[4] we will have to read Scriptures—read writing. The relationship between memory and writing is an ancient one, and some of the moments of its own remembering and forgetting can be read in Jacques Derrida's often quoted "Plato's Pharmacy." Derrida, who has written extensively on circumcision, writes in his "Circonfession" of leaving "nothing, if possible, in the dark of what relates me to Judaism [*ne rien laisser, si possible, dans l'ombre de ce qui me rapporte au judaïsme*]" (1993:154; 1991: 145); he reminds us that memory has often been read as "Jewish." "The people of memory"[5] is also the people of the Book, the same book in which marks of memory, and this peculiar mnemotechnic— circumcision—were inscribed. As one learns from Derrida, circumcision is there to be read simultaneously with the body that reads it, and with the bodies surrounding it too.[6] Jewish mnemonics, whatever they may include, will thus always be entangled in issues of gender. Yet memory "itself" (in Hebrew, *zikharon*) may only be as male (*zakhar*)[7] as the writings of circumcision(s).

The course of my tentative and uncertain readings toward memory, naming, writing, and inscribing has very quickly and provisionally been mapped. It must perhaps be added, though, that what follows will be a circular, yet discontinuous, at times possibly even *painful,* "ride" on a cutting edge (still nothing, in all likelihood, compared to the cutting blade). The driver — the circumciser, if you will — will not necessarily be who *he* seems. This will be so partly because, as hinted earlier, one must try to read the maleness of the inscribing and inscribed (male); but also because part of the question is whether *one* "drives," whether *one* inscribes, engraves, cuts, reads, names, and so on. The ride is therefore not going to be an exploration, an inquisitive and penetrating search toward a unified *explanation* of circumcision, nor an argument for "contextualization." Rather, it will be somehow chaotic, and nothing less than confident in any of the paths it follows. At that point, it could already be said that circumcision, having been named a memory practice and a male practice, inscribes with and onto this naming the forgetting and the remembering that constitute memory. If circumcision is both cut *and* inscription — as well as the inscription of a name, like "Jew" and "male" — it is difficult to see how there could ever be an opening for a smooth reading of these cuts. Possibly, and at times unfortunately, there will be some painful openings. Keep in mind, then, that reading a mode of naming that is also a forgetting is necessarily going to be a reading of disjunctions, folds, and openings: What it is claiming to be is not, nor can it ever be, the *whole* truth, just a few little cuts. Similarly, it will not be possible to simply move from a generality ("naming as forgetting" — our next stop) toward an example ("circumcision is a forgetting") or the other way around, from the particular of circumcision toward the general "rule" of a certain naming and inscribing. Rather than trying to make smooth connections with a cut that (also) disconnects, reading here will try to acknowledge the cuts as disjunctions *and* as connections, leaving inevitably little room for transitions. Reading a cut is necessarily and primarily going to be a reading of who cuts, who and where does one cut? Does *one* cut or many? Is a gesture of cutting (cutting off, cutting out) repeated (and/or avoidable) in the reading of a cut? What does this say about the "inside" or "outside" toward which bodies and body parts are thrown? What could a *smooth* reading of a cut mean? Or, to continue with a more responsible mode of transportation, is a smooth ride possible when *a child is being cut*? Wouldn't the smoothness painfully leave something out? Wouldn't it cut something out too? It is difficult to tell, although we could already note that any reading of circumcision, or its *naming,* will only hardly enable one to *forget* that someone did hold the knife, someone did also scream, even if, especially if, this is not the *whole* story.

Admitting that things will not necessarily "connect," then, we begin again on our route with a difficult detour toward a forgetting of the Jews, toward Jewish forgetting and the problem of naming. We will never be far, then, from circumcision. In *Heidegger and "the jews,"* Jean-François Lyotard (1988a; 1990) inscribes, names, remembers, and forgets. Lyotard tries to think forgetting, and makes use in his texts of many quotation marks. In view of the words that are thus marked — for example, "Français" (1988a:16), "écriture" (ibid.), "présence" (ibid.), "philosophes" (17) — we may be reminded of what Gayatri Chakravorty Spivak referred to as "Culture." In neither case, as both Lyotard and Spivak make clear, could it simply be said that there is an underlying "reality" behind or beyond these words — is there such a "thing" as "Culture" out there? — *nor* are these words simply "empty" words. By now it is the very sharp distinction between form and content that has been interrogated, *not* in order to privilege one term over the other but in order to show that the separating line that cuts between them is always quite complex and easily contaminated. Distinctions — between "Culture" and its "referent," for example — are always problematic even though they are also always at work. If the name (and the namer of) "Culture" forgets, erases the trace of its forgetting *and* builds upon it, what will concern me here is the provisional assumption that there is *now,* and in this particular case, an unretrievable, that is to say, the assumption that, here, the erasure *was* successful (the destruction complete).

Naming, even if it is self-naming — as in "reading as a woman" or "writing as a woman" — is not a one-sided, autonomous, or abstract activity. Indeed, the distinction — the same problematical distinction questioned earlier — that separates and cuts between "sides," and separates "objective categories" — *names* — from their surroundings or contexts is a distinction that masks its "object" when representing it, naming and inscribing it (effacing it,[8] forgetting it). It is therefore also a concrete gesture that may replicate, in ever complex ways, the gesture of violence done to human bodies. It is significant for us here that such violence "must" itself be forgotten in order to *both* eradicate *and* leave "traces": "this slaughter pretends to be without memory, without traces, and through this testifies again to what it slaughters: that there is the unthinkable, time lost yet always there" (Lyotard 1990a:23).

Can and should this forgetting be avoided? Can the *particular* naming that we have briefly explored partake of *less* forgetting? It seems it could not, and yet I would suggest that what Lyotard's text does is, on the one hand, quite different from upholding a notion of naming as remembering; and, on the other hand, the text is precisely trying to refrain from naming-and-forgetting: it tries *almost* not to name "les juifs." "Minuscule pour dire que ce n'est pas à une nation que je pense [Lower case, to indicate that I am not thinking of a nation]" (1988a:13; 1990:3), and closely following, "ce qu'il y a de plus réel dans les juifs réels [what is most real in real *j*ews (translation *slightly modified*)]." *Lower case, again*[9] (and again throughout). Whatever or whoever is named in Lyotard's text, it is possible that the last to be forgotten, that is, here, the last to be *named,* are, indeed, the Jews (capitalized), who are never *completely* named. It could indeed be said that the last time they were, they were *totally* forgotten, literally forgotten to death.

Remember, this process that reads the past, that *inscribes,* names, remembers, and forgets, is a complex one, and cannot be reduced to a swift formula. No simple necessities (rather, possibilities) are asserted here. Indeed, it is against the belief that representations and inscriptions *necessarily* prevent, or protect from, forgetting that Lyotard argues.

It is probably not surprising, especially in view of the English translation, that voices were raised against this text;[10] in ways similar, perhaps, others were raised against men "reading as women" (it is indeed a question of reading). One may have to recognize that these are very complex issues for which no credentials are ever sufficient.[11] Those texts that try almost not to name, not to forget—and nothing has been said here about their "success" and the meaning of its possibility—walk a fine line, a line that is, in many respects, a cutting edge.

Which brings me back to the "cutting around" (*circum-cisio*). It is already a mark (a name) of *oubli* then, and to claim that it is "une histoire de femmes" cannot but also risk the repetition, the recurrence, if simply inverted, of the specific forgetting that concerns me here. This forgetting reads and names (and therefore reinscribes) circumcision as a male practice that, insofar as it marks the male body, founds or confirms male identity. A significant way to try to avoid *that* forgetting is not to stop naming — as if it were possible — but to try *both* to show that whatever circumcision is, it is not male history (nor a story of men) *and* to refuse to state that it is *about* women. The expression "histoire de femmes" borrows from Lyotard's French and quotation marks understood as marking an interrogation of necessity ("never again!") and of righteousness.[12] To *let* silent women speak may too easily lead to — or, indeed, already be a sign of — a persistent refusal to hear within the same language game, a forgetting not unlike a silenc*ing* of women and their voices. It is therefore both forgetting and memory that need to be explored, especially in their reinscribed claims to "success." There may be no guarantees against the *possible* reinscription of silence precisely *while* recovering voices, while representing and speaking *for* "the forgotten" and *about* "the silenced."

To recapitulate, my purpose is to discuss possibilities. The possibility to address an *oubli* and the *oubliés* in a particular configuration of texts while trying to emphasize the silencing involved in one way or another. To read texts and inscriptions as (partly) marking and resisting *oubli*, as (partly) marking and resisting forgetting and oblivion. To attempt, following Lyotard's text, a different reinscription of *oubli* and its marks; to perhaps *cite* silence, if you will, differently. This, however, is a *local* attempt, not necessarily the ground for general claims. Yet because there is here in and with circumcision a recurrence of inscriptions, readings and writings, questions of historiography (one may want to say of "somatography" as well) can, and perhaps must, be raised. These questions and the citations that surround them will only doubtfully *open* the possibility of an alternative; they will never be far nor stand clear from the blade that has made the opening.

In the specific context of circumcision — again, as recurrence and reinscription — reading the texts cannot then be *independent* of how these texts have been read. Here, as elsewhere, there is little sense in trying to read them "as if" others had not read them before. It may be an issue of memory again.[13] At any rate, reading circumcision seems almost to demand such a "reading around." It is for that purpose that I have tried to keep in mind Foucault's "*analyse énonciative*," reading "a specific number of material carriers and techniques" that enable the conservation of texts (Foucault 1969:162). It is a reading of texts that follows enunciations, inscriptions—in this case, circumcision—in their conservation, in the different ways they fit into "groupements" and in their "récurrence" (163).[14]

Zipporah

Georgette Sultana Esther, or Mummy if you prefer...as though the daughter of Zipporah had not only committed the crime of my circumcision but one more still, later, the first playing the kickoff, the original sin against me, but to reproduce itself and hound me, call me into question, me, a whole life long, to make her avow, her, in me.   JACQUES DERRIDA, "Circumfession"

And-it-happened-on-the-way at-a-spending-the-night-place, and encountered-him YHWH and-he-tried to-cause-him-to-die. And-she-took Zipporah a-flint and-she-cut-off the-foreskin-of her-son and-she-touched to-his-feet, and-she-said truly a-'hatan-of-bloods you to-me. And-he-desisted from-him, then she-said 'hatan-of-bloods for-the-circumcisions.   —Exod. 4:24–26[15]

In her comparative reading of the text of Exodus 4 with the Osiris and Isis story, Ilana Pardes seems to dismiss as irrelevant the possibility that the couple the story sets up is not only a husband-wife couple but also a mother-son ("some have suggested that Zipporah addresses her son" writes Pardes, 1992:85). For Pardes, what is important to emphasize in both stories is the heroic role of the mother, which can be read as a remnant of the prominent role of a goddess. It is the role of the mother as heroine that concerns Pardes most crucially. She argues:

> What Freud neglects to take into account both in his depiction of the primal horde and in his treatment of the "family romance" is that women (and mothers in particular)—despite or rather because of their powerlessness—may have an important role in teaching the weak and threatened young sons how to trick hostile oppressors, how to submit to paternal will and at the same time usurp the father's position. (82)

Many points are raised in this statement, yet it may already call for a Nietzschean critique of the notion of powerlessness: "It should be kept in mind that 'strong' and 'weak' are relative concepts" (Nietzsche 1974:118). This statement, as I reproduce it here, may not provide for a complex and differentiated reading of the power dynamics of the kind Nietzsche taught. Nonetheless, it may suffice to make us wonder about Pardes's assertion. Indeed, it is simply not clear what defines the powerlessness of Zipporah in Pardes's reading, although this "powerlessness" does serve to endow *Moses* with a central role: according to Pardes, it is for *his* sake that Zipporah acts ("We have here a violent persecutor, a wife saving her husband" [1992:91]). Although she mentions how Moses is "passive and dumbfounded," and how "he seems paralyzed by the anxieties and doubts that haunt him at this liminal phase in his career" (84), Pardes maintains the wife-husband relation as the only relevant relationship rather than considering the significance of a situation in which a mother relates to, and possibly protects (only?) her son. Pardes's move surprisingly comes after her having admitted that "strictly speaking the identity of [God's] victim is undetermined" (84; see also 92, where Pardes writes of the "blurred demarcation between Moses and his son in Exodus 4"). For Pardes, Zipporah's circumcision "is a blood covenant, which reconfirms the marital bond between Zipporah and her revived spouse" (86).

What remains puzzling, then, is the way Pardes's feminist reading of Zipporah's heroism doubles it with Moses, who is insisted upon as *the* central character—central because the whole action is still seen as revolving around him—of this short narrative. Significantly, the narrative we are reading begins with verse 24 and ends with verse 26, and the name of Moses is never mentioned.[16] The only explanation for the insistence on his presence is the repeated forgetting of a detail: the father and husband (Moses) does not *have* to be part of the story. It remains undecidable if he is there at all. It is the mother who circumcises her son, and possibly—I insist, *possibly*—she addresses her son by reiterating that he is hers *by blood*: "For you are my bridegroom of blood."[17] In anthropological terms, the circumcision and the assertion would mean that in order for the child to be hers, to be part of her tribe, he needs to be circumcised by (the brother of) the mother (see Morgenstern 1963). I write the male actor introduced by anthropologists in parentheses because in our story he does not appear more than Moses, so his putative presence might very well be a consequence of the male appropriation (remember Nietzsche) of a women-instituted ritual. This anthropological insight, which somehow emphasizes the link between the mother and the son by highlighting the assertion to the "bridegroom," is strenghtened by Vincent Crapanzano's description of a circumcision ritual in Morocco. Crapanzano states that, at least in Morocco, "there is frequently a connection between circumcision and marriage" and that, for example, "in some areas of Morocco the boy about to be circumcised is called a bridegroom and the circumcision itself the boy's 'first marriage'" (1992:271).

It might therefore be more helpful to follow Pardes with a difference and read the story of Isis, Osiris, and Horus synchronically rather than diachronically, with Osiris/Horus as *both* husband *and* son, not as first husband *then* son. If we do recognize the relationship of Zipporah and her child as parallel with that of Isis and her son/husband, we might even see in it another version of myths of societies that describe women as the primary or sole instigators of the practice of circumcision *upon the bodies of their husbands and sons.*[18] For Pardes, this synchronic reading does not appear to be a possibility since she holds that Osiris is Horus, the husband, *not* the child. Yet nothing legitimates this conflation *more* than the reading I have suggested, so that it is difficult to understand why, within Pardes's project and given its recognition of the role played by Zipporah, it would simply be dismissed rather than affirmed.

Along with some biblical readings, Pardes's reading may have something to do with what Jean-Pierre Vernant said of memory. According to Vernant, memory is "the progressive conquest by man of his individual past, as history constitutes for the social group the conquest of its collective past" (1985 [1965]:109).[19] The story of the rape of Dinah and its consequences (Gen. 33:18–34:31) is the horrible story of a conquest (the conquest of the city of Shechem), a story that has itself been "conquered" (remembered) in a peculiar way. It has served as prooftext to the legal claim that circumcision was one of the means to enter into the covenant that defines the Hebrew, and later the Jewish, people. Whatever the reasons for the choice of this particular text as prooftext, we shall soon observe that this choice involves some kind of a misreading. Such misreadings, intentional or not, happen often, if not all the time, and concern me here only insofar as one of the central issues raised by the text is, in addition to circumcision, marriage. Meir Sternberg, a close reader of this biblical story, insists on defining the extremely efficient "art of persuasion" of the biblical narrator. Sternberg also claims that the narrator has a clear "goal" (1985:445); in this particular case, it is to present us ("us," the readers defined by this skillful narrator by means of "control strategies"

[444]) with a "balanced response" when we are faced with the violent events of the text (445). Yet, in passing, and with a recurring insight, Sternberg also shows that the story depicts the attempt to establish an alliance by marriage, and the failure to realize this alliance. Sternberg points out that this failure was in fact inevitable, for never "would [Jacob's sons] consider an exogamous marriage" (459). Repeatedly, Sternberg emphasizes the "horror of exogamy" (464, 465, 472, 475) that defines the relations to the "uncircumcised," a horror that will ultimately lead to the murder of the rapist and aspiring husband along with all the males of the city. It thus remains difficult to state that circumcision is the condition of possibility for a marriage into the Hebrew tribe since at no point in the text are we able to see the seriousness of the possibility of such an alliance. Jacob's sons never seem to have intended such a marriage ever to come about.[20]

Let us then just note that here too notions of kinship, the possibility of marriage, and the practice of circumcision are juxtaposed and seem to inform each other. Added to the story of a mother circumcising, we might be able to see how forgetful we have been in thinking that women did not have, did not participate in, *this* story, and why.

Abraham

... all forms of marking within which so-called human language,
as original as it might be, does not allow us to "cut" once and for
all where we would in general like to cut.... We know less than ever
where to cut — either at birth or at death. And this also means that
we never know, and never have known how to *cut up* a subject.
JACQUES DERRIDA, " 'Il faut bien manger' ou le calcul du sujet"

In his essay "L'oubli et la tradition," Paul Zumthor attempts to draw similarities between different conceptions of memory and the way they are embodied in the Middle Ages in Europe. He argues that whether individual or collective, memory is concerned with "the coherence of a subject in the appropriation of her/his duration" (1988:105). The importance of coherence in memory cannot be overstated. Even if not all "effets cohésifs" (ibid.) are the result of memory, and even if one could imagine a memory that would not strive for such coherence, circumcision, as a practice almost inherently linked with memory, certainly seems to withstand the comparison with "tradition" as it is described by Zumthor in more ways than the two just mentioned: "Forgetting is a mechanism used by an hegemonic culture in order to exclude from tradition elements of the collective memory deemed undesirable" (106).

What is important to note in Zumthor's description is that any assertion about or from memory ultimately involves (the risk of) some negation of the present moment, even a "blindness" to it. Such blindness produces the possibility of a new coherence. Zumthor names this process "remembrance."

The addition of necessary forgetting, that is, the selection that can create the gap of creativity leading to an ever new integrity, is likened by Zumthor to "an effacement of any element of memory which could ease an exclusive appropriation" (115), "a putting to death of the fragile personal experience" (117), all for the sake of the community.[21]

Much like Zumthor, who draws from different periods in order to describe the one period and to name the community he is most concerned with, I am pursuing analogies that are of course relevant only to a limited extent. At this stage, and to conform to a recurring image of memory used by Augustine, it may be no more than a matter of "assembling," "collecting" (*Confessions*, X, 11). The themes that appear in Zumthor's description seem relevant in that they highlight the violence of the forgetting involved precisely in remembering specific moments and characters. With this in mind, biblical stories, particularly those dealing with circumcision, may reveal circumcision as belonging to a horizon that is more complex than a *memory* practice. Again, what concerns me here are those elements of the texts that must be forgotten in order to read circumcision as "une histoire d'hommes." That this forgetting also involves a reading of circumcision as somewhat autonomous (disconnecting between nothing?) from a signifying structure in which it is necessarily located seems to be quite plausible by now. My purpose, at any rate, in what follows is not to claim any *new* reading of the story of Abraham. Rather, I simply wish to indicate possible horizons for the different elements of the story.

Having suggested that there are intricate relationships between circumcision and kinship, and between memory and coherence, we may now have to put aside the possibilities of a different coherence, regarding the centrality of male characters, that Zipporah and Dinah could have provided. Indeed, in the words of one scholar, "Abraham represents the adoption of patriarchal rules after separating from 'settled' or 'matriarchal' kin" (Prewitt 1990:32).

Stressing the connection between fertility and circumcision, Howard Eilberg-Schwartz argues that circumcision "symbolized the fertility of the initiate as well as his entrance into and ability to perpetuate a lineage of male descendants" (1990:143). The story of Abraham, as part of the priestly ideology that produced (or re-produced) it, is the mark of an "overwhelming preoccupation with reproduction and intergenerational continuity between males" (144). Presenting what may be called the "point of view of the natives," Eilberg-Schwartz describes how in this male-centered ideology "one must have a member to be a member" (145). This "principle" is the basis for a centralization of the activity of procreation in male hands, confirmed in fact by the covenant of circumcision between God and Abraham in which "fertility is a central issue" (147). The analogies, synonyms, and metaphors linking the world of agriculture, male progeny, and fertility in general, all confirm how "the themes of harvesting a fruit tree and the ripening of fruit are treated as analogous to the harvesting of a woman and the maturing of one's children" (159). Eilberg-Schwartz thus shows that circumcision is not a *recognition* of male descent and male dominance but an *assertion*, a (re-)production of this domination. Such an assertion needs to take place, explains Eilberg-Schwartz, because "paternal identity is never as obvious" as maternal identity (163).

Circumcision is therefore not, nor could it be, only a story of men. Rather, it is part of *making* procreation, genealogy, and, finally, history, a story of men. It may be a male institution, but it involves women at all times for it "also establishes an opposition between men and women. Women cannot bear the symbol of the covenant" (171). Circumcision also represents the "separation of boys from their mothers before and during the circumcision ceremonies" (173). In that respect, circumcision, as Eilberg-Schwartz remarks, is linked, functionally at least, to sacrifice (175). With this Eilberg-Schwartz provides an interesting link with Nancy Jay's work.[22]

In her study of sacrifice and its links to kinship structures, Jay sets out to show that "sacrificial ritual enacts patrilineal descent.... Patrilineal kin know they are kin *because* they sacrifice together; they become patrilineal kin by so doing" (1992:xiii). What this means is that "descent reckoned solely through men is not naturally given but must be socially and religiously created" (xiv).[23] Equally important to understand are the complex relations existing between sacrifice and other signifying practices in the social organization, relations that institute, confirm, or reshape themselves in binary oppositions. Taking the example of the Patriarch narratives, Jay argues that as androcentric as they are, they also include a "continuing tension between descent from fathers and descent from mothers" (97), that is, "a recognition of descent from women" (99). The resolution of the conflict created by this recognition is one "in which sacrifice plays a crucial role" (101). Sacrifice, performed by the father, confirms the inside/outside dichotomy articulated in the relationship between the mothers and the sons (102). The sacrifice of Isaac, for example, is an assertion that Isaac "received his life not by birth from his mother but from the hand of his father" (ibid.). By contrast, the story of Isaac himself, who did not sacrifice, is a story in which "the descent conflict . . . is played out to its full disastrous consequences" (ibid.). According to Jay, then, sacrifice is clearly an affirmation of patriliny.

To conclude temporarily, we can note that these readings too emphasize structural similarities between kinship organization and gender dichotomies, and between sacrifice and circumcision.

The institution of incest, as Edmund Leach shows, is another of the major "tools" that constitute the binary oppositions such as inside/outside that we have just encountered (1969:10–11). Here too the story of Abraham serves as a striking example of an organization of oppositions where the choice between endogamy and exogamy is embodied. Such embodiments in the narrative are found around the characters of Lot (Leach 1969:19) and Pharaoh (Rosenberg 1986:78). Here too we see how the covenant of circumcision is part of a larger concern for descent and genealogy, what Joel Rosenberg, in a structuralist reading, calls "the genealogical framework of the cycle" (1986:85). At the core of this cycle are the two covenants (Gen. 15:1–20, 17:1–27, the latter being the covenant of circumcision). Between the two covenants is the "expulsion and rescue of Hagar," the mother of Abraham's first child, Ishmael (see Rosenberg 1986:84, fig. 2). This expulsion, argues Rosenberg, is extremely important since it inversely prefigures the destiny of Abraham's descent, most importantly, in Egypt (95).

Rosenberg enables us, therefore, to remember how central Hagar is in the story (see also Trible 1984, chapter 1), and how the production of inside/outside categories also requires that these categories be at work *within* themselves. This is why (in structuralist terms) Hagar's son, Ishmael, had to be circumcised as well. For only what is inside can be defined as inside, *or* outside. Analogously, only a woman who was first "kind" (Hagar) can later be defined as "other kind" (Leach 1969:11). Hagar is not just *part* of the story, since genealogy is defined through and with her.[24] There is no necessity to subscribe to the famous Lévi-Straussian assertion that women function like language, as means of communication and exchange; rather, we can see how central—literally central in Rosenberg's diagram—women are in the narrative. This is certainly not to deny the relations of domination and oppression that are inscribed in the text, but to recognize that these relations are much more complex and intricate than they might be remembered if—and as long as—they stay "des histoires d' hommes."

Jean-Thierry Maertens's cross-cultural reading of circumcision (1978) is another confirmation of the links made between this practice and the production of the law of incest.[25] Issues closely bound to memory recur here, issues of control, appropriation, and identity—as they did in the reading of Zipporah, which Maertens also mentions. Reminiscent of Kristeva's "carving of the other sex," Maertens sees the cutting of the male body as an inscription of Otherness. This cut produces the self and its phantasms that control this incontrollable Otherness ("this Other, which I do not control in me more than I control it in the other" [45]). At stake in this control is, of course, not just the individual, but the "cohésion sociale" (97). Circumcision therefore *both* asserts the difference (identity) between the sexes *and* erases the institution of this difference. The erasure is confirmed by pushing circumcision away from the time of marriage, locus of the "horizontalité des rapports entre sexes" (115).

One can see—and one should note the amount of *violent* forgetting involved—how loaded the assertion is, that circumcision is a "male" event. This assertion indeed replicates only one aspect of the movement that characterizes its institution. It erases in a recurring gesture that the "discours phallique" turns the uncontrollable alterity of an Other (*Autre*) into an other (*autre*), that is, into a partner within an economy of the same, even if it is also a relationship of domination. Yet "phallic discourse" also "fills the remaining gap of difference by throwing between the two partners a female body" (132). The result of this dual movement of control of any alterity and of effacement of gaps and differences through violence is replicated in the circumcised who is "cut off from the Other within him in order to be able to measure/erase the difference which founds society" (ibid.).

What is important to note is the way in which Maertens presents circumcision, within a certain Lacanian framework, as one of the rituals that institute the "corps féminin" as a mediator for men to speak "among themselves." To ignore the mediator, the presence *in male discourse* of the feminine element, is to forget this element. Not to forget this feminine element does not mean that the "reality" of women has been recovered, but it does show how male discourse does not *forget* women even when this discourse attempts to produce a ritual that is "about men."

Genealogies

This is because knowledge is not made for understanding; it is made for cutting.
MICHEL FOUCAULT, "Nietzsche, Genealogy, History"

The question is not: what meaning does that inscription carry within it, but what cultural apparatus arranges this meeting between instrument and body, what interventions into the ritualistic repetition are possible?
JUDITH BUTLER, *Gender Trouble*

Circumcision, we have seen, can and has been interpreted as founding or at least confirming the law of incest and the regulation of reproduction. Within this interpretative framework, which I have tried to generally follow until now, circumcision repeatedly draws the limit that separates the mother from the child, nature from culture, the male from the female. This male gesture, understood as male oppression or as "phallic discourse" is thus considered as founding the cultural community. Continuing along these lines a little further, we could add the subsequent view that circumcision feminizes the male.[26] Indeed, as I mentioned earlier, such a view has been advanced, thus showing — but who would doubt by now? — that circumcision *was, when all is said and done,* a male story, a male, androcentric practice that feminized the male by inscribing the feminine onto the penis. This, of course, also confirmed that circumcision is (to be) read first, and perhaps only, from a male perspective.

If these readings have helped to show both written and bodily inscriptions as sites of memory, there remains (at least) one question:

How different are they from the readings of Julia Kristeva and Rachel Biale, from readings that "acknowledged" circumcision as "male"? Do any of these readings *avoid* the recurrence of the marginalization of the "other sex" now "remembered"? *Or* is it conceivable that they constitute also *re*inscriptions of this marginalization? In other words, doesn't their remembering, their naming of circumcision, bear similarities to what they themselves describe as inscriptions of male patriarchy, examples of which they found in genealogies and in circumcision?

In order to begin to answer, we must ask what else a "feminization" of circumcision has come to mean by now or, in Joan Scott's words, "in whose interest is it to control or contest meanings?" (1988:5) There are now a few available reasons that could account for Zipporah's circumcision. One would be that the will of her tribe is at work, making her do what she does. This reading leaves God aside since we do not know what God—if it is God at all and not some demon[27]— wants, nor whom he wants to kill. We could reject this first possibility and see Zipporah instead as an exception to the "universal" rule, since it is a "universal" that only men are actively involved in circumcision, that only men participate in the ritual.[28] A third possibility, alluded to earlier, would be that Zipporah's circumcising her son is simply an act of protection of a mother toward her son, an almost instinctual, maternal act. All alternatives, though, stay within a narrative that sees man as "intruding"—much like YHWH in the Zipporah story—into the first "natural" couple. Since circumcision is one of the most ancient and meaningful human practices, "we" might very well have touched upon one of the earliest traces of culture. Finally, it can thus become "well known" that nothing is more "natural" or "originary" than the relationship between a mother and a child (see Maertens 1978:15). The extent to which such (perhaps not so) careful phrasing still belongs to a historical "search-for-origins" project cannot be overlooked.[29] The way this project temporalizes culture bears similarities to the narrative that articulates the male penis as the surface upon which the feminine cut is inscribed. Indeed, as Judith Butler has pointed out, this "temporalizing" project involves a specific reading of the past, produced by "a strategic tactic within a narrative that, by telling a single, authoritative account about an irrecoverable past, makes the constitution of the law appear as a historical inevitability" (1990:36).

I am not denying that the strategy (or strategies) described here also produces readings that can hardly be dismissed or undervalued. As I hope to have made clear, it would be difficult to inscribe an *entirely* clean cut between readings of circumcision. We may in fact quite precisely begin to see that they are not so distinct from the discourses and categories they criticize. Insofar as they keep their eyes focused on the "male aspect" of circumcision "itself" and therefore read (and reinscribe) the dominant, the first, the male, they do forget about "the rest," the "etc." even (especially?) when claiming to "recover it," making it an "earlier," a "repressed" or "oppressed." Theirs is a strategy that reifies the identity of the "male" out of which it tries to rescue, or simply recognize, "the rest." If, however, the past is—with the biblical text—a more complex text than we have allowed until now, it may be the cut and what it throws out, indeed, the inscription of dichotomies such as nature/culture, male/female, and so on, and the lack of autonomy of each "category" in relation to its "other"—including the dichotomy past/present—that had to be forgotten in order to read, somewhat univocally, the text and the cut as a site of memory.[30]

We have been warned by Judith Butler's articulation of the strategic use of the past. Now Nietzsche's dictum "only that which has no history is definable" (1989:80) may become most helpful. Indeed, when we read the links between circumcision and procreation, we seemed to believe that "procreation" is a clear and well-defined notion that has no history, the "most natural" thing ever.

Howard Eilberg-Schwartz claims that the insistence on procreation as well as on circumcision in the Hebrew Bible is the product of the priestly ideology (1990:146ff.). Following the conclusions of biblical scholarship, this ideology is also the main source for the early chapters of Genesis, which include God's command to "be fruitful and multiply." Regardless, however, of this historical and philological reading, it remains to be seen whether or not there is in this saying—and thus in the notion of reproduction in the text—anything "natural"; it remains to be seen why the Torah

> commanded human beings to engage in sexual reproduction, an activity much like eating or sleeping in which they—along with the members of every animal species—would have engaged anyway?...By interpreting the primordial blessing as legal statute, rabbinic texts may

have altered the meaning of Scripture in no small measure. Yet in so doing the rabbis incorporated the essentially covenantal significance of Gen.1:28 into the Halakhah, *correctly* evaluating the biblical message of "be fertile and increase." (Cohen 1989:164–65; emphasis added)

Cohen is clearly reading procreation as naturally valuable, which explains his judging the rabbis' interpretation as "correct." And yet, at no point is there room to make such a distinction between nature ("sleeping and eating") and culture ("legal statute"). Such a distinction, which interestingly enough the eminent structuralist Edmund Leach does *not* make in his analysis of Genesis, would be based on deciding whether God is a cultural or a natural agent. This distinction would also depend on whether she is setting up nature or culture (Cohen does mention how the commandment was repeatedly linked to the beginnings and condition of civilization). Whichever way we understand the commandment (whether it is or is not a commandment, see Cohen 1989:14), there is no univocal way to grasp what it requires in terms of the division of labor in reproduction.[31] The later intensive discussions about who must fulfill the commandment of procreation attest to the difficulty (see Biale 1984:198–218 and Cohen 1989:144–54).

It is precisely the difficulty of defining and evaluating procreation in the Bible that prompts us, therefore, to read the purpose it might serve in a text like Genesis. Genealogies introduced in this text will ultimately lead to Sarah's barrenness (we learn, before knowing little more than Abraham's name, that his wife Saraï is barren [Gen. 12: 30]).[32] Procreation, in the text, can then also be read as a (perfect?) setup. It "shows" how "natural" it is to have a child, and how the woman is responsible for the fulfillment of this "natural" order. One can still question, though, the *value* of the commandment to be fruitful. What has happened for it to be good? Is this goodness intrinsic to the act of procreation? The commandment and the recurring lists of genealogies show that we are entering a discourse that already (re-) produces a value system. Yet by refraining to ask "what was earlier?" we may be able to remember, as it were, what negotiations and mediations organize this production. By resisting the reading of procreation as *necessarily* "good" for everybody, as was the case in, for example, later rabbinic commentaries,[33] we might be able to perceive what Stephen Greenblatt calls "places of negotiation and exchange"[34] that surround the issue of procreation in the specific context of the biblical texts we have read. We might thus not take procreation — nor the division of labor it includes — for granted even in these texts.

There is, in fact, quite an amount of anxiety in the text over the begetting of children. We do not know to what extent Abraham is anxious, but God is certainly very eager to remind him that she "will make him a great nation" (Gen. 12:2, 7). There are, however, other reasons for wanting children:

> My Lord Yahweh, Abram replied, what do you intend to give me? I go childless. Then Abram said, See you have given me no descendants; some man of my household will be my heir. (Gen. 15:2–3)

An issue of property worries Abraham. In spite of her recurring promises, God has not *given* him anything yet. And his property may end up with someone of lower social status.[35] The economic and legal notion of covenant, of a binding contract, then becomes much more relevant, if also difficult to read. It is at times a gift ("What do you intend to *give* me?" asks Abraham), which the person who walks between the two halves of the sacrificed animals (here God, often a monarch) commits herself or himself to give (Gen. 15).[36] There are no stated conditions to the reception of this gift. At other times, the covenant constitutes, rather than a gift, a two-way contract that legalizes an exchange; it often binds a vassal to a king. It is significant to note that Abraham never seems to enter into the second kind of covenant, which would explain why it is God who must remember the covenant.[37] Further, the covenant seems to require an act on Abraham's part, yet this act is not a form of payment but a sign (rather than a signature) of the contract itself. For Abraham to produce this sign, this reminder, is not yet to *sign* a contract, at least not unproblematically so. To the same extent, the participants in the contract, if not its direct signatories then, need to be remembered as well. For example, in instituting the covenant, God *renames* Sarah (from her previous name Saraï) as well as Abraham (from Abram). Sarah's role and its consequences for reading circumcision can hardly be emphasized enough. Moreover, there is no need to expand on the (cultural? natural?) necessity for a child to be born in order for him to be circumcised. And if it is a child, that is, a boy or a girl, ownership — patrilineal or matrilineal — seems to still have to be asserted, in one way or another. Indeed, it is precisely *Sarah* who makes this assertion of ownership, showing that she is the most actively concerned with progeny, participating also (for better or for worse) in the exchange of Hagar and requesting "to be built" through her. The importance of Sarah's role has already been recognized in feminist readings,[38] but the link with property and its consequences for reading *this* covenant of circumcision would still need to be read. The fact that "Saraï never actually accepts Ishmael as her own" (Prewitt 1990:13; Jay 1992: 98ff.) and thus refuses to appropriate the child hardly leaves Abraham as the *sole* participant in the play of negotiations (gift, promise, or contract) that constitute "procreation" and that bind God to Abraham and to Sarah, Sarah to Abraham, both to the children and to Hagar, and so on.

We may recall another instance of a contract in which the initiative does not necessarily belong to the entering party. In the story of the rape of Dinah, as we saw, whichever interpretations were given for the intent of Jacob's sons, the circumcision was not sufficient to enable entry into the Hebrew tribe. An additional dimension of Dinah's story is that the negotiations between the Hebrews and the Shechemites focus on the possibility of sharing not only women ("Ally yourselves with us by marriage; give us your daughters and take our daughters for yourselves" [Gen. 34:9]), but also property ("Will not their livestock, their goods and all their cattle belong to us, if only we agree to let them stay with us?" [Gen. 34:23]).

The issue of land ownership (or mastery; see Cohen 1989:1–66), it must again be remembered, already appears in the very command to be fruitful and multiply (Gen. 1:28). Conquest—if that is what it is—is by now a familiar theme in our memory search and we should not be surprised at its appearance here. At any rate, there is in "be fruitful" an issue of ownership and of control ("be masters"), a dimension that was not forgotten by Rashi, the eleventh-century Bible commentator, who read the Creation narrative as God's assertion of her ownership over the land, making her the landlord who could dispose of it as she pleases.

With circumcision and the covenant tentatively and possibly set within an economic structure, we see that the "participants" can be identified only by deciding what the relevant system of meaning is. What remains is that we do not know what the covenant "itself" *is*. Its complexity thus forecloses the possibility of "understanding" it simply as a contract between Abraham and God. It is a moment in an economy of ownership, an economy in which all participants negotiate, and in which Zipporah's own assertion of ownership ("You are a bridegroom of blood to *me*") becomes more likely and understandable (if not understood). It is well recognized how economics and gender are related, which is why more of the negotiations and the participants must be addressed, something I have tried to begin to do here.

We seem to have wandered far away from circumcision "itself" only to have established, arguably, little more than the well-known truism that nomad and seminomad societies, such as the nascent Hebrew tribe, make a vital link between issues of economic property and procreation. And yet, remembering that this wandering was prompted by a search into the value of procreation, we might read more closely how, already in the Bible, procreation does *not* appear before a background of "nature." Nor do procreation and circumcision *necessarily* have anything more to do with incest than with economics in which women are not "simply" exchanged but also participate.[39] We have read how crucial it was in the arguments we have examined to link the two (sets of) practices of incest (and procreation) with circumcision, in order to emphasize the foundational dimension of both. This connection can hardly be taken for granted, especially considering the appropriation of culture it bestows on "phallic discourse."

A feminist project that involves a recovery, a retrieval (a remembering) of the voices of women may then have been reinscribing these voices as unretrievably "past." The assumptions at work in the writings of scholars who engage this project, some of whom were mentioned earlier, revolve around successful oppression and successful silencing, so successful indeed that all there is left is "male speech" or "phallic discourse." Such assumptions appear in Ilana Pardes's assertion, quoted earlier, that Zipporah was indeed oppressed, and therefore had to save her husband. The possibility that God would be encountering a woman and her son (her property) alone in the desert, without a husband, a man, being present is almost unimaginable. Freud's famous passage in *Moses and Monotheism* about the "distortion of a text" being "not unlike murder" is quoted by Pardes, and it may explain how, in her own text, it is not "history that has been severely curtailed" (Pardes 1992:97) but the possibility to imagine a different kind of status, a different kind of story for Zipporah, and for "history."

"To put in another place," as Freud describes the text distortion, is exactly what the art of memory, described by Frances Yates (1966), does. But it is still a long way from forgetting as *oubli*, as oblivion. Only when something is, indeed, "put in another place" can it be murdered and *oublié*, can it become unretrievable, absolutely lost. The question remains whether it was ever the case in the texts addressed. Another explanation for Pardes's reading, then, might well be determined by her appropriation of what she names Bakhtin's "*absolute* past" (Pardes 1992:95; emphasis added).[40] Indeed, it is a reading of forgetting as *oblivion* that warrants statements like "it would require some of Zipporah's magical powers to deliver fully a history that has been severely curtailed." (97) Naming the past in this way would be then forgetting how *inoubliable* it *also* is. "Not unlike murder."

Far from univocal, the discourse that (re-)institutes or confirms the many values at work in the texts is leaving traces of heterogeneity, of anxiety, of doubts, as well as recurring reassertions about procreation, ownership, and so on. These traces of struggles, these assertions of jurisdictions are also traces of *oublis*. We (readers) could think that to forget them is up to us, voluntarily helping them glide onto oblivion. Remembering *chronologically*, we were bound to read procreation as independent of any value, as simply God's ex nihilo command in harmony with nature. Reading genealogically, on the other hand, multiplies possibilities. Circumcision now appears as God's assertion, as the priestly writer's (re-)inscription, but also as a different kind of covenant, as a contract and a mark of ownership. Such is, in fact, the circumcision Zipporah *performs* upon her son. In contrast, a reading that sought to retrieve from her story a representation of the original mother-son first couple left intact the assumption that there is a nature upon which culture simply asserts itself (of the kind mentioned earlier: "the emergence of symbolic thought must have required that women, like words, should be things that were exchanged" [Lévi-Strauss quoted in Butler 1990:41]), and the fact that this culture has the form of male oppression. To assume, for example, that motherhood is "natural" might be to forget how it is always already embedded within a set of cultural practices, among which circumcision takes a notable place. Motherhood, as circumcision, is not originally significant (or readable) upon the "natural" body of women; rather, motherhood and circumcision participate in constructing and preserving the always already cultural bodies of women as bodies of mothers. In Judith Butler's words:

> Any theory that asserts that signification is predicated upon the denial or repression of a female principle ought to consider whether that femaleness is really external to the cultural norms by which it is repressed. In other words, on my reading, the repression of the feminine does not require that the agency of repression and the object of repression be ontologically distinct. (1990:93)

Reading the text within the "incest" economy, that is, a phallogocentric view of the institution of culture, may thus reproduce another forgetful mode of reading. Showing Pardes's forgetting was therefore also to reinscribe the "incest" economy within which circumcision "had" to be read. Reading synchronically the son as husband/father, as I have, was in fact strikingly reminiscent of what Jacques Derrida describes in *Glas* as the Hegelian *relève* (*Aufhebung*, following Derrida's translation), a structure that produces "a certain natural family in relieving [*relevant*] already another family more natural still" (Derrida 1986:37). In the Bible, in order to read (cultural) incest as being instituted upon (natural) motherhood, one must indeed remain, like Hegel, with "eyes fixed on a network of philosophemes" (ibid.).

This erection of male autonomy — the realm of the father and the son — is the erection of domination, erection of Babel, as it were, made out of stone, the same stone perhaps that also cuts Moses' son's foreskin. Derrida, however, strikingly shows the difficulty involved in reading the autonomy, the domination, the product of a male *Aufhebung* as entirely successful when he asks: "How does the stone become a child?" (39).

Abraham's knife and Zipporah's stone do not give birth to a child nor to a culture. They are always already within an economy of nature and culture. Without such an economy, there would be no knife, no child. To lose sight of the constant intertwining of the terms would leave only a pile of ruins.[41]

Circumcision, as we saw, is never "decontextualized" in the different narratives we have read. Many similar elements do tend to reappear in each of these narratives. "One" of them, if it makes any sense to speak of one, or indeed if it makes any sense to speak of distinct elements, is the recurrence of "femmes inoubliables." By reading (around) the texts as sites of memory we seemed at first to have recovered the female prominence in some of the biblical narratives dealing with circumcision. However, "recovering" the women in the stories was also to read/reinscribe male domination, with the oblivion in which it had thrown women. By remembering male domination as always successful, one runs the risk of reproducing its premises: there *was* forgetting, there *were* mothers and sons, there *was* earlier. Yet what has been suggested by emphasizing forgetting was its failure to achieve itself. To rephrase Julia Kristeva's statement: "The male, if he exists, does not separate himself, does not ever exist separated from this other." *It was not "simply" a matter of remembering "the Female" or "Woman", but of questioning the implicit assumption that the women in the texts could be absolutely forgotten, as if they weren't (aren't) there, "constitutive" one could say, of/in "men."* That "men" had wanted (want) to forget them and had tried (try) to produce "patriarchy," "patrilinearity," "male domination," and "male speech," that is, to create a world of their "own," has been amply (still is) shown. That this "own" was (is) never successful—which emphatically *does not* mean it was (is) not murderous—but also never "male," has *not* fallen into oblivion. The failure has "merely" (and murderously) been forgotten.

"Men"—who by now deserve quotation marks too—were (are) never "by themselves" however much and violently they might have tried. Circumcision has always remained "une histoire de femmes."

Who Is a Jew?

Nothing in man—not even his body—is sufficiently stable to
serve as the basis for self-recognition or for understanding other
men.   MICHEL FOUCAULT, *"Nietzsche, Genealogy, History"*

Contracts, negotiations, conquests, and assertions of ownership are all notions that make the word *limit* very porous, if only because they involve a constant reshaping of whatever limits there might be. By reading how a specific practice of memory is all but enclosed within its "own" limits, how it is overdetermined and diacritical, I hope to have shown how dealing with this past involves a definition of such limits, that is, a forgetting of the unending process that would define, or more accurately dis-fine, the "present"—yet hardly makes anything "present."[42]

Such a forgetting is part of a striving for coherence (remember Vernant and Zumthor) that finds expression in the reading and the reinscription of circumcision as a male practice. In the Bible, in the book of Genesis, I have tried to read around the *oubliés*. They were so perhaps as part of the intent of a project that Meir Sternberg (1985) calls "foolproof composition" — which could only remain a project — and perhaps as part of a univocal reading of patriarchy, or more simply of "maleness." For the definition of "male" in the Bible, as in many other cultural sites, is far from univocal or comfortably coherent. So much so that there is a peculiar gesture involved in forgetting that the practice of circumcision is at no point disconnected from other practices that situate and produce categories of gender and distinctions that do *not* achieve coherence or produce univocal narratives "units."

I mentioned earlier the importance of a "rhetoric of origins" in the attempt to recover either the origin of the law of circumcision or the silenced women. These attempts assume a point where there is "autonomy," a place where some body stands apart from another, in one place. Our own circular ride — I hope not too incisive, bluntly cutting, that is — takes us back to Jean-François Lyotard, who provides us with yet another detour and argues that a similar theme of distinction is at work in the way "Heidegger's thought remains bound to the theme of 'place' and of 'beginning'" (1990:94). Lyotard argues that Philippe Lacoue-Labarthe's reading of Heidegger and of Europe misses the *oubli* involved in such a bind, insofar as this reading considers that the Jews "play no essential part, have essentially no role on this stage" (87).[43] If I read Lyotard correctly, what he opposes is the assumption of a "Europe" without Jews, as if there was a point (*lieu* or *scène*) or a time (*commencement*) where and when the two were unproblematically distinct and apart, as if the definition of each of the terms was not always haunted by the other. Just as "feminizing" the male was asserting that there was a "male" in the first place, this — now familiar — move still assumes a "before" and a "beyond," a past and an origin, distinct from the "present."

In keeping with the reading of "naming" as forgetting and thus of naming as preserving and reinscribing autonomous distinctions, the body on which circumcision is inscribed has not been considered as distinct in and from the different configurations read ("Qu'est-ce qu'*un* corps, *un* visage, *une* voix?" asks Jean-Luc Nancy [1986a:23]). "The" body was always (part of) these configurations. To ascribe to "it" a privileged position, though, would have been — still is — a possibility only within the early parts of this essay, that is, within a "historical" (versus genealogical) framework. Such a memorable framework is always already at work in trying to define the sub-stance underlying all cultural activity. Calling the body its *essence* might do no more than turn the paradigm on its head (or put it back on its feet, and then, what is the difference?). Yet, because "history" is always already at work, historical readings of circumcision seem to remain unavoidable. With the circumcisions, these readings are texts that must be reread in order to be reinscribed differently, perhaps.

Another reason to refrain from dealing "directly" with the body in these configurations is that it is doubtful to what extent we were dealing here with more than body parts. There are even discussions as to which body part was intended in the institution of the covenant as the cutting of the *'orla* (the Hebrew word translated as "foreskin"). As is well known, the Hebrew Bible describes many body parts as "uncircumcised": Moses' lips, the hearts of the Jews, and so on.

"Parts," as in "body parts," refers at any rate to a "whole," a synecdoche, a trope that Kenneth Burke has described as "representation." Is it the same kind of representation that erases what it represents? No doubt it is also that. Circumcision, read as inscription and representation on a body part, on a body that is a part, is also the inscription and the assertion of the "authenticity" of a whole it represents and effaces *simultaneously.* An autonomous whole, a coherent social and physical body.

Coherence, indeed, just what we always wanted to remember.

'Erev yom kippur 5754
September 24, 1993

Notes

"Men have to learn to pay homage" (Nietzsche 1974:156). I am still learning, so I want to pay without necessarily implicating those I hereby thank. I wish thus to thank Daniel Boyarin for introducing me to the topic, and for letting me read in advance his unpublished "Self-Exposure as Theory" (co-written with Jonathan Boyarin) presented at the American Anthropology Association meeting in San Francisco in December 1992. Without that paper, plus Jacques Derrida's *Circonfession* and Judith Butler's *Gender Trouble,* this paper could not have been written. Doubtful of my "capacity for expressing gratitude," I only hope that in what follows "she has got out a word" (Nietzsche 1974:156). I also wish to thank Jonathan Boyarin for his insightful and generous reading and Howard Eilberg-Schwartz for his time and advice. Also I thank Leora Orent Anidjar, Stephen Greenblatt, Adnan Husain, Istvan Rèv, Avital Ronell, Randolph Starn, and Michael Witmore for fascinating discussions and guidance over earlier versions or parts of this paper, and for much more. The shortcomings that remain and misreadings that persist are, of course, my own.

1. Part of the question that occupies me here is, of course, the question of identity. Although I make no claim to answers—quite the contrary, perhaps—I must mark the circumcisions I deal with as "Jewish" and only as such. There are many reasons for this choice, one of them being that I do not wish to inscribe the plethora of meanings appropriated and constructed by the Jewish tradition(s) over the ages upon different cultural practices. Some similarities in the cutting of the foreskin—which is far from being the only mode of circumcision—do not seem to justify more general assertions than I make. As for "female circumcision," similar reasons could be advanced, and I hope this essay will begin to clarify some of them. Quite importantly, then, and even though I refer in the text to (singular) circumcision, one could only speak of (plural) circumcisions. Also: the conflation of circumcision with memory might be deemed unproblematic insofar as, for example, circumcision "is a reminder of the covenant" (Fox 1974:595). This does not mean, however, that the conflation is necessary or unavoidable. Memory cannot be circumscribed more easily than circumcision.

2. All translations are mine, except as noted otherwise.

3. On the plural meaning of *oubli* as forgetting and/or oblivion, see J. Boyarin 1992:3–4. Lyotard also talks about "un oublié absolu, oublié" (1988a:50) which is close to Boyarin's "oblivion."

4. As Maertens 1978 calls it, it is clearly "une inscription génitale," a text written on the genitals.

5. The expression is Pierre Nora's (1989:22). It should be noted, however, that Jews who might be "a favorite case of a 'people of memory'" are not "altogether unique as a people of memory" (J. Boyarin 1992:93, 101).

6. On the link between reading/writing the body and reading the text, see Wolfson 1987a and 1987b and D. Boyarin 1992, all on rabbinical and Jewish medieval literature.

7. On the etymological link between the two words in Hebrew, see Amos Funkenstein, "Introduction (Collective Memory and Historical Consciousness)" in Funkenstein 1993:6.

8. "Phallogocentrism offers a name to eclipse the feminine and take its place," writes Judith Butler (1990:13).

9. I can find no explanation whatsoever for the most unfortunate rendering of the word *juifs* into (capitalized) *Jews* in the English translation.

10. See, for example, Boyarin and Boyarin 1993, especially 700.

11. It should remain clear that what Lyotard "intends" is unimportant here, which is why I refer rather to "his" text. What is important is that the reading suggested here emphasizes what appears to be a more careful approach to forgetting, and to representing, inscribing, and naming in Lyotard's text. Again, the English translation of Lyotard's "juifs réels" into "real Jews" (capitalized) only serves to show the difficulty (not to say the impossibility) of reading. Reading, or memory, cannot be taken for granted.

12. The tremendous difficulty involved in representation and in naming is exemplified in Halperin 1990; Halperin also uses quotation marks around the word *woman* (117, 117n, 149ff.) in order to show that naming is also already erasing, silencing.

13. This should become clearer below. For now it should be noted that memory is often related to control and order. However, it also ignores chronology, as Freud abundantly shows, making the "past in the present" as relevant as the "real" past. Assuming that these are two models that could serve the work of reading the past, I will make use of both.

14. Note the link that Foucault establishes between the "analyse énonciative" and memory. The analysis, says Foucault, is interested in accumulations (*cumul*), that is, not a form of "souvenir" but "une sorte de mémoire qui traverse le temps" (1969: 161). The "controllable" aspect of "souvenir" as well as the subjectivity it assumes are thus *not* part of the purpose of Foucault's analysis. He also insists on treating the "énoncés" as somehow unique. The "groupement" that is constituted by my readings of circumcision is, to insist on that point, not a claim to a universal understanding of it. It is a reading of this plural yet particular "énoncé."

15. I chose to quote Osborn's "extremely literal rendering" (1988:248) because it presents the text in (almost) all its difficulties. "Almost" partly because the choice not to translate *'hatan* is an enormously overdetermined one, as we will see.

16. On the problems of interpreting this passage, see Osborn 1988, focusing particularly on translation. See also Belz 1975; Belz reminds the reader that Moses is never named, and, hence, that he does not appear, in the telling of the scene (209). He goes on to argue that Zipporah in fact brings her son into the *familia dei* that she already forms with — Yahweh. Osborn somehow agrees with Belz in that "the only clearly identified participants are Zipporah, her son, and Yahweh" (1988:255). Pamela Tamarkin Reis argues for a very different reading. For her, Zipporah, whom she calls at one point "a hysterical woman" (1991:328), addresses Moses as her "bridegroom of blood" in order to insult him (!). Zipporah thus serves a function of a "wake-up call" to Moses: "Zipporah's violence jolts Moses out of his despondency, and forces him to recognize his essential nature" (330) — that is, his Jewishness. Therefore, says Reis, the passage is not about "the supremacy of the covenant of circumcision" (331) but about *Moses*. Fox also reads Moses into the story, suggesting that Moses is "vicariously circumcised" (1974:592). It is the son who, according to Fox, "seems out of place in the story" (593). Osborn, in contradistinction, mentions Gispens's theory, which considers that Zipporah "addressed her son with the ritual formula, 'A blood-circumcised one you are to me'" (1988:249). It is interesting to note how readers who seek to escape the problem of interpreting the three verses that constitute this narrative call for an understanding of it "as it stands in the final text" (Robinson 1986:448; Osborn 1988:255) and proceed to insist on Moses' centrality in the narrative. An alternative is to recognize the importance of Zipporah's role while simultaneously making it a "male role" ("Zipporah's prompt assumption of the role of her absent brother," writes Robinson [1986:449]; the same reader adds later that she "has taken the place of her father Jethro" [458]). "She has in some sense acted in place of the *'hoten* 'father-in-law/circumciser,'" writes Propp (1987:359). It is also interesting to note that some passages of the Babylonian Talmud already "explain" Zipporah away by stating that Moses completed the circumcision. Zipporah only started the procedure (Tractate *'Avoda Zara*, 27a). On another plane, Lawrence Kaplan argues that "the redactor has deliberately built the ambiguity into the present narrative" (1981:66), at least concerning the intended victim of God. Kaplan, though, keeps the focus on the male characters of the story even though from a literary perspective they are in no way active participants. Vermes (1961) provides late-antique literary sources that side with all the interpretations here mentioned, showing that indeterminacy does not yet mean infinity of interpretations, even over the length of centuries. One thing is clear: Zipporah's story, as it is called, is not the story of Zipporah. Ilana Pardes's work is all the more striking for its explicit opposition to such a long tradition.

17. This is one reading offered by the Babylonian Talmud: "Go out and see, who is called *'hatan*? I say it is the child" (Tractate Nedarim, 32a). This is also the thesis advanced by Gispen mentioned by Osborn as accepting "that Zipporah considered the

children to be hers" (1988:250). Still, Moses is considered central in the story and Zipporah reasserts her marriage to him.

18. Maertens (1978) describes such myths; see especially chapter 1.

19. As with other descriptions of memory, the point of Vernant's is not in any kind of universal accuracy, but in its relevance to the following text.

20. Clearly, there are overdetermined reasons as to why they oppose such a marriage. Not only is the practice problematic "in itself," the rape of Dinah makes it even more so (see the controversy between Sternberg [1992] and Fewell and Gunn [1991] on reading the rape as central or not). As to what would have happened if the request had not come from a rapist, it remains sheer speculation. It is at any rate difficult, if not impossible, to state univocally, as Propp does, that "if the Shechemites will circumcise... they may intermarry with the Israelites" (1987:359). To write this, Propp must disregard the deceit that, as Sternberg points out, surrounds the proposal from the very beginning. On the level of source criticism, one would also have to disregard the view that "for the patriarchs (and Israel) to intermarry with the Canaanites would be a rejection of God's promise to give all the land of the Canaanites to them" (Van Seters 1975:277). As Jonathan Boyarin reminds me, the "horror of exogamy" seems to refer only to the marriage of *women* outside the tribe. Men do not seem to be under such a law.

21. The similarities between Zumthor's description and Ernest Renan's "Qu'est-ce qu'une nation?" (What is a nation?), in which Renan states that "l'unité se fait toujours brutalement" (1947 [1882]:891), may raise the question, pointed out to me by Jonathan Boyarin, of whether any construction of group identity is necessarily violent, or whether there is here a "legitimation" of the violence of the hegemonic community, to glorify it (Renan) or to regret it (Zumthor, possibly). Insofar as exclusion is violent, it seems to me that Renan did not even have to glide from *nation* to *patrie* and finally to l'*État* in order to assert the gesture of violence present in the formation and preservation of social coherence. Such issues revolve around thinking the "community" (see Nancy 1986a). What needs to be addressed is the possibility to think ethnicity in ways that would not be ethno*centric,* in ways that would not be "means of enforcing solidarity, often at the cost of repressing internal difference, and... legitimize discrimination against those excluded from the group" (J. Boyarin 1992:90; see also Bhabha 1990).

22. See also Vermes, who mentions different understandings of circumcision as having "sacrificial meaning" (1961:180). Flusser and Safrai (1980) expand on the relationship between the circumcision of Abraham and the sacrifice of Isaac, as well as the link with the Passover sacrifice, use of blood, and so on. This understanding is also present in other instances in rabbinical literature as mentioned in Wolfson 1987b (195, 195n25).

23. Both of these quotations are from Karen E. Fields's reading of Nancy Jay in her foreword to Jay's book.

24. Terry Prewitt also emphasizes that the genealogies at the beginning of the story of Abraham include women for the first time in the Bible (1990:7–8). I insist on the centrality of women in genealogy since it confirms that the story of Dinah, which we saw earlier, is indeed about marriage, if not exogamous marriage as has been read. It is also to reassert the close link between genealogy and circumcision that is in Eilberg-Schwartz's words the assertion that "men cannot reproduce alone" (1992:24). Prewitt argues for the structural necessity of this link.

25. Cross-cultural readings interest me only insofar as they strengthen an aspect of *the particular practice* of Hebrew and Jewish circumcision I am focusing upon.

26. Bettelheim of course, and see also the discussion by Daniel Rancour-Laferriere (1985:333ff.), who also writes about possible links between circumcision and homosexual practices (341ff.). A more relevant reference is found in the work of Daniel Boyarin, who argues in connection with circumcision as perceived in early rabbinical literature, that it "was understood somehow as rendering the male somehow feminine" (1992:496). Boyarin also asserts that "the androcentrism of this formation is of course not affected by this reading" (ibid.). He wishes to show that there is an "alternate reading" to the assertion that "circumcision is a male erasure of the female role in procreation as well" (496n64). Circumcision, which "renders men more like women," repeats Boyarin, may "have been understood not as an exclusion of the female so much as inclusion of the male in filiation" (497).

27. One possibility expressed in the Babylonian Talmud, Tractate Nedarim, mentioned earlier, is that Satan, not YHWH, came down.

28. See, however, Bryk 1934:15; he discusses briefly the (marginal) possibility that women did and do circumcise in some society (Bryk wrote before the American Jewish Reform movement began to facilitate the training of women to become *mohalot* or ritual circumcisers, a decision that as far as I could find was not argued in terms of textual sources, but rather as answering a social demand). It is therefore not at all an impossibility to consider Zipporah's actions just as they are described.

29. See Butler 1990, especially chapter 2, and see also Laplanche and Pontalis, who argue that "l'origine du fantasme est integrée dans la structure même du fantasme originaire" (1964:1853). Dealing here mainly with the book of Genesis ("In the beginning...") it might seem hardly surprising that the claim to recover origins has reproduced itself.

30. I try not to read Eilberg-Schwartz or Pardes as univocal texts on *all* levels. It is their reading of the past, their reinscription of binary oppositions through "recovery," even when this recovery is the recovery of the multivocality of the text, that seems to me to be "univocal."

31. Yanagisago and Collier discuss the politics of the distinction according to "roles" in reproduction and "question whether the difference in reproductive function that our culture defines as the universal basis of the relations between males and females constitutes the structural basis of gender relations in other societies and even in our own" (1990:141).

32. At this point, his name is Abram, later to be changed by God to Abraham. Sarah is so far referred to as Saraï.

33. Although clearly for very different purposes, see Cohen 1989.

34. See Greenblatt (1989), who, however, writes of these places as being "hidden."

35. The *Encyclopedia 'Olam ha-Tanakh* (109) explains that in the Ancient East, it was a known custom for a slave to inherit the property of man with no children. Nancy Jay also mentions the importance of property and control in the Patriarchs narrative and how it surrounds property of land as well as property of house gods and, finally, "control over a line of descent, that is, control over a social structure organized around property" (1992:106–7).

On the plurality of meanings of the notion of covenant (*brit*), see Moshe Weinfeld, who refers to it as "grant," "unconditional gift" (1991[1970]:73).

36. The difficulty involved in reading circumcision, the covenant, the promise, the gift must become most apparent. What, indeed, of the "gift"? It would be necessary to conduct a reading of the Genesis text with Jacques Derrida's *Donner le temps, 1. La fausse monnaie*, which I unfortunately cannot do here. Suffice it to say that Derrida argues—an extremely difficult and complex argument to which I do no favor in "sum-

marizing" one of its moments—that the only possible gift is only the one that is not recognized as such (for re-cognizing would also be acknoweldging, repaying). Perhaps is it the gift of time. It is very likely, I believe, that time is partly what God gives to Abraham. God, at any rate, intends to give ("And I will *give* [*va-etnah*] my covenant between you and me," says God in Gen. 17:2, here translated literally; most versions give: "I will *make* my covenant"). And see the articulations of gift and memory in Derrida's text.

37. Even within the different perceptions of the covenant and/or shifts from one perception to another (see Guinan 1975), it remains that the covenant came to be read as a demand to *men* to remember ("die Beschneidung sollte die Israeliten immer aufs neue in die Pflicht erinnern," says Heinisch quoted in Fox 1974:558), while clearly it is God who commits herself to remember. Fox insists on this aspect of covenants: God, not men, must be reminded (573, 588, 595). Fox emphatically suggests that "circumcision is a cognition sign—like the other *'otot* in P—*whose function is to remind God to keep his promise of posterity*" (595, emphasis in the original). See also Damrosch, who discusses the covenant and states that "hearing and remembrance are the characteristic divine activities" (1987:286). If memory, as Frances Yates describes it, is also about control through localization, it becomes apparent that *men* have appropriated the controls. Remembering Derrida's reflections on the notion of gift, if we do read God as the giver of time, it becomes clearer why it is precisely *this* moment that has been misread, that had to be misread, for it could not be acknowledged *as such*. This *oubli*, though, was clearly overdetermined. At any rate, the "gift" was read as a covenant, a contract, which thus enabled appropriation by men. Whether this appropriation has been *entirely* successful is the problem I am struggling with. Still, the appropriation points toward another analogy (I referred to it earlier) between memory and circumcision, since, as Victor Turner wrote, ritual symbols are "a compromise between the need for social *control,* and certain innate and universal human drives whose complete gratification would result in the breakdown of such control" (quoted in Crapanzano 1992:267; emphasis added). Jorge Luis Borges's *Funes the Memorious* might be one possible allegory for such a breakdown. Finally, the struggle for control, as any bind and contract, depends on at least two signatories. It is only a later reading (which sees man as the actor, victor, and signatory) that actually cosigns on *man's* "first" signature. Such a cosigning, which confirms that "women" are out of the picture, seems to have been articulated by Kristeva, Biale, and, to a certain extent, by Crapanzano, Eilberg-Schwartz, D. Boyarin, and Wolfson, who all seem to accept circumcision as "male" *to begin* with. And yet even talmudic and medieval sources *discuss* the involvement of women in the circumcision; see the Babylonian Talmud, Tractate 'Avodah Zarah, 27a and Tosafot ad loc.; see also Tractate Kiddushin, 29a (I thank Rabbi Nathan Margalit for pointing out some of these sources to me). Also see halakic (legal) writings by, among others, R. Yitzhak Elfassi, the Rif, and Maimonides, who, as Talya Fishman explains, ruled that "a Jewish woman may perform circumcision if no male is available to serve as *mohel* [circumciser]" (1992:241), and see Fishman's notes for sources. There is no doubt that a less phallocentric (and less Eurocentric?) reading of circumcision would open possibilities of rereading the very texts over which rabbis argued at different times, as well as the texts of these different rabbis themselves, a project that would no doubt have to be undertaken in collective research. Elliot Horowitz (1989), for example, provides more sources on the way women already "took back the night" by participating in female-only rituals surrounding the time of circumcision in the Middle Ages and early modern period. I am aware that it could be argued that some scholars—unlike the Talmud—are simply looking at the

body on which circumcision is performed. Yet what would be the purpose of forgetting that rarely does one circumcise oneself and that there are therefore other people present—*not only a father and a son* (see the reading of Hegel in Derrida 1981, to be discussed later)—people who act and react? This is not an exercise in rhetoric. Rather, it is a matter of optics and of *framing*, for there is a recurring frame that always redirects our gaze toward the male. Why? We do not know what *one* body is, as Jean-Luc Nancy reminds us. Why insist then and forget the "rest" of the picture? After all, it is exactly "the rest" that all these readers have taught to read. Although theirs are attempts at understanding male sexuality, it remains in my eyes problematical to assume, again, the *success* of the exclusive male linkage, and therefore to accept the view that "women" are only "brought" into the picture because of some biological necessity (Eilberg-Schwartz). "Women" I argue, were never out of the picture. The distinction man/woman, then, like other names, might here hide much more than it pretends to reveal, as we saw.

It is, however, important to insist again on a nonunivocal reading of the texts of the authors mentioned. As I mentioned earlier, Daniel Boyarin includes as part of his argument the possibility of gender reversal, *for men*. And yet, circumcision remains an "androcentric practice." So much so that in a later essay written with Jonathan Boyarin, they have (almost) nothing to say about "women" since they are speaking about "the double mark of the male Jew," and dealing with "a male Jewish self" (Boyarin and Boyarin 1995). However, it was the very fluidity of gender notions that opened the possibility of a reading of circumcision as rendering "men more like women." It is this fluidity that I believe is "lost" in producing "forgetful" readings of circumcision as, still, male. The (alleged) stability of gender is after all fairly recent and the product of a particular cultural configuration. (See, in relation to circumcision and gender in the perception of the Middle Ages and the Renaissance, Leo Steinberg 1983, especially 49–65, and Caroline Walker Bynum, "The Body of Christ in the Later Middle Ages: A Reply to Leo Steinberg" in Bynum 1991. Both illustrate notions of "gender fluidity.") It is the assumption that stability and "autonomy" (whatever this word means, and even if it is the "autonomy" of a "male realm," as we will see) are found at some or any level of these configurations that underlies, I believe, most of these authors' readings (however opposed their views otherwise might be). Once sexual differentiation is constructed (or even prior to that), it is seen as "complete." An exercise in forgetting.

38. Not by everybody, of course; see Trible 1991. And yet, in Trible's essay and elsewhere as well, the links to and implications for the story of circumcision are not explored.

39. "Incest" has notably never been defined in this essay. Having earlier temporarily endorsed the views of different readers of the Genesis text and readers of circumcision, I must now emphasize the immense problems involved in the very use of the category, not only cross-culturally, but also across time. The narrow perspective on the law of incest as defining the relations between mother and son is evidently problematic, as if this was what incest "eigentlich gewesen ist." From whose point of view? As with Nietzsche's "sacrificial animal," it depends who can "have her say" (Nietzsche 1974:210)

40. Peter Stallybrass and Allon White's adoption of Bakhtin's "grotesque" as "formed through a process of hybridization of inmixing of binary opposites . . . such that there is a heterodox merging of elements usually perceived as incompatible . . . [that] unsettles any fixed binaryism" (1986:44) provides ground for a critique of Pardes's reading of an "absolute past." It must be noted, however, that Stallybrass and White themselves only extend their reading *toward* unsettling the opposition past/present.

41. Which, of course, does not mean that *not* to lose sight of this intertwining would yet guarantee (or would want to guarantee) a "successful" erection.

42. By using the construct "dis-fine" I wish to emphasize a positing of limits that instead of marking a porous border zone, a contact zone, presents itself as a rupture of such contact, preserving, again, "autonomy."

43. This is Lyotard's reading of Lacoue-Labarthe, not the latter's words. It is *at this point* relatively unimportant whether this is an "accurate" reading of Lacoue-Labarthe (in another time and place, Avital Ronell [1989] showed that it is indeed quite important to read how high the stakes are in Lyotard's reading; clearly, I am following another thread here). The distinction of "the Jews" from "Europe" is, I believe, common enough. On the problem of "Europe"'s self-definition, its definition of what its "others" are, see Jacques Derrida's *L'autre cap*, Maria Rosa Menocal's *The Arabic Role in Medieval Literary Theory*, and Ammiel Alcalay's *After Jews and Arabs*.

Bibliography

Alcalay, Ammiel. 1993. *After Jews and Arabs: Remaking Levantine Culture.* Minneapolis: University of Minnesota Press.

Bal, Mieke. 1986. *Femmes imaginaires, L'ancien testament au risque d'une narratologie critique.* Utrecht: HES, Paris: A.G. Nizet. (English edition: *Lethal Love, Feminist Literary Readings of Biblical Love Stories,* Bloomington: Indiana University Press.)

Belz, Walter. 1975. "Religionsgeschitliche Marginalie zu Ex 4 24–26." *Zeitschrift für die Altestamentliche Wissenschaft* 87:209–11.

Bhabha, Homi K., ed. 1990. *Nation and Narration.* New York and London: Routledge.

Biale, Rachel. 1984. *Women and Jewish Law: An Exploration of Women's Issues in Halakhic Sources.* New York: Schocken.

Bloom, Harold. 1975. *Kabbalah and Criticism.* New York: Continuum.

Boyarin, Daniel. 1992. " 'This We Know to Be the Carnal Israel': Circumcision and the Erotic Life of God and Israel." *Critical Inquiry* 18, no. 3 (Spring): 474–505.

Boyarin, Daniel, and Jonathan Boyarin. 1993. "Diaspora: Generation and the Ground of Jewish Identity." *Critical Inquiry* 19, no. 4 (Summer): 693–725.

———. 1995. "Self-Exposure as Theory: The Double Mark of the Male Jew." In *The Rhetoric of Self-Making,* ed. Debbora Bataglia. Berkeley: University of California Press.

Boyarin, Jonathan. 1992. *Storm from Paradise: The Politics of Jewish Memory.* Minneapolis: University of Minnesota Press.

Bryk, Felix. 1934. *Circumcision in Man and Woman: Its History, Psychology, and Ethnology.* Trans. David Berger. New York: American Ethnological Press.

Butler, Judith. 1990. *Gender Trouble: Feminism and the Subversion of Identity.* New York: Routledge.

Bynum, Caroline Walker. 1991. *Fragmentation and Redemption: Essays on Gender and the Human Body in Medieval Religion.* New York: Zone.

Cixous, Hélène. 1986 [1976]. "La venue à l'écriture." In *Entre l'écriture.* Paris: Des femmes.

Clifford, James. 1988. "On *Orientalism.*" In *The Predicament of Culture: Twentieth-Century Ethnography, Literature and Art.* Cambridge, Mass.: Harvard University Press.

Cohen, Jeremy. 1989. *"Be Fertile and Increase, Fill the Earth and Master It": The Ancient and Medieval Career of a Biblical Text.* Ithaca, N.Y.: Cornell University Press.

Crapanzano, Vincent. 1992. "Rite of Return." In *Hermes' Dilemma and Hamlet's Desire: On the Epistemology of Interpretation,* 260–80. Cambridge, Mass.: Harvard University Press.

Damrosch, David. 1987. *The Narrative Covenant: Transformations of Genre in the Growth of Biblical Literature.* Ithaca, N.Y.: Cornell University Press.

Derrida, Jacques. 1981. *Glas, Que reste-t-il du savoir absolu?* Paris: Denoël.

———. 1984. *Otobiographies, L'enseignement de Nietzche et la politique du nom propre.* Paris: Galilée. (Trans. Avital Ronell in *The Ear of the Other.* Lincoln: University of Nebraska Press, 1985.)

———. 1986. *Glas.* Trans. J. P. Leavy and R. Rand. Lincoln: University of Nebraska Press.

———. 1989. "'Il faut bien manger' ou le calcul du sujet." In *Cahiers Confrontations* 20:91–114. (Trans. Peter Connor and Avital Ronell in *Who Comes after the Subject?* ed. Cadava et al. New York: Routledge, 1991.)

———. 1991a. "Circonfession." In *Jacques Derrida* by Geoffrey Bennington and Jacques Derrida. Paris: Seuil.

———. 1991b. *Donner le temps, 1. La fausse monnaie.* Paris: Galilée.

———. 1993. "Circumfession" in *Jacques Derrida* by Geoffrey Bennington and Jacques Derrida. Chicago: University of Chicago Press.

Eilberg-Schwartz, Howard. 1990. *The Savage in Judaism: An Anthropology of Israelite Religion and Ancient Judaism.* Bloomington: Indiana University Press.

———. 1992. "Introduction: People of the Body" in *People of the Body: Jews and Judaism from an Embodied Perspective,* ed. Howard Eilberg-Schwartz, 1–15. Albany, N.Y.: State University of New York Press.

Encyclopedia 'Olam ha-Tanakh, vol.1, ed. Menahem Haran. Tel Aviv: Revivim.

Fewell, Danna Nolan, and David M. Gunn. 1991. "Tipping the Balance: Sternberg's Reader and the Rape of Dinah." *Journal of Biblical Literature* 110, no. 2 (Summer): 193–211.

Finkielkraut, Alain. 1980. *Le Juif imaginaire.* Paris: Seuil.

Fishman, Talya. 1992. "A Kabbalistic Perspective on Gender-Specific Commandments: On the Interplay of Symbols and Society." *AJS Review* 17, no. 2: 199–245.

Flusser, David, and Schmuel Safrai. 1980. "Who Sanctified the Beloved in the Womb." *Immanuel: A Bulletin of Religious Thought and Research in Israel* 11 (Fall).

Foucault, Michel. 1969. *L'archéologie du savoir.* Paris: Gallimard

———. 1971. "Nietzsche, la généalogie, l'histoire." In *Hommage à Jean Hyppolite,* 145–72. Paris: Presses Universitaires de France.

———. 1984. "Nietzsche, Genealogy, History." In *The Foucault Reader,* ed. Paul Rabinow, 76–100. New York: Pantheon.

Fox, Michael V. 1974. "The Sign of the Covenant, Circumcision in the Light of the Priestly *'ôt* Etiologies." *Revue Biblique* 81: 557–96.

Freud, Sigmund. 1967. *Moses and Monotheism.* Trans. Katherine Jones. New York: Vintage.

Funkenstein, Amos. 1993. *Perceptions of Jewish History.* Berkeley: University of California Press.

Greenblatt, Stephen. 1989. "Toward a Poetics of Culture." In *The New Historicism,* ed. H. Aram Veeser, 1–14. New York: Routledge.

Guinan, Michael. 1975. *Covenant in the Old Testament.* Chicago: Franciscan Herald Press.

Halperin, David M. 1990. "Why Is Diotima a Woman?" In *One Hundred Years of Homosexuality and Other Essays on Greek Love,* 113–51. New York: Routledge.

Horowitz, Elliot. 1989. "The Eve of Circumcision: A Chapter in the History of Jewish Nightlife." *Journal of Social History* 23, no. 1 (Fall): 45–69.

Jay, Nancy. 1992. *Throughout Your Generations Forever: Sacrifice, Religion, and Paternity.* Chicago: University of Chicago Press.

Josipovici, Gabriel. 1988. *The Book of God: A Response to the Bible.* New Haven, Conn.: Yale University Press.

Kaplan, Lawrence. 1981. " 'And the Lord Sought to Kill Him' (Exod. 4:24): Yet Once Again." *Hebrew Annual Review* 5: 65–74.

Kofman, Sarah. 1981. "Ça cloche." In *Les fins de l'homme, à partir du travail de Jacques Derrida,* Colloque de Cerisy, 89–112. Paris: Galilée.

Kristeva, Julia. 1980. *Pouvoirs de l'horreur: Essai sur l'abjection.* Paris: Seuil.

Laplanche, Jean, and J.-B. Pontalis. 1964. "Fantasme originaire, fantasmes des origines, origine du fantasme." *Les Temps Modernes* 215 (April): 1833–68.

Laqueur, Thomas. 1990. *Making Sex, Body and Gender from the Greeks to Freud.* Cambridge, Mass.: Harvard University Press.

Leach, Edmund. 1969. *Genesis as Myth and Other Essays.* London: Jonathan Cape.

Lyotard, Jean-François. 1988a. *Heidegger et "les juifs."* Paris: Galilée.

———. 1988b. "À l'insu." In *Le genre humain: Politiques de l'oubli,* ed. Maurice Olender, 37–43. Paris: Seuil.

———. 1990a. *Heidegger and "the jews."* Trans. A. Michel and M. Roberts. Minneapolis: University of Minnesota Press.

———. 1990b. *Vortrag in Wien und Freiburg.* Trans. Clemens Porschelgel and Werner Rappl. Vienna: Passagen Verlag.

Maertens, Jean-Thierry. 1978. *Ritologiques 2: Le corps sexionné.* Paris: Aubier Montaigne.

Memmi, Albert. 1976. *La terre intérieure: Entretiens avec Victor Malka.* Paris: Gallimard.

Menocal, Maria Rosa. 1987. *The Arabic Role in Medieval Literary Theory: A Forgotten Heritage.* Philadelphia: University of Pennsylvania Press.

Morgenstern, J. 1963. " 'The Bloody Husband' (?) (Exod. 4:24–26) Once Again." *Hebrew Union College Annual* 34: 35–70.

Nancy, Jean-Luc. 1986a. *La communauté désoeuvrée.* Paris: Christian Bourgeois.

———. 1986b. *L'oubli de la philosophie.* Paris: Galilée.

Nietzsche, Friedrich. 1974. *The Gay Science.* Trans. Walter Kaufmann. New York: Vintage.

———. 1989. *On the Genealogy of Morals.* Trans. Walter Kaufmann and R. J. Hollingdale. New York: Vintage.

Nora, Pierre. 1989. "Between Memory and History: *Les Lieux de Mémoire.*" *Representations* 26 (Spring).

Osborn, Noel D. 1988. "Circumspection about Circumcision in Exodus 4.24.26." In *Issues in Bible Translation,* ed. Phillip C. Stine, 247–64. London and New York: United Bible Societies.

Pardes, Ilana. 1992. *Countertraditions in the Bible.* Cambridge, Mass.: Harvard University Press.

Prewitt, Terry J. 1990. *The Elusive Covenant: A Structural-Semiotic Reading of Genesis.* Bloomington: Indiana University Press.

Propp, William H. 1987. "The Origins of Infant Circumcision in Israel." *Hebrew Annual Review* 11: 355–70.

Rancour-Laferriere, Daniel. 1985. *Signs of the Flesh: An Essay on the Evolution of Hominid Sexuality.* Berlin, New York, and Amsterdam: Mouton de Gruyter.

Reis, Pamela Tamarkin. 1991. "The Bridegroom of Blood: A New Reading." *Judaism, A Quarterly Journal* 40, no. 3 (Summer): 324–31.

Renan, Ernest. 1947 [1882]. "Qu'est-ce qu'une nation?" In *Oeuvres Complètes.* Paris: Calmann-Lévy.

Robinson, Bernard P. 1986. "Zipporah to the Rescue: A Contextual Study of Exodus IV 24–6." *Vetus Testamentum* 36, no. 4: 447–61.

Ronell, Avital. 1989. "The Differends of Man." *Diacritics* 19, no. 3–4: 63–75.

———. 1994. *Finitude's Score: Essays for the End of the Millennium.* Lincoln: University of Nebraska Press.

Rosenberg, Joel. 1986. *King and Kin: Political Allegory in the Hebrew Bible.* Bloomington: Indiana University Press.

Said, Edward. 1979. *Orientalism.* New York: Vintage.

Scott, Joan Wallach. 1988. *Gender and the Politics of History.* New York: Columbia University Press.

Simonis, Yvan. 1980. *Claude Lévi-Strauss ou la "passion de l'inceste": Introduction au structuralisme.* Paris: Flammarion.

Spivak, Gayatri Chakravorty. 1992. "Acting Bits/Identity Talk." *Critical Inquiry* 18, no. 4: 770–803.

Stallybrass, Peter, and Allon White. 1986. *The Politics and Poetics of Transgression.* Ithaca, N.Y.: Cornell University Press.

Steinberg, Leo. 1983. *The Sexuality of Christ in Renaissance Art and in Modern Oblivion.* New York: Pantheon.

Sternberg, Meir. 1985. "The Art of Persuasion." In *The Poetics of Biblical Narrative: Ideological Literature and the Drama of Reading,* 441–81. Bloomington: Indiana University Press.

———. 1992. "Biblical Poetics and Sexual Politics: From Reading to Counter-Reading." *Journal of Biblical Literature* 111, no. 3: 463–88.

Trible, Phyllis. 1984. *Texts of Terror: Literary-Feminist Readings of Biblical Narratives.* Philadelphia: Fortress.

———. 1991. "Genesis 22: The Sacrifice of Sarah." In *"Not in Heaven": Coherence and Complexity in Biblical Narrative,* ed. J. P. Rosenblatt and J. C. Sitterson Jr., 170–91. Bloomington: Indiana University Press.

Van Seters, John. 1975. *Abraham in History and Tradition.* New Haven, Conn.: Yale University Press.

Vermes, Geza. 1961. *Scripture and Tradition in Judaism: Haggadic Studies.* Leiden: Brill.

Vernant, Jean-Pierre. 1985. *Mythe et pensée chez les Grecs: Études de psychologie historique.* Paris: La Découverte.

Weinfeld, Moshe. 1991. "The Covenant of Grant in the Old Testament and in the Ancient Near East." In *Essential Papers on Israel and the Ancient Near East,* ed. Frederick E. Greenspahn, 69–102. New York: New York University Press.

Wolfson, Elliot R. 1987a. "Circumcision and the Divine Name: A Study in the Transmission of Esoteric Doctrines." *Jewish Quarterly Review,* 78, no. 1–2 (July–October): 77–112.

———. 1987b. "Circumcision, Vision of God, and Textual Interpretation: From Midrashic Trope to Mystical Symbol." *History of Religions* 27, no. 2 (November): 189–215.

Yanagisago, Sylvia J., and Jane F. Collier. 1990. "The Mode of Reproduction in Anthropology." In *Theoretical Perspectives on Sexual Difference,* ed. Deborah L. Rhode, 131–41. New Haven, Conn.: Yale University Press.

Yates, Frances. 1966. *The Art of Memory.* Chicago: University of Chicago Press.

Young, Robert. 1990. *White Mythologies: Writing History and the West.* London: Routledge.

Zumthor, Paul. 1988. "L'oubli et la tradition." In *Le genre humain: Les politiques de l'oubli,* ed. Maurice Olender, 105–17. Paris: Seuil.

Contributors

Ammiel Alcalay is chair of the Department of Classical and Oriental Languages at Queens College and also teaches in the Departments of Comparative Literature and Medieval Studies at the City University of New York Graduate Center. His books include *After Jews and Arabs: Remaking Levantine Culture* and *the cairo notebooks*. He edited and cotranslated *Sarajevo: A War Journal* and *Portraits of Sarajevo* by the Bosnian journalist Zlatko Dizdorevic. Most recently, he edited and translated *Keys to the Garden: New Israeli Writing,* the first anthology of contemporary writing by *mizrahi* Jews to appear in English.

Gil Anidjar is pursuing graduate studies in comparative literature at the University of California at Berkeley.

Daniel Boyarin is the Taubman Professor of Talmudic Culture at the University of California at Berkeley. His most recent books are *Carnal Israel: Reading Sex in Talmudic Culture* and *A Radical Jew: Paul and the Politics of Identity.* His essay in this volume is an excerpt from his forthcoming *Judaism as a Gender.*

Jonathan Boyarin is an independent scholar trained in anthropology. He has published widely in Jewish ethnography and interdisciplinary cultural theory. He currently attends Yale Law School.

Maria Damon teaches poetics and cultural studies at the University of Minnesota. She is the author of *The Dark End of the Street: Margins in American Vanguard Poetry.*

Jay Geller teaches religious studies at Vanderbilt University. He has published numerous articles on Freud, Hegel, Kafka, Nordau, and representations of Jews as well as coedited *Reading Freud's Reading.* His *The Nose Job: Freud and the Feminized Jew* is forthcoming.

Daniel Itzkovitz is a doctoral candidate in the Program in Literature and Theory at Duke University. He is coeditor (with Daniel Boyarin and Ann Pellegrini) of the forthcoming *Queer Theory and the Jewish Question.*

Chana Kronfeld teaches Hebrew, Yiddish, and comparative literature at the University of California at Berkeley. She is the author of *On the Margins of Modernism* and series coeditor (with Daniel Boyarin) of *Contraversions: Critical Studies in Jewish Literature, Culture and Society.*

Jack Kugelmass is professor of anthropology and former director of the Folklore Program at the University of Wisconsin at Madison. His books include *From A Ruined Garden: The Memorial Books of Polish Jewry* (with Jonathan Boyarin), *The Miracle of Intervale Avenue: The Story of a Jewish Congregation in the South Bronx,* and *Masked Culture: The Greenwich Village Halloween Parade.* He is currently completing a book of essays on the public culture of American Jewry.

Benjamin Orlove teaches in the department of environmental studies at the University of California at Davis. He has done ethnographic fieldwork and archival research in the Andean highlands of Peru, Bolivia, Chile, and Mexico. In addition to several academic books and articles, his writings include *In My Father's Study,* a family memoir.

Vivian Patraka is professor of English at Bowling Green State University. A contributor to numerous journals and anthologies, she is currently completing *Spectacular Suffering: Theater, Fascism, and the*

Holocaust.

Ann Pellegrini is visiting assistant professor of women's studies at Barnard College. She is the author of *Performance Anxieties: Staging Psychoanalysis, Staging Race* (1996), in which a revised and expanded version of her contribution to this volume appears.

Naomi Seidman is assistant professor at the Center for Jewish Studies of the Graduate Theological Union in Berkeley. Her study of the sexual politics of Hebrew and Yiddish is forthcoming from the University of California Press.

Marc Shell is professor of English at Harvard University. His books include *The End of Kinship* and *Children fo the Earth.*

Johannes von Moltke teaches film and media studies at the University of Hildesheim, Germany. He is also completing a Ph.D. in literature at Duke University.

Index

Abraham, 299, 369–70, 376–80, 382
Abram, 378
Abramovitsh, Sh. Y., 297–98
Achad Ha'Am, 299–300
Adorno, Theodor, 205, 226–28, 241–45, 247, 250
African Americans, xii; and Jews, xiv–xvi, 1, 134, 151–72; in universities, xi
African American studies, 340
Akhmatova, Anna, 259
Alcalay, Ammiel, xix
Allen, Woody, 3
Aloni, Nissim, 335
Alter, Robert, 338–40
Americanness, 176–95
Andric, Ivo, 341–42
Anglo-Saxons, 182
Anidjar, Gil, xx–xxi
anima, 307
anthropology, viii, 111; and Jews xii, 1–29
anti-Semitism, 93, 189, 111–12, 114, 117, 119, 128–29, 203–5, 211–19, 222, 226–29, 241, 243–46, 247–48, 251, 351; and American racism, xv, 71; and homophobia, 193; and museums, 71; of Third Reich, 93; and "woman," xv, 109
Arabic, 331
Arab Jews, 332
Arabs, 332
Arendt, Hannah, 191
Armstrong, Louis, 157, 159, 169
Ash, Sholem, 300
Ashkenazim, 2, 87, 286, 332, 334, 338. *See also* eastern Jews
assimilation, 98, 120, 134, 154, 203, 205, 212–14, 221, 238–40, 244
Augustine, 370

aura, 204–8, 220, 222–23, 226–29, 231–37, 240, 245–48, 251
authenticity, 330
autochthony, 94
Axis Rule in Occupied Europe (Lemkin), 56

Bakhtin, Mikhail, 308, 313–14
Ballas, Shimon, 335, 336, 338
Barthes, Roland, 47
Bartók, Béla, 150, 152
Barton, Carlin, 316, 318, 319, 323
Bat-Miriam, Yocheved, 294
Baudelaire, Charles, 206–9, 217–18, 226–28, 231–33, 250
Bauer, Ida, 115–18, 125, 130. *See also* "Dora"
Bauer, Yehuda, 55
Bechar, Nissim, 337
Beit Hashoah Museum of Tolerance, 58, 60, 69–74; and Auschwitz, 72; and Black Entertainment Television, 74; civil rights film at, 73; and Simon Wiesenthal Center, 70; Tolerance Workshop, 71
belle juive, stereotypes of, 110, 126, 129–30
Ben-Avi, Itamar, 285, 287
Benjamin, Walter, xiii, xvii, 203–51
Ben-Yehuda, Dvora, 283–85
Ben-Yehuda, Eliezer, 279–303
Ben-Yitzhak, Avraham, 270–73
Berenbaum, Michael, 71–72
Berlin, 79, 206, 218, 220–22
Berlin Museum, 86
Bernays, Martha, 120, 125
Bernhard, Sandra, xv, 110, 130–43
Bernhardt, Sarah, xv, 110, 125–30, 135–36, 141
Bhabha, Homi, 101